AF660062

GLOBAL MARKETING

Gautam Dutta
Faculty, Marketing
Indian Institute of Foreign Trade
Delhi, Kolkata

Pearson

Associate Editor—Acquisitions: Varun Goenka
Editor—Development: Sanhita Sinha
Senior Editor—Production: G. Sharmilee

ISBN 978-93-325-3035-5

First Impression

Published by Pearson India Education Services Pvt. Ltd, CIN: U72200TN2005PTC057128

Head Office: 1st Floor, Berger Tower, Plot No. C-001A/2, Sector 16B, Noida – 201 301,Uttar Pradesh, India.

Registered Office: Featherlite, 'The Address' 5th Floor, Survey No 203/10B, 200 Ft MMRD Road,Zamin Pallavaram, Chennai - 600044
Website: in.pearson.com; Email:companysecretary.india@pearson.com

Digitally printed in India by Trinity Academy for Corporate Training Ltd, New Delhi in the year of 2024.

To my late parents for educating me
To my teachers in school for trying …
And my wife Elora and son Abhishek for their encouragement

Contents

Preface vii
Acknowledgements xi

Chapter 1	Global Market Participation Decisions	1
Chapter 2	Negotiating Cultural Factors	52
Chapter 3	Negotiating Political–Legal Factors	92
Chapter 4	Negotiating Economic Environment	149
Chapter 5	Deciding on International Market Selection	203
Chapter 6	Deciding on Entry Modes	246
Chapter 7	Deciding on Product	303
Chapter 8	Deciding on Brand	351
Chapter 9	Deciding on Pricing	394
Chapter 10	Deciding on Distribution	445
Chapter 11	Deciding on Global Promotion	492
Chapter 12	Research Agenda in Cross-border Marketing	545
Chapter 13	Organising for Global Marketing	595

Index 629

Preface

In most countries around the world, there is a spurt of interest in the globalisation of businesses, whether they are small or big. This trend is visible in developed and also in developing nations. In the first phase of internationalisation, businesses of developed countries resorted to globalisation as a key to business success. American companies led from the front followed by European and Japanese companies. In course of time, there hardly existed a company which considered international interface as a separate, unrelated activity outside its normal business process. The academics of these countries went ahead whole heartedly to support their companies' stride towards internationalisation and contributed heavily by writing articles and books which allowed development and a great deal of understanding in the field. As competition brewed up in the market place across different countries, the writers and practitioners focussed on developing marketing excellence as a tool to achieve competitive advantage. Soon, a realisation dawned on them that to sustain competitive advantage in the realm of acute competition across different economies in the post-internationalisation phase, the practitioners must look beyond the tools and techniques of domestic marketing and expose themselves to specific subject areas such as international marketing or global marketing, which are still in the nascent stage. Thus, from the 1990s, there has been continuous contribution – through books and articles from different writers from different parts of the world – in developing a broad understanding on this important discipline of study known as "global marketing".

I was almost a nomad fifteen years back in this field of study. I first seriously ventured into this field when I was told that my university is considering me as a probable teacher for this subject. At that time I was working as a marketing faculty within the marketing department of a premier national- level institution. Very soon, the time came when I set out to teach global marketing to post-graduate students in the university, which was exclusively offering an MBA degree in the domain of international business.

While delving into the subject, I found a few grey areas. Aspects of domestic business management that were being discussed could easily fit in international business management. There were various other similar overlaps noted, mainly due to the cross border nature of operation. Interestingly, many of these additional aspects are directly dependent on the degree of internationalisation of companies. This makes things difficult for the learners as well as for the teachers because it brings in an ambiguity in understanding the domain of this subject. Another aspect of complexity was to determine a line of demarcation between domestic marketing and international marketing. From where students should start learning international marketing and what should be the coverage of a text book in this discipline? For example, students needed to understand the tools and techniques of executing business research for a domestic company, and hence, writers included them in the text books of business research. While the application may be different, the tools and techniques for domestic marketing research and its international or global counterpart may essentially be the same. Similarly, the fundamental principle of customer value creation is the same in international marketing as it is in domestic marketing, and the same principle is applied in a cross border marketing situation. Because of this overlapping nature, many text books have been written in international or global marketing with varied coverage which appears to be quite confusing for the students as well for the teacher. Also, there are only a few text books written exclusively in the Indian context to depict how Indian companies reach out to other country markets and spell out their marketing techniques. Cases addressing the concerns of American or European companies exclusively cannot be intriguing to students of developing countries like India. These issues prompted me to develop my own content for global marketing, which I use in a typical three-credit course of university MBA curriculum.

This book is an attempt to present the structure of global marketing from the Indian perspective in a cohesive and comprehensive manner. The cases discussed in the book depict the workings of either Indian companies or Indian scenarios to help the students grasp the flavour of cross-border marketing. The opening vignettes are strategically placed to kindle curiosity in students and, more importantly, to create a learning focus. The international market identification process for exporting businesses has never been systematically depicted in the contemporary text books of international or global marketing. Because of the requirement of the class as well as that of the exporting community, I developed a complete framework (which I call Export Market Identification and Selection Process – EMI & SP) as an iterative process of market selection which can be used by students and professional business managers. The framework has been included in this book for the reader's benefit.

Throughout the book it has been my endeavour to place and discuss the different requirements of internationalisation of companies and comment upon the extent of success of their marketing techniques. I have also highlighted the valuable contributions of different researchers in the field of international business and marketing so that students or researchers can immediately identify their areas of interest or relevance for further reading or research. The end-of-chapter questions, exercises, references and further reading sections are intended to encourage the readers in this direction. In addition to providing an in-depth understanding of global marketing, the book also suggests effective tools and techniques that budding managers can adopt in a global company set-up. Further, the book has been written keeping in mind the requirement of a teacher who is offering a three-credit course in global marketing where each chapter of the book can be considered as inputs for each session. However, the world of international business is changing very fast and I would, therefore, welcome any observations or suggestions which would help me correct, update or otherwise improve the text.

While every effort has been made to trace and contact copy right holders, this has not been possible in every case. If notified, the writer and publisher will undertake to rectify any errors or omissions at the earliest opportunity.

Gautam Dutta

Acknowledgements

I am deeply grateful to each and everyone who has encouraged me and helped me to think positively. Some names are so prominent that I will be failing in duty if I do not mention them. First and foremost, I thank my parents for laying the roots of simple living and positive thinking. I am thankful to my colleagues, present and past, for constantly supporting me and providing all sorts of academic inputs.

Prof D.D. Mali of Indian Institute of Entrepreneurship, who was my mentor and helped to channelize my energy to the world of academics from my pursuits in the industrial field, needs special mention. Prof K. Rangarajan of IIFT, who knew my strengths and weaknesses all along, continuously fanned the stronger points, and possibly because of that, I could aspire to write a book on global marketing. My other colleagues of IIFT, Prof J.K. Seal, Prof T.P. Ghosh, Prof R.P. Dutta, Prof B. Roychodhury, Prof S. Tripathy, Prof P.K. Das, Prof R.P. Sharma, Prof D. Sinha, Prof S. Banerjee and Prof R. Bhattacharya, who were always supportive of my work.

I am also grateful to the organisations that have permitted me to use their logo, images and material for illustrations and examples in explaining the concepts.

I am obliged to the editorial team at Pearson for their hard work and encouragement. Mr Varun Goenka, Associate Editor, who always stood by my side and provided continuous support. Ms Sanhita Sinha, Development Editor, and Ms G. Sharmilee, Senior Production Editor at Pearson India, deserve credit for their sustained hard work.

Last but not the least, I acknowledge the contribution made by my wife Elora and son Abhishek, who cooperated extraordinarily while I was writing this book. Understandably, the time I confined myself to my laptop while writing a book of this volume was the time taken away from them.

Gautam Dutta

Global Market Participation Decisions

1

Learning Objectives

After studying this chapter, you should be able to:

- Understand how the international marketers can create customer value better than the competitors.
- Understand the implications of the standardisation vs adaptation debate in customer value creation process.
- Understand the evolution of marketing as a discipline of study in relation with the pace of internationalisation of companies.
- Understand the different drivers of globalisation and their implications on marketing internationally.
- Understand how customer value creation process can undergo changes with respect to the different levels of country market participation.
- Understand the concept of global marketing as efficiency point.

Chapter Overview

This chapter introduces readers with the fundamentals of international business and requirements of international market participation. It first discusses the motives of internationalisation of companies and then highlights on the basic marketing tasks that are required to be performed by international marketers at different level of global market participation. This chapter seeks to answer the question whether marketers can create customer value in different countries with equal efficiency and role of standardisation and adaptation of marketing programmes thereof. In this context, the chapter also highlights the evolving nature marketing in explaining the internationalisation process of the companies. This chapter also introduces the concept of global marketing as efficiency point in the backdrop of different drivers of global market participation.

Opening Vignette

American cookies win over Indian and Chinese markets

The King of Indian Cinema, Amitabh Bachchan once saw the David Fincher's widely acclaimed American film 'The Social Network' and found that the storyline was not as relevant as the contemporary Bollywood blockbuster 'Baghban' for the Indian audiences. He, therefore, did not foresee any threat to Indian cinema from American cinema. But can anyone say the same thing for America's best loved cookie brand 'Oreo' entering India to find a place in its lucrative biscuit market estimated to be of ₹5500 crore ($1.1 billion) size? Particularly when, to its disadvantage, average Indian biscuit lovers neither heard about the American company Kraft Foods Inc nor its billion dollar brand 'Oreo' till it entered India during 2011. What it takes to be the darling of Indian consumers and challenge the existing market leaders like Parley G, Sun feast, etc? Possibly the American company knew the best particularly after its sojourn in China way back in 1996 and re-launching of Oreo during 2005. Initially, the Chinese did not entertain the American brand as they were not historically big cookie eaters. Those who tested it found the cookie to be of peculiar sweet and bitter taste and hence not in line with Chinese choice. Again without any emotional bonding with the American brand name it looked difficult that the Chinese would fall in love for the cookie. As the saying goes "in marketing war nothing is unfair", the American company assembled all the arms and ammunition to fight out the odds. It went on to developed 20 prototypes of reduced-sugar Oreos and tested them with Chinese consumers before arriving at a formula that tasted right. This skirmish with Chinese taste went on and once the 'Chinese relevant' one was found out, the American company fortified it with other weapons to fight out the competitors in the open market. Oreo was introduced with different packages, including smaller packets for just 29 cents to cater to Chinese buying habits. The localisation continued and Oreo products in China came out in different varieties like Oreo green tea ice cream, Oreo Double-Fruit, four layers of crispy wafers filled with vanilla and chocolate cream, coated in chocolate, etc., to the likings of Chinese consumers. After successful alignment with buying habit the next challenge was to align with consumption behaviour. Unlike Americans the Chinese typically do not consume biscuit by twisting open the cookies, lick the cream inside and then dunk it in milk. Here, the American company went head on to change the consumption behaviour of Chinese and launched advertising campaign to popularise the American style of pairing Oreos with milk. NBA basketball star Yao Ming was roped in to enthuse the Chinese youngsters to indulge in the act of 'twist, lick and dunk' while taking Oreo biscuits. These campaigns did wonderful result for the company and eventually Oreo became the bestselling cookies of that country. So, for India entry much latter, the company was ready to prove Amitabh Bachchan wrong. Straightway the company went ahead with product modification through sweetening of the biscuit to suit the Indian palate. Cadbury was a much close brand to the Indian customers because of its long presence in India. In India, therefore, Kraft used its already acquired British brand name and called the biscuits as "Cadbury Oreos" to have clear access to the Indian minds.

Price of the product was strategically fixed to suit Indian pocket and buying habit. Traditional and as well modern like social media like face book, etc., were extensively used to communicate its global slogan based on the concept of 'togetherness'. The result was enviable; the market share went up to 30% from mere 1% at the start up with a year.

When this success story of the American company was told to the students of international marketing in the classroom situation, the students quipped, "that's interesting, it seems that proper marketing strategy can win over any country market irrespective of difference of taste, choice, preference, etc., of the consumers. But does it require company to follow localisation strategy always? What if the reverse, i.e., standardisation strategy is used? What should be the best strategy of a company, localisation or standardisation? How companies can archive marketing success with cost efficiency in the international markets?".

Two vectors shape the world—technology and globalisation. The first helps determine human preferences; the second, economic realities. Regardless of how much preferences evolve and diverge, they also gradually converge and form markets where economies of scale lead to reduction of costs and prices.

—Professor Theodore Levitt

INTRODUCTION

The term "internationalisation" in the context of business is used to describe the outward movement or increasing involvement in a companies' or larger grouping's international operations.[1] The internationalisation of business is not a recent trend of the companies. The outward movement is in fact a very old tendency of business. The Singer Sewing Machine Company of the United States set up a foreign factory way back in 1867. Several renowned companies of today such as General Electric, Ford Motor Company and Unilever initiated their outward movement quite early and had substantial international manufacturing subsidiaries by World War I.These companies even started the process of making their presence felt permanently in the markets of other countries at that early stage. Max Keith, the man in charge of Coca-Cola Deutschland during the Second World War, decided to create a new brand "Fanta" to make its presence in the German market permanent. However, the real rush began at the end of World War II when a number of US companies found in action to win over foreign markets by either sending US-made products to these markets or producing them there. As a result, the investment of US companies in foreign country operations increased from USD 3.8 billion in 1950 to USD 11.2 billion in 1960, and USD 32.2 billion in 1970. This showed the interest exhibited no permission by US companies in manufacturing and marketing products internationally.[2]

Companies originating from other developed countries also followed the pioneering trend of internationalisation set by US companies. European companies were closely observing US companies action towards internationalisation and they soon jumped in to the bandwagon. As it stands today, urgency of internationalisation has not been confined to the US or European companies only. Rather internationalisation has become a primary condition of existence of companies, regardless of size or scope of activities. Indian small companies have shown their worth to the national economy through internationalisation and continuously contributing about 35% of the total export of the country. In fact, internationalisation of business and globalisation has become two sides of the same coin. Both supported each other and promoted a new world order by taking advantage of collapsed country market barriers across the globe. Enterprises are adopting different ways of moving outwards to enjoy the benefits of new market openings in different country markets. The multinational corporations (MNCs) justify their naming by being omnipresent. The quest of these enterprises to spread wings and cross international borders were ably supported by the integration of economies around the world through trade and finance and the resulting ease in movement of economic factors such as capital, labour, technology, and products and services across countries. Smaller companies began sending the excess production beyond the national territory after satisfying the domestic need. Some small- and medium-sized companies began doing the reverse, i.e., first satisfying the international demand and then, if need be, marketing their products in the domestic market. In the changed scenario, the companies in different countries, irrespective of their sizes, started posing a very natural question for themselves, "why should we not go beyond our national border when there are always a group of customers across the world willing to buy our products?"

---

[1] Johanson, J, Vahlne, J-E. The internationalisation process of a firm: a model of knowledge development and increasing foreign market commitments. Journal of International Business Studies 1977; 8: 23-32.

[2] Judd Polk, US Production Abroad and the Balance of Payments (New York: National Industrial Conference Board, 1966, p. 105.

MOTIVES BEHIND INTERNALISATION

Traditionally, companies internationalised due to various internal and external factors. The rapid growth of information and communication technology has always been the invisible external driver behind the internationalisation phenomenon. However, more specifically the following factors can be considered as very active factors responsible for intense internationalisation of companies.

Technology

The development in technology has ensured that the trends exhibited in the latest Paris fashion show spreads instantaneously across the world and, therefore, aiding apparel companies internationalisation. The English Premiere League matches can no longer be called an only British event when every match is telecast and viewed across the world. Now, thirty-three television broadcasters around the world provide coverage of the La Liga, Spanish football's top-level competition for the consumption of the globe. The ESPN Star Sports network broadcasts the La Liga matches across its channels in 18 countries, which include India, Bangladesh, Pakistan, Sri Lanka, Malaysia, Indonesia, Taiwan, Philippines, Myanmar, Cambodia, Laos, Papua New Guinea, the Maldives, Nepal, Bhutan, North Korea, China and South Korea.[3] The spread of information with visuals through television and the Internet has made it possible for the companies to reach to the customers across the world with country specific marketing stimuli designed for a segment. Many companies have been successful in developing a common marketing programme that equally appeals to the identical segments living across the world. For example, Evolution, an advertising campaign launched mainly on YouTube by Unilever in 2006 as part of its "Dove Campaign for Real Beauty" was viewed over 40,000 times in its first day, 17,00,000 times within a month of its upload and 120,00,000 times within its first year. The company was thus able to market its product and expand globally by using the rapid developments on the technology front.

Cost competitiveness

An important internal factor for internationalisation has been the ability to retain cost competitiveness required for global market participation. In the 1980s, when Nike realised that costs were increasing in the US, it closed its US factories and sourced almost all of its production from Asia. In 1982, 86% of Nike's athletic footwear came from Korea and Taiwan and were marketed across the world. Microsoft Corporation could think of developing and marketing gaming gadget Xbox 360 even without having its own manufacturing facility because it could avail cost competitiveness through internationalisation of production. Microsoft simply allowed the product to be manufactured by a specialised contract manufacturer Flextronics in China at a low cost. Xbox 360, thereafter, had tremendous marketing success across the world.

[3] ESPN STAR Sports scores with three-year deal for Spanish La Liga rights, The Business Standard, June, 21, 2011.

Untapped global opportunities

Another external factor behind internationalisation has been the new untapped opportunities present in different countries and interestingly became more pronounced due to the efforts of internationalising companies only. Indian cellular phone operator Bharti Airtel scripted a new chapter in its internationalisation drive by extending its mobile network across 15 new countries in Africa. This move truly heralded the arrival of Bharti Airtel on the global telecom map. It transformed Bharti Airtel into a truly global corporation making it the fifth-largest telecom company in the world, covering over 1.8 billion people across South Asia and Africa.[4]

Technological competence

The technological competence achieved by certain companies is another reason behind rapid internationalisation. These companies have developed strong products or technology that the local competitors are unable to match and hence different market required them. The Scandinavian company Tetra Pak is successfully demonstrating this phenomenon. "Individually, our new technological competence will bring tremendous benefits to our customers, while collectively, they signal a new era in terms of cost, efficiency and environmental performance," quipped Michael Grosse, Executive Vice President, Development and Service Operations, Tetra Pak.[5] He was talking about a new technology developed by the company for enhancing the efficiency and performance of packaging operations. The serial unfolding of new technologies allowed the company to come close to the customers irrespective of its country of origin in a sustainable manner. This has helped them to gain a decisive competitive edge in a world of fast-changing demands and ever-higher expectations.

Entrepreneur's aspiration

Small- and medium-sized companies, in the initial phase of internationalisation, depend more on the entrepreneur's aspiration and dream to be global. Suzlon, the Indian company, began its home country operations in the wind power sector in 1995 with only 20 persons on its pay roll. By 2011, Suzlon had become a global brand with 10,500 turbines and more than 15 gigawatts (GW) of installed capacity in 25 countries due to the push and sheer spirit of entrepreneurship shown by its CEO Tulsi Tanti.

INTERNATIONALISATION AND MARKETING

Whatever may be reasons that encouraged these companies to explore international markets, there is one common ultimate action for all when they are international. All of them needed to market their products/services in the acutely competitive 'market place' by adopting the right marketing strategy. The market place, means here, may have its range of geographical spread from a few foreign countries to all the countries of the world. Companies of different sizes with varied products would be striving to develop right

[4] Annual report of Bharti Airtel, 2012

[5] http://www.tetrapak.com/about_tetra_pak/press_room/news/Pages/new_technologies.aspx

marketing programmes to win over targeted customers living in that target market place. To make things more difficult for them, there would be a number of local companies ready to compete with the foreign companies and drive them out of their countries. Ironically, the local consumers may have more preference for the local producers and even the locals can get local government patronage. The question arises how then the internationalising companies would design their marketing programmes in the midst of such competition? What type of marketing strategy would best suit them? What problems would they generally encounter while designing marketing programmes for multi-country market participation? Is it possible to design a common standardised programme for all the country markets but without compromising with the consumer preferences of individual countries? Or is it wiser to follow 'horses for the courses' policy and resort to different marketing programmes for different countries? If it requires arriving at a trade-off point between these two extremes, then how that point would be decided? What would be the benefits if the company's marketing programme tilts heavily towards standardisation? These are the questions associated with internationalisation required to be understood. This chapter, therefore, introduces readers to the different types of marketing behaviour possible to be exhibited by companies at different stages of internationalisation indicating merits, demerits, and requirements.

MARKETING: THE BASIC TASK

The basic marketing task of a company, whether in the domestic market or in the global markets, is to create customer value. Customer value is defined as the sum total of benefits (economic, functional, and psychological), which a vendor promises a customer will receive in return for the customer's associated payment or other value-transfer (time, effort, and psychological). It is to be understood that when a company enters a market, it becomes imperative that the company has designed its marketing programme in such a manner that it will be able to create the desired customer value better than the competitors in the same market for the target customers. The company needs to base its strategies on customers' preferences to do this. A customer's perceived benefits of a product would come from all the benefits that the customer is expecting from the product as well as in consideration of all the costs associated with the offering and the perceived alternatives. Formally, it may be conceptualised as the relationship between the consumer's perceived benefits, which include functional, social, and hedonic benefits in relation to the perceived costs of receiving these benefits. The perceived benefits are, therefore, relative and subjective involving a whole spectrum of human behavioural aspects towards human value formation. The customer value is often expressed as the ratio of perceived benefits to perceived sacrifice that is involved in getting the product or service. This relationship can be better understood with the help of the following equation.

$$\text{Customer Value} = \frac{\text{Perceived benefits} - \text{Perceived cost}}{\text{Price}}$$

The perceived cost is the price that the consumer is expected to pay for getting the product. A product that is available easily would have less perceived cost for the customers as it is very easy to buy. Thus, the above equation indicates that a marketer has to keep in mind that the price of the product as the denominator of the equation always put pressure on the numerator of the equation to be correspondingly high so that the customer value is increased. It is easy to understand that a marketer will not be able to increase customer value of all the people living in that country or of all the people living in its target country markets with the same marketing strategy. Therefore, the requirement of creating consumer segments comes in to play. The segment could be a group of consumers living in a country or in countries but having the same taste, choice or preferences. The marketer on entry to the new market would need to identify a suitable segment to target and then position the product accordingly to create customer value keeping in mind that the cost of the product will always be there to pull down the customer value creation process as the denominator of the equation. This process is very complicated in the international market as the marketers need to have a clear knowledge of the consumer base and the consumer requirements for that particular category of the product in the country entered into. The selection of the right segment will allow the marketers to position the product and create customer value in the desired way. In addition, the pricing may be comparatively higher in foreign country markets than the domestic one because of transportation, logistics and other costs, which may again put pressure on customer value creation. The customer value creation process, therefore, requires a clear answer for the following questions:

- Who are the customers of the product?
- What are their requirements in terms of different benefits derived from the product?
- What is offered to them?
- What is the distribution channel used?
- How are products priced?
- How is the customer interface managed?
- How are customers served?
- How are customers sustained?

THE STANDARDISATION APPROACH

There have been many discussions over how a company can create customer value in distant foreign markets while internationalising its activities. Many leading thinkers advocated that a new marketing strategy needs to be introduced since a new group of customers are encountered in foreign markets. Theodore Levitt, an American economist and professor at the Harvard Business School, proposed the main argument in favour of the standardisation approach. In his article *The Globalisation of Markets* published in the *Harvard Business Review* in 1983, Professor Levitt argued that the forces of globalisation driven by technology were homogenising the taste, preference and choice of consumers irrespective of the country they belong.[6] Based on

[6] Levitt, T. (1983), "The globalisation of markets", Harvard Business Review, Vol. 61 No. 3, pp. 92-102.

this belief, he literally blamed American multinational businesses for not understanding the same and suggested that marketers need to take advantage of this trend by following a standardised marketing strategy irrespective of the countries that they market their products in. He argued that products perceived as 'classy' such as Monalisa type artefacts, and products strongly associated with the 'country of origin' like Channel perfumes from France or Havana cigars from Cuba can create customer value in an identical way in different countries. The international marketers, therefore, do not require different marketing programme for different country markets. The same is the marketing wisdom for the 'high-tech' products like hybrid vehicles from the Toyota Motor Corporation, smart TV from Sony, etc. Products such as the hybrid cars or LED Smart TV are being marketed worldwide by the concerned companies using a standardised marketing programme. In a sense, the state-of-the art technology itself maximises the customer value and hence international marketers do not need to develop different marketing programme for different markets. Industrial products, where consumers are industries, usually fall in this category and hence candidate for identical marketing programme while marketed worldwide. Products other than 'classy', 'high-tech' and 'industrial', therefore, possibly are candidate for differential marketing programme for different countries. However, if these mass market products are marketed by considering Prof. Levitt's hypothesis of market homogenisation happened due to the forces of globalisation, then the companies can market them with identical marketing programme for various countries. This marketing strategy will also bring additional benefits to the companies with vast multinational presence as they will be able to save considerable amount of money being incurred for country-specific adaptation of the marketing mix. This saving will help them either to reduce prices of the products being marketed or they can be purposefully utilised to enhance the quality of the products further.

Professor Levitt was a staunch believer of homogenisation of the world and hence, according to him, international marketers can consider the world to be flat in terms of tastes, choices, preferences, etc., and hence, mass market products can also be marketed like class market products. He also believed that as civilisation progressed and globalisation became forceful, the ugly face of country culture is no longer creating deep impact on consumers' taste, choice, and preference. Hence, according to Professor Levitt, marketing with globally standardised marketing programme would create an ideal environment for achieving economies of scale. The international company by producing standardised products and marshalling standardised marketing mix elements for a large number of consumers across the world would almost enjoy a mass production scenario accompanied by reduced cost of production. The economies of scale, achieved in this way, would help companies to become more competitive in foreign markets because it would facilitate them to market products of the same or better quality at lower prices. Professor Levitt urged US multinational companies to follow the standardisation approach while deciding on their marketing strategy for countries abroad. He even cursed the US multinationals for not allowing their company to attain scale economics by treading too much on the line of country–specific adaptations of marketing programme and thereby spending more and wasting American stake holders' money.

THE ADAPTATION APPROACH

It did not take a long time for critics to challenge Theodore Levitt's hypothesis of a homogenised world. A number of academicians wrote about the requirement of an adaptation approach as they felt that the world had not been homogenised in the way Professor Levitt imagined. The basic tenets of the adaptation approach, propagated by many writers in response to Professor Levitt's pro standardisation arguments, may be summarised as follows:

- All countries have not been affected equally by globalisation. So, marked differences continue to exist in terms of tastes, preferences and choice of products in different countries.
- Tastes and preferences vary even within the European Union in spite of economic integration. Therefore, a marketer will not be able to adopt a standardised marketing strategy. For instance, the Germans would look to buy a technically correct cars while the French people inherently more akin to buy car that provided them with amusement, fun, etc.
- The gains achieved through economies of scale may not be high enough to provide a competitive edge in the market place and hence cannot be the deciding factor against the adaptation approach.
- The standardisation approach can not cover whole of the world. At best a company can market in a niche segment of few countries in this way. For example, an apparel company can design its marketing mix for the teenagers of India, Pakistan and Bangladesh but the same marketing mix cannot be extended to Thailand or China because of difference in tastes, choices and preferences.
- The economic differences that exist in the world influence the marketing strategy of a company. Coca Cola cannot market its products in Burkina Faso as well as in Luxembourg in an identical way because of the stark economic differences that exist between these two countries. Burkina Faso is one of the poorest countries in the world with an average income per capita of US$300 where as Luxembourg is one of the richest country of the world with average income per capita of US$81,000. This economic difference brought about differences in customer preferences.
- Along with the economic factors, marketers also need to consider country-specific cultural factors. Sometimes, cultural factors are so deep-rooted that the marketing communication positioned to change cultural stereotypes often fall flat. For example, the American multinational cereal company Kellogg's could not replace the traditional breakfast menu of *Rotis* and *Idlis* in India with cornflakes in spite of its aggressive marketing communication campaign.
- The legal and political situation in many countries forces marketers to adapt the marketing mix in accordance with the system. A company is bound to abide by country-specific advertising laws, product labelling and packaging requirements in its marketing communication campaigns. The volatile political situation in some countries forces companies to resort to unique marketing strategies different from the strategies used in politically risk-free countries. For instance, many companies had to restrict their marketing programmes in politically volatile Venezuela and North Korea.

Box 1.1 Has Levitt gone wrong ? KFC experience in India.

India and China were the two markets selected by KFC, the US-based chain of restaurants when it planned its market expansion in Asia. KFC opened its first western-style, quick-service restaurant in the Chinese capital city of Beijing in 1987. By 2001, there were more than 500 KFC outlets throughout China. By 2012, KFC had celebrated the opening of its 4000th restaurant in China.

In contrast, KFC's market expansion in India took off rather slowly. KFC opened its first store in Bengaluru in1985. As of 2012, KFC had about 250 restaurants in India with a target of 550 outlets by 2015. However, KFC has a greater number of outlets in many smaller countries of Asia such as Malaysia, Indonesia and Thailand when compared to India. Was the opening up of the comparatively fewer number of outlets in India linked to the food habits of Indian people and market conditions in India? There is no doubt that there is a sizeable base of Indian customers who are die-hard fans of the chicken dishes introduced by KFC. A large number of first-time Indian customers visit KFC outlets with the predetermined mindset of eating non-vegetarian dishes only. But there also exists a large population in India who still avoid restaurants like KFC for want of vegetarian food served there. Many Indians felt that KFC was not a suitable place for dining out with family because of the lack of choice in vegetarian dishes.

KFC did not have to deal with this issue while expanding its outlets in China or Thailand. The company realised quite early on that its stance on vegetarian food would play a big role in its overall strategy for market expansion in India. KFC's strategy became clear when it started aggressively expanding into Tier 2 and Tier 3 markets such as Guntur, Vijayawada and Visakhapatnam in the south and Guwahati, Siliguri and Asansol in the east. In order to make the KFC brand relevant to all Indians and woo the vegetarian customers, KFC expanded its menu of vegetarian dishes. The company invested in a comprehensive ad campaign focused on the vegetarian dishes on its menu. It added new vegetarian items like Potato Krisper (a potato patty and vegetables filled in a large bun), Twisters (wraps) and salads to its menu. Special efforts were made to earn the trust of vegetarian customers in cities with a predominantly vegetarian population like Ahmedabad. Separate kitchens were introduced to cook the vegetarian dishes. Employees in the vegetarian section wore green aprons and even the tongs used were green so as to make them identifiable and exclusive for use in the vegetarian kitchen. Managers at KFC outlets invited customers to tour their kitchen to showcase the efforts put in preparing exclusive Indian vegetarian dishes. The separate queues at the billing counter for vegetarian food also aggressively communicated how mindful the company was towards the sensitivities of Indian vegetarians.

Strategists at KFC are also trying to learn from competitors in their repositioning attempts to please a large section of Indian consumers. Popular local chains like Haldiram, Nirulas and Bikanerwala have a large following among Indian consumers with the wide variety of vegetarian fast food items on offer. International chains like Subway and McDonald's set the example of brand diversions for the Indian market by introducing vegetarian items. McDonald's exhibited this strategy when it introduced items such as McFlurry, McVeggie, McAloo Tikki Burger and McCurry Pan on its menu and scrapped its iconic beef product, the Big Mac to replace it with the Maharaja Mac chicken burger.

KFC has a different challenge in India when compared to its local and international rivals. It is far from easy to claim a position in the list of specialist vegetarian restaurants after being identified with chicken for such a long time. KFC also cannot plough back its learning from its booming operations in other Asian countries like China, Thailand, Indonesia, etc. The company is also aware that customers will not flock to its restaurants just because of the introduction of a few vegetarian dishes on the menu.

Source: The Economic Times Sep 9, 2012

MULTINATIONAL PHASE IN MARKETING

What were the faces of marketing, as a subject of study and practice, in the initial years of its introduction to the world? Way back in 1936 the *Journal of Marketing* came up in USA as the leading journal of the American

Marketing Association and started introducing marketing to the world. But what marketing content it dealt about? Understandably, during the World War, not much development took place in developing and put forwarding marketing as a discipline of study. Again after the Second World War, a vast majority of the world's nations including all the great powers were busy in reconstruction from damages inflicted during the wars. After the war ended in 1945, the US was found to be at the forefront of the reconstruction activities and even took charge of development of other war devastated nations. The famous General Douglas MacArthur was sent to Japan by the US to take up the work of reconstruction of the war-devastated country. The *Journal of Marketing* during this phase published articles mostly on the importance on post-war planning. A content analysis of 327 articles published in the *Journal of Marketing* during 1939–46 revealed that the majority of articles were on post-war planning, i.e., proposals for marketing's role in preparing for the post-war economy at the firm, community and national levels.[7]

As the world started recovering from the bad effects of the war, in general, Western Europe and America put extra emphasis on the reconstruction of production plant and related infrastructure. International trade which only grew at the rate 0.5% annually between 1913 and 1948 started expanding in the post-war period as many countries, evolving out of the war damage, considered it important for national development. As a result, the volume of international commerce grew at an annual rate of 7% from 1948 to 1973 registering a faster rate than the global economic output.[8]

American companies started showing inclination for expanding their business overseas to take advantage of their comparatively better off position, and hence, their internationalisation subsequently led to the formation of American multinational corporations. These multinational corporations earned their definition as "business organisations whose activities are located in more than two countries through the incorporation and establishment of branches or subsidiaries in foreign countries through foreign direct investment". This brigade of young American multinationals began their journey of exploring foreign markets initially through exports. Later, international divisions were created in the organisational structure to take care of customer requirements in foreign markets and increasing volume of export. The international divisions were responsible for selling products that were manufactured in US primarily based on home country requirements. The US made products used to be exported to the foreign countries and international divisions had the task of maturing sales in target countries at a price calculated on the basis of internal transfer price. In other words, the international division in foreign country used to act as buyer of the products from headquarter in America at a market rate and then added profit mark up, cost of handling, etc., and to sell it further in respective countries. As the sales volume increased with the passage of time and competition brewed up from the local manufacturers, the multinationals felt the need of addressing the customers' requirements of different countries differently. This made them involved in organisational restructuring leading to creation of region-specific

[7] Savitt, R. (2011), "What they wrote about World War II: the Journal of Marketing 1939-1946", 2011 CHARM proceedings.

[8] The Challenge of Global Capitalism The World Economy in the 21st Century By Robert Gilpin and Jean Millis Gilpin, Princeton University Press.

or country-specific area divisions. Area divisions started behaving as individual organisations as if not in any way connected with the parent organisation in USA. The area divisions would not be expecting to get business supports, financial, or marketing from headquarter. It was the responsibility of each division to scan the local environment correctly and device country-specific marketing strategy. There was absolutely no coordination between the different divisions or between divisions and headquarter. Hence, knowledge plough back from different country operation as a whole and dissemination of them amongst different divisions was not there. Multinational corporations, therefore, acted almost as "a group of geographically dispersed and goal disparate organisations that included its headquarters and the different national subsidiaries."[9] Multinational marketing, predominant after World War II, was focussing on marketing to multiple countries through the adaptation of products, services, and other aspects of the marketing mix.[10] Considering the evolving nature of marketing as a discipline of study, it is not surprising that the marketing literature of that time reflected the marketing practices of these multinationals. The word 'multinational marketing' was found to be very popular in the contemporary marketing literature to describe the particular types of marketing practices of the American multinationals. The businesses who looked for support to build their international business strategy after World War II took marketing lessons from these articles and were influenced by the adaptation dominance approach of the multinational corporation.

THE CHANGING CONCEPT OF MARKETING

While young multinational organisations in the US and some European countries were adjusting to the challenges of marketing across different and environmentally dissimilar countries of the world, marketing management as a subject was also developing faster to provide academic insight to the marketing requirements of the companies in a competitive and cross-cultural market place. The multinational marketing approach was getting critically evaluated in order to weigh the benefits as well as the drawbacks. It was also understood that days were going out rapidly when products used to attract customer because of sheer need. Also, there was growing realisation that with competition increasing in the world the marketers cannot attract all the customers with equal intensity by a uniform marketing programme. The segmentation, targeting and positioning (STP) strategy was developed in the mid-1950s when Wendell. R. Smith, an American professor of marketing, emphasised on the need to get close to the customer in competitive market. Under this new methodology of STP it was suggested to divide a market into smaller groups of buyers with distinct needs, characteristics, or behaviours, i.e., segment who might require separate products or marketing mixes[11]. Jerome McCarthy, another American marketing professor at Michigan State University came out

[9] Bartlett, C.A., & Ghoshal, S. 1990. Managing innovation in the transnational corporation. In C.A. Bartlett, Y. Doz & G. Hedlund, eds., Managing the global firm, London/New York: Routledge, 215-255.

[10] Global Marketing: Foreign Entry, Local Marketing, and Global Management, Johny K. Johansson.

[11] Product Differentiation and Market Segmentation as Alternative Marketing Strategies Wendell R. Smith *Journal of Marketing* Vol. 21, No. 1 (Jul., 1956), pp. 3-8.

with the concept of the four Ps of marketing, i.e., product, price, place, promotion in marketing during early 1960. During 1964, Neil Borden, professor emeritus of marketing and advertising at the Harvard Business School, promoted the concept of using the four Ps as a recipe and termed that marketers are mixers of ingredients. Almost simultaneously came the techniques of capturing prospective consumers' preferences through perceptual map and positioning of product accordingly. Phillip Kotler, the marketing guru, came out with his classic textbook *Marketing Management* in 1967, which focused on the changing nature of marketing, i.e., from the production-oriented concept to the marketing-oriented concept.

Robert D. Buzzell, another professor of marketing at the Harvard Business School, looked beyond border and effectively contributed in developing understanding of the cross border marketers. In his article "Can You Standardise Multinational Marketing" published in the *Harvard Business Review* in 1968, he focused on how marketing would look like in cross-border situations. This article proved to be very useful for multinational corporations who were looking at academicians to expand their knowledge and give more insights about the issues in multinational marketing. Eventually his paper was in full agreement with the multinational marketers with emphasis on the point that international marketers can win over country markets through localisation of marketing programme. This, in a sense, justified the "think local, act local" type of marketing strategy practiced by the then multinational companies. This article of Prof. Buzzel published during 1967 along with the article of Prof. Levitt published during 1983 set the two extremes of international marketing strategy for the companies—multinational marketing in line with Prof. Buzzell's hypothesis and global marketing in line with Prof. Levitt's hypothesis. Companies can practice "multinational marketing" following Prof. Buzzell's prescription or can align with 'global marketing' following Prof. Levitt's prescription (Table 1.1).

However, companies have the liberty to shift from one extreme to another, i.e., in a continuum from multinational type of marketing to global type of marketing or vice versa and set their own marketing programme based on internal and external requirements. The external environment pertains to the socio-cultural, political-legal, economic factors, etc., of the target countries covered on which company has no effective control. The internal factors pertain to the company's internal strength like management ability,

Table 1.1 Two extremes of marketing internationally

S. No.	Robert D. Buzzell on international marketing: Multinational marketing	Theodor Levitt on international marketing: Global marketing
1.	Think local, act local as world is not homogenised in terms of people's choice, taste, preference.	Think global, act global as world is fast getting homogenised in terms of people's choice, taste, preference.
2.	Required country specific adaptation of marketing programme as macro environment of one country is different than other.	Required a global standard of marketing programme as macro environment of the countries are fast getting homogenised due to globalisation.
3.	Countries have national culture and consumers are culture bound.	Countries national culture can be overcome by marketing programme.
4.	Customer value creation is primarily essential for multinational companies to attain competiveness.	Economy of scale is primarily essential for multinational companies to attain cost effectiveness and competiveness.

international exposure, degree of rigidity of production system, etc., which are largely under company's control.

YIP'S DRIVERS OF GLOBALISATION

So far, we have understood that the standardisation/adaptation debate has divided international businesses and their marketing into two segments: one, those companies who believe and practice marketing in a standardised way across the different countries that they are involved in; and two, those companies who adapt their marketing strategy based on the local environment of the countries in which they operate in. It is also clear that these companies may change their marketing strategy over the course of time based on their practical requirements.

In 1992, George Yip developed a tool that companies can use to understand their potential for global marketing. Yip's model came as a relief to cross-border marketers trapped between the two extremes in a continuums created by the two professors—Buzzell and Levitt—as it helped them understand their position with respect to the applicability of global marketing. This model enables marketers to understand the potential for globalisation in the industry in which the company is engaged in. A global marketing strategy could be followed by the company if there is a trend towards globalisation. If the trend is towards localisation, the business has limited options and may have to practice multinational marketing or close to that.

In order to understand the potential for globalisation in an industry, it is required to analyse five main categories of globalisation drivers (see Figure 1.1). These drivers are: (1) market drivers; (2) cost drivers; (3) government

FIGURE 1.1 Yip's drivers of globalisation

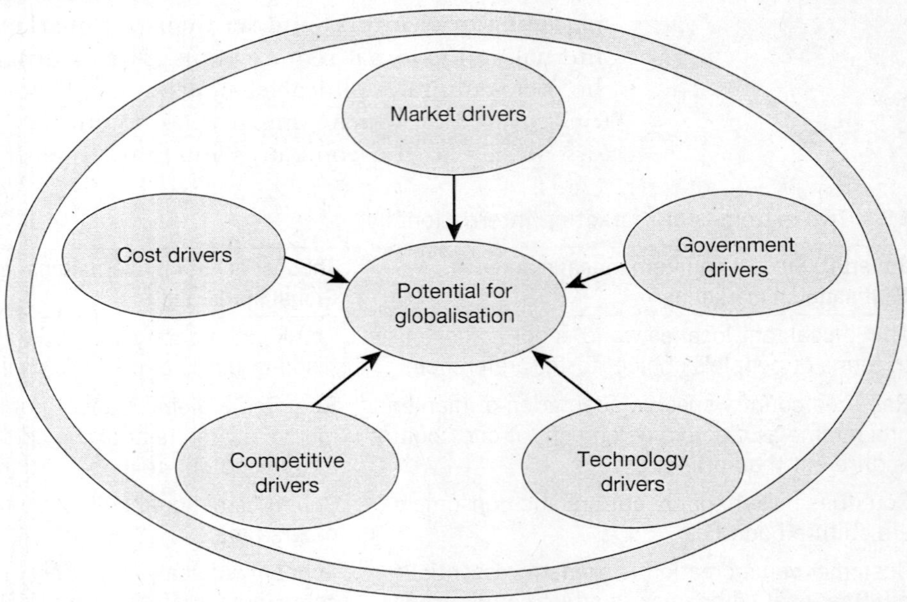

drivers; (4) technology drivers and (5) competitive drivers. The strength and effect of each globalisation driver vary across industries and country markets, thus, influencing the type of marketing that can be best practiced. The five globalisation drivers are explained in detail in the following sections.

Market Drivers

Customer needs are converging very fast across many countries of the world. This is becoming possible because people living there are continuously getting exposed to global standards through globally networked and homogenised media. The isolations existed previously are over due to globalisation. Now the customers across the globe are increasingly coming out of confinements previously created by country-specific variables such as cultural, disposable incomes, consumption habit, etc. All-round changes are being noticed in their behaviour. They are now fast coming out of the stereotypes and embracing global standard. For example, pizzas and burgers were never been in Indian food menu but now even the urban elderly people in India seem to be fond of burgers and pizzas. The Peking duck, a famous duck dish from Beijing and considered the national dish of China, is now popular in many other countries. This dish which received the patronage of the former US Secretary of State Dr Kissinger is now an important item in many restaurants in the US. The Japanese rice wine *Sake* is now popular in the US and Bourbon whisky of the US is now a hot favourite with the Japanese. The Spanish Paella, a very popular dish from Spain, is no longer confined to Spain only but permeated in many other countries and including many restaurants in India (Figure 1.2). Table 1.2 describes the market drivers and their influence on decision making regarding the type of marketing practice ranging from multinational to global. The more the drivers are favouring more will be more the companies will be tilted towards global marketing and vice versa.

FIGURE 1.2 Spanish Paella

Customers are now exposed to well converged standard products regularly because they have access to the outlets of global retailers such as Walmart of the US, Carrefour of France, Metro of Germany

Table 1.2 Market drivers for global marketing

Marker drivers deciding type of marketing	Towards global marketing
Customer need	Look out if the customers are with standard needs and wants. If the needs are converging to a global standard it will be favourable for global marketing. The reverse will take the company to multinational type of marketing.
Channel	Look out if customers' have easy access to global channels of distribution like supermarkets, hypermarkets, etc., then it makes a case favourable for global marketing. The reverse will take the company to multinational type of marketing.
Marketing	Look out if the customers of different countries can be exposed to same marketing strategy in terms of advertising, brand name, etc. Non transferable marketing strategy will take the company to multinational type of marketing.
Countries	Look out if the customers' of lead country have accepted the product. If lag country market acceptances are more then it will be inclination towards multinational marketing.

and 7-Eleven of Japan across the world. Thailand alone has more than 6300 7-Eleven convenience stores with half of them operating in Bangkok city. Advertisers can now run the same advertisement campaign in different countries because of the similar level of understanding among the target customers. More penetration of global channels across the world more will be the urge for global marketing for companies. Marketing strategies that can be transferred to different countries without adaptation is a good sign for resorting to global marketing. This can be practiced by companies participating in the lead country markets with products and successful in getting customers attention. For gaming gadgets lead country markets is Japan where products are experiencing comparatively shorter product life cycle because of acute competition and innovations. In the same way, lag countries are those where marketers can expect a comparatively longer life for their products. Any gaming gadget producing company with marketing success in Japan will not be hesitating to standardise that marketing strategy across other countries but same thing would be difficult for a company participating in lag country markets. The same thing can be said for computer software producers and getting success in its lead country India and thereafter standardise that marketing strategy for rest of the world.

Cost Drivers

Consideration of cost of production could be indicative of type of marketing practice to be resorted by a company. If a company is desperate to achieve economies of scale in production to reduce unit cost of production to become competitive then it would show tendency for global marketing (Table 1.3). The company would expand to cover a larger market and marketing products without much differentiation. This is particularly true when a company operates with high fixed costs. In order to break even early, sales volume will have to be increased proportionally. In this situation, a single country market may not be enough to ensure sufficient sales volume and it becomes important for the company to expand to a large number of countries. For example, companies manufacturing Dynamic Random Access Memory (DRAM) chips used in personal computers have to achieve higher sales volume because of the high fixed cost associated with its production. Characteristically, the highly technology-driven DRAM industry (semi-conductor) has short product cycles but with high fixed costs associated with manufacturing. As the requirement of density (storage capacity) of DRAM increases with the decrease in size of the equipments (chip), the cost required for manufacturing increases. The investment for manufacturing 1GB (gigabit) DRAM (storage capacity is measured by kilobit, megabit, gigabit) was USD 2.5 billion for companies like Samsung of Korea, which was 7.1 times higher than the investment required for 1MB (megabit) DRAM. Samsung had to focus on improving sales through worldwide marketing to cover the high fixed costs associated with the short product cycles.[12]

[12] Kang Joonkyu, "A Study of DRAM industry" Unpublished masters dissertation at the Massachusetts Institute of Technology, 2010.

Table 1.3 Cost drivers for global marketing

Cost drivers deciding type of marketing	Towards global marketing
Economies of scale	Look out if lower cost of production is desperately needed to be achieved through economies of scale then it makes a case favourable for global marketing. If fixed cost of doing business is high as exemplified in case of semi conductor manufacturing, then there will be inclination towards global marketing. In the same way, low fixed cost may provoke multinational marketing.
Economies of scope	Look out if the company can achieve substantial competitive advantage through economy of scope then that would provide push for global marketing. For example, Inter Globe Enterprise was in hurry to economise scope to gain competitive advantage in Indian civil aviation industry sector. If the company not much interested to achieve economy of scope, then there will be inclination for multinational marketing.
Sourcing advantage	Look out if the company can achieve lower cost of production through strategic global sourcing of raw material and intermediate products with efficient supply chain integration, then that would push the company towards standardisation and global marketing. Company indifferent to use global sourcing, may be due to reciprocal interdependence in the production process, would have the option to push the company towards multinational type of marketing.

A related diversification of the product line provides economies of scope, i.e., the lowering of the average cost by producing more than one product. In this case, a company can use its various facilities, tangible or intangible, created for a product to develop other products also. InterGlobe Enterprises, a USD 1.25 billion Indian company in the aviation sector, first shot to fame because of the successful operations of its domestic airline, Indigo, in a highly competitive sector. The company quickly jumped to other businesses across various industries—hospitality, luxury, information technology, and travel—by the smart and efficient use its tangible and intangible resources. Established in 1989, with headquarters in Gurgaon (India) InterGlobe now has a network of 126 offices across 59 cities globally.

Sourcing raw material and intermediate products globally through supply chain integration and modularisation of sourced products can be an important cost driver towards achieving lower cost of production. This tendency would push the company towards standardisation and global marketing. This influence is noticeable in marketing strategy of Nike. This American company was confronted with the short product cycles and volatile fashion trends in the apparels business. Nike, in its desperation to reduce cost of production, started sourcing the different components from countries to be used in the final product. Product design came from USA, zipper from Japan, shell from Korea, lining from Taiwan, lebel, elastic, studs, toggle, string from Hong Kong and finally assembled in China to produce athletic jackets. It orchestrated nicely the sourcing process for the contract manufacturer to produce standardised product to be marketed across the globe.

Government Drivers

Three important factors under government drivers like economic policy of the host country, technical standards applied to products and the stringency of marketing regulations influence the marketing strategies of a company operating in a foreign country. A foreign company can transfer its standardised

Table 1.4 Government drivers for global marketing

Government drivers deciding type of marketing	Towards global marketing
Economic policy	Look out if the countries of presence are open and providing equal treatment to the foreign companies allowing seamless transfer of standard marketing practice then it makes a case for global marketing practice. The reverse would push for multinational marketing.
Technical Standards	Look out if technical standards are uniform in the countries of presence that would provide scope for marketing programme standardisation then it would make a favourable case for global marketing. Otherwise stand alone country specific rigid technical standard would push for multinational marketing.
Marketing regulations	Assess the level of non discriminatory marketing regulations applicable for foreign companies in the countries of presence. If there is high level of non discrimination then it may push for global marketing otherwise a case is built up for multinational marketing.

marketing strategy seamlessly from country to country if the participating countries are open to grant equal rights to the foreign companies under no less favourable term than those available to domestic companies (Table 1.4). The policies of the Indian government towards foreign multi-brand retail ownership put a question mark on the entry of global retailers in India because restricted Indian economic policy will also restrict the companies to transfer their standard successful marketing strategy set to India. Then again stringent marketing regulations enforced on foreign company influences the marketing programme of internati-onal companies. Rigid technical standards may be used by some countries as a means of protecting domestic producers. These countries make these operational by insisting on mandatory product regulations, voluntary product standards and conformity assessment procedures (procedures designed to test a product's conformity with mandatory regulations or voluntary standards). These may create unnecessary obstacles to transfer a successful marketing programme tested in other countries and replicate the same to a new host country.

Box 1.2 Corporate power and free trade agreements

A common element of most international trade agreements is that foreign investors are accorded rights no less favorable than those available to domestic investors. These protections clearly promote foreign investment and can foster economic development. However, some international trade agreements give foreign corporations expansive investment rights unavailable to domestic corporations, and even the power to overrule domestic legislation. Consider the rights granted to foreign investors under the North American Free Trade Agreement (NAFTA) between the United States, Canada, and Mexico. Chapter 11 of NAFTA specifies that no party to the agreement may "nationalise or expropriate an investment" or "take a measure tantamount to nationalisation or expropriation" of a foreign investor without sufficient compensation. While the purpose of this clause appears to be simply to protect foreign investors from seizure of private property, in practice it has had much broader implications: "Since the agreement's enactment corporate investors in all three NAFTA countries have used these new rights to challenge a variety of national, state, and local environmental and public health policies, domestic judicial decisions, a federal procurement law and even a government's provision of parcel delivery services as NAFTA violations. NAFTA permits investors (typically corporations) to sue a host government. In at least 17 cases to date corporations have filed complaints against NAFTA signatories under the Chapter 11 provisions, most of these claiming economic losses related to environmental regulations. In the first claim under Chapter 11 in 1996, the US- based Ethyl Corporation claimed that Canada's proposed ban on the import of the gasoline additive MMT constitutec expropriation. Ethyl Corp. was the world's only producer of MMT, which contains manganese, a known human neurotoxin that has been banned in several US states. The case was settled in 1998 when Canada paid Ethyl Corp. $13 million, withdrew the ban, and published a letter stating that there was no scientific evidence of harmful human health effects from MMT.

The case demonstrated that a foreign corporation could force a national government to change its environmental policies in the interest of free trade. While not all Chapter 11 cases have resulted in victories for corporations other cases have successfully challenged a Mexican municipality's refusal to grant a construction permit for a hazardous waste site and Canada's ban of PCB exports. While the overall economic and environmental impact of these few Chapter 11 cases is relatively minor, the greater impact may be that national and local regulators are reluctant to set new public safety regulations over concerns about corporate challenges, an effect known as "regulatory chill."

Source: Global Development and Environment Institute, Tufts University, USA available at http://www.ase.tufts.edu/gdae/education_materials/modules/Corporate_Power_in_a_Global_Economy.pdf

Technology Drivers

Technology plays an important role when companies make decisions regarding their marketing strategies for different countries. The main bottleneck for a standardised marketing strategy may be the technology use differences that exist in different countries. A company selling soft drinks in Japan would be relying on automatic vending machines, located even in rural places, to reach the consumers. The same strategy will not hold good for a Japanese company in many of the developing and least developed countries. This will prevent the company from adopting a standardised marketing strategy across the world.

The technology effect may be felt by international businesses when they try to reach potential customers in different countries through a standardised marketing communication strategy. According to a research survey conducted on Internet usage, it was estimated that 40 to 60 million people were online in the U.K. in 1998. The number went up to 605 million in 2003 and almost all the citizens had internet access by 2011. Unilever's worldwide Dove campaign for "real beauty" was a grand success in the U.K. because of the large number of Internet users who could view the video on YouTube. The campaign increased the sales of Dove in the U.K. But the same Internet-based marketing campaign released on YouTube did not increase the sales revenue in a number of countries in Africa because the majority of the population did not have access to the Internet. Along with availability of technology use inclination of people living in a country also influence marketing programme. More the people inclined to use latest technology more will be the possibilities of resorting to global marketing as cited in Table 1.5.

Table 1.5 Technology drivers for global marketing

Technology drivers deciding type of marketing	Towards global marketing
Technology base	Assess the level of technological advancements like spread of internet and telecommunication in the countries of presence and if level is high it makes a case of pursuing global marketing. The reverse makes a case for multinational marketing.
Technology use inclination	Assess the level of inclination amongst the potential customers regarding use latest technology. A high level indicates towards global marketing possibilities. If they are less inclined to use latest technology that would make a case of multinational marketing.

Competitive Drivers

In many industries, a company enters a foreign country simply because its rival has entered the country. The Indian automotive sector is a good example of this theory. The entry and subsequent success of Japan's Suzuki Motor Corporation in India heralded the entry of other automobile companies from Japan and Korea. Suzuki Motor Corporation entered the Indian market in 1983. This was followed by Toyota Motors in 1984 in partnership with DCM Limited, Honda Motors in 1985 in partnership with the Hero Group and Mitsubishi Motors in 1986 partnership with Eicher Motor Limited in 1986. That means that in a short span of time almost all the global players put their foot in Indian soil. This led to a huge competition in the market place where everyone was busy to bring out its best to allure the customer. It further led to the development of a global standard practice based on the marketing trend used by these companies successfully elsewhere (Table 1.6).

GLOBAL CORPORATION

Global corporations are the organisations that market their product or products in a large number of countries by owning and operating business subsidiaries. The terms "multinational companies (MNC)," and "global companies (GC)" are used interchangeably to refer to global marketers. MNCs invest in many other countries but has their headquarters located in respective home countries.

Table 1.6 Competitive drivers for global marketing

Competitive drivers deciding type of marketing	Towards global marketing
Competition base	Assess the competitive base in the countries of presence and if level of presence of global players is high then it makes a case for global marketing. Otherwise, country markets dominated by local players would make a case for multinational marketing.
Intensity of competition	Assess the intensity competition in the countries of presence. In case of lackluster and low level of competition amongst local players the inclination would be multinational marketing. Higher level of competition amongst the global players brings out the best and standardises marketing practice and this again provokes for global marketing.

Global companies have also investment in other countries and have a parent location but not necessarily the global operation is controlled from parent locations. In that sense "transnational company" is better word to designate their complex organisational structure and control. Characteristically, a sufficiently large portion of their revenue (both MNCs and GCs) comes from foreign country operations. MNCs traditionally believe in adapting their products and service to each individual country market and without much inter country linkages in the matter of knowledge sharing, etc. GCs are more strategic in this dimension and allow a great amount of inter country linkages and linkages between country operations and global headquarter intensely developed so that global strategy can be framed with emphasis on volume, cost management and efficiency. International companies (ICs), on the other hand, have a specific home country headquarter from where their business interests in export, import, sales management, etc., are carried out. It may be interesting to note that GCs or the MNCs may have its starting point from ICs and in course of time they differentiated themselves on strategic business purposes in accordance with growth.

The revenue earned by some big companies from their foreign operations are given in Table 1.7

Table 1.7 Global market participation of some companies 2011–12

The companies	Foreign sales (Million USD)	Domestic sales (Million USD)	Ratio: Domestic:Foreign	Employee strength
Exxon Mobil Corporation is engaged in the exploration, production, transportation and sale of crude oil and natural gas and the manufacture, transportation and sale of petroleum products.	316,686	150,343	1:21	82,100
Nokia is a manufacturer of mobile devices, which makes a range of devices for all major consumer segments and offers Internet services that enable people to experience music, maps, media, messaging and games.	49.773	412	1:120	113,562
General Motor is engaged in the worldwide development, production and marketing of cars, trucks and parts.	69.045	81,231	1:0.85	243,000
Ford Motor Company is a producer of cars and trucks. Its business is divided into two sectors: Automotive and Financial Services.	54.138	82,126	1:0.66	164,000
Toyota Motor Corp. designs, manufactures and sells sedans, minivans, compact cars, sport-utility vehicles, trucks and related parts and accessories. The Company also provides financing, vehicle and equipment leasing & certain other financial services.	90.119	135,699	1:0.66	325,905
Siemens AG is engaged in electronics and electrical engineering. The Company's operations are focused on three sectors: Industry, Energy and Healthcare.	46.757	51,878	1:0.90	41,200
Kellogg Company and its subsidiaries are engaged in the manufacture and marketing of ready-to-eat cereal and convenience foods.	4959	8239	1:0.60	NA

(Continued)

Table 1.7 *(Continued)*

The companies	Foreign sales (Million USD)	Domestic sales (Million USD)	Ratio: Domestic:Foreign	Employee strength
The Coca-Cola Co is a manufacturer, distributor and marketer of nonalcoholic beverage concentrates and syrups in the world.	27,843	18,699	1:1.49	146,200
3M Company is a global manufacturer, technology innovator and marketer of a variety of products.	19,583	10,028	1:1.95	84,198
iGATE Computer Systems Ltd provides consulting, technology and business process outsourcing, and product and engineering solutions. Its services include application development and management, verification and validation and IT consulting, among others.	742	17	1:44	18,000

Source: Compiled by author from http://www.advfn.com/exchanges/NYSE/XOM/financials

INTERNATIONALISATION OF MARKETING ACTIVITIES

An important question at this juncture is: "What are the characteristics of the marketing practices followed by ICs, MNCs or the GCs? To what extent do they follow the practice 'think local, act local' or the practice 'think global, act global' or strike a position between the two?" Understandably, in tandem with the pace of spreading their activities globally, marketing practices of the companies looking to expand into foreign country markets have also evolved taking into account the requirements of the countries targeted and marketing goals of the respective companies. This evolution led to the development of different marketing concepts such as multinational marketing, global marketing and international marketing. Each of these concepts relates to the number of countries that the company is focusing on and the nature of the marketing programme exercised. We will be describing them in the following paragraph one by one but starting with the basic domestic marketing to capture their differences and similarities.

Domestic Marketing

This is applicable to a company operating within the domestic market of a country where its products are marketed. So, its local or domestic marketing strategy recognises the necessity to consider local issues so that its objectives are achieved. Therefore, it strives exclusively to maximise the adaptation of a marketing mix best suited for domestic conditions. Hence, the products or services are tailored according to the needs and wants of the domestic consumers only. The characteristics of domestic marketing are as follows:

- The marketing mix is adapted to the situation in the local market.
- Products and services are tailored to the needs of the local market.
- The differences that exist in the domestic market are taken care of.

- The focus is exclusively concentrated within the territory of the national market.
- The marketing mix adopted has no or little influence from other countries.
- The marketing mix is flexible and responds quickly to the changes needed.
- Production centres are located within the country.

International Marketing

This term is applicable to the marketing strategy followed by a company, which caters to the specific needs of a few foreign countries as well as home country. International marketing takes place when a company that is based in home country primarily decides to sell its products in another. It may set up sales offices in the other countries to market products effectively. These offices are totally dependent on the home country headquarter and cannot take vital decision unless authorised by the headquarter. The dominance of the home country office is vividly noticed in marketing programme development and implementation. The home country based headquarter is all powerful and hence retain absolute marketing control even if a reasonable number of countries have already been ventured. The executives sitting in headquarter call the shots by making most of the marketing and business decisions pertaining to the foreign country markets. The international marketing strategist located in the home country, however, recognises the necessity to consider the choice and preferences of the overseas markets. However, differentiating the marketing mix for each country that the company expands into will not be considered seriously for implementation. The company produces homogenised products or services that are best suited to the demands of the target markets as well as home country and attempts to enjoy economy of scale at that level. Therefore, it actively looks out country markets with similarities in needs and wants and then expands across the markets of target countries. Hence, the efforts to synchronise marketing activities between the home country and overseas markets can be noticed. The characteristics of international marketing, briefly, are as follows:

- Standardisation orientation: Marketing programme is primarily standardised to the need of the focused market.
- Product and service orientation: Products and services are primarily made for home country consumers and extended across the target country markets with minor differentiation.
- Management orientation: The similarities of needs and wants that demonstrated by the target country consumers are of primary consideration of the management and basically taken care of in devising marketing programme.
- Headquarter orientation: Home country head quarter is responsible for making all the strategic decisions centrally and extends them to the foreign markets.
- Marketing strategy orientation: The marketing activities are coupled with the strategy used for the home country and largely dependent on the environment of the home country.

- Synchronisation Orientation: Deliberate attempt to make marketing activities synchronised between the home country and overseas markets.
- Production location orientation: Production centre is primarily in home country and even while producing from strategic overseas locations high order of synchronisation with home country could be noticed.

Multinational Marketing

Multinational marketing refers to the type of marketing resorted to by multinational corporations, popularly known as MNCs. The MNCs depend heavily on foreign markets for their sales and profits. The MNCs focus on marketing to multiple countries through adaptation of products, services, and other aspects of the marketing mix. Relatively little coordination across markets used to be made as each foreign market was looked at as unique and separate. Multinational marketing, briefly, has the following characteristics:

- Standardisation orientation: The marketing programme is primarily oriented to the needs of the each of the focused markets with polycentric orientation, i.e., each market is different in terms of marketing requirements. Hence, negligible standardisation efforts.
- Product and service orientation: Products and services are conveniently modified for each of the target markets as per actual requirements.
- Headquarter orientation: Strategic marketing decisions are not made at the headquarters but are delegated to the respective countries in which the company operates. Almost total decentralisation except some fundamental matter like yearly financial budgeting and annual reporting of profitability.
- Marketing strategy orientation: The marketing strategies are not synchronised across different countries but are largely independent and country specific. Hence, hardly any knowledge transfer between the organisation to subsidiary or subsidiary to subsidiary takes place. Marketing strategies are flexible too and can be altered according to the specific needs of the respective countries in which the company operates.
- Management orientation: Management thinking is oriented to reap the benefits from the differences that exist in the target markets.
- Synchronisation Orientation: No deliberate attempt to synchronise marketing activities between the home country and overseas markets.
- Production location orientation: Production centres are decentralised and are generally located in respective countries in which the company operates. It does not give much importance of economies of scale but rather strongly believes that extensive differentiation of product and services would suffer from production centralisation.

Global Marketing

Global marketing involves standardisation of marketing program and marketing process and aims at the coordination and integration of marketing approaches across the different markets that a company operates in. The term "program" has an obvious reference to various aspects of the marketing mix while "process" implies operational methods used in program development and implementation. Global marketing is defined by the Oxford University Press as "marketing on a worldwide scale reconciling or taking commercial advantage of global operational differences, similarities and opportunities in order to meet global objectives." Global marketing and multi-domestic marketing or multinational marketing are the two extremes of the marketing continuum while international marketing hangs between the two with the possibility of tilting either way by scaling or de-scaling its operational characteristics.

A company is said to adopt a global marketing strategy when it looks at the entire world as one market, i.e., geo centric orientation. Companies resorting to global marketing take a global view of the country markets where local market and the markets faraway almost considered the same in terms of consumers' requirements. The marketing strategy will not try to adapt to any country specific requirements rather it will try to make consumers behave in accordance with its globally standardised one. Therefore, companies that select global marketing go in for standard products, packaging, identical tag lines and brand names and similar advertising messages and as well as their execution. The knowledge sharing and coordination across the country units is also very high under this type of marketing. Therefore, the global marketing has the following characteristics:

- Standardisation orientation: The marketing programmes are primarily standardised at all levels to reap the benefits of economies of scale.
- Product and service orientation: Products and services are not modified in accordance with any country specific requirements but they are standardised as per global standard.
- Management orientation: Management thinking is oriented to reap the benefits from the similarity and convergence of taste and preferences that exist in the target markets. Management also get actively involved to create homogeneity in the country markets to reap marketing benefits.
- Synchronisation Orientation: Deliberate strategic attempt to synchronise different activities such as R&D, marketing innovations, production supply chain, etc., to take synergistic advantages.
- Marketing strategy orientation: A single and globally focused marketing strategy is considered important for the company. Hence efforts are made to achieve synchronisation across the countries of its presence. It is not possible to respond quickly to country-specific situations. The marketing decisions reflects collective wisdom of different countries and synergistic in nature.
- Headquarter orientation: Strategic marketing decisions are made at the headquarters. A strong headquarter manned with different discipline experts takes the responsibility of decision making voluntarily.
- Production location orientation: Production centres and activities are generally integrated, though located in countries of strategic significance. The production centres are deliberately fed with knowledge collected from

different countries of operation in a systematic way for product and process innovation.

INTERNATIONALISATION VERSUS MARKET PARTICIPATION

A company's sojourn in international market may go through a process from limited market participation to a large number of country markets. It may keep on increasing amount of revenue earned from foreign operations in phases unless it is a born global company who takes birth from foreign country only. The percentage of revenue earned from a company's foreign operations out of its total (Foreign Sales to Total Sales or FSTS) is a good indicator of its internationalisation status. Consider a company A that earns 25% of its revenue from its international operations in ten different countries. Another company B operates only in five countries but earns more than 75% of its revenue from its foreign operations. Both the companies have almost the same amount of total revenue. Which one is more internationalised is a very interesting question to be asked. If percentage of revenue earned out of the total revenue is to be believed then Company B is more internationalised.

Company	Revenue earned in percentage		Revenue earned (Million INR)	No. of country participated
	Home	Foreign		
A	75%	25%	100	10
B	25%	75%	100	5

Who is in a better position to practice global marketing strategy or simply global marketing? The company B who earns more revenue from foreign operation out of its total or A who has more market participation? Answering the question seems to be difficult at this stage. Therefore, another pertinent question is: at which stage of internationalisation does company resort to global marketing practice? As Yip put it, "global level of market participation requires significant global market share, a reasonable balance between the businesses' geographic spread and the market's spread and presence in globally strategic country markets."[13]

The presence of a company in the global strategic markets for the relevant category of business, therefore, is a vital requirement for global marketing. The company B, though it earns a bulk chunk of revenue from foreign operation may simply lacks in terms global market share as wells as critical balance between geographic spread and market's spread. One can simply say that B is more internationalised than A but yet to be fit for resorting to global marketing strategy. Global marketing is best suited for companies having global strategic market participation. According to Yip, a high global market share is important but not the most important requirement for market participation with global marketing strategy. There is a business need for a global company to ensure that its geographic distribution of revenues is reasonably balanced in the worldwide market, i.e., the revenue earned is not coming from just a

[13] Yip, George in 'Total Global Strategy II' Englewood Cliffs, NJ: Prentice Hall, 1992.

FIGURE 1.3 Market participation continuum

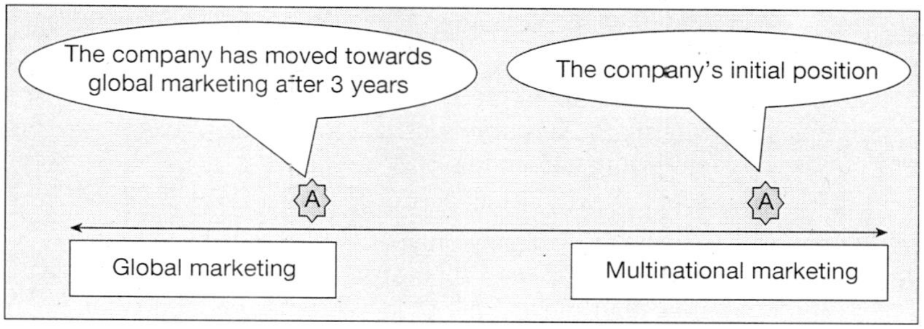

few countries or concentrated and its market share in each country is not too different from its global market share. In other words, the company has almost a market leader like dominance in each participating country. This indicates its capacity as superior marketer to handle dissimilar markets and large market share indicates the outcome. These conditions are extremely important in order to fully benefit from a global marketing strategy. It is understandable that a company comes through different stages of internationalisation before reaching to the global status. At different stages it might have required different approaches of marketing characteristically different but falls anywhere within large variety possible starting from multinational marketing in one end to global marking at the other to optimise its benefits from internationalisation. For example, in the Figure 1.3 above, the company A was practicing marketing which was close to multinational type of marketing with emphasis on country specific adaptation of marketing programme to a great extent in the initial stage. The company A was losing scale economy because of practicing different things for different markets. But subsequently it changed its marketing style and efforts to satisfy customers' need uniformly and hence after three years moved up the scale to some extent towards global marketing but still a long way to go before becoming fully global as shown in the Figure 1.3.

BENEFITS OF GLOBAL MARKETING

In global marketing situation, three important aspects company built in to become competitive in the global market.

1. Economy of scale: Producing similar items more in number reduces per unit cost of production. Reduction of cost of production helps to gain competitive advantage.
2. Economy of scope: Maximising the use of scopes (facilities) created for production and marketing again increases competitiveness of the company. For example, the state of the art leather design centre created in Italy is being used by the company's ten production locations in different countries. This helps in economisation of scope and operating cost reduction.

Table 1.8 Benefits from global marketing

Benefits	Types of marketing and benefits		
	International marketing	**Multinational marketing**	**Global marketing**
Cost advantage	Stand-alone expansion in international markets retards the possibility of achieving economies of scale.	Not much inclination to achieve economies of scale.	International expansion remains largely strategic only to take advantage of economies of scale.
Quality Advantage	Since the company only participate in less competitive countries so the products are not the best in the world in terms of quality.	Different country specific quality standards.	The company is expected to participate in the lead country market. Hence the products are of global standard in terms of quality.
Learning plough back advantage	Only learning from domestic market taken care of. Also ignore the new learning.	The learning from other country operation are not shared.	The leanings from different countries are synthesised purposefully and disseminated across the organisation to get the plough back advantage subsequently. Different country subsidiaries use this learning to get marketing benefits.
Competitive advantage	Face stiff competition from global companies as well as local companies in other country markets. Basically use home grown solutions to fight competition.	Fight out competition from local companies with localisation strategy. But feel helpless against competition from global companies.	Since competitive strategies are globally coordinated, it is possible to tackle competitors with built in globalness.
Scope advantage	Home country based scope advantage only. Limited market participation does not allow much use of scope advantage.	Negligible scope advantage is sought for as there are minimal cross-country interactions.	Conscientious efforts are made to strategically create different facilities so that the entire organisation benefits from them.

3. Learning plough back advantage: A company while operating internationally learns continuously from different markets. These are huge and wonderful if synthesised and reused for strategy formation. The company must be able to gather these knowledge and disseminate them effectively within the organisation. This helps the company to be proactive rather than reactive in the market place. The details of benefits accrued from global marketing and their role in other types of marketing are listed above in Table 1.8.

INTERNATIONAL TO GLOBAL: REQUIREMENTS

Naturally, in the initial stage of internationalisation, companies are more familiar with the marketing mix that is applicable to the domestic markets. Now when a company enters a foreign market for the first time it has two options, either to it retains the marketing mix used for the home country or adapts to the requirements of the target market. It is easy for the entrant company to retain the home country marketing mix. However, with time when the company explores other foreign markets, it realises that the marketing mix needs to be modified to address the needs of the customers in the new markets. Usually the company, in this case, shows inclination to pick up countries selectively based on homogeneous requirements so that the company can specialise in a particular marketing mix. Unlike in multinational marketing, the company does not show tendency to differentiate marketing strategy as per country specific requirements. At a certain stage when the company completed exploring a reasonable number of countries and revenue earning from international operations becomes respectable, the company again tries to enter country markets but this time countries with dissimilarities in the marketing environment. However, unlike the previous stage, this time the company is backed by the experience and learning it has gathered over the years of international operation. Though market dissimilarities pose a great challenge in expanding into dissimilar markets but the company shows confidence and skips shaping the marketing strategy differently for different countries. The traditional management environment, of course, would encourage the company to adapt to the country specific environment through multi-domestic marketing. If the company follows this easy route and act accordingly, it loses the benefits of economies of scale and scope. The other course of action open to the company is to stick to the standardised marketing mix specially developed with full consideration of the similarities and differences in the marketing environment of the target country markets. This standardisation is different from the standardisation used by the company in the initial stages of internationalisation. This is rather an outcome of tortuous evolution of marketing process. The company does not want to drop this new approach so painfully developed over the years. Accordingly, follows the same in other markets as well. This nature of global standardisation continues and the company focuses on bulldosing the differences in the foreign markets by dint of its size, experience, spread and built-up knowledge base. Surely, proceeding in this way is not an easy task at all but only can be achieved through continuous efficient handling of various marketing elements that are candidates for localisation in different country markets.

LOCALISATION CANDIDATES

Every aspects of a marketing programme can easily be susceptible to adaptation in a dissimilar country. The dissimilar country with its country specific taste, preference, choice, regulations, etc., would provoke the different marketing variables to undergo adaptations as per new requirements. The four Ps of marketing individually or in combination are subjected to the pressure of localisation as per foreign market requirements. Clearly, the number of marketing variables that could be subjected or influenced by consumer or country heterogeneity in different country market would be many. Similarly, the influencing factors or the independent variables affecting the marketing variables, i.e., the dependent variables are also large. At this stage a clear understanding of dependent and independents variables are of extreme importance. Table 1.9 lists the important fourteen marketing variables, the possible influencing factors and the broad environmental category they belong.

Table 1.9 Fourteen marketing variables and influencing factors

S. No.	Marketing variables	Influencing factors on marketing variables for a country (Description in the bracket indicates the category of environmental factors influencing the marketing variables)
1.	Product features, use, design, style, etc.	• Climate, topography (Geographic) • Product use condition (Culture) • Per capita income (Economic) • product life cycle stage (Economic) • competition intensity (Competitive) • availability of distribution outlets (Economic and Political) • legal product standard (legal) • patent regime (Legal)
2.	Product positioning	• Perception of the product (Education, Culture) • Affordability (Economic)
3.	Brand name, tag line	• Language differences (Culture) • Symbolism (Cultural)
4.	Packaging	• Purchase quantity (Cultural and Economic) • Colour preference (Cultural) • Legal requirement (Legal)
5.	Retail price	• Income level and purchase volume (Economic and Cultural) • Local tax structure and import duty (Economic) • Legal restrictions,(legal) • Demand elasticity (Economic) • Grey market status (Legal) • Distributor's margin (Economic) • Pricing fluctuation (Currency and Economic)
6.	Basic advertising message	• Media popularity and access. (Cultural and Economic) • Cultural norms (Cultural) • Cost effectiveness. (Economic)
7.	Creative expression	• Education level and globalness (Demographic) • Selection, choice, preference (Cultural), • Advertising agency availability (Economic and competition). • Society restriction (Pressure group)
8.	Sales promotion	• Buying habit (Cultural) • buying behaviour (Cultural), • Legal enforcement (Legal)
9.	Media allocation	• Technology base and access (Technology) • Economic status and affluence (Economic) • Legal enforcement (Legal)
10.	Role of sales force	• Cultural norms (Cultural) • Buying style of customers (Cultural)
11.	Management of sales force	• Remuneration level and satisfaction (Economic and Cultural) • Attitude to learn (cultural)
12.	Role of middlemen	• Distribution system (Economic, Political, Cultural) • Legal provisions (Legal) • Relationship pattern (Culture).

(*Continued*)

Table 1.9 (*Continued*)

S. No.	Marketing variables	Influencing factors on marketing variables for a country (Description in the bracket indicates the category of environmental factors influencing the marketing variables)
13.	Retailing	• Retail structure (Economic) • Legal restrictions on global retailers (Legal, Political, Pressure group)
14.	Customer service	• Customers' uncertainly level (Cultural) • Customer purchase decision system (Cultural)

Source: From various study and compilation by author

FIGURE 1.4 Environmental factors influencing the marketing variables

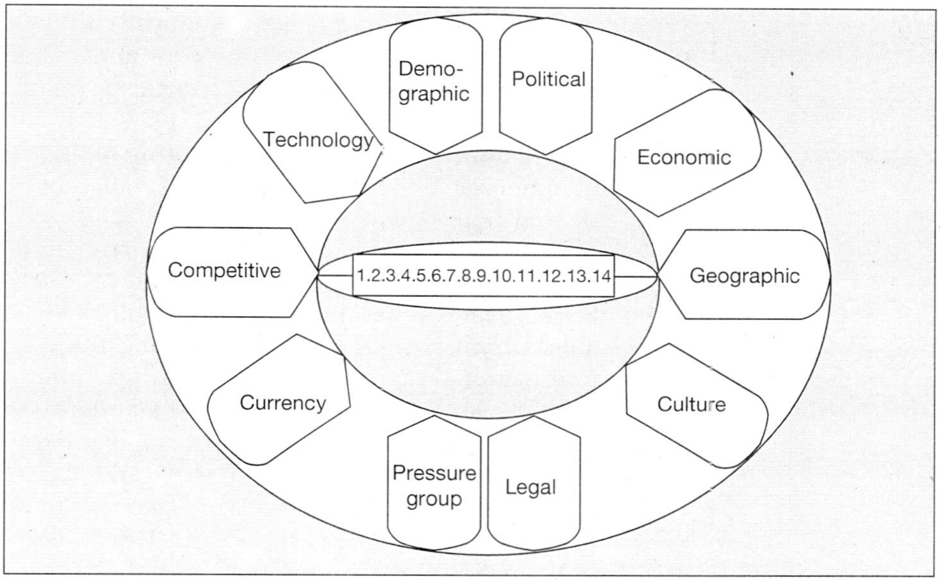

1. Product design 2. Product positioning 3. Brand name, tag line 4. Packaging 5. Retail price 6. Basic advertising message 7. Creative expression 8. Sales promotion 9. Media allocation 10. Role of sales force 11. Management of sales force 12. Role of middlemen 13 Retailing 14. Customer service

Conceptually, standardisation or adaptation of the fourteen factor marketing variables like product design, product positioning, brand name, tag line, etc., are influenced by as many as ten environmental factors identified in the Figure 1.4.

Specifically, these factors are geographical position of the country, prevailing socio-cultural situation, legal environment, pressure group situation, currency environment, competitive climate prevailing in the country, technology environment, demography of the people living in the country and political climate. Individually and collectively these actors affect the degree of standardisation differently in different countries. As a result the company needed to vary its marketing programme individually for a country and collectively for all the countries covered. The marketing program variation means here how the company makes the different recipes using different marketing mix ingredients or specifically the fourteen marketing variables. Understandably, therefore, degree of variation of marketing programmes mostly depends on the ten environmental factors and their impact on target customers' choices and preferences. Therefore, any company desiring standardisation of marketing programme and moving up along the marketing continuum towards global marketing requires careful scrutiny and analysis of these factors.

GLOBAL MARKETING AS EFFICIENCY POINT

Global marketing is practiced when a sufficient high level of standardisation has been achieved in the marketing programme across the countries of presence but without effecting customer value creation process. Again this is possible only when customers are responsive to the standardised marketing mix irrespective of the country of origin and cultural norms. However, factors like economic differences, differences in political and legal characteristics, difference in cultural norms, etc., plays as stumbling block in the way of an internationalising company attempting to drive in consumers' heterogeneity in to homogeneity in different country markets. Practically, given the present skewed heterogeneity pattern of the 220 sovereign country markets of the world, global marketing seems to be really difficult to achieve particularly while marketing FMCG products, food products, etc. Pundits of global marketing believes that though it is difficult to achieve but not totally unachievable. Company may try to tread along the continuum from one end, i.e., multinational marketing situation to the other extreme, i.e., global marketing, in search for achieving global standardisations in dissimilar situations even. Company in desperation to run standard marketing programme and reap the benefits of economy of scope and scale requires using all its expertise and knowledge in the field of management to do so. Let us take an example to pacify the understanding. Yum! Restaurants International (the international division of the world's largest global restaurant company), headquartered in Louisville, Kentucky, operated and franchised the world's largest ensemble of fast food restaurants under the brand name Taco Bell, Pizza Hut, and KFC. Peter A. Bassi, Chairman of Yum! Restaurants International understood that fast food consumption habit was hugely cultural and every country, therefore, would exercise its taste, choice, and preferences differently. Bassi also observed that any company operating in this sector had shown inclination to adapt its marketing for every country differently sacrificing economy of scale and scope. However, when confronted with such issues like adaptation or standardisation, Bassi had articulated one 80:20 rule within the company. According to this rule, the headquarters had retained the right to drive in 80% of marketing programme in the 10,000 restaurants outside the US in a standardised manner, taking cue from the wonderful learning plough back system it had maintained. The state of the art recipe R&D centre the company at New York was of great help in standardising components of marketing up to 80% for 10,000 restaurants without affecting customer value creation process in respective countries. The subsidiaries and the franchises of Yum were required to follow this 80:20 rules in different components of marketing mix also. However, Bassi knew that country-specific preferences were also required to be honoured and, hence, kept 20% open for local adaptation which the country manager in respective country could exercise based on local requirements without headquarter approval. Bassi looked at its greatest competitor McDonald's who was using a similar 95:5 rule to scale up its standardisation to a higher level in multinational–global continuum. Bassi thought that in the coming years his company would also required to respond to that in order to be competitive in the sector[14]. Therefore, in a competitive situation when many other fast food companies were treading along the continuum, from multinational to global marketing, the company who had reached the furthest point possible at that time had the privilege in setting the efficiency point of global marketing in that sector. Therefore, in a sense, global marketing may not require 100% standardisation. The extent of standardisation possible or the furthest point in the multinational–global continuum is fixed by the most efficient company in that sector of the business. Here, in the global fast food business, McDonald has set the efficiency point at 95% which other companies would strive to achieve because of competitive pressure. Hence, in the global marketing situation, different business sectors have different efficiency points. It is also greatly influenced by the inherent sectoral characteristics. For example, in aviation sector, the efficiency point may be as high as 100% because of inherent standardisation characteristics of the sector. But for the handicraft sector, the efficiency point may be as low as 20% given the inherent cultural affinity of the sector. Nevertheless, in all sectors of business, it will be the indicator of competitive efficiency at the level of global market participation.

GLOBAL E-MARKETING: THE DEATH OF DISTANCE

The Internet has transformed the world of communication. It is difficult to believe that the world-wide network of interconnected TCP/IP networks, called the Internet, was introduced only in 1982. As of now electronic mail, instant messaging, skype (two-way interactive video calls), World Wide Web with its discussion forums, blogs, social networking, and online shopping sites have become part of the life. As per the International Telecommunication Union, about 2.7 billion people, or 39% of the world's population, was using the Internet by end 2013. This figure was as high as 77% in the developed world while it was only 31% in the developing world. Europe topped the list with 75% Internet penetration, largely outpacing Asia and the Pacific (32%) and Africa (16%). However, every year internet access rate is growing at a faster pace to cover the balance two thirds of the world's population.[15] Businesses across the world started to become dependent on the Internet. Nowadays, order booking over the Internet, Internet-based advertising, use of social media like Twitter, YouTube and Facebook for advertising, sales made over the Internet, banking and receiving payments over the Internet, etc., have become common and extensively used by businesses irrespective of their size.

---

[14] Tricon Restaurants International: Globalisation Re-examined, A Harvard Business School case prepared by Professors Pankaj Ghemawat and Tarun Khanna. Case no 9-700-030, August, 10, 2000.

[15] ITU press release available at http://www.itu.int/net/pressoffice/press_releases/2013/05.aspx#.Uxv-Vj-SwaY

Table 1.10 The effect of the internet on marketing elements

S. No.	Marketing elements	Type and level of impact
1.	Product	• Facilitates understanding of product customisation requirements. • Greater customisation is possible.
2.	Price	• Decision making on international pricing is easy as the prices of competitors are known. • Ease in allowing customers to know price in other countries and make online payment transactions. • Restricts discriminatory pricing as customers are exposed to the pricing policy followed by the company in other countries.
3.	Distribution	• Easy to reach customers for order booking through the company Web site. • Internet-based merchandising has cut down on distances.
4.	Promotion	• Easy to promote products through Web sites.
5.	Market identification	• Demand for foreign markets can be based on updated Internet-based research.
6.	Foreign country market research and segment identification	• Consumer research and understanding the cultural stereotypes of different countries is now easier based on the information available on the Internet.

The extensive use of Internet in business has impacted cross-border marketing in various ways. Price discrimination in different country markets is not very common now. The price fixed by a company for its product becomes common knowledge to customers irrespective of their location. If differential pricing is practiced, customers become unhappy and express their discontentment again through the Internet. Advertising over the Internet has enhanced the reach of companies by cutting across man-made international borders. Local advertising on the Internet is slowly losing its charm. Companies feel that standardisation of advertising will help them access more countries with ease. Internet-based distribution channels have been able to kill distances successfully. There are many examples of companies who are actively and successfully merchandising their products across the world using the Internet. The effects of internet on marketing elements are stated in Table 1.10.

CHALLENGES OF MARKETING GLOBALLY

There are various challenges when a company opens out for internationalisation. These challenges affect the company deeply because until then, the company has been operating in a thoroughly known domestic marketing environment characterised by low level of uncertainty. Figure 1.5 depicts the situation of a company marketing in the domestic market and extending to two other countries. The domestic company has experience of marketing in A environment only and, hence, require to explore B and C environments to set the marketing programme there. Only X and Y parts of the foreign environment of country B and C are common to both foreign and domestic environments and hence known. Z part, being the common part, is also known to domestic company. However, it requires exploring a vast unknown part of both the foreign country's environment for setting marketing strategy accordingly.

FIGURE 1.5 Internationalisation and unknown marketing environment

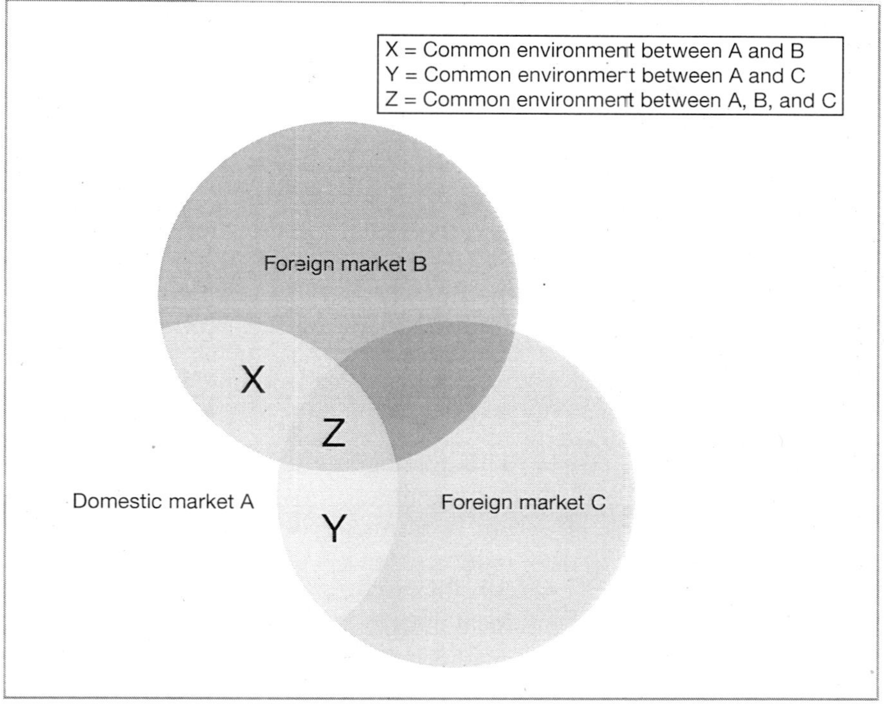

Understandably, when more countries are targeted for marketing, more will be the requirements of stepping in to unknown and different environment. As we have already seen (Table 1.9) that marketing variables get influenced by different environmental factors, the internationalising company would like to adjust its marketing strategy in accordance with country-specific requirements. This, in turn, would disturb its present position multinational-global strategy continuum vis-à-vis competitive position.

Setting Management Orientation

On internationalisation, a company strives to find similarities between international markets and domestic market so that it can standardise marketing strategy and tactics across these markets as much as possible. This is mainly done to push its learning and expertise across markets. It would be natural desire for a company to try its time tested successful marketing strategy of one country in other countries as well. In such situation, there could be some success, particularly in some niche segments, but many a times, market heterogeneity often stands as an obstacle against the further extension of strategy. At this juncture, based on how the company management perceives the differential nature of the foreign country market environment, management orientation can be grouped into three types—ethnocentric, polycentric, and geocentric. The internationalising company faces the challenge of using the right orientation based on the actual requirements.

Ethnocentric

Under this management orientation, the company believes that the marketing practices followed in the home country will succeed in the foreign markets without adaptation. Proponents of this concept strongly believe that whatever the causes of marketing success in the domestic market; it can be easily replicated in the foreign market. A glaring case of management ethnocentrism was Disney World's marketing strategy for the Euro Disney Resort in Paris. The Walt Disney Company strongly believed that the marketing strategy developed for its entertainment complex in the US could easily be carried over to France. The ethnocentrism of the company spelled disaster for the Euro Disney Resort when Paris became a loss-making proposition for the company. However, the company realised its mistake soon and developed a new strategy specifically for Europe.

Polycentric or Multi-Domestic Marketing Concept

This management orientation is just the opposite of ethnocentrism. The management under this mindset readily agrees that each country is different in terms of socio-cultural, political and legal systems. The management believes that each country is unique and hence allows the officials of each subsidiary company to develop their own marketing strategies specific to the local market.

Geocentric Concept

This management orientation promotes the concept of homogeneity across the world. The management firmly believes that there are minimal differences in terms of marketing environment across different countries. Therefore, the company can reap a greater benefit by resorting to a world-orientated approach rather than a country-specific, multi-domestic approach. This orientation helps the company to develop a standardised marketing strategy for the entire world. The geocentric approach is synonymous with global marketing orientation in which a uniform, standardised marketing strategy is used for several countries, countries in a region, or the entire world.

Communications Challenges

Deciding on right marketing communications is very important for a global company. When participating in foreign markets, a company faces several challenges in communicating about its products and their benefits with its consumers. What should be the right marketing communication in a foreign market? The management requires a large amount of data in order to answer this question. The complexity increases when decisions are to be taken regarding adopting a standardised communication strategy for a large number of foreign markets and they are dissimilar in nature.

Targeting the Customers

Consumers' tastes, choices and preferences change more rapidly in the developed countries than the developing or least developing ones. The different segments are also very volatile and get created only to last for a while and are reorganised afterwards at a comparatively faster rate that the developing world. In the developing and least developed countries, consumer segments are often difficult to identify and isolate for targeting purpose. Consumers are inclined to wear different hats at different points of time. Some time they remain ambivalent about their preferences and hence pose considerable challenges for executing the basic marketing task of segmentation, targeting and positioning. This is coupled with the lack of readymade research data on customer preferences, demography, cultural aspects, psychological orientation, etc., does not facilitate to set a multi country homogeneous segment and target them successfully.

Multiple Legal Environment

Each element of the marketing strategy of an international company is a candidate for alteration due prevailing legal connotations. For example, product decisions with respect to labelling, ingredients, and packaging taken for one country may not be applicable for another country due the differences in legal requirements. Often understanding the national laws of each participating country and adjusting the marketing programme in accordance with those pose a big problem for international marketers.

Speed to Market Products

Companies are obsessed with ensuring that their products reach customers in different geographical regions as fast as possible. Speed means more business in the competitive world. Who will be faster to reach the US market, Xbox gaming gadget from Microsoft, USA or PS 4 from Sony, Japan? Obviously, the one to reach the market faster will do brisk business. Here, Sony could do good business in USA market because Microsoft could not match Sony in terms of speed. Therefore, the global company always remains under pressure to complete product development as per the segment requirements and market them speedily in different countries. To be present everywhere at right time with equal speed is, indeed, a great challenge for the global companies.

Tariff and Non-tariff Barriers

Participating in international market requires the entrant company to transfer products/commodities across different national territories. However, these transfers attract different tariffs from different countries. Tariffs are the taxes that a country imposes on the imports of commodities into a country or region. Tariffs have two purposes; first, they are used by a country primarily to earn revenue from the commodities that it imports from other countries. Secondly, tariffs are very important weapon used by countries to provide safeguard to domestic companies and suppliers from the onslaught of foreign imports.

Similarly, the transfer of products/commodities faces stiff Non-tariff trade barriers (NTBs) in the foreign countries. NTBs are the mechanisms used by a country government to further protect the domestic industries when it is not possible to impose tariff barriers or tariff barriers are restricted. NTBs can take several forms. One example of an non-tariff trade barrier is the domestic content requirement clause through which the local government insists that foreign companies use indigenous components in their manufacturing process. Tariffs are widely used to protect domestic Small and Medium Enterprise producers' from foreign competition. The global company, therefore, faces stiff problem on account of tariff and non-tariff barriers, imposed by countries, as they upset the cross-country movement of finished products, work in progress or raw material.

Coordination of Activities

The growth of business across the world poses the huge challenge of effectively and efficiently coordinating activities that are expected to take place in multiple locations. At the global marketing level, the global level value-chain integration provides the requisite competitive advantage over the local and other international competitors. However, decentralised activities across multiple locations must be efficiently synchronised and different business activities are orchestrated in accordance with the requirement. This is quite a big challenge considering the spread of activities almost across the globe. Also additional challenge comes in the matter of deciding how much flexibility is to be provided to the decentralised activities without disturbing the company's objective of centralised control.

LIMITATIONS OF GLOBAL MARKETING

Developed Countries Enjoy Benefits

The global companies put their exclusive attention to the developed countries with high degree of consumerism. They shy away from least developing countries and do not pay much attention to their requirements. It is, therefore, a great challenge to ensure equal sharing of customer benefits across various countries.

Restrictions on trade and commerce

WTO stalemates and rise of non-tariff barriers are detrimental to global marketing. The value of global merchandise exports in 2012 was USD 18.3 trillion nearly unchanged from 2011.[16] The steady trickles of restrictive trade measures are gradually undermining the benefits of trade openness. Global marketers are the worst sufferers of restrictive trade measures and WTO stalemates.

Rapid rise of trade blocs

Countries are forging trade ties with other countries based on the idea that if multilateralism is not achievable or delayed, then minilateralism can do

[16] World Trade Report 2013 available at http://www.wto.org/english/res_e/publications_e/wtr13_e.htm

wonders for them. Under World Trade Organisation (WTO) multilateralism was the principle, i.e., multiple countries were working in concert on issue of removing trade barriers. As result, the world is witnessing the rapid rise of trade blocs. However, WTO stalemates have given rise to minilateralism, i.e., tendency of nations to act on their own, or with only minimal consultation with other nations. Therefore, there is creation of many smaller trade blocks encouraging trade among the member countries while dispiriting trade flow with non- member countries. Global marketing is bound to suffer under the minilateralism scenario.

Dominance of the Arnolds

The Arnold Schwarzeneggers of developed countries, i.e., the big brands of developed countries are expected to dominate the Aamir Khans, i.e., limited famed brands originating from the developing countries. Poor and developing countries are expected to be subdued due to the almost monopolistic situation created by the big Arnolds.

CHAPTER SUMMARY

1. The primary objective of international marketers is to create better customers value than the competitors in the foreign country market.
2. Every country seems to be different in terms of cultural norms shaping the consumer preferences. The technology, political, legal and economic environment are also different in different countries. In multi country marketing situation these differences put pressure on companies to adapt their marketing programmes differently for different countries in search of better customer value creation.
3. By adopting the adaptation approach, a company enjoys the benefits associated with customising its products for the market but sacrifices the benefits associated with economies of scale and scope.
4. By adopting the standardisation approach, a company drives home the benefits of economies of scale and economies of scope. But the customer value-creation process may be hampered because of locale taste and preferences prevailing in every country market were not given due consideration while developing the standardised marketing programme.
5. The various globalisation drivers are very effective in bringing different country consumers to a uniform platform of taste and preferences. These drivers also provide an indication of usability of standardisation or adaptation approach.
6. Companies are resorting to different types of marketing strategies to tackle the challenges arising out of uneven global tastes and preferences. These strategies may exist anywhere in between two extreme points, i.e., multinational marketing emphasising on country specific adaptation and global marketing emphasising on global level standardisation connected by a continuum.
7. The companies work hard to upscale the continuum and move as close as possible to global marketing point. The optimum position or efficiency point in the continuum is decided by the most efficient company or companies dealing with the same or similar products and operating in the same marketing environment.

QUESTIONS FOR REVIEW

1. What is the difference between multinational marketing and international marketing? Explain with the help of an example.
2. MTV Networks (now under **Viacom Media Networks**) are seen globally in 560 million households in 162 countries and 33 languages via

more than 150 locally programmed and operated TV channels. One in four people around the world are in MTV's key demographic segment—ages 14 to 29. Because of India's large youth demographic, MTV soon entered this market via a low-risk licensing agreement with Hong Kong's Star TV. Early on, MTV struggled to gain a foothold in the Indian market due to its lack of shows tailored specifically to the Indian market. Revenues soared when MTV began including Bollywood music in its programming. Other positioning strategies included programming on such topics as fashion and cricket, consumer products such as CDs and clothing, and a Web site that included topics such as "campus life." By the late 1990s, MTV had localised its approach by creating MTV India. Evidence includes the addition of Bollywood music and Hindi-speaking hosts. MTV India also created a Web site and programming tailored to the Indian market. The programming was distributed to viewers in Bangladesh, Nepal, Pakistan, the Middle East, and Sri Lanka as well as India. But recently, MTV has been concerned with the lack of worldwide standardised programming. The management believes that MTV is not benefiting from economies of scale because of its focus on localised or adapted programming. Is it feasible for MTV to arrive at an ideal balance between standardisation of programming and local adaptation? If so, how can this be achieved? Discuss the marketing strategy that the management can adopt to increase the global viewership of MTV channels?

3. The Apple iPod can store and play up to 2000 songs from a hand-held computer no bigger than a cigarette box. Steve Jobs introduced the product in October 2001 in the US market. After its resounding success in the American market, Apple did not lose any time in capitalising on its overseas potential. The iPod was introduced in Europe through its existing Mac dealerships. The sales rapidly rose despite the high price tag. Japan was penetrated through the strong dealership network that Apple already had. Typical of high-tech industries, Apple began to launch new models to suit market requirements. It entered into agreements with major record labels to launch the iTunes Music Store, which enabled customers to download songs without worrying about copyright infringement issues. By 2004, Apple entered the Chinese market after forming an alliance with Founder, China's largest distributor of personal computers.

   The iPod has revolutionised the way people manage and listen to music. Apple was quick in marketing the iPod globally to remain competitive in the market place. Local markets were easily penetrated because of existing dealer networks and new alliances were forged with existing firms where existing networks were absent. Due care was taken to maintain a correct balance between the homogenised needs of the global customer with a right dose of localisation. As far as possible, the company tried to keep major operational activities concentrated in the US but again did not forget to locate some operational activities in countries of specific interests. Can Apple's marketing of the iPod be described as global marketing or international marketing? Why or why not?
4. The history of Häagen-Dazs dates back to the 1920s when Reuben Mattus, the founder, worked in his mother's business in New York, selling ice cream in horse-drawn carriages. Later, he spun-off the business into a company and named it Häagen-Dazs. The business grew rapidly and spread globally as distribution logistics and the popularity of brand increased. In 1983, Häagen-Dazs was bought over by Pillsbury of the US Häagen-Dazs manufactures and markets a wide range of traditional ice creams, frozen yoghurts, gelatos, sorbets and frozen ice-cream bars. Research the spread of business of Häagen-Dazs and understand each of the marketing elements and their standardisation status. Can you call Häagen-Dazs as involved in global marketing? Analyse the fourteen marketing variables of the company used in the text to answer the question.
5. Standardisation is not a clear–cut phenomenon. In the literal sense, standardisation refers to the offering of identical product lines at identical prices through identical distribution systems supported by identical promotional programmes in several different countries. At the other extreme, completely localised marketing strategies would have no common elements what so ever. Obviously neither of these extremes are often feasible or desirable" Why are these extremes not feasible or desirable? Explain with an example.
6. What are the benefits of global marketing over multi-domestic marketing? Does Coca-Cola practice global marketing? Justify your answer.
7. The fast-food restaurant chain KFC has outlets in 110 countries. Debate on the statement that the company is close to global marketing but has not achieved it.

8. What are the benefits associated with global marketing? How can these benefits be availed by a company?
9. What are the main drivers of globalisation? Explain the drivers in detail with examples. What is the relationship between globalisation drivers and global marketing?
10. Discuss the origin of multinational companies. Characterise the US multinational companies after World War II in accordance with their marketing practices.
11. Compare and contrast between international, multinational and global marketing.

EXERCISES

1. Visit the nearest KFC outlet in your city and interact with the management to understand its marketing practice. Also visit the company website to find out whether the American company has really achieved global marketing?
2. Select one domestic company that has not yet internationalised in your locality and assess its potential for internationalisation based on Yip's framework.
3. Undertake online research to find out whether McDonalds follows the standardisation or adaptation approach in its global marketing strategy.

End Case: Indian SUV Scorpio Takes on Global Players in the US Market[17]

Introduction

It was a chilly winter morning of 2008 in Mumbai. Anand G. Mahindra, Vice Chairman and Managing Director, Mahindra Group, was sitting in his office chamber at Mahindra Towers and thinking about the most important meeting scheduled for the day. The meeting was convened to discuss the company's plan to launch three vehicles in the US in 2009—a two-door pick-up, a four-door pick-up and a sports utility vehicle (SUV). The project team was to present the company's business plan to enter the US market. Mr Mahindra, a 1981 alumnus of Harvard University, knew from past experience that planning and execution in the real-world was never as clear-cut as it seemed in business school. He felt that the meeting might not be able to bring out all the issues that the company might confront in the US, but was confident of having a fruitful discussion on the different aspects of the launch plan. The current team was the same team that had shown great understanding and commitment on previous occasions while introducing Mahindra & Mahindra (M&M) vehicles in different countries across the world. However, this time, it seemed that a more in-depth understanding would be required to frame the roadmap to succeed in the highly competitive US market. Mahindra was aware that many of the experienced team members were sceptical about the timing chosen for the entry. Hence, to bring out the best from the team, it would be wise not to give emphasis on the entry decision in the meeting but rather on the issues after entry. Mahindra knew that his leadership skill would be severely tested in keeping the team motivated to enter the recession hit US market. However, one good thing was that the key man required for converting the odds in favour of the company, high profile project manager (PM, M&M) head of Mahindra's Automotive and Farm Equipment sector, seemed to be charged up and ready to take up the challenge. Mahindra knew that PM (M&M), a mechanical engineer with a Ph.D. from leading American University and with vast experience of working with a leading automobile company of the world based in USA, would be his key man during this project.

As expected, the meeting lasted several hours and included a detailed discussion on the threat and opportunity perception of the team members. After the meeting, Mahindra discussed some of the critical issues raised in the meeting in a one-to-one

[17] The case 'Indian SUV Scorpio Takes on Global Players in US Market' has been created by the case writer Dr Gautam Dutta of Indian Institute of Foreign Trade as a basis for class room discussion rather than to illustrate either effective or ineffective handling of business situation.

meeting with PM (M&M), one of his most trusted colleagues.

As Mahindra was leaving the office that evening, he reflected that the majority of the team members nurtured the dream of making M&M a true global player. Most of them felt that the company's decision to enter the US market was a step in the right direction. However, they were apprehensive regarding the timing of the entry. The turbulence in the American automobile sector had forced a number of car manufacturers off the market. Mahindra knew that the launch of a new brand in the volatile American pick-up and SUV market was fraught with challenges. Adding to his agony was the haunting question, "Would the US consumer accept an Indian brand that only a minority of them had heard of?"

Background

Mahindra & Mahindra, founded by brothers K.C. Mahindra and J.C. Mahindra, began its journey in the automobile sector at the dawn of Indian independence. K.C. Mahindra had the opportunity to meet Delmar G. "Barney" Roos, the American automotive engineer and inventor of the general "general purpose vehicle" or Jeep, when he was touring the United States as the head of India Supply Mission. During the meeting, Roos convinced K.C. Mahindra that India would be good market for a rugged terrain vehicle like the Jeep. The seasoned entrepreneurial mind of K.C. Mahindra did not take much time to act on this budding opportunity.

After returning to India, the Mahindra brothers, J.C. Mahindra and K.C. Mahindra, joined hands with a gentleman named Ghulam Mohammad from Pakistan. Mahindra & Mohammad was set up as a as a private limited company to act as a franchisee for assembling Jeeps from Willys-Overland Motors of the US in India in October 1945. The first batch of seventy-five Willys GPU vehicles were rolled on to the Indian roads in October 1947. Mahindra & Mohammad changed its name to Mahindra & Mahindra Limited on 13 January 1948 with the now popular acronym M&M.

Today, the Mahindra Group is a leading manufacturer of multi-utility vehicles with significant presence in key sectors like automotive, farm equipment, financial services, trade and logistics, automotive components, and IT and infrastructure.[18] The automotive business, in course of time, became the leading arm of the Mahindra Group with its product line dominating the utility vehicle and light commercial vehicle segment in India. The Scorpio, the company's flagship SUV, is acknowledged as the right blend between rugged utility and style, while another brand Bolero was crowned with India's Leading SUV Brand award for two years in a row with record sales of over 50,000 units in one year. The USD 4 billion Mahindra Group is now one among the top 10 industrial conglomerates in India. *Forbes* has ranked the Mahindra Group in its Top 200 list of the world's "Most Reputable Companies" and in the Top 10 list of the "Most Reputable Indian Companies."

Journey to Success

The year 1956 was a crucial year in M&M's history. In that year, the company started manufacturing Willys jeep under a license and an agreement with the US- headquartered Willys Motors Inc. M&M was also the exclusive distributors for their entire range of vehicles including utility vans, cargo/personnel carriers and pick-up trucks across India. The manufacturing activities of the company are concentrated in Maharashtra with three plants located at Mumbai, Igatpure and Nashik. The company also has a manufacturing plant in Andhra Pradesh where light commercial vehicles (LCV) and three-wheelers are produced.

The Farm Equipment Sector Division was established in 1963 in the form of a joint venture with International Harvester Inc. and Voltas Limited and christened as the International Tractor Company of India (ITCI). In 1977, ITCI merged with M&M and became its Tractor Division. After M&M's organisational restructuring in 1994, the Tractor Division was rechristened as the Farm Equipment Sector Division. Today, M&M is the largest manufacturer of tractors in India. It designs, develops, manufactures and markets tractors as well as the implements that are used in conjunction with tractors under the brand name Mahindra Tractors.

[18] The company website, www.mahindra.com

Internationalisation of the Company[19]

Mahindra began its journey towards expanding its global footprint by exporting 600 jeeps for the Yugoslavian market in the late 1960s. Mahindra also exported vehicles to Indonesia, Nigeria and other African countries in the 1970s. The 1980s saw Mahindra exporting its CJ5 model as completely knocked down (CKD) units to Iran where it was sold under the brand name Sahara. Mahindra expanded its markets to countries like Nepal, Sri Lanka, Kenya, Namibia, Mozambique in the early 1990s.

The contemporary looks and style of the Bolero, launched in 2001, further transformed the image of the company. In 2002, M&M achieved a major milestone with the launch of India's first indigenous SUV, the Scorpio. In addition to the Scorpio, Mahindra also developed the Mahindra Pick-Up, based on the Scorpio platform, exclusively for the overseas markets. In the early 2000s, Mahindra made its presence felt in Tanzania, Sri Lanka, Congo, Madagascar, Mozambique, Ethiopia, Rwanda, Burundi and Nigeria. In 2004, an SKD (Semi Knocked Down) facility was set up in Uruguay for the manufacture of the Bolero Pick-Up, which was locally sold under the brand name "Cimarron." Mahindra South Africa, a JV company, was also set up in South Africa for the sale of the Scorpio and Bolero Pick-Up. Mahindra Europe was established in Italy in 2005 with the launch of the Scorpio (introduced with the brand name Mahindra Goa) and the Bolero Pick-Up. Mahindra also made a foray in the French market in the same year.

With a growing global presence, Mahindra announced its entry in Spain at the Madrid Auto Show. The Mahindra Goa, the Mahindra Pick-Up, and the Bolero Pick-Up range of vehicles led M&M's debut in Spain. The company soon forayed into Sudan, Morocco, Algeria and Ghana and consolidating its position in the African continent. Mahindra also ventured into Chile in South America with the introduction of the Mahindra Pick-Up. In 2008, M&M's first overseas CKD (Completely Knocked Down) operation was established in Egypt with the launch of the Scorpio. This was soon followed by CKD operations in Brazil for the manufacture of the Scorpio SUV and Pick-Up range followed by the South American markets of Peru and Paraguay.

Globalisation has been an integral part of Mahindra Group's vision. Today, Mahindra vehicles can be found in Europe, South America, Australia, Africa, and South Asia. As part of its vision to become a truly global player, Mahindra recently acquired Metalcastello Spa, a leading Italian independent gear manufacturer and Grafica Ricerca Design (GRD), an Italian auto designing, feasibility and styling company based out of Turin, Italy. M&M intends to use GRD as a "Global Design Centre" for the company and enhance its capability as a global original auto equipment manufacturer.

Automobile Industry in India

After independence in 1947, the Government of India took efforts to create a vibrant automobile manufacturing industry by encouraging the participation of the private sector. However, the Indian private sector had very limited participation in the automobile sector in the 1950s and 1960s. After 1970, tractors, commercial vehicles, and scooters mainly drove the growth in the auto sector. Cars were still considered a major luxury and the sector was dominated by presence of two brands—the Ambassador and the Fiat. In the 1980s, a number of Japanese manufacturers launched joint ventures for building motorcycles and light commercial vehicles in India. It was at this time that the Indian government chose the well-known Japanese automobile company Suzuki for its joint venture to manufacture small cars. Following the economic liberalisation in 1991 and the gradual weakening of the license system, a number of Indian and multinational car manufacturers launched operations in India. As the country made progress on the economic front, the growth of the automotive component and automobile manufacturing industry got accelerated due to the increasing demand in the domestic market. Automobile majors across the globe started looking at India as their potential market. Domestic manufacturers also accelerated their production to meet domestic and export demands. As it stands now, the automobile industry in India is the seventh-largest in the world.

[19] drawn from company website www.mahindra.com

In 2009, India emerged as Asia's fourth-largest exporter of automobiles, behind Japan, South Korea and Thailand. The Indian automotive industry is expected to continue on its growth path because of increasing demand and relaxed restrictions. In February 2009, monthly sales of passenger cars in India exceeded 100,000 units. Several Indian automobile manufacturers such as Tata Motors, Maruti Suzuki and Mahindra & Mahindra are already big players in terms of their domestic and international operations. India's robust economic growth would lead to further expansion of its domestic automobile market and also increase competition from multinational automobile manufacturers wanting to expand their presence in India.

Mid-size SUVs in India[20]

Most SUVs[21] in the world are large-sized with an engine capacity of 3000 cc and a four-wheel drive. A mid-sized SUV, on an average, has an engine capacity of 2000 cc with or without a regular four-wheel drive, and is popular with people living in cities or crowded areas. Mid-sized SUVs are popular in the Indian market because they provide better mileage and are cheaper than the large-sized models. The Indian auto industry is home to a large number of mid-size SUV brands. M&M, with its popular brand Scorpio and its smaller cousin Bolero, is successfully competing with foreign competitors in this segment in India. M&M's Scorpio is among the top five SUVs in India and has a market share of more that 50% in the Indian market.

Tata Safari Dicor: The Tata Safari is one of the oldest and most successful SUVs in the Indian car market. With its excellent styling and comfortable interiors, the car is a hot favourite among the youth. The Tata Safari Dicor has been introduced with a fresh look and an indigenously developed advanced engine, christened as Direct Injection Common Rail (DICOR) engine. This advanced version of the Safari comes with two engine options, a 2.2L VTT diesel and 2.0 L MPFI petrol.

Maruti Suzuki Grand Vitara: Maruti Suzuki is synonymous in the Indian market as the market leader in the manufacturing of small cars. Soon after tasting success in the small-car segment, the company spread its wings to the SUV segment as well. The entry in the SUV market was made with the launch of the Maruti Suzuki Grand Vitara. A 2.0 litre VIS inline-4 petrol engine mated with an efficient five-speed manual transmission powers the car. It also has an optional four-speed automatic transmission.

Mahindra Scorpio: The Mahindra Scorpio, the SUV from Mahindra, created a wave of enthusiasm among young car consumers at the time of its launch. Though today there are many other SUVs competing against the Scorpio in the Indian market, the car has been successful in retaining its loyal following of customers.

Honda CR-V: The Honda CR-V is the only SUV launched by the premium car manufacturer Honda in the Indian market. Honda has positioned its SUV as a dream car capable of delivering a blend of power, performance, and sophistication. The car is designed with elegance and creativity and offers excellent stability, handling and driving experience. This SUV is also available with an engine option of automatic transmission.

Mitsubishi Pajero and Outlander: The Japanese carmaker Mitsubishi entered the fray the lucrative Indian SUV market with its SUV Pajero. Mitsubishi Outlander is a recent addition to the list of SUVs available in India. This SUV has won appreciation in a short span of time with its excellent performance, handling and stability.

Ford Endeavour: Ford, though struggling to cope with the new global competitive regime, was not to lag behind others while vying for a share of the Indian pie. The Ford Endeavour may look obsolescent, but it has user-friendly interiors with plenty of legroom. The car is fitted with five-speed manual transmission and a 2.5-litre turbocharged diesel VGT inline engine.

Hyundai Tuscon: Hyundai Tucson is the first premium SUV from the Korean manufacturer Hyundai Motors India Limited. This compact 5-seater offers a chunky SUV presence, a diesel engine, sprightly performance, spacious interiors, and easy handling.

[20] http://www.articlesbase.com/advertising-articles/top-5-suvs-in-india-691251.html#ixzz0t4B6Hbtj

[21] The SUV category includes midsize SUVs, mini SUVs, and full-size utility vehicles

CASE EXHIBIT 1: Mahindra's Scorpio and its competitors in Indian market

NAME	Tata Safari Dicor	Maruti Suzuki Grand Vitara	Mahindra Scorpio	Honda CR-V	Mistsubishi Outlander
MODEL	LX 2.2 VTT	MT	VLX	2.44WD AT	2.4 MIVEC
ENGINE TYPE	Diesel	Petrol	Diesel	Petrol	Petrol
DISPLACEMENT(cc)	2179cc	2397cc	2179cc	2354cc	2360cc
MAX POWER	140 Bhp @ 4000 rpm	163.5 Bhp @ 6000 rpm	120 Bhp @ 4000 rpm	160 Bhp @ 6300 rpm	170 Bhp @ 6000 rpm
MAX TORQUE	320 Nm @ 1700 rpm	225 Nm @ 4000 rpm	290 Nm @ 1800 rpm	218 Nm @ 1420 rpm	226 Nm @ 4100 rpm
TRANSMISSION	5 Speed Manual		5 Speed Manual	5 Speed Automatic	6 Speed Automatic
TOP SPEED(km/ph)	152	159	155	172	190
0-100 KMPH(S)	16.2	14.4	15.6	9.9	9.6
SEATING CAPACITY		5	8	5	5
MILEAGE(km/l)	9 km/l in city and 12 km/l on highways	16 km/l in city and 22 km/l on highways	10.5 km/l in city and 15 km/l on highways	9 km/l in city and 16 km/l on highways	N/A
GROUND CLEAR-ANCE	195.00 mm	200.00 mm	N/A	185.00 mm	215.00 mm
PRICE(₹)	783,000.00	14,10,000.00	920,000.00	19,80,000.00	20,30,000.00

Mid-size SUV Market in the US

The US market is crowded with SUVs manufactured by different global automobile manufactures and customers have a wide range of vehicles to make their selection from. SUV sales as a share of the US Light Vehicle Market was about 30.3% during 2004, which went up to 30.5% during 2007, but nose-dived to 27.9% during 2008. The drop-off in sales in 2008 can be attributed to the rise in the fuel price. However, the SUV market has shown signs of recovery as indicated by the 31% sales during the first five months (Jan–May) of 2009 with the sale of 538,104 mid-size SUVs. The M&M Scorpio will fit into the mid-size category of SUVs available in the US market. The new entrant Scorpio is expected to compete against the Honda Pilot, the Ford Explorer, the Ford Edge Jeep Grand Cherokee, the Toyota 4Runner, the Kia Sorrento Lexus RX, the Mazda CX-7, the Chevrolet Traverse, the Toyota Highlander, the Chevrolet Equinox, the Nissan Rogue and the newly launched Kia Borrego.

The global warming and energy crisis have promoted the trend in the general automobile market to shift its focus to energy efficient, smaller cars, hybrid cars and fuel cell SUVs. With a market share of 6.2% from January to May of 2009, the Honda Pilot leads the mid-size SUV market. M&M is considering a seven-passenger model with a third row of seating, likely to be a wise move considering that three of the top five best-selling models in the US have this feature.[22] The other contender for market share may be the Chevrolet Equinox with 3-liter engine and 6-speed transmission, every day use positioning, very good fuel economy, and car safety features such as six air bags and diagnostics.

[22] Polk Views, August 2009

The Nissan Rogue is fitted with a Continuously Variable Valve Timing Control System (abbreviated as CVTCS) and a Direct Ignition System, whcih gives the car an optimum performance status and low levels of emission. A specialty of this vehicle is that apart from the front-wheel drive, it has an Intuitive All-Wheel Drive, (AWD). These features give the Rogue a special place in almost every best mid-sized SUV review. The Mazda CX-7 with a 2.5-litre engine and a five-speed automatic transmission is promoted as the best mid-sized SUV for people living in a crowded locality.

The Pre-launch Executive Meeting at M&M

The meeting started at 10 a.m. At the outset, Anand Mahindra spoke for about 10 minutes explaining the need for the company's presence in the US market. He emphasised that the company must be present in leading markets such as the US to ensure global market participation. The experienced gained by the company in its previous forays into internationalisation also needed to be utilised properly to make the entry into the US a success. He also mentioned that the company needed to have a strong presence in the US, which is considered as the Mecca of vehicle markets, in order to achieve the target of realising about 20% of the total revenue from international operations by 2012. He said, "We recently made a bid against Tata Motors to buy Jaguar and Land Rover and we believe that we have a good shot at being a niche global player in the SUVs segment." He also reminded the team that the company's SUV Scorpio had been a runaway success in India and had been accepted well by countries in South America, Europe and South Asia.[23] He then focused on the challenging nature of the task ahead and expressed his full confidence in the ability of his project team under the able leadership of high profile PM (M&M). Following this, PM (M&M) presented the marketing plan prepared for the SUV launch in the US An overview of the plan is given in the following sections.

The Product for the US Market[24]

The US-bound 2010 Mahindra Scorpio will be an upgraded version of the so-called "all new" model unveiled in April 2006, though the basic design dates back from 2002. The innovative design came from Shyamkumar, a rookie IIT-trained engineer at M&M, in 1996 when the company was fighting for survival. The design and development of the Scorpio was a defining moment for M&M as a company and a brand.

The Scorpio is a truck-type, four-door SUV wagon with a separate frame, three-row seating for up to seven persons, and the same general dimensions as a Honda CR-V or Jeep Liberty. The Scorpio's current engine is a 2.2-litre, four-cylinder turbocharged diesel engine that was co-engineered with Austria's AVL. M&M has made an allocation of USD 50 million to upgrade the Scorpio for the US market. The US-bound Scorpio would have a second-generation "mHawk" engine that uses four valves per cylinder and a common rail fuel injection system. The engine would have enhanced MPG (mile per gallon) and minimised exhaust emissions (notably carbon dioxide, the greenhouse gas). The vehicle would comply with T2 B5, the American emission standard. Other modern touches include an aluminum cylinder head, extensive use of recyclable plastics and advanced nano-tech metallurgy. So far, the Scorpio had been sold exclusively with a five-speed manual transmission, but the US version will only offer a six-speed automatic transmission. The new transmission would be purchased from an established outside vendor such as Germany's ZF or even General Motors. Unlike other markets, buyers in the US would expect a standard four-wheel-drive system, which would be taken care off in the Scorpio desinged for the US Others modifications to suit American tastes include the addition of a dashboard and side airbags, plus revisions to upholstery, sound-deadening and assembly quality. The Scorpio would be marketed in the US with a four-year and 60,000-km warranty. The Scorpio marketed in India is already offered with expected "first world" features like antilock brakes, rear-obstacle detection, auto-on

[23] "Mahindra Scorpio," ILoveIndia.com

[24] http://consumerguideauto.howstuffworks.com/2010-mahindra-scorpio1.htm

headlamps and even rain-sensing wipers. These features would be available in the US version too. A four-wheel independent suspension tuned by British sports car legend Lotus is also included. The Scorpio's swing-out cargo door is planned to be replaced with a lift gate. A front-facing bench would replace the pair of inward-facing third-row seats and the dated body side cladding by a less-fussy grille. To match its competitors, the US version would have a leather trim, a navigation system, and similar niceties not currently provided with the Scorpio in India.

Distribution for the US Market

M&M aims to have a well-knit distribution channel so that the US customers can buy the vehicle with ease. M&M has selected the famed Global Vehicles USA (GV) as its sole North American distributor. John Perez, owner of Global Vehicles, has a proven track record of introducing new vehicles in the US market. GV is, from its side, also looking at the task of popularising the vehicle in the US market seriously. Out of the USD 80 million advertising budget GV is to chip in with USD 65 million. This demonstrates GV's seriousness and long-term commitment to the vehicle.

As per plan, GV will import Scorpios into the US from the existing Indian plant. The decision to assemble the vehicle in the US with the help of Navistar's facilities in the US[25] is being considered seriously. Therefore, if Navistar's facilities can be used, there may be a possibility that GV will import vehicles in the form of knocked-down kits. This system would allow M&M to avoid the 25% tax imposed on imports and the Navistar plant will also be utilised purposefully. GV has already lined up 315 dealers in the US who have signed on to sell diesel-powered trucks, i.e., M&M's first offerings in the US and the Scorpio as well. The dealer network will be further enhanced to 400 subsequently.[26] The Mahindra dealers have been carefully selected from the sales networks of companies like General Motors, Ford Motor Company, Toyota Motor Corporation and Nissan Motor Company. Each dealer would pay a sum of USD 195,000 as "initiation fee." This fee would give the dealer an exclusive territory or sales point. Mahindra will require a minimum of 900 sq. ft of exclusive showroom space at its dealerships, which the dealers have agreed to provide. One wall will be devoted to M&M's heritage, with a screen showing highlights of its history. US dealers will not have minimum sales quotas, but M&M has assured dealers that "if you sell them, we will build you."[27]

Pricing for the US Market

A penetration pricing strategy has been proposed for the Scorpio in the US market considering the competitiveness, awareness of target customers and advertising budget. M&M wants to build market share at a slow but steady rate considering that this is the first attempt by an Indian SUV to take on world heavyweights in the US market. Keeping all these factors in view, M&M is proposing to keep the US price of the vehicle competitive. Hence, Americans need to pay only USD 25,000 to be the proud owner of an Indian Scorpio.

Communication Plan for the US Market

"We've never seen an Indian car here. A manufacturing company from India is an unfamiliar thing here. There are not many Indian products of any kind selling in the United States. So there is work to be done," says the CEO of an ad agency in Atlanta.[28] PM (M&M) echoed that US consumers need more familiarity with the Mahindra name. "We are not well-known yet. We must first introduce the Mahindra brand name to the US consumers—nothing to do with trucks manufactured in joint-venture executed between Navistar International (49%) of the United States and Mahindra & Mahindra (51%). Mahindra will solely handle that, and brand building exercise will start two or three

25 The Navistar/Mahindra joint venture first launched in 2005 aiming to build light, medium and heavy commercial vehicles for India as well as export markets.

26 http://www.pickuptrucks.com/html/stories/mahindra/jperez.html

27 WARD'S Dealer Business, August 2008.

28 Automotive News, February 26, 2007.

CASE EXHIBIT 2: Price and millage of scorpio's competitors in US market

Car name	Price	Engine (Litre)	Mileage
Ford Explorer	$28,190	3.5-liter V6 engine	14 MPG
Jeep Grand Cherokee	$19,370 - $23,385	4.0-liter 6-cylinder engine	17 MPG
Toyata 4Runner	$27,500	4.0L V6	18.7 MPG
Kia Sorento	$19,995 - $28,895	2.4 DOHC CVVT gasoline engine	27 MPG Hwy, 20 MPG City
Honda Pilot	$25,895 - $40,245	3.5l V-6 engine SOHC -i-VTEC	20 MPG
Lexus Rx	$39,025 - $37,625	3.5-liter V6 engine	28 MPG City/27 MPG Hwy
Chevrolet Traverse	$29,224 - $39,985	3.6L, V-6 engine 6 speed automatic transmission AWD	16 MPG City/23 MPG Hwy
Ford Edge	$27,420 - $35,770	3.5 I-V-6/265 horsepower and 250 ft pounds of torque	15 MPG City/22 MPG Hwy
Chevrolet Equinox	$23.19	3.0L DOHC direct injected V-6 engine at 264 hp.	25 MPG Hwy/18 MPG City
Nissan Rogue	$20,148 - $22,905	2.5 L 170 hp	22 MPG City/27 MPG highway
Mazda CX - 7	$22,480 - $33,815	2.5 litre MZR 4-cylinder engine that produces 161 hp	24.1 MPG highway/19.8 MPG City

Source: Compiled by the writer from the various company Web sites

months before we start selling trucks from Navistar facility". PM (M&M) said during the meeting.

PM (M&M) informed the team that a marketing office had been set up in Alpharetta, Georgia. This office would be lead by Sanjeev Mahoni, a senior vice president of the company. He would be supported by Bob Mason, a former marketing executive with Ford Motor Company's truck operations.

PM (M&M) also confirmed that the company had zeroed in on Strawberry Frog, a New York-based branding agency, for developing the advertisement campaign after a long search. Only a decade old, Strawberry Frog had worked with Chevrolet in Europe, as well as Pepsi and Heineken. Strawberry Frog came into prominence after it successfully designed the communication strategy of Japanese shoe manufacturer Onitsuka Tiger for the US market. The campaign that focused on the cultural moorings of Japan gave the agency its reputation of going "creatively portraying country background" while designing cross-cultural branding campaigns. The agency is expected to work hard to position the SUV as an "Indian innovative automobile manufacturer with 60 years of rich experience" instead of hiding the fact and trying to sell the vehicle on 'global image'. When quizzed about resource commitment for brand promotion, PM (M&M) said, "The launch spend will be modest compared to what other companies spend. But, it will be a fairly significant spending for us." The company's distributor Global Vehicles has also planed road shows involving test drives, showings at public events, and invitations to visit Mahindra dealers.

Competition

PM (M&M) informed the team that the company would set relatively small sales goals for 2009 and 2010—only 10,000 vehicles in 2009. In 2010, the target would be 46,800 assuming the sale of three vehicles per week per dealer and considering a network of 300 dealers. The total revenue earned from this would be USD one billion.[29] PM (M&M) opined that in the stagnating US auto market, Mahindra would need to compete directly with established rivals like Honda, Ford, etc., for each SUV that it sells. He quoted Rebecca Linland, Research Director of global insight[30] "for American consumer price and fuel efficiency are not the only issues behind vehicle selection."

At the end of the meeting, PM (M&M) reiterated that the company has left no stone unturned to Americanise its Indian SUV and subsequently Mahindra & Mahindra pickups. He said that the 196 recommendations[31] given to improve the company's pickup and SUV by its renowned California-based global automobile consultant J.D. Power and Associates would be put into practice soon. Some of the significant changes suggested by the consultant are different seats, different headliners, more cup holders, a redesigned front console, a larger glove box and a more solid sound when the doors close and restyling the truck's grille from "looked a little sad," to "looking triumphant" are significant. He then read out a list of "odds" that needed to be addressed and a list of "in favors" that needed to be honed. He concluded on a confident note by saying that the company was confident of winning the battle since the "in favours" are more than the "odds."

PM (M&M) listed out the following odds against the launch:

- Mahindra is an ethnic sounding name for Americans.
- The SUV market is overcrowded with the presence of leading brands from General Motors, Ford, Dodge, Nissan and Toyota.
- Consumers in the US tend to be loyal and practical traditionalists. Established foreign players such as Toyota, Nissan and Honda have already had their share of trouble attracting this crowd.
- M&M is coming with clean diesel vehicles by maintaining stringent T2B5 emission levels with requisite engine modification based on latest technology. However, diesel has a historic brown image that many US consumers are associated with.
- Consumers in the US still have the attitude, "Can it really be made well if it comes from India?"
- M&M is not launching the SUV with aggressive advertisement budget but Americans are very impulsive buyers.
- Compared to US standards, the advertising budget allocated is very minimal. The brand building exercise planned before the launch also does not seem to be very intensive.
- It took 25 years for the Americans to believe that the Japanese can manufacture good vehicles. The same could be true for India.

PM (M&M) listed out the following points in favour of the launch:

- It is hard to ignore Mahindra because it is a major company in India, which is making inroads into other countries.
- M&M has historically maintained a good relationship with its partners. An example is its successful joint venture with Renault.
- Navistar already has a relationship with M&M for building trucks for Mahindra.
- M&M is very experienced in the automobile industry since it was founded in 1949.
- With the US mandated new low-sulfur fuel, Mahindra vehicles can produce mileage figures that nearly equal those of more fashionable hybrids at a time of soaring gas prices.
- Despite image, it has used green technology.
- Compact SUV like Scorpio will get about 30 miles per gallon in the city and as much as 37 on the highway. That compares with 30 city/34 highway for the $27,000 Ford Escape SUV hybrid and 21 city/27 highway for the gas-powered $23,000 Toyota RAV4.[32]
- Over the past decade, the company exported more than 50,000 tractors in the US but mostly in the rural areas.
- The large expatriate Indian population in the US may contribute towards spreading the brand's goodwill.

---

29 M&M& Scorpio's US entry is a saga of a man and his machine seeking glory in an alien land Dinesh Narayanan, 11 April 2008.

30 IHS Global Insight is a US based company recognised as the most consistently and accurately forecasting company in the world. www.ihsglobalinsight.com

31 Automotive News, February, 26, 2007

32 Baseball, Apple Pie...and Mahindra? Kiley, David Business; Week; 11/5/2007, Issue 4057, p061-063, 3p

- Mahindra plans to start small but smartly. It will spend only about $20 million on marketing in 2009, less than 10% of what Toyota spent to launch the Tundra pickup. Rather it plans to convince the prospective customer by its quality. The prospective customers will be encouraged by dealers for liberal test drives to satisfy themselves first and then buy.
- Mahindra has already attracted a large number of dealers to distribute Mahindra trucks.
- Its global outsourcing is innovative and supporting supply chain to be cost effective. For example; South Korean company Woosin System does the full body design that earlier had been only been present in Jigs and Fixture for body. This modularisation of supplies has increased supply chain efficiency and reduced cost of production.
- South Africa has accepted the Scorpio wholeheartedly because it is inexpensive and reliable. M&M was able to sell close to 9000 vehicles in three years. This is very good news for the company because the Scorpio was pitted directly against global SUVs from Toyota, GM, Volkswagen, Ford and Nissan and cheaper Chinese models like Geely and Meiya.

CASE QUESTIONS

Q1. How experienced is M&M in the domestic market, particularly in the SUV segment? Will the company's experience in India offer it any benefits when it enters the US market?

Q2. Did M&M make the right decision to enter the US market? Do you think that M&M has attained the status for lead country market participation?

Q3. What type of SUV can be sold in the US market? What adaptation is required to be made? Can the SUVs be shipped from India as it is? Do you think M&M's brand image in the Indian context is tenable in the US market?

Q4. How can the perception in the West that a good vehicle cannot come out of India be changed? Should the brand building exercise of M&M, therefore, be devoid of the "made in India" tag?

FURTHER READINGS

Theodore Levitt's 'The Globalisation of Markets': An Evaluation after Two Decades by Abdelal, Rawi and Tedlow, Richard S., in; Harvard Business School Working Paper No. 03-082. (February 2003).

The authors, in this article, critically analysed the Levitt's understanding of "globalisation" which made him think that "preferences are constantly shaped and reshaped". The authors put arguments in supporting Levitt's way of thinking and opined that interactions change things, rather than leaving them the same. Successful firms and the managers who run them do not leave the world as they found it. Rather than taking consumer preferences as a given, successful managers have treated them as outcomes. Therefore the market is, to some important extent, what firms make of it.

The globalisation of markets by Levitt, Theodore,. Harvard Business Review, May-June (1983).

The article is the base of global thinking in marketing. The author articulated that technology and globalisation are shaping the modern world. Therefore, regardless of how much preferences evolve and diverge, they also gradually converge and form markets where economies of scale lead to reduction of costs and prices. Technology as a force is so powerful that it is driving the world toward a converging commonality. The global corporation need to take advantage of it and operate with resolute constancy – at low relative cost – as if the entire world were a single entity;

"Marketing Adaptations by American Multinational Corporations in South America by Chhabra, Surjitt., Journal of Global Marketing, Vol. 9 No. 4, (1996).

The author made a study to determine the extent of adaptations in twenty-three marketing mix elements in fifty-eight MNC s doing business in South America. The study found that adaptations practices were obligatory, not discretionary. Price and promotion aspects were found to be most adapted, while product and distribution elements remained more standardised.

Diagnosing Global Strategy Potential: The World Chocolate Confectionery Industry by Yip George S and Coundouriotis, George A in Planning Review, January/February, (1991).

The authors used the drivers of globalisation in chocolate confectionery industry to understand globalisation potential and developing a globally integrated marketing strategy. The study found that the four main players in the chocolate industry - Nestle, Hershey, M&M Mars, and Jacobs Suchard - differed widely in their application of global strategy, from market participation to the use of global products, the location of value-added activities, standardising marketing mix elements, and deploying competitive moves. The author also found that in the chocolate industry the market drivers are particularly very strong while and cost drivers are relatively weak.

Conceptualising the global market place: marketing strategy implications by Michael Y. Hu and David A. Griffith in Marketing Intelligence and Planning 15/3 (1997)

The authors provided a theoretical underpinning to the standardisation/adaptation debate. The authors expressed that demand functions across different country markets need to become homogeneous in order for a standardised strategy to be effective. Demand functions are not demand curves, which relate price to quantity, but rather are abstract conceptualisations of consumer wants and needs. Further, the paper presented a three-step process to assist marketing managers in assessing the appropriateness of strategy implementation using the electronics industry.

Standardisation of International Marketing Strategy: Some Research Hypotheses by Subhash C. Jain, Journal of Marketing, Vol. 53, No. 1 (Jan., 1989)

The author forwarded thirteen propositions while developing the framework for understanding the extent to which international marketing can be standardised thus bring it close to the global marketing. Factors effecting the standardisations also discussed in details. The author then developed the further research agenda involved in understanding the core issue of standardisation.

Organisational Dimensions of Global Marketing by Hans Raffée, Ralf T. KreutzerEuropean Journal of Marketing, Vol. 23 No: 5(1998)

In this article the authors placed importance of requisite organisational structure to global marketing. First a comprehensive concept of global marketing discussed and then emphasised on specialised organisational forms to take on the global marketing from theoretical thinking in the mind of the managers to the practical implementation level.

Implementing Global marketing strategy: An interview with Whirlpool Corporation by Ilkka A. Ronkainen, Ivan Menezes, in International Marketing Review, Vol. 13, Issue 3 (1996)

The article is basically an interview that the two authors took with Ivan Menezes, vice president, group marketing, Whirlpool Europe. Whirpool Corporation is the world's leading marketer of major appliances having growth from a mostly domestic manufacturer to a global player. He interview mostly revolved round the cf a customer-driven strategy that actually leveraged the growth of the company around the world.

The fundamentals of standardising global marketing strategy by Nanda K. Viswanathan and Peter R. Dickson in International Marketing Review, Vol. 24, Issue 1, (2007)

The authors in this article basically examined the issues of standardisation and adaptation in global marketing strategy to explain the dynamics of standardisation. A three-factor model of standardisation/adaptation of global marketing strategy, developed by the authors, included homogeneity of customer response to the marketing mix, transferability of competitive advantage, and similarities in the degree of economic freedom. The three-factor model aids decisions relating to standardisation in a global marketing context.

Negotiating Cultural Factors

2

Learning Objectives

After studying this chapter, you should be able to:

- Define culture.
- Describe the characteristics and constituents of culture.
- Explain how culture affects consumer behaviour.
- Identify the tools and techniques used to assess the culture of a country.
- Understand the international marketing implications due to country culture.
- Understand the practical impact of culture in international business situation through case discussion.

Chapter Overview

Consumer behaviour can differ across countries. Marketers have to study responsible factors rigorously before they plan their marketing strategy for a country and decide whether to standardise or adapt there. The marketers' inability to correctly gauge any of these factors can adversely affect their efforts and lead to business losses.

Culture is the primary factor that moulds consumer behaviour. However, it is also easy to misunderstand and misinterpret. This chapter discusses culture in detail and explores the relationship between culture and consumer behaviour. It also focuses on the tools and techniques used to assess and compare cultural environments across countries.

Opening Vignette

Why Brad Pit advertised for Cadillac XTS in China but not for USA?

What it takes to market a luxury car in China? Can an American automobile company sell car in the same way in China as they do in USA? Does the manufacturer of the car need to know about the Chinese culture for successful marketing in that country? These were the some questions asked by the marketers of Cadillac, the leading luxury auto brand since 1902, when it comes to marketing of its new luxury car in China. General Motors of USA has been successfully marketing its Cadillac brand across the globe as luxury car over the years. The company was enhancing its product portfolio with upgradation of design and technology in successive models that came out of its stable. During May 2012 the company began production of Cadillac XTS in at the Oshawa Assembly Plant as a full-size luxury sedan and aimed at to position the car as in a new way. The company depended a lot on XTS model as it would replace both the Cadillac STS and DTS, two previous popular model of Cadillac. The previous models earned brickbats from the marketing pundits on the count that the company was fairly unsuccessful to reposition the brand for younger people. Still young Americans perceives that Cadillac is too traditional and would not fit in to their trendy lifestyle. However, the marketing strategist assured the company that Cadillac XTS was destined to break the jinx. They purposefully developed marketing communications for the XTS sedan focusing on the younger generation. The commercials were created intelligently depicting smart behaviors of trendy young generation. You tube commercials were rolled out to convey a particular message that the new model perfectly match with the youthful aspirations. In one such commercial it was shown that a group of boys jumped in to a spacious XTS sedan during midnight and got complete entrenched in loud music coming out of the CUE (Cadillac User Experience) music system. They drove fast on the highway and on the way a truck driver with dog was picked up in to the cab. The XTS finally landed in a restaurant for dinner where one of the boys, seemingly the proud owner of the car, enjoyed dancing with an elegant looking waiter girl. The commercial was created to induce a feeling to the young generation that Cadillac XTS ownership brings out youthfulness. Obviously, the commercial was developed for world market but wanted to be extra careful of Chinese market as craze for luxury car was increasing with the rise of affluence in the country. Hence, the company wanted to develop its marketing strategy for Chinese market with the involvement of its China market experts. As per production plan, the car was to be assembled at China through their Shanghai facilities in the early part of 2013. There were two models, one 3.6 cc and another 2.0 cc, to be launched simultaneously in China. The launching price decided to be the same as that of USA considering the affordability of the luxury segment customer in China. Cadillac wanted to triple its sales in China by 2015, and to help it get to the 100,000 unit sales per year mark. But, is that USA based marketing communications allow to achieve the target? Would they do the same way as in USA? The company strategist found that culturally the Chinese people are, first of all, very less individualistic in nature, second, they obey the society standard and third, western influence is very high on the consumers when it comes to products selection. Based on the cultural understanding of the country, the company unleashed a customised marketing communication plan involving the great Hollywood hero Brad Pitt. In the commercial for the XTS, Brad Pitt drove the large new sedan around San Francisco, shown off the CUE infotainment system, and looked very pensive, before holding up one finger at the end of the ad. The company never involved Hollywood before for marketing commercial when it was for USA considering the culturally high individualistic behavior of American customer. The same company involved Brad Pitt to inform Chinese customers about luxuriousness of the car. This unique positioning of car and marketing success came only through deep understanding of the local culture of the target country. When this culture based marketing practice of the American company was told to the students of international marketing in the classroom situation, the students quipped, "that's interesting! How the companies would know about the culture of different countries? What are other impacts of country culture on marketing practices? How a country culture is related to consumer behavior?".

> ... *the single greatest barrier to business success is the one erected by culture.*
>
> —Edward T. Hall and Mildred Reed Hall

INTRODUCTION

When companies decide to expand into other countries, their marketing teams are confronted with the dilemma of whether to standardise or adapt. Some marketers accept Professor Theodore Levitt's support for standardisation. They identify similarities in the behaviour of consumers across their target market and choose to customise their offering so that it can appeal to all these consumers. Some marketers accept Professor Robert D. Buzzell's views against standardisation and develop a unique offering for each country in their target market. There are also marketers who take a middle path. They choose to adapt specific features of their offering according to the requirements of each target country and standardise the other features. According to these marketers, the degree of country-specific adaptation should be directly proportional to the degree of difference in consumer behaviour across their target market.

The decision to standardise, adapt or take the middle path is governed by variations in consumer behaviour across countries, and all marketers and academicians accept this fact. However, they still have to reach a consensus on whether the variations in consumer behaviour largely depend on culture. In this kind of scenario, what should new marketers do?

Instead of being swayed by conflicting views and hypotheses, marketers should realise that their primary task is to create better customer value in their target market than their competitors. They can do this only by understanding the needs of their customers, and to best understand the customers' needs, they have to study the cultural aspects that shape those needs.

There are evidences that those organisations who acquainted themselves with relevant aspects of the culture of each country were more successful at achieving their marketing objectives than organisations who did not. For example, the Walt Disney Company exported its theme-park model outside the United States, either through partnerships or licensee agreements, as is, without trying to understand country-specific cultures. This worked well in Japan, where the family-entertainment culture is identical to that in the United States. Like US citizens, the Japanese adore Disney's fairy-tale characters, enjoy North American fast food and are willing to make short family trips at any time of the year. Therefore, Tokyo Disneyland, which started in 1983, saw tremendous success from the outset and could establish itself quickly in the Japanese market. By contrast, Euro Disney Resort, which opened in 1992 in Paris and is now known as Disneyland Paris, had a lacklustre start. The French didn't take themselves to the American-styled theme park at all. In addition to favouring localised forms of entertainment and local food, they preferred to take long vacations. This made the expensive hotels at Euro Disney, which focused on short-term visitors with American tastes, unappealing to them. There were various other Americanised aspects to Euro Disney that did not appeal to the French public in general, and all these combined to push Euro Disney towards loss of sales and ultimately a financial crisis. Ultimately, it had to resort to large-scale localisation in accordance with French culture to pull itself out of this crisis.

Avon, the leading manufacture and marketers of cosmetics, also learnt a lesson while daring to get in to a country without adequate understanding of the country's culture., Avon is also known for its unique business model. This model is based on door-to-door sales of products by locally commissioned representatives, primarily women. By 1969, Avon had successfully used the model in the United States and many other countries. Therefore, when it entered the Japanese market that year, it didn't consider it necessary to make alterations to the model. This was an imprudent decision and caused the company to suffer losses during its initial years in Japan. Avon had not realised that cultural differences prevented the Japanese salespersons from being aggressive and outgoing. Japanese women were reluctant to sell products by approaching strangers, and it was unusual for the Japanese to allow strangers into their homes. This made door-to-door selling almost impossible in Japan, and hence, the Avon salespersons were allowed to operate within the network of their own contacts, which was a marked deviation from Avon's business model.

In addition to forced adaptation of business models, it can also become necessary to customise marketing communication according to the culture of a new target country. The aim of marketing communication is to attract prospective consumers by highlighting the unique features and superiority of a product or service. This aim can remain unachieved if a communication planning does not take culture into account, as was proved in the case of the Toyota Motor Corporation of Japan. In 2003, Toyota ran a print advertisement to promote its new offering, the Toyota Land Cruiser Prado, in the Chinese market. The advertisement showed stone lions bowing to the Prado. Although the advertisement intended to highlight the robustness and quality of the Prado, it only succeeded in incensing the Chinese people. They considered it disrespectful that a Japanese car was being portrayed as more powerful than stone lions, which symbolise power and rank in China. The negative sentiments raised by the advertisement forced Toyota to apologise to the Chinese people. It also stopped using the services of Saatchi & Saatchi, the agency that had created the advertisement, to promote the Prado.

Marketing mishaps, described above, prove how important it is for multinational organisations to demonstrate their respect and keenness in understanding different cultures. But what exactly is culture all about? The next section explores this.

Box 2.1 Country-specific customisation boosted sales of popular work of fiction

It is beyond doubt that Harry Potter series of books, written by the British novelist J.K. Rowling, created a landmark in the history of storytelling. The storytelling style was so perfect that it apparently mesmerised readers of different countries without much of a problem. This was evident when it clocked a record sell of 450 million copies worldwide. The success was so astounding that the international marketers started looking at it as a lesson for them in the field of cross cultural marketing. Can a product be so strong that it can forcefully occupy the minds of the target consumers of different countries by bulldosing the cultural barriers? So to say, can the storylines of a book be so engaging that every child, irrespective of the country they belong, is equally attracted and fall in love with the book? Simplistically speaking, did the Harry Potter books require any adjustment in accordance with the cultural underpinning of the countries when they invaded countries after countries to showcase their incredible marketing success?

Let us look at the history of Harry Potter book marketing to understand the answer to the above questions. Ever since the Harry Potter book came in to the limelight the publishers were engaged in devising suitable international marketing strategy. First step in this direction was language translation as per requirement of the respective countries. Sometime contents of the books were also affected to best suit the country requirements. Most common changes included adaptation of the names of the characters to provide local flavour and use of country-specific dialects for characters who originally spoke in English dialects. Hermione Granger in English version was changed to Hermine Granger and Hermine Grang in the German and Norwegian versions respectively to have a feeling of home grown character. Even the central character Harry Potter became Hali Bote in Chinese.

Particular attention was given while naming of the books so that name itself got close to the heart of the readers. The policy was minimum change but with maximum effect of localisation. The original English name *Harry Potter and the Philosopher's Stone*, originally published in 1997, was changed to, *Harry Potter and the Sorcerer's Stone for US* audience. The word 'sorcerer' is more readily understandable than the word 'philosopher' by the US readers. In short, various meticulous changes were made in the translated versions of the books keeping in mind the cultural tuning of the target audience of different countries. These changes enabled readers from all over the world to accept Harry Potter as their own.

CONCEPTUALISING CULTURE

The word 'culture' came into English from the Latin word *cultura*, which literally means cultivation and is related to another Latin word, *cultus*, meaning cult. In its broadest sense, the word 'culture' may be taken as human interactions in a cult. The study of culture, is therefore, an important component of the curricula of social-science subjects such as anthropology, sociology and psychology. Anthropologists and sociologists, in particular, have suggested various definitions of culture over the years. The following are a few of these definitions:

- **Sir Edward Burnett Tylor (1871):** An English anthropologist, Tylor probably provided the first formal definition of culture. According to him, culture comprises the skills and attitudes that each human being acquires as a member of the society.
- **Ralph Linton (1936):** In his book *The Study of Man*, this American anthropologist described status and role as two different facets of an individual's social position. He then went on to define culture as "the total social heredity of mankind".
- **Melville J. Herskovits (1948):** This American anthropologist studied African culture in detail and stated that "culture is the man-made part of the environment".
- **Talcott Parsons and Edward Shils (1951):** According to these American sociologists, culture is "a symbolically mediated pattern of values or standards of appropriateness". These values lead to the creation and use of significant cultural objects.
- **Clyde Kluckhohn (1954):** Kluckhon is best known for developing the theory of culture within American anthropology. His definition of culture is quite practical. According to him, culture consists of "patterned ways of thinking, feeling and reacting, acquired and transmitted mainly by symbols, constituting the distinctive achievements of human groups, including their embodiments in artefacts; the essential core of culture consists of traditional (i.e., historically derived and selected) ideas and especially their attached values".
- **Geert Hofstede (1980):** According to this social psychologist, culture is nothing but "the collective programming of the mind which distinguishes the members of one human group from another".
- **Jane Sojka and Patriya S. Tansuhaj, (1995)[1]:** These two international marketing strategists defined culture as "a dynamic set of socially acquired behaviour patterns and meanings common to the members of a particular society or human group, including the key elements of language, artefacts, beliefs and values".

[1] Jane Sojka and Patriya S. Tansuhaj (1995),"Cross-Cultural Consumer Research: A Twenty-Year Review", in Advances in Consumer Research Volume 22, eds. Frank R. Kardes and Mita Sujan, Advances in Consumer Research Volume 22: Association for Consumer Research, pp. 461–474.

Box 2.2 Culture influences behaviour

Employees from eleven countries were participating in a week-long convention at their company headquarters in London. By the end of the third day of the convention, the vice-chairman of the company, who had spent almost 8 hours daily with these employees, could identify the nationality of each of them from their behaviour. He recorded the following observations in his notebook:

- Mr John of USA did not want to waste time and expected an immediate answer to every question that they asked.
- Mr Suhail of UAE seemed to be preoccupied with their mobile phones.
- Mr Leonardo of Brazil seemed to be very inquisitive and they were also not averse to arguing with the others about various issues.
- Mr Bo Jing of China seemed to be involved in speaking to his other team members. Furthermore, they spoke to each other only in Chinese.
- Mr Benedict of Germany was more interested in obtaining background information on every problem the company was facing.
- The Mehera of Indian operation was little bit late for meeting and hurriedly entered the room.
- Mr Alessandro of Italy was smartly dressed and made impressive statements.
- Mr Ito of Japan did not talk at all during meetings but generally appeared to be alert and attentive most of the time.
- Mr Carlos of Mexico joined the meeting late, almost half an hour.
- Mr Goran of Sweden when asked about the decrease in demand of the company products, he simply requested for more time to analyze the trend.
- Mr Abedi of Tanzania, throughout the meeting, made very short comments.

Source: Compiled by the author using information available on various websites accessed during 14 to 25 September, 2014 and own experience. http://www.theguardian.com/small-business-network/2015/mar/04/americans-business-brits-challenges-communication; http://nngt.org/digital-library/upload/conference6/nesrine.pdf; www.streesmartbrazil.com; www.quora.com/; http://newsthatmattersnot.com/; http://www.wikihow.com/Dress-in-Italy; http://www.worldbusinessculture.com/Business-Meetings-in-Japan.html; http://businessculture.org/northern-europe/sweden/meeting-etiquette/; www.justlanded.com and www.rooshv.com

In 2001, the United Nations Educational, Scientific and Cultural Organisation (UNESCO) also proposed a definition of culture, which is simple yet comprehensive. According to UNESCO, culture is "the set of distinctive spiritual, material, intellectual and emotional features of society or a social group, and that it encompasses, in addition to art and literature, lifestyles, ways of living together, value systems, traditions and beliefs".

Culture and Marketing

Culture attracted attention of international marketers in the early nineties. As more and more multinational businesses went out to the different countries for marketing purpose, the more requirement was felt to understand the culture backed preference of the people living in that country. Various mistakes in marketing in cross cultural situations were also reported during that time which prompted the international marketers to look in to it more seriously. The rich body of knowledge already developed by the anthropologists, sociologist and psychologist in the domain of culture was of great use to them. Various authors in international marketing have indicated that the definition put forward by C. Kluckhohn[2] and Hofstede[3] in 1954 and 1984 respectively suited most for the understanding definitional aspect of culture in the context of cross cultural marketing. As per both the definitions of culture and contemporary marketing issues, it seems culture and marketing are interrelated because of the following arguments:

(a) Culture is collective programming of human mind and therefore distinguishes members of one human group from another. For all important marketing tasks like segmentation, targeting and positioning a good understanding culture is, therefore, required in order to know each group and communicate the targeted group.
(b) Culture induces a group towards a patterned ways of thinking, feeling and reacting. It is very important for the marketers to have a feel on how target consumer thinks, feel and react to marketing stimuli. Advance information of culture, therefore, helps to shape marketing task related to assessment of consumer behavior.
(c) Cultural values are transmitted on to an individual by other members of the cultural group. One of the vehicles for this transmission is symbol, i.e., objects and process that carry meaning unique to a given culture. This understanding helps the marketers in marketing communication and use of natural elements in advertisements like colour, shapes, locations, materials, animals, and gestures. For example, white symbolises birth or happy life in west but China it is death. Red is prosperity in China.
(d) Examples are at galore when culture of a group of people or community has been highly influenced by exemplary achievements of some persons, alive or dead, of their group or community. Bengali people in India highly appreciate their hero Subhash Chandra Bose and therefore, endeavour to copy behaviour of their hero. Assamese people love to imitate their hero Lachit Barphukan and model their behaviour in that way. So, knowledge of culture of particular community allows marketers to understand characteristics those are most appreciated by them. This would help the marketers in marketing tasks like product/brand promotion through portrayal of a character who serves as model of behaviour for the concerned culture.
(e) The culture based behaviour of a person is highly intuitive which essentially is driven by the person's centrally held value system. This enduring value system builds up person's belief which in turn guides actions in every occasion. So, understanding culture would help the marketers in marketing task like linking consumer value system with the products attributes and communicating the same across the target consumers.
(f) Culture is manifested through expressive, symbolic activity comprising of a number of behaviors occurring in a fixed order, frequently repeated overtime like festivals. Understanding of culture would, therefore, help the marketers to take advantage in deciding on time slot for marketing activities like new product launch in the foreign market, promotional punch for invigorating sales.

[2] Kluckhohn, C. 1954, "Southwestern Studies of Culture and Personality", in American Anthropologist, vol. 56, no. 4, pp. 685–697. American Anthropological Association.

[3] Hofstede, Geert. 1984. Culture's consequences: International differences in work-related values, Abridged edition. Sage Publications.

ELEMENTS OF CULTURE

FIGURE 2.1 Characteristics of culture

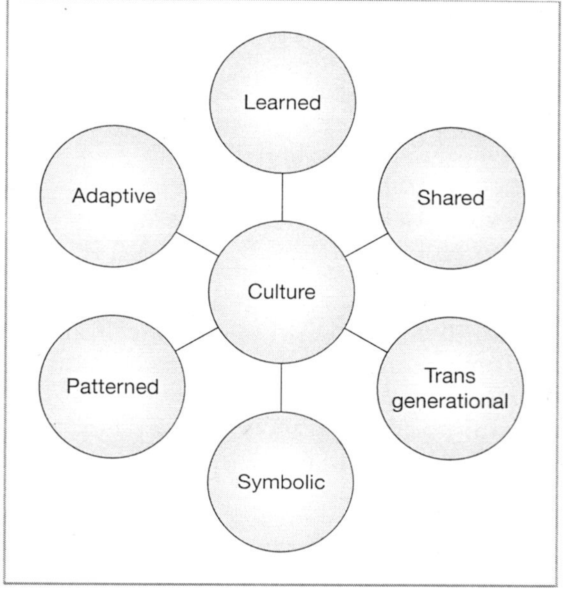

Marketing is a people-oriented function; so, cultural influences on consumers have been identified as critical determinants of marketing effectiveness. Culture and its usual characteristics (Figure 2.1), then being so omnipresent, might exert more influence on human behaviour than what the globalisation prophets expected and, concurrent with much talked about homogenisation tendency. The cultural idiosyncrasies are expected to set the code of people's behaviour in different parts of the world, leading to formation of specific national culture for each country. National culture sets the norms, behaviours, beliefs, and customs of the people living in the country in an identical way.

However, culture and its manifestation on human behaviour are complex, and hence, it is difficult to be understood by marketers. Hence, there is a need for some schema by which marketers could understand and utilise cultural phenomenon to their advantage. One such schema, which has gained wide acceptance, was suggested by Herskovits (1948)[4], who divides culture into five basic elements on which the interpretive framework can be developed.

1. Material culture (including technological and economic phenomena)
2. Social institutions (including social organisations, educational systems, and political structures),
3. Belief systems,
4. Aesthetic systems (including graphic and plastic arts, folklore, music, drama, and dance), and
5. Language of these elements.

Writers, thereafter, developed another cultural framework, which has seven basic elements. They are (1) Religion, (2) Values and attitudes, (3) Aesthetic

FIGURE 2.2 Elements of culture

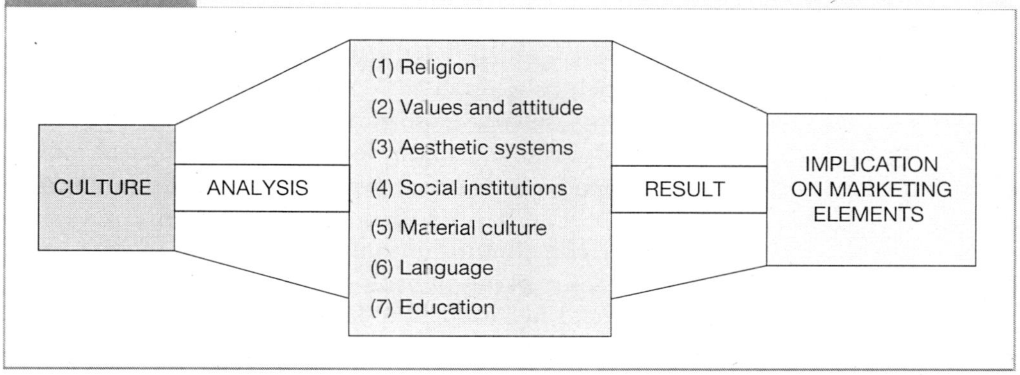

[4] Herskovits, M. J. (1948), *Man and his works: The science of cultural anthropology*, Knopf, New York.

system (4) Social organisations, (5) Technology and material culture, (6) Language and (7) Education (Figure 2.2). Let us examine the cultural elements one by one.

Religion

Religion is an important cultural factor that can have a strong influence on people's attitudes, values and behaviours, at both individual and soci etal levels. Religion manifests in consumer behaviour through rituals and symbols. A series of studies on religious affiliation and consumer behaviour that was done by Hirschman in the early 1980's showed that:

1. Jewish consumers tend to be more innovative and less brand- and store-loyal than non-Jewish consumers (Hirschman, 1981)
2. Catholic consumers are more influenced by price, location, transportation, and mood in making entertainment-related choices than are Protestant consumers (Hirschman, 1982), and
3. Jewish, Catholic, and Protestant consumers use different evaluation criteria for making entertainment, residential, transportation and pet choices.[5]

There are about one hundred different religions across the countries of the world, the dominant among them being Christianity, Islam, Hinduism, Buddhism and Judaism. Of these, Christians make up 33.39% (of which Roman Catholics constitute 16.85%, Protestants 6.15%, Orthodox 3.96%, and Anglicans 1.26%), Muslims 22.74%, Hindus 13.8%, Buddhists 6.77%, Sikhs 0.35%, Jews 0.22%, Baha'is 0.11%, other religions 10.95%, non-religious 9.66% and atheists 2.01%[6]. Different religions have different beliefs, which shape the behaviour of the people following their respective faiths. The companies need to make sure that their products and services are not offensive, unlawful, or distasteful to the people or their beliefs, largely framed by the religion they practice. Nike, the sports shoe maker, antagonised the believers of Islam religion by unknowingly putting stylised "Air" logo that resembled "Allah" in Arabic script. Nike had to apologise to the offended people and pulled the shoes from further distribution and in the process made a huge loss. The US bottle sealing company, Crown Cork and Seal found that their logo of a scantily clad woman is unacceptable to the Islamic societies. Jewish religion prescribes Kosher foods (food that conforms to the regulations of Jewish dietary law) for the followers that conform to the rules of the Jewish religion. The food can be non-kosher due to the presence of ingredients derived from non-kosher animals or from kosher animals that were not properly slaughtered, a mixture of meat and milk, wine or grape juice (or their derivatives) produced without supervision, the use of produce from Israel that has not been tithed (one-tenth part of something paid as a voluntary contribution usually to support a religious organisation.), or even the use of cooking utensils and machinery which had previously been used for non-kosher food. The followers of Hindu religion are usually not expected

[5] Mokhlis, Safiek (2009), "Relevancy and Measurement of Religiosity in Consumer Behavior Research", *International Business Research*, Vol. 2, No. 3, July.

[6] The 2014 CIA fact sheet estimate.

to consume beef as cow holds a sacred place in Hinduism. Consumption of pigs is forbidden among Muslims though pork is the most widely eaten meat in the world. Followers of Jainism, found in India, do not eat root vegetables (such as carrots, potatoes, radish, turnips, etc.) as they believe food grown underground contains more bacteria hence eating them would lead loss of life in some form. Apart from food intake, people's consumption pattern is also influenced by religion. Hindus purchase gold ornaments heavily a few days before the worshipping of goddess Kali and believe that this ritual would bring prosperity to them. Indians like to purchase vehicles on religiously auspicious days and car companies take advantage of this belief by organising numerous marketing events during these days. Some symbols are considered holy symbol in religions such as "786" for the Muslims, "Om" for the Hindus. "8" for the Chinese, "9" for the Japanese and international marketers can take advantage of the impact of these on the consumer behaviour.

Values and Attitudes

Rokeach[7] defined value as an enduring belief that one mode of conduct or end-state of existence is preferable to an opposing mode of conduct or end-state of existence. A value system is a "learned organisation of principles and rules to help one choose between alternatives, resolve conflicts and make decisions". Values set a standard that describe what is desirable or undesirable, good or bad, beautiful or ugly and acceptable or unacceptable. For example, two persons driving their respective vehicle in Indian street when confronted with red signal at a traiffic police point may behave differently. The first person might stop his car well ahead of the white bordered STOP line or GIVE WAY line but the second person might cross the traffic lines without paying much attention to the traffic rules intentionally. Psychologists say that these two persons have two different value system. Possibly the first person grew up in a very much law abiding environment while the this was not the case with the other one. So unknowingly the human beings set their standard of what is desirable or undesirable and act in accordance with that. Many Indian Bollywood movies of yesteryears used to delve with the plot that a person's two sons got separated from each other in a congregation. One son was picked up by a dacoit so when grew up adult he behaved like a dacoit who tried to break the laws of the land. The other son was picked up by police officer and eventually he grew up to protect the laws of the land. The differences in behaviours were because of differences in their values. So, value brings attitude and behaviour is the manifestation of one's attitude. These standards or values also vary from country to country and can be used by the marketers to understand actually how people will behave in a certain circumstances. For example, an average Japanese would respect the seniority of a person by age while an American would go by the official hierarchical position the person enjoys. A simple comparison of values across three countries can be seen in the Table 2.1.

[7] Rokeach, Milton (1973), *The Nature of Human Values*, Free Press, New York.

Table 2.1 Cultural values and priorities across countries

	USA		Japan		Arab countries
1	Freedom	1	Belonging	1	Family security
2	Independence	2	Group harmony	2	Family harmony
3	Self-reliance	3	Collectiveness	3	Parental guidance
4	Equity	4	Age/seniority	4	Age
5	Individualism	5	Group consensus	5	Authority
6	Competition	6	Cooperation	6	Compromise
7	Efficiency	7	Quality	7	Devotion
8	Time	8	Patience	8	Patience
9	Directness	9	Indirectness	9	Indirectness
10	Openness	10	Go between	10	Hospitality

Note: '1' indicates most important cultural value and '10', the least

Source: As per information given in Elashmawi, Farid, and Philip R. Harris. Multicultural Management: New Skills for Global Success. Houston, TX: Gulf Publishing Company, 1993, P-63.

Box 2.3 Can alienate a bit, but cannot make one a stranger to one's own culture

The American multinational food manufacturing company Kellogg, headquartered in Michigan, USA, leant a new lesson in India in the matter of cultural barrier in marketing. Kellogg has been famous all over the world because of its cornflakes based cereal which has its market in over 180 countries of the world. Kellogg's crispy cornflakes is generally consumed with cold milk to retain the crispiness while consuming. Westerners like that crispiness but it is not so for the Indians. Indians have been taught right from their childhood that milk has to be consumed every day and that milk should always be consumed hot. Its suits with the tropical country requirement as well that if not heated once it may become undrinkable. When the company made aggressive marketing of crispy cornflakes in India, on entry, the Indian family started eating corn flakes with hot milk.

When hot milk was poured over the corn flakes it became soggy and they were found less tasty and suitable for eating. The entire marketing team felt helpless to the Indian culture of taking hot milk and watched silently the decline in sales. Kellogg's later had to modify their products to suit hot milk but the damage had already been done. Kellogg's overlooked the cultural factor that Indians have always preferred their milk hot. In addition to the hot and cold debacle, the product was positioned wrongly by not understanding the culture again. Kellogg was positioned as an alternative to the regularly consumed Indian traditional breakfast comprising of oily Parantas, Puris and Dosas. These breakfasts provides a feeling of fullness which the Indians like very much.

Kellogg's Corn flakes, on the contrary, does not give that feeling of fullness and the average Indians when tried with Kellogg's cornflakes as breakfast needed to have some more food in the morning time itself. This made Indians disliking for cornflakes as breakfast item.

Other issue is that Indian breakfast is known for its variety which is missing in corn flakes based breakfast. Indians are not used to same types of breakfast every day. Unlike their western counter part, the Indian housewives love cooking spicy and hot food for breakfast and gets satisfaction when self cooked foods are consumed by the family members. The time spend in getting the food consumed is also different than the westerners. It is not preferred to have a quick breakfast but an elaborate breakfast with variety. Will it not be too much then asking Indians to get satisfied with cornflakes as breakfast though cornflakes has good food value?

Aesthetics

The term "aesthetics" comes from the Greek word "*aesthesis*", meaning a "sense perception". Different people have different sense of perception and hence attach varying levels of importance to design and beauty. The Japanese appreciate, first and foremost, nature and its changes. They enjoy the cherry blossom in spring, the moon in summer and the changing colour of leaves in autumn. The Japanese garden "Bonsai" (potted miniature tree) and "Tokonoma" (an alcove provided in the guest room) among other such arts, reflect the Japanese love for nature[8]. It is interesting to note that all the people from the same culture have the same way of appreciating design and beauty. International marketers take advantage of country specific understanding of what is aesthetically correct for a country. International marketers before entry to a new country endeavours to understand what is fashionable design, what falls under the purview of good taste, what color is liked, and what music or architecture naturally appreciated by the people of the country. This understanding helps them to design marketing programme. John Player, the English cigarette brand took advantage of aesthetic preference of the British people in marketing their product, i.e., cigarette. Imperial Tobaco Company deliberately put efforts to develop 'Navy Cut' branded cigarettes under its subsidiary John Player and Sons in England using the picture of the famous Nottingham castle on the reverse of this packet to convey a sense of pride to the people of Nottingham in particular and England in general .Very soon the castle trade mark strategy of the 'Navy Cut' brand started paying off rich divident. John Player and sons became the largest and most important company in Nottingham providing jobs for thousands of workers from the city. Whenever a British smoker pickup the cigarette packet with the castle trademark in the back the person felt an inevitable link between the brand and Nottingham based heritage leading to a sense of happiness.

In Japanese culture aesthetic dimensions are very active even in day to day life. Seasonable haikus are featured in front page of major newspapers, business letters are written with reference to the beauty of the season, food is carefully arranged in a plate specifically chosen to suit particular food item and season, gifts are wrapped in package that provides the allure of exposing the hidden.[9]

Social Organisation

The nature of social organisations varies from culture to culture. Social organisation in a particular culture is formed by the people of a society so that the members of the society carry out their assigned social roles with an understanding of the pattern of mutual relationship. It indicates how people organise themselves together to meet their shared needs in a society. It is important for the international marketers to understand the assigned socials roles of their targeted consumers in a country market and how they organise themselves as a group for societal activities and roles played by them in the purchase and consumption situations. For example, in East Asia, though China, Korea, Japan and Vietnam have different languages and specific cultures of their own, their social organisations are family-based and primarily patriarchal in nature. Here, the unit of social organisation is family and the

[8] Sai, Ysutaka (1995), "The eight core values of the Japanese Businessman", *Asia Pacific Journal of Human Resourees*, March 35 (2).

[9] Japanese Aesthetics of Packaging, by Yuriko Saito © 1999 The American Society for Aesthetics.

family is headed by a male member who has privileges and responsibilities to the other members of the family. This male member's role is important for the international marketers. For example, the male member who may be husband or father has the following roles:

- He would have the final say on procurements of commodities for family need.
- He would be primarily involved in a purchase function that is required for the family.
- He would decide the restaurant to go to, when hosting a family party.
- He would be the primary earner in the family and decide on the expenses that the family makes for consumer goods.

However, in a matrilineal system, women have a higher status in society than do women in a patriarchal system, as for example in some part of India such as Kerala (communities like the Nairs and Ezhavas and Warriers and in Meghalaya (Khasi, Jaintias and Garo tribes). However, with economic enhancement, social role are fast changing and tends to become ambiguous in nature.

International marketers are also interested to know the size of membership of the social organisation as this forms the primary unit of their market. In Scandinavian countries, the average household size is expected to be the smallest with a substantial number of one-man household. In the US, the basic social organisation, i.e., each household constitutes of limited members such as the husband, wife and a son or a daughter giving rise to nuclear family. In many African countries like Tanzania the parents living in the rural areas play a very limited role in influencing the life style of their urban living adult boys or girls. In India, there is an urban–rural divide in the matter of the size of the households. In rural India, a typical household consists of the joint family of grandparents, uncles, aunts and cousins. However, in urban India, the US type of nuclear family structure is prevalent.

Material Culture

Material culture refers to how people adopt and adapt to technology in a material sense. Technology is becoming increasingly critical to the success of all international businesses. The technological gap between advanced and emerging nations remains vast, and effective international marketing depends how effective the firms are in introducing superior technology products in markets with full understanding of the absorption process by the targeted consumer. Here, culture plays a role in technology absorption by the target consumer of a particular country. International marketers need to take note of the diffusion rate of technology-based products in countries where technology absorption is often hindered by factors such as insufficient income, deficient infrastructure, cultural barriers and lack of information. For example, in Brazil, due to the country's huge territory and complex geographical and cultural formations, a technological innovation is seldom capable of reaching the population as a whole and benefiting the entire society[10]. In two West African capital towns, Ouagadougou and Bamako, bicycle is deemed dangerous in traffic, less efficient, and most of all, is perceived as the transport mode of the poor. Netherlands and Japan has high bicycle transportation allotment rate of 27% and 14% respectively and is increasing, whereas it is only 1.2% in South Korea.[11] Though other factors such as road width, traffic rule, bicycle route signage, etc. play a role in the use of the bicycle, however cultural norms parevailing in the country are also appear to be determinants of its non-utilisation. Changing this kind of negative attitude towards material culture could be an extremely difficult task for the international marketers. Yujie Wei and Salil Talpade, in their study "Materialism of mature consumers in China and USA: A cross-cultural study", found that mature Chinese consumers are more materialistic than their American counterparts[12].

Language

Language is an important element of culture as it aids in gathering information and evaluating it. International marketers operate in different countries having different languages. It is important that firms are capable of communicating to their target customers effectively and consumers are also able to understand the communication and its context. The same words or sentences may have different meanings in different countries. For example, originally a brand name 'hoover' in Britain indicates towards a vacuam cleaners in that country almost unmistakably but can anybody in India will be able to understand it until explained. 'Mash with bread' in British English is simply a dish containing mashed potatoes with bread but in India most people will be asking what mashed 'food item' is added with bread to make it a food dish. 'Doux ' is French word which means soft, cosy and agreeable to touch all at the same time and French company L'Oreal used it worldwide to convey the effectiveness of its hair famous care product ' Ultra Doux'. However, since there is no English equivalent so many Indians could not understand the meaning exactly. In countries of high context culture where non-verbal language is more explicit in communicating people's mood, choice, likings, etc. than the spoken language, international marketers need to be extra careful. Non-verbal communication involves those non-verbal stimuli in a communication setting that are generated by both the source [speaker] and his or her use of the environment. These non-verbal cues have a potential message value for the source or receiver [listener][13].Basically, non-verbal communication is the sending and receiving of messages in a variety of ways without the use of verbal codes (words). Most speakers and listeners are not conscious of the non-verbal messages they send. Such messages may be intentional or unintentional and may include but not limited to elements such as touch,

[10] M. de Holanda, Giovanni, Ismael M.A. Ávila and Ricardo B. Martins (2008), "Mapping users' perspectives and outlining social impacts from digitalisation of terrestrial TV in Brazil", *Telematics and Informatics*, 25(1), 19 – 35.

[11] Chung, Kyung-Ryul, Joon-Ho Hyeong, Chun-Ho Choi, Sa-Yup Kim and Gyu-Seog Hong (2011), "A study on the design strategy for promotion of bicycle use", Wellness Technology Center, Korea Institute of Industrial Technology, Korea.

[12] Yujie Wei and Salil Talpade (2010) "Materialism of Mature Consumers in China and USA: A Cross-Cultural Study". Journal of International Business and Cultural Studies. Vol. 2.

[13] Samovar, Larry A., Richard E. Porter and Edwin McDaniel (1991), *Communication Between Cultures*, Belmont, Wordsworth.

Box 2.4 Non verbal communication across the world

Non verbal mode of communication is also very effective in our day to day live. Remember the famous scene of the science fiction blockbuster movie series 'The Hunger Games' where saluting with three fingers symbolised rebellion against totalitarian rule, signifying thanks, admiration and goodbye to a loved one. When in the recent times Thaliand was brought under army rule the protesters were utilising the three figure gestures in the public place causing lot of uneasiness for army rulers. Possibly, the protesters could not have communicated their dissent in a better way by using spoken language. Since time immemorial people have been using different type of non verbal communications across the world to communicate with each other along with verbal communications. These are gesture, postures, facial expressions, eye contact and gasing, touch differences, smell differences and different paralanguages. The problem that the international marketers face roots from the point that these non verbal communications are not standardised across the countries of the world. Bowing shows rank in Japan but not in US and other western countries. American may use index finger for pointing but Germans like to use their little finger for the same purpose. While at work many Asian workers may suppress facial expression in the matter of discontentment but same is not true with European workers. Japanese, Africans or Latin Americans, would like to avoid prolong eye contact with seniors to show respect but in western cultures direct eye to eye contact is seen as positive spirit. Shaking hands with little pressures may be sign of showing intention of maintaining warm relationship but the same in Japan is a rude behaviour. An Indian may go for frequent bathing to get rid of bad body odour by a westerner may like use more deodorant to suppress offensive natural smells.

glance, eye contact (gaze), volume, vocal nuance, proximity, gestures, facial expression, intonation, dress, posture, smell, word choice and syntax and sounds (paralanguage). A strong verbal persuading ability is considered a suitable quality for a salesman in India. The same may not be true for a salesperson in Japan where customers prefer to be communicated to less through verbal communication and more through non-verbal exchanges like gesture, posture, etc.

Education

Education

Countries of the world vary in terms of drives for attainment of education also. United Nations Educational, Scientific and Cultural Organisation (UNESCO) indicated that few countries of the world are traditionally having higher urge for educational developments and accordingly they are spending high amount for educational development in their countries. During 2007 it was found that education budget of a single country like France or Italy outweighing education spending across all of sub-Saharan Africa. USA, as a country, traditionally found inclined for high drive for education. USA though have only 4% of the world's children and young people but spending of about 28% of the global education budget. In contrast, the UNESCO report on global education revealed that though sub-Saharan African countries had about 15% of the school-age population but they together spend only 2.4% of global education resources. Data from UNESCO Institute of statistics revealed that USA spent more than $11,000 per elementary student in 2010 and more than $12,000 per high school student. Switzerland's total spending per student was even higher than USA with $14,922 while Mexico averaged only $2993 in 2010. The average spending pattern of OECD nations stood around $9313 per young person. UNESCO Institute of statistics continues to present the education statistics of the countries of the globe of which the "The Global Education Digest, 2012" is the latest which covers more than 200 countries of the world. The net enrolment rate (NER) in countries like Pakistan and Ethiopia was dismal with about 72% and 78% respectively while in Japan the NER was 99.5% during 2011. International marketers need to understand the overall level of education of the target group as it may allow them to be sophisticated in their marketing communication. Educated consumers are generally found to be more rational shoppers. The education level of women has been found to influence the food consumption patterns in China. It has led to the consumption of nutritious and preferred foods in a manner independent of the effect of income[14].

CULTURE AND CONSUMER BEHAVIOUR: THEORETICAL CONTRIBUTIONS

Literature on culture has witnessed a number of theoretical contributions made by different researchers at different points in time explaining the relationship between culture and consumer behaviour. We shall now discuss a few prominent theories.

Raju's A-B-C-D Model

Raju's A-B-C-D paradigm model (1995)[15] provided a simple framework that can be used by marketers to understand consumer behaviour within a particular country and country specific differences in consumer behaviour across countries. It considered the purchase and consumption process in any culture along four sequential stages: Access, (A), Buying (B), Consumption (C), and Disposal (D).

Samli Model

Samli model (1995)[16] emphasises that the factors which influence an individual consumer in a purchase situation are already "pre-screened and further modified by culture and other environmental factors" by the individual's culture-bound personality. The buyer's personality is influenced by culture-bound factors when he or she is involved in decision making

[14] Bhandari, Rajika and Frank J. Smith (1998), "Education and food consumption patterns in China: Household analysis and policy implications", *Journal of Nutrition Education and Behavior*, Volume 32, Issue 4, Pages 214–224 (July 2000).

[15] Raju, P.S. (1995), "Consumer behavior in global markets: the A-B-C-D paradigm and its application to Eastern Europe and the third world", *Journal of Consumer Marketing 12*, No. 5: 37–56.

[16] Coskun, Samli, A. (1995), *International Consumer Behavior: Its Impact on Marketing Strategy Development*, Quorum Books, Westport, Connecticut.

FIGURE 2.3 Samli's international consumer behaviour model

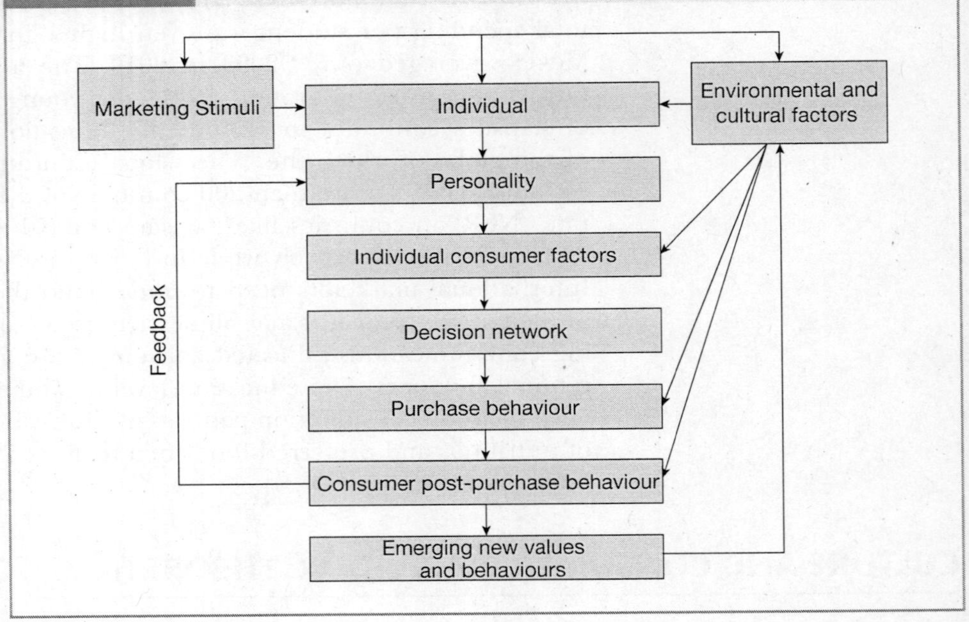

followed by actual purchase. This model shows that an internal feedback emanates from the post-purchase behaviour of the consumer. The personality of the consumer is affected by use of the product and hence, his or her culture evolves with time. The working of the model is as shown in Figure 2.3.

Manrai and Manrai Model

Manrai and Manrai (1996)[17] model of cultural and consumer behaviour considered the components of culture in be categorised into three categories, namely, social, personal and psychological component. Social components are influenced by intermediary variables, i.e., roles and norms; personal components are influenced by lifestyle, personality and self-concept and psychological components are influenced by beliefs, values, attitudes and symbolism. The intermediary variables and the resultant processes such as individualism/collectivism, socialisation and motivation/perception/learning give rise to product acquisition and consumption behaviour, adoption/diffusion of innovations, complaining/complimenting behaviour, responses to advertising/marketing communication and responses to distributional and pricing aspects. However, the resultant consumer behaviour is influenced by political legal, technological and economic environment in which the society exists (Figure 2.4).

[17] Manrai, Lalita and Ajay Manrai (1996), "Current issues in cross-cultural and cross-national consumer research", *Journal of International Consumer Marketing 8*, No. 3/4: 9–22.

FIGURE 2.4 Manrai and Manrai's model of the effect of culture on consumer behaviour

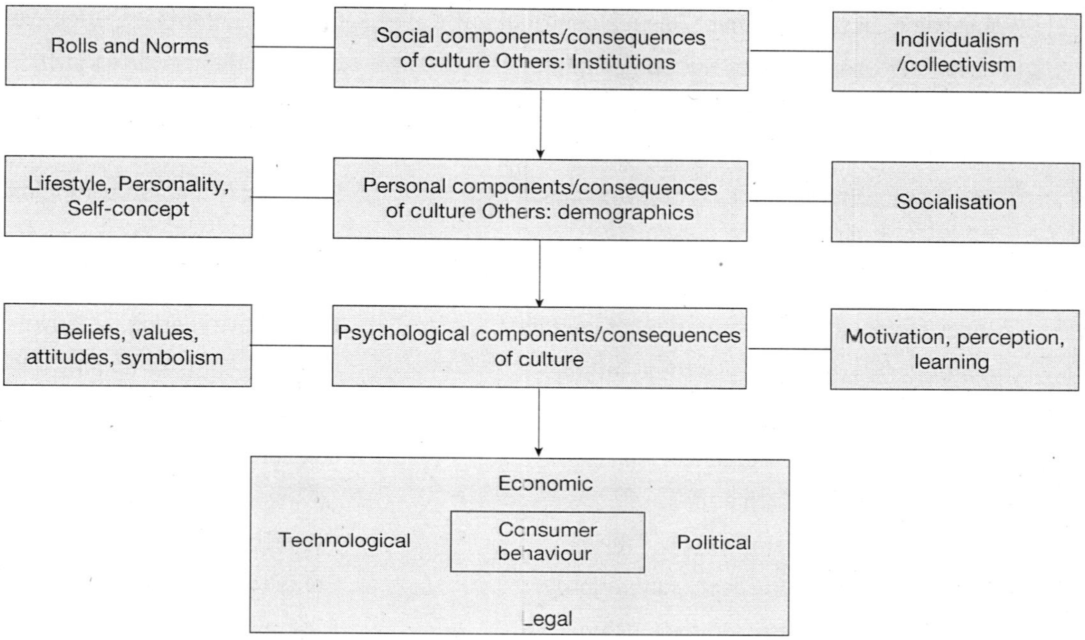

Luna and Gupta Model

Luna and Gupta (2001)[18] postulated that marketing communications influence culture directly and indirectly and hence it is the value system held by the consumer as much as his or her enduring belief that guides actions and judgment across a specific situation. Every culture has unique set of values. Examples of values include 'freedom', 'pleasure', 'inner harmony' and 'happiness'. Rokeach (1973)[19] viewed values at two different levels – terminal values and instrumental values (Table 2.2). Terminal values imply the preferred end states of being and instrumental values indicate the preferred modes of behaviour or means to achieve the end states.

The value system of an individual is constituted of three aspects: heroes, rituals, and symbols. Heroes are alive or dead, who serves as model of behaviour in the society. For example, people living in the eastern part of India

Table 2.2 Rokeach's value system

Terminal values	Instrumental values
A comfortable life (a prosperous life)	Ambitious (hard-working, aspiring)
An exciting life (a stimulating, active life)	Broadminded (open minded)

(*Continued*)

[18] Luna, David, and Susan Forquer Gupta (2001) "An integrative framework for cross cultural consumer behavior", *International Marketing Review 18*, No. 1: 45–69.

[19] Rokeach, Milton (1973), *The Nature of Human Values*, Free Press, New York.

Table 2.2 *(Continued)*

Terminal values	Instrumental values
A sense of accomplishment (lasting contribution)	Capable (competent, effective)
A world at peace (free of war and conflict)	Cheerful (light-hearted joyful)
A world of beauty (beauty of nature and the arts)	Clean (neat tidy)
Equality (brotherhood, equal opportunity for all)	Courageous (standing up for your beliefs)
Family security (taking care of loved ones)	Forgiving (willing to pardon others)
Freedom (independence, free choice)	Helpful (working for the welfare of others)
Happiness (contentedness)	Honest (sincere, truthful)
Inner harmony (freedom from inner conflict)	Imaginative (daring, creative)
Mature love (sexual and spiritual intimacy)	Independent (self-reliant, self-sufficient)
National security (protection from attack)	Intellectual (intelligent, reflective)
Pleasure (an enjoyable, leisurely life)	Logical (consistent, rational)
Salvation (saved, eternal life)	Loving (affectionate, tender)
Self-respect (self-esteem)	Obedient (dutiful, respectful)
Social recognition (respect, admiration)	Polite (courteous, well-mannered)
True friendship (close companionship)	Responsible (dependable, reliable)
Wisdom (a mature understanding of life)	Self-controlled (restrained self)

are greatly influenced by Subhash Chandra Bose who fought almost a lone battle to achieve Indian independence from the British. This may be true for each country where some national heroes are praised and have influencing effects on the countrymen. Now, the term ritual[20] refers to a type of expressive, symbolic activity constructed of multiple behaviours that occur in a fixed, episodic sequence, and that tend to be repeated over time. Ritual behaviour is dramatically scripted and acted out and is performed with formality, seriousness and inner intensity. Ritualistic behaviour is important consumer behaviour as it involves consumption of goods and services that occur in a fixed, episodic sequence and tend to be repeated over time. For example in India, a group of people believe that purchasing gold during "Dhanteras" would bring fortune to the family and celebrate the occasion every year. In Tanzania 'Saba Saba' is a national festival where farmers show the products and produce to international business and it is celebrated on the 7th day of the seventh month every year. Symbols are words, gestures, pictures or objects that carry a particular meaning, which is only recognised by those who share a particular culture. For example, the word 'Bande Mataram' carries the meaning of patriotism in Indian society. The picture of 'Charka' (a simple instrument that spins cotton to thread), in Indian context, represents the value of 'freedom'.

[20] Rook, D.W. (1985), "The ritual dimension of consumer behavior", *Journal of Consumer Research*, Vol. 12, December, 251–64.

FIGURE 2.5 Luna and Gupta's model of culture and consumer behaviour interaction

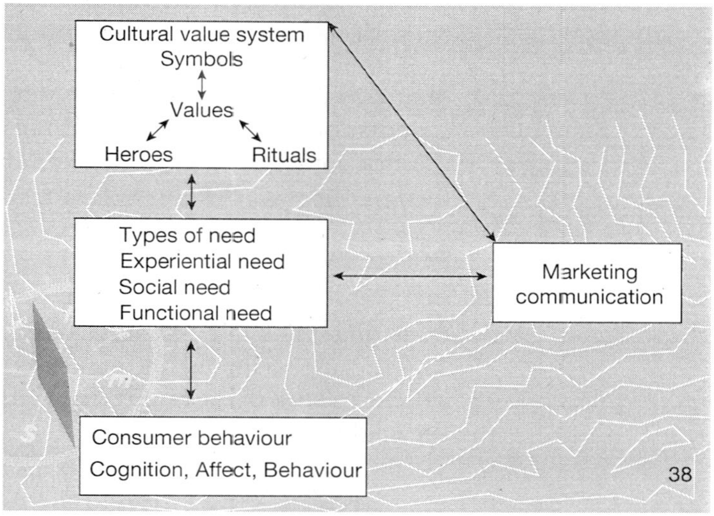

Thus, these three aspects of heroes, rituals and symbols give rise to the cultural value system in a country. The cultural value system influences the different needs of human beings such as experiential need, social need and functional need (Figure 2.5). As a result, consumers belonging to same culture recognise (cognition) a marketing communication in a particular way and develop a like or dislike to a particular product (effect) and influence what they do in a particular purchase situation (behaviour). One interesting point is that any given culture evaluates and reacts to a marketing communication the same way as marketing communication also affects the culture and makes it evolve continuously with time.

CULTURAL DIMENSIONS: TOOLS AND TECHNIQUES

Hofstede's Cultural Dimensions

International businesses require sound understanding of cultural barriers. They also require mechanisms to assess and overcome cross-cultural marketring barriers. Writers and the researchers in the field of culture found that multi-country business success is fairly dependent on breaking the barriers erected by culture prevalent in those countries. For an international business, it is, therefore, important to know how people behave differently due to their cultural background. If a business decides on marketing programmes for a particular country based on the understanding of its home country, chances are that there will be some very bad decisions. In this context, the contribution of Geert Hofstede's[21] research gives insights into different country cultures that can be of great help to international marketers to assess cultural underpinning while deciding on their marketing programmes. Hofstede's research derives from an empirical study of data from about 70 countries with over 60,000 respondents and 116,000 questionnaires. He created four cultural dimensions, and each country received an index on each dimension. Later in 1991, Hofstede added another factor, i.e., Long Term Orientation (LTO) for twenty-three countries of the world. We now describe the first four cultural dimension defined by Geert Hofstede (Figure 2.6) as the last one, i.e., LTO do not have much use in international business.

Power Distance Index (PDI)

PDI is the extent to which the less powerful members of society and institutions (like the family) accept and expect that power is distributed unequally. This represents inequality that exists in a particular society. It suggests towards a society's level of inequality that has been accepted both by the followers and the leaders almost as a rule.

FIGURE 2.6 Five cultural dimensions of hofstede

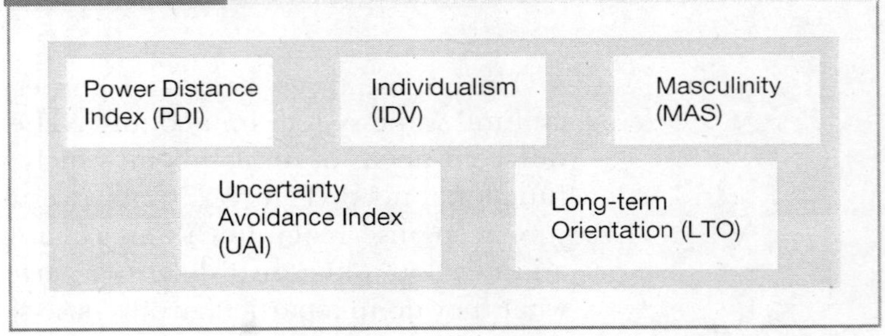

Index	Inference
High PDI	It indicates that inequalities of power and wealth have been allowed to grow within the society. These societies are more likely to follow a system where leaders as well as the followers believe that everybody should not have similar status in the society. Some are there to rule and some are to be ruled. High PDI countries are expected to be hierarchical where the leaders would tend to use force, manipulation, and inheritance as sources of power to remain on the top. **Consequence:** A 'VIP lounge' in New Delhi airports will always be regarded as a place not to be once peeped even by the general passengers as it may disturb the important persons in the society. The concierge in the hotels in Thailand will not be able to match their counterpart in New York by addressing a hotel guest as 'hey Robert, good morning'. A white ambassador car, roaming around parliament house in New Delhi will continued to be looked upon by the general Indians as 'leaders making important decision for the country while moving' even if they are loaded with terrorists. The dresses, the life style, the holiday spots, gadgets, etc. will be cherished by the important people in countries like India, China, Indonesia, Thailand, Malaysia, Korea, Pakistan, etc. because of high power distance exist in these countries. Hofstede's PDI score index for India is 77 and that of Thailand is 64 which may be considered high and in high PDI countries there will be inequalities of power and wealth. An international marketers taking lesson from Hofstede index value will be able to understand the cultural underpinning of the country by understanding the PDI score and develop its marketing programme accordingly.

[21] www.geert-hofstede.com/

Individualism Index (IDV)

Individualism and its opposite, collectivism, stand for the extent or degree to which individuals in the society are integrated into groups. On the individualist side, there are societies in which the ties between individuals are loose: everyone is expected to look after him/herself and his/her immediate family. On the collectivist side, there are societies where people are integrated into strong, cohesive in-groups from birth, often with extended families (uncles, aunts, and grandparents), which continue to protect them in exchange for unquestioning loyalty.

Index	Inference
High IDV	Individuality and individual rights are paramount within the society. Individuals in these societies may tend to form a large number of loose relationships. **Consequence:** 'I want to live my life in my own terms' quipped a teenager in UK who eventually failed to identify with groups, The people around him did not stared at him with a great deal of surprise but rather approved it as a personal matter of a human being. According to the market research firm Euro monitor International, the number of people living alone globally is skyrocketing, rising from about 153 million in 1996 to 277 million in 2011 – an increase of around 80% in 15 years. Who contributed to this growth of individualism? In the UK, 34% of households have one person living in them and in the USA it is about 27%, as per the market research specialist. According to Hofstede individualism dimension the **UK** is amongst the highest of the **individualistic** scores. What the international marketers will do to lure this group of consumers who are individualistic and lives in countries like UK? Can they be treated with the same way as they do in case of a collectivist country?

Masculinity Index (MAS)

Masculinity and its opposite, femininity, refer to value orientation of the people living in the country in accordance with the masculine or feminine nature. Under masculine value orientation, people, in general, behave in an assertive and competitive way. However, under feminine value orientation, there will be inclination of the people to behave in a modest and caring way. Thus, a masculine value-oriented country shows adherence to men's usual values like power assertativeness, achivement, etc.

Index	Inference
High MAS	The country experiences a high degree of masculine values. In these cultures, men values dominate a significant portion of the society and power structure where women values remain subdued. The value orientation in the country will be masculine in nature; for example, strict adherence to rule, less consideration on syspathetic ground, emphasis on self-achievement **Consequence:** Why the Japanese prestigious high speed bullet train 'Shinkasen' always run on time? Why the train always found cleaned enough as if nobody has ever boarded the train? At Tokyo Central Station, a work unit clad in the red uniforms get themse ves ready to with military precision. A bullet train on the Tohoku shinkasen line arrives at Tokyo from Shin Ao Mori every everyday at 16:56 hours and with just 12 minutes the same train will start again as Tsubasa Shinkasen, one out of six train categories operate on the Tohoku Shinkasen line. But the red uniforms Japanese cleaning team has only seven minutes time for the operation clean up. The five minutes will be utilised for passenger disembark and board. During this time the team,

(*Continued*)

(*Continued*)

Index	Inference
	normally 1-2 cleaners each car, would check items left behind on the overhead racks and seats, flip the 100 seat backs in each car, scan the aisles and floor for any refuse, a task generally. wipe off the table tops in front of each seat and adjust the window blinds, exchange the white back seat covers for clean ones. When two minutes of the allotted seven minutes are left they rush for cleaning of the lavatories and washrooms toilets. The last minute they preserve for team meeting at a point to take stock of the situation and final check thereof. At the end they will not forget to bow in unison toward the passengers awaiting boarding. Feeling bad for the team as they are doing these monotonous job 365 days without fail? You may, but average Japanese will not. Japanese because of strong societal masculinity character want everybody for strict adherence to rules and absolute less consideration on sympathetic ground. The same is the case in respect of Shinkasen crews and pilots. They are not allowed to be late or waste time for any personal reasons. How these commonalities in attitude and behaviours can be used by the marketers? May be marketing communications reflects strict adherence to rules, less considerations on sympathetic ground.

Uncertainty Avoidance Index (UAI)

UAI deals with a society's tolerance for uncertainty and ambiguity. UAI refers to how people in the society prefer uncertainty around their day-to-day life. It indicates the extent to which a culture made its members to feel either uncomfortable or comfortable in unstructured situations. Unstructured situations are unexpected, unknown, surprising, and different than what usually happens. People in uncertainty-avoiding countries are more emotional and have structured way of life. In uncertainty-prone cultures, people are generally more tolerant of opinions different from what they are used to and they like to have as few rules as possible. They would not mind different views, and different ways of thinking are allowed to prevail simultaneously in a country. People living under the ambit of this culture are more pragmatic and introspective.

Index	Inference
High UAI	The country has a low tolerance for uncertainty and ambiguity. This creates a rule-oriented society that institutes laws, rules, regulations and controls in order to reduce the amount of uncertainty. **Consequence:** Have you heard Shinkasen or the bullet train in Japan running late? Ask your Japanese co travelers while traveling from Nagoya to Tokyo which is connected by JR Tokaido Shinkansen and it takes exactly 105 minutes to cover a distance of 342 kilometer by Nozomi. The Nozomi is the fastest train category along the Tokaido Shinkansen, serving only major stations and running at a maximum speed of 300 km per hour. Every day the train arrives at Nogoya from Osaka at 7.05 am and reaches Tokyo at 8.42 am. Office goers from Nagoya travelling by Nozomi reach office at Tokyo, therefore, safely just at 9 am on the dot by 5 minutes walk through underground thoroughfare. The follow traveler would reply that he has not heard Shinkasen making late. Even he may ask you what prompted you to think about late running. At the UAI score of 92 Japan is one of the most uncertainty avoiding countries on earth. This country therefore strive to avoid uncertainty in daily life as per as practicable. Everybody wants to behave in a picture perfect style and carryout the designated duty with utmost care. Arriving office in time, keeping the appointment executed in time, even taking coffee at the schedules hours, etc. are some of the norms which the Japanese perform with almost religious accuracy. The international marketers have to be careful about this cultural aspect of Japanese behavior in order to do business in Japan.

(*Continued*)

(Continued)

Index	Inference
	The Japanese would seek for security, assurance, uniformity in marketing intentions and actions. Japanese consumers would like to see that the producers of products are clearly communicating the products benefits and in reality these benefits are achieved consistently while the products are in use. As a result of high UAI this country consumers would initially be hesitant to accept new products on launching unless backed by clear communication and demonstration. The country of origin effect would play a huge role in providing the assurance of surety and consistency.

Culture differences India, Japan, Sweden and UK

India has Power Distance (PDI) as the highest Hofstede Dimension for the culture, with a ranking of 77 compared to a world average of 56.5 (Figure 2.7). This Power Distance score for India explain why this country with huge population is traditionally ruled by few influential persons. Inequality in power and wealth within the society is accepted as natural and not thrown from outside. United Kingdom has a moderately low power distance score of 35 explaining the people's tendency to be equal to each other in all respect. India has masculinity score of 56, with the world average just slightly lower at 51. The higher the country ranks in this dimension, the greater people desire to have masculine values such as power, money, assertiveness, etc. and that prevails in the society. India is not, therefore, a purely muscular country but Japan with a MAS score of 95, maximum in the world, that shows the importance of success and wealth in Japanese society. It is very usual that Japanese workers would spend long hours along the assembly line in Toyota Motor Corporation or elsewhere performing strenuous and repetitive tasks with minimum breaks in between. The UK with MAS score of 66 is above the score

FIGURE 2.7 Hofstede's cultural dimensions – Relative positioning of India, Japan, UK and Sweden

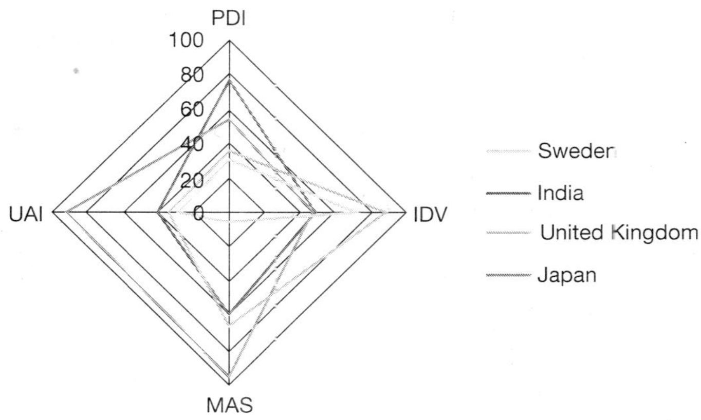

Countries	PDI	IDV	MAS	UAI
Sweden	31	71	5	29
India	77	48	56	40
United Kingdom	35	89	66	35
Japan	54	46	95	92

of India but far below Japan. A high masculinity score also indicates about a gap between values of men and women and acceptance of dominance of men population in the society. At the same time it may also generate a more competitive and assertive female population due to influence effect. Sweden with MAS score of 5 is the lowest in the world and continue to demonstrate feminine values in the society. India is country of uncertainty and hence not surprising that the country scores only 40 at the dimension of Uncertainty Avoidance (UAI) compared to the world average of 65. As indicated, therefore, the country is not a great worshipper of surety, consistency, assurance in the public life. People will be less bothered if the trains and flights are not running on time and would likely to accept as natural one. This lower ranking also indicates that the people will also tolerate ambiguous advertisement from the producers of products and difference being what promised in advertisement and the actual performance. Japan with 92 scores in UAI shows much higher tendency risk aversion, surety, consistency in works and in daily life and the culture will not entertain unstructured ideas and situations. The daily life is bounded by many rules and regulations in order to control of every unknown and unexpected event or situation. Interestingly, Japan and India score very similar in IDV score, 48 and 46 respectively, indicating that a good balance between individualistic and community approaches. These two countries are expected to demonstrate similar cultures when it comes to mutual respect, relationships and greetings. However, IDV score in UK is very high and stands at 89 indicating towards the importance of equality in the societies. The Janitors in a hotel would not hesitate to do breakfast along with the hotel guests in the lounge after the regular cleaning operation. This will not be possible in India as well as in Japan. The Japanese hotel janitor after cleaning may be standing and bowing to the visitors and in India even the same janitor's job would in danger. In Sweden though this phenomenon may not be regular but will be tolerated. All will happen because of cultural differences across the countries!

Cultural distance (CD) calculation

Kogut and Singh (1988)[22] suggested that culture plays a vital role in decisions related to market entry and non-consideration of cultural distance between the host and home country of business may lead to problems, which may be irrevocable. Cultural distance may be defined as 'the degree of difference in cultural norms between countries' and may be measured by a composite index based on deviations from Hofstede's national culture scores to estimate cultural distance. There is a formula for determining CD, which may be given as follows:

$$CD = \sum_{i=1}^{4}[(Iij - Iik)^2 \ / Vi] \div 4$$

Where CD = Cultural distance
Iij = Hofstede index value for cultural dimension i of country j;
Vi =Variance of the index for dimension i;
Iik = Hofstede index value for cultural dimension i of country k;

[22] Kogut, Bruce and Harbir Singh (1988), "The effect of national culture on the choice of entry mode", *Journal of International Business Studies*, 19 (3).

Table 2.3 Cultural distances between countries

Cultural Dimensions	India	Japan	Australia	USA	China	Sweden	Variance for 102 countries
PDI	77	54	36	40	80	31	426.22792
IDV	48	46	90	91	20	71	473.20198
MAS	56	95	61	62	66	5	300.54812
UAI	40	92	51	46	30	29	453.53782
Cultural distance as per Kogut and Singh	(India-USA)	(India-Australia)	(India-Japan)	(USA-Australia)	(USA-China)	(USA-Sweden)	(India-China)
CD (ks)	1.83	2.00	3.07	0.02	3.76	3.12	0.56

It can be seen that the CD calculated for the countries (Table 2.3), US and Australia has minimum cultural distance where as USA- China cultural distance is as high as 3.76 . Cultural distance of China and India is substantially different than that of Japan and India. India – China distance is as low as 0.56 while India maintain a comparatively high distance score of 3.07. USA and India are relatively close with cultural distance of 1.83. In other words, marketers in the US need to be very careful while marketing their products in China compared to when they are entering in Australia. (Figure 2.8).

Hall's Classification

Edward T. Hall, author of The Silent Language (1959), The Hidden Dimension (1966) and Beyond Culture (1976) initiated the concept of 'context' in his seminal works on intercultural communication. Hall introduced the 'context' and 'culture' relationship and divided culture into two types – high-context culture and low-context culture .

High-context culture

One best way to explain the concept of high-context culture is through the communication style of a Japanese worker, "We understand each other, and hence, verbal communications are not much required to know one another working in this office ". Say, you manage assembly line of a factory producing automobiles with all Japanese employees and you can be sure that limited

FIGURE 2.8 Depiction of cultural distances among countries

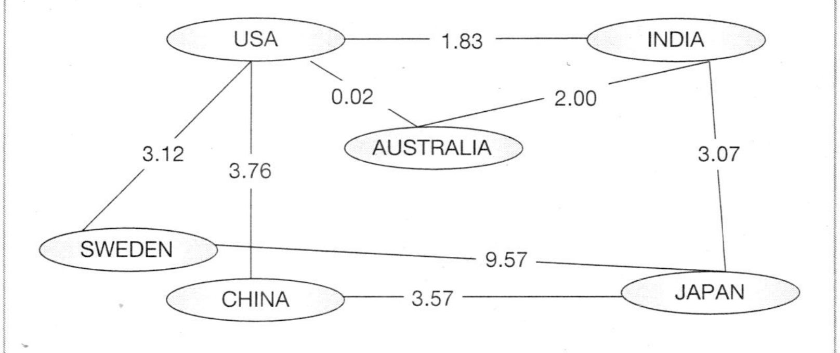

words will be used to manage the assembly line functioning smoothly but there will be extreme production efficiency. When you are entering Toyota Motor's production base in the Toyota city near Nagoya you as a foreigner will be welcome first by the welcome sign at the gate and then a few Japanese girls will approach you to build a context but without explicitly saying that you are welcome to Toyota. These girls would ask you some short questions like, how many Japanese words are there in the name of the owner Toyota or how many people in percentage term living in the Toyota city are actually working in the Toyota Company. It is not important that you click the answer write or wrong but the vistor will be made amused and thereafter the whole atmosphere gets so lively that you do not need someone to tell you that you are welcome. A whole lot of unuttered things are taken care of by the context created around you. When leaving the Toyota city at the end of the visit you feel enthralled. In Japanese culture, therefore, those limited words spoken are extremely important since they are the carriers of a complex message. The entire process, might at some occasion, are not understood by the persons who are totally alien to the Japanese culture. Here, in high-context culture, the orientation to time is important and it lends itself to build up the requisite context. The second important thing is role relationships, since meaning in communication is internalised in the person and it tends to be implicit.

Low-context culture

One Japanese manager of Toyota exclaimed after a meeting in America with the Americans, "These people talk too much and do not bother about the time and situation". Yes, Americans may not like to wait for the context to build up and then speak about it; they would rather desire to let the words used in communication convey the intended meaning. In case of need, they are capable of speaking explicitly and straight. This is because American culture is dominated by people who believe in words as exclusive medium of communication and not the context. This type of culture is referred to by Hall as low-context culture. People living in this culture have the tendency to be logical, linear, individualistic, and action-oriented. So much so, they even admire the very tendency of being logical, facts-oriented, and direct. A person living in this culture would like to approach a problem starting from a thread, lining up the facts related to it for careful evaluation and then after logical analysis come to the conclusion. People in low-context culture use the exact word to convey their feelings without ambiguity. The role relationships in the society are ignored since communications are externalised. The frequency of communication is also very high and directed towards proving a point.

Table 2.4 Countries in high and low context culture

Low-context Culture	High-context Culture
German	French
Scandinavian	Finnish
American	Hungarian
English	Russian
Irish	Italian
New Zealand	Spanish
Swiss	Latin Americans
Norwegian	Greek
Swedish	Japanese

Source: Halls' classification

People of high-context culture behave differently than those of low context culture. This may have business implication particularly in marketing of products in different countries of the world, as marketers need to know how consumers behave in a particular country to set the marketing programme accordingly (Table 2.4). The following behavioural characteristics denote the people of high-context culture.

Social orientation

High bonding: There is a high degree of bonding among people of high-context culture and the bond also extends to family, friend, colleague, community and society.

Commitment

Societal approval: The members show a high degree of cohesiveness and joint commitment for accomplishing something that is considered by the society to be right.

Responsibility

Team work: The team work is easy since all the members shoulder responsibility of all actions taken by individual members.

Confrontation

Less disputes: A confrontation-free environment with peace and harmony prevailing in the society. Learning for cross-border marketers that they would do well if they avoid confrontation with their rival over issues such as comparative advertisements, tall claims of product benefits, etc. in the market place.

Communication

Internalised communication: There are quite a few significant differences between high- and low-context cultures. People in high-context culture keep the communication internalised and overt communication is minimal. Therefore, marketers while executing customer preference survey must take cue from the context carefully to understand the marketing requirements. A prospective customer will not communicate directly about his or her preferences. A Japanese salesperson hardly interferes in to the buyers selection process in a shopping mall as the Japanese buyer will not like it and may even consider it intrusion in to privacy. In general, people of high context culture believe in old Japanese saying, "Hear one, understand ten."

The differences in the characteristics of high- and low-context culture are set forth in Table 2.5.

Table 2.5 Characteristics of culture

Characteristics	Low-context	High-context
Mental process	Logical, linear, individualistic, and action-oriented	Lateral holistic, simultaneous, accepting life's difficulty.
Beliefs and attitudes	Egalitarian, challenge authority, individuals control destiny	Hierarchical, respect to authority, individuals accept destiny and gender roles.
Values and norms	Independence, confrontation, conflict	Harmony, group conformity.
Family and friends	Nuclear, self-oriented, value youth	Extended family, other oriented, respect for old age.

Culture and Marketing Implications

"One of the strongest reasons against Theodor Levitt's standardised marketing hypothesis across different countries was that culture affects consumer behaviour and hence to create customer value marketing needs to be unique and culture-specific. Hence, marketing cannot be standardised across countries since every country has its unique culture. Post Levitt literatures saw open uprising against standardisation hypothesis of Prof Levitt and writers were obsessed with country-specific culture and its effect on marketing across countries. To support these literatures, psychologists and anthropologists openly came out and helped anti Levitt literatures to understand that there is something in the form of 'country specific culture' which can not be seen but can only be experienced through the differential behaviour of human beings". In fact, these literatures have advanced so much that marketers in the post Levitt era strongly believe that international marketers must understand culture well to crack the code of marketing. Now, how does culture affect marketing? To answer this question, McCort and Malhotra (1993)[23] contend that 'culture impacts virtually every construct of concern to marketers'. They proceed to hypothesise that culture influences individual cognitive functions such as perception, information processing, value systems and self-concept. Similarly, Usunier's (1996)[24] great work done in the field of culture also threw light on the influence of culture on consumer behaviour. He proposed that consumer behaviour in the realms of perception, motivation, learning and memory, group influence, age, self-concept, social class, sex roles, attitude change, decision-making, purchase, and post-purchase are all affected by culture.

The possible implication of culture on international marketing are listed below and based on strong empirical research conducted over a period of time by different researchers from specific countries who always believed that only with a great understanding of country specific culture international marketers can be successful in the global arena.

Culture and information search

Consumers across countries vary in their search for information while buying products and that variation is culture dependent. American consumers appear to be less information-savvy – an attribute that is rooted in their culture. The Germans, however, exhibit a characteristic that is quite the opposite of the Americans in their product sensibilities. They carry out extensive research about a product before buying it. So, the marketers need to provide more information to the Germans than the Americans[25]. Countries with high UAI or PDI have been found to show lower use of impersonal consumer magazines. Thus, the uncertainty avoidance and power distance aspects of culture appear to influence the locus of product

[23] Malhotra, Naresh K. and McCort J. Daniel (2001), "A cross-cultural comparison of behavioral intention models: Theoretical consideration and an empirical investigation", *International Marketing Review*, Vol. 18, Issue 3.

[24] Usunier, J.C., 1996. Cultural Aspects of International Business Negotiations. In: Ghauri, P. and J.C. Usunier (eds). International Business Negotiations. Pergamon, Oxford: Elsevier Science Ltd. 91-118.

[25] Anderson, Ronald and Jack Engledow (1977), "A factor analytic comparison of US and German information seekers", *The Journal of Consumer Research*, Vol. 3, No. 4 (March), The University of Chicago Press.

information search[26]. Therefore, the Hofstede indices can be used by the marketers for designing country-specific strategies for deciding on the style and quantity of information dissemination.

Culture and decision making

Country culture can influence the decision making process of an individual. The findings of the study "Does culture matter? A cross-cultural study of executives' choice, decisiveness, and risk adjustment in international marketing"[27] confirm that home culture has predictable significant effects on decision making. Thus, the decision making process varies across cultures and has an impact on the purchase situation as well as managerial decision making. Consumers from countries with high individualism are expected to be quick in decision making in the business scenario than are those from countries dominated by collectivism.

Culture and Intention formation

Lee, Chol and Green, Robert T (1991)[28], in their study of the two countries of Korea and the US found that US respondents framed their purchase based on their own personal attitudes while Korean respondents placed greater importance on social norms. This supports the Hofstede's assertion that collectivist countries would attach more importance on group conformity. This happens in the case of purchase intention formation also. Such collectivist consumer behaviour provides an understanding to the international marketers operating in individualistic countries. Emphasis in individualistic countries would have to be on the individual rather than the society. However, in countries where culture has a deep-rooted impact on the individual, marketers need to differentiate their marketing programme by focusing on the society. This premise is supported by other studies[29] when researchers found that US consumers framed their intention of purchasing a hybrid car for maintaining their self-image in the society whereas for the Koreans the decision was made for the social value associated with green products. This has great implication in marketing, as it showed that different positioning of the same product in different countries was needed for marketing success. Interestingly, many of such insights can be gained by understanding country-specific culture.

Culture and perceived risk

The proponents of cultural traits believe that countries differ in terms of their risk bearing capacities. Accordingly, people of certain countries would be placing more emphasis on safety clauses attached to product uses, warranty/guarantee, etc., than those from other countries. Why? It is expected that in countries

[26] Dawar, Niraj, Philip M. Parker and Lydia J. Price (1996), "A cross-cultural study of interpersonal information exchange", *Journal of International Business Studies*, Vol. 27, No. 3.

[27] Tse, David K., Kam-hon Lee, Ilan Vertinsky, and Donald A. Wehrung (1988), "Does culture matter? A cross-cultural study of executives' choice, decisiveness, and risk adjustment in international marketing", *Journal of Marketing*, No. 52.

[28] Lee, Chol and Robert T. Green (1991), "Cross-cultural examination of the Fishbein Behavioral Intentions Model", *Journal of International Business Studies*, Second Quarter, Vol. 22, No.2.

[29] Jason D. Oliver, Seung-Hee Lee Hybrid car purchase intentions: a cross-cultural analysis Journal of Consumer Marketing, 1984 Volume: 27/2, 2010.

where uncertainty avoidance pattern is culturally high, consumers are certainly conscious about different safety clauses like guarantee, after-sales services, etc., in a purchase situation. Researchers have empirically established that this is true. In a study involving three countries, the US, Jordan, and India, it was found that among cultures where uncertainty avoidance is high, the risk perceived with online shopping is also high, and this impacts online shopping negatively. The practical implication from this insight is that marketers need to take due cognizance of culture and culture-backed uncertainty prevailing in the country to design a marketing programme that best suits them.

Culture and colour association

Marketers attach lot of importance to colour and use it as an effective tool to differentiate their packages in the competitive market, build their brands and sustain logos that can be easily recollected by the customers for repeat purchase, etc. But can the appeal of colour be different in different countries based on their cultural allegiance? If it is so, then the same colour would not be able to appeal to the customers in identical way. Evidences show that the Japanese are fond of white colour while the Chinese may be fond of red. In India, purple colour is associated with intense patriotism. In Spain, the red rose is associated more with lust than love. In Italy, roses serve as a token of affection. In France, yellow roses are inappropriate; it suggests infidelity. This information is very essential for international marketers. Colour can stimulate emotional response, affect persuasiveness, reflect prestige, and certainly affect a consumer's overall perception of a product. Wagner Colour Research Institute experimented with certain colours and stereotyped the association of various colours with their interpretations. For example, blue is associated with wealth, trust, and security; grey is associated with strength, exclusivity, and success; and orange denotes cheapness. However, international marketers are more concerned about the varying colour perception of consumers from country to country.

Culture and information exchange

Literature on consumer behaviour indicates that consumers seek input from others prior to making a purchase. The probable reason for seeking different views is to add to their own information, cover up deficiency and add credibility and objectivity to it. The literature consumers' behaviour also lays considerable importance on information sources as it strongly influences purchase decisions and product evaluations. Generally, the consumer would first try to identify a known person who has the best possible information of the product he or she intends to purchase. Although significant knowledge is essential for sharing information with others as opinion leader, the person with the greatest knowledge of the product may not necessarily be the opinion leader. There are also possibilities that an opinion leader, although not personally involved in the product, may maintain a high degree of category interest in that product category. Because of their personal interest, they read a lot about the category, ask questions to peers, and exchange information with those whom they think as possible information source. How might this vary across cultures? In high power distance society, there exists inequality in the social system and hence, the society is hierarchical. Also, in high power distance society personal initiatives are accepted and appreciated.

Therefore, it can be expected that individuals with high IDV cultures will create an atmosphere around him/her that would serve as the only source of information and dissemination. This would, in turn, provoke the individual to act as an opinion leader and express personal opinions, as opposed to those with low IDV cultures. According to Hofstede (1980), individuals coming from high UAI culture endeavour to avoid uncertainty by adopting a stance of absolute truth seeker and hence may not like to seek the 'truth' in general consumer magazines, periodicals or pamphlets. Rather, they will be very specific in their search and look for evidences.

Culture and product perception

Product perception varies from country to country. BMW car is perceived to be a luxury car in Indian market but not so in Netherlands market where the car is a perceived to be regular car. American consumers perceive that products made in developing countries would not meet the service standard of their own. International marketers are taking advantages of these differentials to become successful in the market place. The same automobile is being positioned as 'amusing fun' in France, 'safety and comfort' in Germany, 'reliable' in Finland, 'road performance' in Italy and 'luxury car' for the Holland. The financial (direct monetary aspects such as price, resale price, discount, investment, etc.), functional (core benefit and basic utilities), individual (customer's personal orientation), and social aspects (perceived utility individuals acquire by consuming products recognised within their own social group) influence the value perception of a consumer towards products. In a cross-cultural context it is expected that these four dimensions that drive the value perception for a product will vary and hence, the same product will be perceived differently by different sets of consumers.

Culture and persuasion

Indian consumers do not generally mind repeated persuasion by the salesman because they consider it is normal practice and nothing unusual. In fact, a number of companies are imparting sales management training by inculcating hard persuasion techniques. This practice, however, will not yield good results to marketing managers in Japan. Japanese consumers are shy and hence hard persuasion would result in loss of sales. Germans are very purposeful in this respect and instead of persuasion they would like to know about the background and technology of the product. The effect of persuasion is not only different on different cultures but the persuasive style used by the presenter may also vary according to culture. An American salesmen would like to provide specific information to customers and help them to make broader generalisation; Russian salesperson prefer to put forward general information first and then help to customer to arrive at specific conclusion. On the other hand, Arabian salesperson would depend on intuition and stress on different possibilities while communicating to customers. In individualistic cultures emphasising on personal benefits would prove to be more persuasive while in the collectivist culture, it is the persuasion based on group benefits. To this effect, Han and Shavitt (1994)[30] found that North

[30] Han, Sang Pil and Sharon Shavitt (1994), "Persuasion and culture: Advertising appeals in individualistic and collectivistic societies", *Journal of Experimental Social Psychology*, 30 (4), 326–350.

American individuals have more favourable attitudes toward appeals that focus on self-reliance, self-improvement, and achievement of personal goals than do Korean individuals, who tend to focus more on family integrity, collective goals and the feeling of harmony.

Culture and product evaluation

Products are evaluated by consumers in the pre-purchase situation based on the desired functional and non-functional parameters which the consumer thinks that products must have. These parameters are dependent on the information access of the consumers. Some information is directly related with the physical characteristics of a product, such as product design, style, colour, size or aroma, while others such as country of origin, brand name, price, warranty and word-of-mouth are indirectly connected and have an influence on the choice exerted by the consumer. Based on the information gathered, the consumer builds up a standard. While evaluating the product, the consumer refers to this standard and self-image and looks for the so-called self-image/product image congruity, which in turn affects the consumer's product preference and purchase intention. Fundamentally, self-image formation is expected to vary in accordance with culture. People from high power distance would also emphasise protecting one's own self-image and seek freedom from imposition by others. They will be selective in information accumulation in building the product standard. Therefore, it is expected that self-image/product image congruity will vary from culture to culture and product evaluation pattern.

Culture and Ad content

The content used for advertising a concept, product or service has to be culturally attuned to get the marketing communication through to the target consumers. The advertisement of the Bank of America which uses cultural differences effectively to communicate the benefit of its products is a case in point. The company communicates the benefits of credit cards to Americans by showing a couple enjoying dinner and paying off the bill by credit card. When the communication is used for Asian countries, the company replaces the sequence of the couple with that of an extended family enjoying dinner.

CHAPTER SUMMARY

1. Culture is a very fundamental force which moulds the behaviour of the people. Every country has its own national culture which is expected to cast its influence on the people's behaviour living in that country.
2. Anthropologists and sociologists mainly worked in the field of culture and have provided a huge understanding on its origin, characteristics and manifestation on human behaviour.
3. The international marketers are largely benefitted from the work of anthropologists and sociologists on country culture. It gave the marketers a fair understanding of not only the culture of different countries but how code of culture required to be interpreted while devising marketing programme as well.
4. International marketing involves understanding the requirements of the target customers living in another country correctly in order to create better customer value than the competitors. This is helped by understanding cultural idiosyncrasies of the people living in different parts of the world. Hence, understanding national culture of a country is important.

5. The different theorists also came out time to time with different models linking country culture with consumer behaviour which again strengthened the understanding of international marketers in the field of culture.
6. The most important contribution came from Geert Hofstede's research which provided various cultural indices to understand the culture of different countries. International marketers have been using these indices to assess cultural barriers while deciding on their marketing.
7. International marketers have been experiencing the effect of country specific culture and hence attempt on standardisation of marketing programme across the countries of their presence is getting stalled to a greater extent. So, culture has, till now, been a very much challenging area for the international marketers. It requires in depth understanding of different country culture first and then moving forward to device right marketing programme and strategy thereof.

QUESTIONS FOR REVIEW

1. The following are the dimensions of culture and cultural distance scores for four emerging markets (Cultural index scores were obtained from Hofstede, 2001; and cultural distance were calculated using the formula by Morosini, 1998). How would you interpret the table below if you are interested in exporting private-label apparel goods to these countries?

Emerging markets	Power distance	Un-certainty avoidance	Individualism	Masculinity	Cultural distance from USA
Argentina	49	86	46	56	61
Brazil	69	76	38	49	69
China	80	30	20	66	83
Hong Kong	68	29	25	57	74

2. What is culture? How does country-specific culture affect consumer behaviour? Explain with the help of a model.
3. The following are the scores of the four dimensions of cultural distance between US and China in Hofstede Model with highest and lowest scores of 74 countries measured. Design the right marketing mix for a credit card to be launched shortly in China that is very successful in US and elsewhere.

Country	PDI	UAI	IDV	MAS
US	40	46	91	22
China	80	32	20	66
Highest	104	112	91	110
Lowest	11	8	6	5

4. The two countries, Mexico and US, scored 81 and 40 in power distance; 83 and 45 in uncertainty avoidance; 69 and 62 in masculinity respectively in Hofstede research. Looking at the scores, comment on how the differences would manifest on the Mexican and US managers in respect of the following: (a) Managerial style (b) Decision-making processes (c) Staffing procedures (d) Interpersonal trust and confidence (e) Enforcing contracts (f) Staff controls (g) Work ethics (h) Balancing work and Non-work interests (i) Gender-based perceptions of work.
5. Explain the role of context in culture. How you would differentiate social orientation, commitment, responsibility, confrontation, and communication in high-context and low-context culture?
6. Describe the four dimensions of culture as given by Hofstede model. Describe the general marketing implications of each of them
7. The table given below are indicative of the characteristics of low power distance society and high power distance society. You are designing the marketing mix for Indian food 'Dosa' for country A (small PD) and country B (large PD) to be launched in these market for the first time. Take cue from each of the characteristics and design two separate marketing programmes for country A and B.

Small power distance (PD)	Large power distance (PD)
Inequalities between people should be minimised	Inequalities between people are both expected and desired
There should be, and there is to some extent, interdependence between people enjoying more power and those with less power	Less powerful people should be depend on the more powerful; in practice, less powerful people are polarised between dependence and counter dependence
Parents treat their children as equals; Children also treat their parents as equals	Parents teach children obedience; Children treat parents with respect
Teachers are experts who transfer impersonal truths	Teachers are gurus who transfer wisdom
More educated persons hold less authoritarian values than less educated ones	Both more and less educated persons show almost equally authoritarian values
Hierarchy in organisations means inequality of roles, established for the sake of convenience	Hierarchy in organisations reflects the existential inequality between higher-ups and lower-downs
Narrow salary range between top and bottom of organisation. Subordinates expect to be consulted	Wide salary range between top and bottom of organisation. Subordinates expect to be told what to do
The ideal boss is a resourceful democrat	The ideal boss is a benevolent autocrat or godfather
Privileges and status symbols are frowned upon	Privileges and status symbols are both expected

8. How does culture affect international marketing? Use your understanding of Hofstede and explaing the effect of country-specific culture on a consumer's (a) risk perception in pre-purchase situation (b) information search and (c) decision making process.
9. What behavioural differences would you expect to find between the sales manager of a large Chinese company and one in an American company in the same industry? What are the factors that trigger the differences?
10. Mr Ito of Nagoya port authority was expecting a business delegation from India. Just at 10 AM, he came to the gate for receiving the delegation. The delegation came late by an hour but Ito kept on waiting for the team standing alone. He was sweating in the sun but seemed to be like a statue unable to move. Actually, when the delegation came he greeted them by bowing and then with a very short welcome speech. The day's agenda was then explained to them clearly. Mr Ito then led the delegation to meet the CEO of the company, Mr Takaki. The delegation could gather that the CEO was the oldest person in the company and also came know that in the highest positions, the company had no female managers. Mr Ito later intimated them that he had not seen a female CEO in the company and it is customary that only after mid-fifties someone can expect to become the CEO. It appeared to the delegation that Mr Ito had been showing great respect to the CEO and was ready to take any order from him. In the meeting that followed, no big business decisions were taken but the CEO mostly indicated of some long-term future potential of business tie ups. The Indian delegation was frustrated as the CEO did not even refer to some immediate business tie-up commitment in the meeting. However, the Japanese present there were all extremely courteous. The delegation came to know from the limited conversation that Mr Ito and others were all working in the same company for a pretty long time period and felt that the workers were really committed to the cause of the company.
    What impression did you get about Japanese culture from the above text? Can you use a framework that may be useful in explaining the cultural dimensions and dynamics of Japanese business?
11. As per Hofstede index, Malaysia is a "high-context" society with high power distance, low levels of uncertainty avoidance and individualism and medium-level masculinity. In contrast, Australia is a "medium-context" society with low power distance, medium levels of uncertainty avoidance and masculinity and high-level individualism. What inferences would you, as a marketing manager intending to market your Ayurvedic product in both the countries, take from the above culture-based information in designing a marketing programme?

End Case: Gangnam Style: The Journey of a Cultural Product Across the Globe[31]

The entertainment trade has emerged as a big business with the spectacular advancements in communications technology. In mid- 2012, the pop single "Gangnam Style," by South Korean musician Psy took the world by storm. Rapper Psy performed it in Korea but almost the entire world overnight became fan of the Korean rapper. The song became so famous that it topped the iTunes chart. The original "Gangnam Style" video was viewed over 200 million times worldwide within three months time of its release in the You Tube during July, 2012 and thereby making it the most liked video in You Tube history. The Korean rapper Psy, (short form 'psycho' aka Park Jae-sang) was an unknown stocky, 34-year-old Korean singer who possibly was not known even to many of his fellow countrymen. However, the "Gangnam Style" video almost did a magic and the ordinary songwriter, rapper, and dancer form Korea overnight shoot to the fame and became worlds most sought after musician. Even the Americans sitting in another part of the world suddenly released that the Korean dance video was a good way to relax and entertained. The Scandinavians, the Arabs, the Europeans along with many others living in different geographic regions tried to believe that the Korean rapper Psy had unique capability to entertain. Many people were curiously looking at the success of Gangnam style of dance in other countries and trying to explain the root causes of this enormous success. It literally broke all cultural barriers and went-in in different countries straight way like bullet piercing the national culture of different countries. Many in the literary circle even opined that Prof Levitt dream came true in terms of this 'cultural product' as it did not require cultural conditioning during its entire journey of marketing internationally.

This case study seeks to explain the factors responsible for the enormous success of the Gangnam Style video across the world. Why people of other nationalities so quickly accepted the video which specifically made with Korean flavor? Whether or not the much talked about cultural differences across the countries of the world erected a barrier for people of other cultures to accept the Gangnam video of Korean origin?

"Gangnam Style" is actually Korean neologism. The term 'neologism' simply refers to one's unique patterns of vocabulary which car generally be understood by the person using them. The Gangnam district of Seoul relates to the Gangnam style neologism and it was expected that people living in that district or acquainted with the particular district culture could only take the actual flavor of this Gangnam style dance. The literary meaning of Ganganam in Korean language is "south of the river". The district is particularly inhabited by the rich people and Psy's parents were one of them. When Psy was in his early twenties, like any other rich person's son in Korea, wanted to be educated in western countries. So he soon landed in USA to study business administration in Boston University. USA. But alas! He ended up spending the entire tuition grant received from his father in purchasing musical instruments. Very soon Psy changed his course of direction and purposefully dropped out of Boston University and freshly enrolled in Berklee College of Music to study music rather than business lessons. However, Psy could not stay long with the music university and his friends at Berklee observed that attaining degree was not the sole ambition of this gentleman. Psy returned to Seoul without university degree but with great passion for music. On his return he started seriously considering taking up music as his profession. His first musical album 'Psy from the Psycho World' was released in Seoul during 2001 but before it fully reached to the target customer segment the local Government banned the album. Further, Psy was reprimanded by Korean authority on the ground of developing a music album with 'improper content'. During 2002, Psy came to limelight again in Korea when his musical album "Champion" became the title song of the Seoul football world cup. Thereafter there was a long lull of almost ten years when Psy kept on struggling to see good days. During August 2012, life suddenly responded to fortune with the

[31] The case 'Journey of a cultural product across globe: A case of South Korean Gangnam Style' has been created by the case writer Dr Gautam Dutta of Indian Institute of Foreign Trade as a basis for class room discussion rather than to illustrate either effective or ineffective handling of business situation.

release of 'Gangnam style' song in his sixth music album Psy 6 (Six Rules). The rest was history!

Should people around the world pay to listen to a Korean song? Mind it, Psy earned about $8.1 million during 2012 out of advertisement, publicity, etc. because people in different countries paid to listen the song and watch Psy dancing. All this fortune came because Psy was able to sell a Korean origin musical album to the countries of the world. Korean history also is silent about any other such remarkable achievement when a totally Korean origin musical album became so famous in other countries. People used to know about Korean high tech electronics products or semiconductors invading different country markets easily- but certainly not about music. Is it some sort of cultural imperialism where one country's beliefs, values, knowledge, behavioral norms, and style of life are imposed on the other countries deliberately? There will be hardly any believer of the notion that Korea had been making rapid stride to engulf different other country cultures through cultural imperialism. It was true that the country had been very ruthless in achieving marketing success across the different countries for different other products like automobile, semiconductor, etc. But certainly, it is not in case of cultural products. However, Korean style of life (or its part) and its depiction in dance form in Gangnam style surely travelled in to different households of different countries almost effortlessly for local consumption. Had Prof Levitt been alive he would have rejoiced to see that cultural barriers of different countries were found broken when Gangnam style invaded them.

Popular belief in the field of cross cultural reception process is that cultural products of one country will find easier acceptance in countries where culture is similar. Simply speaking, consumers from countries of similar culture like that of Korea will find their own values, feelings, and experiences are reflected in the Gangnam style song and hence they will tend to accept the product more readily than those who have different cultures. However, Gangnam style was found to be very popular in culturally dissimilar countries like Australia (cultural distance score 4.11)[32], Canada (cultural distance score 3.18), and USA (cultural distance 4.32) but rather it did not do well in culturally similar countries like UAE (cultural distance score 0.67), Egypt (cultural distance score 0.183), Poland (cultural distance score 1.52). The Gangnam style video was nowhere in the top videos watched in YouTube in the aforesaid countries. In the Middle East countries the top ranked video during 2012 was "Zahgana" sang by a 9 year-old Bahraini pop star Hala al Turk. In India it was Rapper Honey Singh who topped the list keeping Gangnam style in the number two spot.

Let us look back and try to analyse what was there in the Gangnam Style video? What were its lyrics, beats, dance gestures, characters, objects and places? The rapper Psy developed the video in the backdrop of the Gangnam neighbourhood, known as the "Beverly Hills of Seoul", and projected their lavish lifestyle. The lyrics were mostly in Korean but attempted to convey the message through the use of visuals. From blogs of viewers, appeared during the peak of the song, it was revealed that the meaning was not clear even to the South Korean and even the English translation of the lyrics appeared in the different internet pages did not do any good to the non Korean as well[33]. It was also detected that the catchy beats and music videos were not totally reflecting the lyrics. The excess of visual depicting Beverly type of ambience were shown to clearly remind anybody watching the video of western culture through the lyric was in Korean. The horse dance of Psy in the video reflected folk dance of Tibet or Mongolian cultures but certainly not that of Korean where prominent dance gesture used was that of crane. Musical beats of Gangnam style reflects that Psy learnt a great deal of western music during his days at Berklee College of Music, USA. Korean lyric, western type ambience in the visual, alien dance movement but not difficult to be mimicked, upbeat but catchy tune, Asian look of the rapper and on the top the country image of Korea as the producers of many successful global products were nicely ingrained in the video to develop a cross cultural product.

After the global success Psy, the creator of Gangnam style video, admitted that the video was made primarily keeping in view of Korean audience. The global acceptance surprised his as well. It was just like famous Daler Mehndi of India composed a bhangra pop album keeping in view Indian

[32] Kogut and Singh Cultural distance calculated using the standard formula. Less the index score more the countries are culturally close.

[33] See English version at http://www.kpoplyrics.net/psy-gangnam-style-lyrics-english-romanised.html)

population but it caught up the imaginations of international audience also at a later period. The Daler Mehendi's album enthralls Indian audience because it strikes the right cord. Contents and visual of a Daler Mehendi's video developed for India have more melodramatic content than that of the Australian one because Indian audience like in that way. Some more exclusive cultural type Indian dances like Kathakali, Kachupuri would require more intense audience involvement and hence these might not attract western audience at all. Other possible areas where musical video developed for a particular country can be culturally different than another include differences in background scenes, language, storyline, length or duration of video, etc. However, ask any pro Levitt thinkers on the requirement of Daler Mehendi to go global. They will suggest singer Daler Mehendi to go with universality of the contents so that it would go cross border markets without being labelled as 'Indian type'. So, the natural questions came to the mind of the observers – why then Gangnam Style which was basically of Korean nature got marketing success in different other countries? Or, what it requires for Daler Mehendi to do a Gangnam style? Do you have the answer?

A Swedish can enjoy Daler Mehndi bhangra pop if the person can understand it and thereby enjoying the emotions correctly. Otherwise, the contents, in some way, have to be strong enough to drive the audiences of different cultural origin in to certain level of fantasy where the cultural barriers look insignificant. The greater the cultural distance between the producer and audience more push will be required in this direction. So, what will be the antidote for Daler Mehendi album to go global? The basic question at this juncture is how a product attuned to one country culture is to be produced for marketing in other countries with dissimilar cultures? Should then the cultural products producers across the world consciously try to devoid them of the respective culture? Then, if this is the case, Daler Mehndi's Bhangra pop should not take its essence from Punjab and its age old Bangra style. In the same line, Gangnam style should not look like originated from Korea. But see, the great Taj Mahal of India is attracting people around the world because of its Indianness and its embeddedness in great Mughal culture. The Great Wall of China is attracting tourists because it is Chinese. Disneyland has always consciously maintained its Americanness through Mickey Mouse characters irrespective of where they have gone to market internationally.

The existing literature suggest that Gangnam style or Daler Mehndi's Bhangra pop may be comparatively lucky as they use audio visual media where impact of language use on the mind of audience will be less than the print media. The sound/beat created or visual depicted has better transcends across international borders. Gangnam style of musical video is also lucky from the count that viewers exposed to it are not expecting to gather or master new knowledge. Rather, in the first go, the international viewers prima facie are looking for some happiness type of emotions which expectedly are not culturally attuned. At least studies, in this direction, show that audience from both individualistic and collectivist cultures are expected to pass through similar norms in the case of experiencing pleasant emotions[34].

Prior to the era of globalisation, the cultural businesses like Disneyland aimed to generate good feelings within a country to and, of course, in search of a good price. But as the globalisation made progress Disneyland type of cultural businesses aspired to go cross country in search of market to generate more return in monetary terms. YG Entertainment, the label behind Gangnam, had shown a wonderful way of marketing a cultural product across globe. All the four Ps of marketing mix were taken care of in righteous way. The product components (lyrics, beats, dance gestures, characters, etc.) were nicely blended to form a package of offerings and pushed it for distribution through YouTube channels which had 2.5 million viewers across different countries. In order to take care of another P, i.e., price, purposefully Gangnam Style was allowed to be copied (Psy waived the copyright to the song)[35]. The result, we all saw, a grand cross cultural marketing success. Thousands across globe, of different nationalities, deeply drenched in the respective country culture, saw the video as something new and made the song as their own. What else a global marketer can dream of!

[34] M .Eid, E Diener. Norms for experiencing emotions in different cultures: inter- and intranational differences in .J Pers Soc Psychol. 2001 Nov; 81(5):

[35] As noted by Arwa Mahdawi in The Guardian (2012).

CASE QUESTIONS

Q1. Why it is difficult to market a cultural product, like a song/drama of one country, to other countries with different national culture?
Q2. How much Gangnam style video is soaked in Korean culture? Justify your answer.
Q3. What are the factors that helped Gangnam style video to get cross cultural acceptance in different culture? Why it was a grant success in USA but not in Argentina. Is it due to cultural distance? Justify your answer.
Q4. As a student of business management how do you rate the cross cultural marketing success of Gangnam style video? Justify you answer.
Q5. Develop a plan for marketing of Daler Mehendi Bhangra pop so that it can achieve similar marketing success like that of Gangnam style internationally.

FURTHER READINGS

Aaker, Jennifer L. (2000), "Accessibility or diagnosticity? Disentangling the influence of culture on persuasion processes and attitudes", *Journal of Consumer Research*, Vol. 2/5.

The objective of this research was to use Feldman and Lynch's accessibility – diagnosticity framework and offer an explanation towards execution of persuasive appeal in marketing communication across culture. The article took help of three experiments to demonstrate greater acceptance of accessibility explanation. The article allows the researchers and readers to understand the condition under which cultural similarities in persuasion process and effects will happen.

Lee, Chol and Robert T. Green (1991), "Cross-cultural examination of the Fishbein behavioral intentions model", *Journal of International Business Studies*; Second Quarter, Vol. 22, No.2.

This paper researched into the applicability of Fishbein behaviour intention model dealing with an individual's decision to engage in a particular behavior based on the outcomes the individual expects in certain culture. The author carried out this research in Korea and found that the model can effectively be applied in a collectivist culture like Korea for understanding behavioural intentions in Confucian culture as well.

Luna, David and Susan Forquer Gupta (2001), "An integrative framework for cross-cultural consumer behavior", *International Marketing Review*, Vol. 18, No.1.

This article provides a model of linking consumer behaviour with the cross-country culture. The conceptual work portrays how cognition effect and behaviour of the consumer are linked with the cultural value system.

Kim, D., Pan, Y.G., and Park, H.S. (1998), "High- versus low-context culture: A comparison of Chinese, Korean, and American cultures", *Psychology and Marketing*, September, Vol. 15, No. 6.

This article is very interesting because it deals with the characteristics of high and low-context cultures across three countries of the world. Author of the article establishes that China, Korea, and the US differ along the lines of context definition. The respondent Americans demonstrated the characteristics of a high-context culture, while the responents from China and Korea demonstrate characteristics of low-context cultures. The article is useful in understanding the process of conducting cross-country cultural study.

Usunier, Jean-Claude and Ghislaine Cestre (2007), "Product ethnicity: Revisiting the match between products and countries", *Journal of International Marketing*, © 2007, American Marketing Association, Vol. 15, No. 3.

This article deals very important relationship between products and countries based on the consumers' perceptions of a country leading to product ethnicity. The paper starts with investigating product ethnicity at an exploratory level across five surveyed countries for a large set of products and countries. The research found that there exist a "context-centred association tendencies and hence the respondents related goods more closely with their own country. Finally, the paper threw light on why consumers are more Inclined to buy such product offerings that are congruent rather than non-congruent with product ethnicity.

Brown, Lee T., Alan M. Rugman, and Alain Verbeke (1989), "Japanese joint ventures with Western multinationals: Synthesising the economic and cultural explanations of failure", *Asia Pacific Journal of Management*, Vol. 6, No. 2: pp. 225–242.

This paper presents a literature review to develop a conceptual framework which distinguishes between economic and cultural reasons for explaining failure in a joint venture. It emphasised that in order to explain the reason behind the success of cross cultural joint venture between Japanese and Western companies there is a requirement of understanding the combined impact cultural and economic forces.

Tylor, Edward. 1920 [1871]. Primitive Culture. New York: J.P. Putnam's Sons. 16.
Linton, R. 1936. The Study of Man. New York: Appleton.Century.
Herskovits,M.J. Man and his works. New York. Alfred A. Knopf, 1948.
Talcott Parsons and Edward Shils, eds. Toward a general theory of action New York: Harper & Row, 1951.
Kluckhohn, C. (1954). Culture and behavior. In G. Lindzey (Ed.) Handbook of social psychology. (Vol. 2, pp. 921-970). Cambridge, Mass: Addison-Weseley.
Hofstede, G. (1980). Culture's Consequences: International differences in work related values. Beverly Hill, CA, Sage.

Negotiating Political–Legal Factors

3

Learning Objectives

After studying this chapter, you should be able to:

- Understand the country political system of the countries of the world.
- Assess the friendliness of the political systems towards business.
- Understand different political risks and their implications on international business.
- Understand the tools and techniques of assessing and measuring political risks.
- Understand the semi quantitative risk ranking approach and mitigation of political risks.
- Understand the legal system of the countries.
- Assess the product safety and liability regulation in the international markets.
- Understand the legislations related to retail price maintenance and their implications on business.
- Understand how legal systems of different countries forces adaptations in marketing communications.

Chapter Overview

After reading the second chapter the readers will be interested to know about the other environmental factors, other than the cultural one, affecting the standardisation of marketing strategy. This chapter, therefore, introduces the political and legal environment of doing business internationally.

Opening Vignette

Political uncertainty has taken a toll on GMR's business in Maldives

Sidharth Kapur, CFO, of Indian origin GMR Group of companies, could not believe the news that Maldives government was preparing to terminate contract which gave the company exclusive right to build-own- operate the Male airport of the country. Immediate thinking was why the government headed by president Mohamed Waheed was crazy for terminating contract worth 500 million USD. The GMR Group, headed by the great Indian entrepreneur Mr G.M Rao successfully built, owned and operated two major airports in India namely Indira Gandhi International Airport, Delhi and Rajiv Gandhi International Airport, Hyderabad. Both the airports were state of the art and the company won numerous awards and accolades for quality and efficiency in India. The company earned reputation of being a quality infrastructure developer and became a big name in India with no time. The company had to fight out competition from other big infrastructure developer like Larsen & Toubro, etc. in order to win over contracts in respect of different other infrastructural projects in India. The company grew up in a strong democratic system in India where construction bid evaluation and winning them over seemingly happen in transparent way without any direct involvement of government intervention. The company with Indian success in its stride went to repeat the same at the global level. During 2008 the company made test internationalisation through purchase of UK based Power Company Intergen followed by take over of an Indonesian coal firm and a Singaporean Power company during 2009. During 2010 the company continued with internationalisation and successfully contested a competitive bidding process to win over the contract to operate and expand Ibrahim Nassir International Airport of Maldives. The entire bidding process was conducted under the watchful eye of International Finance Corporation (IMF) and the country signed the agreement to this effect during June 2010, which finally brought the GMR group to Maldives. Apparently, till then, no problem of doing business in Maldives could be noticed by the GMR managers. However, it was not known to them clearly that the political opponents of first democratically elected President Mohamed Nasheed were looking for an opportunity to shake up patriotic feelings in the country to garner popular support towards change of government. Just when GMR, after paying the statutory payments to the government of Maldives, started operating the airport and levied a $25 per passenger Airport Development Charge (ADC) for terminal expansion, a turbulent situation surfaced. First, the passengers using the airport declined to pay the tax, and second, a popular 'save country from foreign company's invasion' type of sentiment was carefully allowed to be brewed up by political opportunists. The situation further flared up when the government agreed to pay the lost amount to GMR to honour the agreement. Several igniting public speeches came out from the political opponents and suddenly it started looking as if this was a fight of the people at large to 'reclaim' the airport from GMR for patriotic reason. For GMR, things further worsened when President Nasheed was ousted in a midnight coup. The new government fuelled the anti-GMR campaign further and successfully drabbed presence of GMR in Maldives as anti-nationalistic. Finally, the cabinet decided to scrap the agreement with GMR, which the previous government signed leading to huge financial loss for the Indian company.

When the plight of GMR while doing business in another country and how they caught in between realpolitik and public sentiment was told to the students of international marketing in the classroom situation, the students quipped, "that's frightening ! How the companies would know about the political situation in different countries and risks emanating out of them for the business? What are the way-outs for a company caught in political rivalry in another country?"

How do companies cope? There are no simple rules. Countries that are cavalierly lumped together as emerging markets have very different political regimes. In Brazil you need to understand Congress's multi-party alliances; in China the power dynamics of the Communist Party; in Saudi Arabia the internal relations of the ruling family. Local politics add yet more complexity.

—Schumpeter

INTRODUCTION

Hafez Al-Assad, a strong supporter of Baath party formed in 1947 for promoting radical Arab nationalism across the region, seized power in Syria during 1963. Syria later came out as a socialist republic with a constitution that guarantees a leading role to the Baath Party. Syria has a strong presidential system of government with a powerful executive. The Syrian Parliament (People's Assembly) is elected by popular vote for a four-year term. The last parliamentary elections took place in 2003 and the next elections in 2007. Over the years, however, there has been little change in the political legacy. Hafez Al-Assad left after his thirty-year term. The Baath Party, which enjoys the support of the military-security elite, still dominates Syrian politics with its present president Bashar al-Assad. He took office in July 2000 following his father's death which many thought to be the beginning of change.

But alas! Nothing got changed. Decision-taking was still in the hands of the President and a small circle of people around him. The regime had been facing criticism for a long time, but it seems to have caught momentum from early 2011. Initially, protesters wanted basic reforms, more freedoms, a multi-party political system, and an end to emergency law. Some of these reforms, on paper, implemented by President Bashar al-Assad, but it was far too little and, came about too late. The government was trying to contain popular uprisings, with violent repression, whereas until the size of the security system and the predominance of the Baath party enabled it to maintain a grip on the country. There was a strong popular voice for democratisation but hardly any political action actually took place. Amid political tension, the forecasted growth rate for 2011 was meagre +0.5%. The social measures and the investment expenditure planned by the state following the unrest was not expected to do any miracle. Household consumption was going down with poor performance of the agricultural sector. Only bright part was the hydrocarbons sector, where some growth could be noticed. On the other hand, the tourism sector suffered badly which used to be good contributor of GDP. The ambitious plan of Assad to put Syria as regional hub through requisite infrastructural development like port upgradation, road, air, and rail linkage with neighbouring countries, improving port infrastructures, and easing restrictions on air transport ended up in a whisper without any political action. Oil-based revenue of the government was also showing decreasing trend, and when political tensions stalled the tax reform programmes, there was no money in the government coffer. However, the Syrian regime continued to be stubborn and found battering the pro-reform protesters in the face of international pressure. The story of Syria did not put a bright picture of the country as a destination for doing business. Establishing the correlation between the political events and ease of doing business in Syria may not be that difficult. One can say that this is going to be continued for long term with damaging effect on business environment. The political turmoil effected the business environment with far-reaching effects. It is found to be always true everywhere as well. China's dubious politically provoked action that led four employees of Australian company Rio Tinto put in Chinese jail did not send good message to the international businesses. Rampant corruption and inadequate laws have put international companies like IKEA in Russia in trouble. Hostile political environment of Venezuela has made number international companies to pull out of the country. Ambiguous regulations and partial nature of many countries and their marshalling are really putting international business in bad shape. The political events are often accompanied with legal restrictions in terms of limits on convertibility currency and repatriation of capital, profit, and management leading to discomfort in operation. Therefore, various types of political events in different countries, overtly or covertly may give rise to some sort of business risks to the foreign companies operating in that country. Examples such incidents are many and have been narrated in different business literatures. But still, by nature, international business would require to be continued in many countries with different political system and business risk evolving out of them.

Therefore, it is required that the international business assesses the political environment to find out how much is the risk evolving from a political system of country? How it can be predicted so as to take remedial measure? To what extent it is possible? These are possible questions every international company would like to get answered before going for investment abroad as well as while doing business.

Aon Corporation[1], Headquartered in Chicago, USA which is leading provider of risk management service provider to the companies yearly publishes the political risk map for the countries of the world for the benefit of international investors. Aon's Political Risk Map depicts political risks, as assessed by them, for the countries of the world. For example, the Aon's Political Risk Map 2011 shows that political risks in 19 countries have increased in 2011 while it has declined in 11 countries. Mapplecroft, another leading risk management service provider, in their political risk atlas[2] indicated some significant political risks for business and investors in 2012 and beyond. According to Maplecroft's analysis, Arab Spring countries would face continuing instability and countries like Belarus, Guinea Bissau, Iran, Sudan, Turkmenistan, and Vietnam would be candidate for societal unrest and regime instability. Angola, DR Congo, Guinea, Myanmar, and Zimbabwe would pose risk to the external investors because of demand of resource nationalism coupled with poor or inadequate levels of democratic governance. On the better side, countries like Mexico, Indonesia, Philippines, Thailand, and Liberia are predicted to be blessed with decreased risk and greater opportunity.

All the above discussions lead to primarily two types of understanding. One, foreign companies are attracted to a number of countries, basically in search of business opportunities, who are perceived to be risky due to unpredictable politically motivated events taking place in those countries. These events are not only effecting the general business environment but may be directed to the foreign companies only. Two, these unpredictable politically motivated events are always not explicit like military coup, etc., which more or less predictable and provide time to the companies for appropriate defensive actions. On the contrary, many a time such actions in these days are covert but have enough string to ruin a company in the distant country. Against this backdrop, this chapter, therefore, first examine the different types of political system that exist in different countries with a view to understand the inherent implications of systems followed by a discussion on the types of political risks that may affect international business. Thereafter, the chapter critically discusses the manifestation of major politically designed events on doing business abroad. This chapter also throws light on different ways of assessing political risk of a country.

COUNTRY-SPECIFIC POLITICAL SYSTEM

Every country has a political system. It is system involving government and its politics which manifest the state's sovereignty over a territory and people. The government includes certain formal structures like legislative agencies,

[1] www.aon.com/

[2] The Political Risk Atlas (PRA) of Maplecroft includes maps and risk indices, developed by Maplecroft, to identify and monitor the key issues affecting the investment climates of countries.

for smoothing running of a system of governance. The politics include different parties, lobbying groups, trade unions, etc. The political system may be different for different country.

Different types of political systems are prevailing in the world. Say, the country North Korea, is controlled by a single individual or entity. China, on the other hand is run by a single party. Jordan and Saudi Arabia has different system and run by monarch who are ruled by an absolute leader chosen by hereditary means. Iran is ruled by religion-based leadership. In Israel, representatives of the population operating under a political party rule the country. In United States, a number of directly elected representatives chosen by voters run the country.

While doing business the knowledge of political system is essential for international business as each political system has its own advantages and disadvantages effecting business functions. Many political systems have ingrained characteristics detrimental to smooth functioning of international business. So, at this juncture, it will be worthwhile to build up understanding of different political systems. Some of the more common political systems being practiced around the world are discussed below.

Democracy

This is the most admired and preferred political system evolved over the years. Democracy is actually derived from the Greek language and means as much as power to the people. This is the most admired and preferred political system evolved over the years. In this type of political system, either people govern themselves in a structure of direct democracy, or there are elected representatives of the people who form the government in a representative democracy. There are a few benefits of democracy in relation to doing business in a country. Democracy provides for frequent elections after a specified period of time. This ensures that governments are required to work hard to provide economic benefit to the people or else face the threat of replacement by a new one. Therefore, the government has to implement favourable policies for economic growth and carry out reforms so as to stay in power. In the process, if the electorate are satisfied with the popular and pro-economic development representative, the candidate may be re-elected. Democracy endeavours to ensure that wealth is fairly distributed and economic deprivation is minimised. This, in turn, ensures that there is a certain amount purchase power in every strata of society. Democracy allows for many political parties to compete for power. It therefore gives businesses an opportunity to have their case heard fairly by a like-minded party and tabled before the government, debate on the unfavourable issues and work on the possibilities of rectification, if needed.

Direct democracy

In this type of democracy, the citizen plays a dominant role. Citizens are allowed to participate in decisions making directly by proposing laws or referendums on laws according to their personal likings. They can also vote directly to determine who enters public office or recalling non performing public officials. A classic example of a direct democracy is a unique type of Town Meeting where citizens meet to vote on issues of importance to the community like fund allocation, developmental agenda, etc., or they may propose new laws to make the community run more smoothly. Switzerland is a country with a long tradition of direct democracy. The federal legislations come from the constitution of Switzerland. However, the cantons (federal states) are directly involved to decide on aspects that are required for them. Therefore, based on the citizen provided inputs, the constitution is updated from time to time to take account of required changes. It is firmly ensured that citizens are involved throughout the process. The constitutional changes are affected only if an overall majority of the electorate agrees in a referendum and if the electorate of a majority of the cantons also agree. Scandenavian country Sweden is another good example of countries successfully utilising the benefits of direct democracy.

Indirect democracy

In an indirect democracy, a small group of representatives makes decisions of importance on behalf of their constituents. For example, United States Senate as house of legislature. The members of a legislature are systematically and typically elected by the constituents. However, members may also be appointed in cases, depending on how their government is shaped up. These members are expected to represent all citizens. This ensures that individual citizens are part of the voting process to select their representative who run the country, and hence, they are also encouraged to express their views or issues of concern to their representatives. Furthermore, indirect democracy is divided into two types: presidential democracy and parliamentary democracy. Presidential democracy is practised in the US, whereas parliamentary democracy is practiced in India.

Totalitarianism

As the name indicates a totalitarian government desires to regulate and control all aspects of private and public behaviour in the country. The country may be run by a single political party or one monarch or one dictator. Also the state may be secular or non-secular. The inherent characteristics of totalitarianism plead for leading role of one party in the power and set the stage of philosophical absolutism. Therefore, a totalitarian government works for establishing an universal truth in the country, in line with official ideology. The government takes all measures to make people accept an all-encompassing role of the party even in the public life. For example. Joseph Stalin of erstwhile Soviet Union was a totalitarian dictator during the year 1941 to 1953. This phase was followed by another totalitarian communist government until 1991. China and North Korea are other examples of totalitarianism. Under totalitarianism the government considers itself of having full power to control every aspects of the country including public life. Hence, a person or one party holds absolute control over the affairs of the state. The general population is excluded from the political process. A very bad example of totalitarianism of our days is North Korea where a single-party and the man heading the party considers himself controls everything in the country as totalitarian dictator. The ruler exercises absolute control over the government and the country with allowance of limited freedom of expression and close supervision of people's way of life.

China, in the post-Mao regime appears to have have come out of the 'totalitarian tag' and moved towards authoritarianism by accepting pluralism in the society. The country is no longer that adamant in mobilising the entire population in pursuit of national goals and absolute philosophy it believes. In general, though running of business is difficult in totalitarian country, as businesses may need to involve government in every aspect of doing business. Non-alignment with government may lead to the business venture leaving the country altogether even without its petition being heard. Doing business requires agreeing to government philosophy or at least pretention of alignment with the state philosophy. On the positive side, the state is expected to be disciplined one and free from labour problems, strike, violence, etc., leading to formation of a congenial business environment, thereby creating a pro-productive business environment.

Socialism

Socialism promotes a political system which believes that all the wealth and capital is owned by the state only, or at best commonly owned. In socialistic economies, production, productive system, and allocation of economic inputs are only meant to satisfy the economic demands and human needs. Hence, socialism does not promote the idea of profit accumulation at the hands of a few individuals. It supports to develop equality amongst people, and therefore, produced goods, profits, and other resources can be distributed based on the principle of equality of the people. The socialist system takes great care to ensure that there is no disproportionate distribution of wealth in the society and collective welfare of the people living in the state is achieved. Socialists like to believe that capitalism is not good as it serves the interests of the wealthy people only, and hence, socialism prevents exploitation of the lower class of society. A pure socialist state possibly does not exist today. However, many democratic countries with tinge of socialistic philosophy are not uncommon. In India, the largest democracy in the world, most of the organisations and nation as a whole preach about equal right for the common man irrespective of class or strata they belong. Brazil is another example where tinge of socialism could be noticed. These type of countries are increasingly becoming a great picture of economic exuberance and providing an attractive destination for business investment. Because of their focus on social justice, these countries are expected to have a relatively higher tax structure, some cultural rigidity, and an anti-capitalist pressure group.

MEASURING DEMOCRACY

Democracy is supposed to protect freedom in a country and hence good for everybody including international businesses operating there. Political freedom and civil liberty through inbuilt in the democratic system but quality of those may vary from country to country. Economist Intelligence Unit, therefore, attempted to measure the depth of democracy by computing 'Democracy index' across 167 countries. This index is based on 60 indicators grouped in five different categories such as electoral process and pluralism, civil liberties, functioning of government, political participation and political culture. The index was first produced in 2006, with

Table 3.1 Democracy index across different types of democracy

Full democracies (26 countries) with score		Flawed democracies (53 countries) with score		Hybrid regimes (55 countries) with score		Authoritarian regimes (33 countries) with score	
Norway	9.8	Cape Verde	7.94	Hong Kong	5.92	Madagascar	3.94
Iceland	9.65	Greece	7.92	Bolivia	5.92	Kuwait	3.88
Denmark	9.53	Italy	7.83	Singapore	5.89	Mauritania	3.86
Sweden	9.50	South Africa	7.79	Bangladesh	5.87	Morocco	3.89
New Zealand	9.26	France	7.77	Albania	5.86	Jordan	3.74
Australia	9.22	Slovenia	7.69	Mal	5.84	Ethiopia	3.68
Finland	9.19	Estonia	7.68	Lebanon	5.82	Fiji	3.62
Switzerland	9.09	Chile	7.67	Ecuador	5.77	Burkina Faso	3.59
Canada	9.08	Botswana	7.63	Honduras	5.76	Cuba	3.52
Netherland	8.99	Taiwan	7.52	Turkey	5.73	Bahrain	3.49

Source: http://en.wikipedia.org/wiki/Democracy_Index

updates produced in 2008 and 2013. The countries in this computation are again grouped into four categories – full democracies, flawed democracies, hybrid regimes and authoritarian regimes The 2010 computation put Norway on the top and Portugal at the bottom of 26 full democracies (Table 3.1). Amongst 53 flawed democracies, Cape Verde tops the list while Mali has been ranked as the last country. During 2010, India with a score of 7.28 ranked 40th country in the category of flawed democracy. In the list of 32 hybrid democracies, HongKong tops the list while the bottommost country is Iraq. There are 54 countries marked as authoritarian regimes with Madagascar topping the list and North Korea remaining at the bottom with a meagre 1.08 points.

Measuring Direct Democracy

Direct Democracy Index (DDI)[3] is a unique measure of the quality of direct democracy and its performance. It is based on the procedures that the country's political system applies in proposing, approving, amending, and deleting laws through popular initiative and referendums. The index is a subjective measure of direct democracy that takes into account both the actual referendums and initiatives and the quality of the process. The following table (Table 3.2) classifies the countries in to seven categories: 1) radical democrat; 2) progressive; 3) cautious; 4) hesitant; 5) fearful; 6) beginner and finally, 7) authoritarian.

Table 3.2 Direct democracy rating across countries

Afghanistan	1	Luxembourg	5
Albania	2	Kyrgyz Republic	1
Argentina	2	Lao, People's Dem	1

(Continued)

[3] Fiorino, Nadia and Roberto Ricciuti (2007), Determinants of direct democracy, CESifo Working Paper No. 2035, Category 2: Public Choice, June.

Table 3.2 *(Continued)*

Australia	6	Macedonia	2
Austria	5	Malaysia	1
Bangladesh	2	Malta	4
Belarus	1	Mexico	1
Belgium	5	Moldova	2
Bhutan	1	Mongolia	1
Brazil	2	Netherlands	6
Bulgaria	5	Nicaragua	1
Cambodia	1	Norway	5
Chile	2	Pakistan	1
China	1	Panama	2
Colombia	3	Paraguay	3
Costa Rica	1	Peru	3
Croatia	3	Philippines	6
Cyprus	3	Poland	5
Czech Republic	5	Portugal	5
Denmark	6	Romania	4
Estonia	4	Slovak Republic	6
Finland	4	Slovenia	6
France	5	Spain	5
Ecuador	3	Russian Federation	1
El Salvador	2	Singapore	1
Iceland	3	Turkey	2
Ireland	6	United Kingdom	4
India	4	Turkmenistan	2
Indonesia	6	Ukraine	1

Sources: Kaufmann (2004), Hwang (2005) and Madroñal (2005); Hwang (2005)

Box 3.1 Political risks for business are increasing

Curaçao and St. Maarten have been downgraded on the Political Risk Map 2011 of international financial and insurance broker Aon where it comes to doing safe business. The islands were placed in the risk category "medium-low." Last year the Netherlands Antilles, then still a country, scored "low." Aruba's position remained unchanged: "medium-low." Puerto Rico and Barbados had a similar score. The report makers called it "striking" that of the 19 countries placed in a higher risk group this year compared to the previous year, the majority were located in the Caribbean. Besides Curaçao and St. Maarten, these were: Antigua and Barbuda, the Bahamas, Barbados, Bermuda, the Cayman Islands, the Dominican Republic, Grenada, Haiti, St. Kitts and Nevis, St. Lucia, St. Vincent and the Grenadines, and Trinidad and Tobago. The Dominican Republic and Jamaica were rated "medium-high," Cuba, "high" and Haiti, "very high," meaning that it is highly unsafe to do business in the latter country. Of all countries and islands in the Caribbean, only the US Virgin Islands and Guadeloupe scored better. They were placed in the risk category "low." According to Aon, decreasing tourism numbers have an adverse effect on the economies of the Caribbean nations. Stricter credit conditions at commercial banks increase chances of default and national debts that cannot be paid. "Political risks remain important influencing factors for companies looking for opportunities in upcoming markets in 2011," stated Marc van Nuland, management member at Aon Risk Solutions. Aon Risk Solutions measured the political risk in 211 countries and regions using risk levels of exchanging currency, labour unrest, war, non-payment of national debt, political intervention, disruption of the supplier's chain and risks in the areas of legislation and regulation. The worldwide Aon network comprises some 500 offices in more than 120 countries and has more than 59,000 employees. Aon Corporation specialises in financial and insurance services and is listed on the New York Stock Exchange (NYSE).

Source: The Daily Herald, 6th May, 2011

Box 3.2 Pharmaceutical industry may seek political risk cover

The third world markets are very popular target for the international business development managers of the Indian pharmaceutical giants. They are considering the semiregulated markets of BRIC countries; and un regulated markets or less regulated markets of Africa, Middle East, and Southeast Asia as potential markets in addition to the regulated markets of the United States, Japan, and Europe. Formulations drugs have good demand in these less or unregulated country markets of the former Soviet Union (CIS) and least developing countries of Southeast Asia, Africa, and Latin America. Many markets are found to be lucrative, as most of it is largely unregulated, by the Indian pharmaceutical managers for developing a sustainable export strategy to these markets but they are very unpredictable at times. These unregulated markets are often susceptible to changes in drug laws and approval system, usually emanating from political decisions. The Indian companies has recently seen how two good markets of Uganda and Tanzania have become suddenly rough as rumors spread that fake or substandard, drugs are exported to these countries from China or India. Because of the nature of product, the phama products are always remain very much under the scanner of the country governments, be it developed or underdeveloped. The unpredictability is usually more in case of in politically unstable markets. The reason is pretty simple. In the poor countries the government in power always play with health policy as an important tool for achieving political benefits and hence they may change their drug laws at the drop of a hat. The companies who now may consider themselves to be close to the political powers may found as most unwanted in the next day with the change of course of the political directions. Interestingly, the foreign drug companies are neither a party to the change in the political priorities of the country nor they have the power to reverse it in their favour.

In such situation what a pharmaceutical company can do? It cannot either forgo exporting opportunities for impending political risk of the country or be busy with correcting the risk level of the countries. The industry analysts of pharmaceutical sector in India mostly suggest, in such situation, to go for insurance cover against political risk of the importing countries. However, ground situation in India for availing insurance coverage for international business against international political risk is quite a rarity. Most of the nationalised and private general insurers are reluctant to sell this cover as they are entirely reinsurance driven. The problems of offering such insurance covers are:

- The insurance market is not too equipped to handle such huge risks.
- Any cover against political risks has to be almost reinsured wholly and hence would be very expensive for single company to avail.
- There need to be critical mass seeking for such insurance coverage.

However the globally there are big names in general insurance who are offering insurance cover against political risks with London market being the hub of these covers. As the political volatility of the targeted countries of the 'not so big' Indian pharmaceutical companies are increasing it is the need of the hour to seriously consider the risk coverage issues to make them comfortable to some extent in doing business abroad.

Source: The Economic Times, Apr 15, 2004

POLITICAL RISK

Different authors have defined the term 'political risk', as the term has different interpretations in international business. According to Llewellyn D. Howell[4], "political risk refers to the possibility that political decisions or events in a country will affect the business climate in such a way that investors will lose money or not make as much money as they expected when the investment was made."

David Schmidt[5] defines political risk as "the application of host government policies that constrain the business operations of a given foreign investment." One thing is common to both definitions – the term political risk, in the context of international business, reflects the host country's political decisions which either directly affect or indirectly would affect the business environment and hence may disturb the foreign business in such a way that the company has to undergo a risky phase that may lead to loss of money. Political risk is not, therefore, welcomed by the foreign businesses and hence they put every effort for neutralisation. As countries vary in their propensity to make political decisions that may create disturbance in a business environment, so do foreign businesses in a host country also vary in their preparedness to tackle those disturbances. The preparedness depends upon the business entity's ability to assess the political situations of the host country correctly as it can hardly do anything to reverse the host country's political decision. In general, countries continuously reeling under political instability are supposed to provide a fluid environment for international businesses. But international businesses have learnt over the years about how to conduct there businesses in those countries. Here, the best way to is to treat the 'uncertainty' as 'certainty'. A small African country like Burundi seems to be very stable apparently but there has been a simmering tension in the political front as the ruling party (CNDD-FDD) is constantly under threat from opposition movement of National Forces of Liberation during almost a decade now leading political instability in the country. According to COFACE[6] Burundi is rated 'D' which means that the country is reeling under extreme political and ecomonic situation but companies like Heineken and Coca Cola are doing business there sucessfully. Heineken is developing Nyongera as 100% 'Sorghum' beer marketing in Burundi at an affordable price.

However, in the same way, many big countries that are politically stable can prove to be a risky venture for business houses. For example, Google.com was launched in China in January 2006 with the belief that Chinese population will be increasing their information access through unrestricted use of the internet. The company temporarily agreed to the host countries decision to censor some search results accessed in the country. From 2006, the company carefully monitored the political decisions affecting their business. Then came a situation in 2010 when Google found that a highly sophisticated

---

[4] Howell, Llewellyn D. (1994), "An introduction to country and political risk analysis," in William D. Coplin and Michael K. O'Leary (eds.), *The Handbook of Country and Political Risk Analysis*, Syracuse, New York. Political Risk Services, p. 1.

[5] David Schmidt, as quoted in Poirier, Robert (1997), "Political risk analysis and tourism," *Annals of Tourism Research*, 24(3), p. 667. See also David A. Schmidt (1986), "Analysing Political Risks," *Business Horizons*, 29(4), pp. 43–60.

[6] **Compagnie Française d'Assurance pour le Commerce Extérieur** (COFACE) is a globally operating credit insurer, offering companies solutions to protect them against the various risk.

and targeted attack on their corporate infrastructure originated from China that resulted in the theft of intellectual property from Google. The company found that the host country's political [7]regime was not supportive when the matter was taken up with the government officials. The company decided to review the feasibility of their business operations in China with possible shut down Google.com. The example of Google is a glaring example of how there could be governmental interference while doing business in a foreign company leading to financial loss. There could be Government interference in other ways as well like sudden confiscation of company property, unforeseen restriction in currency, transfer to home country, imposing limits to business turnover and expansion and so on. Political risk can also be there even without direct government interference like in case of politically sponsored communal or racial violence, terrorism and action of underground militants groups causing loss/damage to the company financially or otherwise, say loss of market goodwill.

Classification of Political Risk

Now, it is understandable that different political systems exist in different countries of the world. International marketers would, therefore, encounter different political environments in different countries. While doing so, they may have to put up with different political risks emanating from host government policies. For international business, political risk can come from many directions. Broadly, based on the sources of the political risk, such risk can be divided into three categories – expropriation, transfer and political violence risk.

Expropriation risk

This type of risk arises from the host government's pressure or action, directly or indirectly, on the foreign company's ownership or control pattern, or forceful demand on the company's development rights or facilities or and on its products for the host country's own use. The attempt of expropriation by the host government generally takes place under the pretext of the national interest. Often the people of the country are taken in to confidence by purposeful propaganda unleashed by the government before such action. Nationalisation and domestication are the ugliest face of expropriation where the host country either takes over the control of the foreign company or entrusts the property or development rights of the targeted foreign company to a national company. In these days as the news of such move by any country government spreads very fast and brings bad name for the country so expropriation moves have been reduced considerably. Countries with previous records of expropriation attempts are considered by international business as unfit place for foreign direct investment. Because any move of expropriation brings enough bad names to deter foreign investors investing in the country so some countries may move indirectly in executing towards their goal of expropriation in small steps. This step by step expropriation may

[7] Schmidt, D. A. (1986), "Analysing political risks", *Business Horizons*, Vol. 29, No. 4, pp. 43–50.

take different forms like increased regulations, confiscatory taxes, restrictions on the repatriation of currency, changes in exchange rates and forced re-negotiation.

Transfer risk

This type of risk is very common for international business involving uncertain and unclear system of cross-border flows of capital and know-how transfer. The host country government unexpectedly introduces or bring changes in the legal system in the matter of capital controls rules both for inbound or outbound. The country may introduce changes in system of dividend and interest payments. Sometimes the host country government, in order to earn more tax from foreign companies introduces complex and confusing tax laws which become difficult for the foreign company to avoid.

Political violence risk

This type of risk refers to losses from damage to, or the destruction and disappearance of tangible assets of foreign company due to politically motivated acts of sabotage and terrorism, strikes, riots, and civil commotion, insurrection, coups d'état and outright war. Many foreign companies in countries like Syria, Afghanistan and Pakistan got affected to such kind of politically motivated violence. In these days American multinational and their affiliates are increasingly becoming the target of political violence risks in many countries.

Manifestation of Political Risk in Business

Political risk of any type, whether it is macro, micro or global, can affect the conduct of business in a host country. Generally, the managers of international business perceive that in political stable, developed countries these risks are comparatively less than the politically unstable and developing countries. It is also expected that political risks would be comparatively less in a democratic country than in totalitarian countries. Socialist countries, on the other hand, are expected to perform in a known laid-down path and hence political risks in those countries, through high, are predictable. However, in practice, there is no set rule to assess manifestation of political risk in business and therefore it requires continuous profiling of political risk and assessing their impact on business. The major politically designed events (Table 3.3) that affect business functions internationally are discussed below critically to understand them more closely.

Table 3.3 Different types of events constituting political risk

Expropriation risk	Transfer risk	Political violence risk
1. Confiscation 2. Domestication 3. Local content requirements and import restriction 4. Loss of image due to political transition 5. Politically motivated cyber attacks	1. Currency control 2. Discriminating tax structure	1. Unwarranted action by political pressure groups 2. Labour unrest due to politics 3. Physical damage to assets from political violence 4. Terrorism

Confiscation

This is possibly the worst form of manifestation of political risk. In simple sense, it is the hostile takeover of a foreign company by the host country government without payment. Confiscation is generally considered a drastic step of a host country government. Therefore most of the known circumstances of confiscation involving the host nation have resulted in the foreign business's home nation-to-host nation aggression. For example Cuba and USA was at the logger-heads for a long time when Fidel Castro came to power and American property was confiscated. In the current days, cases of confiscations are not a frequent happening. However, there have been a few isolated cases. For example, the Venezuelan government, during October 2011, took over almost 200,000 hectares (494,000 acres) of land owned by British meat company Vestey Foods Group. The government had been in talks for months to buy the Vestey cattle ranches. But after the confiscation, Venezuela's President Hugo Chavez declared that it was actually a friendly agreement and he was very thankful to the owners of the English company for allowing the property transfer. The Vestey group was operating in the country Venezuela for more than 100 years.

Domestication

Domestication is the step which the host country may take to prove its desire for intense nationalisation. The domestic companies in a country may be poor in terms of technology resulting in weakness and inefficiency and hence they may be unable to compete with foreign companies. The host country, in its desperation to upgrade competitiveness of the domestic companies, may forcibly acquire the foreign companies doing business in that country and transfer ownership of the foreign entity to the domestic one. There are no real and long-lasting benefits of confiscation enjoyed by the host country excepting a very temporary surge of popularity amongst the support groups of the government. Grupo Exito, the leading Colombian retailer with about 262 stores, has a good presence in Columbia and offers a wide range of food and non-food products. The majority stake in Exito is owned by the French group, Casino, while Medellin-based Almacenes Exito SA owns 29%. The company had its presence in Venezuela through six hypermarkets and around 32 supermarkets. During 2010, Venezuela began the nationalisation of French-Colombian supermarket chain Exito. The government announced that henceforth the Exito in Venezuala would be a "socialist mega-stores." where price speculation and hoarding shall have no place. President Hugo Chavez ordered the takeover of six Exito stores into a government-run chain dealing with household goods, clothing, and footwear at discount prices for the Venezuelan consumer. The pretext of this entire takeover was that Exito hypermarkets illegally speculated and raised prices when the national currency Bolivarian currency was devalued.

Currency control

Venezuelan currency crisis is a glaring example of this type of political risk. The democratically elected government declared that foreign debt payments and the import of basic foods and medicines were its top priority.

The government farther artificially pegged Bolivar at a value 17% stronger than what it was last traded to the USD to impose check on movement of foreign currency out of the country. This political move was executed out of the ruling government's fear of shortage of foreign currency and cheaper import of food and medicine to the countrymen. Earlier, the Venezuelan importer of food and medicine had to pay 1853 bolivars against one USD of import; but now, after pegging of currency, the outgo of the same importer would be 1598 bolivars only. Under the new currency rules, foreign companies operating in Venezuela are required to register with the government before they can repatriate profits overseas. A little different manifestation of this tendency of control of foreign currency can be seen in countries like Myanmar. The officially declared Myanmar's currency Kyat (pronounced as 'Chayt') and USD exchange rate is 6 Kyat is equal to 1 USD. However, anyone who walks out of the airport would be able to access unofficial money exchangers who will gladly make a payment of 120 Kyat for 1 USD. Since the country is facing US sanction for a long period of time, it does want to check repatriation of profit through exchange rate manipulation officially and unofficially.

Local content requirements and import restriction

Foreign companies, because of their international spread are expected to globally outsource different components to achieve distinctive competitive-ness while producing in the host country. How much the company would source locally would depend on the company's strategic sourcing decision. But it may not be always true. Locally-sourced expenditures by the foreign company may also be dictated by the local government. Take the case of China in respect of the local content requirements of its wind power industry, which has been in vogue for many years. Any company manufacturing wind turbine equipment is required to use a certain percentage of locally-made components. The imposition of local content requirement began way back in 2003 and with time, it became more stringent. Requirements began with mandating 50% local content in 2003 and increased to 70% in 2004, where it remains today. In addition, the 70% local content requirement now applies not only to the government-run wind concessions, but to all wind farms being developed in China. In the automobile sector, different countries stipulate local content requirement differently. In Brazil, it is about 60% for established automobile manufacturers and 50% for newly-established ones during the first three years of production and 60% thereafter. In fact, all the MERCOSUR (Brazil, Argentina, Uruguay and Paraguay) countries stipulate at least 60% regional content for automobile manufacturing in the region and the member countries allow trade among them with a zero percent import duty.

Physical damage to assets from political violence

International marketers suffer a lot whenever a country is in transition. The same thing happened in Egypt in the recent times when foreign companies suffered a variety of losses as a result of civil unrest. The capital city of Cairo was rocked as a result of political violence rendering the place unfit to run normal business activities. Interesting to note that political violence affects different companies differently. Some company would find that they have sustained physical damage to the company property; some may lost important business hours as well as valued clients. All these ultimately lead to financial loss in terms of increased security expenses, temporary housing and relocation expenses and loss of targeted sales.[8]

Discriminating tax structure

International marketers face a formidable task if, because of political whims, the host country discriminate between local and international companies in respect of levying tax. Let us consider the debilitating effect of such disparate tax structures in two prominent countries.

In the recent times about 13 large foreign-origin companies, doing business in Hungery, said that they are concerned with the move of the government to generate additional revenue by raising taxes on selected and mostly foreign-business dominated sectors of the economy. The Hungarian government was also found desperate to increase its revenue by such unjustified deliberate move. The companies that signed the letter of protest for such discriminatory tax structure were European insurers, energy firms, utilities, retailers, a telecommunications company, and a banking group. On the other hand the country had almost no option to come out of the financial crisis. With the onset of global financial crisis in late 2008, Hungary was with debt levels markedly above those in other central European economies like Czech Republic and Poland. It had asked the EU and the International Monetary Fund for help but was refused. However, later, under the bailout deal, Hungary had to impose tight control on budget deficit. In order to do that, the Hungarian government in 2010 levied high taxes on energy, retail and telecommunications firms.

The foreign businesses elsewhere also were targeted for discrimination. Early on in its reform and opening-up, China's domestic economic climate was more conducive to state-owned enterprises than to international enterprises. This was because the former could secure government support and thus had certain advantages in the market place that businesses from other countries did not possess. Recently, the Chinese government has begun charging foreign companies and individuals who have commercial interest in that country for city maintenance and imposing them with construction taxes and education cess, much to the annoyance of these foreign investors.

Restriction on transfer of profit

Most countries have put rules in place guaranteeing investors an unrestricted remittance of dividends, profits and liquidation proceeds, on condition that payment of taxes and other liabilities has been made according to local regulations. However, there are a few exceptions also. The exemptions include Ethiopia and Mozambique where request prior authorisation is required for transfer of funds. International Monetory Fund's (IMF), knowing this a barrier to do business in different countries, mooted Article VIII of the IMF's Article of Agreement which once agreed upon and signed by a country would disallow the concerned country to impose restrictions on payments and transfers for international current transactions.

[8] http://www.nbcnews.com/id/41351339/ns/travel-news/t/unrest-hits-egypt-during-high-tourist-season/#.Vlx1cNIrKt8

Countries like Ethiopia, Nigeria and Mozambique are yet to accept the spirit of the Article VIII causing problems to the international companies.

Labour unrest due to internal politics

Foreign companies may face labour problem due to internal politics in a country. Recently in China, there was labour unrest in selected foreign companies and government officials were found supporting their actions. A number of suicides at Taiwan's Foxconn, which counts Apple, Dell and Sony among its clients, led the company to double the salaries of its workers. Japan's Honda offered a 24% raise in salaries to buy peace in its main parts factory. Patrick Chovanec, an economist at Tsinghua University in Beijing opined, "The companies are concerned about their image at home and abroad, whereas a Chinese subcontractor making soap possibly wouldn't care what the world thought of them." The US fast-food giant KFC agreed to raise the salary of 2000 staff in northern Shenyang city after months of trade union pressure. There was labour unrest at Suzuki's Indian production facility, which stalled production at the engine units of Suzuki Powertrain India and Suzuki Castings at Manesar and the two-wheeler unit of Suzuki Motorcycle India at Gurgaon. Generally, domestic companies are closely linked with the local politics and have better connections with government officials. Foreign companies may therefore fall prey to the discriminating pattern of labour unrest in their host countries.

Pressure groups

In some countries, there are pressure groups that look upon the foreign companies as oppressors against the national interest. They usually garner huge support as sentiments of nationalism are involved in the issue. Often, political parties take active interest in such issues to project themselves as national saviours. For example, one national level political party in India recently said that they will launch a nationwide movement against multinational companies on the lines of Quit India Movement as they think that their works are detrimental to national interests. They expect that other political parties of the country would soon join them to oust the multinational companies from the country. The Bt brinjal of Monsanto could not enter Indian soil due to active protest from the pressure group. The leader of the pressure group almost singlehandedly ousted the mighty American company from India.

Loss of image due to political transition

Political power transition, hostile or non hostile, in countries and events in the aftermath saw many foreign companies losing their acceptance in those countries. Generally, companies of foreign origin working as 'blue eyed companies' in a particular regime may suddenly become almost 'enemy' of the new ruling party as well to the country. **In countries transition of poltical power takes place due to various reasons. The most probable reasons are** election delay, reforms delay, participation of the military in government decision making, economic reasons like continuing poverty, etc. **However, if transition takes place because of extreme** instability of the ruling political party then possibility of presently favoured companies meted out ill treatment in the post change over scenario increases. However, in an acclaimed democratic country such possibilities are less where foreign companies may look forward to the coming elections as a way out to change existing rulers for a betterment in business environment. For example, during 2005 Kyrgyzstan was in political turmoil as opposition political parties were constantly pressurising President Askar Akayev to make country's judiciary free from political influence of ruling party. However, all the appeals fell in the deaf ear and the President Akayev was openly using the judiciary system of the country to either suppress the voice of political opponents or to remove political challengers. The political opponents were searching for an opportunity to revolt, and they finally united to march into the presidential palace leading to administration collapse and installation of new provisional government (Figure 3.1). The political transition saw that many companies operating in the country falling from gracious position which they enjoyed during Present Akayev's time. This was not the only occasion companies became red faced after political transition. It happened in many countries like Tunicia, Egypt, Libyas, Maldives, etc. In Tunisia, the revolution began during 2010 saw and ouster of the president within a year leading to the setting up of an interim government in the country which threatened the foreign companies who supported the previous government. Similar phenomena happened in other countries too when there were the cases of transition of unstable governments.

Politically motivated Cyber attacks

It is vivid in the human memory how the world biggest search engine, Google complained about a "highly sophisticated and targeted cyber attack" during 2009. It did not take long time for them to claim that the origin of the attack was in China. This resulted in the "theft of intellectual property from Google." Aftermath the attack, the world saw tightening of security system by Google. Again during 2011, McAfee, the wholly owned subsidiary of Intel Corporation dealing with dedicated web security

FIGURE 3.1 The Russian unrest

service, declared that at least five large oil and ga anies were subjected to frequent cyber-attacks. Upon investigation, The hat the attackers targeted control servers located in the US and the Ne gain access to computer systems in Kazakhstan, Taiwan, Greece a whatever may be pupose of these cyber attacks, it was amply clea kers intention was to get in to the confidential information of t gas and oil field production systems, financial transactions, mation. Sony, the Japanese electronics giant, was found to a report reached to them that cyber-attacker had broken its serve and released the personal and billing information of up to 77 millio

Terrorism

Though the multinationals are not likely to be directly effected by terrorism but it is fast becoming a matter of serious concern to multinationals. Very seldom international firms have reported to be directly affected by terrosion and as a result there were loss of life of employees or property. However there were huge indirect effects which include decline in consumer demand, abrupt halt or disruption of supply chain, voluntary resignation of efficient expatriate workers and payment of ransom or protection money. Unfortunately, foreign companies operating in a country, even if they are unwilling to be touched by menace of terrorism, are effected by them time to time. The manifestation happens in the form of employee abduction, ransom claim, huge security concern, employment of protection force, selection of vendors under threat, loss of may days, damage of company property, etc. On the other hand, terrorist groups often try to involve foreign companies by design in the host country to enjoy the undue publicity. There are many example of such occurrences. Way back in 1965 the Revolutionary Armed Forces of Colombia (known by its Spanish acronym, FARC) targeted foreign company by kidnapping its employees in Colombia, Ecuador and Venezuela in an attept to get in to the limelight. Unilever chief executive Patrick Cescau and his successor Paul Polman somehow escaped and saved their life from Mumbai's 9/11' terrorist attack on Taj Mahal hotel.

Schumpeter on political environment

ago, Ahmed Ezz was one of the most powerful business people in Egypt. He controlled % of the country's steel production, played a leading role in the ruling party and, most of all, was a bosom buddy of Hosni Mubarak's son and heir apparent, Gamal. Today, he is a has- sters have demonised him and torched his company headquarters. The old guard has dumped him . He is under investigation, his assets have been frozen and his right to travel has been restricted. npanies that cultivated Mr Ezz wasted their time and money.

e regarded as axiomatic that globalisation would marginalise politics. Theodore Levitt, one of ness School's leading thinkers, argued that "the Earth is round but, for most purposes, it's sensible t". Kenichi Ohmae, a Japanese business guru, published "The Borderless World" and "The End of e". Giant companies such as IBM and Ford played down the importance of country managers o create globally integrated behemoths.

The events in Egypt are a reminder of how foolish such "borderless" thinking can be. Dick Cheney once remarked, "The Good Lord didn't see fit to put oil and gas only where there are democratically elected regimes friendly to the United States." It might be added that the Good Lord did not see fit to put economic growth n equally desirable places. The corporate world is rightly excited by the pell-mell growth in emerging markets, but these are rife with political risks—weak legal systems, makeshift institutions, volatile cities and fragile egimes. A growing number of countries, most notably China but also Russia and the Gulf states, are using business as an instrument of state power. And some of the world's biggest companies, including most of the largest oil firms, are state-run, driven by political as much as economic considerations.

China is the leading offender, using state companies to snap up a growing share of the world's natural resources. It is also using its state-industrial complex to pursue political goals. Google was forced to re-route its servers when it refused to censor e-mails. Four Rio Tinto executives were imprisoned in dubious circumstances. China is not alone: BP's new partnership with Rosneft, Russia's state-controlled oil giant, to develop Russia's Arctic region is complicated by murky political considerations. Political risks can also bite Western companies at home, where governments are increasingly vigilant about corruption. The Obama administration is enforcing the Foreign Corrupt Practices Act with an evangelical zeal—and employing techniques once reserved for fighting organised crime. The British government is introducing tough anti-bribery measures. Executives who adopt what they regard as "local" rules in Thailand or Indonesia can find themselves facing prison sentences back home. How do companies cope? There are no simple rules. Countries that are cavalierly lumped together as emerging markets have very different political regimes. In Brazil, you need to understand Congress's multi-party alliances; in China, the power dynamics of the Communist Party; in Saudi Arabia, th internal relations of the ruling family. Local politics add yet more complexity. The most important advice is t take politics seriously. Oil and mining companies have always done this. Royal Dutch Shell has run a profitab business in Nigeria for more than 50 years despite a dangerous and volatile environment. "New econom companies have tended to be much more naive. The Egyptian crisis demonstrates that they cannot av being caught up in political battles which are now fought over the internet. A Google executive in the reg Wael Ghonim, also doubled as a leading political activist.

Source: Joseph Schumpeter.www.economist.com

Assessing and Measuring Political Risk

There has been a growing interest in understanding and measurin ical risk across the nations of the world, as more and more intern sation of businesses are taking place. In early days of internation the companies that opened their businesses in foreign soil mos on their capacity of resilience in the face of unexpected early pol related shocks. During the initial years of internationalisation, the liked to believed that they stood to gain a lot in terms of develo market and establishing themselves, if they are able to withstan shocks. Naturally then these companies took risk to focus on ex market potential that was available, may be for a limited period with the conviction that gains of doing business abroad would political risks that are being tolerated. However, with the passag internationalising companies became careful towards minimis This is primarily because of two reasons: one, companies lea companies who had assessed risk carefully in advance perform avoided business failure abroad; two, those who had to retur own country, due to business failure abroad, lost huge fina which could not be recovered later.

Therefore, many progressive companies went one step ahead by installing a mechanism to determine the variables composing the political risk and studying them carefully with the aim to find their impact on the planned foreign investment. However, as the companies were becoming watchful, the colours of erstwhile political risks were also changing very fast in many countries. Often the risks are now so camouflaged that a traditional business manager accustomed to understand political risks in terms of some old stereotypes like military takeover, rally against multinational corporations, etc., finds them difficult to understand correctly. The new formats of the political risks are evolving in such a way that are often clubbed with legal and regulatory changes, environmental and human rights issues, etc., which make assessment difficult.

Political risk assessment: Activity based

As US companies were the first multinational companies of the world so the necessity of assessing political risks was mostly felt by them for judging the worth their resource commitment abroad. A survey of leading US MNCs conducted during 1950s revealed[9] that the managers of these companies perceived that political risk was comprised of primarily 13 governmental activities. They host country governments undertook these activities solely because of political compulsions. These 13 parameters are as listed below in order of their ability to affect business.

1. Import restriction
2. Unexpected currency devaluation or revaluation of non-floating currencies
3. Delays in profit repatriation
4. Currency inconvertibility
5. Terrorism
6. Unfair tax laws
7. Labour strikes and trade union power
8. Production or export restrictions
9. Contract repudiation
10. Restrictions on local market access
11. Expropriation or nationalisation
12. Confiscation of property
13. (Lowest) Restrictions on information flow

The first generation risk assessment approach based on government activities was criticised later on two counts. First, political risk was treated exogenously, and second, it was simplified enough to assume them to be confined to certain political activities. Also, these 13 governmental activities vary in their ability to influence business, which may not always be in particular order as elieved. The critiques were of the opinion that a pre-determined set of govnment activities may not decide the negative consequences on business as ferent types of businesses would face different risks arising out of political vities.

, "Importance of political risk assessment function in US multinational corporations," *Global*

Political risk assessment: Event based

The second generation risk assessment attempted towards the identification of events actually disturbing the political stability of a country. These disturbances or events actually provoked a country to behave differently to the foreign investors. Based on this thinking, Dan Haendel, Gerald West, and Robert Meadow[10] worked on zeroing on these events using the following three major data set:

(A) **Socioeconomic:** Ethnolinguistic fractionalisation, GNP growth per capita, and energy consumption per capita.
(B) **Societal conflicts:** Political unrest – riots, demonstrations, and government crises; Internal violence – armed attacks, assassinations, coups d'état and guerrilla warfare, and coercion potential of internal security forces.
(C) **Governmental processes:** Political competition, legislative effectiveness, constitutional changes per year, and irregular chief executive changes.

They collected and analysed hard data for 65 countries for the period 1961–65, in respect of the above characteristics, to understand first, the stability of a political system second, adaptability capacity of a country to a change as adaptability to change is directly related to its political stability. The researchers then generated a "political system stability index" comprised of weighted indicators for socioeconomic, governmental processes and societal conflict risk indicators. They also demonstrated accuracy of the "Political System Stability Index" by calculating the index for countries like Zaire and Dominican Republic which were at that time apparently associated with high political risks.

This event based approach was better accepted by the companies as they found that this technique of assessing political risk of a country yielded better result. Also hard data analysis led to a model with prescriptive ability which can be used by a company as and when required.

Political Risk Assessment: System based

According to Stefan H. Robock[11] it is the political system prevailing in a country that provokes political instability and political risk is only a manifestation of the political system. Therefore, in Robock's framework of identifying and assessing risk consisted of contextual analyses of political system or process that have implications for foreign investors. Again, the implications could be of two types. One, macro political risks, which are non-project specific, and two, micro political risk, which are project specific. Macro political risk can effect broadly all foreign enterprises almost in a similar way (Table 3.4), whereas micro political risks builds up differently for different businesses and are context depended, i.e., the political risk for one company may not be the political risk for another.

[10] Dan Haendel and Gerald T. West with Robert G. Meadow.(1975) , "Overseas investment and political risk" Lexington Books, 1975.

[11] Robock, Stefan H. (1971), "Political risk identification and assessment," *Columbia Journal of World Business*, Vol. 6, No. 4, p. 8.

Table 3.4 Political risks and their influence on international business operations

Sources of political risk	Groups through which political risk can be generated	Influence on international business operations
In fighting between different competing national level political philosophies.	Ruling political party of the country and competing non-governmental organisations.	Confiscation and hooliganism leading to the loss of assets without compensation, loss of working days.
Social unrest	Parliamentary opposition groups	Expropriation due to waves of acute nationalism, loss of freedom to operate, loss of revenue.
Local business, lobby and interest groups like, environmentalists, industry protectionists and national protectionists	Non-parliamentary opposition groups	Forceful restriction on sourcing, recruitment, sales, etc. Foreign ownership restrictions or ceilings, etc.
Impending political independence from dictatorship, authoritarian ruler.	Non-governmental, organised common interest groups; students, workers, peasants, minorities, etc.	Profit transfer problem, change in ownership structure, skewed local content requirement, etc.
Entry into international alliances, membership of international organisation or international organisation. membership obligations, or trade bloc membership	Foreign government or inter-governmental agencies.	Non-adherence of different clauses of contracts by local suppliers and other stakeholders.

Political risk: Semi-quantitative and risk-ranking approaches

During 1979 a new semi quantitative risk ranking approache known as Political Risk Services (PRS)[12] came in to lime light and instantly became popular across the multinational companies. PRS Group of New York had entrusted the work of developing risk ranking system for the countries of the world which could be used by multinationals to Syracuse University, New York. It gained popularity and found acceptance amongst the global companies primarily because of its 'easy to use' nature in quantifying and rating political risk of a large number of countries. Again during 1980 PRS Group launched another approach known as International Country Risk Guide (ICRG) which was highly complementary to already existing PRS system. Both PRS and ICRG continued to coexist till 1993 when finally the two merged to form the present name, i.e., 'The PRS Group'. 'The PRS Group' approach is very popular and is used by about 80% of the world's largest global companies, as well as aid donors and international financial institutions such as the World

[12] Originally, Professors William D. Coplin and Michael K. O'Leary of Syracuse University, New York, developed a system of independent risk assessment in 1979. The system gained popularity as Political Risk Services and has been recognised worldwide as the original system for quantifying and rating political risk.

Box 3.4 Maplecroft identifies political risk hotspots

The Political Risk Atlas of Mapplecroft is a good source of understanding the political risk of the countries of the world. This atlas indicates, based on their analysis, the possible risks for business and investors across the countries of the world. For example according to Maplecroft's analysis, there will be continuing instability in the Arab Spring countries. In countries like Belarus, Guinea Bissau, Iran, Sudan, Turkmenistan and Vietnam there will be potential societal unrest and regime instability. African countries like Angola, DR Congo, Guinea, and Zimbabwe will tightening their control on mineral resources through attempt of resource nationalism. It is very unlikely that these countries would improve their score on parameters refecting good democratic governance.

Maplecroft's risk atlas also indicates the countries who possibly could progress in terms of reduced riskiness. For example, Maplecroft found that countries like Indonesia, Philippines, Mexico, Thailand, Liberia and Bolivia are improving on the count of political riskiness

The users of Mapplecroft political risk atlas can find risk assessment of 197 countries of the world. In order to predict risk of an individual country it considers about 45 risk indices which are the causes of germinating risk towards companies while doing business there. Mapplcroft further analyses these indices for a long period of time to provide an understanding of the trend of the risk prevailing in the countries. From 2012, Mapplecroft has introduced another index in the name 'Forced Regime Change Risk Index' which has been very useful to companies to understand the vulnerability of a country regime.

Bank. The group provides detailed and consistent monthly country level data for almost all the countries of the world which can be used by companies to assess political risks associated with doing business.

The PRS Group, on continuous basis, monitors political, financial and economic risk environments of different countries to provide consistent and comprehensive country wise risk rating. In its unique methodology, adopted for the purpose of risk assessment, the group collects, primary data with the help of pre-set questionnaire covering 22 components of risks grouped under three headings like Political risk, financial risk and economic risk. Thereafter, the responses are analysed critically to produce "total political risk indicators" for utilisation by businesses.

Insuring Political Risk

As per the World Bank's Global Economic Outlook report 2015 there would be slight increases of growth at the rate of 3.5% from 3.4% last year (2014) in advanced economies. But growth is projected to be slower in many emerging countries and oil producing countries. There would be political uncertainty in many countries as a result there could be economic slowdown. An international company is likely to be concerned about the economic and political forecast as they could affect their investment abroad. This is more so when the incidents of politically driven activities effecting foreign businesses are getting reported frequently from developing and least developing countries. For example, a small African country Eritrea is ready with enormous mineral resources but companies from other parts of the world may not be interested to get involved in mining before actually knowing the quantum of political risk involved. Recent example from Democratic Republic of Congo where the mining company Quantum engaged copper mining was expropriated. Oil explorers in Venezuela are constantly under threat because of instability in the political system of the country. Recently one Indian company though won the bidding process to mine a gold mine in Eritrea but could not initiate operation there because of presumed high risk. Such examples shows that the companies investing abroad are requiring to have a safety cover for mitigating risk of foreign operation emanating from political uncertainties. These risk apprehensions were further supported by the MIGA-EIU Political Risk Survey of 2010,[13] which had shown that the global investors, in fact, perceive risks that are driven by political agenda in different countries and are to be on the rise in years to come.

Therefore, market participation by international businesses requires some safety covers. One way out is to mitigate the risks is through some sort of insurance cover for the investors who perceive high risk of operation in certain countries. In this away the investors can pass on the buck to political risk insurers. MIGA (Multilateral Investment Guarantee Assurence or MIGA) is a world Bank initiative to promote multilateral investment of companies in different countries with different risk orientation. MIGA helps investors and lenders to deal with the political risks by providing them insurance cover insuring eligible projects against losses relating to:

- Currency inconvertibility and transfer restriction
- Expropriation
- War, terrorism, and civil disturbance
- Breach of contract
- Non-honoring of sovereign financial obligations

MIGA provides political risk insurance (guarantees) for projects in a broad range of sectors in developing member countries, covering all regions of the world.

Introduction: Legal factors

A global marketer encounters different country markets while making an endeavor to create customer value for its customer segment in the best way possible. Be it standardised marketing practice for country markets covered or a customised one following 'horses for the courses' policy, the marketing strategy must not violet the legal system of the respective countries. Simplistically speaking every country market has its own legal system within which every international business need to operate. In fact, the legal system is an inevitable component of the environment within which a business operates without much liberty for manipulations. The commercial laws, prevailing in the country time, are equally applicable to the international marketers as it is for the domestic marketers. In some countries the international marketers are even subjected to some extent discriminating commercial laws where the domestic companies enjoy certain concessions only. These laws and regulations under which an international marketer operates constitute

[13] MIGA (Multilateral Investment Guarantee Assurence) is an world Bank initiative to promote multilateral investment of companies going abroad for look out of new opportunities.

the legal environment of the country. Companies practicing the standardised marketing strategy are possibly more affected than the customised one as every variable of marketing mix may be candidate for change as per the law of the land. This has a direct bearing on the management of global marketing plan as standardisation of marketing strategy often disrupted by country specific legal rules and principles. For example, one international marketer may be compelled to run different type of advertisements to abide by the legal regulations of different countries. Indonesia during 2007 introduced a rule that required the companies to release advertisements in the country featuring local talents only.

Truly speaking, the international marketers just feel helpless due to lack of a comprehensive internationally applicable judicial and administrative framework or a body of law which can be termed as international legal system applicable to all the countries. Putting simplistically, in absence of a standard "international law" applicable to all the countries, companies are subjected to "country law" of individual nations. Since, every country is empowered to enact its own laws based on their respective requirements therefore laws and regulations greatly vary across countries. Each country specific laws and regulations reflects its socio-political traditions, religious customs, economic-political compulsions, etc. Hence, it becomes extremely difficult for the companies to practice a generalised approach while conducting marketing internationally. It almost appears that company is bounded by the country specific legal system where hardly exist any flexibility of maneuvering. With no way out, the international businesses are constrained to run business operations in accordance with the legal system of the country. Therefore, they organise activities of advertising, pricing, contracting, sourcing, designing product safety standard, setting competition lay outs, etc., within the limit set my country specific regulations without antagonising the law makers of the countries.

Not respecting the country's legal system may attract trouble for the foreign companies. This has been learnt by the international companies sometimes by paying huge price for the mistakes. For example, Henkel, the German multinational company headquartered in Dusseldorf, with its three main business areas such as laundry and home care, cosmetics/toiletries, and adhesive technologies, had to face penal action with another two business giants, namely Proctor and Gamble (P&G) and Unilever for violating legal regulations in Europe. P&G, known for its world class household products Tide, Gain, and Era brands, fights head-to-head with Henkel in European and other markets. The Anglo-Dutch company, Unilever makes its presence felt in the household product category with Omo and Surf brands of detergent powder. Henkel fights with the detergent products of Unilever's and Procter & Gamble's brands with its famous Persil brand of detergent in most of Europe. Interestingly, in the backdrop of apparent market competition, Henkel has also licensed Unilever for manufacture, distribution, and marketing of Persil brand detergent in several countries. These three big companies, in order to avoid direct competition with each other in European market, made a tacit understanding regarding pricing of the detergent. European antitrust regulators caught them and established that during 2002–05, there was a cartel in between these companies for fixing prices of detergent powder which provided marketing advantage in eight European countries like Belgium, France, Germany, Greece, Italy, Portugal, Spain, and Netherland. Intiatailly, the companies denied but had to admit later when investigations threw ample light on the real happenings. As per the law of the land heavy punishment were meted out to the concerned companies. Procter & Gamble had to pay 211.2 million Euros, while Unilever was fined for 104 million Euros by the European antitrust regulators.

However, examples of getting punished for not abiding by the country's legal system are not few. Four companies Procter & Gamble, Colgate-Palmolive, Henkel and Unilever were punished by French government during the end part of 2011 for jointly fixing their laundry detergent prices by manipulating size of the discounts they could offer on their respective brand and mutually adjusting intra brand price differences. The French authority, was very upset with the involved companies as the general consumers of France had to pay more as there was no free competition in the market. In another case, country legal system played havoc with world largest carmaker Toyota Motor Corporation of Japan. US authority almost forcibly kept Toyota out of US market during mid 2010 when it was reported that Toyota was not abiding by the set safety standard of the country. The company was accused of fitting defective accelerator pedals in luxury SUV Lexus GX 460. According to US National Highway Transportation and Safety Administration regulations, Toyota did not disclose information and thereby put the consumers in great danger of accident and even loss of life. Toyota had to surrender to the US authority and paid a hefty fine of record $16.4 million.

Many International businesses understand the reality that legal restrictions are sacrosanct and countries do not tolerate deviations, and hence, violation may put them in difficult position in host country markets. However, mistakes are repeated again, and again while some have learnt. World's popular male grooming brand Axe of Unilever carefully selected the tag line "giving guys the edge in dating game" to communicate clearly to the European customers about perceived benefit of the product. The European regulator was not at all perturbed by the communication. However, the same company would not dare use the same communication in conservative countries of Middle East.

Therefore, it is necessary that companies would like to understand country specific legal system thoroughly and acceptance of its own way of doing business in that country's legal environment. Accordingly, along with understanding of economic, political and cultural environment of the foreign markets, the international businesses also need to know country specific legal system in great details. The academic researchers also had gone to extreme to do research, publish articles, and write business cases depicting the situations of handling legal barriers in global marketing.

In this sub chapter, therefore, we will be discussing legal systems confronted by the companies in different markets followed by legal considerations applicable in areas like product safety, marketing mix decision and product flow which are often found of paramount importance in deriving, formulating, and executing company's strategic marketing plan in international markets.

International Legal Systems

It is important to understand that every country has a basic legal system. Generally, three basic types of systems are there: (a) common law, (b) civil law, and (c) religious law. Broadly speaking, either individually or combinations these three form the legal system of the countries. A country's legal system originates from its unique history keep on taking the shape with the passage of time to form legal system of that particular country and hence the countries not only differ in terms of the basic system but also greatly vary in terms of how the system is implemented in practice. We will now describe the basic three systems.

Common law (Anglo-American legal system)

This is most prevalent system in the world as about a third of the world's population lives in common law jurisdictions. This system actually originated in England in the middle ages and evolved over a period of time. Since it has been originated from England so one would find it the Anglophone countries of the world. The common law applicable countries are India, USA, Pakistan, Nigeria, Bangladesh, Canada, Malaysia, Ghana, Australia, Sri Lanka, Hong Kong, Singapore, Ireland, New Zealand, Jamaica, Trinidad & Tobago, Cyprus and Barbados. The common law emphasises on the opinion formed by judges of court and similar tribunals created in the country. The common law basically believes in rule through precedence and give total emphasise on treating similar facts similarly in different occasions.. Therefore, the common law applying countries believes in upholding history, tradition and usage of the country and desires to see that present court rulings are taking cues from previous happenings in deciding current cases or controversies. Since common law believes in 'history should repeat' type of ideology therefore common law is said to be consistent, stable and predictable legal system. The opinion of the judges reflects tradition and belief of the country. While consistency is the main virtue of common law but the system has been criticised on the ground that it does not have the correcting ability as precedence sets the current issues also. The present case will get verdict based on previous cases even if that was decided. Historical orientation of common law has been favoured by many international businesses, on the ground that it provides some sort of assurance that awkward and unforeseen treatment will not be meted out to them as statutes, codes, and legislation developed over the years will be used to handle new situations also.

Civil law or code law (Continental legal system)

The civil law or code law oriented countries are not many. There are about 70 civil law oriented countries like France, Germany, most of Eastern and Western Europe, Japan, Cuba, Puerto Rico, Quebec, as well as most non-"English-speaking" nations of Africa, Asia, and Latin America. Civil law was originated and evoluted in Western Europe and took knowledge and wisdom heavily from ancient Roman law. It got its alternative name as code law because civil law is extensively codified which makes its applicability rather easy. The extensive codification system governs almost every aspects of happenings in a country in a documented fashion and hence this law is systematic, precise, and understandable to all. The country judiciary also able to follow them without ambiguity. Therefore in comparison civil law system happens to be more rigid but at the same time more predictable than the common law system. Under this system of law, the legislature body of a country first visits various individual statutes pertaining to any designated subject area and then finalises the comprehensive statute or code for the nation. For example, various individual statutes regarding bankruptcy of business establishments will be considered to enact comprehensive bankruptcy Code of the country. In this way, various codes are originated giving rise to laws of the country like commercial law, criminal law, civil procedures, and criminal procedures. While framing various codes the elected political representatives play a greater role than the judges if the country. Under this system political representatives develops various provisions to be included in the system to run the country in a reasonable way and then it is left with the judges to specify the basis for decision-making in the legal system. Therefore, in any practical situation, the role of the judge is simply to set up the facts related to a particular case through applying the provisions of the applicable code and understand the deviations from already codified standard. The judges are at liberty to understand the deviation through detail investigation of the case in hand and according the quantum of deviation frame formal charges. It can be observed that since the codes are evolved keeping in mind the country specific requirements so these codes vary across the countries following civil laws. However, based on commonalities the following four grouping can be made:

- **French civil law** – applicable in France, Belgium, Luxembourg, Quebec (Canada), Louisiana (USA), Italy, Spain and former colonies of those countries
- **German civil law** – applicable in Germany, Switzerland, Brazil, Portugal, Turkey, Japan, South Korea, China
- **Austrian civil law** – applicable in Austria, Czech republic, Slovakia, Greece, Serbia, Romania
- **Scandinavian civil law** – applicable in Sweden, Denmark, Finland, Iceland, Norway

Theocratic law (Religious legal systems)

The dictionary meaning of word 'theocracy'. means a system of government in which a deity is considered the civil ruler. Therefore, foundation of theocratic law is religion practiced in the country and spiritual principles followed by majority population. Hence, conduction of businesses, legal environment surrounding businesses, and individual's way of life are required to follow the religion practiced in the country. The religious heads or authorities, therefore, in such countries are very powerful and could be source of all legislations. These legislations once framed are not generally alterable or questionable but to followed by the people living in that country. The political authority ruling the country shows tremendous respect towards the religious heads and support the legislations to govern the civil society. The middle east countries, countries in Central Asia, many African countries, and Indonesia are the examples of countries subjected to the theocratic law. The legislations of these countries rely on Islam religion so rulings are based on the religious dictates of God (Allah) or the prophetic utterances and practices of the prophet Muhammad. The law takes heaviliy from Shari'a or God's law and Islamic Holy book Koran (Quran).

The way of doing business in countries following Islamic law must follow them correctly to be in accordance with the system. For example, any Indian banks operating in those countries must align with the norms set by Islamic laws while doing commercial transactions. Bankers from other countries must understand that interest earned or 'Riba' during a commercial transaction can be considered as unjust gains. European marketers while advertising in these countries must take a note of the laws and must not cross the boundaries already set by Islamic laws. In general, showing of women is in advertisement is discouraged in many Islamic countries. coraged In these countries it is absolute essential that business houses sacredly honor written agrrements executed with other parties and commercial deals, even if verbal, striked with other business associates are honoured as far as practicable. Food businesses must abide by 'Halal' rules and must not sale food to customers during 'Ramadan' period, Business houses may be cautioned if they sponsor activities leading to business gain of businesses dealing with alcohol or tobacco.

Socialist law

Socialist type legal system was popular in countries where there was communist rules. The believers of Marxist-Leninist ideology endeavoured to make society or country free from existence of any economic class like rich or poor. A person will not be judged based on the economic status he or she enjoys in the country. 'Equality for all' is the main mantra of the socialist ideology of economic status. There countries primarily adapted the civil law system but with different modifications to build in Marxist-Leninist idealogy in the social system. The number of countries under socialist system got reduced when many erstwhile constituents of Union of Soviet Socialist Republics did not continue to follow socialist system. China, Vietnam, North Korea, and Cuba continue to be under the socialist legal system. Businesses operating in social law regime must understand that the single ruling party in the country is all powerful and they will not like any sort of encouragement from the foreign business houses towards bringing multiplicity of political views in the country. The regine feels happy if a company promotes social welfare like free education, free healthcare, etc.

International Law

International Law is an attempt of international organisations to provide a set of common legal rules, regulations accepted by the countries of the world. Therefore, international law finds its applicability in the international level only and in a country specific case. While framing the international laws care were taken to ensure that various international customs; agreements; treaties; accords, charters of the United Nations Charter; protocols; tribunals; memorandums; legal precedents of the International Court of Justice, etc., are duly considered. International will be enforceable to the countries only when the concerned countries agree to the system and accept rulings under the law. The international laws, endeavours to increase its worldwide applicability by including both common law and civil law.

The requirement of international laws surfaces most when there is a distupte between two or more countries or sovereign entities in the matter such as human rights violation by a country, wartime disputes, sea boundary violations by ships one country in to another, etc. However, problem arises when disputes are related to the countries but rather to business houses or related to specific persons with cross country involvement. For example, a contract agreement was executed between ABS export company of India and SGS company of Japan for supply API (used for producing medicine) for the Indian company. The contract specified the conditions under which the exchange is to be performed and details the rights and obligations of the parties involved. The Contract law of respective countries provides sanctity to the executed contract and desires that the contracted clauses of agreement are not violated by the involved parties. Now, the contact was drafted in India following common law and civil law systems and hence it was very much lengthy with every possible details mentioned. However, according the civil law systems prevailing in Japan it should be much shorter and less specific because of the existence of them in the civil code. Therefore, when there was a dispute between the company in the matter of return of poor quality API to the Japanese company, the Indian company failed to explain the differences in Japanese courts.

International businesses, because of its cross country nature, are likely to face this type of problems and question will come as to whose law will be applicable. United Nations Convention on Contracts for the International Sale of Goods (CIGS) is a solution to this direction. CIGS stipulates a set of rules governing certain aspects of the making and performance of everyday commercial contracts between cross country buyers and sellers. CIGS has got importance when came to effect from 1988. Since then a number of countries including USA have accepted it but with the exception of countries like Japan and the United Kingdom. In case of disputes between two cross border companies from countries adopted CIGS, the disputes will be resolved by applying CIGS law and not the country specific law. However, in the dispute between Indian and Japanese company some alternatively arrangement has to be made as CIGS non adopting country is involved. It may be resolved through arbitration process involving International Court of Arbitration under the International Chamber of Commerce in Paris.

Legislations related to Product Safety and Liability

The international marketers market their products across different countries having different legal restrictions on product safety and liability. Not understanding them correctly may lead to legal problems at any stage of the lifecycle of a product. Therefore it is very important to assess whether the product, that is to be marketed in the new country, is subjected to which regulations under the Product Safety and Liability legislation. A "safe product" as one that "does not present any risk or only the minimum risks compatible with the product's use, considered to be acceptable and consistent with a high level of protection for the safety and health of persons[14]". Let's take some examples of product safety and liability related issues between companies and country specific legal standard.

Example 1: Albertsons and Costco is a big retailers in US with 1700 store outlets in 31 states and came in to loggerhead with Taiwan based Sheng Hsiang Jen Foods Co on the product safety ground. The US company declared the popular jelly-like candy made by the Taiwanese company unsafe and banned entry of the products in all its stores until the Food and Drug Administration (FDA) issues a ruling on the safety of the product. The safety issue came in to limelight when a local newspaper reported that two American children died after the sticky gel got struck and could not be dislodged from their throats. The Food and Drug Administration, USA acted first and immediately issued a caution to the purchasers to be careful with the candies and then subsequently confirmed that the candies were indeed a choking hazard which ultimately banned the entry of the product to USA from Taiwan. Encouraged by the turn of events the aggrieved families sued the Taiwanese manufacturer for their loss caused by the imported candies. The legal preceding that followed in California, USA saw that approximately US$115 million compensation was awarded to the aggrieved families which the Taiwanese food supplier and exporter would be liable for payment. More than that the Taiwanese manufacturer-exporter was shattered because of losing a huge market in terms US and loss of revenue stream thereof[15].

Example 2: The US pharmaceutical company Merck & Co Inc researched out Vioxx as a drug for patient suffering from rheumatoid arthritis during 1999 and after availing FDA's approval in 2002 launched the product in US market. But only after two years the company faced a serious charge that the said drug has caused incurable heart related problems for many Americans. The matter was contested in the court of law and Texas jury awarded US$253 million including punitive damages against the US pharmaceutical company Merck & Co[16].

Example 3: Hangzhou Zhongce Rubber Company, a tyre producing company of China, had a reasonable number of importers in USA. The importers located in California, Minnesota, Florida, Maryland and Mississippi was happy with the exporting Chinese company because of good mergin they get in the importation and subsequent marketing them in the country. Unfortunately, after a few truck accident reported in the highways doubt was casted on the quality of the tyres eventually produced by the Chinese company. On investigation, it was found that the Chinese company was miser in using gum strip, a feature that helps to keep the tire belts from separating, while exporting the product, i.e., the truck tires to USA which actually weakened the tyres causing death and injury in the highways. Different lawsuit filed in the US court had

14 European Union's General safety requirement and conformity criteria

15 The Los Angeles Times dated August 17, 2001

16 http://www.justice.gov/opa/pr/2012/April/12-civ-497.html

prompted National Highway Traffic Safety Administration of US to interfere and helped in recalling an estimated 450,000 light truck tires sold under the names Westlake, Telluride, Compass and YKS. In September 2006, Hangzhou also admitted to US authority that it had reduced or omitted the gum strip from an unspecified number of tires.[17]

The three examples stated above are only a few of many cases. In all the cases the producing company not only has face loss but revenue loss as well. As a result, the international marketers while manufacturing or marketing products abroad need to consider product safety and product liability issues in the target countries where it intends to sell the same or similar products. While it will be necessary to at least comply with all of the laws and regulations of each country where it will sell, the manufacturer must also consider the effect of many of these decisions on the extent of liability in host countries, especially in those countries with proactive product liability and product safety systems. The aim of product liability laws, in any countries, is to help protect consumers from dangerous or defective products, while holding manufacturers, distributors, and retailers responsible for putting into the market place products that they knew or should have known were dangerous or defective. As usual USA first mooted and developed the basic concept of product liability during 1960 and was very soon accepted by the other developed countries. As more or less all the other countries of the world became sufferer because of unsafe products, the product liability concepts engulfed them also. European Union adopted the legal concept of strict product liability during 1985. Therefore, the countries of the world irrespective of rich and poor are working to frame their product liability and product safety laws and regulations resulting rise of product liability cases and litigation. A significant part of them could have been avoided had the international marketers aware of country specific rules and regulations. A few country's product safety and liability regulations are described below.

India: Product safety and liability

Laws governing product liability in India are the general statutes prescribing civil liability like the Consumer Protection Act, 1986, Special Statutes pertaining to specific goods prescribing liability, Statutes prescribing Criminal Liability, and Law of Torts. Product liability laws in India attempt to fix the liability of the manufacturers, wholesalers, distributors, and vendors responsible for bringing the dangerous or defective products in the market place for consumption of the consumers leading to injury to a person or property. The aim of product liability laws is simply for protecting the consumers in the market place. In principle, there are three major types of product liability claims that can be made:

Manufacturing defect: The came out of the factory with defect which not allow to functions correctly for which it was produced.

Design defect: Wrongly conceived product and unfit for production.

Marketing defects: The producer or the marketer has failed to prescribe or communicate warning for safer or proper use of a product. There are

[17] CBS News dated February 11, 2009

also three situations where product liability claim may be raised- negligence, breach of warranty and fitness for a particular purpose.

EU: Product safety and liability

The European Union has possibly the most sofisticated and elaborated but comprehensive regulations on product safety and liability which covers all the 28 member countries. The concern for bringing out directives on product liability to ensure adequate laws, regulations and administrative provisions of the use of its member states was expressed in European Union parliament during 1985. As a result the first directive came out subsequently to ensure that consumers are only exposed to safe products.

The General Product Safety Directive (GPSD)

This Directive provides a general understanding of safe product and laid down a generic definition of safe product as applicable to the member states. The GPSD intended to communicate to the producers marketing their products in member states about harmonised European standards. It is necessary that the producers to follow the technical specifications as per European standard to manufacture safe products that are safe and do not expose the Europeans to risks and hazards. The directive covers nearly all products sold in the EU. The Directive further emphasised on the requirements of equipping the consumers with relevant information regarding risks inherent to the product use, store and disposal. In order to ensure that information regarding products use and hazards thereof are reached in time, the EU introduced a rapid alert system called RAPEX (Rapid Exchange of Information between Member States and the Commission) so that all concerned agencies could be alerted in no time.

EU: Across the sector legislations

(a) **Product Liability Directive (85/374/EEC)**

This directive was enacted in EU to clearly specify the extent of liability of all concerned parties where unsafe product use has resulted in consumer's injury or property damage irrespective of location of production. This directive stipulates that the legislation would be free to act irrespective of any contractual arrangement the producers might have made with the injured persons. It also set liability limits to be imposed on the producers producing unsafe products and provisions where member states can apply their options towards varying the liability limits.

(b) **Product Warranty Directive (1999/44/EC)**

This directive was enacted to provide product warranty related clarity to the member states. According to this directive any manufacture marketer is liable to the consumer for any lack of conformity which exists when the goods are delivered to the consumer and which becomes apparent within a period of two years, unless, at the moment of conclusion of the contract of sale, the consumer knew or could not reasonably be unaware of the lack of conformity. This directive was helpful to the consumers as they could get right to claim for unfit products replacement or free of charge repairing, as the case may be, within a reasonable period in the post purchase situation.

EU: Sector-specific legislation

EU came up with various sector specific regulations in order to ensure that only safe products are marketed across the union. These sector specific regulations were needed to ensure that all the sector specific details are addressed keeping in view the sectoral requirements. The some important sectoral regulations important for the international companies to understand and follow while producing products targeting EU countries are as follows.

Chemicals sector: This is a very important sector for EU which always attracted international marketers. The lucrativeness can be expressed in terms of different chemicals used by EU. During 2007, the EU countries together bought different chemical worth 537 billion which was about 30% of the total global sales. Data shows that chemicals industries of EU posted a sales figure of 578 billion euro during 2010 which was about one-fourth of world chemicals sales in value terms[18]. From this anybody can understand that EU is a leading exporter and importer of chemicals in the world. Therefore, to safe guard their citizen from hazardous chemicals EU enacted stringent safety regulations in this sector which are of special importance to the manufacturers and marketers across the world. REACH (acronym for Regulation on Registration, Evaluation, Authorisation and Restriction of Chemicals) enacted by EU during June 2007, is the regulatory framework that put the onus on the company show that the chemicals it produces or uses are safe. The regulations ensure that all chemical entering EU are strictly in conformity with the different REACH clauses and hence safe for use. The regulation also make it manadatory that imported chemicals to EU countries would be subjected to necessary testing in order to establish their conformity to the REACH standard. It stipulates that the cost of such testing would required to be borne by the producer or the importer. It also encourages the replacement of hazardous chemicals with safer alternatives in order to promote innovation in the sector.

Toys sector: The toy sector in EU is also a lucratitive sector for the exporters/international marketers. Many EU member states like France, Germany, Italy, Spain and the UK emerged as prominent consumers of toys in the world. Hence, the EU wanted to ensure that Europeans babies are only exposed to safer toys and not the hazardous one. So the EU acted quite early and the first directive on toy safety regulations were enacted way back in 1988. This directives was replaced with a more refined and stringent one during 2009 with the aim of covering all the safety related issues which can evolve while children under 14 years of age playing with toys. This regulation gave highest safeguard to the children of member states as evident from reducing toy related accidents reported in in EU.

Cosmetics sector: Cosmetic products which includes make-up and perfumes, products for personal hygiene like tooth-care products, shampoos, soaps, etc., have huge demand in European Union. The demand size was about 67 billion Euro during 2010, i.e., about one-third of the global cosmetics market.[19] By looking at the internal demand European Council, way

[18] Cefic (The European Chemical Industry Council) Chemdata International report 2011.
[19] Euromonitor International

back in 1976 promulgated the first regulatory directives governing labelling, packaging requirements and safety requirements. The regulations put the onus of ensuring safety in using cosmetics totally on the producer or the importer of the products in to markets across EU. Subsequent modifications and amendments in the directives saw EU stipulating the ingredients which cannot be used in cosmetics. Further, the European Union, during 2009, made a huge effort in (EU Regulation 1223/2009) harmonising the regulation across the member states. The latest revision of 2013 though simplified various previous provisions but found to be more stringent with the objective of ensuring a total pro active approach on the part of the manufacturers for ensuring product safety.

Pharmaceuticals: The EU offers a lucrative single market covering 28 countries for the pharmaceutical companies. EU shows no laxity in ensuring high level of safety standard for any phamaceutical products marketed in the member countries. The standards and regulations for the development, manufacture and marketing of medicinal products for human and veterinary use are well elaborated in EU's directives and regulations. The European Medicines Agency (EMA), a decentralised organisation, acts as watchdog and evaluator of medicines marketed in European Union.

Machinery: The machinery sector is a very important for all the member states. EU considers that the growth of engineering industries is dependent on the functioning of machinery sector. EU made efforts for harmonisation of the sector across all the member states so that regulations could be developed. The main objective of the regulations were not only to smoothen free movement of machinery within the Single Market but also to ensure that at no cost the machineries were causing harm or injury to the EU workers and citizens. The regulations, therefore, speak about mandatory health and safety requirements as well as the harmonised standards.

Japan: Product safety and liability

Japan governs the issue product safety and liability through its Product Liability Law (Law No. 85, 1994). The Japanese national legislature, the Diet, first enacted this law to provide safeguard to the Japanese people from hazardous products in the market and came to effect from 1995. The law, for the first time brought the concept of strict liability and expanded the definition of a liable manufacturer. The Japanese product liability law drew heavily from the 1985 version of EU's product liability directives.

China: Product safety and liability

In China two major laws namely the General Principles of Civil Law and the Product Quality Law, govern the issues related to manufactures' liability for defective products. The General Principles of Civil Law came in to effect from January 1, 1987 and stipulates that if a substandard product causes property damage or physical injury to others, the manufacturer or seller shall bear civil liability. As the country was fast becoming the destination of many products from international manufactures so the national government enacted the product quality law of China during the year 1993. This law allowed the authority to strengthen the supervision and control over product quality and very importantly to protect the consumers' interests. Any organisation either manufacturing in China or acting as sellers of any product within the country will be under the preview of laws. The objective of the laws was to create an alround awareness about the safety requirements amongst the marketers so that they themselves become proactive in ensuring product quality. The, Chinese law stipulates a compensation maximum up to RMB 50,000 to be paid by a manufacture to the aggrieved person on account of damage caused to the user of the product.

Retail Price Maintenance

"Retail Price Maintenance" or RPM refers to a practice in which a supplier and wholesaler mutually agree and understand the constraint on the prices that the reseller allowed to charge from its buyers, usually ultimate customers, of products or services. As the definition suggest, therefore, RPM is a unique type of vertical agreement between an upstream firm and a downstream firm regarding the terms and conditions governing the price at which the product or service can be sold to the ultimate consumers. The upstream firms include manufacturer, producer, or importer of a good or service while the downstream firms are distributor or retailer. Minimum resale price maintenance (RPM) refers to an agreement controlling retailers' obligation to sell the manufacturer's products to consumers at the manufactures' desired price or above. While maximum RPM is a similar agreement specifying a price above which retailers cannot resell the manufacturer's product.

The various useful characteristics of RPM are stated below.

- Efficient before sales services to the consumers: When minimum RPM arrangement is in vogue the retailers would be encouraged to provide efficient pre-sale services and charge the consumers for the extra service rendered. Also manufactures can motivate the down stream agents by allowing them to earn extra money for the good work rendered to the valued consumers of the products.
- Maintaining price parity in the market: Minimum RPM has the wonderful effect in maintaining price parity by making the retailers to resell the products at certain minimum price and not below that. Indirectly, this discourages the free riding customers who usually tend to understand the nitty-gritty of the products features from full frill retailers and then buy from discounters.
- Maintaining brand image: Minimum RPM prevent availability of the products at different prices at different retailers' outlet and thereby save a brand from a distorted image in the mind of the loyal customers. When some manufactures do not want to compromise on price due to demand slump minimum RPM may work nicely for them.
- Making retailers attuned with manufacturer's objective: Since the multi-brand retailers can sell the products at a desired price so they may feel

encouraged to walk extra mile while selling the products to the ultimate consumers as desired by the manufacturers.

- Allow new product lunching: The retailers may not be interested to stock newly launched product of a company since the market acceptance is yet to be known. In such case the retailers will feel assured that nowhere in the market place the consumers will be able to get the product below certain price since minimum RPM is in vogue.
- Stabilise market price: Under maximum RPM the retailers cannot increase more than a supplier determined price. Imposition of maximum RPM will deter competition of both supplier and resellers to set their respective prices that would maximise their respective profits.

Different countries attach different legal restrictions on RPM. The successful marketing of the products internationally requires a close understanding legal environments governing RPS in different countries. RPM related regulations of a few countries are described below.

RPM in USA

USA is a country of not favouring minimum RPM historically. It is almost considered minimum RPM as 'per se' illegal by the legal authority. It has its root in the type of verdicts given by United States Supreme Court in cases of disputes regarding RPM issues. For example, way back in 1911 in the case of Dr. Miles Medical Co. Vs Park & Sons Co., the United States Supreme Court uphold a lower court's holding that a massive minimum resale price maintenance scheme was unreasonable and thus offended Section 1 of the Sherman Antitrust Act[20]. The impression generated in the business circle that the legal authority in US considered the issues of minimum RPS as almost in the level of horizontal price fixing through cartel type of arrangement. According to them minimum RPM is a mechanism which brings the manufacturer, the wholesalers, and the retailers to a joint understanding to maintain agreed upon prices. The effect of such endeavour was to suppress competition in the market place. There would be no price related competition amongst the retailers for the sale of a particular product if minimum RPM was allowed to be continued, the court opined. Simply speaking, the US legal system almost termed minimum RPM as illegal. This view continued till 2007 when the famous antitrust case between Leegin Creative Leather Products, Inc. and PSKS, Inc was heard and decision came. Leegin was a leather apparel manufacturer located in US and retained PSKS as their retailers to market finished products where the manufacturer asked the retailer to follow minimum RPM, i.e., not to sale below their recommended retail price. However, Leegin observed that PSKS was engaged in selling the products 20% less than the directed price. This made the manufacturer angry with the retailer and snapped supplying of products to PSKS. Aggrieved by sudden stoppage of supply PSKS took legal recourse. The US court gave verdict in favour of PSKS and asked Leegin to suitably compensate the loss of retailer.

[20] The Sherman Act, which is almost 120 years old, is the first, and most important of US federal antitrust laws.

RPM IN European Commission

Traditionally minimum RPM has been treated by the rule makers as an anti competitive practice and almost seems to be consistent in its approach. They found the follows short comings with minimum RPM:

(a) Insistence of minimum RPM by manufacturer prevent decrease of price and makes a ground for manufacturer – retailer union to deprive the consumers.

(b) It will also not allow the manufacturers to put continuous efforts in developing efficient manufacturing process as they will continue to get profit margin without being efficient also.

(c) It may restrict sale of product because of higher price and will therefore prevent manufacture from benefiting from expanded sales.

However, given the above arguments against minimum RPM, EU has always kept an open mind regarding RPM. It is evident from different subsequent verdicts that they are not in favour of imposing a "per se" prohibition on minimum RPM.

RPM in Japan

Japan is also found to against imposing minimum RPM by manufacturer and treated it as unfair trade practices. The document like "Guidelines Concerning Distribution Systems and Business Practices under the Antimonopoly Act", published on 11 July 1991, and amended on 1 November 2005 by Japan Fair Trade Commission (JFTC) shows the legal viewpoint on RPM in this respect. These guidelines noted that any retailing business must have the right to fix its own price as it is almost a basic marketing activity of a business entity. Hence, it is not right for any manufacturer to interfere in the process.

RPM in Mexico

According to the Mexican Federal Law of Economic Competition (FLEC), RPM, whether fixed, minimum or maximum, prima facie indicates towards a practice of monopolistic flavour but should be subjected to the rule of reason as and when such cases come out. Therefore, the FLEC and its Regulations, advocate that it requires thorough examination of individual cases in regards to forms, facts and possible outcome before a conclusion can be drawn. Proper study would bring out the conduct and its real or likely effects on the relevant market. The legality of such conduct, i.e., legal or illegal will then be decided.

RPM in China

China, being manufacturing hub of the world, delivers products to many distribution intermediaries under different contracts or agreements nationally and internationally. Hence how China handles RPM is a matter of interest to business circles. Prima facie, Chinese rules and regulations are against any form of vertical restraints like RPM. Cases related to RPM are subjected to Antitrust or competition law rules. The Chinese Anti-Monopoly Law (Article 14) the prohibits the suppliers in fixing of resale prices (and in particular minimum resale prices) to third parties in general. However, there are some exemptions, based on the motives of enforcing the RPM, where RPM can be practiced. They are:

- Where the objective of RPM is technological improvement or research and development of new products;
- Where the objective of RPM is product quality improvement, cost minimisation, improve efficiency, standardise product specifications and standards or implement specialisation;
- Where the objective of RPM is strengthening of small and medium businesses;
- Where the objective of RPM is serving public interest like energy conservation, environmental protection and disaster relief;
- Where the objective of RPM is rescuing a sector from sudden slump in consumption in times of recession or obvious over-production;
- Where the objective of RPM is for protection of country interest in international trade and economic cooperation.

Box 3.5 Cases of RPM in Chinese Taipei

In 1992, the Fair Trade Commission (FTC) of Chinese Taipei selected cosmetics and six other products for investigation to ascertain if there was any violation of the Fair Trade Law. The Commission found that five cosmetics companies V Hwa Tzu Cosmetics Co. Ltd., Yi Chia Co. Ltd., Chi Jen Hang Co. Ltd., Yi Li Co. Ltd. and Taiwan Pao Li Co. Ltd. had uniform selling prices at their retail outlets. Each of their franchise agreements with their distributors contained provisions, requiring the distributors to sell goods at single retail prices such as "the Promisor shall sell the Franchiser's products for prices set by the Franchiser". The cosmetics companies explained that uniform prices were enforced only as marketing strategy and maintaining the product image.

Judging from the market positions of cosmetics companies, cosmetic market structure and cosmetic product characteristics, the FTC found that cosmetics companies enjoyed certain exclusivity due to strong consumer preference in selecting cosmetics, and higher brand loyalty to cosmetics than to general products. As a result, their distributors dared not violate such restriction for fear of active retaliations or passive boycotts such as discontinuance of goods supply, evacuation of shops, removal of sales representatives, inadequate supply of goods, etc.

The restriction imposed by the cosmetics companies has undermined fair market competition. Their restriction on resale prices and prohibition against any promotional activities of the distributors resulted in uniform retail prices for cosmetics nationwide. As a result, distributors could not engage in retail competition based on their own advantages, nor could consumers enjoy any benefits from competition on the retail level. Under such circumstance where retailers could not engage in any competition, the five cosmetics companies under investigation never had any need to engage in any price competition with other cosmetics companies. This is substantiated by the fact that the prices of the cosmetics were never adjusted primarily for the sake of competition.

Based on the foregoing reasons, the FTC decided that the cosmetics companies shall within 10 days upon receipt of this disposition, notify their distributors (who have been subject to restriction on resale prices and promotion activities) in writing that they may now freely decide the resale prices and engage in promotional activities. Upon issuance of such notification, the cosmetics companies shall also submit a copy of such written notification to the FTC for reference.

Source: Asia Pacific Economic Cooperation, accessed at http://www.apeccp.org.tw/doc/Taipei/Case/Dcosmm92.htm

Box 3.6 The Apple e-books: A RPM story

The US Justice Department was very much upset with the famous American company Apple regarding its Retail Price Maintenance practice in the matter of e- book marketing in US. It was alleged that Apple and five publishing firms namely Simon & Schuster, Hachette Book Group, Pearson's Penguin Group, Macmillan, and News Corp were involved in horizontal price-fixing or minimum RPM . The story goes in this way. Apple was preparing to launch its iPad with iBooks Store for the readers. However, the market strategists at Apple was not sure of the success of iBook because of presence of a great competitor like Amazon who already grasped 80-90% of e book market. Amazon used to sell electronic versions of many new best sellers for $9.99 through its Kindle 2, a black-and-white, text-only, single-use device with page advancing mechanism through use of a button. Amazon was providing the marketing outlet to a number of renowned ebook publishers and was able to capture major market share through aggressive price discounting. The book publishers were not very happy with the pricing strategy of Amazon but could not do anything because of market dominance.

When Apple unveiled iBooks Store during first part of 2010 the aggrieved publishers took it as an opportunity to counter Amazon discounted pricing strategy. On the other hand, Amazon was also looking for a right business strategy to oust the market leader. This possibly brought the aggrieved publishers close to Apple who agreed to link their latest e books to the ibooks store of Apple. To surprise the readers of the e books ibook stores though loaded with the latest books of major publishing houses but with raised prices to the tune of about 17%. This irked the consumers but the publishers were happy because Apple guaranteed a flat 30% commission on each e-book sold. However, the Amazon was running dry and failed to offer new books to the readers at lower price which was previously its forte.

Amazon wanted to get the business back and accused the concerned books publishers of fixing the minimum retail maintenance for conspiring to end e-book retailers' freedom to compete on price. Amazon was first losing its business as the consumers were not interested to get e books which were comperatively older but higher priced,

The US justice department's antitrust division of US looked in to the matter very minutely on getting complaint from Amazon. They opined that consumers had to pay more because of minimum RPM practiced in this case which eliminated the flavor of competition. They further viewed that publishers' power to set the prices to be charged by retailers for e-books was unjust as this would not help market competition to settle the price of a product.

Legislations Related to Marketing Communications

How companies are making their presence felt amongst the target consumers in a foreign country markets? Surely, it is not through their statutory statements appearing periodically in the newspaper of the country. The most visible activity of an international company in a host country market is some form marketing communications like advertising, etc. The foreign company strives hard to get their marketing communications to be noticed almost regularly by the probable consumers so that they are brought under the marketing net. However, many a time such efforts of a foreign company gets boomerang. The company attracts public criticism and even attack if their communication, say TV advertisement displeases or offends the audience. It happens rarely that such public offensive was due to non fulfilment of promise made in the advertisement. But many a time the public offensive come out because the advertisement has not been in line with the norms, l values, customs and social standard. The international marketers sometimes also antagonise the local government if they continue with the offensive advertisements for long time. Sometimes the government interferes in the functioning of a foreign company by imposing a ban from circulating the ill devised advertisement in the country. The country government devices legal regulatory framework, i.e., passes laws and rules defining the ways in which companies can communicate for marketing of products or services in a particular country. Sometimes country government desires that companies exert voluntary restrains so that legal systems of the country are not required to be invoked. For that, industry on their own develops advertising standard to be followed and acceptable to the society as well as to the country.

Self regulatory framework (SRF): These frame works are developed by the peers working in the advertising sector of the country only. While developing the framework ethics, norms, societal system of country legal restrictions, etc., are considered so that published advertisements are not disturbing the basic frabic of the country. The self regulatory system follows the legal framework applicable for the country, However, it may not follow the legal framework in every respect. For example self regulatory framework of USA is comparatively more stringent than the legal one. However, the reverse is also true for many countries. We will briefly describe the regulatory framework, in respect of marketing communications, of some countries.

United State of America

The nongovernmental independent agency Federal Trade Commission(FTC) regulates advertising provides the SRF of the country. The main objective of the SRF is to protect the consumer from misleading marketing communications. The Federal Trade Commission Act ('FTC Act") is the main Statute which governs advertising and marketing of most products and services in the US. The FTC Act intends mainly to protects consumers from false oral or written representations, unsubstantiated claims, misleading claims, untruthful statements, sales of hazardous or defective products or services without adequate disclosures. The FTC acts desires that companies must be truthful about the product claim in advertising and must communicate the details on the label and packaging on products. Under the Fair Packaging and Labeling Act (FPLA), the Federal Trade Commission (FTC) and the Food and Drug Administration (FDA) issue regulations time to time which the company must follow.

Canada

Advertising Standards Canada (ASC) is the national not-for-profit advertising self-regulatory body of Canada. This agency framed the Canadian Code of Advertising Standards during 1963 with the sole motive of promoting professional and ethical practice in advertising. With the passage of time the standards were updated to suit the present day requirements. The standards provides the basic criteria which any company operating in Canada must follow while communicating public for the purpose of marketing products or services The following are the characteristics of advertising regulations in Canada:

Box 3.7 Reebok got punishment for misleading marketing communication in USA

Federal Trade Commission (FTC) was very much upset with the athletic shoe company Reebok when it launched EasyTone shoes in the market with a tall claim about the product benefit. The company's initial advertisement claimed that anyone wearing East Tone shoes will develop "better legs and a better butt". The consumers did not believe in the claim initially but the company was very forceful in making them believe what it claimed in the advertisement. To the rescue of the American consumers the FTC intervened at this juncture and asked Reebok to prove the claim. Inspite of best efforts of the company the advertising watchdog FTC seemed to be unconvinced about the claimed product benefits. Finally, the dispute was taken to the US court and court asked the company to substantiate their claim. The company submitted a detail study report to this effect. However, the US court totally rejected the study report termed it "tiny, anecdotal, unpublished study with lack of representatives sample considéred in the study" and banned the advertisement from public exposure. Finally, hefty fine of $25 million was levied on the company with the charge that the company was engaged in misleading and developing false notion in the public. The court also directed other companies to take a lesson from it and to be abstained from releasing misleading advertisements for public consumption without having proper indepth research studies to substantiate the claims. Reebok learnt a lession by paying price for it.

- All TV commercials are limited to 12 minutes per hour.
- There are some specific legislation(s) governing alcohol, tobacco advertisements. There is a specific "Code for Broadcast Advertising of Alcoholic Beverages, CRTC, 1996" which prescribes the primary regulations in regards to alcoholic advertisements.
- Canada is very strict about advertisement directed for consumption of children and hence came out with a specific act titled "Broadcast Code of Advertising to Children" which governs advertisements to children.

United Kingdom

The Advertising Standards Authority (ASA) is the self-regulatory body of the country which acts as watchdog for the advertisements released for public consumption. ASA has its basic codes as the standards which are to be followed by the advertisers of the country. In UK, the "The Control of Misleading Advertisements Regulation, 1988" gives the legal framework regarding right and wrong with regard to advertising. In addition, the Office of Fair Trading (OFT), also overlooks the advertising standards so that misleading, harmful or offensive advertisements, sales promotions and direct marketing are not reaching the citizen of the country. The OFT invokes different legislations like Competition Act 1998, Consumer Credit Act, Consumer Protection from Unfair Trading Regulations, Distance Selling Regulations, and Enterprise Act while acting against the wrong doers. The OFT has the right to initiate action against the erring companies and levy fine on the offending companies.

Brazil

Brazil came out with its first advertising regulations way back in 1960. These regulations allowed the government agency to monitor advertisements prior their release to public viewing. Up till 1978 the enforcement of advertising code was totally in the hand of Government agency. However, the advertising

Box 3.8 'Sexist' Ryanair ad was banned

Ryan air **Ltd, the Dublin based** Irish low-cost airline company, drew industry attention because of rapid expansion of its no frill airline business. Ryanair was operating its massive fleet of aircrafts consisting of about 300 Boeing 737-800 aircraft across the nation The company was, in fact, scripting the business model of a low cost airline business in a fiercely competitive environment. Therefore, it required to connect the prospective customers very aggressively so that more passengers are flying through Ryan air. The airlines usually advertised in the leading Newspapers of the country and in its print advertisements it reminded the prospective consumers about its low fare advantage. This time the company adopted a very innovative way to do that. Ryan air came up with a print media campaign featuring scantily-clad flight attendants with the tagline: "Red hot fares & crew." The advertising regulatory body Advertising Standard Authority (ASA) of UK came in to sense when a number of complain poured in to its mailbox objecting the use of flight attendants as sexy object to attract customers. Almost simultaneously the another advertising guardian of UK OFT (office of Fair Trading) (OFT) jumped in and made situation difficult for the airlines company. The OFT enquired the case and came to an conclusion not favouring the Ryan air. According to them through the women crew member featured in the ads had consented to appear in the advertisements but it objectified cabin crew and therefore "offensive and unsuitable" from appearing in the public domain as the company wanted to use the same in business purpose. The company was cautioned and was advised to follow advertising code of the country seriously.

Source: The Guardian, 15 February 2012.

Box 3.9 AOL fights with UOL over slogan issue in Brazil

The American global brand company AOL Inc, picked up a fight with CONAR (The National Advertising Self-Regulation Council) of Brazil. This time the fight was between two equals. CONAR over the years had earned good reputation in maintaining ethical standards in advertisements. At the same time AOL became a globally reputed company that developed and invested in brands and web sites. Like any other global company AOL wanted to be always on the top of the mind of its clients and hence released a series of ads. In one of their ads AOL recently came out with a advertising slogan 'The largest because it is the best," and ran through Brazilian television, print and radio. AOL's local competitor Universo Online (UOL), Latin America's largest Internet service provider with more than 760,000 subscribers in Brazil, Mexico, Chile, Venezuela, Argentina and Columbia, challenged the Claim of AOL. AOL claimed to have passed the 250,000-subscriber mark in the region which was largest subscriber based but according to UOL this was untrue. AOL was able to submit evidences to CONOR that in Latin America their customer base was more than that of AOL. Though AOL made counter claim but the advertising regulatory body CONAR supported UOL and asked AOL not to use the slogan in Brazil any more. CONAR also reminded them that AOL could be the world's largest Internet service provider but it was not true in case of Brazil and hence the fact was not expressed in their advertisement.

Source: PR Newswire, 24 August 2000.

industry as a whole did not like the system and actively promoted self regulating code. As a result "Brazilian Advertising Self-Regulation Code" came up with twin objectives. First, reducing the total government control on commercial advertisements and second, install measures for elimination of unethical advertising practice detrimental to the cause of fair competitiveness. A non governmental organisation was created during 1990 in the name of National Counsel of Advertising Self Regulation (Conselho Nacional de

Auto Regulamentação Publicitária or CONAR) to ensure and monitor self regulations in advertisement. Almost simultaneously the Brazilian government enacted the Brazilian Consumer Defence Code (CDC) during 1990 to fully safeguard consumers from simulated, misleading and abusive advertising. CDC rule makes the advertiser responsible, in case of any dispute, for proving that the information provided in an advertisement is correct.

Russia

Federal Anti-Monopoly Service (FAS), a federal agency, is in charge to enforce regulatory control on the marketing communications of the companies operating in Russia. The main objective of FAS is to promote healthy competition amongst businesses. The FAS draws its main power from different Federal laws. FAS basically watch out for the following in the matter of marketing communication:

- Advertisement misleading consumers with disparaging contents, tall claims, etc.
- Advertisements comparing products in unequal terms with implicit or explicit advertising messages.
- Advertisements, released by pharmaceutical companies using comperatative terms.
- Advertisements, direct or surrogated, for restricted products like alcohol.

Box 3.10 FAS of Russia Fined vodka company

During the year 2012 there was a renewed interest amongst alcoholic beverage vodka producers towards capturing domestic market share. These alcoholic beverage companies were marshalling all their resources to fight out the competitors. One such Russian distillery company Vodochnaya Artel "YAT", thought of introducing a very innovative advertisement to popularise its brand through a surrogated type of advertisement. It published an apparently innocent looking advertisement in a magazine with the tagline "Deliver the puck with vodka YAT" where in the company encouraged the Russian to participate in the upcoming men's ice hockey tournament in Slovakia. The Russian advertising watch dog FAS was in a fix as to whether they should term it as surrogated appeal towards the consumers. In that article the company promised some free tickets to encourage Russian hockey team. The members of FAS of Russia mainly deliberated on the issue whether an alcoholic beverage company could make an public appeal through an advertisement with content of national interest but the tag line clearly identifying the brand name of the vodka. Finally, the FAS came to conclusion that the advertisement was indeed harmful for the public because almost the company cleverly synchronised success of players with consumption of vodka. In a sense, the company was encouraging the Russian to drink more vodka to have a fair chance of winning free VIP tickets to witness the hockey championship. So, according to FAS, in all count, the Vodochnaya Artel company violated the regulation of the country and hence liable for publishing inappropriate advertisement of vodka "YAT". FAS, thereafter levied a hefty fine on them and banned any further advertisement of this type. Similar cases of fouling with FAS regulations surfaced when another alcoholic beverage company under brand name "Beluga" started ascertaining public that their product was produced in a ecologically cleaner environment of Siberia and devoid any industrial contamination. FAS pulled up this company for throwing purported and misleading information in the public domain. Further, FAS asked the company to remove the untrue information from its website with immediate effect.

Source: www.fas.gov.ru

China

Chinese government made a cautious beginning way back in 1982 and enacted a series of regulations under the title "Provisional Regulations for Advertising Management" prescribing standard for advertising industry. More latest regulations came up when in 1983 when the State Administration of Industry and Commerce (SAIC) came out with more regulations in the form of the "Interim Regulations on the Advertising Agency System" and the "Interim Advertising Review Standards". Finally, during 1995 the advertising law was passed which required to be followed by international marketers. In addition to SAIC there is Chinese Advertising Association (CAA), as an non-governmental entity working to promote self-regulation in the advertising industry. Under present system an international marketer submits the draft advertisement to CAA for review and if CAA agrees to content, etc., then it is send to the SAIC for final clearance. It has also most become practice that if CAA gives approval then SAIC gives clearance for public viewing without any other questions.

Japan

The Japan Fair Trade Commission (JFTC) is the organisation responsible for maintaining fair competition amongst businesses in the country. In order to carry out responsibilities and discharge duty it draws power from the "Antimonopoly Act" which provides the legal provisions regarding fair and

Box 3.11 McDonald's ad banned in China

American fast food giant McDonald's had a testing time in getting their marketing communications through in China. On entry to China McDonald sensed about a great market potential which required to be unleashed by them through strategic marketing communication. Very soon, therefore, the American company was found very active in unfolding a series of innovative advertisements. In one such attempt McDonald published an ad where it was shown that a Chinese customer in kneeling down position before a McDonald official and begging for acceptance of his expired discount coupon. In the ad the McDonald official assured the Chinese customer that his coupon will be honoured since their validity had been extended for the whole year. The Chinese public, in general, was not feeling happy about the advertisement and there was considerable uneasiness in the atmosphere. The targeted customers of McDonald, per say, could not understand the meaning of the ad. First of all, why a consumer would kneel down for a McDonald burger and second why on earth a Chinese man would be so poor that would compel him even to beg for extension of a simple discounting period. Different questions were buzzing around the big cities like Shanghai, Shenzhen, Chengdu, Tianjin, Xiamen and Xi'an where the advertisement was released. McDonald was waiting for increasing customers after the release of the ad but on the contrary it was going down quickly. The company was soon to realise that they had hurt the feelings of the Chinese customers. Immediately the company issued statement across the country expressing deep regret over the issue and apologised for the mishap. It took the help of Ronald McDonald, the clown character used as the primary mascot of the McDonald's fast-food restaurant chain, to explain to the public that real intention behind the ill fated ad was to create humor. In big size hoarding it was seen that the Ronald McDonald was in a apologetic posture with tag line as "McDonald's humor is 'discounted' this time. On seeing reaction and counter reaction over the ad the China Advertising Association also came heavily on the company. It blamed the company for violation of the conditions of the sanction order. China Advertising Association, in fact cleared the advertisement on the condition that the Mc Donald would not use the kneeling down position in the final version meant for the public.

Source: The China Daily, 23 June 2005.

free competition. It notes that "It is unlawful and prohibited to attract customers unjustly through deceptive and extravagant advertisements with intent to disguise own products or services as extremely superior to those of competitors, and sell them by attaching excessive premiums because such acts distort the proper selection of products or services by customers"[21]. The Japanese Act Against Unjustifiable Premiums and Misleading Representations 1962 describes this as follows: "No entrepreneur shall make such representation by which the quality, standard or any other matter relating to the substance of goods or services are shown to general consumers to be much better than the actual one or much better than that of other entrepreneurs who are in a competitive relationship with the entrepreneur concerned contrary to the fact and thereby which tends to induce customers unjustly and to impede fair competition.[22]"

However, apart from law based regulations, self-regulation is also very strong in Japan. Japan Advertising Review Organisation Inc. (JARO), a non-profit,

Box 3.12 Japan reprimanded the untruthful company

The Japan Fair Trade Commission (JFTC) had to act against Nissho company of Japan for enforcing the principles it preaches for the companies doing business in Japan, i.e., (a) be fair and truthful (b) do not be harmful to consumers (c) show your consideration for youth and children (d) be decent and pursuant to social manners and customs; and (e) be in compliance with relevant laws and regulations, as well as public policy. It so happens that during 2003 Nissho Company introduced a food product named "Perfect Diet" in Japan. It claimed that the product would wonderfully reduce fats in human body even without dieting. The quick slimming process without restricting the normal diet attracted many customers. People believed that companies could be untruthful in advertising oroduct benefits because of first, self restrain and second strictness of law enforcing agency like JFTC. So when Nissho released the advertisements for the product in different newspapers and magazines most of the people did not doubt the claim. Encouraged by initial response the company further enhanced the momentum of publicity for the product. It regularly found to be inserting full advertisement in most reputed women's magazine "ar" of the country as well as other magazines. It claimed there that: (i) Significant slimming effects can be easily achieved by eating the food in question as breakfast without restricting other foods (ii) Taking "PerfectDiet is very simple and easily digestible without causing any problem to the human digestive system (iii) It can be taken as supplement during breakfast so no lifestyle change is required (iv) slimming effect can be achieved quickly as it starts its effect after a week only (v) the food has already been proved through clinical trials (vi) two experts like one doctor of medicine and another nationally registered dietitian respectively claiming that the product in question had made wonderful effect to them as well. In addition, the Nissho company had inserted a narrative text written by a person claiming to be a doctor that "as a result of taking the Perfect Diet, improvement in the metabolic rate and blood-flow amelioration in whole/peripheral parts of the body, which is to fundamental to weight-loss promoting function..... ", etc.

JFTC came to action when a few people put a complain that they have got benefits as per the advertised claim of the company. Immediately JFTC asked Nissho company to submit data regarding constituents of the product and an indepth study report pertaining to the benefit claim made by the company. However, the company could not submit neither any such data nor any study report within the stipulated time limit. Japan Fair Trade Commission (JFTC), therefore, banned the advertisement for public viewing.

[21] http://www.jftc.go.jp/en/about_jftc/role/pdf/1009role_2.pdf

[22] A Note on the Necessity of Rules for Misleading Representation: Experimental Evidence, CPRC Discussion Paper Series, Competition Policy Research Center, Japan Fair Trade Commission available at http://www.jftc.go.jp/cprc/DP/CPDP-38-E.pdf

non-government organisation, is the main pivotal organisation enforcing self regulatory environment in the country.

Australia

Two organisations like Australian Trade Practices Commission (TPC) and Prices Surveillance Authority (PSA) used to ensure healthy competition in Australian market till the job was entrusted to Australian Competition and Consumer Commission (ACCC) during 1995. ACCC draws main legal power from Trade Practices Act 1974 which was renamed as the Competition and Consumer Act 2010 during 2011. The ACCC shoulders the responsibility to oversee the business practices of the companies and ensure that such practices does not cross the barrier set by the provisions of the Competition and Consumer Act. ACCC has the power to impose fine on companies who are wrongfully doing business or running misleading advertisement leading to sufferings of the general consumers of the country It also has the power to run a compliance program in erring company to demonstrate acceptable way of doing business in Australia.

Box 3.13 Can Hyundai do New Zealand in Australia?

"Can 'Santa Fe 4WD' from Hyundai Automobiles be successful in Australia?" asked a new recruit to the company office in Sidney. Already the car was a grand success in many countries of the world and the international marketing managers of the company wanted to repeat the same in Australia too. There was a debate amongst the managers about the marketing communication strategy to be adopted for Australia. Soon it was seen that majority did not want to change the stratergy which made the car so successful in countries like New Zealand and insisted on replicating the same in Australia. In New Zealand the company used a television commercial featuring two young toddlers driving to the beach for surfing. In the ad the viewer saw that a toddler boy wearing a nappy just happily came out from his cot and took the driver's seat of a Santa Fe car parking in the parking zone with utmost ease. The toddler boy then smilingly put the key in ignition slot and drove the car along a highway. On the way he saw a toddler girl hitch-hiking on the road. The boy stopped the car and offered her a lift. The girl got in to the car and both of happily drove the car to the West Coast sea side. On reaching the beach the boy surfed through the waves of the sea while the toddler girl was encouraging the boy while sitting in the car. Then the voiceover: "Hyundai Santa Fe, the next generation is here".

In New Zealand the company conducted survey revealed that the particular ad featuring toddlers was well accepted by the viewers and sale of the car surged ahead as more and more people found the ad very entertaining. The company even praised the creator of the ad when it was rated as the New Zealand's favourite TV ad during the launching year, boosting Hyundai's sales at the time of the Santa Fe's launch. However, the story was different in Australia. The same ad failed to attract not only the prospective customers but in general there was wide spread resentment for showing the underage driving to the Australian population. The common notion was that such irresponsible ad could do no good for the society but rather would have bad effect as a whole. When the public resentment had risen the Australia's Advertising Standards Board (ASB) intervened in to the issue. The Board unanimously decided to clamp ban on the ad with immediate effect so that more public viewing in Australian TV could be avoided. The ASB further opined that since the very notion of a toddler driving a car was fanciful and hence it almost put the very realistic issue like driving in road to the level of fantasy. ASB cautioned the car company to refrain from using fantasy in advertising automobile as it was against the Australian Advertising guidelines for Motor Vehicles. Hyundai had to remove the advertisement from air in Australia.

Advertising Standards Board (ASB), a self regulatory body, supplement the federal control mechanism run by ACCC in ensuring fair competitive business practice in the country. In addition, the Australian Association of National Advertisers (AANA) provided the business organisations with a set of ethical codes of conduct which endeavours to make marketing communications legal, decent, honest and truthful.[23] The Advertising Claims Board (ACB) handles counter claims of the companies who found to have violated code of conduct and provides quick dispute resolution services to the companies.

Middle East Countries

Advertising standards are not very clearly spelt out in middle east countries. In most of Gulf Cooperation Council (GCC) like Qatar, Kuwait, Oman, UAE, Bahrain, Saudi Arabia advertising standards follow the Islamic code of conduct. Dubai is more tolerant than the rest of the Gulf countries. Since legal environments in these countries is fully under the shadow of religious code

Box 3.14 Supermodel Photoshopped for H&M ads in Dubai

The Swedish multinational Hennes & Mauritz AB, popularly known as H&M, is famous for its fast-fashion clothing in over the world. H&M, as its business strategy, wants to communicate its consumers across 57 countries (where H&M has its own store outlets) about the launching of new design, latest dress materials, etc., as fast as possible. Usually they do it by developing innovative advertisements involving supermodels. The famous super model Gisele Bündchen was roped in to popularise its new range of apparel products. She successfully did it in most of the European countries and the company was also very happy with her effectiveness in popularising H&M's apparel products. However, the company was not very sure about the effectiveness of the same campaign in Middle East countries. On scrutiny it was found that in almost all the photo shoots the model was wearing bikini and those campaign were super hit in EU. The company was sure about huge demand of that particular apparel range in Middle East countries too. But the company was not sure about acceptance of an European model in Middle East countries. However changing model and re shooting would take time as well as an expensive proposition. The company first asked its local office to verify acceptability of Brazilian origin super model Gisele Bündchen in Middle East countries. To their surprise it was revealed that Gisele Bündchen is hugely popular in this part of the world and advertising appeal involving her would also be massive in the Middle East. Hence the company decided not to change the model for its campaign in Middle East countries. But the main problem was with the bikini she was wearing as because she need to have full body cover for the advertisements meant for Middle East countries. The company decided to obey the law of the land and put a full body cover on Gisele Bündchen by digitally altering the campaign. The images were, thereafter all subjected to Photoshopping with a t-shirt or vest added under the clothes allowing only revelation of arms. When these campaigns came out for public viewing in magazines circulated in GCC countries there were no controversy regarding disobeying country's legal system. At the same time H&M did a brisk business in the Middle East countries. H&M's recourse through photo shopping was not altogether the new thing amongst international marketers when they came to market their products in to somewhat orthodox countries where legal system is dictated by the region. The Great Barbie did it previously when her usual slim model like body was made to be fully covered with cloths just to go along the legal system of the countries.

Source: The Daily Mail Online, 16 May 2011.

[23] The AANA Code of Ethics has been revised and effected from 1 January 2012. This is available at http://www.aana.com.au/data/Documents/Codes/AANACodeofEthics_1Jan2012.pdf

of conduct so the bindings on advertisements are almost firm in nature. The following are general guidelines to be followed by international marketers.

1. Tobacco and alcohol products can be advertised.
2. Advertisements need to be totally free from political references.
3. Female model used in advertisement campaign must avoid any show of flesh.
4. Sensuality even remotely is not acceptable.
5. Advertisements must avoid depiction of man and woman closeness or intimacy.
6. Money gains in a magical way cannot be shown.

Malaysia

Malaysia enforces a rigid and strict code of conduct in respect of advertisement. The code of conduct draws heavily from Islamic way of life. The basic act which lays down regulations is the 1998 enacted Malaysian Communications and Multimedia Commission Act. The Malaysian Communications and Multimedia Commission is the agency which act as government watchdog and enforcer of the 1998 act in cases related to the matter of marketing communications, fair market competition, etc. Advertising Standards Authority of Malaysia (ASA) complements the government legislations by providing self-regulation codes of advertising in Malaysia.

CHAPTER SUMMARY

1. Political risks are an important consideration for the international business. The various types of political risks active in different countries of the world are affecting companies differently.
2. Political risks like confiscation or domestication are the ugly face of political risks. Fortunately they are not very active now but other political risks in disguise of government action like local content requirements, capital transfer restriction, politically motivated labour unrest, etc., are very active in many countries.
3. Various attempts were made in the past to assess political risk. The methodology varied from activity based system to event based system. Presently a semi-quantitative and risk ranking approach developed and updated by PRS group is popular and useful.
4. The political risks can be insured as well. MIGA (Multilateral Investment Guarantee Assurance), a world Bank initiative to promote multilateral investment of companies in different countries with different risk orientation, helps investors and lenders to deal with the political risks by providing them insurance cover insuring eligible projects.
5. The legal factors are also very important factors to the international businesses because it may affect the standardisation attempt in international marketers There are various legal systems pursued by the countries.
6. Legislations related to Product Safety and Liability are different in different. EU countries have a wide range of Product Safety and Liability legislations. It is important to know the legislation to avoid problems at the later stage.
7. Minimum resale price maintenance (RPM) refers to an agreement under which the retailers are obligated to sell that manufacturer's products to consumers only at or above the prices specified by the manufacturer. Maximum RPM is a similar agreement specifying a price above which retailers cannot resell the manufacturer's product.
8. The successful marketing of the products internationally requires a close understanding of legal environment governing advertisement or marketing communications in different countries.

Countries specific legal bodies are very active today in judging the validity of marketing communications as per their laid down standards.

9. The global marketing efficiency point would be different for different companies. This will be decided by the most efficient company or companies, dealing with same type products and operating in the same marketing environment.

QUESTIONS FOR REVIEW

1. Emami Group is set to acquire an Egyptian personal care products manufacturer. The move is part of the group's corporate strategy to bolster Emami's growth at an accelerated pace of 50-60% CAGR over the next three years. Analyse the political risk of Egypt following the ICRG methodology and suggest the riskiness of the venture abroad.
2. What are the different types of political system prevailing in the world? Do you think that different political system imposes different types of risks for international businesses? Justify your answer with examples.
3. Is democracy as a political system can attract international investors for investment abroad? Is it applicable for all democracy in general?
4. How you would define political risks of a country as it is applicable to international business? What are the different types of political risks relevant for international business? Answer with example.
5. What theoretical and methodological tools allow us to determine the trajectory of domestic politics and regional and internal security contexts in emerging markets? How can the quality and predictability of good governance be analysed and future trends projected?
6. You are a member of a consultancy team that has been employed by a multinational company, doing business in the FMCG category, which is considering whether to invest in Nigeria. Your consultancy is to provide a critical assessment of the political risk present in the country which the company would consider for a 'go or no go' decision.
7. What are the different political risks international businesses can expect in a foreign market? How the political risks can be measured?
8. What is political risk insurance? What is the role of MIGA in mitigation of political risk abroad for international businesses?
9. You are an Indian company producing fabric that are used by your own Bangladesh facility set up for the purpose of stitching different apparel products under the banner 'Four Star'. You have now set up your sales subsidiary in France, Germany, Brazil, Indonesia, United States and Saudi Arabia, who acts as your importer and sales office. Generate a fact sheet about the types of laws applicable to these countries with their characteristics.
10. How easy or difficult was it to identify political or legal forces affecting your firm's proposed entry? Say, you intending to acquire a business in Brazil to start producing sugar from there. Conduct an analysis of political or legal aspects that may affect your business in long run.
11. Describe the different types of legal systems practiced in the countries of the world? How characteristically these systems are different?
12. Characterise the types of investments that are most vulnerable to political risk. Characterise those that are least vulnerable.
13. What is the aim of the product safety and liability law? Briefly describe the product safety and liability regulations applicable in European Union.
14. What are the objectives of international regulations? In which areas these regulations are applicable?
15. What is retail price maintenance? What are its characteristics? Describe the RPM regulations of USA, China and Japan.
16. Why country frame legislations related to marketing communications? Compare and contrast the marketing communications regulations of **USA** and Middle East countries.
17. What role self regulatory bodies play in marketing communications? Compare and contrast the marketing communications regulations of China and Russia.
18. Identify a textile company in your locality with or without a subsidiary in Bangladesh and conduct an interview with the CEO of the company about the possible impending political risks in Bangladesh on the Indian company.

19. The Apple, the smart phone maker's, recently marketed the iPhone 4 in India through agreements with two mobile-phone operators, Bharti Airtel Ltd. and Aircel Ltd. The competition corporation of India felt that it had an adverse impact on the overall industry. Investigate and come out with findings on how the Indian competition law could pull up Apple in this matter.
20. ONGC Videsh Limited (OVL) is operating in South Sudan through its JV Companies, Greater Pioneer Operating Company (GPOC) and SUDD Petroleum Operating Company (SPOC) with stake of 25% and 24.125% respectively. Prepare a country risk profile of Republic of South Sudan and suggest ONGC about possible risk coverage insurance option possible for the company.
21. Select a company with spree for international marketing in your city and develop market risk profiling of the countries of their presence using ICRG framework available at http://www.prs-group.com/ICRG_Methodology.aspx. Submit the report to the company and develop risk Vs marketing impact matrix in discussion with the company officials.

End Case: Is GCPL Facing Political Risks in Indonesia[23]

The beginning:

Godrej Group was founded by Ardeshir Godrej and his younger brother Pirojsha Godrej **way back** in 1897 and was destined to become a house hold name in modern India. Now, this big conglomerate has business interest in real estate, FMCG, industrial engineering, appliances, furniture, security and agricultural value added products. With more than 3.3 billion dollars turnover the name 'Godrej' is now a house hold name and interestingly so much is the power of the brand name that in India people mostly refer steel furniture as 'Godrej' irrespective of their makers. People in India starts the day with Godrej soaps and Godrej shaving cream and go to sleep in night with Godrej made 'Good Knight' mosquito repellent. In between the person uses Godrej furniture in the office, drinks coffee from the Godrej vending machines, eats Godrej food products, uses Godrej fax/conferencing equipment for communication and puts money in Godrej safe. Interestingly all these the person might have done while living in Godrej property condominium. By some estimate about 400 million people across India use at least one Godrej product every day. However, as old saying goes 'Rome can be concquired in one day' these achievements have not also came in a day or two. The foundation of the g journey towards business success was laid about four generations ago when Ardeshir Godrej and Pirojsha Godrej made a humble beginning driven by honesty, integrity but with exemplarily entrepreneurial acumen to reach to the present day success. When one look back the the entire jouney the following developmental milestones could be noticed.

- Ardeshir Godrej began the journey as lock manufacturer. His entrepreneurial orientation allow not only to quickly mastered the technology thoroughly but started capturing the Indian market. He overcame stiff competition from imported locks and established a respectable position for India made locks in the market.
- Ardeshir and Pirojsha Godrej soon looked for diversification and went on to make security equipments of a high quality.
- Quest for more diversifications had gone up and hence in order to manage the same a new spinoff company by the name Godrej & Boyce was promoted. The new company was, manufacturing toilet soaps from vegetable oils. Ardeshir was successful in these business ventures and thereafter moved very fast to establish its presence in other diversified areas like soaps, biscuits and confectionery, canning and processing, and cupboards, furnitures,etc.
- As it is common in business family the next generation entrepreneur Naval Godrej continued with the spirit shown by predecessor and entered in to new businesses like typewriters and refrigerators.
- Then came the luminous third generation, led by Jamshyd Godrej, who changed the rule of the game. Under his able leadership the Godrej group of companies reestablished it self as one of the largest privately-held diversified industrial

corporations in India. The wholly-owned subsidiary attained new height, and two publicly listed companies with promoters holding 88.4% and 68.2%, respectively — Godrej Industries and Godrej Consumer Products Limited (GCPL) – became major players in Indian competitive market. GCPL soon establish itself leader in the Indian FMCG industry with a presence in toilet soaps, hair color, liquid detergents and other toiletries.

Internationalisation Drives

Godrej almost pioneered the FMCG internationalisation for Indian companies. Adi Godrej, Chairman, GCPL recalls the internationalisation drives of the company.

November 2005: GCPL bought Keyline Brands Ltd, a London-based consumer products company which owned brands such as Cuticura, Erasmic and Nulon and had a strong brand portfolio in the cosmetics and toiletry category in the UK and elsewhere. Keyline also had a strong presence in the Gulf, Canada and parts of Europe. It had a strong consumer base in supermarket chains and pharmacies like Tesco, Sainsbury Superdrug and Boots. This gave Godrej trademarks a presence in a large number of countries.

September 2006: GCPL completed the acquisition of South African business of Rapidol, UK, as well as its subsidiary Rapidol International in order to have access to the large and fast growing African hair colour market. Rapidol's distribution network exists in South Africa and other African nations such as Zambia, Mozambique, Tanzania, Democratic Republic of Congo, Swaziland, Ghana, Namibia, Zimbabwe, Mauritius, Seychelles and Madagascar. The Rapidol acquisition gave the company ownership of strong ethnic hair colour brands such as 'Intecto' and 'Soflene' in ten African countries.

July 2007: This year GCPL set another milestone. It entered into a 49:51 joint venture (JV) with Sara Lee of USA. The JV had allowed the company to market Sara Lee's household and body care products for the South Asia markets. Later In 2010, GCPL completed acquisition of balance 51% ownership of Sara Lee but without the brands like Ambipur, Kiwi and Brylcreem.

January 2008: GCPL looked at South African market and acquired Kinky, a South Africa-based haircare company, for 100 million rand (₹55 crore). Kinky had products like dry hair, hair braids, human hair extensions, hair pieces and wigs. It also offered hair accessories like styling gels, hair sprays, oil-free shampoo, bonding glue and bonding glue remover. This enabled the company expand into a new line of business and diversify its hair product portfolio and offerings in South Africa.

March 2010: The company completed its ambition of entering in to west African markets by acquiring a reputed the Nigerian personal care brand Tura. Tura, almost a household name in many African countries, was known for its market-leading personal-care products like soaps, moisturising lotions and skin-toning creams, etc. Its medicated bar soap is amongst the top three in its category in Nigeria. In a press release, Mr Adi Godrej, Chairman, GCPL, said, "Tura helps us leapfrog in our endeavour to build a pan-African presence for our core categories such as personal wash and hair care. Tura is one of the strongest Nigerian beauty brands with a successful and passionate management team with a proven track record over the last two decades. We expect the transaction to provide a tremendous platform for value creation in West Africa."

New Opportunities Abroad

The company was scouting for an opportunity, this time, to spread more in Asia as a part of its 3 × 3 strategy, i.e., make presence felt in emerging markets in Asia, Africa and South America focusing on three product segments - household care, personal wash and hair care. Megasari Group, an Indonesian FMCG company, with an annual turnover of ₹550 crore, manufacturing and sells household products in Indonesia and internationally provided the right opportunity. The company was founded in 1996 in Jakarta, Indonesia. It already had the experience of successfully marketing its products like air fresheners, wet tissues, baby care products, kitchen cloths, car and motorcycle care products, metal polishers, fly and rat glues, and insecticides in local markets. It also had a separate line of business which dealt with canned LPG for outdoor and indoor activities; aluminum foil and plastic wrapping for foods; and drain openers for clogged drainpipes. Godrej Consumer Products Ltd (GCPL), as a leading player in the FMCG sector in India, was not in a mood to waste this opportunity when news came that Megasari Group can be acquired. For GCPL, Indonesia was a target market to enter as it is also amongst the largest consumer markets in Asia. GCPL thought that Megasari Group would provide it the right platform to gain a significant foothold in Indonesia. GCPL finally completed Megasari acquisition process along with its distribution outlets during early part of 2010. "This is a good opportunity which will take the company to the international level along with creating a platform for other Godrej products in Indonesia," Adi Godrej, chairman, GCPL, said after the acquisition. The basic ground work at GCPL revealed the possible benefits out of the acquisition in monetary terms which suggested that when the Megasari Group would operate as a subsidiary of GCPL, the Indonesian operation would add about 25% to GCPL's revenues and about 15% to GCPL's profits.

The Indonesian Political System

Indonesia was under Dutch colonial rule for a long period of time and finally political freedom came during 1945. The Republic of Indonesia came into being with the enactment of the constitution stipulating the rights and responsibilities of citizens. Indonesia started with a central form of government (or unitary state), with the aim to unify the people of many ethnic, religious and cultural backgrounds spread across thousands of islands. However, central form of government did not last long. At the end of 1949, Indonesia adopted a system of federal government under the banner 'United Republic of Indonesia' which lasted for only for seven months. Then again it returned back to the 'Unitary State of the Republic of Indonesia', and revived the 1945 constitution. Again under the central of government the highest political power was rested with elected institution called the "People's Consultative Assembly (MPR). The MPR had the authority to device the state policy. The President of Indonesia, as head of the government, is responsible to the MPR. Time and again during the period 1966 to 1998 the idea of more federal structure of government was mooted to decentralise the power of the country but they were effectively handled by the government. The President of the country is the executive head of the country and discharges duties with the assistance of Cabinet. The government at the provincial level is headed by a governor, and at regency/ municipal level headed by a regent or mayor. There are 30 provinces which are headed by their respective governors and 354 regency or municipal level of government is headed by a regent or mayor The judiciary system is headed by Supreme Court.

Political Environment in Indonesia

Though the political system planned for Indonesia, at the dawn of independence from dutch colonial rule, seemed to be sound one but political environment was vitiated with unexpected turn of events. The beautifully laid down parliamentary system of the country was first disturbed by its first President Sukarno during 1957 when the power of parliament was curtailed to increase his own power. Though his opposition wanted to resist the move but could not do much because Indonesian army was in his favour. His misrule led to a very difficult economic situation for the country and during 1960 the entire country was under super inflation. There was an attempted coup during 1965 by the communist party to through him out of power but was resisted by army. General Suharto of Indonesian army supported President Sukarno to overcome the attempted coup but later took over the political power during 1966 by himself. He introduced a new political system in Indonesia which could be compared with dictatorship only but with the façade of democracy. This continues up to 1998 when General Suharto resigned under tremendous pressure from all front. Democracy returned to Indonesia during 1999 and first pluralistic parliamentary election was held after 44 years of long darkness.

Constitutional reforms were brought in and MPR's institutional role was largely eliminated. A new principal legislative body in the form of House of Representatives (Dewan Perwakilan Rakyat- DPR) formed. During 2004 to give voices to the regional aspirations the House of Regional Representatives (Dewan Perwakilan Daerah – DPD) was formed in the style of US Senate. DPD's members are elected in an individual capacity (not from a party list). DPR plays the legislative role while DPD has consultative role.

Sources of Political Risks in Indonesia

Corruption: As per transparency international's Corruption Perception Index (CPI) Indonesia ranks is 107 out of 175 countries during 2014. This CPI was down to 114 out of 175 countries during 2013. This country has improved its CPI rating but need to go long way to provide environment for foreign businesses.

Subsidy to fuel: Petrol and Diesel oils are continuing to be heavily subsided by the government. It constitutes to about 20% of government expenditure in some years. No one wants to bell the cat as charging market rate price would make the government unpopular which may affect electoral prospects of the ruling party. However, this is taking a huge toll on the current account deficit of the country. It for sure, therefore, that the government programme for off-setting fuel price is unsustainable for a long period of time.

Resource nationalisation: Indonesian government has kick started resource nationalisation. Already nickel, tin and bauxite export have been banned. National government resorting to populist measures of taking controls of natural resources to demonstrate its pseudo patriotism. In general, these type of tendency culminate in to quotas and then finally outright expropriation.

Authority ambiguity: Divisions of power between the political centre and regional governments is not very clear. It is, therefore, obvious that foreign business will be subjected to duel pressure which increases the risk of getting trapped under contradictory rulings issued from different administrative levels.

Domestic market obligation: Confronted with acute shortage of domestically produced oil gas and coal, the government has introduced a domestic market obligations (DMO) measure that would make the foreign companies marketing offerings confined to domestic market only.

Ethnic and Religious Violence: In the past Indonesia saw many violence of ethnic and religious nature. Weak government failed to control

Table 3.5 Indonesia at a glance, 2010

Dimensions	Ranking
GDP rank Nominal GDP ($) 510 billion	19 Out of 191 countries
Per-capita GNI ($) as per world bank	1880
Per-capita GNI rank	145 Out of 210 countries
Population rank (in terms of population size)	4 Out of 224 countries
Geographical area rank (in terms of total land area) as per CIA fact book	16 Out of 250 countries
Global competitiveness rank (World Economic Forum)	54 Out of 131 countries
Economic freedom index rank (Heritage foundation)	119 Out of 157 countries
Human development index rank(UNDP)	111 Out of 182 countries
Doing business index rank (World Bank)	122 Out of 183 countries
Corruption perception index (Transparency International)	2.8, highest 10

them and even sometimes flared them up to satisfy its own interest. At present religious intolerance is rising in Indonesia as evidenced by increasing number of reported cases of this nature.

Terrorism

Although the country believes in pluralism and democratic values but on the fringes there are stints of radicalisation who aspire for a larger role of Islam in Indonesian politics. Occasionally, these are outwardly manifestated through violent acts such as bomb blasts, etc.

Political risks for GCPL: The Indian company GCPL made the entry in to Indonesia through investment mode without retaining any local subsidiary partner. This mode of entry has some inherent risks factors. To minimise risk, therefore, company made a sound preparation through exhaustive information collection and political risk assessment keeping in mind that presently emerging markets are full with business opportunities but also infected with high political risks. The international business pundits were of the opinion, after GCPL's entry in Indonesia, that political risk factors could create disturbance in business strategy execution for GCPL while doing business in Indonesia in future (Table 3.5).

CASE QUESTIONS

Q1. What type of political system exists in Indonesia? How was the political situation of Indonesia during the entry of GCPL? What are the different types of political risks GCPL can expect in the country? Justify your answer.

Q2. Suppose, GCPL wanted to carry out a political analysis of Indonesia before market entry and you were retained as consultant, would you suggested them entry by acquisition? Justify the answer by carrying out a political risk analysis of the target country using ICRG methodology.

Q3. What are the possible ways through which a business strategist of GCPL can predict the political turn of events in the destination country, i.e., Indonesia? What are the ways to safe guard the company from political risks?

FURTHER READINGS

The use of political risk assessment techniques in Jordanian multinational corporations by Adel Abed Rabbo Al Khattaba, Abdulkareem Awwada, John Anchorb and Eleanor Davies, Journal of Risk Research Vol. 14, No. 1, 2011.

This paper articulates the use of political risk assessment techniques in Jordanian multinational corporations (MNCs). The study identified the methods applied by the MNCs in understanding risks. The study also indicates the problem of the MNCs in the matter of correct data availability due to censorship, etc., in some particular countries. This indicates, therefore, problems of using highly sophisticated scientific techniques for risk assessment.

A framework for the identification of political environmental issues faced by multinational hotel chains in newly industrialised countries in Asia by Kim, Chol Yong and Olsen, Michael D. International Journal of Hospitality Management, Vol.12, No.2, 1993.

This paper deals with concentration of travel and tourism industry in some countries than others. This paper is based upon a research project examine hotel investment decision and establishes a comprehensive view of what determine target country's political risk. This article also identifies the importance of variables from the decision makers of international hotel firms. The second part of the paper delves with a framework with 58 political events representing political risk and uncertainty influential.

A stranger in a strange land: Micro political risk and the multinational firm by Ilan Alon, Theodore T. Herber Business Horizons 52, (2009).

This paper discusses the nature of micro political risk within a host country for a foreign firm, illustrating how it stems from economic, societal, and governmental forces. The paper has compiled a number of firm-specific variables which can affect the firm's micro political risk profile, and advance an innovative methodology by which executives can address these variables and develop an assessment of their firm's micro political risk.

Political Risk Assessment: Theory and the Experience of Dutch Firms by Charles Pahud de Mortanges and Vivian Allers, International Business Review, Vol. 5, No. 3, 1996.

This paper first made a review of the literature as to how political risk has been defined along with different assessment methods and management of risk. The paper also investigated few important aspects like various risk elements in order of their effect on firms, assessment of risk, and the implementation of risk reduction strategies in the backdrop of 23 Dutch firms.

Political Risk Management: A portfolio planning model, Business Horizons, by Kennedy, Charles R Vol.31, Part 6, 1988.

This article analyses the concept of political risk, its evolution and conceptualisation, and explores its utility as a means of understanding political events and processes that can threaten order, stability and continuity in International Relations and disrupt the normal practices of interstate investment, trade and commerce. More particularly, the article organises the disparate literature that surrounds the concept of political risk such that it might be more rigorously applied as a social science method for understanding political events and their effects upon commercial and strategic activities.

A Primer on Important Legal Aspects of the International Business Environment by Richard J. Hunter and Robert E. Shapiro in Journal of Money, Investment and Banking, 2008.

This paper discusses the role and function of law in the international business environment. It then discusses a range of issues, elements and characteristics of the legal system which are important for the international managers in order to take correct decision in the globalised economy.

Towards effective advertising regulation: A comparison of UK, Australian and South African schemes by D. Harker and S. Cassim in South African Journal of Business Management, 2002.

This paper reviews the ASR systems in these three countries, using a macro framework for analysis which contextualises advertising in society. The systems have the fundamental process of handling complaints about advertising in common, however there are advantages and disadvantages of each and these are discussed with a view to providing some guidance for Australia's fledgling, reformulated, system. Important insights for the development of regulation of advertising are presented.

Legal aspects of euro marketing by Doris Bydelbrand in European Journal of Marketing, Vol. 28 No. 7, 1994.

This paper discusses the legal issues in marketing products in European Union. The paper highlights on the various marketing issues like promotion, distribution, etc., that were effected in the surveyed firm due to different legal system in different European countries.

Resale price maintenance by Organisation For Economic Co-Operation and Development (2009).

This document comprises proceedings of OECD competition committee debated on Resale Price Maintenance during October 2008. This document contains written documents from OECD member countries along with the OECD circulated analytical note on OECD.

Resale Price Maintenance: Is it Safe to Suggest Retail Prices? by Mary Jane Sheffet & Debra L. Scammon, 84/Journal of Marketing, Fall 1985.

This paper highlights some legal problems associated with Resale Price Maintenance. The paper. describes manufacturers' rationales for using resale price maintenance, discusses the current and probable future legal status of RPM, and suggests steps manufacturers can take in establishing RPM programs in order to avoid legal problems.

Negotiating Economic Environment

4

Learning Objectives

After studying this chapter, you should be able to:

- Understand the changing economic environment across the countries of the world and how it affects international marketing across the countries of the world.
- Understand the changing consumers' demographics across nations and possible economic dividends from the demographic trend and its uses in international marketing.
- Understand the distribution of income and wealth across countries and global wealth formation.
- Understand the nature and process of economic integration of the countries of the world and their implications on international business.
- Understand different theories related to international trade.
- Understand the role of different organisations supporting the trade flow across the countries.
- Understand the currency exchange rate system across the countries of the world.

Chapter Overview

This chapter introduces the economic environment of doing business in country markets.The economic environment is largely uncontrollable for the international marketers. Different countries have different economic environments. Although uncontrollable, this environment plays a very important role for international marketers, as economic progress of the countries determines the market growth. Hence, international businesses need to understand the different factors contributing to the developing of economic system of the countries. This chapter, therefore, introduces different factors related to the economic environment of a country, which the international marketers need to aware of for purposeful analysis.

Opening Vignette

The curious case of Keralite economy and marketing lessons.

Is India rich enough to attract the luxury car makers of the world? If we go by per capita income of India, it was about 54,835 INR per year during 2010–11 at current price which may not suggest the luxury car makers to keep a hope for the internationally repute luxury car brand like Cadillac, Porsche, Audi, BMW, Jaguar, etc. To make the situation worse, one of its southern state Kerala came to the news when the Global Hunger Index 2008, declared hunger situation in Kerala as "serious", which was just better than the grade "alarming" received by many other Indian states. India's GDP growth rate has been struggling and just managed to cross 5%. If India grew at this rate it will take about 30–35 years to reach the Thailand's present per capita income of 5390 USD.

But one would be surprised by the marketing move of one of the greatest luxury car producers of the world. German luxury carmaker BMW's ultra luxury British brand is looking at Indian market seriously. Rolls-Royce sales in the Asia-Pacific region surged 47% year-on-year in 2011, compared with a 17% rise in North America and a 23% increase in the Middle East. China and the US were the brand's largest markets last year. BMW is already upbeat with the sales of its small car Mini, priced at $49,000, in India as the costliest small car in the country, BMW India is also equipping its armory with new models like BMW M3 Coupe, BMW M5 Sedan, BMW M6 Coupe, BMW M6 Convertible, BMW X5 4.8i, BMW 6 series individual and BMW 7 series individual for Indian market. The MINI and Rolls-Royce brands are produced in Great Britain whilst BMW motorcycles are manufactured in Berlin and Husquvarna Motorcycles in Italy. So convinced with the potential Indian market that BMW expressed its intention to introduce its Motorrad range of super bikes, reportedly range from 450 cc capacity to 1300 cc capacity, at a price around INR 1 million in India. "The BMW Group has already established itself very successfully in India with a local BMW automobile production and a sales network for BMW Group automobiles. Now the market for premium motorcycles is beginning to develop, too. The sales activities are now commencing with our two experienced BMW Group partners. We are confident our motorcycles will swiftly become established in timely preparation for the growing market" remarked Hendrik von Kuenheim, General Director of BMW Motorrad.

On one hand the luxury car marketers of the world kept a vigil on how India's central bank is struggling to break the sluggishness of the economy, on the other hand, they did not forget to take a lesson from the news item that a man was arrested in Kerala, for allowing his 9-year-old boy driving Ferrari car. Let's look at some economic parameters of the state which possibly through light on the issue. When the entire country is struggling, the southern state Kerala is surging ahead on the economic front which allowed Kochi, its capital, to beat all the major cities to emerge as the target for the luxury car marketers. Thanks to rising value of spices and rubber and ever-increasing inflows from non-resident Keralites, the state's per capita income clocked at ₹74,620 which is well above than those of other states and union territories of India. The state was the destination of $11.3 billion remittances from nonresident Keralites accounting for almost 16% of the total remittances sent to India during 2012. Kerala continued to be number one in terms of receiving expats' remittances. With the rupee falling against the USD, the inflows have been growing significantly in rupee terms which expanded the state's economic output by nearly 25%. Further to driving up this phenomenon is the international rising price of natural rubber which attained historical highs during 2011 but still hovering around ₹175 per kg and helping the state economically which is producing about 90% of total rubber produced in India. The rubber estate earners are the new keralite sheiks of Kochi with imitating lifestyle of that of Arab world, importantly maintaining a fleet of cars.

Armed with high per capita income the tiny southern state is also attracting super luxury car like Ferrari and Maserati, in the state. Carmakers say Kerala has always been a strong market for cars. The dealership that sells the most number of cars from a single location in the country, Indus Auto of Maruti Suzuki, is in Kochi. Kerala now accounts for 10% of India's luxury car with sales of over 2500 vehicles. Compare this with BMW AG's Rolls-Royce unit sales of 3538 cars during 2011 last year, setting a new annual sales record for the 107-year-old brand and increasing 31% over the 2010 figure.

When the curious case of Keralite economy and how marketers targeted the riches of a state with in developing country was told to the students of international marketing in the classroom situation, the students quipped, "That's intelligent marketing! This is surprising too that even though the national economy is not attractive, the luxury car marketers were targeting the country market. How marketers, therefore, assess the economic environment of a country and link it with its marketing drive? Can the marketers depend only on GDP per capita as an indicator to understand the market potential? Will it be difficult for international marketers to scan economic parameters of different countries on continuous basis to draw inputs for marketing plan? How marketers would accomplish it? Does the economic integration, currency volatility assessment, etc., play any role in conducting economic analysis of a country?

"Marketing affects behaviour, attitudes, relationships, and values, thus stimulating economic development rather than just adapting to it"

—Robert Bartels (1977)

INTRODUCTION

How did Singapore and Venezuela develop in the past 37 years on the economic front? They were almost similar in terms of their economic status with income per capita in Venezuela at $7100 while Singapore slightly poorer at $6500 during 1975. Venezuela was close to the largest market in the world with unrestricted possibilities. The country possessed important oil resources to the extent that revenue from petroleum exports contributed roughly for about 18% of the country's GDP and roughly 95% of total exports during 2010. Venezuela is the fifth largest member of OPEC by oil production It also has other natural resources like iron ore, coal, bauxite, gold, nickel, and diamonds. In simple terms the country has all the ingredients to be an oil-rich country. However, investment rates in Venezuela continue to fluctuate between 15 and 19% and the country stagnated. In 2005, the economy even declined with per capita income less than $6000 per person. During the year 2013, the per capita income increased to some extent to $14,414. While the country increased its income per capita more than double, the people of Venezuela remained comparatively poorer. On the other hand, Singapore's per capita income surged ahead at a faster rate and reached $55,182 during 2013 while it is predicted to grow further to US$58,710 in 2020. Investment in Singapore grew between 30% and 48% and the country multiplied its income per person. While Singapore has been continuously improving its economic environment, Venezuela has seen a significant deterioration in terms of policies and nature of its economy, trade cycles, economic resources, level of income, distribution of income and wealth, etc., although they started almost from the same mark during 1975. The story of economic growth and development of these two countries are totally different. In general terms economic development refers to the increase in standard of living of a nation's population associated with sustained growth, whereas economic growth is merely the numerical increase in activity in an economy, often measured as the rate of change of gross domestic product (GDP). Singapore is a small country with population of 5.165 million (2010) with almost no natural resources. While Singapore can boast of achieving one of the highest per capita incomes in the world, it also suffers from a grossly unequal distribution of that high income. This indicates that Singapore's mammoth GDP value goes to foreign-owned companies and Government Linked Companies, leaving a low share of the GDP to shower on the average Singapore citizen. The result is that Singapore has the second highest income gap between the rich and the poor, as indicated by the Gini coefficient of 42.5 during 2009), according to the 2009 United Nations Development Report. The Singapore government channelises the income through investment in high-technology industries since the small population base of the country enables it to go only for high-tech industries that require only few highly-skilled workers. In comparison, Venezuela is a comparatively large country with a population about six times more than Singapore. Venezuela's economy grew by 9% in 2007; then shrunk in 2009 and further in 2010. Venezuela has one of the highest inflation rates in the world averaging 29.1% in 2010, according to the CIA world fact book. Venezuela is in strict government control, as is evident from the foreign exchange rate system. The currency 'Bolivar' has fixed a dual exchange rate of 2.6 bolivar per USD for imports of essential items such as food, medicine, and industrial machinery, and 4.3 bolivar per USD rate for import of other products, including cars and telephones. In contrast, Singapore has a market-oriented exchange rate regime that perfectly suits its free-market economy with an open business environment that is relatively corruption-free and transparent.

One thing apparently clear from the above discussion is that these two countries, Venezuela and Singapore, offer almost two dissimilar economic environments to the international companies for doing business. Both the countries offer different opportunities and challenges. One of the important factors that international enterprises need to consider while entering the market of a country is its economic environment and how much it is dissimilar from those of countries which these businesses had successfully handled. Different countries not only offer different economic environments but since the economic environment is not static, the scanning and analysis of economic environment becomes a continuous process for a business operating in a foreign country. Moreover, economic factors fall under the "environmental uncontrollables", which puts marketers in a difficult situation while deciding on an effective strategy to handle the odds. It is clear from the above discussion that an international marketer can neither control the economic environment of Venezuela nor Singapore. In fact, many international businesses left Venezuela after the fixed dual exchange rate was introduced as the system affected repatriation of profit and arranging for the USD for sourcing of raw materials. A prosperous and open economy like that of Singapore also offers challenges to international business but differently than the worsening and close economic environment like the one seen in Venezuela. In Singapore, the challenge may come from the high income inequality status of the country which poses a challenge to shape a suitable marketing strategy in a highly competitive environment. Therefore, every country with its characteristically aligned economic environment is a candidate for analysis for successful presence in that country in a sustained way. This chapter, therefore, discusses different factors related to the economic environment of a country, which international marketers need to aware of for purposeful analysis.

THE CHANGING CONSUMER DEMOGRAPHICS

In order to be able to take right marketing strategy at right time and in right countries, the international marketers need keep themselves aware of the change in demographics across the countries of the world and the world as a whole. This will allow the company to keep pace with the demand of the different segments of population by providing right kind of products. The changing demographic trend will require marketers to have a detailed view of what the different segments are being created what they buy, how they buy or what are their spending habits, etc. The job in hand may be difficult because all the parameters will undergo changes, as the focus country of the marketer gets changed. In the next paragraph, we will look into the demographic trend of the consumers across the globe.

Population: The world population during 2014 crossed 7 billion and it is expected that it will increase to 10.1 billion by the end of 2100 according to the

United Nations population projections report prepared by the Department of Economic and Social Affairs (DESA)[1]. Based on the type of population growth countries can be divided in three groups.

High-fertility countries: These are the countries where no fertility reduction or only an incipient decline could be observed until the year 2000.

Medium-fertility countries: These are the countries where fertility has been observed to be declining but whose level is still above replacement level (2.1 children per woman in 1995-2000).

Low-fertility countries: Those countries where fertility stands at or below replacement level (2.1 children per woman in 1995-2000) plus a few with levels very close to replacement-level fertility that are judged ready to drop below replacement level in the near future.

It is interesting to note that, in this increase of world population by 3 billion, Africa as a continent will be playing a lead role. High-fertility 39 countries are located in Africa who will be primarily responsible for the increase in population. Further, 9 high fertility countries are in Asia, followed by 6 in Oceania and 4 in Latin America. Notable high fertility countries, irrespective of the continent they belong, are Pakistan, Nigeria, the Philippines, Ethiopia, the Democratic Republic of the Congo, the United Republic of Tanzania, Sudan, Kenya, Uganda, Iraq, Afghanistan, Ghana, Yemen, Mozambique and Madagascar which account for 75% of the population of high-fertility countries.

According Population Division, Department of Economic and Social Affairs, United Nations, between 2011 and 2100 the populations in high fertility countries would more than triple, passing from 1.2 billion to 4.2 billion. During the same period, the population of the intermediate-fertility countries would increase by 26%, from 2.8 bn to 3.5 bn, while that of the low-fertility countries would decline by about 20%, from 2.9 bn to 2.4 bn. Low-fertility countries include all countries in Europe except Iceland and Ireland, 19 countries out of the 51 in Asia, 14 out of the 39 in the Americas, two in Africa (Mauritius and Tunisia) and one in Oceania (Australia).

It is understandable that the world's population is on the rise due to birth of new born babies. However, it is not only the rise of population which has put the demographic researchers in a fix but in addition the 'ageing of the world' creating an absolute uneasiness. Ageing of the world is happening primarily because of increase in life expectancy and decline in fertility across some countries of the world. As a result the average age of the population as a whole is increasing. In fact, the proportion of older persons increasing at a faster rate is a major deliberating point in demographic conferences. The older persons are registering their increase more in developed countries than in least-developing countries. In these countries older persons have already outnumbered the children. The developing countries where the same trend is being observed are also not far behind. According to DESA prediction, during the next 35 years, i.e., 2050, ageing of world population will be alarming.

[1] The United Nations Department of Economic and Social Affairs (DESA) provides research based inputs on development issues to various agencies. It plays its role successfully to bring together different international community to address issues related to economic and social challenges faced by different nations.

The annual growth rate of number of persons with age 60 years or older registered almost three times more during 2014 than the growth rate of population as a whole. So, going at this rate, during 2050 there will be around 2.03 billion population with age 60 or over in the world.

Most of the aged 60 years or older would be crowding the developed countries of the world. One can think in this way that by the turn of 2050, twenty percent of the population of developed countries would be comprised of people of aged 60 years or older. The situation can be better understood when it is said that there will be two elderly persons for every five persons in the developed world in the days to come. Now, the developing countries would also be effected by the ageing problem but as severe as the developed world. During 2005 there were 9 persons elderly persons out of 100 persons in developing world. This proportion of the older population is expected to rise from about 9 in 2005 to close to about 20 by 2050. The story does not end here. The developed and developing world will also witness notable increase in the number of 'oldest-old' (who are 80 years old or over) people. The total number of the 'oldest-old' pesons was about 86 million in the world during 2005 and this figure is expected to increase by about 5 times (4.62 precisely) in 2050. However, by 2050, most of the oldest-old people will live in the developed and developing countries sparing least developing countries. It is also interesting to know that women oldest old person will surpass the men oldest persons of the world. It is easy to understand the status of older person in a country by knowing the meaning of the index of median age. It simply denotes the age at which 50% of the population is older and 50% younger. For example, during the year 2014 the median age of Indian population was 27 years while that of Japan was 46 years. Thus almost making Japan a country of old population. About 11 developed countries have a median age of over 40. But by 2050, 99 countries will fall into that group. The foregoing discussions establish the fact that different countries of the world are undergoing through demographic transitions. The trend of the transition must be known to the marketers, as it will be required by them while designing marketing mix for specific country. Eventually, the demographic shift may compel a company to change the marketing destination or production destination. For example, Countries like Japan and Germany with median age stands at 46 in 2014 are predicted to decrease their workforce by around 30% by 2050. Hence, a company producing products through a labour-intensive production process may like to shift its production centre from Germany or Japan to elsewhere. However, this change in the demographic transition has not been an overnight affair but a long drawn process depending upon various factors such as country's differential rate of mortality, literacy level, economic progress, etc., and fertility observed over a period of time. Those countries, who are now world's most developed nations, have shown decrease in fertility rates as well as marked increases in life expectancies, resulting in the quick aging of these countries.

However, alongside 'ageing' of the population in certain parts of the world, there are some good news also. Just the reverse of 'ageing', i.e., 'youth bulge' are happening in certain parts of the world. These locations are mainly some developing countries and the least-developed countries. The 'youth bulge' is a phenomenon associated with increasing number younger population in a country say, with median age 15-24 and they can form a very productive human resource for the country in coming days. This phenomenon is happening in those countries where countries have drastically reduced infant mortality rate and mothers are still retaining a high fertility rate. The result of above two happenings is directly related to comparatively larger growth of younger population who today's children but will become tomorrow's young adults and, will be counted as important work force of the country. These blessed countries, for example, are Tonga, Chad, Guinea and Sierra Leone. These countries are expecting to have youth bulge during 2025 with median age of population around 15-24 years. One will understand the importance of youth bulge only when it is mentioned that countries like United States and Singapore had its youth bulge way back in 1978. This indicates that these blessed countries will be located in Africa mostly followed by Asia.

Economic Dividend from the Demographic Trend

Age dependency ratio of a country is the ratio of the non-working age population (people younger than 15 or older than 64) to the working age population (15 to 64 years). In a country with a youth bulge, as the working age population increases, the country's age dependency ratio will decline. This means that if the countries with declining age dependency ratio the working age individuals are put to productive activities with the support of policy measures taken by the respective countries, other things being equal, the level of average income per capita should be increased. In other words, these countries will be then able to reap economic dividend from their demographic trend. Table 4.1 below shows proportion of dependents

Table 4.1 Proportion of dependents per 100 working-age population

Country name	2007	2008	2009	2010	2011
Argentina	56	56	55	55	55
Australia	48	48	48	48	48
Austria	47	48	48	48	48
Bangladesh	60	59	57	56	55
Brazil	50	49	49	48	47
Burkina Faso	92	91	91	91	90
Burundi	75	72	70	69	68
Cambodia	61	59	57	56	54
China	40	39	39	38	38
Colombia	54	54	53	52	52
Comoros	82	82	83	83	83
Congo, Dem. Rep.	99	98	97	96	95
Congo, Rep.	81	80	80	79	79
Ethiopia	87	85	83	81	79
France	53	54	54	54	55

(Continued)

Table 4.1 *(Continued)*

Country name	2007	2008	2009	2010	2011
Germany	51	51	51	51	51
Ghana	75	74	74	74	73
Greece	49	49	49	50	50
India	57	57	56	55	54
Indonesia	50	49	49	48	48
United Kingdom	51	51	51	51	52
United States	49	49	49	50	50

Source: World Bank available at http://data.worldbank.org/indicator/SP.POP.DPND

(non working age population) per 100 working-age population of some of the countries of the world for five years.

However, only demographic trend would not provide the much desired economic dividend to the countries but it should be adequately supported by critical policy making in areas such as public health, education, economic policies that promote labour-market flexibility, openness to trade, and savings. These are important information for the international marketer as it may influence the entry decision as well marketing mix decision in different countries of the world.

Distribution of Income and Wealth

Along with questions such as how big is the population and at what rate it is growing, where the population is located and how dense it is and what is the population age and distribution, another question that haunts international marketers is about the wealth of the countries, how rich or poor

Box 4.1 The "Odour of aging"

International marketers are using demographic trend and economic benefits arising out of that trend successfully. Seeing the population trend in Japan, Shiseido Co, Japan's largest cosmetics producer as well as one of the largest in the world, came out to develop a product that perfectly suits the ageing population of Japan. Because body odour increases as a person ages, researchers at Shiseido spend time on it and in June 1999, the company announced that it had developed a spray and a lotion that chemically suppresses this odour. For older people who have been concerned about their increased body odour, this was relieving news. Even before the products hit the market, the response was overwhelming. Beauty Technology Co., a new company was founded in July 1999 by a Shiseido subsidiary to sell these and other products aimed at senior citizens. There had been sharp rise in sales as well, when sales volumes rose from 4.6 million USD in the first year to 22.7 million USD in the second year. The person who identified a marketing opportunity in tackling body odour was Shoji Nakamura of Shiseido Laboratories. The company supported him for about 10 years when Nakamura had been investigating the distinctive odour gatherings of middle-aged and elderly people. As an olfactory professional, Nakamura felt determined to find the source of this odour. He also wanted to make a contribution to Japan's aging society by devising a means to eliminate or reduce the odour.

Source: Shiseido Co, Japan

Box 4.2 How Brazil's fertility fell

For the first time in half a century, Brazil's population growth rate dipped below 2% according to the country's once-a-decade population census concluded in 1991. The falling growth rate, part of a trend in developing nations, was welcomed by every Brazilian. According to the international observers, it gave Brazil, Latin America's most populous nation, more time to catch up with a yawning social deficit of schools, sewers, and clinics. According to the 1991 population census, which was finally announced its final result during February, the total population of Brazil was 146 million. The Brazilian Institute of Geography and Statistics, the organisation conducting the census operation, at best put the figure as 148 million after adjusting for undercounting. Even with 148 million population, people were happy because 7 million more people were predicted to be there a decade ago. However, with 148 million population, Brazil remained the world's fifth most populous nation, slightly larger than Russia. The four most populous nations were China, India, the United States, and Indonesia.

In order to understand population growth pattern, the policy maker analysed the reports submitted by 189,000 enumerators engaged during the census operation. According to this analysis, there were hidden population movements across a continent-size nation. In the 1980s, the fastest population growth was on the Amazon frontier. In Roraima State of Brazil, where gold miners invaded the lands of the Yanomami Indians, population grew at an annual rate of 9%, the highest in Brazil. Rondonia, another part of Brazil, grew at 7.9% a year, whereas Mato Grosso grew at 5.4%. For the first time, two Amazon cities, Belem and Manaus, broke into the ranks of cities with population over one million. Brazil's 10 other cities in this category in descending order of population were Sao Paulo, Rio de Janeiro, Salvador, Belo Horizonte, Fortaleza, Brasilia, Recife, Curitiba, Nova Iguaçu, and Porto Alegre. The slowest growth rates were detected in the crowded, older states and cities on the Atlantic coast. When the numbers released proved sharply lower than estimates, many mayors and governors were so much surprised that they even demanded recounting. Also, they were apprehensive of cuts in federal revenue sharing in accordance with population size. Census officials reconfirmed them that only to a maximum undercount of 2% could be maximum possible. The analysts attributed Brazil's declining birth rate as to be the major social changes that actually drove down the population of the country. However, those who knew the situation opined that there were many other factors that worked in the backdrop like urbanisation, more women in the labour force, and more access to family planning devices. According to David Wu Tai, coordinator of the census, Brazil's move toward smaller families was responsible for low population growth for sure and this was a global trend. Annual growth rates of population dropped in China to the tune of 1.5% and while in India it was 1.9%. Brazil's Government, which supported population growth as late as the 1970s, celebrated the drop as a step toward improving education and living standards. The slowing population growth was seen as boon because the economy of the country was largely stagnant in the 1980s which would have been under more pressure with rising population. It surprised many in the country that falling fertility rates was observed without any Government programme for family planning or sex education. Although abortion was illegal in Brazil, the Alan Guttmacher Institute of Brazil estimated that 1.4 million to 2.4 million abortions were performed annually. Abortions alone could account for the seven million population shortfall between 1991 actual population and forecasts made a decade ago. In addition, demographers estimated that 30% married Braziliian women underwent sterilisation voluntarily even when they were in child-bearing age. In contrast, the corresponding sterilisation rate for United States women was 17%, and for Latin American women, 7%. It surprised everybody when it made public that Brazil's high female sterilisation rate was due to two important but unusual factors: the high price and unreliability of local contraceptives.

Source: Internet

the inhabitants are and how they are distributed within their countries. In order to understand the wealth of the countries, there are a few standard methods of measurement that are mostly used by analysts. The measure frequently used in this respect is Gross Domestic Product (GDP), which represents the size of a country's economy. An improvised and meaningful method of representing this is per-capita GDP, which is nothing but a measure of the average welfare and affluence, or poverty, of the residents of a country. However, when it comes to comparison of wealth across countries, both GDP and per-capita GDP are less useful because of their association with a country's local currency. When comparing economies across national boundaries the unit of expression has to be similar; hence, to compare the countries of the world in terms of their prosperity or poorness, GDP at purchasing power parity (PPP) is considered as a better way of expression. GDP (PPP) brings out useful information to the marketers by indicating the generalised differences in living standards across countries. It becomes meaningful to the marketers because PPP computation takes into account the relative cost of living and the inflation rates of countries, rather than using just exchange rates, which may distort the real differences in income. Table 4.2 below depicts the GDP per capita (PPP) of top 15 countries, low 20 countries and mid-15 countries of the world.

Distribution of Global Income

International marketers may be interested not only in the purchasing power of the people living in a country but also in country-wise other parameters such as household disposable income, income inequality inside the country since these are important for them to take marketing decisions like pricing,

Table 4.2 GDP per capita (PPP) of top 15 countries, low 15 countries and mid 15 countries of the world. (Current international dollar), 2014

Top country	GDP - cap (PPP) (US$)	Low country	GDP- cap (PPP) (US$)	Mid country	GDP – cap (PPP) (US$)
Qatar	108,228	Mali	1194	Romania	13,809
Luxembourg	80,661	Guinea-Bissau	1216	Brazil	12,994
Singapore	64,883	Rwanda	1704	South Africa	12,238
Norway	58,413	Mozambique	1363	Dominica	15,087
Brunei	58,695	Ethiopia	1334	Saint Lucia	13,680
United Arab Emirates	51,171	Comoros	1346	Grenada	14,320
Kuwait	40,795	Afghanistan	1112	Montenegro	12,566
United States	53,327	Madagascar	1003	Colombia	11,866
Hong Kong	56,404	Togo	1205	Suriname	13,665
Switzerland	47,958	Sierra Leone	1770	Tunisia	10,731
Australia	45,862	Malawi	939	Peru	12,156
Austria	44,746	Niger	898	Dominican	15,087
Bahrain	30,809	C.African Republic	873	Thailand	11,481
Sweden	43,560	Eritrea	801	Belize	9209
Netherland	43,699	Zimbabwe	628	Angola	7063

Source: International Monetary Fund

Table 4.3 Global income distribution by population 1990–2007 in PPP constant 2005 international dollars

Quintiles (20% of a given population)	1990	2000	2007
Q5	75.3	74.4	69.5
Q4	14.9	14.2	16.5
Q3	5.4	6.3	7.8
Q2	3.0	3.4	4.2
Q1	1.5	1.7	2.0
% of global population	97.0	97.6	97.6
% of Global GDP	98.3	98.3	98.1
No of countries considered in the calculations	99	127	136

Source: UNICEF (2011)

product positioning, etc. Household disposable income refers to income of a family from all sources except social transfer in kinds after paying all taxes on income and wealth as well as social security contribution. This data is important for marketers to understand the positioning of expensive category of products, etc. Income inequality is a concept to understand the level of unequal distribution of household or individual income across the citizens of a country. This data again help marketers in their basic marketing job of market segmentation. The marketers can easily understand income inequality or the pattern of wealth distribution in a country very easily to take marketing decision. First, we will take a look on income inequality across countries and then with the country. Table 4.3 shows that as of 2007, only 20% rich persons of 136 country population enjoyed nearly 69.5% of total national income of these concerned countries. On the other hand, in a stark contrast , another 20% comprising the poor population of the world (136 countries considered here) had access to only 2% of the total national income of these countries indicating huge disparity in income distribution across world population. Interestingly, when one considers the bottom three quintiles, it can be understood that 60% of the population of these 136 countries considered in the calculations are responsible for only 12% of the total incomeduring 2007. From the work of UNICEF (2011)[2], depicted in Table 4.3, it can easily be seen that first , there has been a huge disproportionate distribution of income across globe and second, this inequal distribution of wealth has not been happened overnight and third, any change towards making the world a place with equal distribution of wealth is a long drawn process. To support the third point it can be seen from the Table 4.3 that about 10% of the wealth distributed amongst 60% of the population during 1990, which increased to 11.4% during 2000 and finally to 12% during 2007.

Therefore, international marketers have to understand that not many in the population are rich but those who are, are super-powerful because of the wealth they possess. This inequality of wealth distribution has not been a newly identified phenomenon but result of a long process. The nature of country richness or poorness is likely to force businesses to differentiate their marketing mix recipes to suit different brackets of income, if they consider income as a strong criterion for segmenting the market. But at this juncture, it is important for the international marketer to know the geographical location or distribution of the rich and the poor population of the world from the following facts. The Gross Domestic Product per capita(Purchasing Power Parity) in USD (2014 data are estimate of GDP by CIA factbook and 2013 data actual are from World Bank) gives the understanding of distribution of rich and poor in the world.

[2] UNICEF (2011). Global Inequality: Beyond the Bottom Billion – A Rapid Review of Income Distribution in 141 Countries © United Nations Children's Fund (UNICEF), New York, April 2011

Central and Eastern Europe: GDP (PPP) per capita USD 9800 To 26,700 (2014)

This region is composed of 14 countries:

This region is composed of 14 countries: Albania ($11,100), Bosnia and Herzegovina ($9800), Bulgaria ($17,100), Croatia ($20,400), Estonia ($26,600), Hungary ($24,300), Latvia ($23,900), Lithuania ($26,700), Macedonia ($13,200), Montenegro ($15,200), Poland ($24,400), Romania ($19,400), Serbia ($12,500) and Turkey ($19,600).

Commonwealth of Independent States: GDP (PPP) per capita USD 2700 to 24,800 (2014)

This region is made up of 9 Commonwealth of Independent States (CIS) countries and two non members: Armenia ($11,100), Azerbaijan ($17,900), Belarus ($18,200), Kazakhstan ($24,100), Kyrgyzstan ($3400), Moldova ($4800), Russia ($24,800), Tajikistan ($2700), Turkmenistan ($14,200), and Uzbekistan ($5600), The non members Georgia ($7700) and Mongolia ($10,200).

Developing Asia: GDP (PPP) per capita USD 1600 to 77,000 (2014)

There are 26 countries in this region: Afghanistan, ($2000) Bangladesh ($3400), Bhutan ($7700), Brunei, ($77,000), Cambodia ($3300), China ($12,900), Fiji ($8200), India ($5800), Indonesia ($10,200), Kiribati ($1600), Laos ($5000), Malaysia ($24,500), Maldives ($12,400), Myanmar, Nepal ($2400), Pakistan ($4700), Papua New Guinea ($2400), Philippines ($7000), Samoa ($5200), Solomon Islands ($1800), Sri Lanka ($10,400), Thailand ($14,400), Timor-Leste ($6800), Tonga ($5000), Vanuatu ($2600) and Vietnam ($5600).

Western Hemisphere GDP (PPP) per capita USD 4700 to 31,300 (2014)

The Western Hemisphere makes up 32 countries: Antigua and Barbuda ($22,600), Argentina ($22,100), The Bahamas ($25,100), Barbados ($16,200), Belize ($8100), Bolivia ($16,299), Brazil ($15,200), Chile ($23,200), Colombia ($13,500), Costa Rica ($14,900), Dominica ($10,700), Dominican Republic ($12,800), Ecuador ($11,400), El Salvador ($8000), Grenada ($11,800), Guatemala ($7500), Guyana ($6900), Haiti ($1800), Honduras ($4700), Jamaica ($8700), Mexico ($17,900), Nicaragua ($4,800), Panama ($20,300), Paraguay ($8400), Peru ($12,000), St. Kitts and Nevis ($20,300), St. Lucia ($11,100), St. Vincent and the Grenadines ($10,900), Suriname ($16,700), Trinidad and Tobago ($31,300), Uruguay ($20,500) and Venezuela ($17,900).

Middle East and North Africa GDP (PPP) per capita USD 3959 to 136,727 (2013)

The 14 countries that make up this region are: Bahrain ($43,850), Egypt ($11,089), Iran ($15,590), Iraq ($14,951), Jordan ($11,782), Kuwait ($72,000), Lebanon ($17,173), Libya ($21,046), Oman ($44,000), Qatar ($136,727),

Saudi Arabia ($53,644), Syria ($5100), United Arab Emirates ($64,200) and Yemen ($3959).

Euro Area GDP (PPP) per capita USD 25,666 to 91,047 (2013)

This area is composed of 16 countries: Austria ($45,079), Belgium ($41,574), Cyprus ($28,224), Finland, ($39,740), France ($37,532), Germany ($43,883), Greece ($25,666), Ireland ($45,684), Italy ($35,280), Luxembourg ($91,047), Malta ($29,126), Netherlands ($46,162), Portugal ($29,804), Slovak Republic ($26,496), Slovenia ($28,858) and Spain ($33,093).

Low income Countries GDP (PPP) per capita USD below 2000 (2013)

Afghanistan ($1946), Burundi ($771), Benin ($1790), Burkina Faso ($1684), Central African Republic ($603), Congo, Dem. Rep. ($809), Comoros ($1446), Eritrea ($1195), Ethiopia ($1380), Guinea ($1253), Gambia ($1661), Guinea-Bissau ($1407), Haiti ($1703), Liberia ($877), Madagascar ($1413), Malawi ($780), and Myanmar (NA).

Inequality within Country

Next come the situation when the international marketers need to understand within every country, there exist inequalities in terms of income distribution which have to be considered when country-specific marketing strategy is to be decided. Marketers may ask how to know about the status of income inequality that exists in each country. The answers to this question will give an indication of country-specific marketing strategy to be adopted by a company based on people's affordability in different segments of its society. To facilitate understanding of income inequality within countries, economists use a well known measure known as Gini coefficient. This coefficient has a range between 0 to 1 where 0 is perfect equality and 1 (100 on the percentile scale) is perfect inequality indicating that one person has all income. Gini co efficient is calculated with the help of Lorenz curve. This curve is drawn by plotting cumulative percentages of total income received against cumulative number of recipient ranging from poor to reach households living in the country. Then the area trapped between the curve and an absolute equality line gives the Gini co efficient. According to 2008 Gini index estimates based on Solt (2009)[3], Latin America and the Caribbean is the region with the highest levels of income inequality where Gini index stands at 48.3. Sub-Saharan Africa follows the next with index value of 44.2. Asia is not far behind with index score of 40.4. This is followed by the middle-east countries and North Africa (39.2), and Eastern Europe and Central Asia (35.4). Interestingly, the high-income European countries are better off with an index value of 30.9. However, the east European countries like Belarus, Estonia, Latvia, Lithuania, Moldova, Russia are comparatively more equal region. Inequality in the two most populous countries of the world presents a very interesting picture. Both China and India had been showing a trend of increasing income inequality.

[3] Standardised World Income Inequality Database (SWIID), Version 3.0 (Solt, 2009) and Solt, F. (2009), "Standardising the World Income Inequality Database", *Social Science Quarterly*, Vol. 90, No. 2, pp. 231–242.

Box 4.3 P&G found a new America

What the marketers can learn by analysis of the economic data of a country? A nice example of it came out from Proctor & Gamble (P&G). The last recession had created lot of problem for the American middle class population consisting of the 40% of American households with annual incomes between $50,000 and $140,000 a year. The pre recession time was not also good time for the American middle class. There were attacks on them from many directions. Due to the rising inflation the American middle class had a difficult time in keeping up pace with rising cost of college education, health care and housing. The distress was visible. It was reported that the income, adjusted for inflation, of the median family was even lower than in 1998. In addition, the dwindling housing and stock prices further added to the miseries of the otherwise fun loving American middle class. Alas! It took much time for the great marketers like Proctor & Gamble (P&G) to understand the situation. The company was on overdrive to make middle class population of America to buy it products. But all the strategy attempted almost had no result. Fed up with the situation P&G executives attempted to study the US census bureau data on income inequality or popularly known as Gini index. To their surprise, the Gini coefficient of America found out to be 0.468 during 2009, a 20% rise in income disparity over the past 40 years. "Oh my God, America is now similar to the Philippines and Mexico so far as income disparity is concerned" – exclaimed P&G's vice president of consumer market division. P&G, thereafter, realised that the new look America can be better understood by looking at the some economic indices and then developing marketing strategy accordingly. This made sense for them as well. P&G altered its product-development and marketing approach for the 'new found' America successfully.

Source: Internet

The income inequality is an important consideration for marketers since income of the population is an important market segmenting criteria. The more the income segments,exist in a country more will be requirements of differentiated marketing programme. International marketers can consult the Standardised World Income Inequality Database (SWIID)[4], for country specific index value which, in fact, is the most comprehensive attempt at developing a cross-nationally comparable database of Gini indices across time.

Bases for division of world markets

- Different organisation/countries at different point of time divided the countries of the world based on different factors. The initial attempt was made by USA during 1945 to divide countries based on their political intimacy with USA and coined the terms first world, second world and third world countries. Later the World Bank took a more rational approach of dividing the counties based on the level of development. The Human development index during 1990 shifted the focus to human development and attempted to divide the countries based on the aggregate of three

[4] The SWIID (Solt, 2009) is the most comprehensive attempt at developing a cross-nationally comparable database of Gini indices across time. The SWIID standardizes Gini estimates from all major existing resources of inequality data, including UNU-WIDER (2008), the World Bank's PovcalNet, the Socio-economic Database for Latin America, Branko Milanovic's World Income Distribution data, and the ILO's Household Income and Expenditure Statistics, as well as a host of national statistical offices and other sources. Overall, the SWIID includes Gini estimates for gross and net income inequality for 171 countries from 1960 to 2009 and allows examining changes in net income inequality for 132 countries between 1990 and 2008.

indicators: longevity, knowledge, and the command over resources needed for a decent life. The World Bank further attempted to classify countries based on the gross national income (GNP) and arrived at isolating countries in to four segments: low income, lower middle income, middle income, and high income. Then came 'Big Mac index' introduced by economists to classify countries using the price of Big Mac of Mc Donald in different countries to that of the price in USA in purchasing power parity terms. The following Table 4.4 provides further details of the classifications.

Table 4.4 Different ways of dividing world market

Bases	Divisions
This is comparatively old method based on level of alignment of different countries with United States.	First World countries: Market economies having a high Gross National Product (GDP) per capita. Western Europe and Japan as leaders. Second World countries: Centrally planned economies with average GDP per capita and a well-developed industrial structure. USSR was at the center. Third World countries. "Other" nations having diversified political conditions characterised by low GPD per capita and a weak, and sometimes non-existent, industrial structure. Eg Africa, South America and Asia
Based on World Bank used nomenclature	Advanced economies: These are high income countries. Newly industrialised economies: these are the countries where manufacturing goods represent more than 25% of the GDP and 50% of the exportations. Continent sized countries: Economic growth is spectacular e.g. India and China. Least advanced economies (LAE): the per capita income is very low and to the tune of below 700 USD coupled with low level of industrialisation mostly include African countries.
Based on the concept of Human Development and Index (HDI) ratings. A comparative measure of 140 countries	Less than 0.4: Eritrea, Mali, Burkina faso 0.4-0.6: Tanzania, Senegal, Nepal 0.6-0.7: Egypt, Maldives, China 0.7-0.8: Bahrain, Saudi Arabia, Mexico 0.8-0.9: Austria, Singapore, France More than 0.9: Norway, Australia, USA, Korea (S), Hong Kong, Israel.
Based on GNP per capita classification of World Bank.	In this classification, countries are divided in the following income groups: • Low income: $1035 or less • Lower middle income: $1036 to $4085 • Upper middle income: $4086 to $12,615 • High income: $12,616 or more
The Big Mac Index: Economist derived index to measure the purchasing power parity (PPP) between two currencies. Basically an understanding of a Big Mac,(hamburger) cost as per market exchange rates.	Four most expensive: Norway, Sweden, Brazil, Denmark Four most affordable: Ukraine, Hong Kong, Russia, China Three fastest earned: Dubai, Sydney, Tokyo Four slowest earned: Nairobi, Manila, Cairo, Delhi

Economic Integration

The countries of the world, after the World War II, were seemingly interested to move close to each other by way of reducing the barriers of trade between them. As the years progressed, countries felt that goods efficiently produced in one country must gain access to markets of other countries as well so that the consuming countries are benefitted along with the producing countries because of availability of quality products at a competitive price. Therefore, needs were felt for trade level cooperation between countries. In course of time, the need for more intense economic cooperation was felt by the countries which not only included trade of goods and commodities but also considered free movement of human resource, barrier-less sourcing of products from partner countries, relocation of the production centre based on country-specific advantages rather than home country production, etc. As a result, different countries, at different points of time, were found to getting involved in different types of economic integration with varying level of cooperation envisaged under the arrangements. The level of cooperation in economic partnership was mainly depended upon the following three factors:

Culture factors: Countries with similar culture are more likely to form economic partnership. Elements like common language, common etiquette, similar rituals and traditions facilitate interactions between people, which in turn lead to economic relationships between countries. Latin American countries, because of their common Spanish language, feel more close to each other and this has facilitated business collaboration amongst them. Mekong countries, because of similar cultural background, came close to each other without many inhibitions and agreed to form the Greater Mekong Sub-region (GMS) as one of the growth triangles within ASEAN with participation of China's Yunnan province, Myanmar, Thailand, Vietnam, Cambodia and Laos. Many Anglo-phone or Franco-phone countries on the basis of under the dominance of the British or the French respectively have shown greater urgency for integration. In fact, the African Financial Community (CFA) comprising of 14 different countries, sharing the same Franco-phone culture formed two monetary unions with CFA Franc as their currency[5].

Proximity factor: Geographical proximity between countries bring them close to one another. For example, European Union formed by taking advantage of regional proximity of the countries of Europe. Close knitting of countries in a regional set up helps in optimisation of value chain across countries with reduced transportation cost. For example, an optimised textile value chain can be imagined with raw cotton sourced from Pakistan, spinning in India, knitting in Bangladesh before marketing in Europe can be imagined in south Asian context. Therefore, regional proximity acts as a favourable factor towards economic integration.

Development factor: Countries involved in regional integration will look forward to achieve some economic benefits out of it. This means that developing

[5] Fielding, David and Kalvinder Shields (2003), "Economic integration in West Africa: Does the CFA make a difference?", Working paper, Department of Economics, Melbourne University.

countries would be trying to tie up commercially with industrialised countries and industrialised countries would be benefitted from resource endowment of the developing countries. Mexico joined North American Free Trade Agreement (NAFTA) involving Canada and United States and created a successful trilateral economic partnership in North America in order to benefit from the reciprocity. Examples of this type of reciprocity in terms that have brought together countries with dissimilar level of economic development are many. Canada went on to sign free trade agreement with two important Latin American nations: Costa Rica and Chile. Again Chile successfully negotiated another free trade agreement with the US and EU subsequently. The developing countries would primarily be motivated to secure stable access to the developed markets by entering economic cooperation agreements. Of course, there could be other motives as well like attracting some direct foreign investment from developed countries. However, simultaneously, economic interaction drives between countries with similar level of economic development are also taking place for achieving mutual strategic benefits out of the integration. For example, Free Trade Agreement signed between Japan, South Korea, or China. These agreements are executed primarily to avail mutual benefit out of the association. For example, China expects to gain market access for its product; Japan can enjoy the benefits of expanding into China's vast market, whereas Korea would look for some component technology from Japan.

Benefits of regional integration

The world has witnessed a mushroom growth of economic integration arrangements that have been made with varying degree of commitments in the past few years. Countries that are involved in such economic integration processes expect various benefits out of it.

- Access to country markets: The economic partnership enables the participating countries to go beyond domestic markets. This is particularly true for small countries that want to market its products in other country markets. Access to large market allows companies to achieve economies of scale and greater specialisation in production, thus increasing the competitiveness of their products.
- Internationalisation: It increases the possibilities of local companies to extend operation to different countries and reduce vulnerability of the companies if there is a setback in any specific product market.
- Access to technology: Technology cooperation between the participating countries is possible including the application of newly developed technologies.
- Transaction cost reduction: One of the big benefits that companies of the participating countries can expect is reduction of transaction cost which normally exists in the cross-country transfer of products, especially at the international border. In addition, there are also non-border obstacles present inside the country markets which can easily be crossed through economic co operation of countries.
- Access to path of development: Regional cooperation, at the higher level, in trade, transport and other areas like finance, education, etc., can help

the involved countries to build a development-related agenda addressing the region's priorities jointly. The smaller or weak countries can get a way out to reach their developmental dream in association with larger countries in certain higher level of economic cooperation.

Types of Regional Integration

There are various types of regional economic integrations executed by the countries of the world to derive economic benefits that arise out of such integration. These different types generally require different types of commitments from the involved countries. For example, in its basic form of preferential trading type of arrangement, the commitment from the involved nation will be limited. However, in the economic union type of integration the involvement expected from the member nations will be much higher. The different types of economic integrations, observed to be executed by countries, are described below (Figures 4.1 and 4.2).

Preferential trading agreements (PTA)

This is the most basic type of economic integration. Member countries simply enter in to an agreement to mutually lower tariff rates of a few identified products from one another. It is considered as the first step towards initiating much deeper economic integration process between countries at a later period. Generally, in PTA, involved countries reduce tariffs, but not abolish them completely. However, PTA keeps possibilities open to move to the next stage, i.e., with more preferential access to each other's product at a zero tariff rates.

SAPTA (SAARC Preferential trading Arrangement) is an example of PTA. This PTA was signed in 1994 between SAARC countries (India, Pakistan, Nepal, Sri Lanka, Bangladesh, Bhutan and the Maldives). This arrangement

FIGURE 4.1 The economic partnership agreement

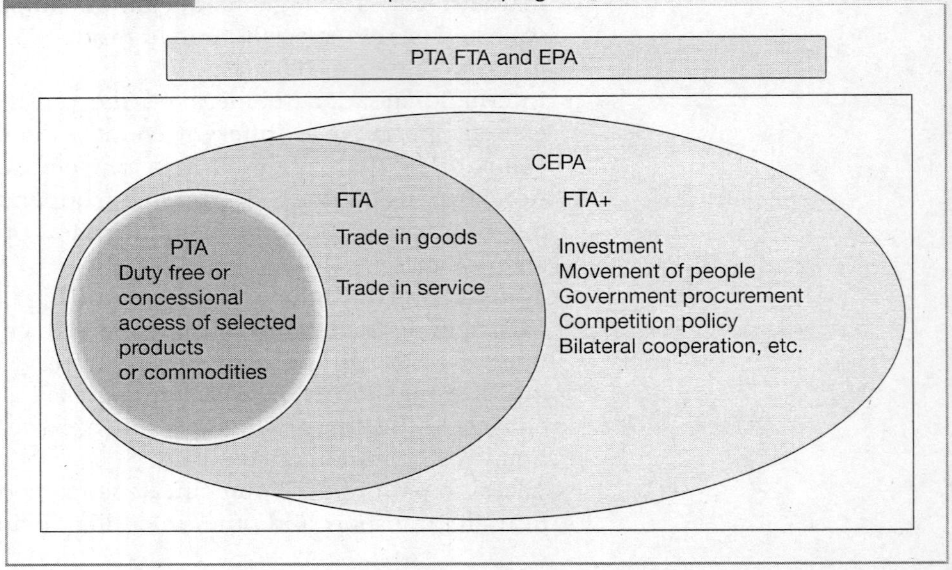

FIGURE 4.2 Customs union, common market and economic union

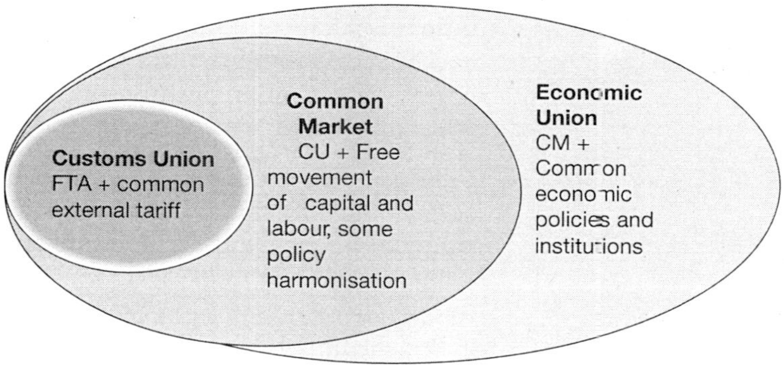

was made to provide tariff concessions to products exchanged between member countries in a reciprocal manner and with mutual advantages of one another so that benefits of integration are equitably availed by all the involved countries. It was decided to give due consideration towards the level of economic and industrial development of the involved countries while deciding on, the tariff policies and systems.

Free Trade Agreement

This is the second step towards economic integration process. A free-trade area (FTA) is signed by member countries to facilitate seamless trade of products, commodities and services by eliminating tariffs and import quotas. The agreement may include a few or many (if not all) goods and services traded between the member countries or prefer a mutually agreed upon list of such goods and services. Generally, free movement of people between countries are not included in FTAs. However, if it is included then it would be considered as an advanced FTA with an open border. But this may happen only when the involved countries show deep desire to be closure to one another and the involved countries' economic structures are complementary.

NAFTA (North American Free Trade Agreement) is an example of FTA. This FTA was signed during 1994, between three countries viz., United States, Canada and Mexico. NAFTA is considered to be one of the most successful FTA in history. This FTA worked out very smothly and hugely contributed to the development of duty-free trade between the three countries. There were noticeable results immediately after execution of the agreement with marked increase in agricultural trade between US and Mexico due to elimination of tariffs on more than fifty percent of Mexico's exports to the US and more than thirty percent of US exports to Mexico. In the post agreement period the involved countries, US – Mexico in particular, were involved in bringing more and more products under the ambit of the agreement. The US–Canada trade also attained a new dimension. The trade between the US and Canada, in course of time, became almost duty free. The major impact in trade dimension between the involved countries came when they made voluntary actions towards elimination of non-tariff trade barriers and strict surveillance for ensuring the intellectual property right of the products. In the side line of this agreement Mexico and Canada further went a step ahead in developing trade intimacy when they executed a separate bilateral NAFTA agreement on market access for agricultural products. The Mexican–Canadian agreement, drafted with similar enthusiasm, also witnessed elimination of most tariffs either immediately or over a period of time.

India and Sri Lanka FTA is another example of this type of economic integration: India and Sri Lanka signed this FTA during 1999. Both the countries, being members to several regional and multilateral organisations such as the South Asian Association for Regional Cooperation (SAARC), South Asia Co-operative Environment Programme, South Asian Economic Union and Bay of Bengal Initiative for Multi-Sectoral Technical and Economic Cooperation (BIMSTEC), aimed to achieve some strategic benefits from the bilateral FTA. The two countries ambitiously included a massive 5112 tariff lines under the preferential treatment on an eight year time period during which the tariffs and non-tariff barriers would be phased out progrssively. The result was found to be encouraging and Indo-Sri Lankan trade rose to USD 2.6 billion in terms of value during 2006 and then to USD $3.4 billion in 2008 which was meager USD 0.55 billion in 1999. Further, in 2011 the trade volume in value terms climed to USD 4.9 billion indicating a continuous journey to the success of FTA. Similarly, India's exports to Sri Lanka went up to USD 4.3 billion during 2011 which was only USD 0.05 billion on the eve of signing the agreement, i.e., year 1999. Encouraged by the growth of trade relation, more closure integrations including corporate investment and ventures in various sectors are being thought off.

Comprehensive Economic Partnership Agreement (CEPA)

CEPA or CECA (Comprehensive Economic Cooperation Agreement, is the third and more comprehensive trade pact between countries with larger in scope and content than just negotiations in the area of trade. Under CEPA the agreement goes beyond traditional tariff focus and additionally includes clauses on the elimination of restrictions on foreign investment, dispute resolution mechanism, and protection of intellectual property rights Therefore, CEPA creates larger markets for the benefit of business organisations who are now facilated to extend operation beyond country border and achieve competitiveness by exploiting economies of scale.CECA or Comprehensive Economic Cooperation is generally considered as the stepping stone for CEPA. CECA mostly deal with reduction or elimination applicable tariffs while CEPA's focus is broader, i.e., it considers not only integration in terms of easy market access but also acceleration of inter-country investments and services.

India-Japan CEPA

India- Japan CEPA is an example of this type of economic integration. The Indo – Japan CEPA was executed during April, 2011 with the ambitious target of elimination of tariffs on 94% of goods over a period of 10 years. It is envisaged that that the CEPA will bring these two Asian countries closer to each other through sustained facilitation of trade and investment between the two nations. From the Indian side, the CEPA was considered to be extremely important for the country as this agreement could open vistas for Indian companys' entry in to lucrative Japanese market. It was expected that in the post agreement period the Indian companies will be able to forge more cross-country business tie up with Japanese companies as result of elimination of almost all the tariffs on industrial products. The India-Japan CEPA would also facilitate Japanese investment in India. More importantly, the trade-in services clause in the agreement may change the level of Indo – Japanese collaboration in the information technology area in the upward direction.

India-Singapore CECA

India–Singapore CECA provides a good example of this particular type of economic partnership model. The CECA was signed during June, 2005 with the intention of bringing the two involved countries closure in terms of trade of goods and services. In addition, a bilateral agreement on the matter of bilateral investment promotion and cooperation in the areas of mutual interest were also executed. The two countries agreed to take measures to avoid double taxation, granting of mutual recognition of quality certificates issued by the involved countries, liberalising visa rules, facilitating easy movement of professionals, fixing modalities of frequent customs interactions at different levels, simplifying dispute settlement procedure and installing mechanism to safe guard intellectual property rights, etc.

Customs union

Customs union (CU) is the next level of integration which is similar to FTA or CECA or CECA but in addition, the member countries of the CU agree to frame harmonised and common trade policies which will be applied by the member countries to all non-member countries. This clause in CU make the involved countries, covered in this type of agreements, much more united and therefore, fight for achieving common interests in the matter of cross border trade and enhancing economic efficiency. Since external policies are jointly decided so the involved countries almost in a designed way establish closer political and cultural ties. In CU, therefore, the member countries mutually agree on a common tariff schedule, decide on non-tariff barriers in a participative way and actively apply them while importing from non-member countries. Since the member countries use common tariff so in practice the markets of the involved countries behave as common market for the exporters dealing with the customs union. On the negative side of CU, the member countries of a customs union keep on fighting amongst themselves while finalising a common tariff keeping the interest of all the participating countries intact. So, it takes long time to establish a CU. After forming of CU, the comparatively smaller countries complain about not getting equal opportunity to get their interest represented. In addition, the member countries go through a long process of negotiations to develop consensus about an acceptable way to share the benefits of integration equally through acceptable means.

Salient features of a C.U

- A common and mutually agreed upon external tariff (import duty) rates for all the countries included in the CU. The CU members would applied these rates while importing goods from countries outside the CU.
- Duty-free and quota-free trading of goods among the member countries.
- A set of common uniform rules in terms of phyto-sanitary requirements, food safety standards, rules of origin, etc., for regulating the importation of goods from third parties.
- An uniform customs rule and procedure for the all the countries under CU.
- A common harmonised system of tariff nomenclature and description of tradable goods for the CU as whole.
- A common customs valuation method for tariff duty calculations.
- A common central administrative body with adequate representation of member countries for management of the CU.
- A common trade policy, jointly decided and reviewed from time to time, for the member countries for carrying out trade with non member countries outside the customs union,

East African Community Customs Union

East African Community (EAC) is an example of Customs Union. This CU has five member countries, namely, Kenya, Tanzania, Uganda, Burundi and Rwanda. The CU was originally formed in 1967 by three East African countries – Kenya, Uganda and Tanzania but it collapsed within ten years. However, during the year 1999 Tanzania snapped its relationship with another CU, i.e., common market for Eastern and Southern Africa (COMESA) in 1999 and rejoined EAC to strengthen its existence. The CU was further strengthened, two more African countries Rwanda and Burundi joined it in 2007. In its new form, removed all internal tariffs between member countries and initiated a five-year long process to establish common external tariff for the CU. The EAC secretariat at Arusha, Tanzania, finally established a three-band common external tariff (CET) with a minimum rate of 0%, a middle rate of 10% and a maximum rate of 25% for external trade with the non-member countries. The EAC secretariat at Arisha took up a number of initiatives to make the regional grouping in line with the characteristics of an ideal CU. For example, it establishes a common customs administration mechanism for EAC, harmonised trade documentation system and customs procedures, drafted policy for promotion of exports from the member states, and systemised the procedure for trade statistics collection and dissemination system. It introduced a common East African passport which allowed the citizens of its member states to freely visit any place within the EAC. For movement of goods across member states it introduced interstate passes and harmonised vehicle transit procedures.

Southern African Customs Union

The Southern African Customs Union (SACU) is the world's oldest customs union, established way back in 1910. It has five member countries viz., Botswana, Lesotho, Namibia, South Africa, and Swaziland. The SACU Secretariat is located in Windhoek, Namibia. SACU, after its formation, initiated measures to eliminate tariffs and other barriers substantially between the member states for easy movement of goods. SACU successfully fixed a common external tariff for trading of goods with non-member countries. Though the secretariat was located in Namibia but during the initial years the CU was led by and administered by South Africa, being the economically strong country in the group. As a customs union, SACU adopted a formula for sharing revenue from the collected duties on imports from non-member countries. The member countries sat together to address the various contentious issues to cropped up in course of time and a new agreement was executed in 2002 by the member countries to provide the CU a modern look.

GCC Customs Union

The Gulf Cooperation Council (GCC) was founded on 26 May 1981 by six middle east countries like Saudi Arabia, Kuwait, Bahrain, Qatar, the United Arab Emirates and the Sultanate of Oman. GCC countries came quickly close to each other because of common culture. All GCC countries are Islamic states with all countries having a significant economic dependence on oil exploration business, especially in respect of Kuwait, Saudi Arabia, Abu Dhabi and in the UAE. In the recent times, Saudi Arabia is pushing hard to make the GCC customs union a more meaningful co-operation amongst the member countries but failed to gather enough support from all its member states, especially from the Sultanate of Oman.

Common Market

A common market (CM) is an advancement of customs union where the member countries agree to the provisions of free movement of two basic resources of production, i.e., labour, and capital within the jurisdiction of member countries in order to achieve regional production efficiency. In addition, CM has all the characteristics of CU. Hence, a CM endeavours to affect significant policy harmonisation across member countries for facilitating free movement of labour and capital within the CM area. Therefore, a common market, in its successful form, has increased economic interdependence amongst the member states. There would be marked harmonisation of fiscal and monetary policies within the region because of the inherent requirements of economic interdependence. As a result almost seamless mobility of labour and capital amongst the member states supported by efficient allocation of resources in the production sector could be noticed in a CM. So, any small member nation, once admitted to a vibrant CM, has the possibilities of stepping in into a big league of united member nations striving for achieving economic efficiency.

MERCOSUR

MERCOSUR (the Common Market of the South), made up of four member states viz., Argentina, Brazil, Paraguay and Uruguay, is an excellent example of CM. Argentina and Brazil led the move towards formation of the common market during 1991 and continued to act as the nucleus of this group. Venezuela entered the CM and got full membership during 2012 and thus making this CM as the largest trade bloc of this kind in South America.

The founding agreement between the four member countries, popularly known as the Treaty of Asuncion, and later (1994) amended and updated version the Treaty of Ouro Preto laid down the aims and objectives of the CM. The aim set for the CM was to achieve regional economic integration through free flow of goods and services, establishment of a common external tariff, adoption of a common trade policy and coordination between the macroeconomic and sectorial policies of the member states. The CM strictly follows the founding aims of the trade block and even suspended Paraguay in June, 2012 following the violation of certain principles of MERCOSUR. The headquarters of this bloc is located in Montevideo, the capital of Uruguay, and the official languages are Portuguese and Spanish. Attracted with the success of MERCOSUR five countries like Chile, Bolivia, Ecuador, Peru and Columbia applied for membership of the CM. These five countries were allowed, in a phase manner, to be the associated members of MERCOSUR and enjoy preferential tariff benefits. In order to make the CM vibrant one, it executed numerous trade agreements with various other successful trade blocks such as NAFTA and DR CAFTA (The DR-CAFTA is a trade agreement between the United States and the countries of Costa Rica, Dominican Republic, El Salvador, Guatemala, Honduras, and Nicaragua. This Agreement is currently in force. As per this agreement, consumer and industrial goods exports from USA to the CAFTA-DR countries have zero tariff from 2015 and tariff duty on agricultural products will be phased out by 2020.), etc., and actively pursued trade linkage development with them.

COMESA

The Common Market for Eastern and Southern Africa (COMESA) is another example of CM. The move to form some kind of economic partnership amongst eastern and southern African countries was initiated during mid-1960s which gained momentum along with the pan-African solidarity mood. The United Nations Economic Commission for Africa (ECA) first mooted the formal proposal during 1965 for a sub-regional economic integration. It helped to shape a sub-regional preferential trade area (PTA) during 1978 but only during 1981 a formal (PTA) agreement was signed by 10 countries like Burundi, Ethiopia, Kenya, Madagascar, Malawi, Mauritius, Rwanda, Somalia, Tanzania, and Zambia. The PTA format took long ten years to finally culminate in to the Common Market for Eastern and Southern Africa or COMESA. An agreement to this effect was signed on 5th November 1993 in Kampala, Uganda, by 16 countries like Burundi, Comoros, Democratic Republic of Congo, Djibouti, Eritrea, Ethiopia, Kenya, Madagascar, Malawi, Mauritius, Rwanda, Sudan, Swaziland, Uganda, Zambia, and Zimbabwe. COMESA has an ambitious plan of forming a Monetary Union, a step towards developing it in to an Economic Union of Africa, by 2018.

The Andean Community

The Andean Community is also an example of CU located in South America. This CU has four member countries like Bolivia, Colombia, Ecuador and P eru. The Andean Community first took the shape of a Free Trade Area (FTA) during 1969 and finally culminated in to a CU during first part of 1995. Venezuela joined the community during 1973 but withdrew itself as two member countries like Peru and Columbia inked a FTA with USA during 2006. For free movement of people across the member countries it created common Andean passport for all four member countries during 2001. Its headquarters is located in Lima, Peru.

Economic Union (EU)

EU is almost the ultimate sort of economic integration people witnessed in this world. In this type of integration, the participating countries go to the extreme of harmonising a number of important policy areas. EU extends itself beyond CU by installing common monetary and fiscal policies, labour market, regional development agenda and transportation and industrial policies. Economic union has common currency for the member states. With the introduction of common currency the member states enjoy the benefit of trading amongst member states without the problem of currency exchange rate fluctuation. This further pushes the growth of trade flow. Cross border businesses get space to expand and flourish in member countries freely by availing the facility of free movement of capital and labour. Since it require harmonisation, co ordination, implementation and monitoring of many common policies across the member states, so the EU must be effectively administered with the help of supranational institutions.

European Union (EU)

The European Union is a unique example of economic union with 28 member states tied in economic and political partnership. This economic union geographically cover much of the European continent. The formation process of EU dates back in post Second World War period when six countries like Belgium, France, Germany, Italy, Luxembourg and the Netherlands began to unite economically and politically. The desire of unification came in to reality when these six countries signed a treaty to run their heavy industries – Coal and Steel Treaty – under a common management during 1951. Benefitted by unification, the first European common market plan was drafted during 1956. In the next year the European Economic Community (EEC), or 'common market' was formed allowing free movements of people, goods and services across the borders. The six country EEC continued to draw unification benefits in trade and commerce until 1973 when three more nations like United Kingdom, Denmark and Ireland joined it to take membership to nine countries. Greece, was found to be desperate to enter the union, but the Commission of the EEC stalled it. Finally, Greece joined the EEC, as its tenth member, only in 1981. Spain and Portugal also became members of the EU in 1973 making the strength to 12 countries. In 1993, EEC came out with a stringent norms in respects of level of democracy, rule of law, human rights, protection of minorities, etc., for the new candidate countries waiting to be member of EEC. In 1995, the Scandinavian countries, Finland and Sweden found to be fulfilled the laid down membership norms and joined the EU. Austria was also maintaining its neutrality during the cold war along with Finland and Sweden but was finally allured by the example of the two Scandinavian countries and became the 15th member of the trade block during 1995. There was no increase in EU's member countries from 1996 to 2003. However, 2004 turned out to be a historic year for EU with ten new countries joining it, taking its size from 15 to 25 members. First three countries were Estonia, Latvia and Lithuania (of former Soviet republics), followed by Poland, the Czech Republic, Hungary and Slovakia (four former satellites of the USSR) and finally three more countries like Slovenia Cyprus and Malta. The new look trade block, popularly named as EU – 25, almost resembled a re-united Europe. EU- 25 was found to be lucrative enough with a 450-million-strong population. Then came the turn of two former communist countries of Central Europe to join EU like Bulgaria and Romania. However, initially they were denied entry on the ground of poor economic and social environment. It was finally during 2007 these two countries were allowed to be the members of EU. During July 2013 Croatia, a country from ex-Yugoslavia, joined the EU to make the tally to 28 member states under EU.

As a result of a part of economic union the member countries are can avail the following benefits:

Barrier-free access: The member states made both the tariff barriers and non-tariff barriers non existent in the matter of trade of product and services across the member countries. This helped the EU companies to market the products and services to a larger market. The rules of origin were set to favour the manufacturing and value addition activities across the member states which incentivised the producers.

Enlarged market: With free movement of man, capital and technology across the member states the producers can set their production location more strategically and market products to a much bigger market than before.

Standard harmonisation: European standards were created to ensure that everyone like the manufacturers, suppliers , consumers and regulators of a particular material, product, process or service follow them. The set standard allowed every stakeholders to clearly know what is expected and therefore lowered the transaction costs and prices.

Streamlining of transport and logistics: EU took maximum efforts for ensuring smooth and efficiency based movement of products and people across the member states. The EU companies took maximum advantage of that and produced world class products and services for marketing across the world.

Other Notable Economic Integration

CARICOM

The Caribbean Community (CARICOM) is a common market now with the participation of 15 Caribbean nations namely Grenada, Guyana, Haiti, Jamaica, Montserrat, Saint Lucia, St. Kitts and Nevis, St. Vincent and the Grenadines, Suriname and Trinidad and Tobago. The initiative to form CATRICOM was take by four Caribean countries namely Barbados, Jamaica, Guyana and Trinidad & Tobago during 1973. The administrative headquarter of CARICOM is located at Georgetown, Guyana.

ASEAN

Association of South-east Asian Nations (ASEAN) in it present format is a common market in the Asian region. It was created in 1967 initially with five member states, namely, Indonesia, Malaysia, Philippines, Singapore and Thailand. Later five more countries, namely, Brunei, Darussalam, Cambodia, Lao PDR, Myanmar, and Vietnam joined to increase the number of member countries to ten. It has ambitious plan to create a customs union by the name ASEAN Customs Union (ACU) first and then finally to an economic union by the name ASEAN Economic Community by 2020.

NAFTA

The North American Free Trade Agreement (NAFTA) is a free trade agreement between three important countries of the world namely USA, Canada and Mexico. It achieved exemplarily success as a trade bloc in the America region. The NAFTA agreement was signed in 1992 and was quickly enforced during 1994. The involved countries felt the need to enhance trade between them by elimination of high barriers existing at that time and as a result the trade volume immediately rose after signing of trade agreement. In addition, NAFTA encouraged companies to consider cross-border investment, which had a particularly positive effect on Canada and Mexico. USA exported its agricultural products to Mexico and Canada while Mexico exported products like beef, corn sweeteners, beans, apples, etc., to USA taking advantage of NAFTA. NAFTA also helped services trade between member countries by eliminating trade barriers in nearly all service sectors.

EFTA

European Free Trade Association or EFTA is an economic partnership agreement signed by seven countries namely Austria, Denmark, Norway, Portugal, Sweden, Switzerland and the United Kingdom. This FTA was initiated during 1960 by the 'outer seven' countries to counter the move to form European Economic Community (present EU). Finland joined the Association in 1961 followed by Iceland in 1970 and Liechtenstein in 1991 making the total strength to ten. However, countries like United Kingdom, Denmark, Portugal Austria, Finland and Sweden left the trade bloc one by one and by 1996 it had only four country members namely Iceland, Liechtenstein, Norway and Switzerland. These four countries are still continuing with the EFTA.

THEORIES OF INTERNATIONAL TRADE

Why does trade take place between countries of different geographic locations? Why should one country, say India, sell its cotton that the other country China will buy? When one strives to find out the answers of these questions the economic rationale of trade becomes apparent. In the above example, the selling nations, i.e., India must have gained from the sale while the buying nations, i.e., China must have realised the gain without suffering economic loss. This two way gaining process is essential to ensure that trade and investment between the countries can continue continuously.

In addition, India as a nation must have enjoyed its comparative better position in terms of resource endowment than not only China but many other countries of the world. This comparative advantage allowed India to make gain from sale of cotton to China. In fact, this comparative advantage acts as root cause of trade between the nations. In general, a country can have comparative advantage over the others in many ways that provide unique benefits in the competitive world. These unique benefits may come from possession of various factors by a country such as resource endowment, skilled labour force, favourable climate it enjoys, arable land it commands, etc. For example, Gabon, a small African country in Western Africa, has huge petroleum deposits, Senegal has phosphate deposits while countries like Singapore, China and South Korea enjoy the comparative advantage of the entrepreneurial orientation of their people.

The Mercantilist View

The mercantilist view provides a sixteenth century explanation towards drives and motives of international trade between nations. According to this view point a country's prosperity depends on its export dominance. Therefore, naturally countries will strive to increase export and minimise its import so as to enhance economic prosperity. This sole desire to enhance economic prosperity will acts as driver for the countries to get involved in trade with other countries. Therefore, in a sense, increase of export will bring prosperity and that prosperity will help the country to increase wealth. As during sixteenth century wealth creation was synonymous with creating stock of gold so countries will engage in trade to increase their gold reserve. With an increase of gold reserve, countries could put themselves in an advantageous position in relation to the others in the matter of financing war, managing adversities as in the case of draught or other natural calamities, etc. However, the mercantilist view was criticised latter and the critiques did not buy the argument that mere possession of gold will bring development to a country. According to them, possession of gold does not enhance the welfare of a people and hence only increase of export may not lead to development. In fact, country should focus attention to increase production efficiency which would allow them to dominate in international trade and thereby earn prosperity. The theory of mercantilism was also discarded by noted economists like Adam Smith and Ricardo on the ground that this theory emphasised on wealth creation out of trade between countries in a very straight jacketed way.

Theory of Absolute Cost Advantage

This the great economist Adam Smith's theory which was propounded by him way back in 1776. This theory revolved round on production advantages of the nations which drives the trade flow. Adam Smith argued that countries would gain from trading if they specialise according to their production advantages. For example consider Country Brazil (B) that has an advantage in producing Goods X and Country China (C) that has an advantage producing in Goods Y

Table 4.5 Labour cost of production (in Hours)

	1 unit of goods X	1 unit of goods Y
Country Brasil	10	30
Country China	30	10

when there is no trade between them (Table 4.5). The country specific advantage mentioned here is purely in terms of cost of production determined by the labour costs required in the production of the respective goods.

The pre-trade exchange ratio in Country Brazil would be 3X = 1Y and in Country China, it would be 1X = 3Y. In this scenario it is evident that Brazil should not produce the product Y and China should not produce the product X. However, Brazil would be benefitted if it confine itself only in producing product X where it has absolute cost advantage in the production while China would be benefitted it produces only Good Y. If one unit of Good X is produced in Brasil it would have consumed 10 hours of labour, that would have costed 30 hours of labour in China. Similarly, if the production of a unit of Good Y costs 30 hours of labour in Brazil, that would cost only 10 hours of labour in Country China. It will be beneficial, therefore, that Brazil and China would be engaged in trading of goods. Brazil would export good X to China and China would export good Y Brazil and both of them will then wisely gain from the trade as they will be able to save hours of labour, i.e., cost. Here, in this theory only one dimensional advantage, i.e., labour cost has been considered but in reality this is not true. In actual setting, it is multi-dimensional as advantages may come up in international trade setting from many factors like economic strength of the country, the force of requirements and the bargaining power.

Theory of Comparative Cost Advantage

The well-known British economist Ricardo put forward this theory of trade in 1817. In the theory of comparative cost advantage, Ricardo fully acknowledged that countries differ in terms of absolute cost advantage as laid down by Adam Smith. However, he was of the opinion that the absolute cost advantage would not be the only factor for countries to involve in trade. Ricardo's view point can be explained with the help of a simple example.

The following table indicates that when India produces 1 tonne of soybean it consumes 80 units of labour while China does so by consuming 240 units of labour. In case of 1 tonne of cotton production, India spends 90 units of labour whereas China spends 180 units for the same amount of production. Now, the question is why do these two countries trade with these two commodities? Table 4.6 reveals that India is comparatively more efficient in producing soybean. It can produce three times as much soybean as China (240/80) with labour cost remaining the same but in case of cotton, it is only two times (180/90) more than China. Therefore from a point of view of country-specific advantage, India must devote its resources in producing soybeans. On the other hand, China should concentrate on producing cotton and import all its soybean requirements from India because of comparative advantage.

Table 4.6 Theory of comparative cost advantage

Country	Labour cost of producing	
	1 ton of soybean	1 ton of cotton
India	80	90
China	240	180

Now, this can be illustrated by computing the opportunity cost of producing soybean and cotton in the following way. The value lost for not taking up an alternative activity is termed as opportunity cost.

If China produces 1 tonne of soybean it foregoes 240/180 = 1.33 tonnes of cotton

If India produces 1 tonne of soybean it fore goes 80/90 = 0.89 tons of cotton

Here, the opportunity cost for not producing 1 tonne of soybean is 1.33 ton of cotton in case of China. However, the opportunity cost for not producing 1 tonne of soybean is 0.89 tons of cotton in the case of India. This implies that opportunity cost is less for India than for China. It is now easy to understand that any country would engage itself where the opportunity cost is comparatively less. Here, in this example, India incurs less opportunity cost than China when it produces 1 tonne of soybean.

Therefore, in a nutshell, this theory was talking about that trade between countries might not take place on the basis of real cost differences of the production in two countries only but the comparative cost differences amongst the countries would decide the trade flow.

The economist Paul Samuelson provided another well-known example in understanding the Ricardo's theory. This example looks like this. Suppose in city of Kolkata the best management teacher Mr Dutta is also to be the best cook of Indian food. Suppose in the city Delhi Mr Rao is considered to be the most productive management teacher as well as equally good cook. However, if Mr Dutta of Kolkata focused on the task of being an management teacher and retained a cook, instead of pursuing both occupations simultaneously, then his fame as teacher would have increased. On the similar note, if Mr Rao concentrated on cooking wholly rather than teaching he would have been prospered more. The result of these changes would be fantastic. When Mr Dutta visiting Delhi he would have been benefitted by Rao's food more and vice versa, i.e., Mr Rao would have been enlightened by Mr Dutta knowledge more while visiting Kolkata.

Factor Endowment Theory

The factor proportion theory marked the beginning of the modern theories of international trade during the 1920s. Eli Heckscher, a Swedish economist, propounded this theory during 1919. But it was written in Swedish and later Bertil Ohlin, a student of Heckscher, worked on the basic model and translated the work into English thirty years later. Bertil Ohlin, in his work, elaborated the factor endowment theory and got Nobel Prize in 1979. The Heckscher–Ohlin theory differentiated the products based on the requirements of labour, capital and natural resources consumed during their production process. It also differentiated countries based on the possession of production factors. According to them a country could be termed as a country with production factor abundance or scarcity only when these production factors are relatively weighted in terms of abundance or scarcity across the factors. Also they are to be weighted across the comparing countries on relative terms and not on absolute terms. This means that one factor is regarded as scarce or abundant in a country in relation to the quantum of other factors as well as in comparison of their availability in the comparing countries. Simplistically speaking, a country can be regarded as richly endowed with capital only if the ratio of capital to the other factors is higher when compared with other countries. The Heckscher–Ohlin theory suggests that a country will do well in producing and thereafter exportation of such products where the production process utilises a relatively large amount of factors with which the country relatively well endowed.

Heckscher–Ohlin's theory makes some assumptions in deciding the international trade flow. The following three assumptions are important.

1. There are two countries involved with two production factors namely labour and capital.
2. Each country produces two commodities or goods (labour intensive and capital intensive).
3. There is exist a perfect competition in both commodity and factor markets.

Limitations of Heckscher-Ohlin's (H-O) theory

- The theory considered on the two factors. Its missed out a very important factor, i.e., transport efficiency as a deciding factor for the ascertaining direction of trade flow. Ohlin's theory also silent about the qualitative difference of the factors of production.
- H–O theory consideration of only a two commodities, two countries and two factors horizon, is too simplification which in real terms will not happen.
- In real life situation, a capital abundant country may export labour-intensive goods because of high demand of such goods in the market. In practical situation the demand of the product plays a deciding role as regards to its production in a country. However, the H-O theory is silent about the role of demand in deciding trade flow.
- The H–O model is static in nature and can not take care of change in factor condition with time. American economist Dr Wassily Leontief, tested H–O theory to find out its accuracy under the conditions prevailing in the USA. He researched out that USA exported labour-intensive goods and imported capital-intensive goods. However, being a capital-abundant country USA must export capital-intensive goods and choose to import labour-intensive goods than to produce them at home. This situation is called Leontief Paradox which negates H–O Theory.

ORGANISATIONS SUPPORTING TRADE

International trade has its impact on economic development of different countries. The exchange of goods, services, and capital among various countries are required so that mutual interdependence can bring out the best of every country which in turn provide synergistic benefits to everybody living in this world. In today's world, no country is completely self- sufficient, and hence, it requires that different countries are involved in exchanging skill, technology, products, services, scarce resources, etc. in a continuous and unrestricted way. However, time and again, flow of international trade got hampered due to different barriers it encountered in the form of government-sponsored restrictions like tariffs, quotas, non-tariff barriers, etc.

Factors like transport and logistics inefficiencies, political risks, knowledge deficiency, etc., are also active in slowing down the momentum of trade between the countries of the world. There are different trade support organisations that are mandated to work round the clock in the international level so that the effect of trade barriers on international trade are minimised, if not totally removed.

World Trade Organisation

The World Trade Organisation (WTO) was created during 15th April, 1995 at Marrakesh in Morocco as important international organisation to ensure smooth and barrier free trade across the countries of the world. The 1948 creation GATT (General Agreement on Tariffs and Trade) preceded WTO. The GATT was mandated to dictate the rules of trade in the entire world. During almost its existence of half a century GATT was somewhat successful in ensuring existence of a strong multinational trading system but many other things were needed to be done. The GATT member countries realised that much more was needed to be done in the context of the multinational trading system getting hugely complex. As a result WTO came up to overhaul the entire system of trade practice. Therefore, the member countries wanted to provide more teeth to WTO so that complex issues can be handled by the newly set up organisation. The notable differences between the GATT and WTO are mentioned below.

- In WTO the signatories are "member countries" where as signatories to the GATT were "contracting parties". The members were expected to play more voluntary role with full understanding of their responsibilities unlike the contractual nature, of job under GATT.
- GATT was merely a provisional legal agreement framed jointly by countries. However, WTO was created as organisation with physical presence of its headquarters in Geneva, Switzerland.
- WTO was given a larger mandate to cover goods, services and intellectual property rights issues as well. Whereas GATT was restricted to deal with only trade in goods.
- GATT was functioning more like a facilitating agency. It was acting as instrument to listen to cases of disputes but without any enforcing power. But WTO was given the power of ruling enforcement was well. It has a dispute settlement system with effective ruling enforcement mechanism.

Ministerial conferences of WTO

The Ministerial Conference is the supreme decision-making body in the WTO. The conference is generally organised once in every two years. Under the banner of the conference all the member country representatives meet in a place to discuss and deliberate on issues pertaining to trade. At the end of the threadbare discussions the Ministerial Conference takes decisions on all matters related to trade. So far, after the origin of WTO there were eight rounds of conferences which are briefly described below.

First conference: The first ministerial conference under WTO banner took place in Singapore during 1996. The issues that were deliberated were popularly known as the "Singapore issues". The Singapore issues basically dealt with four important areas, namely, transparency issues in government procurement, trade facilitation or the customs issues, trade and investment issues, and trade and competition issues. A clear decision on these four important areas could not be arrived at because of disagreements between representatives of developed and developing economies.

Second conference: The second ministerial conference was held at Geneva in Switzerland during May 1988. There were expectations that stalemate issues would be finding an way out but it did not happened. No agreement was reached among the members. Even it could not be finalised whether multilateral trade talks would cover only the Uruguay Round "built-in agenda" or a wider range of issues would be brought in the discussion table. The EU representatives were in favour of a comprehensive Millennium Round, where new issues would be covered. But the developing countries, in general, were of the opinion that existing issues should be covered first before bringing in new issues. The US representatives took a neutral stand on both these aspects but had shown tremendous interest for an agreement on electronic commerce.

Third conference: The third ministerial conference of WTO was held in Seattle, Washington, during November 1999. Not much break through made in the conference. USA and Europe wanted to execute an agreement on agriculture which the developing countries protested for not taking them in to confidence. In addition there were massive demonstrations from different non governmental organisation and situation became chaotic. The conference ended without any concrete result.

Fourth conference: The fourth ministerial conference was held at Doha, Qatar during November 2001. The representatives of member countries agreed launch a new round of discussion known as Doha Development Round. However, major divide was observed between developed and developing nation representatives which made the progress of discussion very slow. European Union, United States, and Japan became the leaders of the developed country group while developing countries were led by Brazil, China, India, South Korea, and South Africa. Issues related to agriculture, industrial tariffs and non-tariff barriers, services and trade remedies were the mostly debated areas but without any conclusive result. Maintenance of agricultural subsidies was also a contentious issue that remained unresolved. The conference also approved the joining of China as the 143rd member of the organisation.

Fifth conference: The fifth ministerial conference was held in Cancun, Mexico during September, 2003. The conference attempted to resolve the contentious issues that surfaced in the Doha round. Again there was tough battle between the developing country alliance and developed country alliance. Brazil, China, India and South Africa were very critical of the move by developed countries on the issues like cross-border investment, competition policies, trade facilitation, and government procurement. Literary threatened by the pressure from developed group of countries a new unification move by the developing, least developed and civil society organisations from around the world could be noticed on the contentious issues in Cancun. They put a is stiff resistance to the attempt of the developed group during the discussions leading to finding a consensus on the so-called "Singapore issues". The third world countries continue its counter pressure to end the agricultural subsidies within the EU and the US and make world a level playing field for the farmers. The standoff continued until the fifth round was closed without progress.

Sixth conference: The sixth WTO ministerial conference was at Hong Kong in December 2005. After the breakdown of the Cancun meet, a hopeless situation emerged where arriving at some agreement at WTO ministerial conference looked almost impossible. Hence, there was an renewed realisation to pave ways for things to move in WTO for greater interest of the world as a whole. Hong Kong conference, therefore, attempted to break the stalemate and settle the unfinished agenda of the Doha Development Round negotiations. Two important decision were made thereafter; one, phasing out all their agricultural export subsidies by the end of 2013 and two, abolition of subsidies to cotton exporters by 2006. However, the third world countries reiterated their demand on removal of high domestic subsidies in agriculture by the developed countries in addition to the abolition direct export subsidies already agreed upon. Regarding tariff reduction the developing countries agreed to adopt the Swiss formula to cut industrial tariffs. Swiss formula is a simple mathematical formula, basically introduced by the Swiss team to WTO, which can be used to cut and harmonise tariff rates. The linear Swiss formula reduces the high and low tariff at the same percentage rate while non linear one discriminate between high and low tariff rate. An agreement was reached in the matter of allowing entry of duty free, tariff free goods from the least developed countries (LDC) to the developed one. There was a great deal of negotiations in the context of Non-agricultural Market Access (NAMA) which basically began during 2002. NAMA deals with all products that are not covered by the agriculture negotiations or the services negotiations.

Seventh conference: The seventh WTO ministerial conference was held in Geneva during 30 November – 3 December 2009. The conference was serious about trade reforms in the services sector and wanted to deliberate on the issues related to trade rules and trade facilitations in services. The conference in principle agreed to the requirements of allowing duty-free, quota-free market access of products (like cotton etc.) and services from the least developed countries of the world to the developed world. There was discussion on mushroom growth of bilateral and regional trade agreements between various countries and the forum agreed on the point that these regional trade blocks must complement each other.

Eighth conference: The eighth ministerial conference of WTO was held in Geneva, Switzerland, from 15 to 17 December 2011. However, though the 153-member country representatives looked serious to proceed with solving the contentious issues but could not make much concrete moves forward. The US and China fought over a bilateral issue related to levying

Box 4.4 WTO in action: The Shrimp-Turtle Case

Mexico has a huge coastal line of 8475 km along pacific ocean and 3294 km along Atlantic ocean. On the Atlantic side as well as on the Pacific side there are at least 21 commercially important varieties of shrimps available. However, throughout the entire coastal line shrimp distribution is uneven due to natural reasons and, in general, commercial fishing is more active in the east coast than the west coast. A large chunk of Mexican population lives on shrimp fishing. They get a very readymade lucrative market nearby and off load the product in bordering US markets. Mexico, knowing well the importance of US market to them, complied with the standard set by the United States National Marine Fisheries Service (NMFS) regarding the use of TEDs (Turtle Excluder Devices) while shrimp fishing. The Mexican shrimp exports were, therefore, free from any possible embargo by US for the catch. However, during 1998, US Government restricted imports from Mexico on the ground that shrimps were caught by trawler without TEDs. The restriction was very much damaging for Mexico as many fishermen were set to lose their livelihood. Detailed enquiry revealed that the poor fishermen might simply had not enough money to use fishing nets with TEDs as one such trap door fitted net costed more than the yearly income of a fisherman. The US ban on Mexican exports alarmed many other shrimp exporting countries to US including India, Pakistan, Malaysia and Thailand. These four governments challenged the US ban in the floor of WTO by arguing that the US could not apply its laws to foreign process and production methods. Also in earlier occasions the US government subsidised TED fitted nets for the US fishermen under the pressure from environmentalist groups. Therefore, attempt to restrict imports from Mexico was discriminatory in nature. The Shrimp–Turtle case was heard by the WTO Appellate Body in 1998 and found that United States discriminated between countries by providing "financial and technical assistance," to some fishermen to exclusively of a country but not all countries. According to them this was a clear case of discrimination and hence ruled against the United States. But later in 2001 US corrected the discrimination observed in this case by discontinuing the TED subsidisation process. Now, WTO appellate body observed the US law actually encouraged other countries to adopt sea turtle conservation programs and was thus a measure relating to conservation only and rejected the arguments made by the complainants in the matter of discrimination. The final verdict in favour of USA had significant ramification as the WTO permitted the US to restrict an import based on its production process (catching of shrimp) and not the product (shrimp) itself. In this particular aspect WTO opined that sea turtles were migratory enough to classify them to be belonged to certain ocean only and hence fell outside the scope of Article XX (g). The WTO also observed that turtles were really "exhaustible natural resources" and any attempt, overtly or covertly, to cause damage to them contradicted the preamble of the 1994 WTO agreement regarding ensuring sustainable development. Having observed these, the WTO corrected its earlier decision when found US actions were not discriminatory.

punitive duties on large cars and SUVs exported by USA to China. The conference approved the inclusion of Russia, Samoa and Montenegro in the WTO fold.

Ninth conference: The ninth ministerial conference of WTO was held in Bali, Indonesia during 3-7 December 2013 which saw the member countries broadly agreeing to 'Bali Package'. The package had altogether four core areas (trade facilitation, agriculture, cotton and least developing country development) and seven decision points. Out of the seven, the most important one was that developed countries agreed to abolish import quota on agriculture import from developing world. The second important one was that of streamlining customs operation by removing bureaucracies.

United Nations Conference on Trade and Development (UNCTAD)

UNCTAD is an United Nation's agency mandated to work for economic and social development of the third world countries in particular through trade and investment. The UNCTAD was established during 1964 with the objective of facilitating the trade, investment and development opportunities of developing countries. For the purpose of achieving its objectives the organisation acted as the permanent intergovernmental body of the United Nations in the matter of trade, investment, and development issues of the developing countries. The headquarters of UNCTAD is located in Geneva, Switzerland, and it has 194 member States. UNCTAD, in periodic interval, organises seminars and conferences for highlighting and deliberating on issues related to trade and economic development of the developing countries. It strengthens the research capacity of the member countries, organises capacity development training and renders policy advice on issues related to trade, aid, transport, finance and technology. Some important initiatives of UNCTAD are briefly discussed below.[6]

Generalised System of Preferences (1968)

The Generalised System of Preferences or GSP was the brainchild of the first Secretary General of UNCTAD to provide easy access of goods produced in developing or least developing countries to the developed country markets. The modalities of GSP proposal was placed in the first UNCTAD conference in 1964 for deliberations. Looking at the overwhelming response of the third world countries it was accepted in the second conference held at New Delhi in 1968. Under the GSP scheme, the developed countries agreed to levy either reduced or zero tariff to the products produced in the developing and least developing countries. For example, Indian handicraft products will have access to German market at zero percent import duty under the GSP scheme.

International Commodities Agreements (ICA)

ICA facilitates a number of countries producing or dealing a particular commodity to come together and jointly agree to a particular norms of trade. The norms of trade set under ICA includes commodity pricing system to be followed, quality standard applicable in trade, quantity to be brought in to trade, etc., deemed fit by the participating countries in order to stabilise the international trade with respect to particular commodity. The system works on the consensus developed between the countries participating in the ICA. For example, UNCTAD successfully facilitated the international Coffee Agreement.

Research and Dissemination

UNCTAD strengthens trade research in number of developing countries and hand hold the local researchers in producing world class reports. A number of such reports like The Trade and Development Report, The Trade

[6] For more details see http://unctad.org/en/Pages/Publications.aspx

and Environment Review, The World Investment Report, The Economic Development in Africa Report and The Least Developed Countries Report are contributing to the latest understanding towards trade and development.

UNCTAD Statistics: Being a part of United Nations UNCTAD has access to trade data of the countries of the world. Also UNCTAD by itself compiles data from various sources, uses trade data in conducting state of the art trade research and endeavour to provide raw data for the use of the researchers around the world. UNCTAD collaborated with International Trade Centre (ITC) and World Trade Organisaton (WTO) in providing raw trade data to the researcher through the website www.trademap.org.

IMF and World Bank

The IMF (International Monetary Fund) and the World Bank are the two pivotal organisations of the world. These two organisations, formed in 1944 , were entrusted with the responsibility of managing global financial system and making monetary resources available on loan basis to the countries in need of them. In addition to the lending support to the nations the banks provide effective policy and technical supports. The Bretton Woods conference recommended the formation of these two organisations for speedy development of the 184 member countries in the post world war era. While granting loans these two organisation differ on the loaning characteristics. The IMF collects membership contributions and disburse the same to the needy countries generally on short and medium term. On the contrary, World Bank almost act as investment banker and collect deposits from different countries, corporations or individuals against issuance of bonds or membership fees for loaning the collected amount to the needy countries usually on a long term basis. However, while loaning to the countries both of them follow a single criteria, i.e., the loan amount must be used for development of the countries, say for infrastructure development, ailing public sector privatisation, curtailment of undue subsidies, installation of free trade regime, building efficiency in the power sector, etc. In addition, both the organisations have a developed a package of support services for particularly the poor countries of the world. Management consultation (MC), staff collaboration (SC), special assistance scheme (SSS), poverty reduction programmes (PRP), millennium development goal achieving (MDG) services are some of them. Under MC, the banks depute their consultancy team to the countries who in turn use the service of the team in achieving a breakthrough of the problems faced. Under SC the banks voluntarily depute their experts to the loan receiving countries who in turn collaborates with the real-time ground condition in order to ensure smooth and effective utilisation of the loan amount. Under SSS the banks render voluntary services to the heavily indebted poor countries and allow these countries to set their home in order through enforcing fiscal discipline and reducing heavy debt burden on the economy. PRP is a special programme of both the banks directed towards poverty elimination in the member countries. Under this programme the banks endeavor support poor countries developing effective linkage between national policies, donor support, and periodic outcome assessment. Under MDG scheme the banks have single agenda of equipping the member countries to actively prepare themselves so that the United Nations' Millennium Development Goals could be achieved by them.

Asian Development Bank

The Asian Development Bank (ADB) came to existence during 1966 when necessity was felt to have an exclusive multilateral development financial institution for the Asian and Pacific countries. ADB, after its birth, is actively engaged in rendering its support services to promote economic and social development primarily in the designated region. The bank has its headquarter located in Manila, Philippines. Like IMF or World Bank, ADB also extends loans and technical assistance to its 67 member countries. Out of the total members 48 are from the designated region and 19 from other parts of the globe. In search of achieving its mandate of promoting economic and social development in the target region, the Bank extends grants, loans, and guarantees for the projects which are aligned with its mandated objectives. In order to guide the financially supported countries though the right way, the bank uses monitoring and evaluation (M&E) approach. Under M&E approach the bank first ratify the path envisaged to achieve the desired outcome and then realign them if required, understand the outcome and correct deviations, if any. There could be two types of M& E process for the developmental projects funded by ADB: independent and self-evaluation. Depending upon the criticality in the projects under consideration ADB enforces either of the two options. Under independent evaluation process ADB involves its Independent Evaluation Department (IED) in the projects and make all-round efforts to transfer latest and updated knowledge to the policy makers, designers, and implementers of the project. Under the self evaluation approach ADB involves its concerned operation department to design and implement country strategies.

FOREIGN EXCHANGE AND EXCHANGE MARKET

The countries of the world exchange their financial resource while getting involved in trade (export and import). While exporting, a country invites inflow of financial resources from another country, whereas importing allows financial resource to flow out of the country. The export dependent country like China earns a stockpile of foreign currency and builds its foreign exchange reserves. On the other hand, Burundi, a small country Africa, is an import dependent country which allows financial resources to out flow from the country. Table 4.7 below indicates the 11 best performing countries of the world that have created impressive forex reserves.

As revealed from the above table countries like China, India, Switzerland, Hong Kong, etc., are increasing the forex reserve while some like Russia, Saudi Arabia, etc., are losing it. Countries with depleted forex levels feel the agony of depletion while nations that have gained forex levels become cheerful of their increased exchange reserves. The cheerful countries know that in case of an national emergency, these reserves are an extremely good source of wealth to fall back upon. Not only through export but foreign exchange

Table 4.7 Best performing countries of the world in terms of Forex reserve

Rank	Country	Foreign exchange reserves (Millions of US$) as of	Foreign exchange reserves (Millions of US$) as of
1	China	30,00,000, Jun 2012	38,99,285, Dec 2014
2	Japan	12,72,777, Jul 2012	12,50,073, April, 2015
3	Saudi Arabia	989,592, May 2012	686,431, April 2015
4	Russia	510,543, Jul 2012	360,500, May 2015
5	Switzerland	446,005, Jun 2012	582,487, March 2015
6	Taiwan	391,110, Jul 2012	419,608, March 2015
7	Brazil	376,153, Jul 2012	364,473, April, 2015
8	Republic of Korea	312,378, Jun 2012	369,900, April, 2015
9	Hong Kong	294,957, Jun 2012	343,213, April, 2015
10	India	289,737, Jun 2012	351,557, May, 2015
11	Singapore	243,383, Jun 2012	251,921, April 2015

Source: Foreign exchange reserve, IMF data

can come to a country in the form of foreign investments, loans and bilateral aid among other things. The countries while striving for earning foreign reserve build up also require to spend them while making payments for imports, payment of interest, repayment of loans and repatriation of investments and profits. The difference bewteen incoming and outgoing builds up the reserves for a country.

Foreign Currency

It is natural that countries will have their own national currencies. India has Rupee, USA has the USD, China has Renminbi, Thailand has Bhat, etc. However, there are about 50 such countries that do not have their own currency but utilise those of others. For example, some small countries like Andorra, Kosovo, Monaco, Montenegro, San Marino, and Vatican City do not have their own currency but use Euro of European Union though they do not belong to Euro zone. Some countries use a common currency because of some sort of economic integration. For example, fourteen countries like Benin, Burkina Faso, Cote d'Ivoire, Guinea-Bissau, Mali, Niger, Senegal, Togo, Cameroon, Central African Republic, Chad, Republic of the Congo, Equatorial Guinea, and Gabon decided to have CFA Franc as their own currency. Zimbabwe had its own currency up till 2009 but now accept currency of Botswana, South Africa, UK, and US.

USD US Dollar	NZD - New Zealand Dollar
GBP British Pound	MYR - Malaysian Ringgit
INR Indian Rupee	EUR - Euro
AUD Australian Dollar	NZD - New Zealand Dollar
CAD Canadian Dollar	MYR - Malaysian Ringgit
AED Emirati Dirham	THB - Thai Baht
CHF Swiss Franc	JPY - Japanese Yen
CNY Chinese Yuan Renminbi	PHP - Philippine Peso

Now, the currencies of the countries may have its differences in terms of convertibility. A convertible currency can readily be exchanged for other currencies while the non convertible currency can be exchanged. Some currency may also qualitatively differs with other in terms of ease of ease of convertibility. The easily convertible currencies are characteristically strong and stable and therefore other countries find no problem in accepting them readily. For example, the USD is the most convertible currency as it readily acceptable by any country of the world. Japanese Yen, British Pound and Euro are also examples of a currency that is fully convertible. However, there are many countries whose currencies are non-convertible. For example, the respective currencies of Russia, China, Brazil and India are much less convertible than USD. The more a currency non convertible more will be the problem for international trade. Yuan, the Chinese currency, is a case of strong currency but lack full convertibility. The Chinese government execises strict controls on the currency which makes it difficulty to covert in to other currencies and vice versa. For strategic reasons the Chinese central bank shows tendency to buy whatever foreign currency flows in into the country and exchanges them to Yuan to keep the Yuan away from rising against the dollar.

Currency exchange and exchange rate

Suppose, Mr Ramesh of India exported tea to the US and New Zealand and after the exportation realised the value for the tea remitted by the respective importers in USD and New Zealand dollar respectively. Now, how much USD the Indian exporter realised? Similarly, how much New Zealand Dollar was deposited by the New Zealand importer to the bank account of Indian exporter? Who decided these? Would the same amount be paid if the Indian exporter repeats the export after say, six months? The answer lies in the price of the exporter's currency, i.e., Indian rupees expressed in the importer's currency, say, in USD or in the New Zealand Dollar. Again, the price equivalent of one currency expressed in another, i.e., the exchange rate does not remain the same over time as it is evident from the Table 4.8.

Table 4.8 Exchange rate for the Indian rupee against a sample of currencies

Indian rupee	Currency per 1.00 INR as on 23.08.2012	INR per unit of currency as on 23.08.2012	INR per unit of currency as on 02.05.2015
Euro	0.014427	69.313595	70.998
US Dollar	0.018130	55.156096	63.756
British Pound	0.011402	87.703519	97.703
Australian Dollar	0.017227	58.047749	49.433
Canadian Dollar	0.017927	55.780467	51.266
Emirati Dirham	0.066593	15.016602	17.358
Swiss Franc	0.017329	57.706018	68.201
Chinese Yuan Renminbi	0.115153	8.684094	10.286
Malaysian Ringgit	0.056138	17.813321	17.280
New Zealand Dollar	0.022172	45.102372	45.671

Source: X – rates.com

Therefore, the exporter is required to use the currency exchange rate prevailing at the time of transaction execution to know the exact value the export will fetch. In addition, the exporter will also needs to assess the possible fluctuation of the exchange rate as this may increase or decrease the sale proceed. If the Indian rupee value appreciates against the USD, it would mean that the dollar is now cheaper than what it used to be earlier. For example, INR - USD exchange rate was 65 INR = 1 USD during January , 2015 and now on May 2015 the exachage rate is 55 INR = 1 USD. This means that Indian rupee has appreciated against USD. It may not be good for the Indian exporter as for export proceed of 100 USD he will get now 550 INR. On the other hand if rupee value depreciates against the USD after a year, the Indian exporter would stand to gain from the transaction. Previously he expected to get 550 INR for 100 USD transaction but now he will get 650 INR against 100 USD sale proceed. This is depicted in Table 4.9 for a sample export value of USD 2000.

Now, how does the appreciation or depreciation of a currency affect the trade, i.e., both export and import? Consider, Mr Ramesh as an Indian importer importing textile machinery which costs $1000 from the US Let us assume that Ramesh had to pay the US exporter ₹50,000 ($1 = ₹50) to buy the machinery. Ramesh felt the need of importing the same machinery just after one when INR appreciated with exchange rate standing at ($1 = ₹40). Now Ramesh paid 40,000 to buy the same machinery and was very happy. However, after another month, he imported the same machinery when the rupee had depreciated against dollar ($1 = ₹60). So Ramesh had to pay ₹60,000 this time.

Now, think of the Indian exporter Mr Shyam exporting machinery to the US at $2000 and getting paid in dollars. So, Shyam would receive an amount equivalent to ₹10,000 as per the basic prevailing exchange rate ($1 = ₹50). However, while executing the second order, the rupee had appreciated against the Dollar ($1 = ₹40) and hence, the rupee proceeds from the transaction would be ₹8000. But if the rupee had depreciated ($1 = ₹60) the same exporter would have got ₹12,000 from the deal. Therefore, exporting companies continues to demand the government for control of the appreciating rupee. A countries with huge export proficiency would naturally not desire that their local currency appreciates against the USD. The same is the case with China where companies are against the appreciating Yuan against the USD.

Table 4.9 INR appreciation or depreciation effect

Rupee–US dollar base exchange rate	Rupee value appreciates against the US dollar after a month	Rupee value depreciates against the US dollar after a year
Export value in USD: 2000	Export value in USD: 2000	Export value in USD: 2000
Exchange rate $1~₹50	Exchange rate $1~₹40	Exchange rate $1~₹60
Exporter will get INR 10,000	Exporter will get INR 8000	Exporter will get INR 12,000

Foreign Exchange Market

In the world of many country-specific currencies there is a genuine requirement of establishing a specific system towards acceptability of each other's currencies. This is required because countries are involved in exchanging good and services, human movement across different countries, purchasing of another country property, etc. But for all these things to happen it requires that the country or the individual, or the company, as the case may be, is in a position to buy the currency of another country first. The foreign exchange market addresses the issue of availability of the necessary currency with a built-up exchange mechanism. The foreign exchange market is essentially a market where currencies of different countries are bought and sold. In a practical sense, the foreign exchange market function like an 'over the counter' (OTC) market. It is more like an informal system operating without any specific physical place where the participants, say individuals, bankers, brokers, etc., meet to settle their deals. The physical location of such places could be a finance centre, exchange counters having facilities to meet, communicate and exchange information with the help of telecommunication system like telephone, fax, computer with internet facility. The Society for Worldwide Interbank Financial Telecommunication popularly known as SWIFT provides a wonderful platform for exchanging financial transaction related information on a regular basis. SWIFT communication network facilitates more than 9000 financial institutions in 209 countries worldwide to send and receive information about financial transactions in a safe and standardised way. The SWIFT network is highly used by different country users and it was estimated that in a single day the number of the transactions generally exceeds $5 trillion It is used by traders, commercial banks, post offices , central banks, institutional investors, currency speculators, corporations, governments, other financial institutions and retail investors for generating messages effecting money transfer.

Table 4.10 Exchange rate between INR/USD/EUR

Year	Average USD/INR	Average EUR/INR
2014	61.013055	81.0339112
2012	52.905811	67.732711
2011	46.659403	64.871760
2010	45.712259	60.611361
2009	48.362283	67.343146
2008	43.461696	63.624028
2007	41.210051	56.403761
2006	45.251373	56.842993
2005	44.046621	54.811882
2004	45.251080	56.237604
2003	46.648882	52.720717
2002	48.539477	45.887973

Source: Compiled from different internet sources

Exchange rate

The USD–Indian rupee exchange rate is getting changed significantly in recent times. The same is true for most of the other currencies as well. In particular, Indian rupee had a significant fall against the USD in the past 10 years period. In the year 2002, the Indian rupee used to be traded at about ₹48 to a dollar. During 2007, the average exchange rate was ₹41 to a USD. By 2012, one required about ₹52 to purchase a USD which went up to ₹63 during 2014 (See Table 4.10). It is not difficult to understand the business implications of these huge fluctuation of transaction rate. As the rupee continued to get weaker the imports bill of the companies also had risen. The Indian companies who depended on the imported raw material found it tough to run businesses profitably. Higher cost of production did not allow them to compete with other countries pricewise whose currencies arrested currency depreciation faster. Government of India also suffered as its import bill of crude oil continued to be fatter as the country depends on imported crude oil heavily. A weak rupee also influenced the transportation sector cost and industry as a whole.

Now, how are these exchange rates are determined every time? Ideally speaking , the exchange rate is the function of demand of the particular currency and supply of the same at a particular time in the market. If the demand for a particular currency is more and its supply is less, there will be a hike in the price of that currency. Similarly, less demand for a currency in an excess supply condition will lower the price of the currency. For example, suppose US made products, in general, become hot favourite for the Indians and a large number of Indian are after buying American products like fast food, laptops, I phones, etc. The suppliers of these product in India will rush to have more USD to buy product from USA and make them available in India. This means that the total expenditure by the Indian people outside US would create a demand of USD rise. What would be the status of the supply of US currency in India at that time? In a short supply situation coupled with an increased demand condition, the USD will become expensive for the Indians. The reverse is also true. That is, in an excess supply situation coupled with decreased demand condition, the USD will become cheaper. However, the foregoing explanation is a very simplistic explanation of exchange rate determination. In practical terms the following factors, in a complex combination, influence the demand of a particular currency and the exchange rate thereof.

Economic factors: This is a very important factor influencing the exchange rate of a particular currency. A country's economic progress is directly proportional with the increasing volume of economic transactions. To sustain higher rate of economic transactions the country will require more money supply in the market and hence there will be an environment of demand created for the particular currency. At this juncture it is to be seen what role the central bank of the country plays. It may be the attempt of the bank to restrict money supply in the market and allow the demand to build up more. The central bank may act in this particular way because of monetary policy it has adopted for the coutry. With the increase of interest rates the assets denominated in that currency will give more yield. This, in turn, will create increasing demand of the currency both internally and externally. Investors of home country and abroad will be in need of money for the purpose of investment. The value of the currency in question will also go up by the process. However, it may be noted that if central bank restricts money supply to the economy by increasing the interest rate where the demand is fast increasing, it would lead to inflation. This inflation is inflicted in the economy by high interest rate imposed by the central bank. The producers of goods and services will be asking more prices from the consumers to cover their higher cost of capital. At this juncture it will be interesting to see the impact of the situation on the exchange rate. With high interest rate the buying power of the people will be somewhat reduced and hence less money supply in the economy. However, since the economy is still hot there will be continuing production of products and services, although they are highly priced. In such situation, the demands for the currency will be high as many people still have the hunger to buy products or services and for that they want to have currency. There will demand for currency from the investors to take advantage of higher yield on investment. This will create a scenario towards the possibility of currency appreciation in the exchange rate market.

Market psychology: This is another important factor influencing the currency exchange rate. The super Forex trading trio of the world, Deutsche bank, UBS AG, and Barclays Capital will be as usual busy in handling about 4 trillion USD turn-over per day. These transactions are mostly happening in London exchange centre (about 40% of the total), followed by New York, Tokyo, Hong Kong and Singapore. Different trading slots are created in a day like Asian trading session, the European session and North American session coming one after another for better addressing to the regional needs. In every slot news and rumours run high about the regional problems and prospects. Experts further tries to built up the understanding of the forex traders by supplying news and views about a country, its economic development policy, role of central bank, sectoral outlook, etc. Interestingly, expectations and perception of the traders about a country build up in the process and the traders react accordingly during actual transaction sessions. Favourable news about important developmental parameters help to create the right perception in traders and enhance their confidence in the nation's economy and currency, leading to aggressive buying of that country's currency in exchange for others. Similarly, mood will be dampened because of continuous inflow of bad economic news coming from a country. First, in such situation, traders' confidence on the country will be eroded and second the traders will be cautious in taking risk and hence play safe. For example, a series of remarks by American president on Indian dwindled the traders' confidence. "It is still too hard to invest in India. In too many sectors such as retail, India limits or prohibits the foreign investment" or "Bade Bade Deshon Mein Aisi Choti Choti Baatein Hoti Rehti Hai. ..."types of observations by American president raised concerns over "problematic" investment climate in India in the recent times. The market psychology, therefore, was not in favour of India. The result was as expected. Indian currency traded nearing the all-time bad rate of about ₹64 per USD.

Political stability: Forex market has always a standard perception of political ucertainity in developing and least developing country. Many small African countries are also demonstrating that they are highly politically vulnerable. Forex market always very sensitive towards political disturbances in a country. The political situation in a country can affect the exchange rate in short, medium and long term. Political instability or turmoil not only disturbs the business environment but also the country's economy as a whole. Successful projection as a country devoid any political risk and uncertainty will help to build up correct impression of growth potential and hence forex market will react favourably to it. When the BJP came to power with a thumping majority it did indicate political stability and in the initial period of BJP forming government the currency exchange rate reacted favorably. Russia is perceived to be a country of continuous political unrest till today and hence the currency Rouble is facing very bad days so far as exchange rate is concerned.

Trade Financing

Trade finance includes activities related to the financial requirements of international trade like letter of credit, working capital credit related to export and import, factoring services, insurance, etc. This comes under the trade facilitation services positioned to reduce transaction cost of traders in a country. Trade finance infrastructure means facilities both physical like banking institution, credit guarantee institutions, etc., and otherwise like efficient systems making the physical facilities truly functional. According to United Nation Economic and Social Commission for Asia and the Pacific (UNESCAP) trade finance infrastructure is a requirement for a country and its absence is equivalent to the existence of a barrier to trade. Trade initiatives of a country are hurt if the traders have limited or clumsy access to working capital finance, cumbersome procedure to obtain credit guarantee or insurance and shrouded banking activities delaying the buyer- seller financial transactions. According to World Trade Organisation, some 80% to 90% of world trade depends on trade finance. Hence, it is described as the 'lifeline of trade', a method to facilitate international commerce. For example, almost in every developing and least developing countries. Small and medium enterprises (SME) constitute the vibrant industry segment responsible for cross-country trading of raw material, intermediate products or finished goods. A sorry state of trade financing infrastructure mostly effect these segment and hence affects the trade potential of an economy. It is essential that these SMEs to reduce the transaction cost and time with the support of a streamlined trade financing procedures and processes in order to become competitive internationally. In fact, more faster the traders get access to finance to carry out the transactions, come under credit guarantee schemes, make insurances, etc., the more trade will be facilitated.

Pre-shipment finance

The traders falling under SMEs require finance to materialise trade. Exporters require working capital (i.e., short-term financing) to mature their export orders. Generally, after receiving the purchase order from importers the export oriented manufacturers initiate manufacturing of the desired product and during the process they require short-term finance. The working capital cycle time of an export oriented manufacturer is usually shorter because once the exporter materialises an export order and receives payment from the importer, the financing need gets settled. Such financing is known as pre-shipping finance. In the case of an importer, there is also a financing requirement. An importer imports raw material from overseas seller and then put to use in manufacturing finished products for the export markets. Here, the importer usually requires a line of credit during the time when raw materials are purchased, manufacturing processes are completed, a right importer is found out and payments are received against finished good dispatched to a foreign country. In many cases, requirements of finance is very much urgent. Say, the manufacturer- importer is required to make up front payment to the exporter of raw material without waiting for the goods to arrive. After the completion of manufacturing the manufacture requires also some time for identification of the right buyer of finished products from the right country to avoid distress sell with less margin. The more the delay in executing a right export order, the more will be the requirements for the manufacturer -exporter to have some sort access to finance. Therefore, countries with pro-trade policy facilitate pre-shipment finance for traders through the development of an efficient financial infrastructure.

Trade Financing Instruments

Documentary credit or commercial letter of credit

Documentary credit or commercial letter of credit (L/C) is the most popular and practised methods of payment in international trade. The process is also very safe and best way to receive payment by a novice exporter. The issuing bank say B-1 located and approached by the importer of Britain makes the payment to the exporter from India upon the presentation of stipulated documents. Therefore, the Indian exporter does not have to wait until the goods reach the British importer or the importing country Britain. The issuing bank B-1,upon request from importer, sends the L/C to the advising bank B-2 in India with whom the Indian exporter is in touch. Upon completion of the export order documents like shipping and insurance documents, commercial invoices, etc., are submitted to the advising bank say B-2 for necessary payment as stipulated in the L/C. The B-2 later claim the amount from B-1 bank. The L/C is a documentary credit arrangement with international acceptability and is governed by the International Chamber of Commerce Uniform Customs and Practice for Documentary Credits (UCP 600 being the latest version). However, efficiency in handling L/C with a clean system differs from country to country. Some countries handle L/C related issues more efficiently than others and therefore contribute to the facilitation of trade. In many countries, traders face problems with L/C operation like advising bank is not recognising the issuing banks, banks' red tapism delays the process of transaction of goods and money, banking officials are not fully conversant with UCP-600 complaint procedure, etc.

Counter trade

This is a not frequently used system of payment in international trading of goods. Under the system counter trade, the value of goods to be exchanged between importer and exporter is stated in the agreement with specified currency but payment is made without actual money transfer. After actual transfer of exportable goods through the border the buyer pays the seller the cost of the goods sold not in cash but in kinds. The buyer may dispatch some other goods and commodities worth to the agreed amount to seller in lieu of cash. Counter trade offers an ideal solution for countries that do not want to spend USD holding or wants to manage trade balance in a more respectable way. Traditionally, the border areas are involved in 'barter trade' involving the exchange of goods and services against other goods and services of equivalent value across the border. This is also a form of counter trade.

Factoring

Factoring is an innovative way through which commercial bank allows the exporter to sell the accounts receivable to the bank itself and receive the sale proceed immediately in cash. The bank later realises the payment from the importer. Since the bank takes the risk of non-payment by the importer so the account receivables will be discounted with an appropriate risk adjusted rate which means that the exporter will receive a risk-adjusted return. The actual discounting rate depends upon the risk involvement in the transaction.

Pre-shipping financing through banks

In this system bank directly takes the responsibility of making payments required during pre shipment period to support pre-export activities like payment of wages and other overhead costs of small scale manufacturer – exporters. It may so happen that a developing country, in order to develop efficiency in pre shipment financing of the small scale sector, may commit a fund specifically for the purpose of rapid export growth and chanellise the pre shipment finance for small scale sector through its banking system. Pre shipment finance is more needed by the exporter who uses imported inputs for production. In such cases the length of working capital cycle is usually longer requiring additional working capital and hence pre shipment financing through banks will be a very useful strategy.

Export Credit Insurance

Trade is full of risk and the traders may not be well prepared to take high risk. For example, the exporter has exported the consignment but the importer failed to keep the commitment of making the requisite payment due to financial limitations or outright rejected the material on the ground of quality issues. The exporters, particularly from small scale sector, find the commercial risks of these types dampening the spirit of the business. In addition, some times the small scale exporters face tremendous political risks while executing a lucrative export order from some countries like Somalia, Venezualla, Burundi, Burkina Faso, etc. The example of risk manifestations are: the exported material may face a ban in the importing country for political reasons, terrorism or riots have not allowed the export consignments to be cleared from the dock, the central bank of the country imposed temporary ban on remitting payments, etc. Exporters may be protected from such risks through export credit insurance. The level of support towards enhancing the risk taking capacity of the exporters from least developing or developing countries is not very encouraging. However, the developed countries very strongly support theirs exporters' risk taking capacities. Even developed countries proactively support and safe guard interest of their exporters during entire pre-shipment and post-shipment periods as well as in foreign investments in business purpose through adequately devising insurance schemes. Many developing countries have neatly chalked and planned their export credit guarantee schemes to safeguard export-financing banks from losses but implementation has not been up to the mark.

CHAPTER SUMMARY

1. The economic environment is considered as uncontrollable variables by the international marketers because the company can hardly to anything to alter it. However, the international business must understand not only the economic environment of the countries of its presence but the factors influencing it so as to develop marketing strategy accordingly.
2. The current world population is close to 7 billion which is projected to be increased to 10.1 billion by the end of 2100 and in the increase of 3 billion populations Africa as a continent will be playing a major role. Among the 59 High-fertility countries, 39 countries are from Africa, followed by 9 in Asia, 6 in Oceania and 4 in Latin America. This has marketing implications.
3. Along with shift in location of population growth, there will be change in the ageing pattern in the different countries. The number of persons in the world aged 60 years or older is expected to almost triple, increasing from 668 million people in 2005 to nearly 2.03 billion of older persons by 2050. There will be an even more notable increase in the number of 'oldest-old'
4. Along with understanding of the population trend another question haunts the international marketers, i.e., what is the wealth of countries and how rich or poor its inhabitants are along with its distribution pattern within the countries.
5. Income distribution pattern of the world shows that as of 2007, the wealthiest 20% of mankind enjoyed nearly 69.5% of total global income when total national income of 136 countries was considered.
6. There are huge income inequalities inside the countries as well. The Gini coefficient which measures the income distributions pattern within a country reveal that income inequality exists in every country but level varies across the countries.
7. In order to enjoy the benefit of unity, the different countries, at different point of time, are executing different types of economic integration pacts. These are very important considerations for the international marketers as company may be expected to get big homogenised markets with the active support from trade facilitating organisations.
8. Another important consideration for the international marketers is to understand the exchange rate mechanism and make themselves conversant with the factors affecting the currency exchange rate movements of the countries.

QUESTIONS FOR REVIEW

1. Discuss how changing consumer demographics globally will impact on consumers and their expectations of products and services.
2. "For decades, second-hand garments from the West have created a thriving business in India, as cheap clothing for millions of the country's poor. The trendier lots routinely resurface in urban flea markets such as Sarojini Nagar in New Delhi and Linking Road in Mumbai, where fashionable collegegoers and their mothers pluck bargains at dirt-cheap rates. But now a huge amount of discards from well-heeled consumers in the US, Canada and South Korea are ending up in Panipat, Asia's biggest textile recycling hub, to get a second life."
   Evaluate the linkage of population change with importation of second hand cloths. Do you think that all top five populous nations will be the dumping ground for second hand garments? Research out the economic trend of top five population nations and possibilities developing textile recycling hub in those countries.
3. What is age dependency ratio? How it is related to the economic dividend? "Countries like Congo, Burkina Faso has age dependency ratio more than 90" What would be its possible implication in economy? What marketing lessons would be drawn by company like Coca Cola while deciding its future marketing strategy for these countries.
4. "Megasari provides us a strong platform to establish a significant foothold in Indonesia, which is among the largest consumer markets in Asia," said GCPL chairman Adi Godrej in a statement. Do you think that GCPL has made a right investment in Indonesia? Analyse the economic situation of the country and justify the statement made by GCPL chairman.

5. What is income inequality? How this can be measured? “The distribution of consumer incomes is a key factor in determining the structure of a vertically differentiated industry when consumer’s willingness to pay depends on his income”. Take a country where income inequality is high and justify the statement.
6. “Consumers’ income distribution in a country has the effect on firms’ entry, product quality, and pricing decisions.” Why it happens? Suppose, your company is contemplating entering in a country A where Gini index value is 23 and Country B with index value of 67.5. Your company produces and markets luxury product. How the high and low Gini Index would affect entry, product quality, and pricing decisions for these two markets? Explain with reasons.
7. What is economic integration? What are the economic and political arguments for regional economic integration? List out and explain with example the benefits international companies can take through Customs Union types of economic integration.
8. What are the differences between FTA and Customs Union? Select an Indian company and identify the exportable product and find the international markets for the product through systematic market selection procedure.
9. Explain the difference between a free trade area and a common market. State the areas where negotiations be held between the involved countries in a common market agreement.
10. Are economic blocks supporting the cause of World Trade Organisations? Why or why not?
11. Why trade will take place between countries? Explain with the help of trade theories
12. China has the most foreign exchange reserve. Why then it had pegged its currency?

EXERCISES

1. Visit Standardised World Income Inequality Database (SWIID) at http://myweb.uiowa.edu/fsolt/swiid/swiid.html and assess the income inequality in Sweeden, South Africa, India and Egypt and use the finding to develop marketing programme for Luxury motorcycle Bajaj Auto intend to develop.
2. Emami is developing perfume for the ‘oldest old’. Identify 15 good countries to market the product by demography profiling.
3. Assess the economic potential of the countries under Caribbean Community and Common Market (CARICOM) and thereby suggest whether a spice exporter from India intending to market product in these countries can benefitted due to the economic integration.
4. Visit an exporter of your locality exporting to countries with pegged currency and prepare a case towards advantages and disadvantages faced by the exporter.

End Case: Carrefour Could Not Carry It In Greece[7]

Entry of Carrefour in Greece

Today’s Carrefour, the second largest retailer (2013 ranking) of the world in terms of global sales, was a small family business of Fournier and Defforey family of France during 1960s. It made a modest entrepreneurial beginning during 1959, to eventually become today’s ‘Carrefour’ group. In 1960, the group was searching for location to expand and found a place in the south-eastern France and opened its first super market in Annecy. At that time no body even thought of that it was the starting point of growth only. Carrefour group, as the years passed, grew in size to become the world’s second-largest retailers. The group now operates through about 9500 stores worldwide under different retail formats like hypermarkets, supermarkets, Cash and Carry, and convenience stores. The company grew through internationalisation which was always the mainstay for the company and hence it became a pioneering entrant in so called risky countries such as Brazil (1975) and China (1995). Currently, the group is present in 32 countries with 26,369 employees world over and earns over 57% of the group turnover from international operation. Although the group made an entry to an

[7] The case ‘Carrefour could not carry it in Greece’ has been created by the case writer Dr Gautam Dutta of Indian Institute of Foreign Trade as a basis for class room discussion rather than to illustrate either effective or ineffective handling of a business situation.

Asian country like China during 1995, it restricted itself from entering Greece until 2000. The group justified its entry in to China as the country was showing all the prospects of economic growth during year 2000. Huge population of the country and growing affluences attracted the retailer to China. However, in case of entry in to Greece the company was little bit sceptical. In comparison to China, Greece population was miniscule and stood at about 10.6 million and growth rate was almost stagnant at around 0.5%. GDP percapita with 16,627 USD (PPP) during the year 2000 looked somewhat impressive and was growing at around 4% year on year. However, the household consumption level per head in Greece was decreasing. It was 8080 USD during 1998 which came down to 8050 USD in 1999 and then to 7339 USD during 2000 registering a negative growth of 8.88% (yoy basis). The managers at Carrefour were certainly perturbed by the economic indicators of Greece before entering the country.

Table 4.11 provides an understanding of Greece economy in comparison with Chinese economy before entry of Carrefour into the respective countries, whereas Table 4.12 provides the Greece economic parameter in the post entry situation.

It was decided at Careefour headquarter that instead of entry by creating a wholly owned subsidiary there should be a joint venture to share the risk of investing. The Greek Marinopoulos group, a diversified privately held company with holding in retail and manufacturing, provided the right opportunity. During the year 2000, a 50–50 joint venture was created between the Greek Marinopoulos and the French Carrefour Group. Soon, it became the biggest retail chain in Greece in terms of both turnover and number of stores. Group Carrefour Marinopoulos, as named after the JV, grew quickly in Greece with an impressionable chain of hypermarkets, supermarkets and convenience stores across the country. Carrefour invested its huge retailing experience, excellent organisational planning acumen and modern technology to earn the good will of Greek customers. The managers at Carrefour, in fact, were very happy with their performance and started offering excellent services and high quality products to the customers. The retail environment in the country was also found to be favourable.

Table 4.11 China Vs Greece; Economic parameter comparison before entry of Careefour

	Economic parameters	**1995**	**1996**	**1997**	**1998**	**1999**
GREECE	House hold consumpt in US$	10,773	11,015	11,298	11,768	12,133
	GDP (current US$) Billion	137.38	146.56	143.31	144.92	143.00
	GDP per capita (current US$)	12,918.80	13,685.3	13,298.5	13,375.2	13,140.1
	% share of income held by highest 20%	43.30	NA	NA	NA	NA
	Population growth rate (annual%)	0.8	0.7	0.6	0.5	0.4
	Population ages 15-64 (% of total)	68	68	68	68	68
	Economic parameters	**1990**	**1991**	**1992**	**1993**	**1994**
CHINA	House hold consumption in US$	260	271	303	332	346
	GDP per capita (current US$)	260	329.7	362.8	373.8	469.2
	GDP (current US$) Billion	314.4	379.46	422.66	440.50	559.22
	% share of income held by highest 20%	40.70	NA	NA	43.2	NA
	Population growth rate (annual%)	1.5	1.4	1.2	1.1	1.1
	Population ages 15-64 (% of total)	65	65	65	65	65

Source: World bank data

Table 4.12 The Greece economy (1998–2003)

	1998a	1999a	2000b	2001b	2002b	2003b
Nominal GDP (US$ bn)	118.5	120.2a	112.4a	117.3a	133.5a	172.7a
Population (m)	10.5	10.6	10.6	10.6	10.6	10.6
GDP per head (US$ at PPP)	15,119	15,727	16,627	17,589	19,041	20,178
Household consumption expenditure per capita (US$)	8,080	8,054	7,338	7,549	8,449	10,849
Number of households ('000)	3549	3579	3632a	3667a	3706a	3743

a: EIU estimates; b: EIU forecasts; c: EIU actual

Source: Economist Intelligence Unit (EIU).

The Retail Sector of Greece

Characteristically the retail sector of Greece was dominated by small retailers. It was estimated that during 2001, there were about 188, 132 retail outlets in Greece which earned the country reputation of being the highest retail density country (number of shops per head) in the entire EU. These small retailers were not at all ready to face the onslaught of the giant retailer and started declining in numbers rapidly. Inspired by the success of Carrefour more supermarkets and hypermarkets joined the sector. According to an estimate the supermarket and hypermarket chain of retail shops grew in number by 11.5% and 10% respectively during 2002 itself. The market further witnessed drop in numbers of small retailers because of either consolidation or winding up of operation. According to 2003 data from the National Statistical Service, the average annual turnover per retail outlet amounted to €175,654. In the same year, 75,859 wholesalers became active in the country, with an annual turnover of €56,489 million and an annual turnover per business of €744,658. Small retailers were increasingly making themselves located in small shopping centres following the "shop-in-shop" concept prominent in many countries. As it was expected, by 2006, the supermarket sector had completed its total dominance in Greece and became the main player in the retail sector by capturing 50.7% of total sales, followed by the motor trade and apparel-footwear sectors with shares of 16.8% and 11.8% respectively.

On the consumers' side, the Greeks characteristically spend more on food, beverages and tobacco which accounted for about two-fifths of total consumer expenditure in 2003. Basically, Carrefour attracted the Greeks by demonstrating a wave of modernisation in retail environment. The country was yet to embrace e retailing as internet penetration rate was just over 20% during 2004. This was the lowest rate of internet coverage in the entire Western Europe. Along with low internet accessibility another factor like reluctance of Greek consumers to provide details of their credit cards over the Internet or over the telephone hindered the progress of e-retailing. So, without any major challenge the Carrefour group was doing its business in Greece. The group also easily handled the local competition. The largest retailer in the market was Alfa-Beta Vassilopoulos which was actually a 50:50 JV between local Alfa-Beta Vassilopoulos company and Belgium's Delhaize Group had only 10.3% market share in 2003. The company operated through 101 supermarkets and ten ENA cash-and-carry stores. In 2002, it launched A-B City convenience stores and is continually expanding the market share of its own label but in totality no match for Carrefour. Carrefour also did not spend much time in deciding its fighting strategy with the nearest competitor because of its much higher level of market share. Sklavenitis was another retailer, specialised in grocery business, in the Greece market. This group had its most retail outlets located in and around Athens and as per estimate by total sales it was the third-largest retailer in 2002. The fourth place was occupied by the Germany's Metro Group with a market share of 7.3%. The group was not directly competing with Carrefour as it operated its six cash-and-carry warehouses in B to B style. However, another German retailer Schwarz Group's Lidl was giving a brief fight to Carrefour by running its discount stores across Greece since 1999.

Retail Demand in the Country

Greece proved to a good country for Carrefour. Retailing market as a whole expanded rapidly in Greece and during 2002 retail sales alone accounted for 25% of GDP. Greece was also doing well in the economic front with GDP growth rate clocking at about 3.9% per year, on average, between 1998 and 2003. During 1990s the average Greek households did not have a much respectable personal disposable income. But the situation went under substantial change during 2000 when the average personal disposable income of the Greece citizen also increased by 36% to reach US$12,772. However, this figure was comparatively not great when matched with that of other West European countries. For example, disposable income for average German was US $19505 during that time. However, the rise in disposable personal income always in the past helped the big retailers in increasing their sales in any country. Therefore, almost everything was going very smoothly for the French retailer after entering Greece. A matter of concern suddenly cropped by when a survey reported drop in demand for white goods in the country. Survey also indicated that Greece, in the past, also recorded to have the lowest ownership of household appliances in the entire EU which did not change much even after presence of world's best retailer in the country. However, the manager at Carrefour wanted to have more information on this issue. The same was the situation with sales of personal computer. When every other EU nations were encountering a record demand of personal computers, Greece had a very poor demand situation because of some unknown reason. The penetration of cable television in the domestic Greek households continued to a matter of concern for the retailers. Greek cable subscriptions were far below EU averages and hence some of the finest communication strategy of Carrefour to induce market demand in the slump areas could not reach target audience. Only solace came for the retailers came from rise in demand from apparel products, cosmetics and toiletries, bath and shower products, oral hygiene and deodorants which registered steady demand sector during 1998 to 2003.

The Change in Economic Scenario

Greece successfully treaded in the right path of economic growth in the post world war period. The country registered consistent GDP growth rate of about 7.7% in between 1960 and 1973. The country was even been compared with the Asian giant Japan for its success of registering high GDP growth rate in successive year. Interestingly. when Greece was growing at the rate of seven plus GDP, the EU–15 grew at the rate of 4.7% and OECD countries at the rate 4.9%. Greece successfully managed to nurture its main industries like tourism, shipping, industrial products, food and tobacco processing, textiles, chemicals, metal products, mining and petroleum for maintaining the GDP growth rate. Then came the 1990s when the Greek companies was facing tremendous competition from outside due globalisation. But the country was able to clock GDP growth rate higher than the EU average since early 1990s. However, many EU insiders were very critical of the country's rising unemployment levels, hopelessly inefficient and bureaucratic public sector, rampant cases of tax evasion and corruption and hence sceptical about future. They were casting doubt on the sustainability aspect of the economic growth rate. In fact, it really did not take much time to become reality. By the end of 2009, the Greek economy was clearly signalling a troubled state of affairs (Table 4.13). The Greek government was found to be inside a huge debt trap with external debt soared to about 160% of the country's GDP in 2009. The prevailing low interest rates in the Eurozone forced the annual domestic credit expansion in Greece to tune of 30% per year during 2004–2008. Consequently, the current account deficit signalled an alarming double digit figure of 10% of GDP. The government was trying desperately to get a way to come out of the peculiar economic situation. EU came out to stall the free fall of the Greece economy but with some stringent condition. The Greek government had no other option than to implement a drastic fiscal austerity programme in early 2010 in exchange for bail-out funds from the EU and the IMF. This programmes came along with various stings like a significant rise in tax structure, decrease of real wages of workers, decline in household wealth, limited credit availability, etc.

The Exit

Mr Lars Olofsson, the chief executive of Carrefour since January 2009, was busy in fighting his own battle in it's headquarter. The shareholder of the company was not very happy with the performance of the Swede CEO as under him the share price of the company was halved. In addition, the news of bad economic condition of Greece and its effect on Carrefour reached him. Sales at Greece Carrefour were sharply dropping as consumers were heavily burdened with government austerity measures. The consumers preferred to visits small retailers and that too only for basic daily requirements. Helplessly, the big reail giant Carrefour was observing consumers turning away from hypermarkets. In 2011, Carrefour's total sales fell by 8.1% to €2.5 billion registering a loss of 440 million Euros.

At the the end of year 2011, the Carrefour headquarter was also on turmoil over the issue of recruiting a new CEO. Finally, Carrefour named veteran Mr Georges Plassat as new chief executive replacing Mr Lars Olofsson who promised for a turnaround for the company. On the Greece front, the first quarter sales of 2012 also welcomed the new CEO with a saddened note. It did not take much time for the business veteran like Plasssat to understand that the Greece business had turned to become a loss-making venture and its continuence will further aggrevate the situation. Georges Plassat was desperate to get rid of the Greece operation as quickly as possible. According to him the future of the country economy as well the joint venture retailing already crossed the limit. He reminded the Marinopoulos family about their commitment for the country and advised not to leave the sinking boat at this juncture. The local partner finally agreed to break the JV and take the responsibility of running the retail chain on its own strength. Mr Plassat formally announced that Carrefour was rejigging its plan for international business. It would leave Greece by transferring entire Greece operation of 463 shops (41 are hypermarkets and 252 are supermarkets, with the remainder a mix of other formats) to Marinopoulos at a cost of one Euro only and move to Argentina to buy 129 stores in supermarket chain Eki.

Table 4.13 The Greece economy (2007–2012)

	2007a	2008a	2009a	2010a	2011a	2012b
Nominal GDP (US$ bn)	311.2c	348.4c	326.4c	305.6c	300.3	259.3
Population (m)	11.2	11.2	11.2	11.3	11.3	11.3
GDP per head (US$ at PPP)	28,328	30,177	29,335	28,300	27,184	25,709
Private consumption per head (US$)	19,969	22,914	21,455	20,444	20,744	17,303
Number of households ('000)	3900c	3937c	3973	4010	4047	4084

a: EIU estimates; b: EIU forecasts; c: EIU actual.
Source: Economist Intelligence Unit (EIU).

CASE QUESTIONS

Q1. What was the economic environment when Carrefour decided to enter Greece? Outline the economic parameter which made the decision possible for the company to invest in Greece. You, as the then CEO of Carrefour, justify the decision through economic analysis of the country.

Q2. What was the economic environment when Carrefour decided to exit Greece? Outline the economic parameter which made the decision possible for company to exit the country. You, as the present CEO of Carrefour, justify the decision through economic analysis of the country

Q3. Would it have been possible for Carrefour to get an early signal of the economic ailments of the country rather than to wait till 2012? What are those signals that the company should have taken into consideration?

FURTHER READINGS

Oh, Chang Hoon and Alan M. Rugman (2012), "Regional integration and the international strategies of large European firms", *International Business Review*, Vol. 21 Issue 3, June.

This paper uses 1100 firm-year observations to explore the variation in strategy from regional to international from the perspective of regional economic integration. This paper also examines firm-specific factors that affect global strategies.

Alhorr, Hadi S., Kimberly Boal, and Briton J. Cowden (2012), "Regional economic integration and international strategic alliances: Evidence from the EU", *Multinational Business Review*, Vol. 20, Issue 1.

This is article throws light on environmental changes as a result of economic integration between countries. It discusses market issues and currency commonality issues, etc., that take place within members of the economic community. The article suggests that whenever there is economic integration, there will be change in the pattern of relationship that gets formed at the firm level amongst the member countries.

Austen, Siobhan (2002), "An international comparison of attitudes to inequality", *International Journal of Social Economics*, Vol. 29, Issue 3, pp. 218–237.

This article examines the economic inequality issues and attitude of the people living in those countries. The articles covers six countries such as Australia, West Germany, the UK, the USA, Hungary, and to highlight the attitude of people and compares the attitudes in each of these countries in respect of economic inequality pertaining to 1987–1992 period and draws some conclusions on the important relationship between culture and the economy.

Pol, Louis G. (1986), "Marketing and the demographic perspective", *Journal of Consumer Marketing*, Vol. 3, Issue 1.

This paper throws light on how demographic data can be used in marketing and formulation of some marketing strategies. The article observed that use of demographic perspective in marketing strategy formulation has not been forthcoming. The article, therefore, offers an explanation of the demographic perspective in order to make demographic data more useful to marketers when marketing in country markets.

Agarwal, James and Terry Wu (2004), "China's entry to WTO: Global marketing issues, impact, and implications for China", *International Marketing Review*, Vol. 21, Issue 3.

This paper discusses the very important happening in the history of WTO, i.e., China's entry into WTO and the country's successful transition from a command economy to a market-based economy. This article also examines the possible impact China's entry into WTO and its impact on global level marketing of the country. It reviews 11 specific WTO policy issues and offers several global marketing propositions in terms of WTO's impact on and implications for China.

Deciding on International Market Selection

5

Learning Objectives

After studying this chapter, you should be able to:

- Understand the motives of international expansion, both the proactive and reactive, for the companies.
- Understand the different types of market selection process demonstrated by the companies while selecting country markets.
- Assess the problems encountered by the companies while resorting to systematic market selection process.
- Understand a systematic export market selection process.
- Understand systematic market selection process applicable for a company while expanding to foreign country with hierarchical entry mode.
- Introduce different information sources to be utilised by the companies while deciding on the market selection.
- Introduce the problems of market selection in case of emerging country market and solutions thereof.

Chapter Overview

This chapter introduces the international market selection process for the companies. As the countries of the world are increasingly becoming more accessible, the companies of different sizes are showing desire to have a pre-entry match making between their capabilities and foreign country market potential before final selection and actual entry is made. Past trends amongst the small and medium-sized companies (SMEs), from developing countries in particular, are found to be more ad hoc in market selection and depend more on intuition and/or qualitative market data only. This chapter, therefore, deals with the salient issues of market selection and highlights on methodologies used for selection that can come handy for the international marketing managers in deciding the international markets for entry.

Opening Vignette

Is Addis Ababa providing good business opportunities for Kajaria Ceramics of India?

Kajaria Ceramics is the largest manufacturer and exporter of floor and wall tiles in India. It is the successful start up of Mr Ashok Kajaria, a technocrat from California University, who visualised that with the increase in number of Indian middle class in the country the demand of designer tiles would also be increased. Mr Kajaria's entrepreneurial acumen rightly pushed him to enter into technical collaboration agreement with Spanish company Todagres, the second-largest maker of tiles in the world. With their technical support Kajaria ceramics started manufacturing of Glazed Tiles and Listello Tiles, under the Kajaria brand name, using latest manufacturing technology. The products were rolled out in the market and with no time It did make a solid presence in the market. The market success did not allow them to look back and the company went on for further expansion of manufacturing capacity. Started with mere 12,000 tonne per annum (tpa) in 1988, the total installed capacity of its production units located at Sikandrabad, (Uttar Pradesh) and Alwar (Rajasthan) jumped to 160,000 tonne per annum by the end of 1999. Presently, the company possesses a manufacturing capacity of 43.60 MSM (million squire miles) across its seven manufacturing plants located at Rajasthan, Uttar Pradesh, Gujarat and Andhra Pradesh. This includes a 2.60 MSM vitrified tile capacity, added in April 2013, by way of purchasing another plant at Morbi, Gujarat by its subsidiary Jaxx Vitrified.

The ceramic tiles manufacturing capacity of world stood at 10,512 MSM during 2011 and out of which about 46% was produced in China. The rests were produced in countries such as Brazil (8%), India (6%), Iran (5%), Italy (4%), Spain (4%), Vietnam (4%), Indonesia (3%), Turkey (2%), and Mexico (2%). A very interestingly feature of the sector is that the producing countries are also good consuming countries of the products. For example, during 2011 China consumed about 39% of the world consumption followed by countries such as Brazil (7%), India (6%), Iran (4%), Vietnam (3%), Indonesia (3%), Saudi Arabia (2%), USA (2%), Russia (2%), and Mexico (2%). So, the Indian company apart from taking keen interest in the domestic market requirements of ceramic tiles was also in look out of export markets. Accordingly, the company started exporting tiles to the Gulf countries, Europe and Bangladesh during 1989. The Chemical and Allied Export Promotion Council of India (Capexil) special export award (given for the highest export made in a year) was awarded to the company three times in succession from 1992 onwards to testify export marketing excellence of the company. In course of time, the company further started exploring marketing opportunities in different countries of Europe, West Asia and nearby South Asia. Very soon its products were seen to be exported to Australia, South Africa, Vietnam, North America and Singapore. However, as it is associated with exportation of heavier products, the transportation of finished goods seemed to be eating up the profits. Then, a time came when the company was looking for more intense internationalisation through manufacturing presence in foreign country. At that time, Ethiopia government was actively looking for inward flow on foreign investment in that country. In 2010, Mr Ashok Kajaria, managing director of Kajaria, was briefed about of an investment opportunity in Ethiopia by the then Director General of the Ethiopian Investment Agency (EIA), Abi Woldemeskel. Mr Abi convinced Mr Kajaria, about the business opportunities in the ceramic sector and assured him of full cooperation from Ethiopian government. Further discussion between the company and EIA saw allotment of land in Debre Berhan, 130 km north east of Addis Ababa, capital city of Ethiopia, for factory construction. The Company initiated preliminary actions to put up a ceramic tiles unit in Ethiopia and accordingly incorporated a subsidiary, Kajaria Ceramics Addis Pic. in Ethiopia. The Company invested an amount of ₹3.03 crore in the subsidiary by way of Equity and Advances. However, all was not well in the post investment period. The company did not appreciate the deteriorating business environment of the country. Finally, the company decided not to proceed further and abandon the project. The newly opened subsidiary was declared closed and in the process the company lost the money as well as valuable time which the officials put for the project abroad.

When this foreign market selection mishap of Kajarias were told to the students of international marketing in the classroom the students quipped, "That's strange! Why not the Kajarias had collected enough information about the host country before committing investment? This is natural that companies would constantly look out for new markets but why Kajarias had shown urgency of international expansion when home market was growing faster? What were its motives behind expansion abroad? How companies, then, should look for systematising the international market selection process so that such loss of investment does not occur?"

"When a company decides to go international, it faces a host of decisions. Which countries should it enter and in what sequence? What criteria should be used to select entry markets: proximity, stage of development, geographic region, culture and linguistic criteria, the competitive situation, legal and banking system or other factors?"

—Warren J. Keegan

INTRODUCTION

It is natural for businesses of all sizes, in this age of globalisation, would look for internationalisation of their activities through cross-country business. The countries of the world have also realised the importance of opening up more and more and welcoming cross border businesses with open arms. Both cross border inter and intra company transactions of products are soaring up indicating their requirements away from production centre. At the same time, the countries are increasingly embracing cross border trade as pathway to the desired level of development. The World Trade Organisation (WTO) has noted that, since its establishment in 1995, both the number of free trade agreements (FTAs) and the pace of signing new FTAs are increasing. From 1995 to 2003, there was an average of seven FTAs signed yearly. In 2004–09, this number rose to a yearly average of 15. During April 2015 there were 612 bilateral or regional FTAs notified to WTO and perhaps there could be many more which have not been officially brought to the notice of WTO. Another indicator in this respect may be the terms of change effected by those countries which were found not so good in terms of 'openness to trade' and 'ease of doing business'. The 'doing business report' of World Bank ranks, every year, countries of the world in terms of easiness of carrying out business operation, i.e., ease of doing business rank by using a particular methodology. These ranks, when compared for successive years, indicate changes effected by 183 countries in the business regulations enforcement dimension. The findings of the successive reports are encouraging and indicative of increasing easiness of doing business in many countries with the passage of time. The report recorded that countries such as Georgia, Rwanda, Belarus, Burkina Faso, Saudi Arabia, Mali, the Kyrgyz Republic, Ghana, Croatia and Kazakhstan have made largest strides in making their regulatory environment more favourable to business[1].

From 2006 World Bank's "doing business ranking" system has added a new topic in its report under the heading "trading across the border" that compiles the procedural requirements for exporting and importing a standardised cargo of goods. Accordingly, countries of the world are ranked based on easiness while exporting or importing of goods. While computing rank of an individual country it gathers information on the complete procedure from the beginning, i.e., contractual agreement between two parties to the finish, i.e., delivery of goods to the destination of another country. Information on the time taken to execute the procedural formalities such as pre-arrival documentation for loading of cargo in ship/train, port and terminal handling at the destinations, customs and inspection of cargo, and finally delivery to the warehouse of the importing country are also recorded. The trading across ranking of 2014 when compared with that of 2010 for 183 countries indicates that some countries across the world are turning to be serious about easing the process of product and commodity transfer across international borders. Table 5.1 indicates the changes in respect of 34 countries.

[1] http://www.doingbusiness.org/reforms/five-years

Table 5.1 Trade across border indicators

Countries	Trading across borders rank		Countries	Trading across borders rank	
	2010	2014		2010	2014
Singapore	1	1	United States	20	16
Hong Kong	2	2	Mauritius	24	17
Estonia	3	6	Portugal	23	29
Finland	5	14	Ireland	22	5
UAE	6	8	Latvia	16	28
Denmark	7	7	Saudi Arabia	19	92
Sweden	4	4	Austria	26	19
Korea, Rep.	8	3	France	25	10
Norway	9	24	New Zealand	27	27
Panama	10	9	Australia	28	49
Israel	11	12	Lithuania	29	21
Thailand	12	36	Egypt, Arab Rep.	30	99
Netherlands	13	13	Georgia	31	33
Germany	14	18	Luxembourg	33	35
Cyprus	16	34	Bahrain	35	64
United Kingdom	18	15	Taiwan, China	15	32
Japan	21	20	Djibouti	36	56

Source: http://www.doingbusiness.org

Now, in the backdrop of a country's willingness to encourage foreign business, companies of different sizes are also strongly making a move towards the internationalisation of business activities.

It is understandable that with increased ease of doing business abroad and decreasing trade barriers, internationalising of the companies would continue. However, from the marketing point of view, the importance and need of systematically evaluating and selecting an international market before entry has been stressed by many researchers. This is primarily because market failure of a commodity or service is mainly attributed to poor market selection committed by international marketers in their rush to enter a new country[2]. On the other hand, companies increasingly desire to have a pre-entry match making between their capabilities and foreign country market potential before final selection and ultimate entry in order to avoid any post entry mishaps. But, in reality, examples are at galore when companies failed in the foreign markets because of poor market selection. Small and medium-sized companies (SMEs), in particular, are found to be more ad hoc in market selection and depend more on intuition and/or qualitative market data only which led to failure in foreign countries[3].

---

[2] Dalgic, T. and Heigblom, R. (1996), "Educator Insight: Marketing blunders revisited- some lessons for managers", *Journal for International Marketing*, Vol. 4, No. 1.

[3] Papadopoulos, N. and Denis, J. E. (1988), "Inventory, taxonomy and assessment of methods for international market selection", *International Marketing Review*, Vol. 5, No. 3, Autumn, pp. 38–51.

The above discussion clearly makes us understand that internationalisation is the order of the day. However, while internationalising, companies vary efforts in terms of their market selection process. This chapter, therefore, deals with the salient issues of market selection and highlights the methodologies used for selection which can come handy for marketing managers in deciding on the international markets for entry.

INTERNATIONALISATION OF INDIAN COMPANIES

India emerged as the world's 21st largest outward investor during 2010 with more than US$75 billion overseas investment in the past decade. In the same way the country became the world's 13th largest FDI host country during 2008. With 2008 inflows of $42 billion and 2009 inflows of $27 billion, it proved to be top-three preferred investment destination globally. The country liberalised its FDI policy in several economic sectors, provided a globally competitive workforce, and hosted a growth oriented business environment to attract foreign investments. As a result, India had received some $169 billion of cumulative FDI inflows by the end of 2009 since it first opened itself to foreign direct investors in 1991[4].

Many Indian firms are increasingly showing their inclination to go aboard and make their credible presence. This phenomenon is not restricted to a particular sector but span across different segments such as automobiles, pharmaceuticals, hotels, textiles, engineering goods, entertainment, etc. Table 5.2 lists some of the recent internationalisation of Indian companies.

Table 5.2 Indian companies going abroad

Indian business organisation	Approach to internationalisation
Adani Power Ltd	Formed a wholly owned subsidiary Adani Shipping Pte Ltd in Singapore with investment of 23 million USD
Dabur India Ltd	Formed a wholly owned subsidiary Dabur International Limited in UAE with an investment of 21.5 million USD
Biocon Ltd	Formed an wholly owned manufacturing and research subsidiary in Malaysia with an initial investment of around 160.38 million USD
Paharpur Cooling Towers Limited	Formed a wholly owned subsidiary Paharpur (Mauritius) Ltd.in Mauritius with an investment of 2 million USD
Siva Ventures Ltd	Formed a wholly owned subsidiary Siva Group Shipping and Trading Projects Pte Ltd.in Singapore with an investment of 39.5 million USD
Suzlon Energy Ltd	Formed a wholly owned subsidiary Suzlon Energy A/S in Denmark with an investment of 125 million USD for wind turbine manufacturing
Tata Steel Ltd	Formed a wholly owned subsidiary Tata Steel Asia Holdings Pte Ltd, Singapore with an investment 529.million USD
House of Pearl Fashions Pvt Ltd	Formed a wholly owned subsidiary Multinational Textile Group Limited in Mauritius with an investment of 100 million USD

(Continued)

[4] India: World's 21st largest outward investor: Report. *The Economic Times*, September 23, 2010

Table 5.2 (*Continued*)

Indian business organisation	Approach to internationalisation
Piramal Healthcare Ltd	Formed a wholly owned Subsidiary Piramal Healthcare Ltd in United States Of America with an investment of 41.25 million USD
Sintex Industries Ltd	Formed a wholly owned subsidiary. Sintex Holdings BV in Netherland with an investment of 17.29 million USD
Simplex Infrastructures Ltd	Formed a joint venture Simplex Infrastructures (Thailand) Limited In Thailand with an investment of 0.03 million USD
KEC International Ltd, an RPG group company	Acquired Texas-based power transmission infrastructure company, SAE Towers Holdings, for an enterprise value of 95 million USD
Arvind Fashion Ltd	Formed a wholly owned subsidiary Arvind Textile Mills Ltd in Bangladesh with an investment of 0.28 million USD
GMR Infrastructure Ltd	Formed a joint venture Istanbul Sabiha Gokcen Ulusarasi in Istanbul (Turkey) with an investment of 121 million USD
Varun Shipping Co. Ltd.	Formed a wholly owned subsidiary VSC International P.Ltd in Singapore with an investment of 172.5 million USD
The Metal Powder Co Ltd	Formed a wholly owned subsidiary Copper Bronze Powder Sdn Bhd in Malaysia with an investment of 53 million USD
Mahindra & Mahindra Ltd	Formed a wholly owned subsidiary Mahindra Overseas Investment Company (Mauritius)Ltd. in Mauritius with an investment of 4.32 million USD
Ashok Leyland (ALL)	Formed an wholly on subsidiary Avia Ashok Leyland Motors Sro in Czech republic with an investment of 1.5 million USD
Tata Motors Ltd.	Formed a wholly owned subsidiary Tata Motors Thailand Ltd in Thailand with an investment of 15 million USD

Source: RBI data on outward Foreign Direct Investment: 2010-11

REASONS FOR EXPANSION ABROAD

Why do firms want to expand overseas? The motives are varied and some of them act as primary or proactive motives and others are secondary or reactive motives that trigger international expansion. It is always a combination of motives that bring company expanding to other country markets.

Proactive and reactive motives: The proactive motives are strategic in nature which primarily allowed a company to take decision for internationalisation, say, grabbing a new business opportunity in a particular country. The reactive motives are supportive in nature, for example, may be if that company is present in the particular market it may serve a key customer. A company can have a horde of motives but some reasons become the primary followed by the reactive motives that support the internationalisation move. Some of the motives of company's internationalisation are as stated below.

Tap Market Opportunities

To grab market opportunities abroad by far remain the most common motive of the internationalising companies. For example, take the case of

Emami Group. This group is a business conglomerate with pan India presence through its battery of brands and business initiatives since 1974. With an aggregate group turnover of about ₹3000 crore, Emami Limited, the flagship company of the Group, is a coveted ₹1100 crore business entity, a leading player in the personal and healthcare consumer products industry in India engaged in manufacturing and marketing of health, beauty, and personal care products. It attracted Indian consumers more because the company claimed that the products were based entirely on ayurvedic formulation. Emami has over 30 brands under its portfolio and maintained revenue at the compounded annual growth rate (CAGR) of 27% during 1990s. During late 2000, the company made a plan to enter Egyptian market by acquiring a local personal care products manufacturer. The move was a part of the group's corporate strategy to bolster Emami's growth at an accelerated pace of 50–60% CAGR over the next three years. The strategy was straightforward – acquiring a small company and commencing operation in the country. The rationale behind the move is to tap business opportunities of the region arising primarily out of a rising population that is predominantly youth, increasing demand for personal healthcare products, and improved purchasing power. The acquired unit would also allow the Indian manufacturer to market products in the Common Market for Eastern and Southern Africa (COMESA) and Arab Common Market (ACM). Besides, the group will also save import duty that it is currently paying when exporting products to these countries. Manufacturing abroad would also save on delivery time and logistics cost. "We also feel that a regional manufacturing base will help us to become a leading player in this market. We have already reached out in the Middle East, CIS, Europe, North America, and Africa, clocking a growth of over 50% from these markets and contributing to about 20% to Emami's total turnover" Emami Director, International Business Prashant Goenka said.[5] Hence, internationalisation of Emamai was triggered by primary motives and supported by proactive motives such as serving niche customers, saving of import duty, etc. The key motive for business expansion of many companies, like Emami Limited, has been the opportunities abroad. In fact, producers of many high tech products have gone to other countries by sheer market opportunities in the foreign markets. Toyata Motors of Japan took their hybrid vehicles to USA only because that country offered more market opportunities than anyone in the developing and developed world.

Box 5.1 China alluring companies with market opportunities

Chinese market has always allured foreign companies dealing with consumer products. FMCG Marketers around the world also had shown tremendous urgency to reach China as fast as possible. The country is all set to become the world's largest consumer market by 2020. This process is being helped by the increasing income of the Chinese population, in general, and income of the bottom level population in particular. Data shows that China's household income of the bottom 20% of earners rose by 5% during 2003–04. During the same period per month income of the top ten percent rich population surged 255% to about 34,000 Yuan (4978 USD) as per Credit Suisse's China Consumer Survey data. The marketers'

[5] The Economic Times April 19, 2010

internationalisation process became more faster when they came to know that the increase in income was accompanied by a trend of less saving. Based on the trend, Credit Suisse expects China's consumer spending will climb and its share of global consumption will increase from 5.2% at USD 1.72 trillion in 2009 to 23.1% at USD 15.94 trillion in 2020, overtaking US as the world's largest consumer market. Further, the internationalising companies moved faster in China when the news spread that the government was taking all measures to sustain the buying spree of the consumers and even provided subsidies for rural buyers for buying of big ticket items such as TV, AC, washing machines and refrigerators. Apart from FMCG companies, the automobile companies of the world also felt the same rush for entering Chinese market. China had gone to the extent of granting sales tax concession in small engine vehicles that allowed the country to surpass US as world largest automobile market. The other reactive motives of internationalising companies built up from the information that the Chinese households had shown savings tendency inversely proportional to their income rise and demonstrating the same in practical as well through purchase of new cars, TVs, personal computers, etc.

Source: Internet

Saturated Domestic Market

Demand saturation in domestic market has been the reason for many company's internationalisation. For example, take the case of American company Gerber Products Company. The company, located in Michigan USA, was the leading player of USA baby food market since 1927. The company symbol 'Gerber baby' became well-known very quickly across the states of America. However, confinement in domestic market led Gerber baby to become well known in USA but completely unknown to other parts of the world. The company continued, after its successful introduction as quality to dominate the baby food market in the United States. Very soon the Gerber baby trademark and the lovely baby face became the symbol of vitamin-rich, pressure-cooked, sealed and 100% safe baby foods and liked by the parents of new born of USA. Hence, in the initial years at least, the company did not feel like going international. But this phase did not last long. Competition from other producers started brewing up. By the year 1935 there were about sixty other baby food manufactures in USA who started to put their products in the same country market. Initially, Gerber resisted the competition and safeguarded the market share. But the company soon noticed that that overall market size is shrinking as the birth rate of babies started declining in USA. The company noticed that about 98% of the world's births occur outside the United States. In order to avoid domestic market saturation, the company looked towards international markets. As a result, the company embarked on a new mission of expansion and diversification. It first entered Mexico in 1959 where baby birth rate was quite high. By 1991, Gerber became a common baby food name in many foreign countries such as USSR, Thailand, Brazil, Chile, and Sweden. Now the company markets its baby food in 80 countries, with labeling in 16 languages. The primary or proactive motive of internationalisation, in case of Gerber Products Company, was that of saturation in the domestic market.

Access to Emerging Markets

Emerging markets are those country markets of the world where business activities are showing rapid growth with fast expansion of market demand backed by increase of income level of consumers. Many a times the lucrativeness associated with market growth has brought out foreign companies to these markets. For example, Toshiba elevators of Japan entered Golf region with a market ambition that can be only be fulfilled by the rapid economic growth of the gulf countries. Toshiba elevator took full advantage of the economic progress of the Golf countries and executed projects worth more than Dh 300 millions in first five years of its existence with well-knit marketing plan. The company further has planned to achieve a 100% growth in turn over in the Gulf region in the next five years. According to Mr Sunichi Kimura, its CEO, marketing scenario in the current year is looking bright as the UAE property sector is recovering fast. The company also successfully entered to other nearby emerging countries like India and performed reasonably well. It also opened subsidiaries in places such as Saudi Arabia and Qatar with local partners to take advantage of fast infrastructural development.[6] The company headquarter in Japan fully backed the proactive motive of internationalisation of the local offices in regards to taking advantage of the economic growth of the emerging markets.

Achieving Economies of Scale

Achieving economies of scale sometimes becomes the root cause of internationalisation. Take the example of semi conductor manufacturing sector which is characterised by high fixed cost investment in bringing the products to the market. This is again linked with the high technology obsolesce rate associated with the end products such as personal computers, cell phones, automotive and other electronic devices. To remain competitive in the sector it is very important that a company to lower its breakeven point by selling more in larger market. Therefore, companies operating in such sector need a larger customer base to achieve economies of scale. Semiconductors manufactures of South Korea, Malaysia and Taiwan had to set up sales subsidiaries at Phoenix , Mesa, Chandler, Oakhill, Tempe, Toronto to capture markets of USA and further to South America. Companies with high fixed cost can ensure sales growth if they have larger number of country markets to increase sales. Sales growth allows the company to achieve economies of scale in production and also to spread advertising and marketing costs over a larger output. In such cases, the urge in achieving scale economics becomes the proactive motive for market expansion to other countries of the world.

Access to Lower Cost of Production

Labour costs vary from country to country. As reported by the bureau of labour statistics, US department of labour, the hourly manufacturing compensation costs in the United States in 2009 were lower than in 12 European

[6] Khaleej Times, March 28th 2010

countries (Norway, Denmark, Belgium, Austria, Germany, Switzerland, Finland, Netherlands, France, Sweden, Ireland, Italy) and Australia, but higher than in countries such as UK, Japan, Singapore, Korea, etc. The 8 countries with the highest costs in Europe had their cost levels 30–60% higher than the US level, but costs in Canada and Japan were about 10% lower than in the United States (Table 5.3).[7] This is an important consideration for the internationalising companies with Greenfield projects.

The manufacturing cost differentials becomes the proactive motive for many company's international expansion. Take the case of the extrusion technology Company X Tech, based at Boston USA, producing extruded telecommunication parts which fit in the global supply chain of telecommunication major Lucent Technologies. X Tech entered China with a wholly own subsidiary at Xiamen with the primary motive of reducing cost of the manufactured products with low labour input cost.

Access to Raw Material

The companies also internationalise to become closure to the raw material sources. Let us take the example of Shri Renuka Sugar's internationalisation drive to demonstrate the point here. Shri Renuka Sugar has one of the largest sugar refining capacities in India and was struggling to utilise the full capacity due to shortage of raw material. Brazil, blessed with ample land and rainfall (in excess of 1000 mm per year) topped the list of sugarcane production globally. The country is the lowest-cost sugar producing nations accounting for more than 50% of the world sugar exports. It is precisely for this reason Shri Renuka Sugar entered Brazil, the largest producer of Sugarcanes in the world. Similar is the case with French Cosmetics Company L'Occitane founded in 1976 by Olivier Baussan of France. It shoots

Table 5.3 Hourly compensation costs in manufacturing, USD

Country	Compensation costs in manufacturing, USD	Country	Compensation costs in manufacturing, USD
Norway	53.89	Singapore	17.50
Denmark	49.56	Republic of Korea	14.20
Germany	46.52	Argentina	10.14
Finland	43.77	Brazil	8.32
France	40.08	Tawan	7.76
US	33.53	Poland	7.50
UK	30.78	Mexico	5.38
Japan	30.36	Philippines	1.50
Canada	29.60	Australia	34.62

Source: MIT study

[7] MIT IPC Globalisation Working Paper 00-004 reported about country specific productivity variations. Using the Taiwan productivity rate as an index of 100, China was a 95, Indonesia 40-45, and Cambodia 55-60

in to the limelight internationally as manufacturer and retailer of skincare, body care, fragrance and hair care for the up market consumers. The company markets its product in over 85 countries around the world, through a wide network of boutiques and strategic partners. L'occitane brand earned the reputation of producing high quality, efficient and sensorial products formulated with traceable, natural and active ingredients. L'occitane has been proudly advertising the fact that these natural ingredients such as shea butter, etc., are being produced by the company in its own land with great care. Shea is one of the main resources of Burkina Faso, a small country in the heart of West Africa. L'occitane entered in to Burkina Faso 25 years ago for producing Shea butter, extracted from nut of the African Shea tree, for the use in their cosmetics, body care, hair care and skin care product lines.

Develop Global Image

Starbucks, the leading American coffee retailer, wanted to become the most recognised and respected global brand of coffee by availing business opportunities around the world. For this, Starbucks expanded internationally at a furious pace since it was purchased and transformed by the renowned entrepreneur Howard Schultz. The company grew from a local Seattle company to a global enterprise with more than 5000 retail stores on four continents. In 2001, the company opened a record number of stores, had posted its highest net earnings in history despite the recession, and was named as the fastest-growing global brand by the Business Week. The speed with which Starbucks had managed its expansion in different countries was almost as remarkable as the changes it had brought in traditional conceptions of brand marketing. Starbucks, in its race of being the global retailer, converted the world's oldest commodity into a differentiated, lasting, value-laden brand. The proactive motive of Starbucks behind the expansion was to be the truly global brand.

Global Competitive Advantage

Companies may enter into different country markets to enjoy scope advantage. Presence in multiple locations allows the firm to optimise every activity in the value chain. Suppose a textile firm operating from four locations – India, Pakistan, Bangladesh and Italy. Presence in these four strategic locations provides the firm with leverage to develop the value chain at optimum level – cotton sourcing in Pakistan, spinning and design of textile can be done in India, knitting in Bangladesh and marketing in Italy. Pakistan has resource advantage that allows the firm to source quality raw material at low cost. The cotton can then be passed to its Indian location for spinning as the country has excess capacity for spinning. India has so many centres of excellence in textile design, which provides the firm the ability to have world class design at comparatively low cost. The design and yarn may then be passed to the Bangladesh location of the firm for knitting them in to garments. Finally, the knitted garments can be dispatched to the Italy office for marketing. This firm is then said to have availed the global scope and utilised them optimally to be globally competitive. The firm managed to have enhanced performance, reduction in cost, and risk reduction through cross-country coordination and leveraging of country-specific benefits to its favour.

Downplay the Trade Barriers

Companies may enter in to another country in order to overcome the trade barrier. Let us take the case of automobile manufacturer Hyundai to illustrate this point. The Chennai manufacturing facility of Hyundai in India produces small cars and has the capacity to produce 0.6 million units a year. Out of the production, exports accounted for about half of the company's sales. The wholly-owned Indian arm of the South Korean company exported about 0.14 million cars in the first six months of 2009, a 22% increase over the previous year. The i20 model car accounted for over 40% of exports from 2009–10 onwards. All on a sudden the company decided to shift part of the production of its i20 model to Europe from Chennai to save on logistics costs and import duties in Europe. By December 2010, India's largest car exporter shifted the production of the Hyundai i20 to its joint venture facility Hyundai Assan facilities (Izmit plant) in Turkey to take production closer to its large overseas markets such as Germany, France, Italy and the UK. The company saved logistics costs and import taxes which constituted to about 10–15% of price of cars exported from India. In absence of any FTA between India and Europe made unfavourable for Hyundai to continue exporting from India. Therefore, the expansion to the other countries as planned by Hyundai was based on proactive motive of downplaying with the trade barrier and high transportation cost only.

SELECTION OF COUNTRY MARKETS FOR EXPANSION

The companies which felt the need for internationalisation may demonstrate different ways of market selection. How the Dutch company Heineken, who in these days calls itself as world's most international brewer, selected its international markets for expansion could be of great interest. Around 1873 the company began its journey from Amsterdam. By 1900 it exported beer to Africa and during 1923 the first brewery outside Netherlands was set up at DR Congo. During 1946 it further expanded to Nigeria followed by expansion to Egypt during 2003. The expansion continued to Sri Lanka (then Ceylon), Singapore, Indonesia, and West Indies. The natural question asked as to what strategy the company adopted for market selection. Egypt is located in the north-eastern region of Africa, well connected with other parts of the globe through the Mediterranean Sea in the north of the country. Sri Lanka is an island nation in South Asia and in the path of major sea routes. Singapore consists of the island of Singapore and fifty-eight smaller islets and is blessed with a vast coastline. It is separated from Indonesia, an archipelagic country, by the Singapore Strait. The West Indies is a large group of islands that separate the Caribbean Sea from the Atlantic Ocean. What is common to these countries apart from all of them having sea connectivity? Why did the Dutch brewer Heineken select these markets for expansion? The expansion to these markets was carried out possibly because they were either former Dutch colonies or easy to reach through sea route. Next, the company expanded to African small country DR Congo when a Belgian brewer company wanted to sell off its business to Heineken. Therefore, in a way, one can term the expansion and market selection process of Heineken as 'based on situational convenience' at least in those early years.

In contrast, Japanese companies demonstrated a more purposeful approach in selection of markets for expansion. For example, Suzuki Motor Co., Ltd. opened its direct sales subsidiary in USA way back in 1963 to market its product. Then it moved to Thailand during 1967 to open Thai Suzuki Motor Co., Ltd. to assemble its first motorcycle plant outside Japan. During 1974, the company entered Indonesia to produce automobile parts to reduce cost of production further. During 1982, the company started overseas car production from Pakistan and India to tap the huge market potential of Indian subcontinent. During 1990, Suzuki took first step to enter Eastern Europe by signing a basic agreement on a joint venture for car production in Hungary. Production of Suzuki cars and motorcycles began in Vietnam during 1996. In order to take the benefit of marketing in Latin American countries, Suzuki began cars manufacturing in Argentina during 2000. Thus, Japanese companies showed more strategic orientations in their moves for internationalisation.

The German international retailer METRO Cash and Carry, the fourth largest retailer of the world behind Wal-Mart, Carrefour and Tesco, began its successful international expansion forty years ago by opening a wholesale store in the name of "MAKRO" in the Netherlands. After 40 years, this German B2B wholesaler now operates in 31 markets and thus in more countries than any of its competitors. The latest expansion moves of the retailer have been to Kazakhstan and Egypt at the same time. Metro Cash and Carry sees potential for 10 to 15 wholesale stores in Kazakhstan with an average investment of about 15 to 20 million Euros per store. The opening of the first store in Egypt is planned with further horizontal expansion of around 10 stores in this North African country in the medium term and for more than 20 outlets in the long term. For market selection process, the Cash and Carry division (MCC) of the retailer has developed a model that all its group companies apply and adapt according to their specific requirements. The retailer, initially, did not follow any particular process of international market selection and simply was guided by managerial experience and wisdom. But from 2003 onwards, the retailer developed a detailed framework of market selection. The starting point of its international market selection framework is evaluation of the countries (other than those where the MCC exist) in accordance with corporate principles and goals. One such principle is to evaluate competitions from other retailers in the prospective country before making entry decision. If other big retailers already dominate the market and occupy lion's share, then there is little possibility of MCC entering the market and those countries will be automatically eliminated. The remaining countries will then be subjected to evaluation in terms of legal standing, taxation, and financial data collected through extensive secondary research. This stage will further eliminate some countries. The remaining countries will then be scored on the basis of predetermined weighted factors such as GDP per capita, private consumer spending, population, city/urban agglomerations with population level, retail concentration, etc.

The preliminary ranking of the countries so obtained will be pipeline countries for country specific feasibility study considering **PESTLE (Political, economic, social, technological, legal and environmental) factors**. At the end, the company executives will make visits to the top countries (those that have passed through the process successfully) for final selection.

The above three examples showcase three different ways of market selection process. Heineken's market selections in initial years were very much ad hoc in nature. Japanese were more strategic in comparison but MCC was fully systematic. A number of well-developed literatures in international marketing have favoured systematic market selection process in comparison to stand-alone or ad hoc selection of country market. These studies have indicated inadequate or inappropriate evaluation of markets before entry as the key reason for failure in foreign market in subsequent time. These literatures have also favoured systematic evaluation of markets to ad hoc processes as the loss of misadventure, in most of the cases, will be more than the cost associated with systematic market selection process. Therefore, thinkers in international marketing have emphasised on the need of resorting to systematic evaluation and selection of the market before entering into new country market. This makes sense also as companies, after systematic selection of market, not only develop a full knowledge of the market before entering but also, at the same time, get preparation time to effectively deal with uncertainties of the new business environment.

Factors Affecting Market Selection Process

Now when a company contemplates an expansion into a foreign market, it is natural that it would want to judge which country/countries would provide the best of opportunities. This matchmaking between what the company can offer to the market and which country is the best fit for such offer is an important consideration that the company needs to decide on before making a serious move for expansion. At this juncture, the company faces a task of selecting the countries in terms of potentiality from around 220 sovereign countries in the world. This poses considerable difficulty not only for the SMEs but for bigger companies also. The following are the problems while resorting to systematic market selection process, in general terms.

- What makes a systematic market selection process and what is standard procedure?
- What information/data is required?
- How to collect first-hand information about the countries? Will it involve country visits?
- What different analyses need to be done using the secondary data?
- How much in-depth analysis one would do? Will it be too academic?
- What criteria one would adopt to compare international markets and short-list suitable countries for market entry?
- How much would depend upon the factors like personal experience or personal preference, rather than on data such as market size, growth rate or accessibility?
- What would be the best methodology that can be applied for selection of market by using the data that would be collected in the process?

Companies, looking to get answer to these questions, also vary in terms of their effectiveness and efforts they put in to get answers to the above questions because of a number of reasons. These reasons are varied in nature but mostly related to the internal capabilities of the company. The reasons are discussed below.

Organisation's orientation

"An organisation's response to global market opportunities depends greatly on management's assumptions or beliefs, both conscious and unconscious, about the nature of the world"[8]. Different writers' in international marketing, at different times, have pointed towards the fact that companies can be categorised in four different ways in terms of management orientation.

Ethnocentric Management of an organisation sees the home market as superior, but sees similarities in other markets to their own.

Polycentric Management views each country as unique and outlines the differences associated with each new country.

Regiocentric Management views both the similarities and differences of each country in relation to the world.

Geocentric Management have a worldwide view and can see the differences and similarities between home and host countries

The differences in the orientation induce the companies to involve in the market selection process differently. It is understandable that a company with ethnocentric orientation would pursue less rigorous methods to select a foreign market because its perceived difference between home country and foreign country is usually less. However, a company with polycentric orientation views each country as unique and is expected to put lot of effort in the market selection process.

International exposure

A Company's exposure in the internal market would be an influential factor in deciding its involvement in the market selection process. Companies with huge presence in domestic market but negligible experience in one or a few foreign markets would be highly specialised in terms of dealing with specific type of markets only. The domestic competitive pressure would make them primarily occupied with domestic problems than focusing attention to the international market selection process. The managerial experience of such companies would be primarily with the domestic markets and hence that may discourage them to resort to extensive international market selection research as the result may be deviating from management's practical experience. Generally, such company would open an international office in strategic location with responsibility loaded on the incumbent manager to internationalise the company. Since the main thrust of launching a systematic market selection is necessarily to be backed by top management's formal decision and active support therefore the absence of that make the incumbent manager unable to make any headway in this regard.

[8] Keegan, W. J. and Schlegelmilch, B. B. (2001), *Global Marketing Management – A European Perspective*, Pearson Education Limited, Harlow.

Time for research

Alon[9] (2004) argued that the time allotted for market selection decision is a key variable in deciding the market selection process. The successfully internationalised company like Metro Cash and Carry has demonstrated that the selection process could even run continuously like any other task of the company. Most of the time, the decision to enter a new foreign market is associated with long term strategy of a company and not just a reactive decision to certain spontaneous market happenings and hence requires quick action. In such hurried cases the decision maker can not resort to an extensive research in deciding the market as time at their disposal for analysis is limited. The company is, then, all set to enter a country which seems the easiest and less risky for decision-making. On the other hand, a company who takes the task of market selection proactively and accordingly install a machinery to carry out a formal selection process ahead of its competitors is expected to perform better. Thus, the time allotted in making the decision would be crucial factor in selecting the methodology for market selection.

Resources

Since international market selection involves looking across the international border, the data required for assessing foreign markets may not be easily available. It may require conducting both secondary and primary research to have a clear market perspective of the targeted foreign markets. In some circumstances, the company may have to outsource some research activities to professional research agencies to avail the expertise of the agency with a given market. Companies differ in terms of resources it can allocate for internationalisation. Some companies keep the agenda that makes market research a continuous process and thereby stand to benefit from updated information on right market entry at the right time. However, it all depends upon the resources the company is likely to spend on the selection process, which largely varies across companies.

Niche market specialisation

Some companies may operate as specialists of dealing with a niche product for a market sub group. For example, a company which markets only halal food may not be interested in countries where halal food is not much in vogue. Therefore, naturally market research activities of the company would be confined to those countries where particular demand exists or may exist. Moreover, in such cases, as the geographic spread for executing market research will be reduced the product demand determining factors will also be reduced.

Export Market Selection Process

How do export-oriented firms select market from a country? How do they assess the export-market opportunities? What specific market research they

[9] Alon, I. (2004), "International market selection for a small enterprise: A case study in international entrepreneurship", *S.A.M. Advanced Management Journal,* Vol. 69, Issue 1, pp. 25–33.

need to do when looking for a country of probable export destination? The small and medium enterprises (SMEs) recognise that there would be some countries across the world where their products would be of great demand. But which are the countries that may accept their products and allow them to earn profit through export? Only a few small enterprises intending to off-market their output abroad know about the other country's details such as geography, culture, and economics. Access to internet resources has allowed a window of knowledge but what exact information is to be looked for is not known. These difficulties compel enterprises to go for reactive mode of market opportunity identification through responding simply to unsolicited orders from foreign customers. This creates a sense of uncertainty about the size of the market and frequency of exports. At this juncture, the possible resource commitment to tap the market more aggressively is perceived to be risky and enterprises resort to wait-and-watch measures. On the other hand, identifying and analysing foreign market opportunity in a systematic way may allow enterprises to be proactive rather than reactive in pursuing the opportunity with more commitment. Studies in the literature report that the lack of information or insufficient information about foreign markets is one of the most commonly cited reasons preventing companies from exporting.

A systematic way of deciding on the export market opportunity may be executed step-by-step by the SMEs in the following manner.

Deciding on objectives

How important is exporting for the enterprise? The more importance is attached to exporting, the more likely it is for the firm to look for more detail about foreign market opportunities before sending products abroad. The depth of analysing also depends on how much time the entrepreneur would possibly be able to spare for desk work. Many small firms are 'all in one', i.e., due to smallness it is difficult to distinguish between the enterprise and the entrepreneur. In that case it may be difficult for the entrepreneur to spare time for this particular task by dissociating from day-to-day business activities. Comparatively bigger SMEs may have the ability to employ experienced international marketing managers who have the requisite feel of markets abroad and understand well about the informational requirements. So, in this step 1 of the selection process the objective of market selection will be set.

Decide on the product code

Harmonised System (HS) codes are an international method of classifying products for cross border trading purposes. World Customs Organisation (WCO) provides this classification system and is used by customs officials around the world to determine the duties, taxes and regulations that apply to the product. The Harmonisation Code (HS-Code) approximately covers 5300 articles/product descriptions put progressively under headings and sub headings for identifying specific product or commodity and they are arranged in 99 chapters, 21 sections. The HS Code number is an aggregate of a series of codes starting with a broad category and assigned a 2-digit identifier. It is then assigned a 4-digit identifier and likewise it goes down further.

For example:
Chapter 04 deals with dairy products, bird's egg, natural honey and edible products of animal origin (2 digits).

0401: Milk and cream, neither concentrated nor containing added sugar or other sweetening matter (4 digit).
04011000: Milk and cream containing fat not exceeding 1%.
04012000: Milk and cream containing fat > 1% but < 6% by weight.
04013000: Milk and cream containing fat > 6% by weight (6 digit).

Another example:
Chapter 16 deals with preparation of meat, of fish or of crustaceans, molluscs or other aquatic invertebrates

1602	Other prepared or preserved meat, meat offal or blood
1602 10 00	Homogenised preparations
1602 20 00	Of liver of any animal
	Of poultry of heading 0105 :
1602 31 00	Of turkeys
1602 32 00	Of fowls of the species Gallus domesticus
1602 39 00	Others of swine
1602 41 00	Hams and cuts thereof
1602 42 00	Shoulders and cuts thereof
1602 49 00	Other, including mixtures
1602 50 00	Of bovine animals
1602 90 00	Other, including preparations of blood of any animal

The HS coding system has world over acceptability and is used by more than 200 countries as a basis for their Customs tariffs and for the collection of international trade statistics. In order to be amenable to new product introduction or scope enlargement WCO prepares amendments updating the HS every 5 – 6 years. So, in step 2, the company, intending for export, would decide on the exact HS code/codes of the product/commodity being made ready for export.

Countries of possible destination

Once the product/products is/are decided and the relevant HS codes are known, the exporter may look for the country market. The exporter, at this stage, must think of all the countries of the world as possible market for exportation. Since in many cases it would be difficult to correctly assess consumption demand for the product so import demand could act as dummy for the purpose. High import of a particular product by a country indicates insufficiency of local production to meet consumption requirement. The idea of using import value as filtering criteria stems from the fact that import does indicate some void of the product in a particular country. Therefore, arranging the possible countries in order of their import value in USD terms, either descending or ascending, of the particular product and dropping out the countries with nil or negligible values may reduce the number of countries to a manageable one.

Huff and Sherr (1967)[10] presented the technique, popularly known as 'shift share approach', as a method of determining regional growth rates of markets.

[10] Huff, D. L. and L. A. Sherr (1967), "A measure for determining differential growth rates of markets", *Journal of Market Research*, Vol. 4, Issue 11, pp. 391–395.

This simple yet very useful technique that can be applied to screen high opportunity export markets for product/products of interest. This technique identifies the export opportunity differentials of product/market based upon the changes that have occurred on an imported product at the beginning and end of a specified period of analysis in the country/markets under consideration. For using the method, the following information are needed.

1. Time period for which growth comparisons of imported demand are made
2. Geographical unit (countries) for which analysis for relative measure is to be done
3. Variables, to measure relative gain or loss (import data)

The process involved calculation of the following:

Actual change: Suppose there are ten countries known to have demand for a specific product of interest as evidenced by the import demand over the years, for which the firm is looking for external market. The growth in the import value for a given time period for each of these countries will give the actual change. It is the actual change of the import value for the particular product of interest for the ten different countries under consideration. So,

$$\text{Actual change: } \Delta V_i = V_i,\ t - V_i\ (t-1)$$

Total growth: This is the summation of the growth variable of all the countries under consideration at the beginning of the time period and at the end of the time period. So,

$$\text{Total growth} = \Sigma V_i,\ t \text{ and } \Sigma\ V_i\ (t-1)$$

Rate of growth: The growth rate of all the market under consideration, K, is equal to the ratio of the total value in the terminal time period to the corresponding value in the initial time period. So,

$$\text{Rate of growth } K = \frac{\Sigma V_i,\ t}{\Sigma V_i\ (t-1)}$$

Expected value: If, for a given market, the import had grown at the rate achieved for all the markets, the expected value of the growth variables at the end of the terminal period $E\ (V_i,\ t)$, is the product of the actual value for this market at the end of the initial time period and the rate of change for all markets. That is

$$\text{Expected value} = E\ (V_i,\ t) = KV_i(t-1)$$

Expected change: The expected change in the value of a growth variable for a particular market in a given period of time is the difference between the expected value and the actual value for this market at the end of the initial time period. So, the Expected Change, $E\ (\Delta V_i,\ t)$ is given by

$$\begin{aligned}\text{Expected change} = E\ (\Delta V_i,\ t) &= \text{Expected value} - V_i\ (t-1)\\ &= KV_i\ (t-1) - V_i\ (t-1)\\ &= K - 1 \cdot V_i\ (t-1)\end{aligned}$$

Net shift: This is the difference between the actual change and the expected change for a given market and is denoted by N_i. Hence, N_i is given by

$$\text{Net shift} = \text{Actual change} - \text{Expected change}$$

$$N_i = \Delta V_i - E(\Delta V_i, t)$$

Sum of net shift: The sum of net shift of all the markets under consideration is zero, i.e., ΣN_i for all markets = 0. This implies that if all the shifts for the market under consideration are separated into ones that are greater than or equal to zero and into those that are less than zero and denoted as ΣN_i positive and ΣN_i negative respectively, then

$$\Sigma N_i \text{ positive} + \Sigma N_i \text{ negative} = 0$$

Total absolute net shift: This is either the sum of positive net shifts or the negative net shifts and is represented by S where $S = \Sigma N_i$ positive or ΣN_i negative.

Percentage net shift: This figure is arrived at by dividing net shift of the individual markets by absolute net shift, i.e.,

$$\% \text{ Net shift} = \frac{N_i}{S} \times 100\ \%$$

Application of the method

This example illustrates the application of the shift share method for identifying the market for conveyor belts. Consider a manufacturer of conveyor belts with its plant in Bangalore looking for marketing opportunities abroad. The product, i.e., conveyor belts consist of two end-pulleys and a continuous loop of material that rotates about them. They are used in a variety of material handing applications, including food and beverage processing, manufacturing, mining, packaging and power transmission. Some conveyor belts are designed to transport commercial goods, construction materials, forest products, or pulp and paper. Others are designed for agricultural, general-purpose or inclined conveying applications. Elevator belts are designed for vertical applications and have attachments such as buckets or trays. High-temperature conveyor belts are made of materials that are suitable for use at high ambient temperatures or that are designed to handle high-temperature materials. Often, these products are used in oven conveyor belting and the conveyance of heat-treated parts. Belt material is the most important consideration when selecting conveyor belts.

With wide variety of applications, conveyor belts have a good international marketing potential in several countries of the world which the manufacturer-exporter is looking for. The product carries the six digit ITC HS code of 401012. Table 5.4 presents the import value of the product against the HS code 401012 in Column 1, for the year 2003–04, for top forty countries as have been obtained from trade data base[11]. Column 2 gives the import values in USD terms of the same product (in six-digit ITC HS code) for the year 2007–08 for the same countries. Column 3 shows the actual change and is the difference between the values of Column 2 and Column 1. The K factor, i.e., the growth rate is then calculated by dividing the sum of Column 2 by the sum of Column 1. Column 4 has the expected value that has been arrived at by multiplying the values of Column 1 by K. The difference between the values in Column 4 and Column 1 is given in Column 5 and represents the expected change. Columns 6 and 7 give the negative and positive net shift

[11] www.trademap.org or World Integrated Trade Solution (WITS) data base

Table 5.4 Shift share calculation

S. No.	Country name	Import value (₹ lacs) period 1 (2003–04)	Import value (₹ lacs) period 2 (2007–08)	Actual change Value (₹ lacs)	Expected value (₹ lacs)	Expected change value (₹ lacs)	Net shift (–) Value (₹ lacs)	Net shift (+) Value (₹ lacs)	Absolute shift value (₹ lacs)	% Ns
									(*S*)	*N/S* × 100%
1.	Algeria	223.48	20.38	–203.10	385.15	161.67	–364.77		–3921.98	–9.301%
2.	Australia	323.17	1158.20	835.03	556.96	233.79		601.24	3921.98	15.330%
3.	Bangladesh	24.84	3.13	–21.71	42.81	17.97	–39.68		–3921.98	–1.012%
4.	Canada	98.43	431.93	333.50	169.64	71.21		262.29	3921.98	6.688%
5.	Chile	1.13	141.07	139.94	1.95	0.82		139.12	3921.98	3.547%
6.	Denmark	11.51	550.49	538.98	19.84	8.33		530.65	3921.98	13.530%
7.	Djibouti	1.12	1.84	0.72	1.93	0.81	–0.09		–3921.98	–0.002%
8.	Finland	12.68	60.78	48.10	21.85	9.17		38.93	3921.98	0.993%
9.	France	2.18	175.62	173.44	3.76	1.58		171.86	3921.98	4.382%
10.	Germany	97.74	216.91	119.17	168.45	70.71		48.46	3921.98	1.236%
11.	Ghana	12.24	13.20	0.96	21.09	8.85	–7.89		–3921.98	–0.201%
12.	Greece	0.59	16.25	15.66	1.02	0.43		15.23	3921.98	0.388%
13.	Guyana	3.13	5.84	2.71	5.39	2.26		0.45	3921.98	0.011%
14.	Italy	136.41	614.77	478.36	235.09	98.68		379.68	3921.98	9.681%
15.	Japan	1.42	1.83	0.41	2.45	1.03	–0.62		–3921.98	–0.016%
16.	Jordan	0.36	16.31	15.95	0.62	0.26		15.69	3921.98	0.400%
17.	Kazakhstan	198.70	589.42	390.72	342.44	143.74		246.98	3921.98	6.297%
18.	Kenya	10.66	16.59	5.93	18.37	7.71	–1.78		–3921.98	–0.045%
19.	Malaysia	46.01	26.07	–19.94	79.29	33.28	–53.22		–3921.98	–1.357%
20.	Mauritius	2.86	1.46	–1.40	4.93	2.07	–3.47		–3921.98	–0.088%
21.	Nepal	6.40	3.42	–2.98	11.03	4.63	–7.61		–3921.98	–0.194%
22.	Netherlands	158.27	701.43	543.16	272.76	114.49		428.67	3921.98	10.930%
23.	New Zealand	29.39	1.04	–28.35	50.65	21.26	–49.61		–3921.98	–1.265%
24.	Nigeria	0.36	33.26	32.90	0.62	0.26		32.64	3921.98	0.832%

(Continued)

Table 5.4 (*Continued*)

S. No.	Country name	Import value (₹ lacs) period 1 (2003–04)	Import value (₹ lacs) period 2 (2007–08)	Actual change Value (₹ lacs)	Expected value (₹ lacs)	Expected change value (₹ lacs)	Net shift (–) Value (₹ lacs)	Net shift (+) Value (₹ lacs)	Absolute shift value (₹ lacs)	% Ns
									(*S*)	*N/S* × 100%
25.	Peru	30.17	161.47	131.30	52.00	21.83		109.47	3921.98	2.791%
26.	Portugal	8.84	99.37	90.53	15.23	6.39		84.14	3921.98	2.145%
27.	Russia	19.08	23.71	4.63	32.88	13.80	–9.17		–3921.98	–0.234%
28.	Saudi Arab	209.12	108.63	–100.49	360.40	151.28	–251.77		–3921.98	–6.419%
29.	Singapore	67.45	11.02	–56.43	116.24	48.79	–105.22		–3921.98	–2.683%
30.	South Africa	2216.96	874.26	–1342.70	3820.74	1603.78	–2946.48		–3921.98	–75.127%
31.	Spain	3.28	128.42	125.14	5.65	2.37		122.77	3921.98	3.130%
32.	Sri Lanka	4.55	1.47	–3.08	7.84	3.29	–6.37		–3921.98	–0.162%
33.	Thailand	19.13	15.20	–3.93	32.97	13.84	–17.77		–3921.98	–0.453%
34.	Trinidad	54.76	128.94	74.18	94.37	39.61		34.57	3921.98	0.881%
35.	Uganda	0.48	0.11	–0.37	0.83	0.35	–0.72		–3921.98	–0.018%
36.	U A. E	95.00	325.53	230.53	163.72	68.72		161.81	3921.98	4.126%
37.	U K	79.70	397.13	317.43	137.36	57.66		259.77	3921.98	6.624%
38.	U S A	623.78	1312.59	688.81	1075.03	451.25		237.56	3921.98	6.057%
39.	Vietnam Soc. Rep	3.11	4.19	1.08	5.36	2.25	–1.17		–3921.98	–0.030%
40.	Zambia	35.77	7.08	–28.69	61.65	25.88	–54.57		–3921.98	–1.391%
	GRAND TOTAL	4874.26	8400.36	3526.10		3526.10	–3921.98	3921.98		

Table 5.5 Short-listed countries

S. No.	Country name	% NS	S No.	Country name	% NS
		N/S × 100%			N/S × 100%
1.	Australia	15.330%	6	Kazakhstan	6.297%
2.	Canada	6.688%	7	Netherland	10.930%
3.	Denmark	13.530%	8	UAE	4.126%
4.	France	4.382%	9	UK	6.624%
5.	Italy	9.681%	10	USA	6.057%

Source: Author

values respectively, which is nothing but the difference between the expected change of Column 5 and actual change Column 3. Column 8 gives the absolute change, while Column 9 expresses the net shift as a percentage of absolute change.

It may be observed from the above table that some countries are showing positive shifts while others are showing negative shifts. The countries with substantial positive shifts are shown in Table 5.5 and these could be selected for exporting conveyor belt from the company. The countries whose net shift value is negative do not attract the manufacturer exporter at present. The ten countries with positive shift are short-listed as the countries of attraction and put under further tests.

So, at the end of step 3 of the selection process, the analyst will get to know the short listed countries having demand for the product and their rank in accordance to the demand.

Establish the trend

Once the countries are short listed, it becomes possible for the company to subject them for further tests towards their suitability as export destination. In the next step, therefore, the company may want to know the trend of importation of the product/products under consideration of the short listed countries from the home country of the intending exporting company (Table 5.6). This basically serves two purposes; one, to determine if the country of intending exporter has a history of exportation of the selected product/products to the short listed countries and two, to further isolate the countries out of the shorted listed countries who are over the years good importers of the product from the home country of the exporting company. This can be done easily by collecting trade data between the concerned countries in dollar terms from the free to use trade data base like www.trademap.org (Table 5.7).

Table 5.6 Home country position in the short listed countries

Short listed countries	Ranking of the countries based on yearly import value from India			
	2005	2006	2007	2008
Australia	1	1	1	2
Canada	2	3	2	1
Denmark	3	2	3	3
France	4	5	4	6
Italy	5	6	6	5
Kazakhstan	6	10	10	4
Netherland	7	9	9	10
UAE	8	8	5	9
UK	9	7	7	8
USA	10	4	8	7

Source: Author

So, at the end of step 4 the analyst will be able to identify and rank countries in terms of their possible demand sustainability. Here, in the table,

Table 5.7 Trade intimacy with the target country market

Product ginger	Trade intensity Index 2005	2006	2007	2008	Remark
Australia					An index of more (less) than one indicates a bilateral trade flow that is larger (smaller) than expected, given the partner country's importance in world trade.
Canada					
Denmark					
France					
Italy					
Kazakhstan					
Netherland					
UAE					
UK					
USA					

Australia, Canada, Denmark seems to be the countries with stable demand for the product.

Trade Intimacy

After establishing market fluctuation trend of the short listed countries, the exporter will be further interested to know the level of trade intimacy of the short listed countries with home country. Here Trade Intensity Index (TII), formulated by Frankel (1997)[12], can be used. The TII is based on an actual observation of bilateral trade flow, and it measures the intimacy of the trading relationship between any given two countries.

$$I_{ij} = (X_{ij}/X_i) / (M_j/W)$$

Where, X_{ij} denotes exports from Country i to Country j,
Xi equals the total exports from Country i,
M_j is the total imports of Country j, and
W represents the world trade volume
In this way, the TII of the countries under consideration can be calculated by collecting yearly export –import data in dollar terms between the concerned countries from free to use website like www.trademap.org.

For those trading partners that have TIIs greater than unity, their trade relationship can be defined as 'intensive'. An analysis of the changes in TII over time can show whether two countries are experiencing an increased or decreased tendency to trade with one another. An increasing TII can assure the exporter of apparent increasing easiness being experienced by the exporters of his country while exporting to the target country in question.

So, at the end of step 5 the analyst will be able to re - rank the short listed countries based on trade intensiveness.

[12] Frankel, J., Stein E and Shang Jin-Wei (1997), "Regional trading blocs in the world economic system", *Institute for International Economics*, Washington DC, ISBN-0-88.132-202-4

Table 5.8 Further information for marketer to decide on target market

Market access requirements	Remarks
The product-specific entry tariff rate to be charged by the destination country, Any quota that may have been imposed on the product.	Tariff rate applicable updated information are available from www. Trademap.org under market access tab.
Any existing or possible trade agreement such as RTA, FTA, etc.	Trade agreement related updated information are available from www. Trademap.org under market access tab.
The non-tariff barriers practised in the country.	Non tariff barriers related updated information are available from www. Trademap.org under market access tab.

Final decision on target market

Once the countries of interest are identified and their relative attractiveness ranking are made in the previously mentioned successive steps, the next task for the marketers is to ascertain the market access issues such as tariff rate, possible non tariff barriers, tariff concessions expected by different countries The various issues the marketer would like to know for further screening of the short listed countries are detailed below in Table 5.8.

Market Selection for Setting up Own Subsidiary

Country market selection process for setting up own subsidiary requires more detail investigations because of more intense involvement with the destination country than entering the country through export. Hence, the previously described export market selection process will not be applicable. Market selection for setting up own subsidiary in foreign country would require, therefore, more detail investigations of the countries before final selection.

In the matter of market selection for setting up subsidiary Johansson, (1997)[13] and Root, (1994)[14] opined that companies follow two fundamental patterns in market selection process: expansive and contractible. Expansive process: In this process, company will select its neighbouring countries as the country to enter to take full advantage of its acquaintance with the country markets. In other words, the selection of country market will depend on psychic distance and least psychic distance countries will be selected for setting up own subsidiary. Psychic distance refers to the knowledge and experience of company officials, responsible for foreign market selection, about foreign country markets in the matter related to doing business there. This distance acts at the individual level. Generally, neighbouring countries provides least psychic distance to the managers of the entering company.

Contractible process: In this process, the company does not keep any prejudice to any geographic location but rather looks at the world with an open

[13] Johansson, J.K. (1997), *Global Marketing, Foreign Entry, Local Marketing and Global Management*, McGraw-Hill, Chicago, IL.

[14] Root, F.R. (1994), *Entry Strategies for International Markets*, Lexington Books, San Francisco, CA.

mind for selection of the most suitable country market to enter. It install a process which possibly considers most, if not all, country markets that have possibilities of becoming target market and then the process sequentially evaluates the country markets with the help of pre determined criteria best serve the purpose of the company. At different stages of evaluation different countries come up which are put to test with specifically selected criteria to ascertain the suitability of the country in terms of its marketing requirements. At the last, a manageable number of countries remains for more thorough investigation before actual entry is made.

A typical contractible market selection process may have the following sequential process.

Decide the objective of expansion

The mainstream perspective in international business assumes that companies are strategy oriented and hence they have some definable motives when looking for expansion internationally. These motives are in tune with long-term objectives that the firm desires to achieve and hence bear the cost and risk associated with entering and operating abroad. For example, Metro Cash and Carry (MCC), the German retailer while embarking on country selection for expansion, bears the motive of becoming one of the top three retailers of the selected country amongst countries where it has an existing presence. The company wants to be first of its kind, in terms of its innovative B-to-B business model, when the countries where the company has no previous presence are considered. So in the first stage of contractible process it is required that the company clearly spells of the objective of expanding abroad. The objectives are further translated in to operational terms so that it set the tune of the selection process. For example, MCC says that do not consider those countries under selection process where the big retailers already occupied forty percent of the market share.

Decide on country basket

At the initial stage, it should be decided that how many countries would be there in the basket of candidate countries. Literally, all the 200 countries of the world should be there in the basket. However, based on the objective set in the previous step, the company typically decides to consider a particular trade area, a particular economic grouping or a group of countries which satisfy the broadly the company objective already documented. MCC's objective of regional focus allows them to start with countries from Europe, Asia and to a lesser extent from North Africa. North America, South America, UAE and Oceania would not there in the MCC's country basket the reason being either the markets are too competitive or there are inflicted with entry barriers.

Preliminary screening

After deciding the country basket the next step is necessarily a preliminary screening process. At this stage, the countries under scanner are subjected to evaluation through scoring on different parameters such as political stability, geographic distance from strategic locations of interest, and economic development. The countries that fare poorly in this evaluation are eliminated.

At this stage, requisite weights can also be assigned to the parameters under consideration based on the type of products to be marketed. For example, a company that deals with a product such as voice processing software would assign more weight to parameters like ethnic diversity of the country than geographic distance. In a sense, the company at this stage must be able to identify the parameters under the four broad headings of economic environment, political environment, demographic/physical environment and socio-cultural environment. The score will then be allotted to the individual countries under the radar of this exercise against the pre-determined parameters. In addition to data searches across various publications that are used for scoring the countries, many of the ratings may came from subjective judgment of the experts. For example, Tables 5.9 to 5.12 are the sample formats for scoring individual countries based on four broad criteria. In this example, five fictitious countries, Free Mania, Closed Mania, Develop Mania, Developing Mania, and Market Mania have been taken to demonstrate the evaluating techniques in preliminary scoring stage.

Table 5.9 Economic environment of country 'Free Mania'

S. No.	Economic environment	Weight	Multiplied with the score on a scale 0–4[1]	Final rating[2]
1.	Overall level of development	3	3	9
2.	Economic growth: GNP, industrial sector	2	2	4
3.	Role of foreign trade in the economy	1	1	1
4.	Currency: inflation rate, availability, controls, stability of exchange rate	0.5	1	0.5
5.	Balance of payments	0.5	1	0.5
6	Per capita income and distribution	1	3	3
7.	Disposable income and expenditure patterns	1	2	2
8.	Monetary Inflation	1	1	1
	Total	10	× 4 (Max)	21(Max 40)

1. 0-unacceptable; 1-poor; 2-average condition; 3- above average condition; 4-superior condition
2. Maximum point that a country can score is 40.

Table 5.10 Social/Cultural environment of country 'Free Mania'

S. No.	Social/Cultural environment	Weight	Multiplied with the score on a scale 0–4[1]	Final rating[2]
1.	Literacy rate, educational level	3	3	9
2.	Existence of middle class	2	2	4
3.	Similarities and differences in relation to home market	1	1	1
4.	Language and other cultural considerations	0.5	1	0.5
5.	Religious bias	0.5	1	0.5

(*Continued*)

Table 5.10 *(Continued)*

S. No.	Social/Cultural environment	Weight	Multiplied with the score on a scale 0–4[1]	Final rating[2]
6.	Gender values	1	3	3
7.	Attitude towards entrepreneurship	1	2	2
8.	Attitude towards foreign business	1	1	1
	Total	10	× 4 (Max)	21(Max 40)

1. 0-unacceptable; 1-poor; 2-average condition; 3- above average condition; 4-superior condition
2. Maximum point that a country can score is 40.

Table 5.11 Political environment of country 'Free Mania'

S. No.	Political environment	Weight	Multiplied with the score on a scale 0-4[1]	Final rating[2]
1.	System of government	3	3	9
2.	Political stability and continuity	2	2	4
3.	Ideological orientation	1	1	1
4.	Government involvement in business	0.5	1	0.5
5.	Government involvement in communications	0.5	1	0.5
6.	Openness to trade (trade restrictions, tariffs, non-tariff barriers, bilateral trade agreements)	1	3	3
7.	National economic and developmental priorities	1	2	2
8.	Terrorist activities; Riots, frequency of bomb blast, etc.	1	1	1
	Total	10	× 4 (Max)	21(Max 40)

1. 0-unacceptable; 1-poor; 2-average condition; 3- above average condition; 4-superior condition
2. Maximum point that a country can score is 40.

Table 5.12 Demographic/Physical environment of country 'Free Mania'

S. No.	Demographic/Physical environment	Weight	Multiplied with the score on a scale 0-4[1]	Final rating[2]
1.	Population size, growth, density	3	3	9
2.	Urban and rural distribution	2	2	4
3.	Climate and weather variations	1	1	1
4.	Port efficiency; Shipping distance	0.5	1	0.5
5.	Product-significant demographics	0.5	1	0.5
6.	Physical distribution efficiency, retailing network.	1	3	3
7.	Natural resources	1	2	2
8.	Communication network; Mobile penetration	1	1	1
	Total	10	× 4 (Max)	21(Max 40)

1. 0-unacceptable; 1-poor; 2-average condition; 3- above average condition; 3-superior condition
2. Maximum point that a country can score is 40.

Table 5.13 Overall countries score

S. No.	Countries	Score				Final score (Max 160)
		Economic	Socio-cultural	Political	Demographic / Physical	
1.	Free Mania	21	21	21	21	84
2.	Closed Mania	14	13	15	16	58
3.	Develop Mania	12	15	12	13	52
4.	Developing Mania	25	25	25	25	100
5.	Market Mania	3	4	5	2	14

For other countries such as Free Mania, Closed Mania, Develop Mania, Developing Mania, and Market Mania are scored in the similar way and the respective scores are plotted in the Table 5.13

In this example, out of the five countries under consideration, the country Developing Mania has scored more than the other four and hence in terms of attractiveness tops the list.

Deciding on the opportunities

The scoring done in the previous step will allow the company to focus its attention on some countries that appear to be attractive at this stage. However, a big question requires answering at this juncture: which of the short-listed countries fit perfectly in terms of opportunities required by the company. To get answer the question, the company has to first understand its strategic requirements and expectations from the countries and then set up criteria through which it can judge the countries in accordance to the suitability dimension. The comparatively less suitable countries may then be relegated to 'waiting list'. For example, say a mobile handset manufacturing company found ' Developing Mania' as a candidate country. In the country basket during preliminary selection process, However, the company set a strategic consideration that if a single handset manufacturer dominates the country market with more that seventy percent market share then it will adopt a policy of 'wait and watch' and hence that country will not be considered as market. Thus, the company decided to put a criteria in this direction and 'Developing Mania' was tested against it. It was found that Nokia totally dominated the country market and hence strategically decided not to take a very strong rival 'head on' because of its certain shortcomings on competitiveness. This stage, therefore, creates two separate lists of countries: one, a list of **focus countries** for further investigation and two, a list of **wait listed countries** for consideration the next year.

Desk research for the focus countries

This stage entails close observation of the focus countries and extensive desk research. In this stage country profiles are made for focus countries by exploring different possible information sources. Countries are profiled in more details than in the preliminary selection stage with data on parameters such as market potential, growth rates of market, strengths and competitive factors, ease of entry, distribution possibilities, cultural distance,

Table 5.14 Parameters for desk research of focus countries

S. No.	Focus countries A, B, C, ...	Weight on a scale 0-4[1]	Multiplied with the score on a scale 0-5[2]	Final score
1.	Market potential	4	4	16
2.	Growth rates of the market	2	3	6
3.	Strengths and competitive factors	1	3	3
4.	Distribution possibilities	3	4	12
5.	Cultural similarity	1	2	2
6.	Technology absorption	1	2	2
7.	Ease of entry	3	3	9
				50 (Max 140)

1. 0-least important; 1-important to some extent; 2-important; 3-very important; 4-absolutely important.
2. Scores are on a scale 1 to 5 where 1 indicates poor condition on that parameter and 5 indicates outstanding. Maximum score that a parameter can have is 20.

technological development, legal system, tax structure and financial environment. The basic idea at this stage is to know the countries more closely and rank them in the order of attractiveness. Parameters that are considered here are both macro and micro in nature but strategically selected so that they reflect the company's possible match with the market (Table 5.14). Based on these data, the focussed countries are to be scored. Apart from searches across various data sources many of the ratings may also come from analyst's subjective judgment because of difficulty in getting accurate data on every selected parameters.

In this way, the focus countries are rated to find out their relative attractiveness for the company.

Deciding on the operational issues

The desk research of the previous stage has led to selection of a few countries which offer opportunities for international expansion. The parameters selected so far have tested these countries from all direction including the match between firm's objectives and country opportunities. However, some operational issues need to be addressed such as the availability of office space, components of cost of production, difficulty of hiring human resources, work cultures, port efficiency, forecast of sales revenues and projected profit. So, in this stage both primary and secondary information are collected to understand ease of operating business after getting in to these countries.

Country visit and final choice

One important aspect to be noted at this stage is that desk research done in the previous states would not provide the actual feel of the country prospect. Therefore, in the final stage, a team from the company need to visit the country of best prospect to validate the desk research findings with the ground situation. The team may try to understand the immediate environment of business in question such as suppliers, presence of pressure groups, distributors, law and order enforcement, modalities of approval of foreign business, functioning of chambers of commerce and industries, banking efficiency, etc. The report of the visiting team will ultimately trigger resource commitment, both financial and human, for international expansion.

SOURCES OF INFORMATION

The systematic market selection process requires both micro and macro data of different countries which are be far away from the company's existing location. There are various websites which may prove to be very handy while looking for various data. Few of such websites are discussed below.

Business Environment Risk Index (BERI): BERI is a risk rating for country risk created by the Business Environment Risk Intelligence SA. It analyses the country situation and forecast the country risk for over 140 countries of the world. Experts retained the company carry out the analysis. The index is primarily useful as a handy tool to understand a country situation in terms of political stability, economic growth, currency convertibility, attitude towards foreign investors, enforceability of contacts, local management or partners, etc. The index attach high importance on the political stability of the country out of the many other factors considered for index preparation. The index value ranges from 1 to 100. A score below 40 indicates high risk country where as a score above 80 indicates favourable environment for investors. http:// www.beri.com/ is the website address.

Export. Gov: Export.gov is an American government website managed by the International Trade Administration of USA in collaboration with various other US department such as Small Business Administration (SBA), Energy, Export Import bank, The US Trade and Development Agency (USTDA), Overseas Private Investment Corporation (OPIC), etc. The US Government has also strategically partnered with major corporations to help small and medium-sized US companies begin and/or expand their export sales. http://export.gov/ is the website address.

Global edge: This website is maintained in the Michigan state university and funded in part by the US Department of Education. globalEDGE delivers a comprehensive research tool for academics, students and businesspeople. Connect with over 47,000 people using the gE Network while tapping into a directory of over 5000 quality resources. globalEDGE provides tools and resources to efficiently research nearly any international business question that one can have. One can find sector detailing, insight research of industries, trade law, trade data, tutorials, etc., http://globaledge.msu.edu is the website address.

The world fact book: The World Fact book or the CIA World Fact book is a useful website for knowing the information of the countries of the world. This is developed and maintained by the Central Intelligence Agency of the United States with almanac-style information about the countries of the world. The Factbook is available in the form of a website, which is partially updated every week. It is also available for download for use off-line. It provides a two- to three-page summary of the demographics, geography, communications, government, economy, and military of

267 entities including US-recognised countries, dependencies, and other areas in the world. It is frequently used as a resource for academic research papers also.

Federation of International Trade Association (FITA): FITA, founded in 1984, engaged in fosters international trade by linking local, regional, national and global associations that have an international mission. FITA provides useful resources, to the international trade community desiring to upgrade their business globally. http://www.fita.org/ is the website address.

CBI (Ministry of Foreign Affairs of Netherland)

CBI is the website maintained by the Ministry of Foreign Affairs, Government of Netherland and contributes to sustainable economic development in developing countries through the expansion of exports from these countries to the European countries primarily. The website contains various reports pertaining to various sectors such as agriculture, fishery , forestry, consumer goods, industrial products, and services as well in respect of the EU countries. These reports helps to understand the market access requirements, legisialtions, market survey and marketing giudelines. It also offers services to the European importers to access to hundreds of suppliers in emerging markets in various sectors through its database. These supplier are screened, trained and have access to the latest information regarding market developments, norms, import regulations, etc., http://www.cbi.eu/ is the website address.

Emerging market companion: The Emerging Markets Companion provides comprehensive review of news, closing prices, and research from the major emerging markets financial and regional centers. The Emerging Markets Companion was founded in 1996 and is based in River Edge, New Jersey. USA. Many freely available information about the emerging markets such as news, analysis, commentary, and data for investors of Eastern Europe, Asia, Latin America, and Africa are available in this website. There are links to other emerging-market sites, including excellent online country- and region-specific financial resources. http://www.emgmkts.com/ is the website address.

WTO tariff analysis online: This WTO site helps to research and analyse tariff data for the WTO member countries. The member countries binding commitments and maximum tariff are feely available in this website. This operates in question – report mode where the researcher or entrepreneur can enter the "queries" in the " ask Tariff Analysis Online" which will produce some answers in the form of reports. The reports can be viewed and manipulated online or downloaded and printed. http://www.wto.org/english/tratop_e/tariffs_e/tao_help_e.htm is the website address.

Emerging Markets: Assessing Market Potential

One major problem of contractible market selection process surfaces from the fact that it will now allow emerging country markets to be selected unless the analyst purposefully picked up specific criteria favoring the emerging country markets during successive evaluation stages. In general, the emerging country markets are not expected to fulfill all the criteria of evaluation and score high while rated. The political situation in most of the emerging countries markets will not attract good score when compared in the same table with a develop country. So, neat result would be settling in the bottom in the selection process. However, how an international marketers can forget that these emerging countries are in the process of rapid economic development by restructuring their economies along market-oriented lines and can offer a good opportunity to them in the long run. According to the World Bank, the five biggest emerging markets are China, India, Indonesia, Brazil and Russia who offer great marketing opportunities to the international marketers. The emerging markets such as Mexico, Argentina, South Africa, Poland, Turkey, etc., also attracting the international businesses with growth opportunities that possibly no longer exist in highly competitive developed country markets. But these countries may not score high when macroeconomic parameters are evaluated. But one internationalising company could visualise the tremendous long term possibilities emanating from their demographic dividend and spending patterns in spite of rough political and legal environment. The political system of these countries may be considered acceptable to the company even if branded as flawed democracy by the democracy index of the Economist. The legal system may be not strong enough to save guard intellectual property rights. A huge income inequality in the country may be the characteristic by default. However, for a particular company looking for long term potential, these countries may be perceived to be attractive countries inspite of many odds. Malaysia and Mexico has majority of population below 18 years which remains as attraction for businesses. The strength of Indian middle income population in terms of purchasing power entices international marketers even if the political and legal systems are not up to the mark. Therefore, briefly, the attractiveness of the emerging countries are on account of such parameters such as large young populations, untapped resource bases, and growing per capita income, which cannot be captured by normative stage by stage screening process using macro economic and political factors. However, companies do not want to miss them as well. Arnold and Quelch (1998)[15] proposed a simple method for assessing the potential of emerging markets. This method considers demographic and economic data available for emerging markets as well as data specific to both product and country markets and predicts long term market potential Q.

$$Q = (P + NP) \times (\text{Dev GDP} - \text{Adj GDP})$$

Where Q, total market potential of the emerging country;
P is national population;
NP is new population, i.e., population growth in the planning period;
Dev. GDP is average per capita GDP in developed markets; and
Adj. GDP is GDP in the measured country market adjusted to purchasing power parity level.

[15] Arnold , D.J. and Quelch,J.A.(1998), "New strategies in emerging markets". Sloan Management Review, Vol. 40, pp 7-20

Table 5.15 Market potential of emerging markets

Emerging markets	National population 2030 in million (P)	2010 population in million	NP to be added by 2030 in million	Dev.GDP, in USD in 2011	AdjGDP (GDP PPP per capita) 2011 in USD	Dev GDP – Adj GDP per capital in USD	Market potential (Q) 2030 in million USD
India	152.35	122.46	29.89	29,500	3652	25,898	39,45,301
Indonesia	27.97	23.99	3.98	29,500	4668	17,831	498,733
Brazil	22.05	19.50	2.55	29,500	11,719	17,831	393,173
Russia	13.64	14.30	–0.65	29,500	21,248	8302	113,239
Mexico	13.54	11.34	2.20	29,500	15,270	14,280	193,351

Source: Author's calculation

The following example will demonstrate the use of Arnold and Quelch method in understanding the market potential for emerging countries such as India, Indonesia, Brazil, Russia, and Mexico. The planning period taken in this example is 20 years, i.e., up to 2030 from 2010. The GDP per capita data adjusted to purchasing power parity has been obtained from CIA fact book. Using Arnold and Quelch (1998) formula, the market potential (Q) by 2030 in respect of five countries, namely India, Indonesia, Brazil, Russia, and Mexico has been calculated out and placed in the Table 5.15

The method allows computation of market size of the emerging market by relating growth of population of that country with the difference between GDP per capita averages between developed markets and an emerging market. This long term market potential would act as an additional indicator while the company takes recourse to normative market section process of emerging markets. It can be seen from the above table that India is the top potential country followed by Indonesia, Brazil, Mexico and Russia.

CHAPTER SUMMARY

1. The motives for the company's expansion are varied and some of them act as primary or proactive motives and others are secondary or reactive motives that trigger international expansion. It is always a combination of motives that bring company expanding to other country markets. The proactive motives are strategic in nature while the reactive motives are supportive to the key strategy.
2. When a company contemplates an expansion in to the foreign market it is natural that it would want to judge the potentiality as to which country/countries provides the best of the opportunities. This matchmaking between what the company can offer to the market and which country is the best fit for such offer is an important consideration that the company needs to decide before making a serious move for expansion. At this juncture the company faces a task of finding out the best suited country market in term of market potentiality from around 200 sovereign countries in the world. This poses considerable difficulty not only for the small size companies but for bigger one also.
3. The companies, while resorting to market selection, encounter a number of influencing factors which ultimately decide the selection process. These influencing factors are mostly related to the internal capabilities of the company such as organisational orientation, time for research, and resources committed for the purpose.
4. Export market selection process follows through a number of steps stating with ascertaining the HS code of the product/products for which the market is sought for. A mathematical procedure, like

shift share method, allows the marketer to use the trade data base more effectively and efficiently. The process ultimately focuses on few country markets which then are extensively investigated further with various economic analyses to zoom on the best markets.

5. In case of market selection with hierarchical mode of entry, more detail investigations will be involved in the process. In expansive mode the companies generally will look for and enter country market having least psychic distance. In contractible methods of foreign market selection a sequential process of evaluation of more promising markets is followed through pre determined criteria and rejecting the countries at different stages who do not pass through the selected criteria. The criteria are specifically selected that allow the company to judge suitability of the country in terms of its marketing requirements. At a certain stage, when a manageable number of countries emerged, a more thorough investigation of the countries is done to arrange the countries in terms of preference of entry.
6. The emerging country markets are not expected to fulfill all the criteria of evaluation adopted in systematic market selection process and such markets will not attract good score when compared in the same table with a develop country. Assessing the potential of the emerging markets, therefore, requires a different perspective. These markets can be further judged towards their long term market potential, cultural distance between the emerging market and country of origin, competitive strength of the specific industry in the emerging market and customer receptiveness to the product of the foreign country. However, these assessments are not an alternative method of systematic market selection but rather as a tool to complement the normative selection process only.

QUESTIONS FOR REVIEW

Short Answer Questions

1. How is systematic screening and assessment of countries performed for export market identification? What different types of information are needed for this process?
2. Do you think a company can use systematic market selection process in case the target markets comprises of emerging markets? Justify your answer.
3. Select an Indian company and identify the exportable product and find the international markets for the product through systematic market selection procedure used in export market selection process
4. What are the different web-based trade data sources useful for export market selection process? What information is available in the www.trademap.org data base?
5. What are the benefits of systematic market selection process? Answer with the help of examples.

Descriptive Questions

1. In December 1995, Beverages India released its energy drink, Boosta in India. This product proved a great success in the Indian market and now dominates the company's sales. In addition to the quality of the product, a major reason for its success has been its eye-catching packaging and effective branding. Boosta is a lightly carbonated, new age beverage containing a uniquely balanced blend of pure spring water, natural amino acid, vitamins and caffeine. Boosta, as a product, provides an immediately discernible boost when an energy lift is needed. The CEO of Beverages India on his recent tour to South Africa got attracted as its potential market. His initial research on the market revealed the following; the total value of the South African energy drinks market was AUD 134 million during 2008, total consumption was 204 million litres and total production was 218 litres; disposable income is increasing but this may be within a small segment of the population; black empowerment is a key consideration in South Africa, but there are concerns that this movement will benefit only a certain black elite; unemployment is still rife at approximately

30%; achieving effective distribution in township areas is a key concern, especially as far as physical distribution in the face of criminal activities is concerned; high levels of illiteracy exist in the country. Segmentation is complicated because there are a multitude of black cultures and subcultures with no clear regional delineation.
Evaluate the target market selection process of the company **Beverages India?** *What further market research (if any) would be required to consolidate the decision to enter the South African market?*

2. Toyota, the Japanese automaker, exported overseas first to its Southeast Asian neighbors, then to Australia. As a former export manager of Toyota remembered: "The Asian markets were familiar with us and expansion were natural. Australia, we did not know very much but it was a sort of rehearsal for entering the US. We had decided that Toyota needed to be in US market because of its market potential and status it carried here at home. Europe? Well that is different" He smiled sheepishly. "A Danish Businessman came to Tokyo in 1958 and wanted to be our representative in Denmark. We did not know what to do, but he simply ordered few cars from us, pre paid and we had to ship then. That is how Europe got started. No systematic planning, as you can see. The Danish businessman was a very good entrepreneur and we became very successful in Denmark" He further added.
Do you support the way Toyota expanded in international market as stated above? Why? or Why not? What would you think the benefit would have been in case of systematic market selection and expansion process?
3. Four Star International produces knitted garments in a factory at Kolkata. Usually, the products are exported to Dhaka, Bangladesh. However the owner of the Company is not satisfied with the margin earned from Bangladeshi importers. Now ABC international is looking for export markets other than Bangladesh.
You are approached as consultant to find top five lucrative export markets for the product. Work out on the assignment and submit a market selection report to the owner of the Four Star International. Use www.trademap.org for data requirements.
4. Brio air international of China deals with different types of air purifiers. Now, the company is looking for exporting products to emerging countries such as Brazil, South Korea, China, and South Africa. Find out the market potential of these countries.
5. Emami Group is set to acquire an Egyptian personal care products manufacturer. The move is part of the group's corporate strategy to bolster Emami's growth at an accelerated pace of 50-60% CAGR over the next three years. Prepare a market attractiveness report of Egypt by considering the political, economic, social-cultural and legal factors for the Emami group.
6. Star Export International of Delhi found out the following trade data in respect of Indian export and world export of following six commodities. On the basis of the data in table below, indicate which is the commodity, at HS code 6 digit level, where the country has most comparative advantage?

		Country's exports in m USD		World exports in m USD	
		2012	2013	2012	2013
030751	Octopus, live, fresh or chilled	0.06	1.88	150	142
040790	Bird's eggs in shell, preserved or cooked	0.91	0.99	121	132
160419	Fish nes, prepared or preserved, whole or in pieces but not minced	0.11	0.09	112	110
843629	Poultry keeping machinery, nes	0.01	0.2	42	69
020312	Hams, shoulder and cuts thereof, of swine bone in, fresh or chilled	0.32	0.95	64	32
030613	Shrimps and Prawns, frozen, in shell or not including boiled in shell	4.67	17.55	1561	1003
Total aggregate export		5067.18	4861	356,828	397,383

7. Visit the website www.trademap.org and find the top ten most important markets for Spices (HS code 091099) for a spice exporter from India. Find out top five exporting countries and the top five importing countries of the world in this product category. Indicate India's position in those countries in terms of its export. Comment on India's high or low share of export in those top five countries.
8. What factors would you consider when suggesting an American global manufacturer of household vacuum cleaners while choosing one from three countries such as Mexico, India, and China as next new country to enter? You can use trade data base or any other data base for extracting specific information and developing your suggestion paper thereof.

EXERCISES

1. Mr Shah of Rajdhani Exports, Delhi is looking for exploring international markets for exportation of Imitation Jewelry under HS code 7117 from India. Prepare a detail market survey report indicating best international markets to be targeted for submission to Mr Shah.
2. LT Foods of India markets its 'Daawat' branded basmati rice in major markets such as USA, UK, Germany, France, Spain, Middle East, South Africa, Mauritius, and Australia. Now, the company wants reassess its selected markets to know whether they are present in the best markets of the world in terms of branded basmati rice demand trend or there are other lucrative country markets where the company can export. Install a market selection process and indicate top markets for rice exporter of India.
4. Pick up a company from the list of Indian companies recently ventured out of India and assess appropriateness of the country selected for entry in to international markets. Use Company related data from respective company's website and annual reports to judge the appropriateness.

End Case: AB Pharmaceuticals Finds Its International Markets for Exporting[16]

AB Pharmaceuticals (ABP) is a small but vibrant pharmaceutical enterprise located in industrially active zone of Ahmedabad (Gujarat), India. The enterprise came in to existence in the year 1970. With long credible existence exclusively in sector, the company won many awards from government to mark its competency in business. ABP believed in quality tenets of its founder Mr Vijoy Mehta throughout the decades of its existence and therefore earned good name in the market covering whole of India and the subcontinent. This way, till now, helped the company not only to develop loyal clientele in India but a number of companies from neighboring countries such as Bangladesh, Nepal, and Bhutan regularly imported products of the company. Recent years have seen the opening up of markets in many countries which have made the new generation owner of ABP, Mr Gautam Mehta, curious about the possibilities of sending products in to these markets. Mr Mehta, in recent management meeting, remarked, "exporting has been crafted as a policy level strategy to foster economic development of India, so ABP expect to get many sops from the government for being able to identify a good potential market for their products and successful marketing thereof". In the meeting, he further advised his managerial team to identify country markets, beyond subcontinent, through following a systematic market selection process. According to him, "ABP can show better export performance than those that do not have a well knit export market identification and selection process" He advised his team not to put too much emphasis on the macro level analysis like PEST or PESTIL in the beginning. Rather, the export market selection should be started straightway with demand analysis for the products ABP produces in 220 country markets of the world and then look other aspects through PEST or PESTIL.

[16] The case 'AB Pharmaceuticals finds its international markets for exporting' has been created by the case writer Dr Gautam Dutta of Indian Institute of Foreign Trade as a basis for class room discussion rather than to illustrate either effective or ineffective handling of business situation

"I understand that our small company will not be capable enough to break the regulatory shackles of developed country markets and PEST environment of other countries having demand for our product will not be much admirable. I like to see the demand oriented countries first, irrespective of their PEST environment" He quipped.

Mr Mehta himself took the lead to initiate a systematic market selection process in the company. "Export Market Identification & Selection Process (EMI & SP), as I fondly call it, is an iterative process of market selection which can be completed in easily in our office. We will use this in the future years also for export market selection of our company", he told his managerial team members. Mr Mehta then explained the process to the team in the following way.

THE EMI & SP

The EMI & SP can be taken up as a group work in the team. The ABP managerial team has an objective to explore different country markets for export opportunities not only for this year but continue to evaluate opportunities in the subsequent years. At first, consider all the 220 countries of the world as the possible countries to export out products. You can take a single or an assortment of quality products which are apparently in demand in the international markets, but as of now our company does not have the information about the optimally best 20 markets which are comparatively more attractive than the others. At this stage the EMI & SP starts with a series of steps which the team will execute till the optimum markets are identified for product/products. The following steps our team need to execute in each year to find out the possible countries of our best interest.

Step 1: Product Selection for Export

The step one of EMI & SP is for product identification and exportability development scenario where our team members will discuss amongst themselves about the export feasibility of the products which primarily surfaced as selected products for international markets. This step allows the members to judge exportability of the products in a threadbare manner for which international markets are being identified. This step is basically a brainstorming session wherein team members would try to develop consensus about product/products for which export markets are to be selected. Say, here at this stage, one member of the team identified pharmaceutical medicaments (put up in packaging for retail sale) as possible product that can be exported from our company in India. Efforts will be made to develop primary consensus within the team about projecting it as exportable product from our company, the next step automatically will be to develop an understanding towards competitive advantage of the selected product in the international markets.

Step 2: Assessing Product Competitiveness

Step two allows the team to understand the challenges of international markets where many comparable products will be competing for market share in the same country. So, step two will begin by accessing trade data (both export and import) country-wise and year-wise recorded by aggregators (like www.trademap.org) at the international level. He explained the team members about the International Trade Centre (ITC) website www.trademap.org and various features of it. Mr Mehta further helped the team member to

Table 5.16 Competiveness with RCA

Particulars	2008	2009	2010	2011
Total Export of '300490' from India to the World	26,05,582	29,25,700	39,54,777	52,82,830
Total Export of '30' from India to the World	50,05,349	50,11,360	60,96,125	82,59,853
Total World Export of '300490'	24,43,82,089	24,82,83,050	25,62,56,488	26,64,05,387
Total World Export of '30	39,98,33,127	42,09,79,930	44,36,39,461	45,97,17,675
RCA	0.85	1.0	1.12	1.1

download the annual export import time series data in respect of product medicaments (selected by the managerial team of ABP as foremost exportable product of the company) with the designated six digit HS code of 300490 from the trademap.org for all the countries of the world for the past years. Mr Mehta himself explained the process of calculating index like Revealed Comparative advantage (RCA) by using trade data downloaded from www.trademap.org website in the following way.

- Export of medicaments from India in 2008: 2605.582 million USD
- Total pharmaceutical exports from India in 2008: 5005.349 million USD
- Total export of medicaments from the world in 2008 : 244,382.089 million USD
- Total pharmaceutical export of the world in 2008 : 399,833.127 million USD
- So, the Revealed Comparative Advantage Index (RCA) for medicaments for the year 2008 will be (2605.582/5005.349)/(244,382.089/399,833.127) = 0.852

Similarly, proceeding in this way, the team members calculated RCAs for other years also as shown in the Table 5.16. It is 0.85 during 2008, 1.0 in 2009, 1.12 in 2010 and 1.10 in 2011. The RCA index has increased from 0.85 in 2008 to 1.10 in 2011. So, in this product category, the team members expected to enjoy increased competitiveness in the world market as the index value not only increased with time but also exceeded unity in the more current years.

Step 3: Identifying countries with import demand

Once the product was assessed for competitive advantage in the world market, Mr Mehta drew attention of the team members towards market identification for the product next. Here, the team members downloaded yearly time series data of import (in USD terms) in respects of the identified product for approximately 220 countries of the world freely available in www.trademap.org for previous 8 years. The team applied a simple mathematical technique like Shift Share Method on the downloaded time series import data for isolating relatively better country markets in terms of import demand for the product under HS Code 300490.

Table 5.17 Short listed countries with relative growth characteristics for product medicament under the HS code 300490

Importing Countries	Imported value in 2008*	Imported value in 2013	AC (2013-2008)	K $\Sigma 2013 \div \Sigma 2008$	EV (K × 2008)	EC (EV-2008)	Shift(N+) (AC-EC) If +ve	Shift (N–) (AC-EC) If -ve	%Shift (N/S)×100%
Germany	172,03,458	239,46,429	67,42,971	1.135	195,32,856	23,29,398	44,13,573	0	18.38562
Japan	74,16,988	110,64,874	36,47,886	1.135	84,21,270	10,04,282	26,43,604	0	11.01246
Russian Federation	51,23,409	78,55,692	27,32,283	1.135	58,17,133	69,37,243	20,38,559	0	8.492024
Saudi Arabia	99,447	19,11,146	18,11,699	1.135	112,912.4	13,465.41	17,98,234	0	7.490902
China	29,12,096	50,38,457	21,26,361	1.135	33,06,402	394,306.2	17,32,055	0	7.215221
Australia	51,94,234	74,42,371	22,48,137	1.135	58,97,548	703,314.2	15,44,823	0	6.435268
Ireland	15,40,073	32,71,507	17,31,434	1.135	17,48,603	208,530.3	15,22,904	0	6.34396
Italy	114,72,203	137,99,138	23,26,935	1.135	130,25,572	15,53,369	773,565.7	0	3.222443
Switzerland	85,60,783	101,88,246	16,27,463	1.135	97,19,938	11,59,155	468,308.3	0	1.950832

* All import values are in thousand USD downloaded from www.trademap.org

The Table 5.17 given below was the result of the analysis where in accordance with the descending order of net shift, the top 10 countries got highlighted. The top countries had shown more growth in demand relative to the other countries of the world for the product, i.e., medicaments and hence ABP team prima facie considered these 10 countries as the possible target country for exportation of the selected product.

Step 4: Assessing Trading Relationship

Through the ABP team focused, at this stage, on the ten countries selected in the step 3 as comparatively better countries in terms of growth in import demand but remained undecided as to which of these ten countries needed to be targeted more. Mr Mehta introduced the requirement of understanding the strength of trade intimacy between India as exporting country and the emphasised ten countries at this stage. He went on then in explaining the concept of Trade Intensity Index (TII) which can be computed using a trade data and utility of the index in grading the emphasised ten countries. The member used the following import data downloaded from trade-map in calculating the index TII.

- Export of medicaments from India to Germany in 2009: 103,098 million USD
- Total pharmaceutical export of India in 2009: 151,268 million USD
- Total import of medicaments by Germany from the world in 2009: 172,03,458 million USD
- Total pharmaceutical import of Germany in 2009 from the World: 446,76,014million USD

So, the trade intensity Index (TII) calculated out to be: (103,098/151,268)/ (172,03,458/446,76,014) = 1.77

In this way the TII of the countries under consideration were plotted as shown in Table 5.18 Mr Mehta explained that those trading partners of India with TIIs greater than unity could be termed as 'intensively related countries and ABP could consider these countries as "comparatively easy countries for exporting" and accordingly rearrange the team's preference.

When TII related exercise was completed the members rated altogether eight countries such as Germany, Japan, Russia, Saudi Arabia, Ireland, Italy, Switzerland, and Panama as to be the better countries where ABP must send its product under consideration. The ABP team rated Saudi Arabia as the best country to focus its export attention.

Step 5: Assessing Competition

At this stage Mr Mehta reminded the team members that it was not enough to understand attractiveness of the countries by looking at TII only because there would be other strings attached like competition. He casted doubt whether a small company like ABP could actually break in to these countries by thawarting the competition. In order to understand

Table 5.18 Trade intensity index

Product medicament	Trade intensity Index			Remark
	2009	2010	2011	
Germany	1.77	1.98	1.63	An index of more (less) than one indicates a bilateral trade flow that is larger (smaller) than expected, given the partner country's importance in world trade.
Japan	1.29	1.23	1.66	
Russia	1.11	1.12	1.07	
Saudi Arabia	6.39	14.95	21.34	
China	0.47	0.2	0.41	
Australia	0.86	0.9	0.91	
Ireland	2.08	1.21	1.44	
Italy	1.28	1.13	1.37	
Switzerland	1.74	1.59	1.76	
Panama	2.31	1.51	1.00	

Table 5.19 Competitivenes in target countries

	Competition in target market (India's rank in the destination market in product medicament)		
	2009	**2010**	**2011**
Germany	23	15	15
Japan	22	22	18
Russia	5	4	5
Saudi Arabia	Nil	25	28
China	26	27	26
Australia	13	13	14.
Ireland	13	15	14
Italy	25	20	22
Switzerland	26	28	27
Panama	15	18	18

the countries in terms of level of competion likely faced by its product, the team members again visited www.trademap.org data base and found out who are the other countries presently exporting to the identified countries and position of India there. The ABP team worked it out and readily came out with Table 5.19 which indicated India's position as exporter to the top ten countries for the years 2009 to 2011. The team member easily understood from the table that India, as exporter, improved its competitiveness in medicament export only in Germany and Japan. In Russia, it maintained a very stable position. Presence of India in Switzerland was almost negligible against the competition. At this stage, based on the competitive position of India, the ABP team opined that five country markets seems to be attractive, viz Russia, Japan, Germany, Ireland and Australia from competition point of view.

Step 6: Understanding the Market Access Requirements

Pleased with the progress, Mr Meheta further drew attention of the team members to the fact that possibly India could improved its position as exporter to many of these ten country markets had there not been various barriers to export. He them emphasised on the requirements of knowing these short listed countries in respect to tariff and non tariff barriers imposed by them while importing from India. He demonsrtated, then, to the team members how to use Market Access Map (MacMap) of the trademap data base and World Bank's "Doing Business Index" in order to understand the level of tariff and non tariff barriers faced by an Indian exporting company. The ABP team understood and explored the websites as told by Mr Mehta and further ratified the shortlisted countries with new information on expected tariff and non tariff barriers. The Table 5.20 was the resultant table prepared by the ABP team in respect of all the ten countries considered.

While analysing the result, the ABP team felt that that Russia and China were charging higher tariffs while importing medicament than the other countries under consideration. Also, Russia's 'doing business rank' gone down in the recent

Table 5.20 Tariff and non tariff barriers

Countries	Total ad valorem equivalent tariff (%)	Doing business rank		Import procedure (days)	Documents to import	Cost (USD)
		2010	2011			
Germany	0	25	22	7	5	937
Japan	0	15	18	11	5	1060

(Continued)

Table 5.20 *(Continued)*

Countries	Total ad valorem equivalent tariff (%)	Doing business rank		Import procedure (days)	Documents to import	Cost (USD)
		2010	2011			
Russia	10	120	123	36	13	1850
Saudi Arabia	0	13	11	17	5	686
China	2.58	89	79	24	5	545
Australia	0	9	10	8	5	1119
Ireland	0	7	9	12	4	1121
Italy	0	78	80	18	4	1245
Switzerland	0	21	27	9	5	1540
Panama	0	77	72	9	4	915

years along with clumsy 'trading across the border' procedures casting doubt on it as possible importing country.

Step 7: Final Selection of Target Market

Mr Mehta was very happy with the progress of the team. He joined the team to finally decide on the countries which offered ABP best exporting opportunity based on four parameters such as trade intimacy, competitiveness, tariff and non tariff issues, and rank them in terms of export attractiveness. They looked at the shortlisted countries again and assigned scores. It was decided that if a country found to be as most attractive country comparatively on account of any of the four parameters, the country would be awarded three stars (***) which means excellent country, followed by two stars (**) for very good country, and one star (*) for good country. If assessed as a 'bad country,' it would be marked with a # mark. For every * mark assigned, the country would get one mark as score. In this way the ABP team scored the shorted listed countries and presented the result to Mr Mehta in tabular form (Table 5.21) for his final comment.

Table 5.21 Selected countries for export

Countries	Ranking of countries				Score
	Trade Intensity	Competitiveness	Tariff	Non Tariff	
Germany	*	*	***	**	7
Japan	**	**	#	**	6
Russia	*	***	#	*	5
Saudi Arabia	***	*	#	**	6
China	#	*	#	*	2
Australia	*	**	***	*	7
Ireland	*	*	***	***	8
Italy	*	*	***	***	8
Switzerland	*	#	***	**	6
Panama	*	**	***	*	7

Mr Mehta was delighted to see the efforts put by his team in the matter of export market identification and remarked, "Let us then prepare ourselves to export out the product medicament to Ireland, Italy, and Germany as the company's first export consignment out of Indian subcontinent".

CASE QUESTIONS

Q1. Do you think that the international market identification process adopted by ABP was capable enough to identify the best possible export destinations? Why or why not?

Q2. What are the merits and demerits of the market identification process adopted the company ABP?

Q3. Can you suggest a modified process of market identification to make the selected countries as the best in terms of export destination?

FURTHER READINGS

Koch, Adam J. (2001), "Selecting overseas markets and entry modes: Two decision processes or one?", *Marketing Intelligence and Planning*, Vol. 19, Number 1.

This paper argues that market selection and market entry modes are two aspects of one decision process and not separate decisions. It suggests that such an integrated process requires consideration of many factors that can influence the outcome. It then presents a new market and market entry mode selection model (MEMS) which conforms to the proposed inclusive spectrum of the market selection analysis.

Cavusgil, Tamer S. (1985), "Guideline for export market research", *Business Horizon*, Nov.–Dec.

This article opines that export market selection process be should continuous and systematic and that is required for access to the best markets in the world. Accordingly, the article provides a guideline for export market research indicating an exhaustive list of factors to be considered in each stage of the process.

Sakarya, Sema (2007), "Market selection for international expansion: Assessing opportunities in emerging markets", *International Marketing Review*, Vol. 24, Number 2.

This article discusses the four criteria specific to the preliminary assessment of emerging markets (EM) as international expansion opportunities which do not rely on macroeconomic and political factors as used in traditional market selection analysis. Case application of the four factors, viz. strong future market potential, manageable level of cultural distance, supportive and developing local industry and positive customer receptiveness for foreign products and business, provides a tool for IMS for emerging markets.

Rahman, Syed H. (2006), "International market selection process: An investigation of the relevance of business operating environment" *Journal of International Business Research*, January.

This paper provides a partial test of those frameworks that different researchers recommend towards different decision frameworks for international market selection process. It deals specifically with factors such as the host country's business operating environmental variables recommended by different researchers in deciding the target market.

Deciding on Entry Modes

6

Learning Objectives

After studying this chapter, you should be able to:

- Understand the various modes of entry with the pros and cons associated with each of the entry modes.
- Assess the basic features of the entry modes such as controllability, resource requirements flexibilities, and marketing efforts.
- Understand the theories of internationalisation and their relevance in explaining the choice of entry mode.
- Understand the entry mode selection process for a company and data requirement thereof.
- Closely understand the factors influencing the entry mode choice of a company.

Chapter Overview

It is very important that companies enter a country with an optimum entry mode, i.e., a mode that allows them to attain best performance abroad. Literature in international marketing has regarded pre-entry decisions on mode of entry as a "crucial issue" for international marketers and advised them to resort to in-depth analysis before actual entry. This chapter introduces the different entry modes possible for a company on internationalisation and throws light on the critical issues involving the entry mode selection of a company. This chapter also introduces different theories of internationalisation. Broadly, it deals with different issues related to entry mode of internationalising companies.

Opening Vignette

L&T decided to pull out of China due to low growth and stringent competition

Larsen & Toubro (L&T) entered in the Wuxi new district of China by establishing a wholly-owned foreign enterprise (WOFE), L&T (Wuxi) Electric Co. L&T Wuxi (LTW) was set up to manufacture high-end air circuit breakers. L&T entered in to an agreement, during 2006, with Wuxi new district for the establishment of the green-field manufacturing project on a 25,000 square meter plot. L&T, being the largest and most respected company of India's private sector, was looking for internationalisation. Before entering the country with WOFE, the company supplied critical and sophisticated equipment for various heavy engineering installations in China through exportation of the products. The change of entry mode from export to wholly-owned subsidiary was preferred to play a big role in the high-end switchgear sector in China and more so because the air circuit breaker was a part of L&T's expansive range of electrical and electronic products. With magnificent progress of the Chinese economy, the company set a target for itself to do a business of 40 to 50 million USD by the fifth year of operations in China. In addition, L&T decided to explore opportunities to cater to the requirements of circuit breakers in other Southeast Asian markets such as Taiwan and Malaysia through exportation from

Wuxi production facility. However, things did not turn up as planned and LTW was facing a hostile situation in the host country. The level of competition was uneven and small-scale producers were often found calling the shots with low cost – low price advantage. The company management in India, deciding on the future of LTW in China, had several meetings but with a single agenda: to analyse whether the company had gone right by setting a wholly owned subsidiary in China. In fact, the company could have considered other options in venturing out to a risky but lucrative market in China. One option was to be a minority partner with a Chinese big company dealing with similar product line and gain experience of Chinese market criticalities. The second option could have been to find out a comparatively smaller company with switchgear manufacturing facilities in China and forming a majority joint venture with them. The third option for L&T was to take over existing manufacturing facilities of a Chinese low-cost switch gear manufacturer in China and enjoy the benefits of its existing clientele. Finally, the fourth option was to export components from India in semi knocked-down (SKD) form and assemble them locally by either hiring a facility there or through outright purchase of an assembling space of a Chinese manufacturer. But, alas! It was too late to think about the options for L&T to enter China.

When the details of this foreign market entry mishap of L&T was told to the students of international marketing in the classroom the students quipped, "That's surprising! Why did the company want to enter China with wholly-owned subsidiary straightway? Why not JV? It could have entered into a minority JV with a local partner to test the market first and then jump in to WOFE. How did they decide on the entry mode? Did they follow any process? Were those pros and cons of different entry modes assessed prior to investment commitments in China? Can the companies, in general, have a procedure to assess the implication of different entry modes before actual entry into the country markets so that such loss of investment does not occur?"

"The choice of market entry mode has a strong impact on international operations and it can be regarded as a "crucial issue" in international marketing"

—Wind and Perlmutter, Columbia Journal of World business.

INTRODUCTION

K•Swiss is an American footwear company founded way back in 1966 in Los Angeles, USA, by two Swiss brothers. The company designs, develops and markets an array of athletic footwear for high performance sports use, fitness activities and casual wear under the K•Swiss brand. They are also involved in designing and manufacturing of slip-on, lace-less footwear using another brand name, i.e., Royal Elastics brand through its wholly owned subsidiary. K•Swiss excelled in marketing its product because it believed in design originality to capture the heart of its users across the countries of the world. For example, it designed and produced a high-performance athletic shoe "Classic", when entered the market initially which still accounts for a significant portion of the company's sales. Thereafter, the company did not deviate much and kept its shoe design relatively unchanged with peripheral add-ons only. The original owner could not retain the ownership of business for long as popularity increased and finally during 1986 it was purchased by an investment group led by Steven Nichols. The new management soon realised that production cost was spiralling up and if something was not done immediately then it would affect the business performance. The company rightly understood that if it could become as cost competitive as it was design competitive, then only it would be able to enter and establish markets in emerging countries in particular. Accordingly, the new management took initiatives and shifted its manufacturing base to low-cost economies like China. Soon it started producing about 78% of the production from its manufacturing base in China followed by 12% in Thailand and 1% in Taiwan. K•Swiss brand shot to a new height when it was ranked number one in quality by 500 athletic shoe dealers and chosen as official footwear of the 1994 US Open lawn tennis tournament. In the present days K•Swiss is a sought-after product in the Classic category (casual), training, basketball, tennis and children's footwear in many parts of the world. They took measures continuously in production components outsourcing so that cost of production remained in the low ebb. Also, it believed in intense internationalisation in terms of marketing its finished products as the US footwear markets were getting saturated resulting decreasing revenue from US market in particular. Lately, the company looked towards the Indian market for marketing its products because of the following primary reasons.

- K•Swiss would have cost advantage if it enters India as the production facilities are in close vicinity (China and Thailand) and can also address the market saturation problem in developed countries.
- From the financial perspective, India is also open for foreign investment. It is one of the fastest growing emerging markets with real GDP growth of around 8.9%.
- India's adoption of western culture has made foreign sportswear firms such as Nike, Reebok, Puma, Converse, and Adidas quite popular.
- The GDP growth and overall industrial growth in India means that the people have more buying power and K•Swiss can see India as a good market from the revenues perspective.

The company management considered the prospects of Indian market in full and entrusted the work of formulating the entry strategy to its South Asian management team. The team was pondering with a set of question to be answered in order to develop entry strategy that would provide the company maximum advantage in Indian market. The questions at that stage were: How should the company enter the Indian market? Is it through exporting the product to India or setting up a wholly owned subsidiary in the Indian soil? Can it be through executing a joint venture agreement with an Indian company? What entry mode is optimum for the company? The objective of any entry strategy is not only to provide minimum risk exposure to the company in the foreign market but also to give the company maximum marketing advantage. Managing these two extremes has often proved to be difficult for many companies since the decision about strategy of entry depends on various factors, many of which are unknown. As for K•Swiss, various internal company factors like capability of the company to manage a wholly owned subsidiary would surely play a role in entry mode selection for India entry. At the same time, the macro and micro business environment factor prevailing in India also influence the company while deciding on the entry mode. It can also be said that a company could also consider the entry mode of its arch rivals to the Indian market and entry strategy makers would likely to have a better look at them. Therefore, the choice of market entry mode would depend on various factors and a company needs to consider them while entering into selected markets. Deciding on the optimum entry mode for a company has always been regarded as a "complicated process" by the international marketing manager because of requirements of decision making in so many areas. But without doing it a good markets may be wasted causing a great loss to the company. The literature on international business has testified to this fact frequently. This chapter, therefore, discusses and throws light on the critical issues involving the entry mode selection of a company.

POSSIBLE ENTRY MODES

When companies identify opportunities in the foreign market, the next natural decision would be to decide on the entry mode. In this respect, companies have many choices involving simple decision making to complex decision making. The products can be sent to a selected foreign market in exchange for money through a middleman located in home country. This constitutes a simple exchange with low level of risk as such exchange includes neither require extensive marketing planning, nor any investment commitment in the foreign country. However, suppose the home country producer finds that transactions through middleman is not rewarding enough and wants to execute the transaction directly with the foreign country buyer then involvement will be increased. It may also so happen that distance between the production location and importing country is very high causing transportation cost to become a deciding factor on competitiveness and hence likely that exportation is not preferred. The home country producers would have to think of some other options like licensing or franchising as preferred mode of entry where more involvement will be required. The risk factor will be increased for the home company as it involves sharing of its proprietary technology and other know-how with the foreign affiliates in return of fees or royalty on revenue. The home company may, at certain stage, think of collaborating with a foreign company to share some valued activities beneficial to each other through formation of a strategic alliance. The home company may even consider setting up of a manufacturing facility or sales office of its own by way of foreign direct investment in the host country to avail long term opportunities there. This action of the home company not only increases its involvement but also risk to a higher level. Therefore, a variety of options are available to an internationalising company, from which the company has to select one that suits it perfectly. Figure 6.1 details the basic entry mode options available to the company.

Exporting as Entry Mode

For small- and medium-size enterprises (SMEs), internationalisation is generally not an easy process because of its smallness not only in size but in the skill level as well. So, for them, internationalisation rather takes place gradually through a learning process. However, this is not applicable to those small companies that are born global. They start business in foreign soil to take advantage of the external country markets right from the beginning. These born global companies get their initial internationalising motivation from small or constrained domestic market insufficient to provide the desired growth momentum. So, in that case, they take risk head on by launching risky

FIGURE 6.1 Principal entry mode

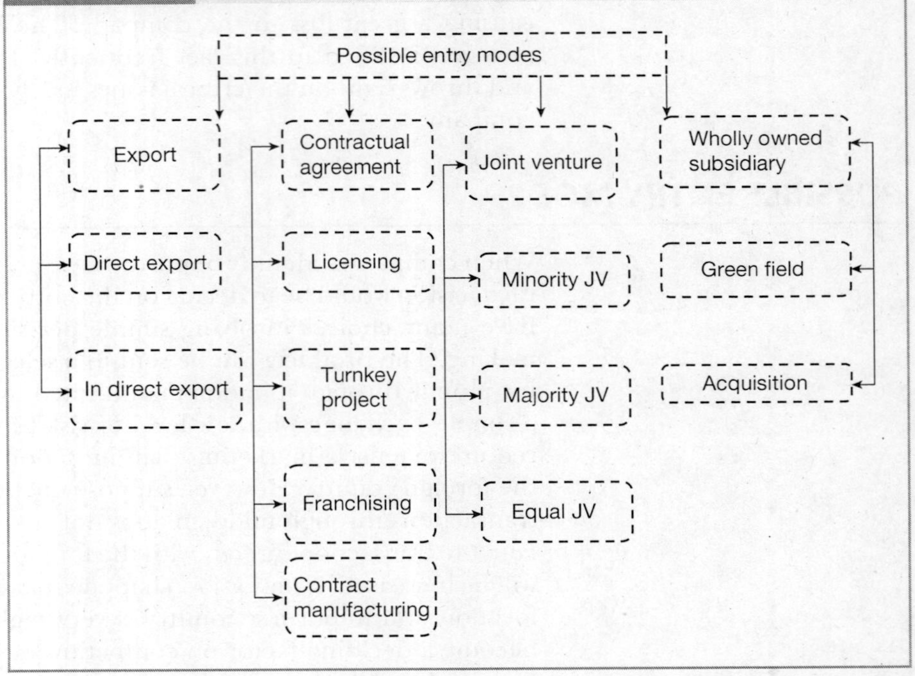

wholly owned subsidiary in the foreign soil. The risk, referred here, is related to the possibilities of losing monetary investments while entering into a new country. However, unlike the born global, the usual process of internationalisation of SMEs is through exporting. It involves lowest risks in the process of internationalisation and hence, it is popular process for small companies even if they have a very strong presence in the domestic market. In India, the small- and medium-sector companies are responsible for about 34% of the total export from the country[1]. SMEs of India, in general, treaded through the gradual learning process of internationalisation. While availing opportunities of different countries, they resorted to export as entry mode, particularly in the initial stage of internationalisation and achieved considerable success. Basically, the exporting process is opportunity driven. The small company first necessarily be lured and believed by the export marketing opportunities of distant markets and then it would take active interest in them. The opportunity recognition process may not always be system driven and may take the shape of an ad hoc process. In the trial run thereafter, the company transfers the centrally and domestically produced product to the country/countries of the buyer/buyers. On transfer of products the exporter collects the sales proceed as per the contract agreement with the buyer and evaluate the outcome with the initial expectation. If the outcome matches the expectation, then the company continues to export. The exporter, in the entire process, learns from experience and eventually expands foreign buyers in other countries as well. The risk is inherently low in this mode of internationalisation

[1] http://dcmsme.gov.in/sido/export.htm

because the exporter does not required making any large financial commitments in export operation. Hence, there is very less chance of losing money in the process. However, there are many benefits of internationalisation through export that the company can avail. Some of them are as follows:

- The production location of the exporter remains in his own country or in a country where manufacturing has been undertaken. For example, Hyundai, the Korean car manufacturer, produces its flagship car i10 in India and exports it to other countries in Europe. This provides the company a known environment where production functions can be accomplished with considerable ease and low cost.
- The exporter gets encouragement from home government through various policy decisions as exporting brings home the valuable foreign currency which, in most cases, is the USD. The host country government may also provide incentives for importing a few intermediate products if those are used for production of the exportable products. This is very much prevalent not only in India but in other developing countries of the world.
- The exporting company centralises production function in home country or in any other country of its interest and cater to the multi-market demand of the products. This centralisation allows the exporter to achieve economies of scale which eventually help in increasing profit volume through reduced cost of production.
- The exporting company usually do take advantage of its existing home country facilities and hence does not make huge financial commitment for international markets and hence, the risk of marketing abroad is very low.

There are two possible ways of tapping overseas markets with operations based in the home country. These are: (a) indirect export and (b) direct export.

Indirect export

This is the simplest form of internationalisation and it often looks like pseudo internationalisation. In this process, the manufacturer does not required to know much about any foreign market opportunities or the buyers but the products are exported out to international markets through intermediaries who are also located in the same country as that of the manufacturer. The customer who could be the buying agent of another company is located in the foreign country. The manufacturer shoulders the responsibilities of R&D, production and marketing of the products so produced to an intermediary located in its own country only. At this stage the manufacturer is not even aware of the foreign countries and buyers of the products the intermediary has planned to despatch. The intermediary is greatly experienced in exporting and in touch with foreign department stores, individual foreign buyers or branch offices of foreign buyers. This allows the intermediary to update continuously the foreign requirements and act as conduit to off load the home country manufactured products to different foreign destinations.

FIGURE 6.2 Indirect export

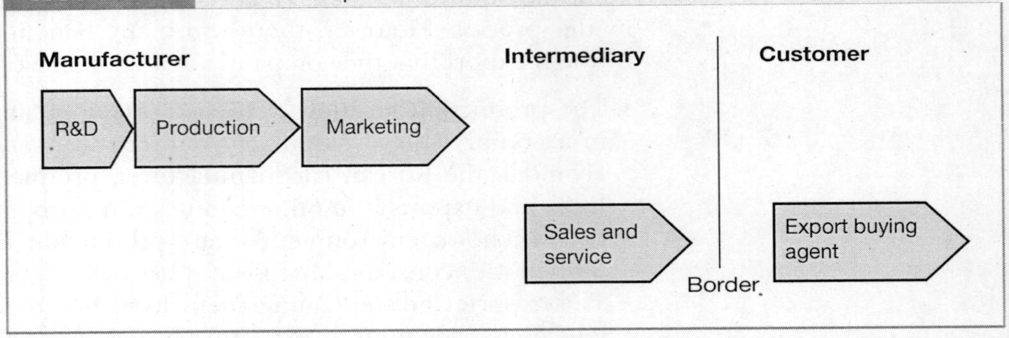

In indirect export the manufacturer completes the sales by transferring the products to the intermediary in the host country itself. It will be the job of the the intermediary then to take possession of the products and execute the task of cross-border transportation to the customer by finding out suitable foreign buyers and building up necessary assortments as per buyer's requirements.

It is very common practice that under the format of indirect export, the manufacturer transfers the products to the export houses or merchant exporters located in the country. The merchant exporters/export houses are well versed in handling foreign buyers and markets. So they execute the task of looking for buyers in the foreign country and follow-up negotiations on price, delivery and others terms of sale with the foreign buyers to complete the process of exportation as specialist. This is suited for the small-scale manufacturers as it saves them from carrying out the task of cross-border interactions and transferring products to foreign countries. This, in a sense, also allows the manufacturer to concentrate more on the manufacturing process rather than performing the functions of a marketer or a logistics expert.

Although indirect exporting allows the products of a manufacturer to be sold in foreign countries, but it does not allow the manufacturer to gain experience in cross border marketing with time resulting total dependence on the intermediaries. Hence the product development or modification required for exploring different foreign markets is totally dependent on feedback from the export houses. The manufacturer even remains in the dark about the destination country of the products his company has produced. The most important disadvantage of indirect export is that the manufacturer never gets graduated to become manufacturer exporter and there by limiting the requisite growth of exporting community of a country. So, in short, the following are the advantages or disadvantages of indirect exporting.

Benefits of indirect export:

1. The manufacturers get time to specialise in production activities. They do not require spending on maintaining export department or export personnel.
2. The specialisation of the intermediaries like export houses or merchant exporters are put to maximum use leading to achieving efficiency of highest order.

3. Assortment building of requisite sizes is possible. Products may be collected from several parties from time to time and despatch them together in accordance with the requirement resulting in saving unit cost through consolidated shipments.
4. The country government always recognises and incentivises the export houses in accordance with their contribution in enhancing exports from a country and ability to earn of valuable foreign currency. In India, export houses are encouraged to move from single-star category to five-star category; the star ratings dependent on total FOB (Free on Board)/FOR (Free on Railway) export performance during the current plus the previous three years. The encouragement comes in the form of some incentives such as duty draw back, etc. In India, the following privileges are granted to star export houses.
   (a) Licence/certificate/permissions and customs clearances for both imports and exports on self-declaration basis.
   (b) Fixation of input–output norms on priority within 60 days.
   (c) Exemption from compulsory negotiation of documents through banks. The remittance, however, would continue to be received through banking channels.
   (d) Retention of 100% foreign exchange in exchange earner's foreign currency (EEFC) account.
   (e) Enhancement in normal repatriation period from 180 days to 360 days.
   (f) Entitlement for consideration under the Target Plus scheme.
   (g) Exemption from furnishing of bank guarantee in schemes under this policy.

Therefore, the urge to increase export sales, in turn, benefits the producers through quick materialisation of the sales. In addition, the reputation of the export house will enable the manufacturer to get a better representation for his products abroad. In case the export house is selling complementary products, the sales of such products may also increase.

Drawbacks of indirect exports

1. The producers never get exposed to the foreign markets and their knowledge about the foreign markets remains rudimentary throughout.
2. A total dependency of the manufacturer on the export house without developing its own export expertise.
3. The export house/merchant exporter does not believe in specialisation for the sake of earning more through commission. They simply are willing to transfer products from one country to another with business dealing developing across too many unrelated lines.
4. The foreign customers may not be acquainted with product manufacturers at all and hence the country is not likely to get the reputation as manufacturing country quickly. It is a common practice that while marketing the product abroad the export house will do it under its own name and reputation,. Sometimes export house may also use its own brand name to sell products in the foreign markets.

Direct export

Direct export is executed by manufacturer and hence the manufacturer plays all roles that include manufacturer of products, market selector,

FIGURE 6.3 Direct export

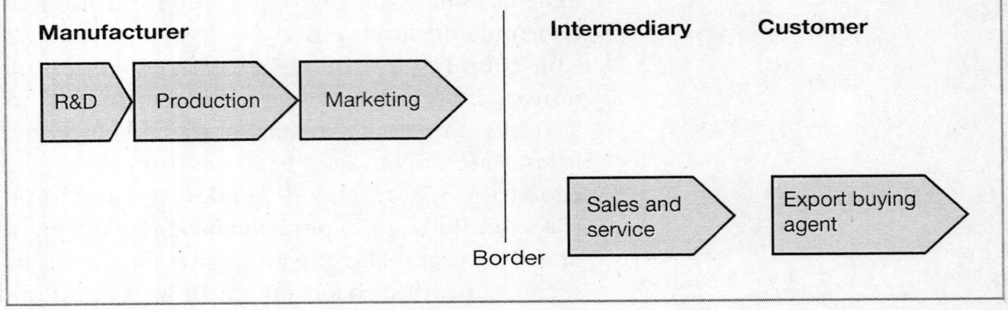

communicator to buyers abroad, price negotiator, facilitator for international transfer of products, payment receiver, and feedback acceptor from the buyer on possible areas to make products more marketable abroad in future. Obviously, as the role of the manufacture increases risk also considerably increases in direct export than in indirect exporting. However, the risks are compensated through better sales proceed realisation since the whole process is executed without the involvement of export houses or merchant exporters and hence, there is no sharing of profits.

Benefits of direct exporting

1. Direct exporting to a foreign country entails manufacturer or the exporter to have considerable involvement in the exporting process. It starts form searching of business contacts abroad, zeroing on one or more importers, deciding on terms of sale, arranging logistics, settling the documentation requirements, etc. Handling this nitty-gritty allows the exporter to get a close understanding of the foreign markets and its requirements.
2. In direct export, the manufactures exporter can control price aspects in manufacturing based on the negotiated price with the foreign customers.
3. In direct export, it is a direct product transfer from manufacturer exporter to the foreign customers by avoiding the intermediary which makes the distribution chain shorter leading to better margins in the transactions for the involved parties.
4. Success in the foreign market builds up reputation and goodwill for the manufacturer exporter which allow it to pursue more intense internationalisation in course of time.
5. Varieties of information such as marketing opportunities abroad, trend of market demand, level of product acceptance, etc., are accumulated around the manufacturer exporter which at later period comes handy in taking more strategic and pre-emptive actions.
6. It would not take much time for the companies to fully understand the fact that control on local marketing effort in a foreign country is low with exporting as mode of entry and hence in the long run the company would not be able materialise its marketing ambition fully. So, in order to gain some amount of control in their hands, they may resort to various hybrid entry strategies such as exporting through independent

agents and distributors in the foreign country, export through alliance with local marketing partners, and export through a wholly-owned sales subsidiary. It is a common for manufacturer–exporters to export products to be marketed by independent agents and distributors. A number of premium segment cars such as Mercedes Benz, Rolls-Royce, and BMW are exported from their manufacturing base to India through independent agents and distributors. On the other hand, European and Japanese car makers (Volvo, Toyota) export cars to the US and market them in the US through wholly owned sales subsidiary. Audi, the German luxury car manufacturer, enjoys considerable success in India by establishing its own sales company for India. The sales subsidiary listens to the needs and wants of the local market and decides on advertising, pricing, market research and importantly distribution management. Exporting firms may develop alliance with a local partner instead of opening own sale subsidiaries or contacting independent agents for effective marketing of the product.

Organisational forms of direct exporting

To carry out exporting process in a company, there could be broadly two types of organisational structure in a small or medium size company.

Export cell: In this form, one export cell is created within the organisation and entrusted with the responsibilities of export management. It reports to the domestic marketing head of the company. Depending upon the volume of export, the department size may be varied with reinforcement from the main marketing department. This method is very popular because of its simplicity, low maintenance cost and flexibility in using human resource within the organisation in accordance with the requirement time to time.

Dedicated export department: A dedicated export department is created when export is in focus in an organisation. This is possible when the company has a set an export earnings target and it is strategically important for the company to excel in long term. Generally, large companies are expected to have a dedicated export department. It is common that the department acts as a separate profit centre with exclusive focus on export and export management.

Drawback of direct exporting

1. Exporting does not lead the company close to the customers in a foreign country. In true sense, therefore, it may not be considered real internationalisation through full exploitation of foreign market. In reality, it is only sending products in foreign market which has resembles with domestic market.
2. More intense internationalisation through other modes of entry such as licensing, strategic alliances, and foreign direct investment in wholly owned manufacturing subsidiaries may not be possible even after long experience in exporting because customer's needs and wants have not been transferred to the manufacturers by the importing agents.
3. So, in a way, manufacturing exporters are at a difficult position to acquire true international marketing skills.

Entry through Contractual Agreements

Contract manufacturing

Contract manufacturing is another mode entry which is becoming increasingly popular in recent days for the companies who do not want produce on their own but take the help of some specialist manufacturing concern, generally located in countries with low labour costs, for production of the desired product. This arrangement, popularly known as contract manufacturing, helps marketing as well as manufacturing companies both. Under this arrangement a contractual agreement is executed between the contract manufacturer and the hiring company detailing the terms and conditions of the process. The contract manufacturer, being a specialist manufacturer, easily understands the requirement of the client and agrees to a payment term which not only covers the labour, tooling, and material costs, etc., related to the production but also own profit margin. The signed agreement between the hiring company and the contact manufacturer thereafter governs the behaviour of the involved parties. The agreement stipulates different issues related the manufacturing process such as raw material sourcing procedure, involvement of the hiring company in sourcing process, original equipment design procedure and involvement of contract manufacturer in it, key component sourcing procedure, etc. In case of certain key components where the hiring company has exceptional skill and which also provides them competitive advantage in the sector may not be left in the hands of contract manufacturer. For Example, famous diesel engine manufacture Cummins inc. never allowed fuel pump manufacturing by the contract manufacturers but closely retained with them only. However, in all cases, contract manufacturers are exclusively responsible for shop floor manufacturing responsibilities. In some extreme cases, the hiring companies may even entrust the responsibilities of continuous R&D activities with the contract manufacturer. However, generally, tasks such as technology input, research and development, and marketing in particular will be taken care of by the hiring companies. The hiring company ensures that products, so manufactured, are marketed with the brand name of the hiring company to retain the competitive advantages at the market place. The time frame of the contract is generally as stipulated in the contract agreement.

FIGURE 6.4 Contract manufacturing

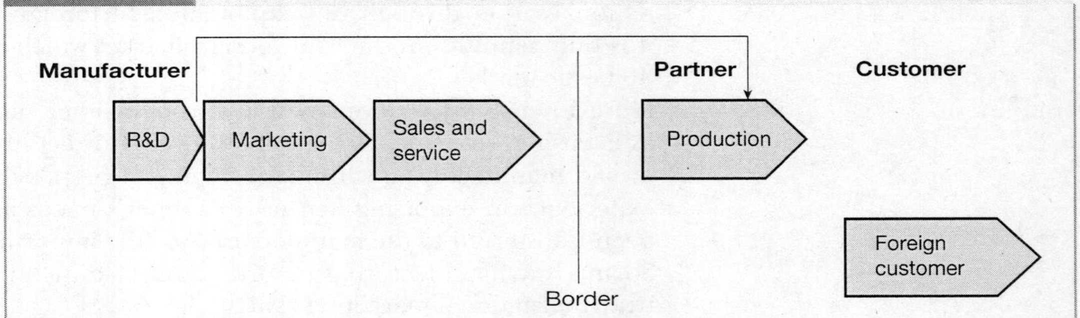

In some sectors such as computer, pharmaceuticals, semiconductor, medical equipments, video gaming gadgets, automobiles components, etc., contract manufacturing has prevalence. Many pharmaceutical companies use Indian companies as contract manufacturers to enter into other country markets. A Mumbai-based Indian drug maker, Indoco Remedies Ltd, became a contract-manufacturer of a South Africa-based company, Aspen, the largest pharmaceuticals manufacturer in Africa. As per the agreement the contract manufacturer Indoco was required to produce tablets, liquids and creams for Aspen. Aspen took the advantage of low cost manufacturing in India to be competitive in foreign country markets such as Brazil and other Latin American countries[2]. Though Indoco Remedies, in the process, would learn about the technology related to manufacturing of the drugs, entrusted to them by Aspen, but it would be difficult for the Indian company to become competitor of the hiring company when the stipulated contract period comes to an end. This is simply because Indoco do not have as credible brand name as Aspen in the global arena. Very few people will purchase the drugs if they are not branded with the name Aspen. It is, therefore, difficult for the contract manufacturer to compete with the hiring company on the expiry of contract period simply because of brand power the hiring company possesses. The Taiwan-based IT company, ACER, struggled at one point of time to recreate itself from a contract manufacturer to a competitor for the hiring companies. At that time, ACER was a simple contract manufacturer of the renowned laptop computer brands of the world. To come out of the contract manufacturer frame, ACER had to develop its capability aggressively in R&D to develop innovative technology and brand building. ACER struggled to build brand and compete with heavyweights in the market and later this struggle became a well-documented example to describe the value-adding potentials of various industries in a production value chain. The hiring company initiate value addition through R&D to design a suitable product and then only it is passed on to the contract manufacturer. The contract manufacturer does the dirty job of manufacturing and adds further value through fabrication. Finally, the hiring company takes it back from the contract manufacturer to add further value through branding and make the product ready for sale. When ACER struggled to upgrade itself from contract manufacturer to branded producer it found that most of the values were added in the first and the last phase. It also observed that during the middle phase when ACER acted as contract manufacturer through fabrication least values were added. Soon ACER understood that since the hiring companies retained the patent, technology and branding with them and handover only the fabrication part to contract manufacturer it would be extremely difficult for ACER to climb up value chain and compete with a hiring company. For the same reason a contract manufacturers, generally, would never be in a position to bargain with the hiring company for a higher share of profit than what was agreed upon.

Benefits of contract manufacturing

Cost savings: This is the most important benefit of entering in to a foreign country through contract manufacturing. Companies just enter in to a

[2] *Business Line*, Tuesday, Oct 26, 2010

country look for already build up manufacturing facilities owned by a contract manufacturer. When they handover the production responsibility to contract manufacturer they do not pay for the facility or equipment needed for production. Otherwise, investment in developing own manufacturing plant and building would have been a major part of total investment made in the foreign country. It also allows them to make considerable savings on recurring labour costs such as wages, training and benefits.

Mutual benefits: Once the contract between the contract manufacturer and the hiring company is executed the contract manufacturer is ensured of a steady flow of business until the set-up cost for assembly lines are recovered fully. Similarly, as most of contract manufacturers are strategically located in low cost countries such as India, China, Bangladesh, Thailand, etc., the agreement of contract manufacturing assures the hiring company of a steady flow of low cost finished product in to its warehouses.

Specialists in play: Contract manufacturers are very much seasoned and possess advance skills in manufacturing which the hiring companies do not have. Also the contract manufacturers enjoy special relationships with raw material suppliers required for maintaining supply chain efficiency. On the other hand, the hiring companies have strong market accepted brand image as well as well developed R&D facilities which makes marketing easy. For example, Microsoft is a big name with a clear advantage in marketing, but it does not possess enough competencies in manufacturing computer gaming consoles. So, it took the help of a contract manufacture in China in producing the video gaming gadget XBOX 360, while keeping the marketing right exclusively with Microsoft. The company Microsoft uses three specialist contract manufactures namely Flextronics in China, Wistron in Taiwan and Celestica in China for production the modern gaming consoles.

Quality enhancement: Hiring companies like Microsoft while manufacturing its Gaming gadgets X –Box 360 installs own methods of quality control to help them to pass on only quality products in the market. Hence, two quality checks, one at contract manufacturer's end and another at hiring company's end, allow enhancement. In fact, the Japanese hiring companies do not leave their contract manufacture alone throughout the manufacturing process but get involve along with them in ensuring quality. The American hiring companies , on the other hand, believe in checking quality at critical points only. But, whatever be the ways followed, the quality gets checked and ensured.

Low cost focus: The contract manufacturer is a specialist in low-cost manufacturing while the hiring company specialist in marketing. This method is perfectly suitable for companies that enjoy a huge marketing advantage but devoid of any production specialisation in the chosen line at a low cost. Reputed contract manufacturer sets up its own industrial park to source raw material and other supplies so that save money on transportation and inventory. For example, Flextronics maintains industrial park in four countries such as China Brazil, Hungary, Mexico, and Poland.

Box 6.1 XBOX 360 Story

Flextronics International Ltd has manufacturing facilities networked in over 30 countries. This Singaporean electronics manufacturing services provider came in touch with Microsoft to write a different story of manufacturing. That story, in fact, started a few miles northwest of Guadalajara, the capital city of the Mexican state of Jalisco, when Microsoft officials met the officials of Flextronics at Parque Integral de Tecnologia, an industrial park complex owned and operated by Flextronics. Microsoft was searching for someone for off-loading the entire manufacturing of their new gaming gadgets. Some people like to think that if Microsoft would not have met Flextronics, then the world would not have seen Xbox. May be Microsoft had the money but they would not have taken up the dirty job of manufacturing. Flextronics chair and CEO Michael Mark openly expressed his pride by saying "If guys like us didn't exist, guys like Microsoft wouldn't do a hardware product. The risk would be too high." Jobs like what Flextronics handle for companies like Microsoft, in the parlance of manufacturing, is known as Electronics Manufacturing Services, or EMS, which assembles things such as PCs and consumer gadgets for clients. This is also a contract manufacturing for the electronics companies of all stripes. The contract manufacturers enjoy the specialised manufacturing job. Demand for this type of dirty job handlers went up and up across countries as those have money focussed more on marketing with big brand images like that of Microsoft. Therefore, the demand of Flextronics went up continuously and now it has about 80 factories in 28 countries around the world, Flextronics makes cell phones for Ericsson, routers for Cisco, printers for Hewlett-Packard, and PDAs for Palm. Its Indian facility is located in Chennai.

Source: Internet and www. Wired.com

Economies of scale: This is another major benefit of contract manufacturing. Usually, the contract manufacturers have multiple customers for whom they produce different products from different suppliers. This entails them sourcing of bulk raw material at a time with reduced costs leading to attainment of economies of scale advantage. The more units there put in one shipment, the less expensive the price per unit becomes resulting shipment advantage as well. Sometimes, hiring companies also lend their support to contract manufacture to ensure global sourcing of raw material with scale economics in place.

Flexibility: Products produced by a contract manufacturer makes it possible for the hiring company to market products without upfront investment in plant and machinery. This may allow a company to reach a country market quickly and also to pull out at short notice in case of trouble. This method, therefore, is advantageous in situations where market uncertainty is there.

Demerits of contract manufacturing

1. The hiring company, in a way, has to depend on the manufacturing company (contract manufacturer) and its efficiency. It is a common practice that the manufacturing company does not restrict itself to the jobs of one manufacturer but a number of similar jobs for other manufacturers. A mere written agreement may not be enough to safe guard the design secrecy of product and maintaining exclusiveness in the market place. So, sharing of R&D and design with the contract manufacturer may be risky.
2. The contract manufacturers are not in touch with the market and hence cannot hear the voice of consumers asking for any modification/

alteration in product. So, the hiring company takes time to effect any market desired change in product.

3. In these days a contract manufacturer requires versatility to cater to the different requirements of the hiring companies. Otherwise, they may look like 'general' and 'one solution for all'. In that situation it may be difficult to find out right type of contract manufactures for right type of hiring company or so to say match making between two.

Licensing

Licensing is a contractual mode through which a company may enter in a foreign country. In this mode of entry the entering company (licensor) agrees to allow a host company (licensee) in foreign country to use the relevant technology developed by it for commercial production of product or products for a certain period of time. In return, the licensor asks for a payment which is known as 'royalty'. The term 'royalty' is generally used to designate the fees associated with licensing. The terms of association between the licensee of foreign country and licensor of the host country are detailed out in a document known as licensing agreement that includes details of products to be produced, time frame of the association, royalty related clauses, technology revision clauses, etc. Both the licensor and the licensee need to formally agree to the clauses of the agreements and provide legal status to the document before embarking on the main process of production and marketing. In general terms, the royalty to be paid by the licensee could be an on-going payment calculated as a percentage of sales of products or a one-time payment. The range of products to produced by the licensee is as mutually agreed and included in the agreement. The duration of the association, as mentioned in the agreement, generally varies from industry to industry and even from case to case within a particular industry. In this mode of entry the licensor feels happy because the licensee without much hesitation agrees to market finished products under the strong brand of the licensor and then the goodwill generated by the product in the foreign market automatically accumulates to the licensor's account. Companies that excel more in technology than marketing find licensing as an appropriate method of entering into the foreign market and as it saves them from setting up own expensive production facilitates. There had been over 15,000 known technology licensing transactions worldwide with a total value of over $320 billion in the period 1985–1997, implying an average of nearly 1150 transactions worth $25 billion per year[3]. Developing countries like India are also proving to be good destination for technology oriented companies of developed countries. The famous German semiconductor chip manufacturer in the automotive sector Infineon Technologies AG, with excellent reputation of more than 40 years and a broad innovative product portfolio of outstanding quality, wanted to enter India using licensing mode. The Indian semiconductor market was lucrative enough with market size of about $3.25 billion during 2006 and was forecasted to become $36 billion during 2015, Infineon wanted to enter the prospective market

[3] Arora, A., Fosfuri, A. and Gambardella, A. (2001), *Markets for Technology: The Economics of Innovation and Corporate Strategy*, The MIT Press, Cambridge, MA.

FIGURE 6.5 Licensing

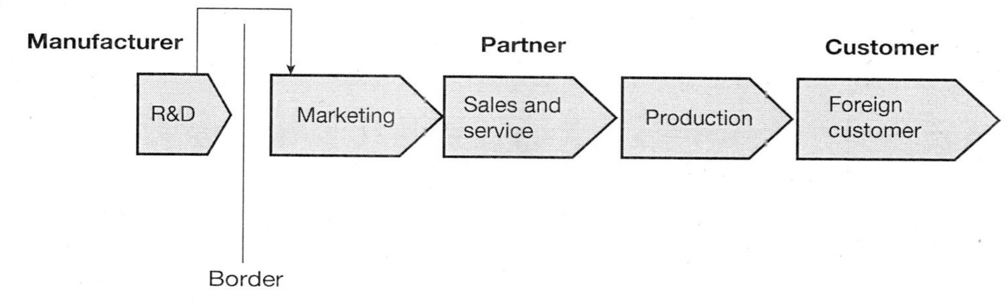

without any further delay.[4] It found Hindustan Semiconductor Manufacturing Corporation (HSMC), an Indian company based in Hyderabad, as a good match to execute licensing agreement. These two companies entered into a licensing agreement allowing HSMC to manufacture integrated circuits (IC) in India using the technology from Infineon. Infineon Technologies AG, signed a Memorandum of Understanding (MoU) with (HSMC), to license its leading-edge 130nm CMOS process technology. This MoU helped to build a foundation for the production of integrated circuits for mobile phones, ID cards and automotives in India for the Indian market. Infineon, as part of the agreement, offered expertise and advice for the technology transfer and setup of the HSMC facilities. Infineon also licensed its fully qualified and silicon/product-proven design libraries to for faster product development at HSMC.

In licensing arrangement, the status of technology holding of the licensor plays a big role. The licensee will be basically attracted by the technology knowhow status of the licensor. It will execute the licensing agreement so that the technology knowhow along with the licensor's patent right, trade mark or copy rights, as the case may be, can be used while marketing. In fact, more the updated technology knowhow of the licensor the licensee will be attracted in spending financial resources for developing the production set-up in the host country. This, in a sense, also influence the duration of the licensing agreement. The more updated the technology knowhow of the licensee the more the licensee will be eager to extend the duration of the agreement. However, in return of technology knowhow of the licensor, the licensee also has a responsible role play. The licensee must do justice to the technology and produce products to the full satisfaction of the licensor in terms of product quality standard. In addition to providing the expected performance standard the licensee should not delay in making royalty payments as agreed upon to the licensor for the use of technology. It has been seen in the past that a licensing agreement usually survives for a long time if there exist reciprocal relationship between the licensee and the licensor. The way licensor desires that the licensee must produce the products at par with its own production standard, in the same way the licensee must be adequately

[4] http://www.hsmcindia.com/pdf/hsmc-infineon.pdf

supported with technical advice. Any violation to this effect is not expected to be tolerated by the licensor as it may lead to dilution of licensor's own brand internationally. It may be noted that the licensee markets the products of the licenser in addition to producing it, whereas contract manufacturing covers only manufacturing.

Advantages of entry by licensing

1. A low cost entry into the international market without much capital outlay on the part of licensor. Since direct financial investment of licensor in the foreign country market is considerably low so this method provides somewhat flexibility with low risk. It also provides fast track entry in to the foreign market where immediate entry is required to take advantage of the market opportunities. With low risk and flexibility, this method is considered excellent while entering into countries where the market is attractive but with a certain amount of risk.
2. By this method, the licensor gains easy access to the country market knowledge already acquired by licensee.
3. In general, host country government welcomes any licensing agreement executed in the country. It considers such agreements as inflow of new technology in to the country.
4. The licensors find that licensing mode of entry is advantageous to them instead of exporting products from their home country in terms of savings potential. They could save money through licensing arrangement which otherwise they would have been spent for shipping freight, marine insurance, custom duty, etc.
5. Little bit more marketing control in licensing than exporting enjoyed by licensor.

Disadvantages of entry by licensing

1. There may be a genuine reluctance on the part of the licensor to share the latest technology with the licensee. This tendency gets developed out of licensor's acute desire of not sharing the latest technology but retaining the expertise needed for direct marketing, if required. This type of situation may lead to dispute between two involved parties.
2. The licensee may have tendency to quickly learn a new technology from the licensor and at the end of the licensing agreement period start marketing similar products under own brand name. This, leads to a possibility that the licensee might become competitor to the licensor with the advantage of being in home country market.
3. A very careful drafting of the licensing agreement is required to tackle the future eventualities. In case of any loophole in the agreement the licensee may take advantage of the situation.
4. Marketing control, in this entry method, is not as efficient as in contract manufacturing. We find a good example of this lacuna in marketing control in the Disneyland licensing arrangement. Disneyland launched the Japan Disneyland project in Chiba (Japan) through a licensing arrangement and the Japanese licensee enjoyed the marketing control almost totally. Possibly Nike learnt to recover from the lacuna and expanded

their business in Asia through licensed manufacturing but retained the control of marketing with them. Microsoft took the middle path while entering Japan initially by entering a licensing arrangement with ASCII and exercised marketing control jointly with alliance partner.

5. In presence of written agreement, the licensor may find it difficult to convince the licensee even if something going wrong in production or in marketing during the agreement period.
6. A licensor may execute several licensing agreements with different licensees in the same country. A difficult situation may be brewed up while distributing the marketing jurisdiction of each licensee. Each licensee may come up with their own demand, overlapping, etc.. leading to conflict.

Franchising

Franchising is a popular form of entry mode for companies that possess marketing excellence comparatively better than technology excellence. This entry mode is currently very popular amongst restaurants and hotel chains of developed countries while entering in different developing and least developing country markets. In licensing arrangement, the technology is licensed to be used by a partner organisation; but in franchising, a well-set business model, popular brand name, and efficient marketing management techniques are transferred to the franchisee from the franchisor. This transfer is governed by an agreement known as franchisee agreement which sets the rights and responsibilities of both the involved parties.

Under the agreement, the franchisee is required to pay a fee, popularly known as 'franchising fees' to the franchisor on a monthly basis calculated on possible revenue generation in the venture. It may also sometime involve paying of an initial fee to the franchisor. In return, the franchisor supports the franchisee with a complete marketing plan towards managing and operating the establishment. Since the franchisee depends solely on its brand image of the franchisor so the franchisor leave no stone unturned in equipping the franchisee with a complete business management guide to be followed while doing business. The local franchisee typically invests money in the local operation and operates business as per directives and guideline provided by franchisor. So, the franchisor continues to be the de facto manager of business.

FIGURE 6.6 Franchising

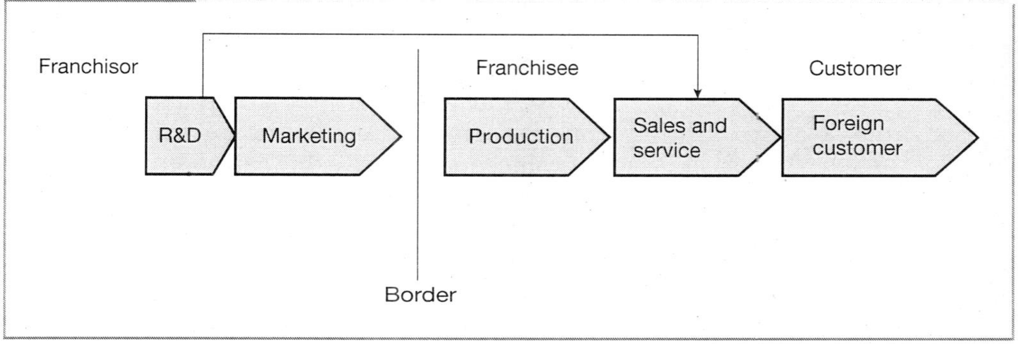

Table 6.1 The franchisee business: 2012 rank

Franchise	2012 rank	Country of origin	No of country present	No of franchisees	2015 rank	Industry/Category
SUBWAY	1	USA	98	36,223	1	Food franchises
McDonald's	2	USA	119	33,517	2	Food franchises
KFC	3	USA	108	16,853	3	Food Franchises
7-Eleven	4	USA	16	44,700	5	Convenience store franchises
Burger King	5	USA	76	12,300	4	Food franchises
Pizza Hut	6	USA	92	13,432	7	Food franchises
Wyndham Hotel Group	7	USA	70	7637	9	Hotel franchises
Ace Hardware Corporation	8	USA	70	4440	8	Home improvement franchises
Dunkin' Donuts	9	USA	32	10,083	14	Food franchises
Hertz	10	USA	147	8518	6	Car rental franchises

Source: Franchisee Direct

According to Franchisee Direct, an international agency who ranks the global franchise operation of companies every year, food franchises are the largest in number followed by convenience store franchises, cleaning franchises, child educational franchises, hotel franchises, car rental franchises, fitness franchises, health and beauty franchises and real estate franchises. In fact, six food franchises figured in the top ten franchises of the world according to the list of 2012 prepared by Franchisee Direct.

Advantages of entry by franchising

1. The franchisor can enter in a country without making much investment as the local franchisee shoulders this responsibility. The franchisee also enjoys requisite support from the franchisor, as per franchisee agreement, to set up and run the business operation. Accordingly, the franchisor smoothly transfers business model, product and brand image to a new country. This way the franchisor can increase its presence in many foreign countries very fast.
2. This mode enjoys flexibility since the franchisor need not invest much financial resources in foreign country. So, in case of need, the franchisor can wind up the foreign operation easily.

Disadvantages of entry by franchising

1. During the agreement period the brand and marketing excellence of the franchisor are managed by the franchisee located in another country. This requires careful and continuous quality control from the franchisor's headquarters so that reputation of the brand name is maintained and not diluted. As the number of franchisee increases in a country it becomes increasingly difficult to enforce standardised operational procedure across all the franchisees operation.
2. The franchisee agreement requires careful drafting in accordance with the franchisee law of the target country. The objective is to focus on standardisation of products and operational procedure so that brand image of the franchisor is not hurt in any way in foreign country.

Box 6.2 Regulation for Indian franchise sector

In India, sectors such as food, lifestyle, retail, business services, healthcare, communication, education, entertainment and travel are increasingly getting franchisee businesses. According to some sources, because of the boom, the Indian franchise market has become the second largest in the world. Increasingly more foreign companies are becoming interested in entering the country with franchising as entry mode. India, among other countries, has certain rules which make entry of foreign players difficult in the retail and education markets with FDI. However, the laws governing franchising operation in India are not very clear. There are ample ambiguities that make foreign companies uneasy to enter into franchising operations in India. This is a matter of concern for the Franchisee Association of India (FAI). FAI as the representative body of franchinee operation in India also desire to have transparent and adequate legal framework that can make the sector grow at a rate of 50% annually from the current 30%. The foreign companies expect legislation and also a clear code of franchisee conduct in the same lines as prevalent in developed countries. Proper legal cover and transparency in the legal system would make many other foreign companies to take this route for Indian entry. Major brands such as Jockey, Dominos, KFC, Mc Donald, Starbucks, etc., are all operating in the franchising mode in India. However, with the presence of clear and transparent regulations, the franchisee businesses of foreign origin will grow even more in the years to come.

Source: http://articles.economictimes.indiatimes.com/2011-01-27/news/28427507_1_franchise-route- accessed on February 20, 2011

Franchise laws across the Globe

Many countries of world have developed comprehensive legislation for smooth running of franchising businesses in their respective countries. In USA, the Federal Trade Commission's Rules on Disclosure Requirements and Prohibitions Concerning Franchising and Business Opportunity Ventures (1979) provides necessary requirements in conducting franchisee business in the country.

For Canada, it is the Arthur Wishart Act which governs the franchisee–franchisor relationship since 2000. This act governs all important aspects of franchisee business in Canada such as fair dealing by each party in an agreement, right to action in case fair dealing is violated, expected performance and enhancement.

In the United Kingdom, an agency like British Franchise Association (BFA) acts as regulatory body to ensure that the basic norms of running franchise business are followed in the country. The same agency is also responsible for setting of norms as well as updating them from time to time. In Australia, a mandatory franchise code of conduct along with the Trade Practice Act 1974 governs the franchisee industry in the matter of minimum standards for franchise agreements, dispute settlement procedure, facts disclosure requirements, etc., in the country. In Japan, Japan Fair Trade Commission (JFTC) took the responsibility of enacting the guidelines on franchising business during 2002. It is still in force and provides the basic frame work for running a franchise operation in the country. In China, the government came forward during 2004 and enacted a legal framework governing franchise businesses in the country which came in to effect from February 2005.

Franchising Vs Licensing

Both franchising and licensing are contractual mode of entry which provides a way for a company to enter foreign countries with comparatively lesser financial commitment in terms of foreign direct investment while entering.

Table 6.2 Franchising Vs Licensing

Franchising	Licensing
It is considered as entry mode when the franchisor considers its marketing excellence to be superior to that of their technology excellence.	It is considered as entry mode when the licensor considers its technological skill to be superior to that of their marketing excellence.
Almost whole business model, brand name, and management style are transferred to the franchisee from the franchisor.	Only a part of the business, i.e., product or products related technology knowhow is transferred.
Period of contract is generally shorter, but renewable	Period of contract is generally longer, even up to 15–16 years are common
Usually the franchisors do not look at established businesses as the possible franchisees.	Usually the licensors consider established businesses as the possible licensee.
The payment made by the franchisee to the franchisor is known 'management fees'. Generally the fee is standardised and not much negotiable.	The payment made by the licensee to licensor is known 'royalty'. Generally, royalties are open for negotiation.
The franchisee transfers the entire goodwill of the franchisor.	The licensor retain the entire goodwill associated with the product/products

While this is a similarity between the two types of entry modes but there are many dissimilarities as well which are depicted in the Table 6.2 below.

Exporting Franchising Combination

This mode of entry is beneficial for the companies who wants to retain the exclusiveness of its central production location but wants to market in different countries of the world. The production location also provides these companies country of origin advantage in marketing the product across globe. For example, the famous Leonidas Chocolates of Belgian produces chocolate covertures in its only Brussels Factory and then distributes them 1400 'Leonidas Chocolate Boutiques' all over the world using franchisee mode. As per company statute if the products are not produced in company owned Belgium factory, the brand name Leonidas, Belgian cannot be used. In end of 2007, Mr Darshit Shah of Premium Pralines, India availed the opportunity to be become the franchisee of the largest Belgian Chocolate company Leonidas and brought the brand "Leonidas" to India. This entry mode makes both the involved company happy as the producer is able to maintain exclusiveness and at the same time the franchisee able to use the marketing advantage of the country of origin of the product. According to Mr Shah it was only 6-8 months time required to attain the break even in such business.

Joint Ventures

In Joint Ventures (JV), an international company enters a new country with equity participation in a local company. The international company then becomes a partner of the local company and thereafter a new jointly owned business entity is formed. The entrant company thereafter reinforces the new business entity with transfer of technology and management expertise.

The entrant company benefits from the local company s in-depth knowledge of the market and existing channels of distribution. This allows the entrant company to understand local marketing requirements easily. The entrant company, on the other hand, contributes in terms of new technology or better management practice duly transferred to new business entity. Both the contributions, from the entrant company and the local company, expected to create complementariness and based on which the newly formed joint venture excels in marketing in the target market. It has been observed in the past that the success of any joint venture depends upon the merit of complementariness. Therefore, while entering in to a country as joint venture the entrant company must ensure that its objective of forming the joint venture is complementary to the local company's objectives.

Integrated JV

In integrated JV, the entrant company makes equity participation in manufacturing as well as in sales and distribution facilities to join with a local partner in a foreign country. The manufacturing partnership allow the entrant company to avoid trade barriers, gain access to local raw material resources or skilled manpower, operate at lower overall costs, and satisfy local content requirements specified by country government. At the same time, the entrant company ensures that improved technology and manufacturing process, it possesses, are transferred to the jointly owned new manufacturing entity. Similarly, the new entrant company also makes equity participation in developing the distribution system of the jointly owned company with local partner for smooth delivery of the finished products. Basically the foreign partner brings new technology to the local partner and makes world class products available to the local customers. It also avoid government wrath of bringing sophisticated products from abroad by locally manufacturing them and remains at low cost by eliminating shipment cost and import duty. Manufacturing in local country allows the foreign partner to better adapt products and services as well.

Joint operation of the sales and distribution also brings the foreign manufacturer more nearer to the market leading to better service to the customer. The entrant also enjoys a great advantage in terms of utilisation of the existing distribution set up of the local company. The jointly owned sales and distribution system further get enriched with the marketing expertise of the entrant which readily transferred to the local new entity. In the initial period of creating an integrated JV the entrants likely to make huge commitment for the local market in terms of transfer both technical knowledge as well as marketing expertise to the local partner. Therefore, such big involvement with the local markets are only made by the entrants when they can foresee a long term benefits commensurate with the commitment. However, the initial financial involvement is expected to be much less than the investment and commitment required to establish a wholly owned local sales subsidiary. Where country market is full with regulations imposed by local government and market knowledge is difficult to acquire from distance then integrated JV will provide substantial manufacturing and marketing control of the local marketing channels and accessibility with a local company flavour.

FIGURE 6.7 Integrated JV (Entrants jointly own an integrated set of production and distribution.)

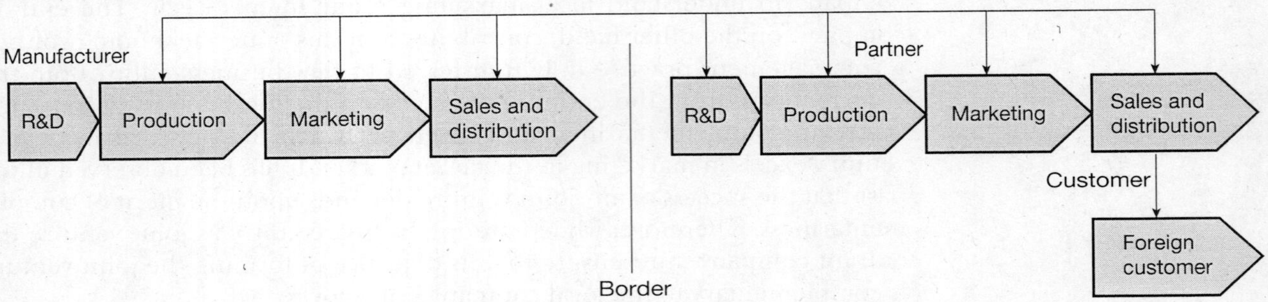

Box 6.3 Hero, Honda part ways after 26 years

What are the similarities between the Hero group of companies in India and the Honda company of Japan? In one word, it is the modest beginning and sharp rise to the top to dominate the market. The Munjals, behind Hero Group, made a very modest beginning as suppliers of bicycle components in the early 1940s in India. True entrepreneurial spirit saw a continuous journey towards progress leading to a nationally and internationally known company under the brand name 'Hero'. There are many achievements made by the Hero Group in its long presence in India. One of the Hero Group's bicycle company, Hero Cycles, is acknowledged as one of the world's largest bicycle manufacturer producing 16,000 units. Similar beginning and progress, one can see for the Honda motor company. Honda also made a modest beginning in 1946 as the Honda Technical Institute by Mr Soichiro Honda as bicycle manufacturer of Japan. There was no looking back from that time, as the company grew to dominate the global automotive market with over 100 plants in 33 countries selling 11 million product units as of 2002.

People were not surprised when these two companies came together to dominate the world. The entire world witnessed Hero Cycles, India, and Honda Motor Company, Japan, inking a joint venture agreement and constituting the world's single largest motorcycle company during 1984. In two decades, Hero Honda has built two world-class manufacturing facilities at Dharuhera and Gurgaon in Haryana. A third plant at Haridwar, Uttaranchal, also started production by April, 2008. Some of the most likely reasons for Honda to enter India through the joint venture route with Hero are:

1. India was the second largest manufacturer of two-wheelers in the world but had very low penetration rates (less than 10%) resulting in enormous market potential.
2. The two-wheeler industry was a typical seller's market with customers often forced to wait for 12 months to buy a scooter.
3. In the mid 80s, the Indian government started permitting foreign companies to enter the Indian market through minority joint ventures.
4. Honda has a preference for high control entry mode (bargaining power approach) and would thus have preferred to set up a wholly owned subsidiary. This was prevented by Government regulations at the time.
5. Low-end technology and lack of marketing skills by Indian brands provided sufficient incentive for world-class manufacturers like Honda. Both of them enjoyed the synergies of JV.

Advantages for Honda

1. A JV was the only legitimate route for a foreign firm to enter the Indian market at the time.
2. Hero had a more or less aligned business model (bicycle manufacturing) focussed on delivering products of superior value at reasonable prices.

3. Hero's mission was to bring transportation to the masses, thus recognising the enormous untapped potential of the bicycle market.
4. There was an opportunity to tap into Hero's extensive dealer network that was spread not only in high-density urban centres but also in rural outlying areas untapped by other two-wheeler manufacturers.
5. A flourishing bicycle business and strong moped business meant that it enjoyed strong brand loyalty with customers and had insights into the customer psyche.
6. Supply chain efficiencies were achieved by expanding into areas such as manufacturing of subassemblies and components and some of the raw materials. Many of these firms were run by members of the promoter family ensuring co-operation and quick response to demand shifts.

Advantages for Hero

1. Honda is a pioneer in manufacturing the first bicycle engine, which became the centrepiece of its global expansion.
2. Honda is a great believer in the "glocalisation" strategy which implies building plants locally to meet local demand.
3. Honda prefers to use the bargaining power approach in entering foreign markets due to which there is a preference towards high-control entry modes.
4. The Japanese culture of building alliances on the basis of trust and relationship meant that Hero would gain from Honda's technology and R&D capabilities.
5. Honda's innovation would enable Hero to deliver India's first ever bike with a four stroke engine and an unmatched mileage.
6. There was an incentive for Honda to assist Hero in building supply chain capabilities through backward-integration as the Indian government regulations required firms to indigenise production within a short period of time.

The termination of JV

Technologically, Honda was superior to Hero, and hence new technologies had flown from the former to the latter through technology transfer arrangements. Honda, was on the other hand, was getting the benefit of receiving high royalty payment from Hero. In a way, both were playing complementary roles to each other. The Hero group understood the requirement of Indian consumers very well while Honda was supporting them continuously with new technologies that were very much required for the fast-developing Indian market. However, this relationship did not continue for ever.

Slowly, Honda started showing reluctance to transfer the technology developed by it. Sometimes, the technology transfers to Hero were found staggering and not up to date despite a technology tie-up agreement in force. Hero was uneasy over high royalty payouts to the Japanese company. Honda Motorcycle and Scooter India, Private Limited (HMSI) was set up during 1999 as a wholly owned Indian subsidiary of Honda Motor Company. Hero was not that happy with that as cannibalisation of Hero Honda's market share by HMSI was evident. After a lull of uneasy calm in December 2010, finally both the companies decided to terminate the 26 years joint venture in a phased manner.

Source: Internet

JV in production

In this mode, the entrant company makes equity participation in manufacturing only to join with a local manufacturing partner in a foreign country. Therefore, it looks like almost similar to the licensing arrangement; but

FIGURE 6.8 Entrants jointly own foreign production facility but use independent distribution channels

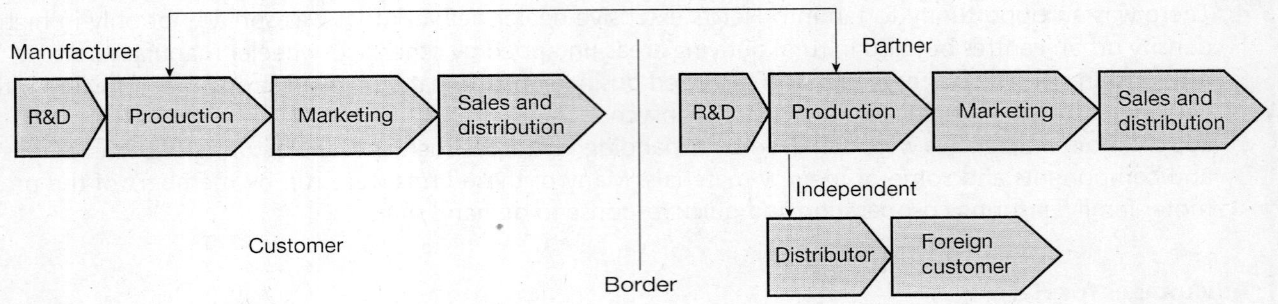

unlike licensing, the entrants here have ownership stake in the production facility of the local partner company. For example, consider a Japanese company that manufactures some electronic equipment by utilising the production set up of an Indian company through executing a JV agreement. As per the agreement the Japanese company makes equity investment in the production set up of the local company and upgrades the local production set up to suit the requirement of producing world class electronic gadgets.

However, the Japanese company have neither transferred its marketing knowhow nor partnered with the existing distribution set up of the local company. On the contrary, the products jointly produced are marketed through an independent distributor company of a foreign country. The basic rationale behind this type of entry behaviour is that either the entrant did not find the existing distribution channel of the local company attractive enough or the independent distributor is comparatively more efficient. Also it may require considerable financial outlay to invigorate the existing sales and distribution system of the local company and take to a level at par with the selected independent distribution channel.

JV in distribution and production subcontracting

In this mode, the entrant company makes equity participation in sales and distribution facility only to join with a local distribution company in a foreign country. This happens when the entrant finds that the reach of the local company's distribution structure is very much suitable for the gaining access to local customers of the foreign market. In regard to production, the company may have various options. Sometimes the company may be attracted to send products to the newly formed distribution JV through exporting from its home country facility. However, products may not be viable for long distance transportation either because of high transportation cost or perishable nature. Therefore, the company may think of subcontracting of production as an option and hence make suitable arrangement to this effect. For example, a German confectionary company Infinity Confectionery Limited developed JV with an Indian retail company to get access to the market through the existing set up of the retailer. A subcontracting arrangement was made with a local confectionary making unit which had spare capacity to produce the product. The product is best produced in the local set up with the specification supplied by the German company.

FIGURE 6.9 Entrants jointly own foreign distribution but subcontracts production

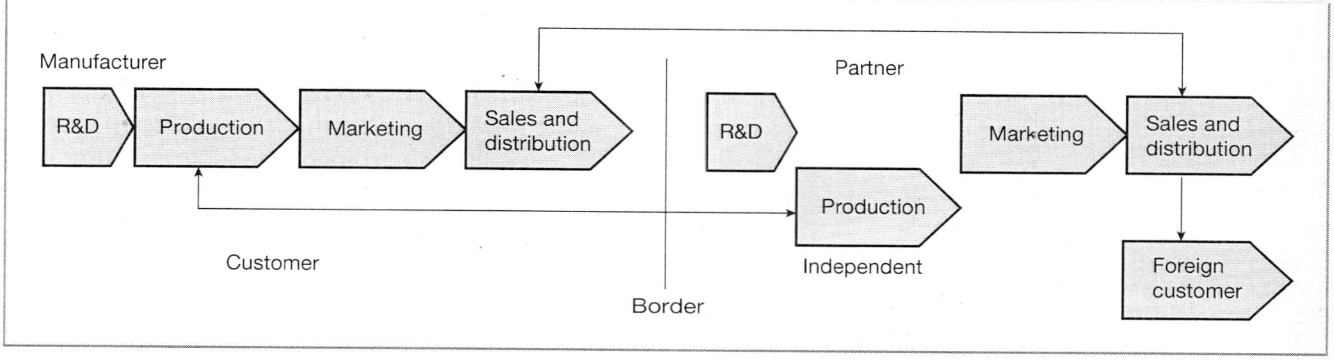

JV exporting combination

This entry mode saves considerable amount of financial resources of the entrant company since here, the entrant takes a conscious decision of not going for any joint move for setting up production facility in the foreign country. There could be several reasons for that but prominent one could be considerable amount of locational disadvantages because of high labour cost, scarcity of raw material, etc., in the destination country. So, the entrant company does not consider setting up of a production facility in the foreign soil. However, the destination market requires partnership with a local distribution company which has a wide reach across different parts of the country in terms of distribution network. At the same time, exporting a product to that country is found to be a possible proposition since import tariff of the destination country is favourable. So, the company opts for exporting the finished products directly to the jointly owned distribution set up in the foreign country. For example, General Motors of USA set up a manufacturing plant in Rayong, Thailand as wholly owned subsidiary to cater to the ASEAN market. From this plant it exports automobiles directly to Malaysia where it had inked a distribution JV with a local reputed company DRB – HICOM for marketing of its car in the country.

FIGURE 6.10 Entrant exports to a jointly owned distribution facility

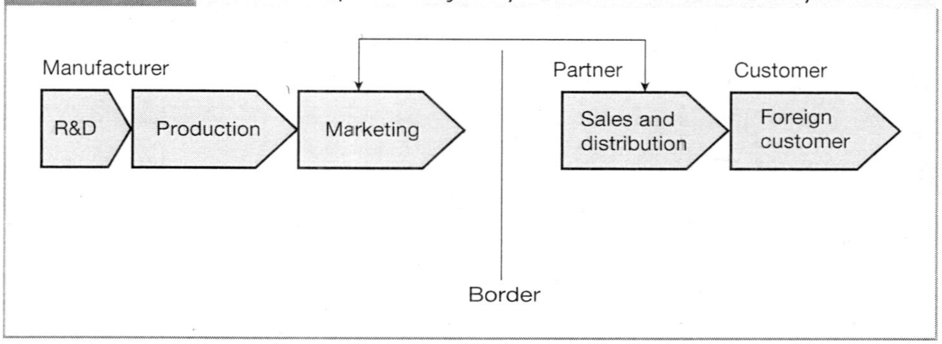

FDI/JV combination

As the name suggests, this entry mode requires the entrant company to go for foreign direct investment (FDI) in setting up a wholly owned production facility in the foreign market. Also the same entrant company requires another distribution joint venture (JV) with a local company to efficiently distribute the finished products coming out of the wholly owned manufacturing facility recently set up in the foreign land. The rationale behind such combination move could be to achieve cost effectiveness in production, which the foreign country can provide, as well using the efficient distribution channel of an existing local company. So, the option of manufacturing the products with cost advantage and getting access to the nook and corner of the country through partnership with a local distribution partner is thought of as the best way of entry in to the country market. For example, the Italian car manufacturer FIAT produces cars at their own facility but for distribution it went with distribution joint venture with another established Indian company Tata Motors which enjoyed a considerable good distribution network in the country.

Advantages of Joint Ventures

As compared to the earlier stated forms of overseas investment, joint venture has the following advantages:

1. Equity participation leads to greater control of different operations such as marketing, production, etc., in foreign country. This could be attractive proposition to many companies in comparison with exporting or licensing. JV allows the entrant to be benefitted from its own marketing understanding transferred to the new business entity.
2. The knowledge and experience gathered from the foreign operations with the active support of the local partner provide the company the vital exposure needed for a future expansion plan. The local partner, who understands the local sentiments better, also helps in dealing with start-up problems such as government clearance, labour problems, etc.
3. The local partner helps the entrant company to enter into trade relationships with critical suppliers for smooth running of production.
4. In comparison to wholly owned enterprises, capital investment is comparatively lower in joint ventures. Thus JV is an attractive proposition for a company who is not very sure of long term opportunity in the foreign market.

FIGURE 6.11 Entrants owns foreign production and jointly own foreign distribution

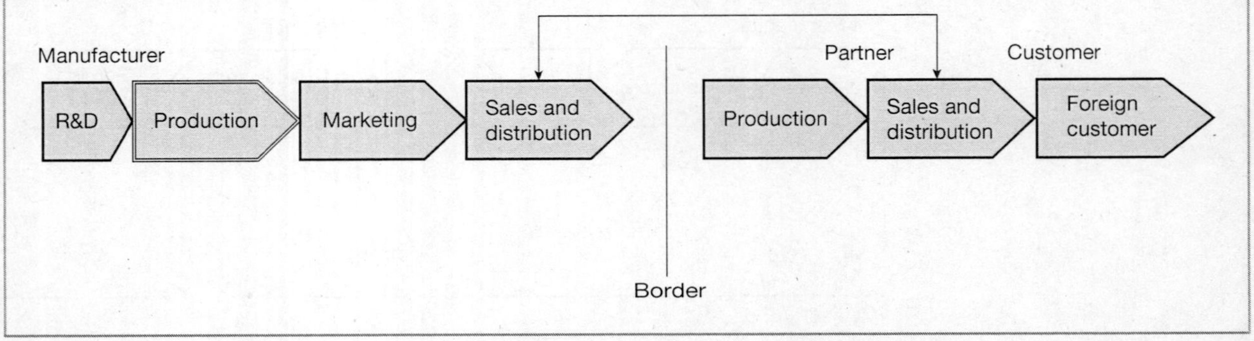

Disadvantages of Joint Ventures

1. In joint ventures type of arrangement there will be greater risks in comparison to franchisee and licensing as initial investment is much high in this mode. Therefore, the entrant company surely would like to be in the driving seat in the matter of controlling important marketing and operational issues. The traditionally oriented local company may find all these things difficult to digest leading to inefficiency and drop in profit generation.
2. It involves judicious selection of a JV partner. Unless a right match is made in terms of selecting the right JV partner conflict over technology transfer, investment pattern, channel control, etc., even in the short run, cannot be ruled out. Past cases suggest that such conflicts create operational problems such as man management, product planning, marketing, etc.
3. The companies involved in JV bring their own expertise as well as assets to be invested in the new business entity. Generally, it is difficult to correctly assess the worthiness of such investments as well as establishing equivalence of contributions made by the respective partners. This may invite misunderstanding leading to conflicts which are difficult to be sorted out.

Wholly Owned Foreign Enterprise

A Wholly Owned Foreign Enterprise (WOFE) involves greatest financial commitment to a foreign market. For entering using this mode of entry, a company has two options; one, initiate actions to develop a new facility in the foreign country and two, acquire a local business operation by outright purchase. However, company makes investment for the inherent benefits attached to this mode of entry: first, complete control of business operation including marketing and second, closeness to the market.

Apart from the fact that the entrant company needs to commit considerable financial resources in the foreign country, this mode of entry is also time consuming because to start up a new foreign operation involves various formalities. However, in the second option, i.e., acquiring a foreign company with all its resources the start up time will be much lesser since it gets a readymade set-up in the foreign country. It also the quickest because the entrant need not to go through the formalities like application to the Foreign Investment Promotion Board (FIPB) of the country asking for permission, procuring land, building, etc. In addition, acquisition allows the entrant company to use qualified management personnel and labour of the acquired company. It also provides advantage in gaining instant local knowledge and contacts with the local market and government through established relationship of the acquired company. When an entrant company is put to the task of making a choice between acquisition and starting a new company, it requires scanning of various types of factors. However, reasons to start a new company could be that (a) non availability of suitable local company exactly matching the requirements; (b) those that are somewhat suitable are not willing to sell out their company; (c) the existing market liability of the suitable companies are huge and involves a huge investment.

FIGURE 6.12 WOFE (Entrants jointly own an integrated set of production and distribution.)

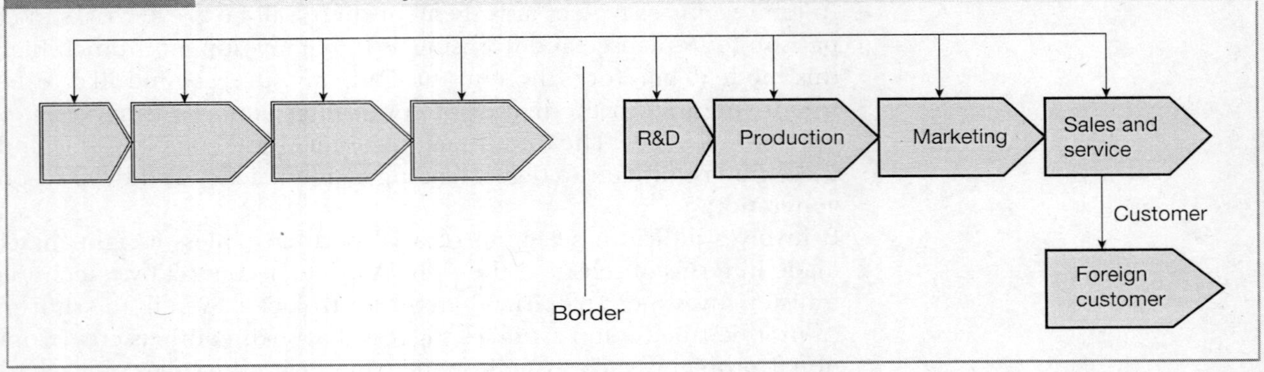

The following example of an American company XTech illustrates the above point. XTech opened its first wholly owned foreign enterprise *XTech Mechanical Assembly-Xiamen*[5] in Xiamen.

Extrusion Technology (XTech), based at Boston, USA is a leading manufacturer of mechanical solutions for circuit-board mounting systems. Enclosures and front panels manufactured by XTech are used in a wide range of industries such as electronics, telecommunications, GPS, wireless equipment, and networking industries. XTech sells its products to well-known companies such as Lucent Technologies, Motorola, Marconi, Juniper Networks, Ciena, and others. It was a natural desire for XTech to come close to the customers and thus achieve productivity gains and value-stream improvements. Accordingly, the management of the company at Boston decided to go to China and produce from there. The biggest customer of XTech, i.e., Lucent welcomed this decision as this relocation would help them to improve supply chain efficiency. However, the company management of XTech was not very sure about the mode of entry in China. A number of proposals were on consideration. Initially, the company thought of opening the China operation as a majority joint venture with a local company as XTech lacked China experience. The company also did not want to share the assured market, in terms of its clients which it had built up and nurtured over the years. Thus, wholly owned foreign subsidiary appeared to be the only option the company had. Cultural and political analysis revealed that there was nothing similar between China and USA and hence, company strategists perceived this mode of entry as risky. So when the company got the assurance of all-out support from Chinese investment promotion board there was no second thought and the company straightway went for wholly owned subsidiary in China. XTech opened its first wholly-owned foreign enterprise in Xiamen, China, in the year 2006. XTech facility in China had 20,000 square feet shop floor with a vertically integrated manufacturing capability for producing front panels and enclosures. Later, after two years of Chinese entry, the management board of XTech in a review meeting of company performance in China appreciated its then CEO Reinhold Hesse for taking the right decision on entry mode selection for China entry.

---

[5] http://www.prnewswire.com/news-releases/xtech-opens-manufacturing-facility-in-china-55273612.html

Advantages of WOFE

1. WOFE provides full ownership of the foreign establishment; so, the profit generated from foreign operation need not to be shared with any local company.
2. The desired marketing control will be highest in this operation. This, indeed, is a great requirement in these days. A company requires tackling ever changing market place dynamics with the ability to change marketing mix in accordance with the requirements of the market place.
3. When entering a country with WOFE, it does not require a technology-oriented company to share its cutting edge technology with a local company.
4. WOFE also helps a company to get involved in any international alliance with other establishments as per its own requirement without taking concurrence from a partner company.

Disadvantages of WOFE

1. WOFE requires a company to commit considerable amount of resources in terms of capital and management in a foreign country.
2. Every country has its own business dynamics and hence it is difficult for a new entrant to achieve a local flavour in the short run in the absence of a local partner. This may be particularly true where doing business ranking (business environment ranking of countries by the World Bank) of the destination country is not very high.
3. Some countries may be reluctant to welcome a foreign business entity and hence impose mandatory requirement of local partnership where WOFE is not a feasible option of market entry.

In conclusion, it might be said that there is no one best way to enter foreign markets. One entry mode could only be considered as optimum in a particular circumstance favouring that mode than the others under consideration. Hence it requires that a company intending to enter foreign markets should analyse carefully its strengths and weaknesses and the opportunities and conditions in each market and thereafter select the optimum mode of entry.

Box 6.4 Continental Tyre's entry in India: JV to WOS

India is surging ahead with its vehicle population. The rich middle class of India are after acquiring one vehicle after another. The country once dominated by only two brands, Fiat and Ambassador, now has become home for almost all the global brands. With the growth of demand of vehicles, there will be an increase in demand of high quality vehicle tyres. In fact, during 2010 India became the world's fourth largest (€26 billion sales) tyre market. So, it is not surprising that Germany-based Continental tyre would like to have its permanent presence in India. Now the questions arise about how the company should enter India – whether it should be a JV with a local partner or a WOFE? The leading German tyre company Continental supported the Indian company, Modi Tyres Company Ltd (MTCL), with a technology licensing to make Continental branded truck and bus tyres for the Indian market way back during 1971. But the desire to have permanent presence in Indian market came after India opened up automobile sector for the foreign manufacturers. The German company ended its relationship with MTCL when the Indian company stopped production operation during 2001 due to its internal problem. Meanwhile Indian economy got the taste of liberalisation and Continental was again interested to enter Indian market. What entry mode it will use for Indian entry? Should it go for setting up a wholly owned subsidiary? Or should it look for a minority JV partner? The management in Germany wanted to retain the management control in its own hand at any cost. So, during 2011 when MTCL restarted operation Continental brought Modi Rubber and create a JV with Modi Tyres on 85: 15 basis. In the process, the German company with 85% of MTCL, acquired the management control but also kept the local partner to retain local flavour. After completion of the transaction, Continental used its management control and focused on local production and distribution of radial truck/bus as well as radial passenger car tyres for the Indian market. Continental Tyres India, thereafter, continued to fight out competition from other global players such as Bridgestone and Goodyear in Indian market. At the same time, domestic players such as MRF, Ceat, JK Tyres and Apollo were also trying hard to gain market share by increasing their competitive spirit through technological progress.

Partnership with local companies in the form of majority JV or entering the country with more intense presence through WOS has been the path of entry for Continental Tyres elsewhere also. It took over the European tyre company Uniroyal, Inc., USA, to have a wider base in Europe during 1979. Continental Tyres entered the North American tyre industry with its 1987 purchase of General Tire and converting it into WOS. In 1990 Continental Tyre set up a joint venture with the Portuguese company Mabor for the production of tyres in Lousado and fully acquired it during 1993. Continental strengthened its position in the ASEAN region and Australia by establishing a joint venture together with Malaysian conglomerate Sime Darby Berhad during 2003. The company, thereafter, is operating under the name of Continental Sime Tyre Sdn. Bhd., with two tyre plants in Malaysia. So, it is likely that Continental Tyre will buy the entire stake of MTCL soon to convert it from JV to WOS.

Source: Business line April 18, 2011 and Website of Continental Corporation.

WOFE by Acquisition

This mode of entry is a deliberate action of an entrant company to buy the most, if not all, of another targeted company in the host country. The objective is to gain full control of the target company. This provides the entrant company quick access to a foreign country market. So, if a company wants to expand in international market faster, on its own, then acquisition mode of entry benefits the entrant company in terms of quick presence in a foreign country market. However, this mode of entry requires considerable financial resources to be paid in cash to the stake holders or for acquiring company's stock or a combination of both. The primary merits of acquisitions are: (a) It relieves the entrant company from the problems connected with setting up a new business establishment in a foreign country. (b) The entrant company gets the local flavour and access to local marketing channel. The demerits of acquisitions are: (a) it may requires for an entrant company to get involved in an all-cash transaction situation while acquiring the host country company. (b) It is difficult to assess the right worth of a cross border company and set the actual price and hence the acquiring price many a time more than it actually deserve. (c) Sometimes the entrant company lands up in paying 'control premium' so that it can have full management control on the acquired company. Some examples of cross border acquisitions are as follows: Suzlon Energy of India acquired the Hansen Transmission of Denmark, for ₹2350 crore to enter into non-conventional energy sector of Denmark which included the control premium. The Indian company Aban Offshore limited (AOL) acquired the first 33.76 %of Norway's Sinvest for ₹2100 crore in 2006, and subsequently made a

Box 6.5 Godrej Consumer Products Limited extends operations abroad

During March, 2010 leading Indian FMCG player Godrej Consumer Products Limited (GCPL) announced its plan to enter Nigerian market by acquiring a leading West African beauty brand "Tura". 'Tura' brand had a well established market in Nigeria and in other African countries for a long time. With the purchase of 'Tura' GCPL was all set to start its innings in Africa. The company historically preferred acquisition as entry mode. Between 2005 and 2008, the company acquired UK personal care products company Keyline Brands, the South African hair colour business of UK's Rapidol and South African hair accessory maker Kinky. However, in the past, Godrej Household Products (GHPL), a 100-percent subsidiary of GCPL had a JV with Sara Lee of USA to become Godrej Sara Lee. During 2010, GCPL acquired the stake of Sara Lee in their JV to make Godrej the biggest home-grown consumer goods maker and thereby ending the Godrej Sara Lee joint venture of 15 years. The latest acquisition of GCPL was the Megasari Group of Indonesia for ₹1200 crore in an all-cash deal. This acquisition will allow GCPL to set a firm foot in the growing Indonesian market. Indonesia, which is among the largest consumer markets in Asia, provide wonderful opportunities for GCPL to market its personal care products such as Cinthol soap and Colour Soft hair colour. With this acquisition, Godrej extended its product portfolio to products such as HIT insecticide, Stella air freshener and instant foods products earlier marketed by Megasari Group. Godrej also got a readymade market to extend its Indian best sellers in the category of hair oil, shaving cream and dish wash to Indonesian market.

The host country economic environment looked very promising to Godrej with 6.6 to 6.8 GDP growth rate predicted by the Indonesian government for the year 2013. During 2012 the country clocked GDP growth rate of 6.5% backed by a steady domestic consumption. Pre-acquisition research in Godrej revealed that investment banking division of the British multinational Barclays ranked Indonesia third after China and India amongst the 10 emerging Asian nations in terms of economic growth. As per demand, potential-wise, this market suits GCPL as Indonesia is the fourth-largest household insecticide market among emerging economies after China, India and Brazil.

The Indonesian government is also welcoming foreign businesses by allowing them to operate with full financial flexibility and access to international technology and resources. Repatriation of profit is also allowed by the foreign companies with right to employ expatriate workers. With the proclamation of the Capital Investment Law (2007) by the Indonesian Government, the differential treatment between foreign and Indonesian investors was removed excepting in a few sectors that are closed to, or only partly open to foreign investors.

Source: The Economics Times, April 7, 2010 (http://articles.economictimes.indiatimes.com/2010-04-07/news/27600084_1_south-african-hair-hair-colour-megasari-makmur-group)

complete acquisition exemplifying step-by-step acquisition. In the history of Indian pharmaceutical sector, the biggest acquisition happened when Dr Reddy's Laboratory acquired Germany's Betapharm for ₹2600 crore. Microsoft made its largest ever acquisition when it took over Skype for $8.5 billion which could be because of the valuation of Skype including its resources such as employees, management team, customers, or intellectual property, business model, etc.

Exporting -WOFE Combination

This is a popular mode of entry as presently companies are inclined to manufacture products only in strategic locations. So, they are likely to export the products from such locations to the countries of marketing interest. Under this combination mode, the company utilises its strategic production locations and then extends marketing operation in other countries through setting up of a wholly owned distribution subsidiary. In this way, both production control as well as marketing control is achieved. This is an excellent way

Table 6.3 Top 10 acquisitions by Indian companies

Acquirer	Target company	Country targeted	Deal value ($ mn)	Remarks
Tata Steel	Corus Group plc	UK	12,000	Steel
Hindalco	Novelis	Canada	5982	non-ferrous metals company
Videocon	Daewoo Electronics Corp.	Korea	729	Electronics
Dr. Reddy's Labs	Betapharm	Germany	597	Pharmaceutical
Suzlon Energy	Hansen Group	Belgium	565	Energy
HPCL	Kenya Petroleum Refinery Ltd.	Kenya	500	Oil and Gas
Ranbaxy Labs	Terapia SA	Romania	324	Pharmaceutical
Tata Steel	Natsteel	Singapore	293	Steel
Videocon	Thomson SA	France	290	Electronics
VSNL	Teleglobe	Canada	239	Telecom
Bennett Coleman & Co	Virgin Radio	UK	$53.2 million	Media
Sterlite Industries	Asarco copper mining company	USA	2.6 billion	Sterlite is a part of the Vedanta Group

Source: Siliconindia.com

to remove the drawback related to low marketing control inherent to export mode. For example, Haribo, the famous German confectionary company produces products in strategically located 16 plants in Europe and markets across many countries through setting up of wholly owned distribution subsidiaries. From these production locations the company exports its confectionery products to its wholly owned distribution subsidiaries purposefully set up in Poland, Slovakia, Portugal, etc.

Basic Features of Entry Mode

Controllability in entry mode

In deciding the mode of entry of a particular company in a foreign country, the most important influencing factor is the degree of 'control' it can exercise. Here 'control' simply means the extent to which the entrant company has its say on the host country operations and in strategic decision making. In this respect, different entry modes can be differentiated in terms of levels of control it provides the entrant company over the foreign operation[6]. For example, WOFE provides highest control of foreign operation since the entrant company operates in the host country on its own and company management takes all decisions as per its own strategy. However, in licensing, the entrant company has the least liberty to exercise marketing or management control since the local licensee retains them fully as per licensing agreement and in lieu of royalty. Interestingly, in joint venture (JV) the

[6] Anderson, E. and H. Gatignon (1986), "Modes of foreign entry: A transaction cost analysis and propositions", *Journal of International Business Studies*, Vol. 17, Fall, pp. 1–26.).

entrant company can vary the level of control in accordance with the ownership pattern it preferred while entering in to the agreement with the local partner. In majority JV the entering company has more control that minority JV while in 50:50 both the entrant company and the local company enjoy equal control. Therefore in short, the more the ownership of the foreign company, the more will be the control and vice versa. However, with more control as the investment gets increased the riskiness of foreign operation also increases.

Resource requirements in entry mode

In deciding the mode of entry of a particular company in a foreign country, the second most important influencing factor is the degree of 'resource requirement' while entering the country. There is a resource commitment, financial, managerial or both, involved in each entry mode for an entrant company for the use of its host country subsidiary. But the degree of resource requirement varies in accordance with entry mode selected under a specific context. Also there is high probability of irreversibility of committed country-specific resources which possibly cannot be redeployed elsewhere without loss of its value. This creates concern for the entrant company since the entrant company will definitely be evaluating the investments against possible future benefits. The resource commitment of, the entrant company is minimum in export mode. Whatever resources are committed for the purpose of export are not invested in any foreign subsidiary but they mostly are confined within the home country. In licensing also the resource commitment, in financial terms, are not much since the licensee bears major costs related to opening of foreign operations and making them operational for revenue generation. The licensor generally requires to commit human resources to do the supervisory role to ensure the righteous way of use of license. Here the commitments can vary and directly proportional to the depth of the requirement of capacity building of the licensee through training, etc., so that proper use of the licensed assets is possible and therefore in a position to earn revenue. The resource commitment is the highest in case of a wholly owned subsidiary. In JV, the entrant company commits considerable amount of resources, both managerial and financial but depends on the types of JV executed. The minority JV the entrant company can helps the host company in developing both tangible and intangible assets meant for generating revenue and thus bearing only a part of all the costs of opening up and serving the foreign market. However, in majority JV the level of resource commitment is correspondingly high.

Flexibility in entry mode

In deciding the mode of entry of a particular company in a foreign country, the third most important influencing factor is the degree of 'flexibility' while entering the country. Here, flexibility means the manoeuvrability the foreign company possesses in case it desires to withdraw from foreign operations after entry. Interestingly, different entry modes provide different operational flexibility level. In many cases it is directly proportional to the quantum of resource commitment. Export has least financial

Box 6.6 BMW's entry modes in Asia

Advancing its international market strategy, the BMW Group made a formal entry into India way back in 2006. The company from it headquarter planned a wide range of activities for the country like India with huge marketing opportunity. The company flagged off Indian ambition by entering the country with a wholly owned subsidiary BMW India Pvt Ltd during 2006. Under BMW India a wholly owned sales subsidiary in the national capital Delhi and another wholly owned assembly plant for BMW automobiles in southern India (Chennai) were planned. The assembly plant in Chennai commenced business operations at the beginning of 2007. It made initial investments of 20 million Euros for Indian operation. The plant was planned to produce BMW 3 Series and 5 Series saloons for the local market. The sales subsidiary was entrusted with the responsibilities of developing the dealer organisation, deciding on pricing and product strategy, etc. In the medium term, the company expected to employ about 650 people in India which excluded 600 additional employments generated through the dealer and service network.

"The Indian automobile market offers significant growth potential in the long term. With our increased presence there, we will be well positioned to fully tap into this potential. This marks a further important step in our Asia strategy", said Helmut Panke, the then Chairman of the Board of Management of BMW AG. The company had a target of an annual sales volume of 150,000 units of BMW, MINI and Rolls-Royce cars in the Asian markets by 2008. Just before the entry in India the company clocked a sales volume of 95,482 automobiles in Asia during 2004 fiscal. With the set up Indian unit, BMW Group almost completed its presence in all the strategic nodal points in Asia to cater to the requirement of AFTA (ASEAN Free Trade Area) markets. It appointed an exclusive retailer in Japan way back in 1994. The wholly owned Thailand assembly plant was set up during 2000 followed by another one in Indonesia (2001). BMW entered Malaysia with is a joint venture with local partner Sime Darby Berhad. Also in China, the company had gone for setting up a production JV by the name BMW Shenyang plant as well as a distribution joint venture.

The Singapore-based regional office of BMW Asia was entrusted with the responsibility of managing of importation of knocked down parts by the wholly owned assembly plants.

Source: BMW press releases

commitment and hence provides the highest flexibility than any other mode.

Contractual mode such as licensing involves long term commitment of the entrant company with lesser financial and management commitments for the foreign operation and hence withdrawal from foreign country not much difficult. However, during the contractual time period the entrant company required to be present in the foreign country. Flexibility is least in investment mode like WOFE, where the foreign company makes considerable financial and managerial investment in the foreign country. In the same line, comparatively high level of resource commitment than contractual modes as well as mutually agreed upon time period of joint operation make JV based entry modes less flexible. As a way out, the entrant company can progressively reduce ownership form from majority JV to minority JV, with the passage of time, in case exit from the country is planned. Therefore, to start with a minority JV in foreign operation provides more flexibility and strategic in nature.

Marketing control in entry mode

In deciding the mode of entry of a particular company in a foreign country, one of the most important strategic influencing factors is the 'marketing control' while entering the country. What is marketing control? Marketing control implies the ability of the foreign company to listen to the requirements of the foreign customers minutely and exercise marketing tools it commands in order to capture the foreign market share more than the competitors in its own strategic way. Exporting, being in the lower order of mode of entry options, an exporting company is considered to have lowest marketing control. It is generally the importing agent or firm that listens to the customer's needs and wants and usually remains hesitant to pass them on the exporting company. Hence, manufacturing exporters endeavour to go up the ladder of entry mode by opting for licensing, strategic alliances or wholly owned manufacturing subsidiary in order to have more marketing control. Ideally, in terms of marketing control WOFE is the best option. WOFE brings the entrant company close to the market to grasp the exact requirements of the customer and take marketing actions. In franchising as entry mode, franchisors never desire to compromise their marketing excellence when extending operations to the foreign country; they strive to ensure transfer of marketing knowledge straight to the franchisee. Hence, with the adequate support of the contractual agreement retains marketing control. Licensing, as an option of entry mode, is inconvenient in respect of marketing control. The entrant company is almost totally dependent on the licensee for exercising marketing control. In joint venture there could be two situations: Situation A where the foreign company's marketing excellence is superior to that of the local partner; Situation B where the foreign company's marketing excellence is inferior to that of the local partner. Situation A requires the local company to accept and learn to change as per the competitive requirements to reap the maximum benefits. Situation B can be advantageous in terms of adaptation of marketing requirements as per the local need since the foreign company's marketing skills would now be strengthened due the partnership with the local firm and joint venture can look for a synergistic effect.

Since control on local marketing effort is vital for efficient marketing of products, companies resort to various hybrid-entry strategies such as exporting through independent agents and marketing in foreign country with franchised distributors, exporting to a local marketing partner built through alliance and exporting to a wholly owned sales subsidiary in order of increasing marketing control. Manufacturer exporters often export products to be marketed by independent agents and distributors. A number of premium segment cars such as Mercedes Benz, Rolls–Royce, and BMW are exported from their manufacturing base to other countries like India, and they reach to Indian customers through independent agents and distributors. On the other hand, European and Japanese car makers (Volvo, Toyota) export cars to the US which are marketed in the US through wholly owned sales subsidiary. Audi, the German luxury car manufacturer, is enjoying considerable success in India by establishing its own sales subsidiary company in the country. The sales subsidiary listens to the need and wants of the local market and decides on advertising, pricing, market research and importantly, distribution management. Similarly, licensing arrangement can be made with independent agents for production in a foreign country and agreeing to an alliance with a local company for marketing. Disneyland launched the Japan Disneyland project in Chiba (Japan) through licensing arrangement and entrusted marketing control on the Japanese licensee. In the Euro Disney, Disneyland entered in to a joint venture with local European partner and entrusted marketing under the control of local European partner. Nike expanded their business in Asia through licensed manufacturing but retained the control of marketing with them. Microsoft entered Japan initially by licensing with ASCII and marketing control jointly with alliance partner. Companies with foreign direct investment can also try with different control on marketing. LG had the FDI route in the US but entrusted marketing control to some independent agents. Japanese car maker Mitsubishi entered the US through FDI route and started manufacturing automobile in Illinois and then marketed through it joint venture with Chrysler. Entering a foreign country through JV and then marketing the product through own marketing subsidiary is also very common. Mercedes–Benz India that set up as a joint venture between Daimler–Benz and Telco for production and marketing of Mercedes–Benz passenger vehicles in India is a case in point. Mercedes–Benz India also set up its dealer network in India through its own sales subsidiary for its Actross range of off-the-road mining trucks exported to India by the company.

Country barriers in entry mode

In deciding the mode of entry of a particular company in a foreign country, one important influencing factors is the 'country barrier' while entering the country. Prominent country barriers here include tariff barriers, government level regulatory barriers, distribution access, natural barriers like customer allegiances, and country norms like local content requirements. These barriers influence the entry mode decisions of the entrant company. Countries with high tariff barriers are not considered as good countries for entry in export mode. The entrant company will be compelled to decide towards hierarchical entry mode and resort to set up foreign subsidiaries in foreign country. Toyota Motor Corporation of Japan otherwise believes in exporting its vehicles from Japan, but in those countries where it is confronted with high tariff on the vehicles imported into the countries from Japan, the Toyota automobiles had opted for FDI. The same is the case of Japan's Suzuki Motor Corporation, which decided to enter India through Joint Venture Agreement (JV) with Maruti Udyog Ltd. Government regulations also influence the entry mode. For example, India does not currently permit foreign direct investment (FDI) in multiple-brand retailers; thus, global firms such as Wal-Mart Stores and Carrefour are restricted from selling directly to customers in the country and compelling changing their usually preferred entry mode. Again foreign holdings in single-branded retailers capped at 51% in India influencing a number of foreign retailers' entry mode choice for India. Natural barriers like customer allegiance expected in the host country also influence entry mode choice. Because of assured market success following Chinese consumers' continued rush to buy foreign luxury cars, especially in the mass luxury segment, BMW Group readied itself to enter the country with a 50: 50 JV with local Huachen Auto.

Strategic alliance

Strategic alliance, in these days, is fast proving to be a popular mode of entry in to a foreign country for many companies. Under strategic alliance two or more business entities get united to support each other in order to perform better in the market through cost reduction and improved service to the customers. Alliance could be worked out by companies in the similar line where they mutually agree in sharing technology, trademarks or other assets to improve market performance. However, they do not go for setting up of a separate business entity under joint ownership like Joint Venture Company where profits are shared. Two or more companies may agree to go for partnership types of strategic alliance in order to achieve a common objective. They may also go for co-branding for helping each other in markets to realise synergistic effect. Companies may also share their physical resources with each other to excel in their respective business. It has been observed that several types of alliances are worked out by the international businesses. Fiat and Tata Motors signed an alliance agreement in 2007, which allowed the companies to go together in the Indian market with the principles of complementariness. Fiat will be using well developed Indian distribution network developed by Tata automobiles and Tata will have access to the improved diesel engine technology of Fiat. Star Alliance is an alliance of 25 airline companies and under this alliance co-branding has been encouraged to rope in more customers across 150 countries of the world. Microsoft and Intel jointly decided in investing financial resources in two university research centres, Berkeley and University of Illinois, USA, in order to develop multi-core computing.

THEORY OF INTERNATIONALISATION AND MARKET ENTRY

It is required that companies are making optimum entry mode choice while entering in to a foreign market in order to excel in international business. Therefore, entry mode decision making has always been considered of paramount importance for companies for achieving success in a foreign country. Considering it as a frontier issue in the field of international marketing, the academics in different universities also worked hard to understand the actual process, as it happens in businesses and implications of various entry modes on business performance. A number of researchers, over the years, researched on the entry mode choices to develop further understanding in the field. A number of such understandings got developed in course of time which led to the development of few theories popularly known as theory of internationalisation. A few of them, like the process approach, the transaction cost approach, the eclectic paradigm and International Networks approach is discussed here.

Process Approach or Uppsala Model of Internationalisation

The process approach is also popularly known as the Scandinavian stage model or Uppsala model of internationalisation because a few professors from famous Uppsala university of Sweden developed it. These academicians put forwarded the model by studying the internationalisation process of Swedish small and medium manufacturing enterprises (SMEs). Two researchers Johanson and Wiedersheim–Paul[7] first studied the internationalisation process of four Swedish SMEs and identified the following successive possible stages followed by them during inter-nationalisation.

Stage 1: No regular export activities
Stage 2: Export via independent representative
Stage 3: Establishment of a foreign sales subsidiary
Stage 4: Foreign production/manufacturing units

Based on the above findings of the research, Scandinavian researchers Johanson and Vahlne[8] further studied the pattern of internationalisation of the Swedish manufacturing SMEs longitudinally and with extended sample size. The whole study, when completed, detailed the internationalisation behaviour of the Swedish manufacturing SMEs and commonalities observed in the process provided evidence of the process approach or incremental approach. The process approach states that manufacturing companies extend their activities in the foreign country in an incremental fashion which is directly proportional to the quantum of knowledge they gathered during previous internationalisation activities. Simplistically speaking, according to process approach, one small enterprise would initiate internationalisation through exporting process only and that too in the neighbouring countries where it has quite a good understanding of the business environment. It would continue to gather market knowledge from the neighbouring country while exporting there. The knowledge is termed as 'experiential knowledge', i.e., the knowledge which the enterprise gathers through personal experience only and not by hearing or reading a lot about the country in question. In this way, the small enterprise continues to gather and accumulate experiential knowledge of foreign market operation and matures with time in conduction of international marketing. According to the Uppsala model researchers, because of the requirement

FIGURE 6.13 Experiential knowledge increases with increased internationalisation

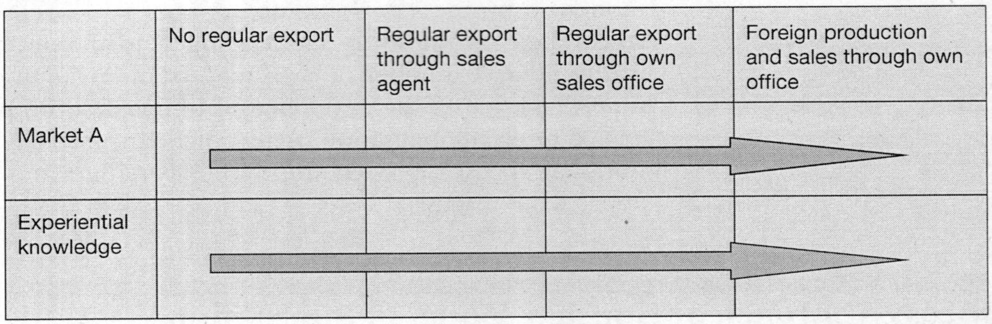

[7] Johanson, J. and Wiedersheim–Paul, F. (1975), "The internationalisation of the firm – Four Swedish cases", Journal of Management Studies, Vol. 12 , October, pp. 305–322.

[8] Johanson, J. and Vahlne, J.E. (1977), "The internationalisation process of the Firm – A model of knowledge development and increasing foreign market commitments", *Journal of International Business*, Vol. 8, Spring/Summer, pp. 23–32.

of experiential knowledge while taking the move for internationalisation, the internationalising enterprise would select neighbouring country market where the experiential knowledge is expectedly to be high. The business would not try the next higher mode of entry even in case of the neighbouring country till gaining sufficient experiential knowledge.

So, in this process as the experiential knowledge increases, the mode of entry of the enterprise would undergo changes from simple export to complex wholly owned subsidiary. This process holds good in case of internationalisation through the countries located at a distance instead of neighbouring countries. The basic understanding from this theory suggests that internationalisation requires experiential knowledge and at certain stage the accumulated experimental knowledge provides enough courage to take the risks associated with hierarchical mode of entry. The experiential knowledge has acted, therefore, to overcome the psychic distance which the managers of any business keep in their 'psyche', i.e., mind or the soul. According to this theory, the managers of the internationalising business feel about psychic distance because of the unknowns and unfamiliarity attached with doing business in a foreign country. Usually, the perceived difference amongst the business managers of an enterprise in respect of language, culture, political system, way of doing business, etc., between home country and a foreign country gives rise to psychic distance. Characteristically, therefore, psychic distance would be different for different countries and neighbouring countries with short geographical distance expected (but not necessarily) to have minimum psychic distance. Therefore, going by this Uppsala model, enterprises begin internationalisation in countries in which the enterprise have the lowest market uncertainty or highest experiential knowledge level or lowest psychic distance. There could be some exceptions to this step-by-step internationalisation based on experiential knowledge development. First, where the enterprise commands substantial financial or managerial, resources to face adverse circumstances arising out of internationalisation and second, international expansion is directed towards a very stable and homogeneous country. For example, a resourceful company like Nissan or Toyota, when entering into a country like Cambodia will not practice step-by-step entry because of their ability to face any adverse consequences of foreign commitments. In a mostly homogenised and stable business environment such as that prevailing in countries of the European Union, an internationalising business also may not follow incremental pattern of entry. Researchers in Uppsala University, who continued researching on process approach, found further that the process approach would not be followed on a continuing basis by a business entity, i.e., a limit to process approach. To exemplify their understanding in this direction, the case of an Chinese business can be cited that has been doing business in India, Bangladesh and Pakistan markets for long time and following process approach it has already set up a wholly owned subsidiary in India and Bangladesh followed by a JV in Pakistan. This Chinese enterprise recently entered Sri Lankan market straightway with wholly owned subsidiary without following the incremental approach. In a sense, therefore, an enterprise after having been earned enough internationalisation would not wait to follow step by step approach of internationalisation.

The Transaction Cost Approach

When a person considers buying a house in a competitive market, he or she pays not only for the cost of the house but also for the cost of search and information of sellers selling houses, apart from the monitoring and enforcement costs. When such sellers are identified, the buyer bargains with them about the price, quality, etc., and takes possession of the house within the desired time. Search and information cost will be the financial resources that are spent to find out the most desired house at the best suited price. For doing this, one needs to look for information and spend time on them to make a conscious decision in terms of availability, price, location, etc. Bargaining costs are due to the efforts needed to come up to an appropriate contract with the sellers regarding the price and payment terms. Monitoring and enforcement costs are incurred for making sure that the seller sticks to the terms of the contract, and taking timely and appropriate action to hand over the house in time. These additional costs are to be incurred apart from the cost of house. These costs are again may be grouped under two broad headings: Ex ante cost (Search and information costs) and Ex post cost (Monitoring and enforcement costs). The term friction was used by Williamson[9] as a metaphor to understand the reason behind these additional costs between the seller and buyer. This friction is responsible for occurrence of transaction costs. Therefore, without any friction the buyer-seller are perfect friends resulting zero or minimum transaction costs. The amount of friction or transaction cost depends on the behaviour of buyer and seller in an exchange situation. However, in the real life both the involved parties in an exchange process demonstrate opportunistic behaviour in order to optimise respective benefits.

FIGURE 6.14 Transaction cost: Low and high

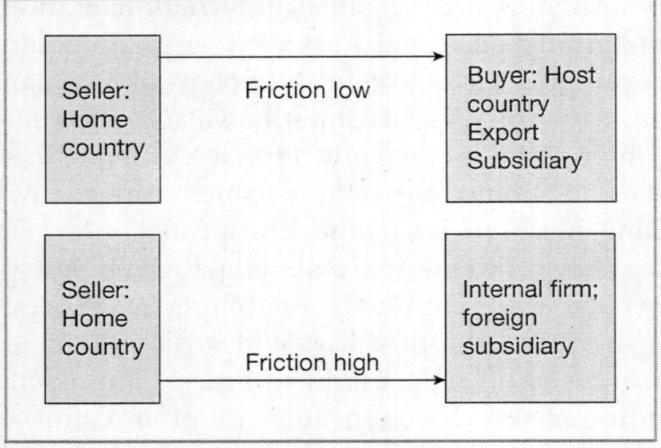

While executing a cross-border transaction it is expected to have more friction than a domestic transaction. In a cross-border exchange process, because of the presence of international border, information does not flow freely from buyer to seller or vice versa resulting the exchange process shrouded under cloud of misunderstanding. Let us imagine that an Indian firm wants to extend the market for its products to Bangladesh. In Bangladesh there are many buyers (here agents, distributors) for the products. The competition in Bangladesh is high and hence the concerned product has to build up its market share under an acute competitive environment. Hence, the seller from India will desire to get into Bangladesh market through low control mode, i.e., export.

[9] Williamson, O. E. (1975), *Markets and Hierarchies: Analysis and Antitrust Implications*, The Free Press, New York.

The export of products also provides the benefit of replacing one buyer/importer by another in case the present one creates problems in agreeing to the terms of sale. Also, the threat of replacement acts on the present buyer and ensures seller's expected behaviour. If a situation turns up where the Bangladeshi buyer performs as per the expectation of the Indian seller, then the disagreements or 'friction' between the two countries is expected to be low. However, when the Bangladeshi buyer does not perform efficiently and shows signs of increasing disagreements in business matters with the Indian seller, then there is a build-up of friction. The Indian seller looks out for information on the possible alternatives, tries to bargain with the seller, and makes an effort to monitor and enforce activities that the buyer is reluctant to perform. Because of these efforts, the seller incurs some costs. For example, search and information costs will be incurred for finding alternative importers or import houses. There may be a need of enhanced monitoring of the importer's activities, for which the seller may have to send an Indian employee to Bangladesh which again results in cost to the seller. In addition, to enforce the buyer–seller contractual relationships, the Indian seller may have to seek legal opinion from time to time which also comes at a cost to the seller. In a sense, the seller could observe that transaction costs associated with low-control modes like exports are increasing day by day. At this stage, the Indian seller would compare the benefit of integration of his Bangladesh operation with the cost of integration (cost of resource commitment arising out of probable internalisation of the Bangladesh business). Again, the transaction cost depends on three factors related to transaction – asset specificity, degree of uncertainty involved and frequency. Asset specificity is the extent to which an asset can be used for alternative purposes without losing any of its value. Hence, wherever asset specificity is high, the transaction cost will be high as well and the price to change transaction partners in terms of transaction cost will be high. The second factor determining the height of transaction cost is the uncertainty or complexity of a transaction under information asymmetry situation. Poor quality of enforcement system and costs attached to seeking information further increases the transaction costs. So, the greater the uncertainty or complexity of a transaction, the higher is the transaction cost. The third factor determining the transaction cost is the frequency of transaction that has positive relationship with the transaction cost. Higher the frequency of buyer–seller interaction in an unclear environment, the more will be the transaction costs.

The eclectic theory

John Dunning[10] put forwarded a three-factor theory, best known as Dunning's eclectic paradigm or OLI approach, which considered a combination of three advantages, namely, organisation-specific advantages (OSA), location-specific advantages (LSA), internalisation-specific advantages (ISA) to understand the process of entry mode selection of a company. OSA relates to the internationalising companies armoury of advantages which specifically

[10] Dunning, J. H. (1977), "Trade, location of economic activity and the MNE: A search for an eclectic approach", in B. Ohlin et al. (eds.): *The International Allocation of Economic Activity*, Macmillan, London.

Table 6.4 Dunning's eclectic paradigm

Entry mode	Firm-specific advantages (FSA)	Country-specific advantages (CSA)	Internalisation-specific advantages (ISA)
Export (Market)	•		
Licence	•	•	
FDI (Hierarchy)	•	•	•

Adapted from Dunning, 1977, 1988

could be utilised by a company while in foreign country. For example, a company's possession of superior technology or a characteristic such as multinationality can provide huge advantage to the company in the post foreign entry situation. According to Dunning, these types of organisation specific advantages help the company to reduce transaction costs in dealing with various agencies in foreign countries. So, in a sense, a company by dint of its possession of OSA will be in a better position to deal with cross border transactions and that too at a lower transaction cost. So, if a company posses OSA then it will be inclined to execute cross border business through exportation at a low or without any friction with the agencies like importers. CSA is of two types: structural and transactional. Structural advantages relate to the differences in the factor cost between host country and the targeted foreign country. The transactional advantages refer to the "enhanced arbitrage and leverage opportunities" to be enjoyed by the entrant country while operating in the foreign country. If the company can foresee CSA, it would like licensing types of entry options by forgoing export type of option. ISA implies the internationalising company's possession of the very ability to transfer its ownership-specific advantages in the targeted foreign country. According to Dunning, when an internationalising company has all three types of advantages, the company would go for setting up of a wholly owned subsidiary in the foreign market. These possibilities are outlined in table below.

Industrial Network Approach (INA)

In both the transaction cost approach and the eclectic approach of internationalisation nowhere role of individuals were emphasised as a factor influencing internationalisation activities of companies. The industrial network approach (INA), on the other hand, focuses on the role of individuals in the internationalisation process. The industrial network approach was put forwarded by the Scandinavian researchers of Uppsala University and Stockholm School of Economics, Sweden. The network approach details out how a company becomes a member in an industrial network and the process of internationalisation taking shape with the involvement of individuals involved in industrial network. Basically, the network approach considers industrial system as a network of companies engaged in production distribution and facilitation. Buyers and sellers actively participate in interactions taking place in the network to realise each other's objectives. The INA promoted the idea that in such interactions not only products or services are exchanged but it takes the shape of a platform where social relationships are also developed amongst the perticipants[11]. So, apart from product or service exchange, information exchange and financial exchange in business sense, social information is also exchanged. The addition of the social exchange process in an industrial network of businesses makes INA different than other theories of internationalisation. INA argues that business organisations and entrepreneurs cannot exist in isolation and hence they are very much embedded in social context. Various types of relationships are building up amongst the industrial networks participants such as buyers, sellers, and suppliers in the backdrop of products or service exchange[12]. Now, the internationalisation process of a company is characterised and influenced by relationships developed by the individuals affiliated to the companies involved in the networking process. According to INA, international extension of a company into new countries is the result of its relationships with foreign country networks.

MODE OF ENTRY: GOODNOW FRAMEWORK

Entry decision is of paramount importance for a company. Any international marketing plan must pay serious attention to proper entry mode analysis in order to decide the optimum mode of entry. When the company has correctly understood the reasons for going international, decided on the products or services to be offered in the foreign market and the market segment to be targeted, a proper entry mode analysis can be considered to have been adequately executed. A good understanding of the techniques of entry mode analysis is required so that managerial time and financial resources are spent fruitfully for the purpose ensuring efficient performance in a foreign country. James D. Goodnow, in his article "Developments in international mode of entry analysis"[13] has suggested a framework for entry mode analysis which could be very handy for any internationalising company. The framework is simple but provides an extensive analysis-based understanding to the practitioners about the preferred mode of entry. This framework uses information, which can broadly be classified into major nine categories.

The Goodnow's framework will be best understood by considering the possible entry of Wal-Mart in India. The Wal-Mart Stores Inc. or simply Wal-Mart is a globally famous chain of large discount department stores operating in about 15 countries through 8500 stores. Mike Duke, the present CEO of the company who saw the company growing since 1995 in different capacities, was a staunch supporter of more intense internationalisation for the company. Historically, Wal-Mart used different modes of entry while entering in different countries in which they are already in. In some countries, it acquired an existing player or built an alliance with an existing player or started a Greenfield operation, either alone or in partnership with another player. The Wall-Mart entry modes in different countries are listed below in tabular form.

---

[11] Nooteboom, B. (1993), "Networks and transactions: Do they connect?" In: J. Groenewegen (Ed.), *Dynamics of the Firm: Strategies of Pricing and Organisation*. Edward Elgar: Aldershot, 9–26.3

[12] Johanson, J. and Mattsson, L. G. (1987), "Inter-organisational relations in industrial systems: A network approach compared with the transaction-cost approach", *International Studies of Management and Organisation*, Vol. 17, Issue 1, pp. 34–48.

[13] James D Goodnow (1985), "Developments in international mode of entry analysis", *International Marketing Review*, Vol. 2, Issue 3, pp. 17–30.

Entering country	Mode of entry	Justification
Canada	Acquisition	Acquired Woolco because of a high degree of local competition in the mature market.
Mexico	50-50 joint venture	The company preferred to form a JV with Mexico's largest retailer Cifra, which eventually allowed them to learn and acquire operational expertise.
Brazil	60-40 joint venture	Wal-Mart preferred a majority JV (60–40 joint venture) with the Brazilian partner Lojas Americana after Mexico experience.
Argentina	Wholly owned subsidiary.	The company got matured with Latin American market so , in case of Argentina, Wal-Mart did not look out for partners to start with but was quite confident of operating alone.
United Kingdom	Acquisition	ASDA was the number three retailer of the country was acquired and upgraded the company in respect of technology.
Germany	Acquisition	In 1997, the retailer acquired the Wertkauf stores followed by acquisition of Interspar in 1998.
Japan	Minority partner	Purchase of 6.1% ownership of Japanese diversified retailer Seiyu to experience the market already occupied by powerful retailers such as Costco, Carrefour, Takasiama, etc.
China	Green field investment	To take benefit of huge opportunity on long term basis. As of March 1, 2012, Wal-Mart had owned 370 units in 140 cities in 21 provinces and four municipalities across China.

While in China, how can the company like Wal-Mart overlook the Indian market? The company was actively looking for opportunity to creep into the Indian market. It may be pertinent to mention here that not all entry strategies practised by the company to enter different country markets were successful in providing marketing benefits. It achieved great success in the United Kingdom, South America and China whereas ventures in Germany, Indonesia and South Korea were unsuccessful. Therefore, the company had to bank on its long experience and plan its Indian entry strategically, reflecting on the contextual parameters. Here, Goodnow's framework may be useful in deciding on the right entry mode using contextual parameters. To work out the framework, first, each of the nine parameters in the order of the company's priority needs to be discussed.

1. **The firm's policies** — Surely a company, big or small, enters into country market with motives. Generally, one common pre-decided motive has been to capture a certain portion of the market share and earn profit. Naturally, if the desire of the company to make substantial profit over a long period of time in the destination country market then it would not like to enter the country through export mode. Therefore, issues like how much market share the company wants to grab in the foreign market also influences the entry mode. Another important aspect here about the motive of the company in terms of time it wants to get elapsed in order to recover its initial investment from foreign market operation. In fact, these motives are required to be clearly spelt out by a company in order to have the requisite entry mode. An export mode or licensing mode, where initial investments are less, could be a good choice of entry modes if the company desires to recover the investment very quickly. While deciding on the company policy it is also important that how management level officials of the companies perceive the level of risk towards

the primarily targeted countries. It also important to understand if the managers of the company showing any preference or bias towards certain countries, etc.

2. **The company's strength and competitive position:** Under this heading it is required to quantify the strength of the company in the home country market in terms of its sales volume, current market share, number of product lines, etc., also influences entry mode. This is important to understand because of the fact that a strong enough company in the domestic market would not likely to enter foreign markets with export as entry mode. In addition, a big and strong company is likely to have a complete range of product line which can be leveraged out in a foreign market with long terms presence only. This could be an important deciding factor in the entry mode selection. In the same line the size of the company, the resource it commands and the level of vertical integration are the other factors that can influence entry mode. Companies with size advantage, resource advantage, and supply chain integration advantage are likely to prefer the hierarchical mode of entry. A technologically superior company also enjoys certain competitive advantages which are not restricted by an international border line. Hence these types of companies with technology superiority would again like to enter a foreign market with the intention of retaining its exclusive beneficiary status and enjoy marketing advantages. The managers' experience with certain countries provides the company of benefit of acquiring experiential knowledge in the matter of target country business environments. This allows the company to take risk associated with opening up wholly owned subsidiary with foreign direct investment.
3. **Product Characteristics:** What types of products are being produced by the entrant company is an important consideration influencing the entry mode of a company. It is easily understandable that a company manufacturing highly voluminous products are likely to be attracted by the either JV entry mode or wholly owned subsidiary entry mode while entering to a new country. Therefore, cements will continue to be produced where major raw materials are available and the choice of entry mode is through FDI only. The same is the case for products that inherently have a low shelf-life. Thus, the product and its characteristics also influence the choice of the entry mode.
4. **Domestic government policies:** This is a very important consideration in deciding on entry-mode choice. Many countries of the world actively support internationalisation of their companies and accordingly design support or incentive programmes. Supportive home country policies include profit repatriation facilities, import tariff concession when foreign-made products are exported back, easy availability of foreign exchange, etc. Countries like Sweden are actively encouraging their companies to pursue the path of internationalisation by arranging trainings/seminar on cross cultural management/marketing, etc.
5. **Comparative cost variables:** Possibly this is the most important factor influencing entry mode decision. The countries can be very well differentiated in terms of cost of production. Countries enjoying low cost of production have been the destination of many companies to set their wholly owned subsidiary particularly where cost of labour or raw material influence the total production cost heavily. The comparatively low

cost structure provides competiveness which the manufacturing enterprise looks for. Therefore, the task of analysing mode of entry involves analysis of comparative cost advantage between the home and host country. In general, the more the comparative cost advantage than the home country, the more will be the inclination of a company to enter the country with hierarchical mode of entry.

6. **Host country marketing opportunities:** It is an understood fact that companies look for marketing opportunities in foreign country markets. This is must for every company and hence in the market selection process, companies attach a lot of importance to this single factor only. If the depth of the marketing opportunity is huge, then the company may put an all-out effort for internationalisation at a faster rate. Naturally, a big country with versatile opportunities would be a candidate for hierarchical entry for an internationalising company than a small country with limited market opportunity.
7. **Host country economic development:** Host country economic progress or rate of progress allow an entrant company to do business with comfort. An economically progressing country always remains eager to host good and efficient companies irrespective of their country of origin. The simple reason behind such motive is that such company provides various benefits to the country such as introduction of new technology, employment, etc. At the same time the company also gets benefitted due to better business infrastructure, increased spending power of the target consumers, etc. The companies entering into growing economy, therefore, are expected to have long-term commitment, which would again influence the entry mode decision towards foreign direct investment.
8. **Host country legal and political environments:** The political, legal and regulatory environment of the host country often have direct influence on a companies' entry mode. A country with low politically certainty will be very attractive for companies to enter it foreign direct investment. In the same line, a company with FDI route intention will be judging the country about the friendliness of legal environment in the destination country. The international ratings of the countries in terms of political, legal and regulatory environment, published by specialised agencies, therefore, are indication towards their ability to attract foreign companies with FDI commitment.
9. **Geo-culture environment:** A company with the intention of setting up a wholly owned subsidiary would look for cultural similarity and harmony in the destination country. In a similar cultural environment or multi cultural environment, prevailing in the destination country, it would be easy to manage and retain its multicultural workforce, promote understanding, tolerance and flexibility, along with shared values, beliefs and goals. These benefits, availability or otherwise, therefore influence a company while taking decision on depth of investment.

Country evaluation process

Also there would be sub-criterion under each of the nine parameters will be evaluated by giving them points on a scale of 1 to 10, where 1 indicates 'very low' and 10 indicates 'excellent' on that count. Each of the nine parameters will have weights which are judged and fixed by the company in accordance with their preferences and long-term marketing objectives. The weight of each parameter is in the range from 1 to 4 where 1 indicates 'minimum importance' of that criterion and 4 indicates 'maximum importance' attached to this parameter. Say, a company wants to enter a country where political stability is questionable but the concerned company traditionally has shown tremendous ability to operate in those countries of less political stability. Therefore, for this company, political stability of the target country is not that important. Going by this consideration, the company would attach less importance to this parameter and hence possibly get the weightage as 1. Hence, by taking the weighted average score of all the sub parameters, under nine parameters, one can arrive at an overall entry index score which will help Wal-Mart in selecting the right entry mode for Indian market or verify its present mode of entry towards correctness. All the nine factors of Goodnow framework are elaborated below in the backdrop of Wal-Mart's entry in to India.

1. **Enterprise Policy** **(Weight 4)**
   (A) Enterprise goal: Wal-Mart is a big company that does not look for immediate results in this venture but would look for long-term profits that can be extracted from India. Hence, it would not be looking for immediate payback. In addition, initially, the desired market share would not be a criterion. The value as well as weightage of this parameter is very high for the company.
   (B) Desired control: This value as well as weightage of this parameter is far above average, as Wal-Mart would desire control over the proceedings. However, it cannot have total control due to some factors such as production, R&D, etc. in Indian situation because of opaqueness in Indian business environment.
   (C) Perceptual biases: This value is below average, as Wal-Mart does not hold any biases against factors such as plant location, risk opportunity, etc. They just want a good platform to begin with, which can be provided to them by way of executing partnership with an Indian company. When the management of Wal-Mart scores for each point and average score was calculated, the average points scored for Parameter 1 was found to be 8.34, which was quite high in a ten-point scale, which was quite high in a ten-point scale.

2. **Enterprise strength** **(Weight 3)**
   (D) Enterprise size: Score is very high, this can easily be said by looking at the mammoth size of the company aiming for further rapid expansion in terms of sales and diversification in the retailing sector.
   (E) Technological uniqueness: Being a well-established company, Wal-Mart has achieved extraordinary expertise in technological matters. This strength can convert even a bad retailing situation good for the company in Indian market.
   (F) Relative enterpriser experience: This value is above average because Wal-Mart is very much experienced in organised reta-iling in many countries of the world and achieved relatively high share in sales abroad compared to home market.

(G) Financial flexibility: Since Wal-Mart would more or less use their own funds for expansion and, hence, would have much financial flexibility, this parameter can have a high score.

(H) Relevant management experience: This value is very near to the average because Wal-Mart would be a retail outlet in the Indian context where possibly not much of its international management experience would be copied in. However, some areas would surely benefit from the China experience.

(I) Competitive position: Wal-Mart enjoys a highly competitive position in the world market to keep its reputation and competitive positioning intact in rest of the world. This score would, therefore, be high.

Average points scored for Parameter 2 is 9.51.

3. Product Characteristics (Weight 2)

(J) Product characteristics: Wal-Mart would be playing in the retail filed, and hence, not much product sophistication and differentiation will be applicable. However, in keeping with its international reputation, the company would be able to maintain quality and sophistications at par with its outlets in the rest of the world. So, the score is above average.

Average points scored for Parameter 3 is 7.3 .

4. Domestic Government Policies (Weight 3)

(K) The score on this parameter will not be very high since the US government would not directly rally behind the company in the matter of changing host country policy in respect of multi-brand retailing. In addition, the level of US government trade promotion measures in the home country would not have much effect on entry mode since Wal-Mart is already a well-known brand across the world.

Average points scored for Parameter 4 is 6.67.

5. Comparative Costs (Weight 3)

(L) Comparative cost of labour, etc.: Maximum of these factors have been given a high ranking as labour, R&D, and transportation are important factors that will determine the selling cost, which is an important factor for the retail chain. In Indian operations, these factors would be favourable to the company to a great extent.

Average points scored for Parameter 5 is 7.

6. Host Country Marketing Opportunity (Weight 4)

(M) Market size: These factors are important determinants of the entry mode strategy as it is essential to know the potential and the size of the market the company is entering. India's middle-class population is more than the European population. Hence, this customer base is an important determinant for Wal-Mart's success as a retail chain in the country. With the affluence level of the middle-class population increasing, it would be a lucrative market for the company with long-term potential. There are a good number of local players who are right now reaping the benefits but the market is far from saturation as the rural population is still untapped and local players are technologically weaker that Wal-Mart. On this count the score, therefore, would be high.

Average points scored for Parameter 6 is 9.

7. **Host Country Economic Development and Performance** (Weight 4)

(N) Economic performance: Better the economic performance of the country, better the opportunity. On this count, India is showing a great prospect with GDP growth rate and its sustenance. Economists and specialist agencies expect the growth story of India to continue and, to a great extent, be untouched by the global recession due to its strong domestic demand. However, the country has many things to be done in terms of poverty alleviation, tackling high level of corruption, etc. This may have an effect on the full blossoming of economic performance. Hence these are ranked high.

Average points scored for Parameter 7 is 7.22.

8. **Host Country Legal/Political Environment** (Weight 2)

(O) Political stability: India is the largest democracy of the world. The legal system is well established. The country is also politically stable. However, the enforcement of law takes a long time and often proves as good as denial of justice. Patent and copyright, though strong on paper, are difficult to enforce. These factors may affect the business scenario. There are operating restrictions in place on foreign companies in the retailing business, which have direct effect on the mode of entry of a company. The host government is yet to make a firm decision on multi-brand retailing by foreign companies. However, it is being felt that the sector would be opened up soon going by the liberalisation momentum of the country. However, the silver lining is that the mood of the government is changing and it looks for a big leap in the reform process.

Average points scored for Parameter 8 is 6.73.

9. **Geo-cultural Environment** (Weight 1)

(P) Cultural environment: The increasing affluence and openness of the country's middle class towards Westernisation has influenced the buying behaviour of the consumers and they are now showing increased inclination to buy in supermarket environment. However, there is large chunk of population which continues to patronise the weekly 'sabji hat' and road side 'kirana' store. Generally, people tend to buy fresh vegetables for day-to-day requirements and therefore avoid coming to supermarkets for vegetables. However, the company thinks that this would change soon and hence, it is not considered very important for making the entry mode choice.

Average points scored for Parameter 9 is 2

The next step in this framework is to find out the weighted average of the scores obtained from the framework obtain the entry index score in the following way .

Entry index score = $\sum W_i P_i / \sum W_i$ where W is the weight and P is the points scored.

= 197.84/27

= 7.33

The next step is to understand the entry index score obtained through this process. Here index score 1 indicates export and 10 wholly owned subsidiary and in-between scores are required to be interpreted accordingly. For example the score of 7.33 suggests may suggest entry of Wal-Mart to India as a joint venture with a majority share.

CHAPTER SUMMARY

1. When companies identify opportunities in the foreign market, the next natural decision would be to decide on the entry mode. In this respect, the companies have choices that range from simple to complex. The products can be shipped to the selected market in exchange for money. It may also so happen that the foreign company sets up a wholly owned manufacturing subsidiary by way of foreign direct investment in the host country in plant and machinery. In fact, a company has several entry methods and the company selects the one that suits it optimally.
2. For small- and medium- sized companies, internationalisation is generally not a straight-forward process but one that takes place rather gradually; hence, exporting as entry methods suits them initially. This exempts those small companies that are born global because the basic purpose of founding 'born global' small company is to take advantage of the external country markets right from the beginning possibly because small or constrained domestic markets are often insufficient to provide growth momentum. So, in such cases, the gradual process of entry may not be followed.
3. Entry through contractual agreements like contract manufacturing and licensing are becoming very popular these days as some of the countries are fast becoming the production hub because of low labour costs. Some hiring companies take the benefit of approaching a contract manufacturer to get its products manufactured on a cost plus profit basis. Many technologically superior companies are also selecting licensing as an easy route of entry into countries where technology is not updated and markets products through the licensees.
4. Franchising is a popular form of entry mode for companies that have marketing excellence. This entry mode is being extensively used by restaurants and hotel chains for entering in different country markets.
5. Companies enter foreign markets through a suitable mode of hybrid entry that may be a combination of basic entry modes such as exporting and JV in distribution or JV in Production. Similarly, a mix of FDI and JV entry methods are also tried to capture the foreign market. Such hybrid entry methods allow the company to enjoy the advantages of multiple entries in practice.
6. Entry choice strategy has been considered as a frontier issue in the field of international marketing. Over the years, a number of researchers contributed to this field leading to development of four selected fields, namely, the process approach theory, the transaction cost theory, the eclectic paradigm theory, and the international networks theory. These theories provide a theoretical understanding of the factors that have to be weighed by a company when deciding on optimum mode of entry into a foreign market.

QUESTIONS FOR REVIEW

Short Answer Questions

1. What are the different modes of entry into a foreign market? Discuss the merits and demerits of direct and indirect export.
2. What is the difference between joint venture and wholly owned subsidiary?
3. What is franchising? What are the differences between licensing and franchising?
4. What is optimum entry mode? What are the different parameters to be considered in deciding the optimum entry mode for a company?
5. What is integrated JV? Explain with the help of an example.
6. What do you understand by 'JV Exporting Combination' as a method of entry in international market? Explain with the help of an example.

Descriptive Questions

7. A neophyte US firm decided to avoid managerial and research expense to explore foreign markets and simply license the manufacturing and sales of their product to a UK firm. The English firm was granted the right to sub-license the process knowhow to other parts of the world. After a few years, the foreign markets for the company's product increased greatly in potential but the US Company gained only a small share of the increase in revenues. It had already "sold" its markets to the UK Company and could only watch as that company's sales took off. Early in the phase of global expansion, American Gillette licensed its razor blade manufacturing technology to British Wilkinson. As a result, Gillette had to fight a long battle with Wilkinson to gain dominance in the European market. Do you think licensing is an attractive option for foreign market entry? Explain your views with the help of example. What steps, according to you, should a company take to make licensing an attractive foreign entry mode?
8. While Disney World entered the Japanese market by licensing a Japanese company, Euro-Disney (now Disneyland Paris) was established as a joint venture with European backing but with Disney holding majority control. To what would you attribute the difference in entry mode? Given the lack of early success in Europe, do you think another entry mode would have been better? Why or why not?
9. The following are the six options that your company of apparel manufacturing is considering for entering into a foreign market. For selecting the best possible mode of entry, it is required to indicate cost implications for each of the four entry modes. Suggest the possible cost implications, advantage and disadvantages of each of them for considerations of the company
   (a) Production is WOFE and Distribution is also WOFE
   (b) Production is acquired and distribution is acquired
   (c) Production is WOFE and distribution is acquired
   (d) Production is acquired and distribution is WOFE
   (e) Production is export and distribution is majority JV
   (f) Production is sub contracting and distribution is WOFE
10. "Licensing is an attractive option for entering into a country market." Detail a step-by-step approach on how a firm can safeguard from the disadvantages of licensing.
11. As per Dunning's eclectic paradigm, three conditions – ownership-specific advantages, location-specific advantages, and internalisation advantages determine whether a company will engage in FDI. Explain with the help of a firm you are aware of.
12. FH Faulding & Co. Ltd. is a successful Australian pharmaceutical company with operations in over 50 countries and extensive operations in Asia. The Faulding business provides solutions in two key areas: (a) branded consumer health and beauty products; (b) prescription drugs that are sold directly to hospitals, clinics, doctors or are formulated for consumer use and sold through pharmacists. Its method of Asian market entry requires that orders for pharmaceutical products be sent to Australia for direct export to the required destinations of 18 Asian country markets it has its presence. The Singapore office opened in 1987 and today, the office acts as a regional hub to 18 Asian markets. It also oversees the Asian marketing effort. However, with more focus in Asian markets in recent days, ideally the total ownership and manufacture in local markets is seen to have commercial and logistical advantage. The management of Faulding seems to favour a majority joint venture operation both in production and in distribution on the ground to leverage the expertise of the local company, and hasten distribution to hospitals and influence the medical fraternity in each country. Faulding's country-in-charge of Japan recently put forward his view in favour of technology licence to a local manufacturer in a business meeting while the China-in-charge seemed to favour a 50-50 joint venture in product manufacturing only. What were the benefits availed by the firm under the existing entry method? What disadvantages can you identify in having a local joint venture partner? Which mode

of entry, according to you, would best satisfy the marketing objective in China? Justify your answer.

13. India's health and wellness segment is expected to touch ₹55,000 crore by financial year 2015. PepsiCo in India is all set to take this opportunity by establishing a joint venture with Tata Global Beverages for launching a glucose-based beverage, 'Lehar Gluco Plus' (a lemon-flavoured, noncarbonated drink). The JV is expected to roll out more health and wellness beverages in the coming years. What benefits are expected by PepsiCo out of this JV? What would be the expectations of Tata from this JV?
14. What are the different entry methods open to a firm that decides on international entry? What benefits, in general, can a firm avail with JV as entry method? What disadvantages can you identify in having a local joint venture partner? Analyse the pros and cons of JV as entry mode of an Indian company you are aware of into China.
15. Bajaj, country's second largest bike maker recently picked up 14.5% stake in KTM Power Sports AG, Europe's second largest sports bike maker, through its wholly owned Netherlands subsidiary, Bajaj Auto International Holdings BV. KTM and Bajaj agreed upon joint projects for the development of engines as well as vehicle platforms. KTM has agreed to provide Bajaj the know-how for the joint development of highly efficient water-cooled 4-stroke engines of 125 cc and 250 cc capacities, while Bajaj will provide KTM entry into a whole new segment of street motorcycles by sharing the technology it has been using for its own products. With the introduction of the new EU driving license allowing bikes up to 125cc being ridden with a car driving license in all EU member states, KTM will have an advantage with offerings in this segment. KTM plans to source the production of these bikes from India while Bajaj will take care of the distribution of KTM products in South East Asian countries. Bajaj CEO Rajiv Bajaj commented, "KTM's sharp brand positioning, differentiated designs, and hyper performance have inspired Bajaj to invest in this participation. Bajaj is delighted with this opportunity to co-develop a range of products for manufacture by Bajaj for both KTM and Bajaj brands. Bajaj is equally excited to access the European market via KTM."
    Analyse the possible benefits of Bajaj from the JV. Analyse the possible benefits of KTM from the JV. What is your prediction for the JV? Will it be a success or a failure?
16. What is the difference between franchising and licensing? "Pierre Cardin has lent his name to just about everything – at the expense, say some, of much of his credibility. He is known all over the world for his penchant to stamp his name on everything from golf clubs and frying pans to binoculars and orthopaedic mattresses. While most designers content themselves with fragrance, accessories and underwear, Cardin has amassed more than 800 licensees around the globe, and earns royalties on Pierre Cardin luggage, ceramics and cooker hoods". How can a company safeguard itself while entering foreign market through licensing? Explain in the context of Pierre Cardin.

EXERCISES

1. Visit the Web site of ONGC Videsh Limited (www.ongcvidesh.com) and identify three countries it had entered lately. Then, establish the optimum mode of entry for the company in respect of entry mode into these countries following Goodnow framework. Comment on the correctness of mode of entry actually practiced by ONGC Videsh Limited with possible marketing implications.
2. Research on the distribution alliance between Tata and FIAT at the secondary level and then resort to a primary survey for finding the advantages and disadvantages of such alliance through interactions with Tata automobile officials. Based on the findings build up an international marketing plan for FIAT's future use.
3. Renault and its joint venture in India with Mahindra & Mahindra (M&M) did not last long. It was termed as a failure as it posted a huge loss of ₹490 crore in the year ending March 31, 2009. Conduct a research on the requirements for developing a successful JV in the automobile sector, in the back drop of Renault–M&M JV failure.

End Case: L'Occitane is Re-entering in India[14]

The begining

L'Occitane is a $612 million French skin care brand producing cosmetic products for both man and women since 1976. L'Occitane, was founded by Olivier Baussan with the purpose of creating a company that celebrates and preserves the traditions of his native place Provence, located in south east of France. L'Occitane, literally means 'the woman from Occitania'. From the very initial days of its journey the company aspired to be the market leader in the product category it caters, i.e., body, face and home products. Accordingly, it nurtured and developed the brand image which can be understood from its three brands essence statement; "authenticity and naturalness", "effectiveness and pleasure", and "respect and responsibility". Inspite of its coverage of a number of country markets it never felt encouraged to produce products in destination countries except the Brazil sun range beauty products which is produced in Brazil only and for local market. All of L'Occitane's products are developed and produced from its French with base in a place called Manosque. The company openly declared that most of the ingredients used for producing its beauty care products were sourced from either its own backyard garden or from garden of local producers who relied on the traditional production methods of L'Occitane.

A Global Brand

L'Occitane did not take much time to market its products across Europe. In course time it not only increased its presence in different countries of the world but at the same time it launched different product lines in the same product category. Now, L'Occitane is a well-recognised international manufacturer and retailer of different skincare, body care, fragrance and hair care products. L'Occitane products are sold in over 80 countries through over 1600 retail locations which sell exclusively L'Occitane products. It also uses independent distributors and travel retail operators to reach the target customers. In addition, the company distributes its products via complementary channels such as internet shopping Web sites, mail orders, spas and home shopping television networks, as well as sales outlet located in big hotels. L'Occitane was successful internationally in projecting an image as producer of high quality, efficient and sensorial products formulated with traceable, natural and active ingredients inspired by Provençal traditions. The consumers of different countries now not only identify the standardised L'Occitane logo but also distinguish the products from others in the market. By dint of its international reputation, the company presently occupies about 30% of market share in big markets such as Russia and China. In Japan, it has a market share of about 25% and maintains a steady share in the ever-competitive home country, i.e., French market. But the intense competition in the cosmetic segment in the global market keeps L'Occitane busy in looking for greener pastures in the overseas markets on continuous basis.

Entry in to China

Apart from successful business operation in Europe, the company wanted to have a big presence in two populous and growing countries such as China and India. It planed entry to booming cosmetic market of China during 2004 and finally entered the country next year. The company was very successful in China instantly as the affluent population of the country, particularly residing in the Tier II cities, fell in love with the brand. In 2010, the company was listed on the Hong Kong stock exchange and the company raised US$687 million through initial public offering (IPO) as the first French company to do so.

Home Country Advantage

The reputation of French perfume and cosmetics industry has always played a significant role in the internationalisation of companies like L'Occitane. Historically, the French perfume and cosmetics

[14] The case 'L'Occitane is re-entering in India' has been created by the case writer Dr Gautam Dutta of Indian Institute of Foreign Trade as a basis for class room discussion rather than to illustrate either effective or ineffective handling of a business situation.

industry maintained a steady growth momentum due to the presence of a strong network of small- and middle-sized enterprises (SME) producing products for not only the country but for the entire world. The year 2006 saw a milestone achieved when the perfume industry clocked a sales record of 15,229 million euros and the growth rate of French perfume and cosmetics industry was found to be faster than the economic growth rate of the country. A few statistics would help one to understand the magnitude of the industry. Export of French perfume and cosmetics brands reached new record high (a total of 8686 million euros), an increase of 7.4% during 2006. In 2006, the French perfume and cosmetics income offset three-quarters of its energy imports expenditure; it also offset one-third of French trade deficit that year. Good performance of the sector continues and till today the French perfume and cosmetics sector usually considered to be top line export oriented sector following aerospace industry, automobile manufacturing and the soft drink industry. The experts agreed that the growth story of French perfume and cosmetic sector would continue and it would be difficult for other countries to replicate. The international dominance of French perfume has been so pervasive that "made in France" perfume and cosmetics has become the quality statement in the entire world. In fact, the French perfume industry dominates the world market of perfume with about 57% of the international market share.

Home Country Support for Internationalisation

France is open country and traditionally participates in bilateral and regional trade agreements as a member of the European Union. France received a score of +0.58 for the factor "Political Stability" in the World Bank's Governance Indicators 2009, which signifies a less violent and politically more stable society. The country always encouraged its perfume and cosmetics industries for internationalisation and intense use of the carefully built up 'Made in France' image. The COFACE (Compagnie Françoise d'Assurances pour le Commerce Exterieur) is the arm of the country through which it takes measures for supporting cross-border marketing of domestic products. COFACE offers credit guarantees to exporters for market research and promotion, including participation in trade fairs in countries outside the EU, insures loans made to foreign purchasers of goods to promote the export of goods of French origin and facilitates tax incentives for French companies investing abroad.

Entry in India

India, since 1991, in principle took a stance that projects its image as a liberal country open to internationalisation. The Indian government desires to increase trade relation with countries of the world as evident by increasing number of trade agreement the country executed with other countries. India also saw a phenomenal increase in GDP growth accompanied by increased foreign direct investments (FDIs) and foreign institutional investments. In the post 1991 period, the country has witnessed dramatic swings in the policy measures governing foreign investments in different sectors in response to changing global environment. India now encourages foreign companies to set up their wholly owned subsidiaries in India. Almost all sectors are now open to FDI in India through the automatic route under which the foreign investor or the Indian company is not required to obtain approval from RBI or the Government of India for investment. Foreign investors have the option to do business in India by opening liaison office/representative office or a project office or a branch office by registering themselves with the Registrar of Companies. Many foreign companies are taking the route of forming joint venture with Indian companies also to do business in the Indian soil. Joint venture is increasingly becoming the entry method of choice for the foreign companies because of considerable operational ease arising from the fact that they are not required to face different rules and relations and are treated at par with the Indian companies. Foreign companies operating with branch office in India are allowed to operate throughout the country. The easy availability skilled workers at comparatively lower compensation rate have also made India an attractive destination to invest. In addition, the country has the second largest population in the world and very fast becoming the most lucrative consumer market with rising income of its population. The big global names in the cosmetics and skin care sector such as Germany's Beiersdorf with iconic Nivea brand and L'Oreal, the world's largest cosmetics company with its own and acquired iconic British skincare brand 'The Body Shop' are all doing brisk business in Indian soil.

L'Occitane in India

As India is rich in traditional cultivation of ayurvedic medicines and beauty products, the entry of L'Occitane in the Indian market was inevitable. L'Occitane took a low-risk mode to test the market in India and initiated exporting of its skin care products in 2002. For this, it engaged the Delhi based lifestyle chain Ravissant as exporter - distributor. Ravissant, initially, focussed mainly on Delhi and Mumbai markets and decided to extend marketing to other big cities such as Chandigarh, Pune, and Bangalore. L'Occitane products in India were placed with under price tag in the range of ₹250 to ₹2000, which was 15% lower than those of contemporary products marketed in the US market at that time. L'Occitane, with all its global experience, was supporting its exporter-distributor to raise the popularity of the brand in India. But around 2004 the company noticed very poor off take of its products from different outlets. The entry to China, almost during that time, diverted the attention of the company management from the problems in Indian market. But early success in Chinese market made the company to be insightful about Indian affairs. It quickly had several rounds of meetings with the exporter- distributor both in India as well as in Paris in regards formulation of new strategy for Indian market. Ravissant took steps to open up three boutiques Delhi to bring some exclusivity factor to the luxury brand which was missing at that time. Meanwhile, the French company became unhappy with the distribution deal with Ravissant. The company noticed that Ravissant was not doing justice with brand like L'Occitane and failed to provide exclusivity to the products. Rather a few non luxury cosmetic products brands were attempted to be marketed simultaneously with luxury brand L'Occitane. Finally, the sales reached such a low level that the company decided to snap the exporting distribution deal with Ravissant during 2008 end. Towards the end of 2009, the company in its board meeting decided to attempt re-entry to India. The CEO of the company visited India for exploring the options of re-entry in India. In any case the company did not want to miss the opportunity of reaping huge benefit from the growing affluence of its target market population. After the visit of the CEO, a Kolkata based group, Beauty Concepts, executed a contract with L'Occitane to set up a 49:51 joint venture with L'Occitane during 2010. As a majority partner in the JV, L'Occitane had its right to decide on the Indian marketing strategy. Very soon during first part of 2011 the French company came out of danger zone and started operating as a successful brand in India. With the active support of its new JV partner the further spread its retail operation to the Tier II cities during 2012 onwards.

CASE QUESTIONS

Q1. Should the group L'Occitane agree to re-enter India through JV mode or come prepared for a wholly owned subsidiary? What lesson can the company take from its previous entry?

Q2. Use Goodnow's framework to understand the correctness of entry mode of L'Occitane in India during 2002.

FURTHER READINGS

Hill, Charles W. L, Peter Hwang and W. Chan Kim (1990), "An eclectic theory of the choice of international entry mode", *Strategic Management Journal*, Vol. 11, No. 2.

This paper argues that a firm's choice of entry mode depends on the strategic relationship the firm envisages between operations in different countries. A particular entry decision cannot be viewed in isolation. It must be considered in relation to the overall strategic posture of the firm. Further, the paper argues that different variables often suggest different entry modes and that resolving these differences involves accepting trade-offs. The paper places a unifying framework that identifies three underlying constructs which influence the entry mode decision.

Cumberland, Fleming (2006), "Theory development within international market entry mode – An assessment", *The Marketing Review*.

The market penetration problem has been subject to much consideration in the research literature. This paper critically evaluates and compares the basics of these theories with a meta-theoretical argumentation that has methodological flaws.

Johanson, J. and J. E. Vahlne (1977), "The internalisation process of the firm: A model of knowledge development and increasing foreign market commitments", *Journal of International Business Studies*, Vol. 8, Spring/Summer.

These Swedish researchers studied the internationalisation process of Scandinavian firms and suggested a hypothesis on incremental process of market entry. This paper critically analyses the internationalisation process of the firms adopting incremental approach.

Demirbag, Mehmet, Ekrem Tatoglu, and Keith W. Glaister (2008), "Factors affecting perceptions of the choice between acquisition and greenfield entry: The case of Western FDI in an emerging market", *Management International Review*, January.

This article investigates MNE's investment in Turkey and their choice of entry mode. Thereafter, it draws hypothesised relationships between adopted strategies of entry, country-specific motives and the selected mode of entry. The results of logistic regression modelling provide insight to the relationships.

Luo, Yadong (2002), "Product diversification in international joint ventures: Performance implications in an emerging market", *Strategic Management Journal*, Vol. 23, No. 1.

This paper deals with 134 JVs created in China and their performance. A basic hypothesis, i.e., relatedness of a JV's products with that of its foreign and local parents is positively associated with the performance of the JV. The performance is tested to prove that product relatedness of foreign and host partner affects JV performance. A JV maintaining bilaterally related diversification (i.e., with both parents) performs better than a venture maintaining a unilateral related linkage (i.e., with one parent), which in turn outperforms a JV which is unrelated to either parent.

Dow, Douglas and Jorma Larimo (2011), "Disentangling the roles of international experience and distance in establishment mode choice" *Management International Review*.

This article empirically determines the role of international experience in establishment mode choice decisions. This paper indicates that experiential knowledge (cluster-specific experiential knowledge and general internationalisation knowledge) are both significantly related to establishment mode choice, but in opposite directions.

Deciding on Product

7

Learning Objectives

After studying this chapter, you should be able to:

- Understand the different components of product and how component mix is related to the value creation process of the target customers.
- Assess the advantages and disadvantages of product standardisation and adaptation of products in the international markets.
- Understand the different types of product adaptations followed in international markets and their implications on marketing.
- Understand the requirements and implications of component-wise adaption process in the international markets.
- Understand the various options of standardisation and adaptations of products and their implication on the competitive efficiency of a company.
- Assess the factors encouraging product adaptations in international markets and the strategic consideration in product strategy.
- Assess the factors influencing the timing of entry in country markets.
- Understand the requirements of managing the product line and product mix in international markets.
- Understand the criticalities involved in launching new products in international markets.

Chapter Overview

This chapter deals with product decisions that one international marketing manager requires to make in order to be competitive in cross-border markets. Product is the first and foremost component of the marketing mix, and product strategy is very important in order to create right customer value in different country markets. However, product decision has not been easy for international marketers, given the diversity of environmental factors across the countries of the world. In this chapter, different aspects of product management in the international markets will be discussed highlighting issues such as product standardisation vs adaptation and timing of entry into foreign markets for ensuring marketing success.

Opening Vignette

Kellogg decided to accept product adaptation for Indian market

Kellogg Company's strategists in Michigan were wondering what went wrong when its wholly-owned Indian subsidiary, Kellogg India Ltd or shortly Kellogg, reported a gradual drop in sales in the Indian market. This was a setback to the company as it always considered India as a huge potential market. The company did some homework before entry and calculated the potential market size as massive when at least

30% of nearly a billion Indian populations would resort to eating corn flakes for their breakfast. This was further reinforced by a market research report prepared by a professional research group. The report highlighted that about 250 million middle-class Indian population were almost ready to accept products such as cornflakes, wheat flakes, and Basmati rice flakes. This made the company director Avronsart pretty sure of achieving marketing success in India. However, things did not unfold as it was expected. The subsidiary headquarters at Mumbai reported stagnation and then decline in countrywide sales almost within a year of launching during 1994. The whole company machinery was searching for the cause of failure. What went wrong? In order to popularise its products, the company made a high-profile launch backed by hectic media activity to attract its target segment of middle-class consumers. The company launched its products keeping the price comparatively higher than that of other brands in the market. The company justified its pricing by opining that the targeted segment was health conscious a neo-rich middle-class population that would not hesitate to spend extra in order to purchase a global brand. The initial sales after launching the product made company officials happy when out of curiosity many purchased the Kellogg cereals. However, repeated purchase, which should have happened for a daily consumption product like breakfast meal, was not through. The company started worrying but failed to understand the reason. In a rush to defuse the situation, Kellogg further extended its product line and introduced various flavours such as Wheat Flakes, Rice Flakes, Honey Crunch, All Bran, but alas! None of them managed to result in increased consumption. Report poured in from various Indian cities that out of every 100 packets sold, only two were being bought by regular customers, the remaining 98 being first-time buyers. On further enquiry, it was revealed that Indians were not accepting the products which they could use as breakfast and, hence, not purchasing regularly. Kellogg, over the years, learnt to depend on a few product attributes such as crispiness, nutrition, etc., which actually allowed the company to fight with local preferences in countries such as France, Italy, and Korea, where its targeted consumers were obsessed with croissant, biscuits, and noodles, respectively.

Kellogg realised in a hard way that it was not only fighting the traditional preference for roti and chapatti of Indian consumers, but at the same time, something was wrong with the product itself. Indians were pouring boiled hot milk, unlike in the West, which instantaneously converted the crispy flakes to soggy flakes. The Indians also did not like the taste of added sugar in their breakfast meal. If one tried having it with cold milk, it was not sweet enough because the sugar did not dissolve easily in cold milk. However, the company was not interested to modify its product but rather came out defending the standardised version. In early 1996, Managing Director Avronsart of Kellogg openly came out defending the product failure and expected that at some point of time the Indian food habits would change.

Disappointed with the product mishap, Kellogg decided to be extra careful and introduced its time tested two products, Chocos and Frosties, in quick succession in Indian market. This time, the company was more optimistic of its success as chocolate in Chocos and sugar frostings in Frosties were in line with the taste and preference of the Indian consumers, particularly with the children. As expected, the sales picked up this time but with a strange feeling to the company as it noted that these products were being consumed as snacks contrary to the positioning efforts. Finally, the company learnt a lesson and came away from 'standardised global product' to 'adapted local product' concept and launched a series of totally 'Indianised' products. Kellogg introduced Mazza series in August 1998 – a crunchy, almond-shaped corn breakfast cereal in three local flavors – 'Mango Elaichi,' 'Coconut Kesar,' and 'Rose', which were specifically developed for Indian market after a one-year extensive research and development effort. These products were also positioned as a tasty, nutritional breakfast cereal for Indian families so as not to repeat the yesteryears' failure.

When this product adaptation and positioning mishap of Kellogg was told to the students of international marketing in the classroom, the students quipped, "That's perplexing! It is natural that a global company like Kellogg would enter India with globally standardised products. Why were they required to launch adapted products? Why did the company not foresee the requirements of product adaptations before entering in India? If adaptation is required at all, what are the different types of variation possible in the product? How will this lead to positioning of the products? Can the companies, in general, have a procedure to assess the product adaptation requirements before entering a country?

"Today, nearly every industry has a significant global segment in which consumers prefer products or services that are much more global than they are local... The global segment is increasing in size in nearly all cases.

—George Yip, Global strategy in the 21st century (2000)

INTRODUCTION

Product decision is a very important decision that an international marketing manager makes in order to develop a marketing strategy best suited for cross-border markets. The product is the first and the most important component of the marketing mix. However, product decision has not been easy for international marketers. Differences in taste, choice preference, life style, etc., across the countries of the world demanded product differentiation from the international marketers. Many a times these compelling factors forced marketers to develop customised products for different foreign markets. Though a standardised product policy had been the first choice of the internationalising company but the same company managements decided to push product customisation to gain market share in the foreign market. Consider the case of big names in the world dealing with white appliances such as Samsung, Whirlpool, and LG, and their product policy dilemma. The product microwave oven came out of their stable and proved to be a convenient and efficient gadget to cook particularly for the people living in the western countries. After a fair stint of success in the USA and Europe these international big names dealing with white appliances turned towards India with marketing dream in mind. What was the result? These companies soon realised that these products were not invented keeping Indian eating habits and kitchen in mind. Hence, Indian curry, the main item in lunch or dinner, could not be cooked in these wonderful gadgets. Over the years Indians typically cooked in a pan with fire below it, which remains open during cooking for stirring and adding spices from time to time. It is a common belief that more the stirring during cooking, more it will be tasty for the Indian tongue. Unlike western way of life, Indian society sees it as normal that, in general, Indian women would spend time in the kitchen and cook food for their family. In fact, the women folk in India derive huge satisfaction when the food prepared by them are consumed and appreciated. So, naturally, all the marketing attempts of the microwave oven producers went in vein. The Indian women found not convinced to bring out frozen sandwich or readymade porridge from refrigerator and heat them in the microwave for serving breakfast in the family. Therefore, the reaction of average Indian, on seeing the working of the microwave oven when it was first introduced in India was not encouraging for the producers at all. The reaction of the rural India population was even more unwelcoming. They stubbornly declined to bring this gadget into their homes based on their perception of uselessness. Multinationals such as Whirlpool, P&G, IFB, etc., were trying to finding a niche segment in terms of the neo-rich Indian middle class and their liking for westernisation and push the product into their homes. According to them, this segment is populated with the husbands and wives as working couples and, hence, hard pressed for time. So, they were expected to relish the benefit of saving time for cooking and welcome the product in to their homes. Slowly, the other customer segments would follow the suit due to word of mouth publicity about the product benefits. All, therefore, would require launching the product with big fanfare and waiting for the good times to come. However, it was taking more time to be accepted by even the richer segment of Indian middle class. The companies were struck by the turn of the events. The market strategist suggested that the product had to be adapted to suit Indian cooking as otherwise it had no future. This type of failure of a product in a specific market in spite of its huge success in another country is not uncommon. Differences in region-specific or country-specific taste, choice and preferences, etc., have made many big companies fail in some specific markets. Consider the case of Sony, the Japanese electronics giant, marketing its products in the Indian market. Sony was forced to adapt their electronic products for India to retain its market share in the third largest market in Asia next to Japan and China. During September 2008, Mr Yoshiki Yamanokuchy, the Sony India marketing manager came out openly advocating for the company's exclusive product policy for Indian market. "Our research in the small screen LCD TV highlighted some features which the Indian consumers seek. This includes side speakers, black cabinets, FM radio, PC adaptability, and round design". The important consideration for Sony, at that juncture, was to recreate products or product lines that were best suited for the country-specific market. The world's largest electronic company, Royal Philips Electronics, had the same problem in India and hence decided to restructure its consumer lifestyle business to suit the Indian way. The company reworked its plan to evolve the Indian business into four categories – healthy living, home living, interactive living and personal care. Under healthy living, products such as water purifiers and mother and childcare items were serious candidates for adaptations. A whole range of other products such as mixer-grinder, food processor, home theatre, hair dryers, electric shavers, etc., were also brought under study to make them more Indianised. "Our team is studying the cooking style of Indian ethnic cuisine to roll out such kitchen appliances," remarked Mr Elwin de Valk, the Philips global head[1]. In fact, the product adaptation requirements have been more demanding and complex in the case of food products. Food companies like McDonald had to work very hard for McDonaldisation of the world. They had to make several changes to their product line based on the country-specific requirements. The first encounter of McDonald during 1996 with Indian food culture was even more interesting than a Hollywood blockbuster movie. In McDonald style the company made a quick make over and introduced adapted vegetarian food items with no-pork, no–beef for Indian customer. First, the Indian customers had to be convinced that the hamburger company can make fast food free of beef and pork. Second, very fast, they had to learn to introduce Indianised food such as mutton-based "Maharaja Mac", "McAllo Tikki burger", etc., to tempt the middle-class customers of urban India. Presently, many food items McDonald serves in India are skilfully adapted to the Indian taste.

However, not all products require adaptations; the famous T model vehicle of Ford Motor Company conquered the world market without any country-specific modifications. The 'high touch' products such as "Channel perfume" from France, Cigars from Havana, etc., do not require any modifications

[1] Philips to restructure consumer lifestyle business in India, *The Economic Times*, 26th June 2009

for cross-country acceptance. A survey noted that a bottle of Channel perfume is being sold somewhere in the world every 30 seconds without any references to product adaptations. It can be understood in this way: a high-touch product like, say, a Mona Lisa painting does not require adaptation for any market of world. 'High tech' products like hybrid cars, sophisticated new generation video games, high definition TV are not also candidates for adaptation in any part of the world. However, it is not true for other categories of products. It is a fact that international marketers had to resort to customising products according to the needs of different markets across the world, but standardisation of the products attracted much of the fascinations of both marketers and researchers. The concept of product standardisation in the international markets has the blessings of the Harvard University professor Theodor Levitt (1983)[2] who through his seminal article 'globalisation of market' called for developing 'global products' for similar markets across the countries of the world. He cited the famous example of T model of Ford motor company and called for American multinationals to return to sense by stopping product adaptations.

Quest for product standardisation

Literarily, the standardisation of product means a situation when a total uniformity is maintained in developing the product with market acceptability across the globe. Therefore, it implies that there is homogenisation of demand in the country markets place, at least to a considerable extent.

On the international level, if 100% standardisation of product can be achieved and practised then it may provide a lot of benefits for the company. These major benefits include the following:

Marketing advantage: The standardised products can be marketed across the globe. As the products are then produced in bulk and if, simultaneously, quality level can be enhanced, then companies can be better benefitted by catering to the needs of global customers and global segments. Global brand development will be easier for the companies as well.

Easier internationalisation: The products would also have seamless access to many markets of the world. Whatever the preference of the automobile for the Americans the same would be for the Chinese. As a result, internationalisation of Ford Motor Company, for example would be much easier.

Knowledge development and transfer: Since continuously companies would marketing the similar products for the globe so knowledge about marketing or production would be easily transferable from one country to another country.

Cost advantage: It means that McDonald will have same food items for all the 100 odd countries of the world. This would benefit the company in achieving scale economics and cost reduction. The company can locate it production plants in more strategic locations and gets benefits of strategic sourcing of raw materials also.

Because of the charm of the proposition of globally standardised products in terms of marketing and cost advantages, many academician and business

[2] Levitt, Theodor (1983), "Globalisation of markets", *Harvard Business Review*, May–June.

managers were found inquisitive of knowing how this can be materialised in a practical sense. The urge to go for product standardisation became more pronounced after the clarion call of Professor Levitt for development of global products only. The CEOs of the American multinational companies were found eager to know the implication of such strategy more clearly. This had its global effect and researchers across the world interested in analysing the various facets of product standardisation. In fact, subsequent research in international marketing, during early 1990s, revolved round the questions of how products can be standardised, partially or fully, when marketing them globally and to what extent it can be done.

In this chapter we shall look into different aspects of product management in the international market by highlighting issues such as product standardisation vs adaptation and timing of entry into foreign markets for ensuring marketing success.

Forces for product adaptation

The research based knowledge and experience, pouring all over from Europe and USA in particular, the multinational companies understood that due to various market-specific environments or circumstances, they might not be able to resort to product standardisation in many product categories right way and modifications and alterations are the alternatives in the prevailing situation. The multinationals, through their practical experience, learnt the following in terms of product alteration/modification.

(a) Different country markets require the marketers to abide by different statutory rules and regulations governing the product standards. These entail them to do compulsory changes in products.

(b) Customers' demographic differences across countries also, in several ways, make adaptation necessary to sustain competitiveness in country-specific situations. 'One size for all' cannot be practiced when marketing in different markets in Asia, Europe, or other region because of demographic differences.

(c) Even economic differences across the countries are so pronounced in the would that compel the marketers to launch products with different features according to the affordability of the target customers.

(d) Cultural/social customs and taboos are deeply impregnated in people of different origin influencing consumer preferences, consumer purchasing habits and product use pattern which in turn exert strong influence in deciding the level of modifications in product attributes. National culture's effect on product acceptance is well-documented in international marketing. Even the success of a new product introduced in a foreign market is found to be dependent on the host country's cultural norms and beliefs[3]. Coca Cola had to introduce a modified product Spritea (green tea + sprite) because of local preference for green tea to bolster its marketing in China.

[3] Takada, Hirokazu and Dipak Jain (1991), "Cross-national analysis of diffusion of consumer durable goods in Pacific rim countries", *Journal of Marketing*, April, Vol. 55 Issue 2, pp. 48–54.

(e) Marketing infrastructure, level of competition, and technology preferences of a country-specific market are also acting as compelling factors to introduce modifications in product features. For example, Philips India introduced a crank-up, or free-power radio in the rural Indian market to counter the problem of scarce availability of electricity.

(f) Another important consideration in product decision is the level of consumer ethnocentrism. Ethnocentrism is a belief of consumers living in a country that home country products are the best in the world for their consumption. Although the people across the world are increasingly accepting the 'best product' irrespective of their bias towards products made in their home country, contrasting cases are also known to be in existence. In India, a marked preference could be noticed for ethnic 'Khadi Product' at least in some specific segments. In a longitudinal study conducted in Finland, Darling (1987)[4] found that Finnish consumers were ethnocentrically oriented and hence preferred the European products despite the fact that several product attributes were of non-European countries.

(g) In addition, at different stages of product life cycle the products are entering in to different country markets requiring product modification. The product life cycle theory of marketing simply says that a product is just like human being, and hence, it would undergo different stages like introduction, growth, maturity and decline and marketers should accordingly be prepared to take marketing action. International marketers need to know the exact stage in which the product is released in different country markets and product modification required. For example, LED TVs will not to be introduced in Belgium and Bangladesh simultaneously. The different product life cycles stages in different countries would make the all-important call for product modification decision.

In a nutshell, therefore, several factors influence product adaptations and hence, they require careful attention of international marketers who decide on the product strategy. All the points discussed thus far have important implications in international business. International marketers must be aware of the functioning of the very important first P of marketing mix, i.e., product in the international markets while deciding on the product strategy.

PRODUCT COMPONENT MIX

Although at a simple look a product may be looked upon as a single entity but on a closer look it may be seen as consisting of several layers or components. Each one of the layers or components are added purposefully to play a specific role while satisfying consumer requirements in terms of the expected benefits emanating out of the product as a whole. These benefits, in

[4] Darling, John R. (1987), "A longitudinal analysis of the competitive profile of products and associated marketing practices of selected European and non-European countries", *European Journal of Marketing*, Vol. 21, Issue 3, pp. 17–29, 13p.

one way, may be categorised as tangible or intangible. Tangible benefits are those benefits which are real, actual, material, and substantial having actual physical existence. Intangible benefits are subjective benefits that cannot be measured in monetary terms or in a quantative way easily. These benefits are imaginary but create important positive effects in consumers' minds about the product. The components, whether tangible or intangible, in totality are responsible for atrracting the target consumers enough so as to induce them for initiation of purchase process leading to consumption. Thus, for marketers, every component of the product is important. It is highly required that the marketers understand them correctly so that a right proportional mix of the components is ensured in developing a product on offer. A right product component mix for the right consumer segment would be absolutely important to ensure the product's marketability. Therefore, it is the task of marketers to build on each of the required components of the products on offer, its tangibility or intangibility along with the features and benefits so as offer a product complete in all respect. Theodore Levitt[5], in his model, grouped the components of the product into three layers or components; each consisting of important product sub components. Various authors on marketing, at different times, have come out with different nomenclature for the layers

FIGURE 7.1 Product component mix

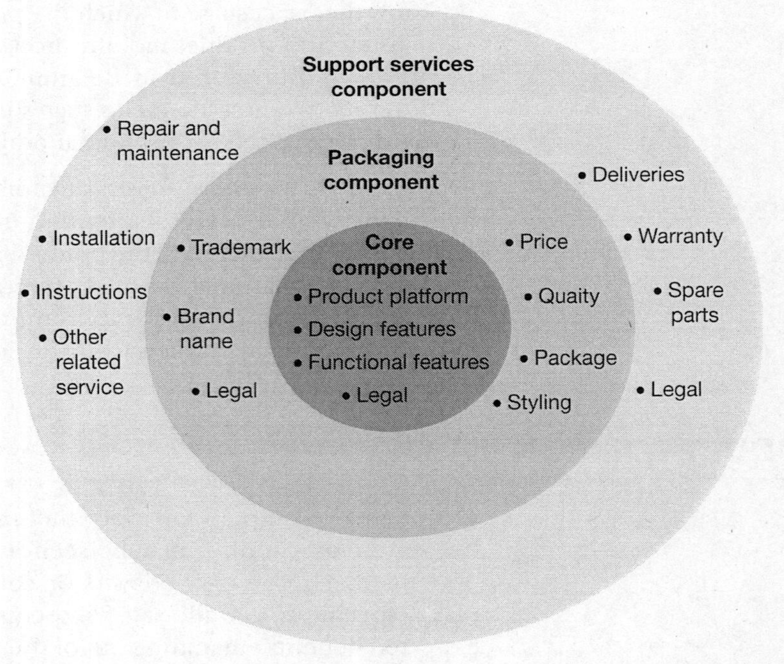

Adapted from Philip R. Cateora and John L. Graham (2007), *International marketing*, McGraw-Hill.

[5] Theodore Levitt, "Marketing Success Through Differentiation—of Anything," Harvard Business Review (January –February 1980).

or components. However, for simplicity, we shall refer to these layers as core component, packaging component and support service component (Figure 7.1). There can also be one additional layer at the top of these layers, called augmented products component, to provide the customer with information about forthcoming products being developed by the company and their possible features. We shall discuss each of the components separately one by one as stated below.

Core Component

This core is the basic components or starting point of a product formation. The core component builds up the basic essential features of the product and hence a marketer must be very careful in understanding it as other components will be formed around it. The core components is responsible for providing the basic benefits to the consumer. It should be as per the requirements consumers are looking for while purchasing the product. The consumer must be able to receive the desired basic benefits for which the product has been purchased. There is usually a core reason or benefit which not only makes product identifiable but also satisfies the consumer's need. For example, the core component of a car consist of various sub-components such as engine size in cubic centimetre, doors, windows, etc., functional features like horse power that the car is supposed to produce; legal features like right hand drive or left hand drive. This basic foundation of a product must be able to make the desired impression on the customer. Adequately designed core component can handsomely contribute to the process of total customer value creation by the company.

Packaging Component

It is certain that no customer will purchase a car that has only the basic components. Therefore, there would be requirement to top up with a second layer, i.e., packaging component. This second layer is also very important as it is purposefully designed to fulfil customers' expectations in a competitive market. For example, the packaging component of a car consists of a well-recognised and publicised brand name that is identifiable with the product category and features that enrich the quality of the ride such as in-car entertainment system, safety system such as air bags, adequate boot space to accommodate luggage, mobile phone holder and GPS screen, colour scheme as per choice of customer, air conditioning, aesthetic body styling relevant to time, power brakes, rear window wiper, etc. All these ingredients are put together to build up the packaging component around the core component already formed. Thereafter, the formed packaging component is offered to the targeted customers at a reasonable price. Both the components together, i.e., packaging and core component now would allow the target consumers to perceive the product as a consolidated offer. This, in turn, provide the producer the required competitive advantage and the customer of the product more satisfaction.

Support Service Component

The support service component, which is added as the third layer above the packaging component, is meant to provoke the target customers to walk an extra mile towards possession of the product by paying the price it worth. This support service component and its constituents are strategically designed, keeping in mind the offerings of the similar products in the competitive market, so that it can provide the competitive edge over the rivals in the product category. The aim of the support service component is to garnish the product with those features which would uniquely satisfy the targetted customers. Say, a prospective buyer of a car making a choice between ten similar cars offered by different other producers and decided that easy availability of spare parts in addition to driving comforts would be the deciding factors for the purchase of a car. Here, the company can easily develop an edge over its competitors by devising the support service component in an innovative ways to satisfy the customer's need. For example, the automobile company can set up a home delivery of spare parts telephone call, which is unique to the product. While devising the support service component, therefore, care should be taken to select the sub components which can outperform the competitors' products. For a car, as an example, support service components could be: warranty clause, facility of repair and maintenance, before sales service, after sales services, etc. Warranty or guarantee clause may work wonders as sub component of support service component for the marketers as it can enhance customers' confidence in product. Introduction of complementary offerings such as steering cover, wheel cover, body designing accessories, etc., as sub component in support service component may further extend the attractiveness of support service components.

Therefore, a product is a bundle of the above three components designed in such a manner that in totality it satisfies the target customers needs and wants. This is a very important step in the direction towards developing product–market relationship through understanding details of product component mix.

Future Component

The art of providing product related consumer satisfaction is a continuous process for the marketers. Companies are continuously working to provide the best and updated product to the consumers so that it can beat the competition in the market. Accordingly, companies would be devoting resources to bring more and more new product features as the time progresses. The newer version of the product would surely come up with improved performance because of use better components or materials. Subsequently developed technology innovations would be applied to the newer versions of the product. However, it is the task of the marketers to make the customers aware of the future products in the pipeline which would be launched in the coming days. The customers must know that the added features would ensure better product performance as well as customer satisfaction. For example, automobile companies launch improved versions of car models continuously with improved features such as engine performance, air conditioning system, design modification, hybrid system, safety features, etc., which can lead to better driving satisfaction. The task of the marketers is to keep the future expectations of the customer alive all along so that they remain loyal to the product or the brand. The last layer of product or component takes care of these requirements. The projected future developments in the product system are introduced to customers at this level. These enhance the customer's perception of a product. For example, a provision of replacing the present cast iron wheel with a forthcoming alloys wheel with easy instalment-based payment option would create an enhanced perception of the automobile's value in the present buyers. Other examples of sub-components in this fourth layer could be easy and comfortable buy-back arrangement with purchase of an hybrid model and automatic upgradation with time or possession of some specific parts of the automobile absolutely essential for driving safety.

Product Components and International Marketing

A clear understanding of the product component mix is considered important based on the fact that before a product is made ready for international market, the marketers must know what different components and sub-components constitute the offering and their impact on the target customers' value creation process. A particular component of the product may be looked upon as the value creator in one country while the same component may be perceived to be the value destroyer in another. For example in India, the customer may over-emphasise on the fuel efficiency of an automobile whereas in Thailand, the customer may consider it as a destroyer of driving comfort. For the Swedish, neither fuel efficiency nor driving comfort matter as much as the vehicle's the safety aspects. When a product travels from country to country, therefore, it may require adaptation of existing components or introduction of new sub components as per the requirements to the local market condition and the target customers' satisfaction. However, a company may not like to make adaptations in a majority of the sub-components while introducing its product in a new country market as it will increase the cost of production. It will be better to understand the distinctive need of the consumer and accordingly effect the adaptation to those sub-components best suited to the requirement. LG may sell LED TV with seven years' international warranty in Portugal but not in Singapore, as customers in Portugal are more uncertainty avoidant than customers in Singapore. In this case, therefore, the change has been effected in the support service sub-components keeping the core components of the product, LED TV, unchanged. The company, naturally, does not like to make significant changes in the core component as the product travels from country to country. The reason is simple. Changes in the core component are likely to be associated with cost and may even affect the scale economics if it leads to change in the product platform itself. Changes in the outer components such as warrantee clauses, etc., would not be so difficult for the company to bring about and would therefore be readily agreed to. That is why more the competition in a country market, more will be the differentiation in the outer components of the product offering being made by the competing companies in that particular country market.

Box 7.1 Vertu: It has different components

Vertu, the mobile phone, came from the stable of Nokia. Vertu is basically built on GSM platform. After introduction, Vertu quickly became a sought after mobile handset particularly for the people in the affluent segment. The product found well acceptance in countries such as China, HongKong, Russia, Middle-east, etc. The company made the products available at special outlets and not in the general Nokia stores. The company made all efforts to elevate the prestige of the phone in the perceptual space of the prospective customers. Surely, the consumers were not attracted to this gadget because of its mobile communication ability. They were rather hankering after the product's exclusiveness purposefully nurtured by the company. The price of the product was set at a very high range and some of the products were hand-crafted with platinum and gold body which were priced even up to USD 50,000. According to company strategist, every phone was created exclusively. Some Vertu handset came out in the market with exclusive leather body cover to increase their visual appeal. It also used ceramic to built exclusive sleek look with razor blade like smoothness. However, the products were not made readily available off the shelf of a mobile store. If someone wanted to gift such a mobile phone to dearest one, the person had to wait even if affordability to buy the gadget was not the issue. They were required to be booked in advance and the company might even take about six months for the product to be delivered. There were about 350 Vertu outlets across 35 countries which the company used for booking and delivery of the product. Interestingly, the company did not provide any warranty for the product, but simply hands it over to the purchaser in an expensive gift pack.

However, the company was not at all hard-pressed to produce the products in the factory in accordance with the market demand. However, it was made purposefully as a part of Nokia's marketing strategy. Think of a person who had to wait for six long months keeping in mind the birthday of the person's beloved one and ultimately on the special day, he could gift out the 'Vertu'. This type of event had hedonic value associated with it, which both the giver as well as the recipient relished. Marketing director Chris Harris of Vertu gladly confirmed that the strategy worked nicely for the company. According to him, though it took about seven days to create a single hand-crafted high-end Vertu with titanium, diamonds, and rubies, but delaying was required to position them as sought after luxury brand. To retain aspirational value of the product, it was important to keep supply always less than the actual demand. The company also launched different mobile phone accessories such as leather carry bag, desktop, and Bluetooth. To further strengthen the marketing campaign, the company purposefully created credible and interesting stories around the product and product-related consumers' satisfaction.

Source: Patience is a Vertu, The Economic Times, Sept, 6. 2006

Case Questions

Q.1 What are the different product components of Vertu?

Q.2 Which component would you possibly suggest to the company for adaptation, in case of need for a particular country like China? Justify your answer.

Therefore, country specific market knowledge and understanding of product components and sub-components allow the marketers to adapt their products more effectively and efficiently while still achieving economics of scale, at least in a component-specific way.

Standardisation or Adaptation of Product

Product standardisation, in the international context, means that the marketers are not required to vary and/or adjust the components of product, partially or fully, according to the differences in needs and wants of the different country consumers that they serve. American Marketing Association defined product standardisation as a system of identification that describes products by their equal quality standard. Standard quality of product provides two advantages; one, ease of comparison by the buyers and two, labelling advantage by the administrator. From the company perspective it is beneficial in the sense that they can produce large number products of similar type but for different countries. This allows them to enjoy economies of scale. Scale economics refers to reductions in unit cost of produce as the usage levels and size of a facility and other inputs increase. Product standardisation is also expected to benefit the company through economies of scope. Here, scope economy refers to a situation when, as a result of marketing similar products in different countries, some of the common facilities can be conveniently shared to bring about a decrease in the total cost of operation. Say, Company A produces and markets all similar and standardised cars for EU, Asian countries and America. The company has a car research and development centre in Italy, a state-of-the-art sales training centre located in New York and IT centre at Bangalore to provide back-office support. The production centres of the company are located in Bangkok, Delhi and Detroit. The R&D facility in Italy provides the necessary inputs to all its production centres. The New York training facilities provide training services to the company globally, whereas its back-office support services are provided by the Bangalore centre irrespective of the part of the world the requirement comes from. Since the company is not producing different products for the different markets, the scope of the support services could be economised by allowing them to service the requirement of different places. However, when the company started producing Hybrid cars from the Detroit location based on an entirely new technology and looking at the requirements of US markets only, the R&D centre at Italy could not handle the requirements. Thus, the scope economics of the situation was disturbed with the introduction of different products for different countries.

The advantages associated with product standardisation are listed in Table 7.1.

However, soon companies began to feel that there is a growing requirement of understanding the unique characteristics of each market being targeted because of acute competition. The understanding of different country markets revealed that the requirements of the target consumers

Table 7.1 Advantages of product standardisation

Advantages	Remarks
Homogenisation of needs	Global need will allow the development of global brand
Scale and scope economies	Cost advantage is essential to get the competitive advantage. A single common facility can be created for activities like R&D to cater to the global market, and hence, balanced resource distribution can be ensured
Easy sales and distribution	The cost can be reduced through unique marketing programmes.
Homogenous technological process	Use of the same technology may lead to homogenisation and hence rising technological capability.
Support to consumer mobility	Increasing global movement of consumer can be supported adequately.
Avoiding high adaptation cost	Adapting to each country will be expensive hence may not be desirable

in respect of product characteristics are different from country to country. This understanding compelled many companies to modify the product through redesigning, rebranding and relabeling. For example, Shiseido, a major Japanese hair care and cosmetics producer, found that it had to change the container shape while marketing some of its skin care products differently from Japan while marketing in other countries as customers there would not be so fussy about aesthetic part of containerisation. To address the country-specific requirements more, Shiseido launched AUPRES in 1994 as an exclusive brand for China and targeting the upscale population there. Then in 2006, in order to cater to the requirement of Chinese women more closely, it came with another exclusive country specific skin-care product line under URARA brand. Sony of Japan extended the warranty period while marketing LCD televisions in Scandinavian countries to suit to their requirements which it did not do for other countries. In fact, there are innumerable examples of product modification in different product sub-components as practised by many international companies. The extent to which the product would be modified depends on various factors such as the demographic characteristics of target population, habits and culture, economic condition, mandatory condition, etc., for each market. For example, an Italian automobile company (now owned by FIAT) found that their 800 cc car under brand Romeo requires change in shape to 'tall boy' for African countries to facilitate an average African driver to use the car comfortably. This change was purely driven by demographic requirements as the average African body size is bigger than that of Italians. Also, the mandatory provisions have required converting the car from right hand drive to left hand drive. It is for sure that if had these two changes were not affected; the car would not have been able to get through to the desired market. Thus, adaptation of the product according to the requirement of the target market/markets enables satisfactory market penetration. The different advantages of product adaptations are stated in Table 7.2.

Types of Adaptation

Broadly, product adaptation can be categorised into two types: discretionary adaptation and mandatory adaptation. Under discretionary adaptation, the company decides about the requirements and also retains the authority to effect modification in a product whereas under mandatory adaptation the specific country dictates the requirement of adaptations and a company is bound to follow it. Basically, the discretionary adaptations are

Table 7.2 Advantages of product adaptation

Advantages	Remarks
Mandatory product modifications	The mandatory requirements of different countries can be taken care of.
Local culture and tradition	Adapting according to local culture and tradition makes product diffusion easy
Adapting to the conditions of use	Differential usage in different countries will not be a limiting factor for international marketing.
Consumers ethnocentrism	Ethnocentric consumers would love to use products adapted to local condition
Beat the competition from big multinational	Close to local preference provides competitive advantage

forced by competition in the market but mandatory adaptations are enforced by the prevailing legal system of the countries. Apart from these two simple grouping of adaptations effected in products, there could be other types of adaptations, which generally fall under the discretionary type of adaptation. We will discuss them one by one.

Convenience adaptation

As the name suggest some adaptations are required for products to make them a perfect fit to the local market conditions. In convenience adaptation the root cause of effecting adaptation is the convenience of the users or the consumers. It is done by purposefully inducing localness in the products so that the products attract local consumers because it is now convenient to use. For instance, Kraft Foods of USA (now known as Mondelēz International, Inc.), which is principally engaged in manufacturing and marketing packaged food and beverages with world famous brands names of Kraft, Maxwell House, Oscar Mayer, Oreo, LU, Jacobs Coffee, Tang, Toblerone, etc., learnt the lesson of convenient adaptation quickly while entering Chinese market. Kraft found that one of its flagship products Oreo was too sweet for the Chinese taste as well as the packaging size was bigger than actually what they preferred to carry. These made the Chinese consumers refrain from buying while product launched. Kraft's facility in Suzhou Industrial Park, near Shanghai, for Cookie Research and Development came to the help of the company and facilitated Kraft to create new product platforms tailored to suit local tastes. Kraft, thereafter, reduced the size also from its usual 14 cookies a pack. The repacked smaller size now contained seven cookies only. The price also got reduced to 2 Yuan (29 cents) for seven cookies from 5 Yuan (US 73 cents). This further encouraged the consumers. The company was very happy with the adaptation and launched new Oreo products such as Oreo Wafer Sticks, Oreo Wafer Rolls, Oreo Soft Cakes, and Oreo Strawberry Crème with such convenience adaptation. Kraft then made an extensive advertising and marketing campaign to promote the new range of products. These adaptations made China as the world's largest Oreo market outside the United States. The subsequent company survey confirmed that convenience adaptation helped to increase its sales. Chinese consumers ate about 42% more Oreo cookies after the adaptations were affected. The Kraft experience suggest that convenience modification may affect the technical specification, specification such as size/length, etc., weight and constituents of the material, product get up, etc., per the country-specific requirements. Examples of such convenience adaptations are plenty. In developing countries, vehicles produced by foreign automobile companies usually adapt vehicles so as to sustain the local rough condition of driving by strengthening the body, suspension, steering, etc.

Economic adaptation

In this type of adaptation the economic value of the product take the driving seat and become the root cause of effecting adaptation. Such adaptation requires changes in price and payment adjustment, changes in distribution, changes in energy input/consumption and packaging with an objective of enhancing the economic value of the product. Simplistically speaking, economic adaptations are effected based on consumers' willingness to pay against the benefits they considered to have received. For instance, middle class Indians desired to have more fuel economy in cars against the price paid. Hyundai cars when it launched Hyundai Gen i10 with mileage of 19.81 km per litre, the middle class Indians found it to be costly. The company then launched new i10 variants with 1.2 litre petrol engines having fuel economy of 20.36 km per litre. This economic adaptation created economic value of the product leading to increase in sells.

Performance adaptation

The performance adaptation is basically brought by a company when local condition demands for performance enhancement of a product besides its efficiency. For instance, a study undertaken to understand performance of German-made washing machines to Indian conditions showed that the normal cotton washing time was of 120 minutes. This was considered 'high' by the Indians. The Indians participated in the study opined that 120 minutes was far too long for Indian house holds and insisted that the machine must perform faster to complete the washing within maximum 60 minutes. The German company looked back to analyse its rated time duration and found that program time was long because it took time to heat up the water (clothes come cleaner in warm water). Also, the German households may not mind about the time elapsed while washing but they were very particular about ensuring that the detergent used during washing were fully drained off. This required additional spinning cycle and hence time. At first, the company failed to understand why longer time was not desired by Indian housewives; but later, they came to know that Indians were not very fussy about total cleaning of detergent. In addition, the frequency of washing is almost daily in Indian middle income households and not weekly as in the case of Germans. The use of maidservants for washing clothes had been common before the purchase of the washing machine in Indian situations and some household continued to use them in case of power failure, malfunctioning of machine, etc. So, the traditional method of quick washing acted on them and thereby the demand of a higher performance in washing than the German one surfaced. Based on the study report, the German washing machines were made to adapt to the Indian situation of improved performance.

Social significance adaptation

This type of adaptation is brought by companies to take advantage of materialistic appeals prevailing in societies. In many societies, possession of certain products increases a person's relative status in the society. Companies would like to bring modifications in product, or its parts, that would allow the owner to demonstrate his/her the relative pre-eminence in status to the observer while he/she uses the product. Hence, marketers of such products would be eager to find out such issues prevailing in countries/societies and think of possible ways to effect adaptation in products to get advantage in marketing. For instance, in earlier times, the refrigerator was meant for households as a device to keep food items under cold condition to avoid keep them from decaying. With time, marketers have brought product modification in several ways. A little product modification in terms of keeping provision of ice cube preparation in refrigerator brought about social significance in Indian middle class society. Now, Indian hosts are using the product modification to project their status as 'upmarket hosts' in a social function. The marketers are taking full advantage of the same by effecting requisite product modification. In this way, therefore, many products become candidates for adaptations based on their social significance in different countries.

Aesthetic adaptation

Different people living in different countries have different aesthetic sense. How people living in Tanzania appreciate beauty would not be same as how the Japanese do it. Aesthetic adaptation deals with these finer aspects. This adaptation considers the local elements which eventually create pleasure in people and marketers incorporate them in the product so as to increase their marketability.

Therefore, marketers on entry to a country always try to understand the clues which can develop products on aesthetic line and accordingly bring about modification leading to enhanced marketability. The local people feel more closeness to these adapted products because these finer changes, according to them, represent beauty, artistic expression and finer taste. Interestingly, these modifications seldom improve product's functional features but still have the ability to enhance marketability in the concerned country. For instance, refrigerators may be decorated with traditional Indian painting to attract the Indians more. Hannspree, a Taiwanese manufacturer, introduced a 28-inch LCD screen in an apple-shaped casing for pleasure adaptation of TV.

Component-wise Adaptation in International Market

With the full understanding of different components or layers of a product, international marketers may go for component-wise adaptation of products. It may work well when the product is not subjected to adaptation in totality as per the country's requirement but only some components are required to be adapted to suit the local tastes and preferences. This may save the costs associated with total adaptation. The story of the adaptation of Japanese vehicle Wagon R will demonstrate adequately the requirement and stages of component-wise adaptation of products in international markets.

Product components when in Japan

1993 version: The original Suzuki Wagon R was developed as Japanese category of small vehicles (in Japan known as 'kei' car) in Japan way back in 1993. According to Suzuki Car Company, the 'R' stands for recreation and the word 'Wagon' justifies the "tall wagon or tall boy" design of the car. The car had a unusually tall feature, short bonnet and a vertical hatchback, comparatively bigger cabin space within the legal provision of Japanese 'kei car' dimensions. The car was fitted with a 1000 cc engine. Length was 138.6 inch and width was 58.1 inch width.

1998 version: The second-generation Wagon R car was introduced in 1998 under the brand name 'Wagon R+'.

2003 version: The third generation Wagon R was fitted with a small engine of 660 cc.

2007 version: Model name was changed to 'Stingráy' build on the same product platform but length was bigger (145.51 inch length and 58.1 inch wide). Sportier look was provided which was absent in previous versions. An aggressive looking front bumper was fitted in the car and extended taillights. Alloy wheels and an aero kit were also fitted in the car.

2008 version: Two sportier variants of Stingray – AZ-Wagon and AZ-Wagon Custom were launched but were marketed by Mazda motors. Also a new fourth generation Wagon R with 600 cc engine was launched side by side. It had larger rear doors fitted with quarter glass eliminating the need for a D pillar arrangement. The pillars are the vertical supports of an automobile known respectively as the A, B, C or D-pillar moving in profile view from the front to rear. The same car produced in Europe under the name Splash imported in Japan and continued to be marketed along with Wagon R.

Product components when in Europe: Entry to the European market during 2008 was made with a new name Opel Agila. This was built in Hungary plant on the Wagon R+ product platform. In UK it was fitted with a 1289 cc petrol engine, anti-lock braking system (ABS), electronic break force distribution (EBD) and air conditioning as options. The model had the dimension of 139.4 inches length and 63.8 inches width with 21.1 cu ft of cargo space. The model was jointly produced with Opel using Opel's engines and transmissions. In late 2008, the Opel Agila was renamed as 'Splash' and marketed in Europe and elsewhere.

Product components when in Indonesia: In Indonesia, the Wagon R was launched as Suzuki Karimun fitted with a 1000 cc petrol engine during 2006. During 2007 e petrol engine was upgraded to 1100 cc.

Product components when in China: Jiangxi Changhe Motor of China and Suzuki made a joint venture company in China and the company launched two models, namely, Changhe–Suzuki and Changhe–Suzuki F–MPV, where both models used the basic Wagon R platform.

Product components when in India: The Wagon R, first introduced in India during 2001, was fitted with Suzuki's 1100 litre petrol engine. The size was 138.58 inch length and 58.07 inch width. This model was replaced during 2010 with the K series 998 cc engine. The 2010 version was built on a newer platform with more interior space, and new features such as an under-seat tray below the front passenger seat. Its looks were also changed to cover up the previous boxy look at the back. The size was 139.33 inch length and 58.07 inch width.

The component-wise adaptations at different times in different country markets allowed the company Suzuki to retain the core components as far as practicable while marketing in different countries. This allowed the company to at least achieving scale economics in core component manufacturing. However, in order to fight competition and indulge in country specific localisation, the company had gone for adaptations in the sub components of outer layers to take the advantage of adaptation theory.

Box 7.2 Product adaptations for India

Philips India thought of getting in the minds of rural Indian consumers by introducing a crank-up, or power-free radio that does not require battery or electricity. This radio works on mechanical power through the movement of a rotary arm. By turning the arm for one minute, any rural Indian can listen to the radio for 30 minutes. "This has huge benefits in the power-starved regions of the country. It saves on energy consumption and running costs in the small towns," says Gunjan Srivastava, director, audio-video business, Philips India. Now, a farmer of Punjab will be able to enjoy Hindi or Punjabi songs while working in his paddy field not connected by any power source. Within Philips there has been talk of taking this product to its other markets in the Asia-Pacific region. Philips India is working on another product, a special DVD player which won't require any power. "You can connect it to an inverter or your car battery," says Srivastava. He expects the product to hit the Indian market within the next six months. In launching adapted products for Indian market, Unilever's Indian subsidiary, Hindustan Unilever Ltd (HUL), is also not far behind. HUL as India's largest consumer goods company with a formidable track record in R&D, recently introduced a detergent which reduces water consumption by 50%. This soap, the company claims, will provide significant benefit to Indians since it enables them to wash clothes with comparatively less water. Considering the fact that many parts of India suffer from acute water scarcity particularly during summer, this soap is expected to squarely address the consumers' requirement. HUL and Unilever scientists have also developed and patented a low-cost device, which makes water as safe as boiled water, besides removing pesticides.

Source: http://www.frostwave.com/

Standardisation Vs Adaptation: Options

The product adaptation may not be a primary motive for a company because of cost implication unless it is required for being in the competition. In general terms, therefore, standardisation practice provides benefits of scale economics as well as straight forward marketing management practice across different countries of the world. However, the difference in marketing environment would keep on exerting pressure on a company to go for adaptation. At this stage, looking from the point of view of options available to the international marketer, it can be seen that any company primarily has four options for setting out its product strategy. The options are discussed below, one by one.

Option 1 - Ethnocentric standardisation

Under this option the entrant company may opt for standardisation of its product with all its components as per the home country requirements and push a single uniform product to the world market and thereby take adaptation requirements head on. Medina and Duffy (1998)[6] proposed one very interesting and effective definition of product standardisation which suits this option very well. According to them, a company can practice the process of extending and effectively applying product standards dictated by the domestic country requirements – tangible and/or intangible attributes – to markets in foreign environment. Therefore, a standardised product in

[6] Medina J. and M. Duffy (1998), "Standardisation vs globalisation: A new perspective of brand strategies", *Journal of Product and Brand Management* Vol. 7, Issue 3, pp. 223–243.

the context of international marketing, under this option, will be one where the subcomponents of the core, packaging and support service components are tailored as per the domestic market requirements but expected to have international/global appeal. This type of product standardisation has advantages as product made for domestic market can be pushed to the global market. This has happened in case of high-touch products like handicrafts reflecting country's specific culture. Cigars produced in Havana, perfumes from France, etc., are all pushed in global markets based on their home country standard. However, this option has not been proved very effective in the case of FMCG products. The electric oven made for USA did not appeal much to the Japanese consumer. The Chinese, in general, prefer to have big cars, which may not have sweeping success in India. The company may require continuous and persistent communication in order to change the traditional and cultural preference of consumers of another country in order to make them accept the home country standard of the company.

Option 2 – Polycentric standardisation

Under this option the entrant company may opt for Standardisation of the product with all its components as per the global requirements and push a single uniform product for the world market and take adaptation requirements head on. This strategy seems to be effective when globalisation is the top priority. In fact, this may be the impact of globalisation on the company's desire to understand the commonalities of consumers' requirement and offer a global product around the world. In many sectors such as automobiles, electronics, etc., the strategy of "global product", i.e., the same product being produced and commercialised in several countries at the same time, is a strong tendency. The global products, however, may not be able to satisfy specific needs of local markets arising out of social, economic or political conditions, different climate, conditions of usage, acquisitive power of population, local content needs, environmental laws, etc. Therefore, global products strategy is based on the assumption of convergence of taste and preference of the consumers across the globe.

Option 3 – Geocentric adaptation

Under this option the entrant company may opt for customising the product with all its components and sub-components as per the discretionary requirements of the host country and push different customised product to different countries to take advantage of becoming local in local markets. Here, the core component's attributes may be the same as those of the standardised product or even altered as per the country requirements. But the support service or packaging component attributes are modified to incorporate discretionary requirements from the viewpoint of country environment. For example, the way McDonald has adapted its products based on country preferences.

- USA: Serves hamburger with chicken
- Japan: Chicken Tatsuta, Teriyaki chicken, Teriyaki Mc Burger
- India: Replaced its traditional Big Mac with Maharaja Mac
- Germany: It serves beer
- New Zealand: Serves Kiwi Burger with beetroot sauce

- Singapore: Serves chicken rice with chilli sauce cooked in vegetable oil
- Italy: Serves varieties of salads featuring Mediterranean flavour

These adaptations of McDonald proved useful to make the consumer feel that the foreign product is close to his/her own traditional preference and ensures marketability. The adaptation has to be more pervasive in the case of food products. However, the company may not show too much inclination to do it unless faced with competition. High tech products such as HD TV and hybrid car may avoid customisation altogether because of their acceptance based on sheer technological advantage.

Box 7.3 Chinese demand longer cars

China's luxury sedan market is very difficult to be understood by the foreign marketers. The tag 'L' fitted on the luxury sedan attracts the customers more. Customers usually have inclination for a car with long wheelbase. So the letter "L" in the name of their model not only provides individual satisfaction but also, to a certain extent, prestige in the society. "A big car not only brings comfort, but also indicates taste and wealth of the owner" an "L" car owner in Shanghai said. The western marketers understood the local preference, through their acquaintance with Chinese vehicle market, that if the car body was not extended to provide enough inside space then it would be difficult for them to convince the luxury segment consumers. This sentiment is also very active in the high-end official car segment as well. In the official as well as personal car segments, the consumers feel that the high spending associated with buying a luxury car can only be justified in terms of its inside space availability. German luxury car brand Audi understood the Chinese preference and made their offer ready for the target consumers. It started with its model Audi A6 as the first luxury car tailored for the Chinese market during the year 2000 by extending the wheel base. The company also did not forget to put the word 'L' to designate the model while advertising the car to the Chinese rich customer segment. The result was as expected and Audi maintained its dominant position in the sector with around a 40% market share. The 10-centimeter longer Audi A6L managed to achieve amazing sales of 25,368 units in 2005. The company even performed much better afterwards when they could double their sales to more than 57,350 units. In 2007, just after two years after the company first learned about the requirement of extended version, the company reached a landmark of rolling out the 100,000th Audi A6L model using the same production line on the Chinese soil. The success story of considering the demands of local consumers did not end here. In 2008, the A6L model became the first luxury car to break the 200,000 sales barrier. The success of the A6L was a typical example of winning the local customer by supplying them with products of their preferences. 'Bigger is better' was the Chinese consumers' philosophy when they purchased luxury vehicles. Audi understood this through their research on the Chinese customers' taste of luxury vehicle. In the social sense, the research indicated that the 'bigness' was also associated with prestige. In particular, when buying a luxury car, affluent Chinese and officials liked to show off their wealth and social status by having a bigger car. They would feel great when a common man in the street can appreciate the luxury enjoyed by the car owner and easily identify them by their car size and the 'L' tag with the model name. The car company simply wanted to capitalise on this psychological satisfaction specific to their target customers and build its marketing programme around it while marketing in China. The company ensured that the space and comfort for rear-seat passengers remains the top priority while manufacturing luxury sedans because most official cars are those owned by businessmen and are chauffeur-driven in China. The extended wheelbase should also make the person seated in the backseat feel roomy with more leg room. The company also observed that Chinese usually buy their first car for use of the entire family keeping in mind the comfort of the all seating in the car. But as they become richer, they buy additional cars keeping in mind the social prestige that they can earn by possession of a car distinctly different from the common one. This time, the leg space and comfort for their rear seat passengers become foremost along with the experiential pleasure of being in a luxury car. In 2006, BMW also understood the market requirements and launched its elongated 5 Series in China, with a wheelbase 14 centimetres longer. The extended version increased the 5-Series' sales by 50%, during 2010. Buoyed by the success, Audi launched another improved lengthened series A4L during 2010 with high hopes of replicating the success of the A6L exclusively for the Chinese market. Volvo launched the long wheelbase version S80L sedan during 2009 exclusively for the China market. Even the conventional and orthodox German premium car brand Mercedes-Benz embarked on the business of localisation of cars. From 2010 Mercedes-Benz started producing the extended version of the New E Class locally for exclusively China and thereby winning the Chinese consumers.

Option 4 - Mandatory adaptations

Under this option the entrant company may opt for adaptation of the product with all its components as per the host country's mandatory requirements and push the adapted products into different country markets. Under this option then, adaptations are limited and undertaken only as per the regulatory requirements prevailing in different country markets. Here, the core component's attributes may be the same as those of the standardised product. But the packaging and support service component attributes are modified to incorporate the mandatory requirements of the countries. For example, a processed food manufacturer may comply with EU regulations on processed food products such as compulsory country-of-origin labelling (COOL) for processed food made from meat and fish ingredients while marketing such products in EU markets. A foreign apparel marketer may comply with Chinese regulations on clothing and label its products with details of the factory of origin, including telephone and fax numbers. An automobile manufacturer may only be concerned about the emission norms and right hand/ left hand drive modifications before launching its products in specific country markets.

Standardised to Global Product

A standardised product benefits a company in a number of ways. Following this philosophy, there are two options a company can follow out of the four described above – ethnocentric standardisation and polycentric standardisation. It may so happen that because of lack of understanding of the exact needs and wants of foreign country customers, the company resorts to manufacture the product as per its own country requirements and then push such product to other countries. It may also be possible that the company has understood the commonalities of needs and wants of different countries and then produced the product as per global standard and introduced it to other countries. Since, in a practical sense, it is not possible to have need convergence across the countries of the world, proceeding with the polycentric standardisation may be difficult for companies in many sectors. So, even if the company realises this to be a better option, it will find such standardisation practically impossible to follow. So, the company may follow ethnocentric standardisation in its quest for standardised product and move forward by exploring other country markets through a process of evaluation of the home country product by the other country's customers. In order to ensure marketability, the company will subsequently modify the home country product's

Box 7.4 Philips in India

The world's largest electronic company, Royal Philips Electronics, has decided to restructure its consumer lifestyle business and rework its distribution strategy in India to gain more market share. The company plans to evolve the Indian business into four categories - healthy living, home living, interactive living and personal care. Under healthy living, Philips has products such as water purifiers and mother and child care items. The home living items include small domestic appliances such as mixer, intelligent food processors, home cleaning, and floor cleaners. The interactive living port folio will be consumer electronics, products such as home theatres and flat panel TVs that bring cinematic viewing experience at home. Under personal care, Philips will expand its present range of hair dryers, electric shavers and epilators to include skin care and sleep products like morning wake-up lights. The company does not want to take any chance of not being able to attract the attention of Indian consumers. Therefore, before the launch of the products, the strategists of the company study the lifestyle of Indian consumers and come up with products that suit their needs. In particular, the company would like to understand the Indian cooking style well and then roll out its Indianised kitchen appliances for the consumers.

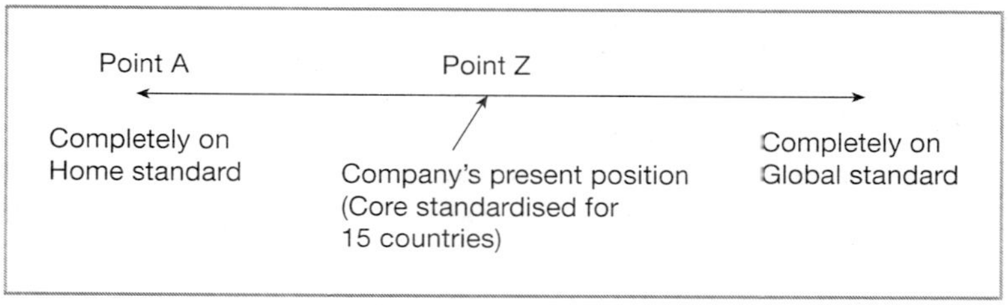

standard to set new standards until it gains acceptance in target country markets. It may so happen that after each successive evaluation, the company is able to achieve at least few components of the product standardised for say, 15 countries. This process will be continued and the more the number of countries the product has travelled, the more will it have its characteristics modified to meet the global standard.

Thus, it may be seen that home country standardisation and global standardisation exist in a continuum. Say, a company starts along the continuum from Point A and reaches the Point Z in Time X. Another competing company in the product category completes the same journey along the continuum in Time Y and X > Y. This, in a sense, indicates better marketing efficiency of the latter firm since it will fare better than the first one in reaping the benefits arising out of product standardisations.

Adapted to Customised Product (Geo-Centric to Mandatory)

A product may have to undergo several changes to meet the mandatory requirements of a new country market. These may vary from simple changes to total redesign of the physical core product. Adaptation starts with mandatory modification, which the company has no other way than to comply with. For example, if the regulation stipulates certain norms for the product, the company has to adhere to them. Customisation appears to start after the mandatory modifications or adaptation requirements have been complied with based on competitive requirements. For instance, a car manufacturer

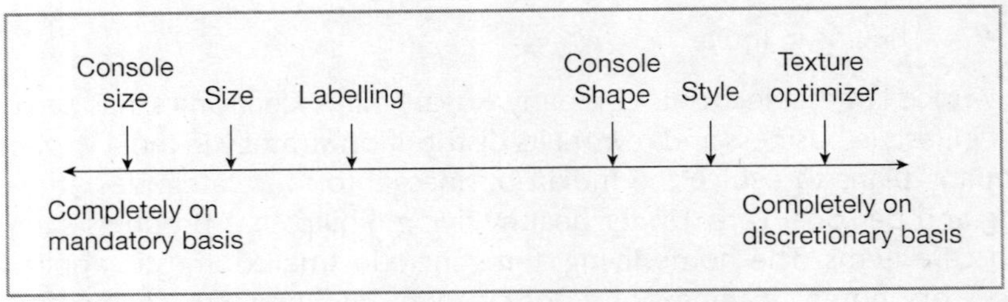

first set right the mandatory modifications such as car length, engine size, emission requirements, etc., before focussing on aesthetic features and fringe attractions such as fitting coffee mug holder, car colour, leather seats, ash tray, etc. The process of the company's journey from mandatory modification to customised modification appears to exist on a continuum. Based on the competitive requirements of the country market, the company will fix its own position along the continuum.

Let us take a practical case. Say, an electronics product manufacturer of Japan started production of a new type of gaming device based on home country standard, which is on a comparatively smaller product platform. After successfully marketing the product across Japan, the company was tempted to market it in ten other countries. Subsequently, it was observed that to make the product suitable for the targeted ten countries, the company had to change the product platform to a comparatively bigger one, which is more or less acceptable to all the ten countries. So, the company achieved standardisation on the core component by trading on the evaluatory process of standardisation to globalisation. Next, the company will travel along the next continuum, i.e., from adaptation to customisation. The company first made all mandatory modifications on the

Box 7.5 Think global. Be local.

Pizza Hut, the American restaurant chain and its international franchises, offers different styles of pizza across 94 countries of the world. Pizza Hut's learning came quickly that the restaurants' success was directly proportional to its product adaptation capabilities. Pizza Hut also tried to put the valuable learning into practice and went on to customise pizzas to the local palate. Initially, the process of adaptation was not easy because the Italian concept of fast food was alien to other countries. In India, the company struggled to capture the market primarily because the standard Italian toppings were completely alien to the Indian taste. It was also a difficult task to break the Italian tradition and walk a distance to become close to Indian food like Tandoori. But with the launch of a Tandoori Pizza the results were amasing and store traffic flourished dramatically. The Indian new generation felt comfortable with the local taste under the much sought after American environment. Pizza Hut, in order to bring more success home, gradually experimented with more flavors to satisfy the Indian tongue. Today, Pizza Hut has more than 150 restaurants in India, and the marketing to Indian customers suddenly started looking very easy. Another American chain, McDonald, also learned it quickly and dispensed with its most prominent ingredient in order to respect, and to please its Indian customers. Now, Mc Donald's menu is dominated with local creations such as McAloo Tikki Burger, Curry Pans, Wraps Pizza, McPuff, and McVeggie leaving aside its usual meat based items. Today, 70% of McDonald menu is 'Indianised', and the McAloo Tikki burger is its highest selling product. In India, if you run an international chain of food products, you only need to be close to the local taste.

Source: The Businessweek May 07, 2006

components and then went ahead with customisation based on country-specific requirements such as change of console shape, style, texture decoration, culture dictated warranty, etc. Interestingly, the more the company travels on this second continuum, the more it travels back in the first continuum. However, because of competitive pressure, the company cannot slow down its journey on the second continuum. Therefore, for practical purposes, irrespective of the marketing options available, the company has to travel across two strategic continuums, i.e., standardisation to globalisation and adaptation to customisation in terms of product decision. Over the past several decades, these two divergent international marketing strategies concerning product offerings have been debated upon to arrive at the exact position most suitable for a company. It has been indicated that the exact position in the continuums to be captured by a company depends on the objective set by the company.

FACTORS ENCOURAGING ADAPTATION

Product adaptation, i.e., modification of the existing products differently for different country markets, entails additional expenditure. However, product adaptation is important to ensure that marketable products are produced, which not only creates customer value in the competitive market place but also ensures all the legal obligations are adequately met for the target country customers. The different factors that compel the international marketers for product adaptation are stated below.

Usage Conditions Driven Adaptations

In different countries different usage conditions are generally noticed for the same product. Consumption of beer with lunch and dinner may be common in Sweden but it is not common in India. Corn flakes are taken for breakfast in many European countries, but Indians like to take corn flakes at a time other than during breakfast. Based on the usage pattern, the products are therefore modified. For example, since the Swedish take beer during lunch or dinner, beer with 3% alcohol is common in Sweden. On the other hand, since Indians drink beer during party time only, beer with 8–9% alcohol is common in the Indian market.

Economic Factors Driven Adaptations

The economic environment in the country influences not only the incomes level of the people living in the country but also their taste and preferences. Canned food, canned fruit juices, tinned fish, etc., are sought-after products in the developed world particularly because of their busy lifestyle, but not in the developing and least developing countries where people generally have time to have fresh fruits instead of canned ones. However, with rising income level, the taste preferences are seemingly have undergone a subtle change particularly for affluent middle-class Indians. This led to the introduction of canned food by many companies in the Indian market for consumers who did not like them previously.

Trade Restrictions Driven Adaptations

Trade barriers put definite pressures on manufacturers to produce products/commodities to suit country-specific requirements. For example, all producers for the EU market must adhere to product requirements that are established by the EU law. Failure to meet legal requirements would mean product withdrawal if and when the non-compliance is discovered. Canned pineapple in light syrup produced in Thailand was detected and rejected when tin used for packaging the product was not found to be at par with the EU legislation on contaminants. Poland rejected entry of juice drinks made in Philippines as the colours used in the juice were not as per EU legislation requirements.

Tradition Driven Adaptations

Sometimes as a result of long tradition, products are produced in a particular way. For example, if Japanese Sake is made in USA, it will also take clues from Japanese tradition and adapt to that particular procedure. Takara Sake USA, a member of the Takara Group of Japan, is the USA based leading company famous for alcohol-related business and biotechnology products. Takara has great experience in producing Shochu, Mirin and Sake type of Japanese alcoholic liquor for more than 150 years. Because Takara's main business endeavours depend heavily on the mastery of natural processes such as fermentation, the company feels a strong responsibility towards preserving the natural environment. As a self-proclaimed 'harmonist', Takara is also engaged in activities aimed at educating people about the importance of sustainable co-existence with nature. Its work in this area is embodied in Takara's corporate philosophy: "Contributing to the creation of a vital society and a healthy lifestyle for its members through our fermentation technology and biotechnology in a way that achieves harmony with nature." Takara Sake USA, established in 1982 in Berkeley, California, follows the same Japanese tradition in sake-making craftsmanship though it produces the products mainly for US consumers. The main products produced in Berkeley such as the "Sho Chiku Bai" brand of Sake, "Takara Mirin" and Plum wine have containers, packaging, etc., reflecting the Japanese tradition.

Local Considerations Driven Adaptations

Local considerations remain in the minds of company managers during the process for product adaptations. In order to acclimatise with the local conditions, the company may have no choice but to adapt its products. For example, Volkswagen never sells its Passat car in the US and EU with wheels below 18 inches. But in China, the Passat cars are fitted with wheels not more than 15 inches to provide comfort while driving. The reason is that the smaller wheel save the passenger from jostle in China's bumpy road. Local consideration in China forced Volkswagen to use wood like material for internal decoration of car trim. However, for the German market they do not do this. Volkswagen also increased the length of the Passat car by 4 inches in China because this car is mainly used to transport Chinese executives. Cases where local considerations are the root cause of adaptations are many in the food category, where the producers had to keep local considerations in mind before presenting their product to the local customers.

Standards Driven Adaptations

Different countries set their production standards in their own way. These countries want foreign companies to follow their country standard and produce products accordingly if they wish to market them in the country. These standards are to be followed on a compulsory basis.

The following are examples of some popular standards followed in different countries

UL Marks: The underwriters laboratories, headquartered in Illinois USA, is a safety-related certification company that gives standards for different products such as electrical gadgets, and products entering the country need to adapt to it.

CSA International: The Canadian Standards Association (CSA) International develops product standards for the Canadian market. The CSA International Division tests and certifies products that are marketed in Canada.

CCC Marks: The China Compulsory Certification (CCC) is a compulsory safety and quality mark for 132 product categories marketed in China.

- **NOM Marks:** Mexico insists products to contain its NOM safety mark and ensuring that products adapt as per their standard.
- **CE Marks:** The *Conformité Européne* (CE) mark indicates that a product has met essential health, safety and performance requirements by design or testing. It is required for a wide range of products, including machinery, electronics, toys, medical devices and telecommunications equipment. Most companies have to meet CE mark requirements in order to sell their products in the European market. The European Commission describes the CE mark as a "passport" that allows manufacturers to circulate industrial and consumer products freely within the EU.
- **TÜV Marks:** Technical Inspection Association of Germany provides certification standards to validate the safety of products for marketing in Germany.

Specific Regulation Driven Adaptations

From time to time the countries of the world come out with some specific regulations that companies need to follow in their production for marketing their products. For example, the RoHS, WEEE, and REACH regulations are required to be followed and met for marketing products in the entire European Union.

Restriction on hazardous substances (RoHS)

The European Parliament and the Council of the European Union initiated the RoHS on July 1, 2006 to protect human health and the environment from environmental contamination that arises out of manufactured products and residual waste. It applies to a wide range of manufacturers selling products in Europe. Under the provisions, there are key restrictions on the use of hazardous substances such as lead, cadmium, etc., in the manufacture of electrical and electronic equipment.

Waste electronic and electronic equipment (WEEE)

The WEEE directives were set out by EU in 2003, outlining the responsibilities of electronic and electrical equipment manufacturers with regard to the collection and recycling of waste. The EU has restricted the use of hazardous substances in manufacturing electronic and electrical equipment and promoted the collection, recycling, and re-use of such equipment to avoid health and environmental risks.

Registration, evaluation, authorisation and restriction of chemicals (REACH)

REACH regulations of the EU, effective from June 1, 2007, are intended to ensure safety of human beings and the environment from rampant use of chemicals in household and industrial processes. The objectives of REACH are to:

- Reduce the risks posed by chemicals to humans and the environment
- Enhance the competitiveness of the EU chemicals industry, a key sector of the economy
- Promote alternative methods for the assessment of hazards of substances
- Ensure the free circulation of substances in the internal market of the EU

Packaging and Labelling Restriction Driven Adaptations

Both enterprises and the government have a common interest in the purpose of labelling and packaging. Enterprises endeavour to achieve marketing benefits in terms of creative, consumer-oriented containers for delivering a product in a visually appealing and safe manner. However, while some of the communications expressed in the labelling are voluntary, others are mandatory. The respective country government may also impose restrictions on packaging type, material, and durability and thereby forcing adaptations by the companies. For sensitive items such as food products, medicine and cosmetics, the country may opt for laying a strict standard to be followed by the manufacturers. The government has specific interest in labelling to ensure that the in terms of mandatory communication requirements for public safety and environmental concerns are followed. A producer may vary the voluntary communication from country to country based on the country-specific requirements. The mandatory communications in labels usually requires the producers to indicate the contents, measurements (units, weight, and volume), pricing, expiration date, and any warnings associated with the products' use. In many countries, labels must be in the host language only. Often, manufacturers minimise costs by printing packages with labels in multiple languages so that the product can be sold in multiple markets. Heavy costs are associated with language translations of instructions, user manuals and computer software.

Text adaptations

The language written on the packaging is very important for communication about the product features to the customers. In many countries, English is not understood by a large section of the population. Hence, the company has to translate the text into the local language to be able to provide a clue as to what is being offered. For example, not all the Chinese have good understanding of English and hence communicating to target consumers can best be done with text translation in Chinese. Average Indians have a good understanding of English, which allows companies to market products to a specific section of society that has a fair exposure to the language. Pringles, from P&G, markets its products around the world with sales in over 140 countries and uses text translated in 37 languages.

Packaging size adaptations

Product packaging size is often one of the first things international companies need to adjust when entering another market. For example, the average Japanese home too small to store western-sized jumbo packages. Also Japanese do not believe in purchasing in bulk and consuming like Americans. These reflections are seen in the packaging of Japanese companies. Kewpie, the Japanese condiments giant reduced the volume of its salad dressings from 200 to 170 millilitres and was surprised to see a 5% increase in order volume. For pre-packaged product the EU regulations stipulate that the weight or volume must be at least 5 grams or 5 millilitres for the smallest packages and no more than 10 kilograms or 10 litres for the largest packages.

Colour adaptations

The colour of the package is very important for creating a positive impression in the minds of the consumers. Certain colours evoke certain emotions in the minds of the customers. These colour-based emotions may be different in different countries. Abashiri Brewery came up with blue, green and red beer with requisite packaging so that the Japanese consumers can pick them up depending on their mood. PepsiCo tried to take advantage of a new packaging colour phenomenon by offering Pepsi in a crystal clear bottle when they launched Crystal Pepsi. They expected that the consumer will feel confident of consuming fewer calories with this drink than with other cola drinks when the product is packaged in crystal clear bottle. However, the company found that it was not very effective as the colour evoked different emotions and sent out different meanings to the targeted country populations of different countries. Green packaging did not seem to do a great job in China. Green is the colour in the national flag of Egypt; so packaging of disposables in green colour is not well accepted. The same is true in India where saffron is regarded as a sacred colour and hence it is not accepted as the packaging colour of disposable products.

Label adaptations

The content and the composition of the product inside the package are communicated to the consumers through labelling. Other aspects that a label may communicate are origin, production process, guarantee, etc., which are often subjected to country-specific regulations.

For instance, textile labelling directives of EU specify a particular type of label only. All textile products must carry a label which indicates the fibre content on the product. A textile product consisting of two or more fibres must be marked + %. The EU has enforced strict rules for food products to be marketed in the countries under it. The objective is to ensure that customers should exactly know the ingredients and nutritional information before eating them.

Country Specific Import Regulations Driven Adaptations

US regulations on processed food product

- Label formats must be adjusted to provide nutritional analyses
- Cannot claim the presence or absence of a dietary property can treat a disease or its symptoms—for example, the effects of Vitamin E in a food on skin complexion—even if the claim is valid.
- Competitor criticisms of the growth, distribution, or preparation of foods as detrimental to the diet will not be permitted

EU regulations on processed food product

- Compulsory country of origin labelling(COOL) for meat and fish ingredients in processed food
- Front pack freezing dates

China regulations on clothing

- All clothing is labelled with the factory of origin, including telephone and fax numbers.

Right-hand traffic and left-hand traffic regulations

- Vehicles are manufactured in left-hand drive (LHD) and right-hand drive (RHD) configurations. Seventy-six countries of the world comply with left-hand traffic while 163 countries, with right-hand traffic.

Country Culture Driven Adaptations

Product packaging, labelling, physical characteristics and marketing have to adapt to the cultural requirements when necessary. Religion, values, aesthetics, language and material culture all affect product purchase and consumption decision. Some countries are culturally inclined to avoid uncertainty and hence may desire more assurance in product usage. Many companies accordingly change the warranty clause to make their products attractive for such countries.

Green Product

Green products come to existence when manufacturers follow a developmental process keeping in mind the environmental considerations. The product developmental process takes into account all stages of the product life cycle in order to reduce its total environmental impact. Thus, the product development process undergoes modification based on a holistic view. The raw material used, number of components added, the adapted design and finally disposal of products after expiry of life cycle all come under scrutiny as part of the holistic view of the product's impact on environment. Green product is a novel way of delivering value to the customers who are environmental conscious. In the long run, it can change the basis of competition in the market place. The respective government policies of different countries towards sustainable development has an influence on the company's effort to resort to eco design for development of green product. However, there are also many companies which resort to green product development on their own. For example Philips has set a specific goal for green product development in light and bulbs category. It set a target of generating 30% revenue of total turnover by 2012 from green product sells and 50% by 2015. So the company clearly believes in sustainable development through achieving a balance between social and environmental performance. The company believes that emerging and other least developing country markets are also inclined towards producing greener products though the pace of such development may be slow and steady.

Strategic Consideration in Product Marketing

The product strategy revolves around the standardisation and adaptation dilemma. The adopted strategy should ideally enhance marketability of products in the different international markets. It will be the best if this can be achieved minimum or no product adaptation. However, product strategy can be best understood in combination with the strategy for marketing communication. The product adaptation–standardisation strategy is directly linked with the approach to communication adopted by the company Accordingly, Warren Keegan[7] suggested five major product strategy marketers have in international marketing.

Strategy 1: One product one message

This strategy promotes the understanding that a product should be extended to international markets without modifications. The same strategy can be adopted for communication also. The communication made for a particular country can pass on to another country without modification along with the unmodified product. This strategy is expected to be less expensive as the same product and communication strategy are passed into other markets. However, it can be risky if the communication is not understood. Definitely, the type of products being marketed would have an influence on this strategy. It may not work well or prove to be failure in case of food products, automobiles, cosmetics, etc. But, it may work well for airlines, tobacco, etc., where fairly common universal needs are addressed. Products of these types may go with context-free information that is easier to standardise when accompanied with standardised products.

[7] Keegan, Warren (1969), "Multinational product planning", *Journal of Marketing*, Vol. 83, January, pp. 58–62.

Strategy 2: Extended product-communications adaptation

In this strategy, the product is extended without modification as it can serve almost in the same manner as in the home country in every country market. However, it may so happen that the consumers of different countries are to be addressed differently to market it. This is suitable for the products that are used differently in different countries. For example, Kellogg corn flakes may be the same when it is marketed in India or the US. However, Indians prefer to take the product as a mineral supplement along with hot milk. So the company has to communicate differently about the product to Indians than it does with the Americans.

Strategy 3: Product adaptation–communications extension

The premise of this strategy is that one product produced for a country may not be used in the same way in another country. For example, McDonald's compromised with its original Americana to please its Indian customers. Beef and Pork are alien for many Indians and hence the firm had to adapt its products as per local preference with products such as McAloo Tikki Burger, Curry Pans, Wraps Pizza McPuff, and McVeggie. However, the campaign 'I am loving it' was designed to run in any of the 100-plus countries where McDonald's has restaurants. The assumption is that although the product will be different in foreign markets because of adaptation, communications can be made with a single voice across all countries where McDonald's restaurants are functional.

Strategy 4: Product adaptation–communications adaptation

In this strategy both product and communication would be adapted according to the typical need of the country market. Ward[8] found in his study of 97 foreign products in the US market that 66% were made to adapt while they are marketed in the US. The modifications were in respect of pattern of usage, labelling, quality, packaging and styling. Interestingly, about 71% of the samples studied were found to adapt their promotions also in respect of media used, sales force incentives, volume of advertising, distributor incentive, special promotion and publicity. For example, one foreign cereal marketer had to adapt its products for the US market as the target customers' profile got changed due to the declining birth rate of the country. The marketers noticed that the number of children below the age of 13 was falling and the number of people in the age group of 19 and above was steadily increasing. As a result, the product cereal had to be adapted with high fibre content and relatively low fat and calories to suit the requirement of the new target group. Promoting the new 'adult cereals' was a challenge and the company's previous advertising message and theme was not effective to handle it. So it demanded an entirely different approach. TV advertisements were put in early evening shows or in afternoon soap operas rather than in Saturday morning cartoons. The marketing slogans were also modified accordingly:

[8] Ward, James J. (1973), "Product and promotion adaptation by European firms in the US", *Journal of International Business Studies.*

- "The Big G Vitamin Cereal"
- "One Bowl, 100%" (typically shown with commercials showing people having to eat a whole stack of bowls of other cereals to get the same 100% nutritional value)
- "100 Calories. 100%"
- "Are you getting 100%?"

Strategy 5: Product invention

This needs a totally new idea to fit the exclusive conditions of the market. Companies like 3M are doing good business with it. Since the innovative company is coming out with small or big radical innovations time to time, it does not require any adaptations. Their marketing communications are also very standardised since the products speak for themselves. However, marketers need to place high informational content in their communication in such a way that it is understood by the prospective customers. In this strategy the product development costs will be high, but the marketing advantages are also very high.

Strategy Selection

Out of the five strategy options which one is best applicable for a company? The best option to be used will depend on a detailed analysis of both the product and the market. Product analysis would revolve round understanding of the different product components and their adaptability quotient.

Box 7.6 McDonald's advertising adaptation

Literal meaning	Country
I am loving it. (English)	American Samoa, Andorra, Australia, Austria, Azerbaijan, The Bahamas, Bahrain, Belarus, Belgium, Brunei, Bulgaria, Canada, China, Croatia, Cyprus, Czech Republic, Denmark, Dominican Republic, Estonia, Fiji, Finland, France, Georgia, Gibraltar, Greece, Guam, Hong Kong, Hungary, Iceland, India, Indonesia, Ireland, Isle of Man, Israel, Italy, Japan, Jordan, Kazakhstan, Kuwait, Latvia, Lebanon, Liechtenstein, Lithuania, Luxembourg, Macau, Macedonia, Malaysia, Mauritius, Mexico, Moldova, Monaco, Montenegro, Morocco, Netherlands, New Caledonia, New Zealand, Northern Mariana Islands, Norway, Oman, Pakistan, Poland, Portugal, Qatar, Romania, Russia, Samoa, San Marino, Serbia, Singapore, Sint Maarten, Slovakia, Slovenia, South Africa, South Korea, Spain, Sri Lanka, Suriname, Sweden, Switzerland, Taiwan, Thailand, United Arab Emirates, United Kingdom, United States, Yemen
It enchants me (Spanish)	Argentina, Chile, Colombia, Costa Rica, Ecuador, El Salvador, Guatemala, Honduras, Mexico, Nicaragua, Panama, Paraguay, Peru, Puerto Rico, United States, Uruguay, Venezuela
I love all this a lot (Portuguese)	Brazil
That is what I love. (Russian)	Russia

Source: http://en.wikipedia.org

Market analysis on the other hand, delves into both micro and macro issues associated with market dynamics of the target country. The choice of strategy will depend on the outcome of the analysis when linked with the following questions:

- What function or need is the product expected to serve in the target market?
- Under what conditions the product would be used?
- What are the preferences of the potential customers?
- What is the ability of the customers to buy the product in question?
- What would be the costs of adaptation and manufacture?
- How the adaptation would be matched by existing or desired promotion?
- How will the new adapted product affect the competition favourably?

Timing of Entry

The starting point in the timing of foreign market entry has been elaborated by Professor Raymond Vernon in his pioneering thesis on international product life cycle. Prof. Vernon developed the international product life cycle (IPLC) theory in the 1960s. Although the model was developed with the US as the target, it can be generalised and applied to any of the developed and innovative markets of the world. According to this theory, a product may exist in different country markets at different stages of the product life cycle. This differential presence brings challenges as well as opportunities for international marketers and complicates the product strategy. As shown in the Figure 7.2 below, it is possible to enhance a product's life when its existence is considered in markets of varying economic status.

FIGURE 7.2 International product cycle

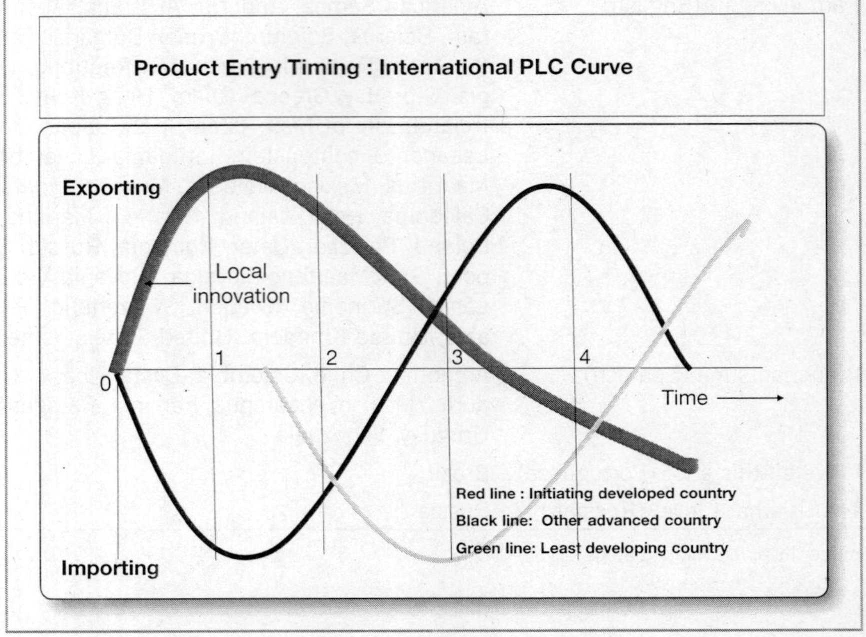

In developed countries

During the introductory phase, a product is expected to be launched in a developed country and refined, and made more usable through incremental innovations. This can be best done in advanced country where capability of doing research exist in a active stage. This stage, therefore, witnesses the refinement of marketing approach as well based on the refined status of the product. At this juncture, the product is new, and hence, market is not ready for it; so, it requires efforts for development. It may be noted that at this time, there hardly exists any demand in the markets of underdeveloped countries. So, the company launches the product in developed markets at a price that helps it to recover the huge product development cost. Therefore, in the introductory stage, the product will be having limited availability in the most advanced country markets, often than the company's domestic or home market.

With the passage of time, the product would be made available in different other similar countries of the same economic status. The product will be continued to be developed although those developments are mostly incremental in nature. As more and more customers come to know about the product, the customer size continues to increase both in domestic market as well as in foreign markets. Exporting is the usual process followed at this time to send the product out of the home country. The company actively pursues market expansion in different segments also and reduces the price of the product. Competitive pressure from companies also exert pressure and challenge the supremacy of the product. This leads to further reduction of the price. At this stage, the company looks for a way out through international marketing and starts to investigate opportunities of developing country markets. Soon the opportunities are seen and products are exported to the developing country markets. Thereafter, products are also exported to the least developing country markets where it will be again in the introductory stage of product life cycle. In order to capture market in the economically dissimilar countries, there would be communication adaptation to ensure unleashing its foreign market potential.

In developing countries

The export marketing will be continued in this way till the product reaches maturity stage in the developed country. In the maturity stage, the sales growth gets slowed down. It is no longer in demand in its own country market or in other developed country markets, which were primarily fed through importation. At the same time, the product is now not worthy of much more incremental innovation to boost the particular product life cycle stage. At this juncture, the originating company look out for starting its own production base in the least cost developing country market or pass on the technology to an associate company. This further reduces the cost of production, which becomes advantageous and pumps some amount of life in the product. Thereafter, the developing country production set up continues to satisfy its own market need as well exporting the product to the least developing country market where the product is almost in the introductory phase and market potential still to be fully explored. This phase continues for some time, but eventually with the passage of time, the price gets further declined.

In least developing countries

In course of time, the demand of the product also starts declining in the developing country market either through product maturity or due to introduction of better products. Now, in order to maintain a profit margin, the company further feels the requirement of reducing cost of production which only the least developing country could offer. So, the producing company either shift its own production base to a least developing country or pass on the technology to a subsidiary company in that country. Thereafter, whatever would be the residual demand that exists in the developing country will now be met through importation only from least developing country production.

Deviations: A few questions were mooted in course of time, while applying the theory into practice

1. Why companies cannot be proactive enough for resorting to global Sourcing ?
2. Why there would be stretched lead time between new product development and introduction in the foreign market ?
3. Why the lead market and lag market domination would be in phases? It may cause the innovator company to lose marketing advantage in the developing and least developing country markets.
4. Why all the companies would be following the theory in practice?. For example, now a days, companies may not at all produce in developed country but start producing the product in the developing country and import the product back to ensure better profitability to start with.

MANAGING PRODUCT LINE AND PRODUCT MIX

A company may have just one product, whilst others may have a large number of different products positioned for a country market. Most of the companies deal with a number of related or assorted products in the international markets constituting their product lines and product mixes. The company carefully selects the product mix for each country keeping in view the competitive environments, economic parameters, need choice and preferences of the target consumers. Thereafter, the company strategically develops product lines by splitting its product mix into groups (Table 7.3).

The most important decision the company has to take is to select the most appropriate product mix, its width, depth and length that will be offered in a particular country based on factors such as competition, product life cycle, and customer preference. Product mix is defined as the set of all product lines and items that a particular seller offers for sale to buyers. It is also known as product assortment. For example, Proctor & Gamble has a fairly large number of product lines such as food products, households, cosmetics products, personal care products, cleaning, etc., for each country market. This makes the width of the product mix. The depth of the product mix is ascertained by the number of varieties are offered in each product lines. P&G offers many varieties in the product lines. For example, the toothpaste comes in different sizes with options of adopting from gel or paste types. The consistency of the product mix refers to how closely the various product lines relate in end-use, production requirements, distribution channels or in some other way.

Table 7.3 P&G's product line and product mix

S. No.	Product	Product line present in US market
1.	**Health Care**	Fibersure, Metamucil, Pepto-Bismol, Prilosec OTC, PUR, Therma Care Vicks
2.	**Baby Care**	Charmin, Children's Pepto, Dreft, Luvs, Pampers, Pampers Kandoo
3.	**Hair Care**	Aussie, Head and Shoulders, Herbal Essences, Infusion23 Pantene, Physique
4.	**Deodorants**	Old Spice, Secret, Sure
5.	**Dish Care**	Cascade, Dawn, Ivory, Joy
6.	**Hair Colour**	Clairol, Herbal Essences
7.	**Feminine Protection**	Always, Tampax
8.	**Household Cleaner**	Bounty, Mr Clean, Mr Clean Auto Dry Carwash, Scent stories
9.	**Oral Care**	Braun, Crest, Crest Whitestrips, Fixodent, Gleem, Glide, Scope, Oral-B
10.	**Cosmetics**	Cover Girl, Max Factor
11.	**Laundry**	Bounce, Cheer, Downy, Dreft, Era, Febreze, Gain, Ivory, Tide
12.	**Prestige Fragrances**	Baldessarini, Boss, Boss Skin Bruno Banani, Dolce & Gabbana, Escada Ghost, Hugo, Lacoste, Naomi Campbell, Puma, Valentino
13.	**Personal Cleansing**	Camay, Clairol, Herbal Essences, Ivory, Noxzema, Olay, Old Spice, Safeguard, Zest
14.	**Prescription Drugs**	Actonel, Asacol, Dantrium, Dantrium IV, Didronel, Macrobid, Macrodantin
15.	**Snacks and Beverages**	Folgers, Home Café, Millstone, Pringles
16.	**Skin Care**	Braun, Gillette, Complete Skin Care, Noxzema, Olay
17.	**Shaving Care**	Braun, Gillette Fusion, Gillette M3 Power, Gillette Satin Care
18.	**Paper Products**	Bounty, Charmin, Puffs
19.	**Pet Health and Nutrition**	Eukanuba'Iams

Sources: http://www.pg.com

Product-mix Decision

A company decision of product mix strategy for international markets revolves round the following strategic points.

Expansion of product mix in a particular country

A company may decide to expand its present mix by increasing the number of lines or the depth within the lines based on the demand created in the market. Product lines may be related or unrelated to the present products. The company may also increase the number of items in its product mix.

Contraction of product mix in a particular country

A company, in certain adverse circumstances, may prune or thin out the product mix for a particular country. This is done either by eliminating entire lines or by simplifying the assortment within a line for a particular country. The shift from fat and long lines to thin and short lines, is generally invoked to eliminate low-profit products and to keep marketing attention to few products and earn more profit from them. During 1993, KFC introduced 'Rotisserie chicken' called Rotisserie Gold to capture Boston market of USA. However, the customers did not like it, and hence, the company withdrew it during 1996 and introduced another product line called 'tender chicken' for the US market.

Alteration of existing product

Developing a complete new product may take time; so, the management may take a decision in some country market to take a fresh look at the company's existing products in an effort to improve an established and matured product. For example, Maruti Suzuki modified its matured Zen car model to take on the tall boy shaped car from other companies and improved it to create 'Estilo' for the Indian market.

NEW PRODUCTS LAUNCHING

Apple introduced its new product iPhone on June 29, 2007 and thereafter launched its generations of iPhone models, each accompanied by one of the six major releases of iOS series, for people around world. While launching the products in USA, the company expected that the new product would get acceptability in different country markets as quickly as possible to achieve targeted sales. They planned accordingly and after the first launch in the USA the products were made available in the UK, France, Germany, Ireland and Austria subsequently. However, many other countries of Europe, Latin America, and South Africa came to know about the product and there was a latent demand was created. From 2009 onwards Apple made the product available there also. Apple put all round effort so that products are accepted throughout the globe and achieved considerable success. How long it would take for such a products to become popular in every other countries? Marketers at Apple tried to get an answer to this question and found that for a communicating instrument like Apple mobile phone, it would not take much time. In fact, past experience of marketers suggest that different products take different time for spread across the consumers of the globe. The five important factors influencing the diffusions of new products are:

- Relative functional advantage: Apple iPhone offered a huge advantage over the other types of mobile phone during its launching in 2007. Just like when MRI (Magnetic resonance imaging) came in the market replacing X-rays instrument. MRI had considerable comparative advantage over X -rays. So, it should be expected to be diffused at a faster rate amongst different consumers. The iPhone product line provided a considerable advantage over the previous products used for a similar purpose and hence they got acceptance across the consumers of the world very quickly.
- Social compatibility: Social acceptability also matters in diffusion of products. How much is the adaptability of the product in the social system? A product which is difficult to get along with the social system would face problem of quick diffusion. A social networking website 'perfspot' could not get requisite acceptability of the users as it was not secured enough. Genetically Modified Seeds could not be spread in many countries because the concerned society rejected them.
- Ease of use: The menu driven operating system like windows XP got acceptability throughout the world in a rapid pace because of easy to

use nature. But window server could not spread fast because of the difficulties associated with command driven system. Basically, the complexities of use restrict movement of the product across consumers and countries.

- Trialability: An automobile company when launching a new car allow its prospective consumers to drive the car and get acquainted for a limited period of time. Many cosmetic companies allow free sachets to be distributed to the consumers so the new uses get acquainted with the product. This allows new users to know the product without committing a huge financial or personal investment. This reduces unfamiliarity with a newly launched product and hence acceptability of a product.
- Observability: When desk top computers were introduced there was tremendous resistance from the typewriter users to switch over. However, in course of time these typewriter users saw others using computers and enjoying much greater benefits than the typewriters can provide. This made them switchover from using old machine to new machine, i.e., computer. So, in a sense, convenience experienced by the people who used computer influenced the typewriter users and converted them new users of computer. Companies launching new product in market arrange demonstration of the possible benefits so that others can also observe and start believing in the benefits it offered.

International Product Positioning

A product launched in a competitive country market place has to attract the attention of the target customers. This requires a strategy on the part of the marketers to position the product in a manner that it fits in to the exact need of the target consumers. Product positioning has been defined as the act of designing the image of the firm's offering so that target customers understand and appreciate what the product stands for in relation to its competitors. Product positioning, be it in national or international level, offers a steep challenge to marketers because a product may require different positioning at different stages of its life cycle. It requires building up the position in the customer's "perceptual space", which is clearly not under the control of the marketers to a large extent. Therefore, marketers strive to use purposeful internal and external communication to develop a creative, persuasive effect on the consumers' mind based on the most competitive, distinctive and convincing feature of product or brand.

Product position in the international market becomes more difficult if it is required to be positioned differently in different countries because of country-specific differences. Many companies are lucky in this sense. Consider the case of energy drink brand, Gatorade, which is marketed across 100 odd countries of the world. The manufacturer practised a standardised way of product positioning across all the countries without differentiating the countries in terms of usage difference, cultural difference, etc. Gatorade is positioned as a new category of energy drink, a premium product, and a unique functional drink promising and delivering benefits that no other drink can offer. However, there are differences when target group of consumer of one country perceive a product's benefit differently from another country. It may also happen that a brand's personality is being perceived differently in different countries due different cultural setting. Country stereotypes have also played role in perception build up, evaluations and purchase. In a stereotype way, BMW branded car was found to be more popular in the UK while Mercedes was traditionally more popular in Thailand although Mercedes cars are more expensive than BMW cars in both countries. This is the reason that Thailand has been the country where Mercedes–Benz has the largest market share outside Germany. A lesser known Japanese electronics brand may be perceived by an average Indian customer as being better than a well-established electronic brand of India due to country of origin stereo type. In India "Made in Germany" instantaneously commands respect from customers because they perceive anything made in Germany would have reliability, strict engineering and superior design. in many countries. India's VIP luggage or Kingfisher might face difficulty in creating the same product perception in Brazil as it has done in India. LG had to introduce a new design of a walkman-cum-speakers in China only to find that the slim speakers of the product have not been perceived well by the target consumers. Possibly, it is the automobile industry that suffers the most from the perceptive differences across the countries of the world. Consider the case of an automobile company intending to position its new model in three country markets. This automobile company traditionally positioned its cars on the lines of comfort in the domestic market as well as in a few countries where it exported previously. The company did some research to diagnose the differences in perceptual aberrations in the three targeted countries to understand them more closely before deciding on the full-fledged internationalisation drive. In Country A, it appears that the car model will do good business than competitors if it is positioned as a car which is superior in terms of fuel efficiency, value for money and after sales service, but not for look and comfort. However, in Country B the same product is likely to be accepted more easily by the prospective consumers if is positioned with a superior look and updated technology, but not on other count like fuel efficiency, etc. In fact, Country B is found to be obsessed with technological up-datedness of cars and any compromise on this account will be detrimental to the marketing success. In Country C, surprisingly, the requirement was found to be only for the brand image of the car followed by the fuel efficiency. Figure 7.3 below depicts the differential requirements of the positioning of the car in the three different country markets. The research had many implications.

For instance, the research shows that it will prove to be costly to the company to pursue a line of standardisation policy across the countries where they have the presence. If the company wants to stick to a standardised policy, then has to unleash a purposeful communication campaign in the three country markets. The more widely or differently perceived in different countries, the more would be the pressure on the company on communication adaptations. The case of Kellogg's corn flakes in India is a glaring example to this effect. The product was perceived by the Indian consumer as mineral supplement that can be consumed at any time but certainly not as breakfast whereas half of the world looks upon corn flakes as breakfast material. This compelled the company to resort to a different kind of advertising campaign exclusively for India. Therefore, the standardisation agenda of the company also suffered.

FIGURE 7.3 Perceptual differences in three countries

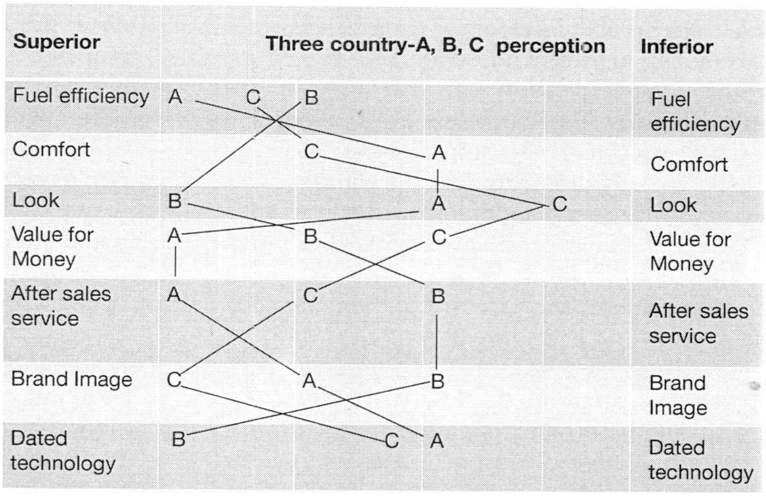

Perceptual mapping

How would consumers of the country of Brazil perceive the Kingfisher branded beer? Surely, the company would like to know about it before launching the product, so that its communication to the target consumers becomes meaningful and purposeful. Say, the next target country for Kingfisher, after Brazil, is Korea. Can the company go to this country using the same marketing that was maintained in Brazil? It is obvious that such strategy will not work and the reason is simple. The target groups of customers are different in different countries in term of culture, product exposure, taste, preference, etc. So, the key to a product's acceptance lies in understanding the customers well and positioning it flawlessly. In this respect, perceptual mapping techniques are widely used by the marketers as a strategic tool. It offers a unique method to understand the complex relationships between market place offerings and the criteria used by buyers in making purchase decisions and recommendations. Perceptual mapping provides a powerful graphic simplicity that can appeals to senior and junior management alike for strategic thinking about product positioning in competitive markets. The objective of such mapping is to judge how the competitive offerings of the company are perceived by the target consumers. Each brand or product in a competitive market is thought of as occupying a certain position in a customer's "perceptual space." Perceptual mapping techniques attempt to graphically represent this product space. The three usual techniques applied to draw perceptual maps are (1) factor analysis, (2) discriminant analysis, and (3) multidimensional scaling.

CHAPTER SUMMARY

1. Although a product is simply looked upon as a single entity on offer, a closer look reveals its constituents or components. Each of the components has a specific role in satisfying consumer requirements by providing the desired benefits. These benefits, whether tangible or intangible, provoke

the target consumers to purchase the product and consume. Thus, every component of the product is important and a right proportional mix would be absolutely important to ensure its marketability in international markets.

2. Product standardisation, in the international context, means that marketers are not required vary and/or adjust the components of product, partially or fully, according to the differences in needs and wants of the different countries where they market their product. Standardisation of products offers various benefits to international marketers. The most important of them are economy of scale and economy of scope.
3. On the other hand, due to the difference in the country environment, the international marketers also enjoy certain benefits through product adaptations. The most important of them is that adapting according to local culture and tradition makes product diffusion easy.
4. Product adaptation is basically of two types: Discretionary adaptation and Mandatory adaptation. Apart from these two simple grouping of adaptation effected in the products, there are other different other types of adaptations which generally fall under the discretionary type of adaptations. There are several factors that influence product adaptations in the international markets.
5. In order to compromise with the requirements of different country-specific needs and to tilt balance towards standardisation to some extent, the companies resort to component-wise adaptations.
6. Along with solving the Standardisation vs Adap tation dilemma, international marketers also need to understand the correct entry timing in different country markets, Vernon's international product life-cycle theory provides a base to understand it.
7. Managing product line and product mix in the international markets is another important decision which requires timely expansion, contraction and alteration strategies in place.
8. Launching of new products in the international markets requires clear understanding of the diffusion process in the target country market and assessment of differential perceptual position of the product in multi-country marketing situation.

QUESTIONS FOR REVIEW

Short Answer Questions

1. What is the standardisation–adaptation dilemma in international marketing?
2. What are the different types of product adaptations? Explain with the help of an example.
3. What are the factors that encourage product adaptation in international markets?
4. What is perceptual mapping? Why it an important tool for the international marketers?
5. What are the different components of a product? Explain with example.

Descriptive Questions

6. "As a practical matter, standardisation is not a clear-cut issue. In literal sense, standardisation would mean the offering of identical product lines at identical prices through identical distribution systems, supported by identical promotional programs, in several different countries. At the other extreme, completely localised marketing strategies would have no common elements whatsoever. Obviously, neither of these extremes is often feasible or desirable." Why the "extremes" are not feasible or desirable? Explain with example.
7. Describe the international product life cycle concept indicating its implication in product marketing internationally
8. Pick a product with which you are acquainted with and describe the adaptation process practiced by the company for marketing it internationally.
9. The MTV Network draws a worldwide audience, as 80% of its viewers live outside of the United States and it broadcasts in 17 languages in 140 countries. In 1987, MTV expanded internationally with MTV Europe. One in four people around the world are in MTV's key demographic age group

of 14 to 29 years. Because of India's large youth demographic, MTV soon entered this market via a low-risk licensing agreement with Hong Kong's Star TV. Early on, MTV struggled to gain a foothold in the Indian market due to its lack of shows tailored to suit the preferences of this region. When MTV began including Bollywood music in its programming, revenues soared. Other positioning strategies included programming on such topics as fashion and cricket, consumer products such as CD's and clothing, and a Web site that included topics such as "campus life". By the late 1990's, MTV had localised its approach by creating MTV India, which included Bollywood music and Hindi-speaking hosts. MTV India also created a Web site and programmes tailored to the Indian market. The programmes were distributed to viewers in Bangladesh, Nepal, Pakistan, the Middle East, and Sri Lanka in addition to those in India. However, of late MTV has been concerned with the lack of worldwide standardised programming. The management believes MTV is not benefiting from economies of scale because of too much localised or adapted programming.

Is it feasible for MTV to reach an ideal balance between standardisation of programming and local adaptation? If yes, how? Thinking in terms of the marketing program elements and marketing strategy, what can management do now to make MTV succeed around the world?

10. Kraft Foods of USA (It is principally engaged in manufacturing and marketing of packaged food and beverages with world famous brands names such as Kraft, Maxwell House, Oscar Mayer, Oreo, LU, Jacobs Coffee, Tang, Toblerone, etc.) entered China more than 20 years back. But for many years, it was not doing well and thus, it shook the company's original belief that what was good for one market would also be good for all other markets in the same product line. To win over Chinese customers, Kraft realised that even a global corporation must transform itself, letting local managers make decisions based on their understanding of the market. Kraft learned that building up a local management team to maintain solid connections with the Chinese distributors is a major part of doing retail business in China. The local team assessed the situation and found that Oreo was too sweet for Chinese consumers. They found the US price of 5 Yuan [73 cents] for 14 cookies was too heavy for them and that the package was too big. Kraft opened a new facility in Suzhou Industrial Park, near Shanghai, for cookie research and development which allowed Kraft to create new product platforms tailored to suit local tastes. Kraft, thereafter, made a radical move by launching new Oreo products like Oreo Wafer Sticks, Oreo Wafer Rolls, Oreo Soft Cakes and Oreo Strawberry Creme. The price was reduced and the packaging was readjusted to make it small (in a smaller size at 2 Yuan [29 cents] for seven cookies). Kraft then began an extensive advertising and marketing campaign to promote the new range of products. Thanks to these reforms, China, thereafter, became the world's largest Oreo market outside the United States.

    Do you support the localisation effort of Kraft? Why or why not? How will it affect the company's global marketing strategy considering the fact that Kraft Foods operates in over 70 countries and sells its products in over 160 countries across the world?

11. How would you use the international product concept to ensure better marketability? Explain your answer with the help of possible product adaptation for a German confectionary firm entering into the Japanese market.
12. Select one particular product segment, say the SUV segment of an automobile company having markets across the globe and conduct an in-depth investigation of product offerings, features/benefits, design elements, etc., across multiple country markets. To what extent are localisation and adaptation evident? What factors drive the relative levels of standardisation or adaptation?
13. What is product diffusion? What are the different factors affecting product diffusion in the international market?
14. Hyundai Motors does most of its engineering work in Korea, engine calibration and testing in Michigan, vehicle styling Southern California and high-temperature testing in California desert. The company adopts new technology from its research centres in Frankfurt (for diesel engine technology) and in Tokyo. Research the new product development process in Hyundai with the involvement of the multi-specialty locations and analyse how they overcome the diffusion barriers in country markets.
15. Produce a perceptual map of Tata indigo car in two countries, say, Tanzania and India. Bring out the product positioning strategy differences and suggest the positioning strategy the company should pursue in African markets for its vehicles.

EXERCISES

1. Collect raw data through a survey of foreigners in your city to understand their perception of Tata Nano car and develop them into a perceptual map. Indicate the most important attributes in consumer decision making while this car is marketed abroad.
2. Conduct a primary market research in your country to understand the competition in the beer market and find the product attributes such as heavy or light, bitter or mild, gaseous or non gaseous. Also demonstrate how the leading foreign and local brands are differentiating according to these dimensions, with the support of a perceptual map.
3. You have been approached by a processed food manufacturer cum exporter, intending to export your country's products to the US, to prepare a report for them on the food labelling requirements in US. Visit the Food and Drug Administration Web site of the US government (www.fda.gov) to understand the requirements and prepare a detailed report.
4. Break down the product Scorpio (SUV of M&M) into components and sub-components, both tangibles and intangibles, into different layers as per the product concept. Identify the components that could be candidates for possible adaptation while marketing the product in the US considering the culture, norms, use condition, regulations, etc.

End Case: Microwave oven adaptation[9]

The innovative mind of Mr Percy Spencer for the first time introduced the concept microwave after the World War II but commercialised during 1955 by Tappan Appliance (which became a subsidiary of Electrolux in 1979) of USA. Thereafter it spread very fast in kitchens of USA and Europe because ease of use. Its popularity went up fast because the appliance matched very well with the lifestyle of western countries. In Asia, Japanese first welcome the product in their kitchen as the fast life style of industrialising country perfectly matched with the product characteristics. The global demand of microwave oven during 1990 was 22.3 million numbers (Table 7.4). The USA topped the list and interestingly Asian country Japan ranked third and countries such as China and India were not in the list. This global demand is expected to reach 72.5 million units at the end of the year 2015. The demand is primarily generated by various factors such as replacement demand, niche market product developments, adapted product lines and incremental product innovations, etc. The geographical reach of the product enlarged across the developed markets of North America and Western Europe, rising income industrialised countries and developing markets of Asia Pacific and Eastern Europe.

In the early 1990s microwave oven was almost alien to China but as the country started becoming the manufacturing hub for the entire world micro oven found access to Chinese market. The middle class population bulged in China along with growth in affluence during 1990s facilitating it to become a lucrative marketing place for multinational home appliance manufacturer. Later many Chinese manufacturers entered in to the market and as a result it became a very competitive market but with the rise

Table 7.4 The global demand of microwave oven, 1990

Rank	Company	No of units produced in million
1	USA	8.8
2	Europe	7.0
3	Japan	3.6
4	Asia and Oceania	2.1
5	Canada	0.8

Source: Japanese Engineering Industry (JEI) (November, 1990 issue)

[9] The case 'Microwave oven adaptation' has been created by the case writer Dr Gautam Dutta of Indian Institute of Foreign Trade as a basis for classroom discussion rather than to illustrate either effective or ineffective handling of business situation

of market size. India, on the other hand, was not influenced by the Chinese story of rapid entry of the gadget in to kitchen because of altogether different household cooking style of these two highly populated countries of the world. Unlike the Chinese or Western countries, Indian food items such as curry, etc., are required continuous stirring while being cooked. This was not at all possible in microwave oven. On the top, culturally the Indian housewives want to spend time in kitchen and any idea of reducing time spend on kitchen was not readily acceptable to them. Indian housewives prefer to cook for the entire family and take lot of pride when the family members appreciate taste of the cooked items served during dinner or lunch. Traditionally, society also accepted it as a norm that kitchen jobs such as cooking, etc., are mostly to be done by the women members of the family. The multinational marketers, when peeped from China, because of the above reasons, became indifferent to the Indian market opportunities.

It was only during mid 1990s when more and more Indians were getting into the earning spree in search of economic prosperity. Double income families in urban societies also kept on increasing. Kitchen gadgets such as microwave ovens, etc., were started to be looked at as a tool of convenience and to minimise time spent in kitchen by sacrificing Indian taste preferences. A general perception was going around that those who were bachelors or double income couple would be more inclined to use such gadgets since they would not mind sacrificing taste preference. Anyway, this thinking gave the international marketers a ray of hope for Indian market.

The leading microwave oven producers of the world such as Matsushita, Toshiba, Tappan, Whirlpool, Gold Star, Samsung, Daewoo, Electrolux, etc., felt that with the passage of time the affluent Indian middle class people would be inclined to use this easy and time saving gadget in their kitchen purely because of change in lifestyle brought by economic prosperity. They were simply allured by the sheer possible size of Indian market in case the Indian housewives started accepting this product.Without waiting these companies hatched strategic plan to enhance market size in India. They resorted to various techniques of convincing the Indian consumers. Multi-pronged strategy was devised by different companies to educate Indians about the benefit and usage of microwave oven in daily life. The reputed chefs, established recipe writers, television personalities of kitchen shows, etc., were engaged to teach the housewives about utilising the microwave oven for their day-to-day cooking. Every day, through shows, TV programme, FM channel, etc., they taught about how to cook very basic Indian foods such as 'dal', 'tarka', etc., to special dish such as 'Biriani', 'Hilsa Fish curry', etc., using the microwave oven. Further, the companies felt that direct marketing oriented approach would be much more effective when attacking the culturally driven cooking habit of Indian women. Sales women were engaged to visit door to door and convince middle class families to use the oven. However, there was a realisation that had the product been modified to Indian condition more would been the acceptance of the product in the market. This also provided the key to further extend the market beyond urban area to the vast rural India and ensure a long time presence in the market. This led to the all-round effort by the companies for introducing Indianised microwave oven. Multinationals such as Haier, Electrolux, Whirlpool, etc., started looking for product innovation exclusively for the Indian market. Some manufacturers were also seen at putting tremendous efforts in customising microwave ovens in accordance with Indian style or to make them compatible with Indian tastes and preferences. Whirlpool introduced an Indian-adapted version, 'MagiCook' microwaves, with the option of MicroTawa that ensured food could be cooked as per a variety of Indian recipes. All the efforts put together brought the result in terms of increasing sales revenue. Buoyed with the success Indian companies such as Onida, Godrej, Videocon, etc., enhanced their marketing efforts. Competition brought forth decrease in price coupled with a gradual rise of acceptability powered the rise in sales further.

The initial success was cherished by the companies, both domestic and multinational. Business school cases were written to highlight new product introduction and success in a new market. Seminar and conference were organised to showcase the marketing success over consumer habits. In one such marketing conference organised in New Delhi company representatives were engaged in discussing the root cause of success in Indian market. "The company would have the last laugh that will be able to replace the rural 'chulla' in the villages of Punjab with microwave oven. For this you require a good look at your product and ask yourself whether the product still resembles more like an American gadget or rural Indian kitchen appliance." said Mr Khosla, senior level executive of Whirlpool in the back drop of a marketing conference in New Delhi.

At the end of the conference while returning to his office in his official car Mr Khosla was attracted towards news item appeared in the leading business newspaper which read, 'Microwave ovens sales have gone down, consumers bought only about one million microwave ovens in 2014.' Mr Khosla was remembering his own comment and realised how the microwave manufactures have failed to change food preparation habit of Indian as a whole. He remembered the famous quote of Mahatma Gandhi, "India lives in her villages" and found how it still true. Conquering a few urban Indians do not necessarily mean pan Indian acceptance of the product. On the top the neo rich urban consumers are getting infected with health hazard bugs spread by western media about ill effects of microwave cooking. Mr Khosla realised that unless new market window in terms of India's vast rural sector is opened the microwave oven marketing in India will not see its real good days. The next day, sitting in his chamber, Mr Khosla invited a small group meeting of company official and put in front of them the outcome of the yesterdays marketing conference and his thinking how to really get in to rural household of India with product modification and marketing thereof. As the group agreed in the meeting, the next day he engaged a group of business school students to list down the product components of microwave oven available in the market through secondary survey. Basically, he wanted to critically understand the product and its adaptation process locally in Indian situation. The following were the product components listed by the students as per available products in the market (Table 7.5). On looking at it the Whirlpool executives quipped, "We have to understand the different layers of components completely and bring out the features and benefits of each of the constituents of the components for effective marketing in Indian scenario in order to make Indian product adaptation story permanent".

Table 7.5 Different components of microwave oven

Core Component:	
Product platform	Cavity size: 0.5 cu. ft, 1.0 cu. ft. and 1.4 cu. ft. Frequency: 2450 MHz, Power output of 600-800 watts, Quartz Grill, Stainless Steel Cavity, Magnetron
Design features	Solo, Grill, Convection
Functional features	Reflector system, Power Levels Child Lock Jog Dial Forced Air Crisp Function MicroTawa Stew timer Boom-rang turntable Doneness control Air circulation fans Turbo defrost Automatic reheat Humidity sensors Quartz heater Three stage memory Frozen food keys
Packaging component	
Price	3000-12,000 INR
Quality	3, 4, 5 star rating
Packages	Box paper packaging
Styling	Boxlike
Trademark	Whirlpool
Brand name	Whirlpool
Support service components	
Deliveries	Within a day
Warranty	1-3 years
Spare parts	Available on order
Repair and maintenance	Within warranty period only
Installation	Free service
Instructions	24 page in English
Other related services	Recipe booklet, Cooking manual

CASE QUESTIONS

Q1. Break the product, i.e., Microwave Oven into different layers of components anc bring out the features and benefits of each of the constituents of the components towards marketing in rural India.

Q2. Assess, assuming you were the marketing manager, what component adaptation you would have sought for the product to make it more acceptable to the Indian rural market.

Q3. Assess the rural Indian preference and develop a full proof marketing plan for the company indicating the constituents of the components where adaptations were not effected. Show reasons and possible implications.

FURTHER READINGS

Johansson, Johny K. and Hans B. Thorelli (1998), "International product positioning", *Journal of International Business Studies*, Vol. 16, No. 3.

The authors of this article used a framework of international product positioning by considering the factors related to firm-specific and country-specific advantages. This article emphasised on the importance on developing clear understanding about product perception in the minds of international customers. This understanding can be used to measure the relative disadvantage or advantage possessed by a product as compared to those of its competitors from other countries.

MacKay, David B. and Robert F. Easley (1996), "International differences in product perception: A product map analysis", *International Marketing Review.*

This article provides an example analyses of weakness of traditional product mapping methods for product positioning analysis. This article, therefore, delves on the high and rapid variability of product preferences within each country and the lack of a common product perception among countries and went on to compare product perception difference that exist between Japanese and US consumers in case of gift products and proposes a new method for overcoming these problems.

Watson, John J. and Katrina Wright (1999), "Consumer ethnocentrism and attitudes toward domestic and foreign products", *European Journal of Marketing*, Vol. 34, Issue 9/10, February.

This article investigates thoroughly the relationship between consumer ethnocentrism and consumer attitudes toward foreign manufactured products among product categories in which domestic alternatives are not available. In order to understand consumer culture-backed attitude, it uses the values of classification of Schwartz. This article is useful for students to understand how cultural-backed attitude drive highly ethnocentric consumers in the evaluation of foreign products.

Janda, S. and C.P. Rao (1997), "The effect of country-of-origin related stereotypes and personal beliefs on product evaluation", *Psychology and Marketing*, Vol. 14, No. 7, October.

This article reviews how cognitive structure influences consumers' use of the country-of-origin factor in product evaluation. This article establishes the relationship between three useful concepts, i.e., cultural stereotypes, personal beliefs, and country-of-origin perceptions.

Hoffman, James J. (1997), "A two stage model for the introduction of products into international markets", *Journal of Global Marketing*, Vol. 11, No. 1.

The paper deals with test marketing of a product in a country where it is required to identify country and selection of the best city to launch the product. This article present a two-stage model combining the elements of marketing strategy, goal programming, and microcomputer technology for the purpose of developing an effective method for making product entry determinations. The companies in the need of product introduction in international market will get a good understanding from this paper.

Yamin, M. and R. Altunisik (2003), "A comparison of satisfaction outcomes associated with adapted and non-adapted products: Domestic versus imported washing machines in Turkey", *International Marketing Review*, Vol. 20, No. 6.

This paper deals with customer satisfaction associated with the consumption of adapted products related with non-adapted imported products. Several hypotheses were tested on data based on a customer satisfaction questionnaire administered to a randomly selected sample of households in Turkey in order to answer several questions related to product adaptation. The result indicates that, after all, it is quality of the products that brought satisfaction for both groups of consumers.

8

Deciding on Brand

Learning Objectives

After studying this chapter, you should be able to:

- Understand the basic brand vocabulary in the context of international marketing.
- Understand the standardisation vs customisation issues in the context of brand internationalisation.
- Understand the brand categorisation process based on geographic coverage and product coverage used in the international context.
- Understand the different types of branding based on geographical coverage and product coverage in the international markets.
- Understand the various problems associated with brand internationalisation such as image, logo, name, and portfolio transfer in the international markets.
- Assess the various factors affecting the brand performance in international markets.
- Understand the brand positioning and brand communication system in the international markets.

Chapter Overview

This chapter deals with different branding issues in the context of marketing internationally. Companies require a well-knit branding policy while competing internationally. It is always a challenge for companies to transfer a home-grown brand in the initial phase of internationalisation into the international arena. The brand will be alien to the foreign consumers, acceptability of the brand image will be in the low ebb, and various issues may crop up to create barriers to product acceptability such as language differences distorting the meaning of the brand name, tag lines suggesting unintended meanings when translated, the logo acquiring a negative connotation, etc.

Opening Vignette

'Nirula' possibly is the oldest Indian brand in the 'Indianised' fast food sector

'Nirula' possibly is the oldest Indian brand in the 'Indianised' fast food sector. It started way back in 1934 when a Chinese food restaurant was opened in Connaught place, New Delhi, by two brothers, LC Nirula and M Nirula. Nirula's restaurant got a facelift during seventies when it added more product variety such as pastry, ice cream, and different Indian snacks, and it became a landmark in the Connaught place locality for anybody travelling to New Delhi. During the next two decades, the company was busy in expanding to various locations in Delhi and linking them with a central kitchen. The brand became more familiar as this family-style restaurant continued serving quality Indian foods to the residents living in the Indian capital city. Post 2000, there was proliferation of many MNC food chains in Delhi and other parts of India threatening the existence of Indian type fast food restaurants. However, Nirula was able to maintain its market share in a thoroughly competitive market by sheer focus on 'Indianised' menu and went on to open more restaurants under Nirula brand.

The expansion was largely based on the franchisee structure. Navis Capital Partners, a Malaysian private equity firm, was attracted by the brand image of home-grown fast food chain 'Nirula' and invested aggressively in it to acquire management control. Under the active support of Navis Capital, Nirula attempted to expand more to the smaller but rich Indian cities such as Meerut, Pune, Mussoorie, Surat, Patna, etc. Then came a time when the management thought about internationalisation of the Nirula brand. With globalisation of the fast food sector, the demand for Indian food kept growing phenomenally in the international market and Nirula's management was keen on extending the brand internationally. Foreign expansion plan was hatched to step in to neighbouring countries first and then further to the Middle East, the UK, and even the USA. The company was even not discounting possibilities of a presence in Europe in the near future as young generation Europeans also developed liking for Indian fast food. However, the company management wanted to be sure of expected popularity of Nirula brand outside India. It was also a question in front of the management if at all the company would be successful in transferring the home-grown brand identity to the other countries. A related question came at this juncture whether the company should harp on transferring the existing brand image of Nirula's to other countries, which has been nourished over the years based on Indian values, attributes, trait, and personalities. The management was thinking whether the brand name "Nirula" and the tagline "It's delicious!" were transferable to other countries. More significantly, the question was whether its brand positioning as a fast food restaurant chain that serves hygienic, good quality food at an affordable price specialising in Indian-style western fast food tenable in the targeted foreign country markets.

When this brand positioning dilemma was told to the students of international marketing in the classroom, the students quipped: "That's disturbing! Can a company which has diligently built its brand image over a period of more than sixty years requires changing its positioning on entry to a new country market? It is also true, at the same time, that the concerned company does not enjoy the 'global brand' status which can have the acceptability throughout the globe in a similar fashion. So, can the 'Indianness' attached to the brand attract customers from other countries? If not, then it will remain as a fast food restaurant catering to the expat Indians only. If adaptation is required at all, what are the different factors to be considered to arrive at a decision? How this will lead to repositioning of the brand? Can the companies, in general, have a procedure to assess the brand adaptation requirements before entering a foreign country?

International managers confront difficult questions when developing the ideal international brand portfolio. They must decide not only how to build their international brands but also which local brands to build, which to eliminate, which to sell, and even which to assimilate under an international brand name. These are important decisions that significantly influence any company's success

—Isabelle Schuiling and Jean-Noël Kapferer (2004)

INTRODUCTION

The simple word 'Nestlé' does not carry any meaning to an average Indian. But today, the same word seems to have enough strength to mould consumers' perception of the value of the product/products coming from a particular company not only in India but almost throughout the world. However, about two hundreds and fifty years ago, the name 'Nestlé' was alien to almost everybody in the world. In Switzerland it made a very humble beginning during 1866 to let the world know about the meaning of the word. It was all started by a Swiss gentleman by the name Henri Nestlé, a pharmacist by profession, who was desperately thinking about the ways to reduce high infant mortality rate of the erstwhile Switzerland. He was highly touched by infant death and wanted to do something to improve the situation. Being a pharmacist it was easy for him to enquire with the parents about the root cause of infant death in his locality. To his surprise, Mr Nestlé found that the infants of Switzerland had no access to good quality baby food, which to a great extent, was found to be responsible for the abnormally high infant mortality rate in that country. His entrepreneurial instinct coupled with social empathy led him to form his own enterprise for producing an infant cereal under the name 'Nestle'. Within a short period of time the cereal became very popular as it promised good health of new born babies. Incidentally, this was the first Nestlé product in the world. There was no looking back thereafter. It continued for next hundred odd years, and the name 'Nestlé' became most sought-after name for the young mothers of the world. The product was accepted as a safe food for children, and the name 'Nestle' was taken as guarantee to that. While extending the product to Germany, it was found that "Nestlé" in German language means "little nest", which in literal sense symbolising all the good values of nurturing such as family, warmth, and caring. 'Nestle' got the opportunity to capitalise on the meaning and build an image that resemblance a safe and caring 'little nest' where the babies of the world can stay without fear. Nestlé uses this image still today. In course of time, Mr Nestlé felt proud about it and quipped, "It will be my seal of quality world over". As the time progressed the word 'Nestle' became the umbrella brand for the company and continued to enjoy its status as a symbol of "family, warmth, and caring" for the company products throughout the world.

The first Nestlé factory came up in Vevey, Switzerland which eventually became the global headquarter of the company. After the success of milk product, Nestle added another product category under the 'Nestle' umbrella, chocolate, followed quickly by Nescafe coffee. Then the time came for internationalisation of the products. Nestlé acted very carefully to ensure that the same image of "family, warmth, and caring" was transferred along with product/products when marketed in other countries. The international success of Nestlé was evident from the fact that, at a later period, more than 90% of the total company turnover started coming from overseas operation. The company did not take a long time to understand that behind the successful overseas operation the role of the name "Nestlé" had been the key factor. In a cross country survey, taken up by the company, it was revealed that wherever the products were marketed the people living in that country could feel the same warmth of the Nestle image. The management of the company understood that the ability to transfer the value proposition of the brand Nestle consistently to the customers irrespective of their country of origin brought the marketing success. The knowledge and experience gathered in terms of the process and requirements of extending the brand image to those countries helped the company in further internationalisation. Of course, this was a task of difficult nature. The consumers of different countries with diverse cultural backgrounds had different preferences for the products' intrinsic feature such as size, designs, consistency, etc., and extrinsic features such as name and country of origin. Even in the culturally dissimilar countries the brand image of Nestle did wonder in consumers' attitude formation process favourably. In some countries the company was struck with the name 'Nestlé' as people were facing a lot of pronunciation difficulties. But, the company managed to have considerable success sheer by the brand image of Nestle. However, as the competition in some countries became acute, the company felt that, to suit the local requirements, it may be required to adapt the brand as per the country-specific need. This put the company in to the dilemma of standardisation vs adaptation of brand when marketed in those countries. In such situation the company decided not in favour of diluting the existing brand image of 'Nestle' too much through local adaptation and image alteration. Confronted with such challenges of localisation, the company had to launch or acquire various localised brands in different countries. This helped them, in some specific countries, to thwart intense competition from the local products. For example, Nestlé acquired pasta brand Buitoni in Italy and actively positioned the brand as "share the Italian love of food" through innovative positioning and promotions. The process of acquiring brands from local and regional markets in different categories of products favoured the company to face tough local competition successfully. But, at the same time, the number of brands in its kitty went up and became a sizable number in course of time.

All these experiments led to the understanding that deciding about geographical reach of the brands is also an important consideration. The company thereafter allowed some of its brands such as Nestlé, Nescafe, Maggi, Friskies, Buitoni, Carnation, KitKat, etc., to travel globally because of their geography neutral acceptability. However, strategically, the company restricted some of their brands such as Perugina, Findus, Stouffer's, etc., within some specific geographic regions. At the same time there were thousands local brands doing good business within a geographic territory of a country. For example, Brigadeiro brand covering chocolate truffle candy business was acquired in Brazil only for Brazil. These local brands were proved important for the company to compete in local markets. In fact, these local brands provided a very effective weapon to the company to deal with ethnocentric consumers having a strict home country product bias. In this way the story of Nestlé continued and it became the largest food company in the world measured by revenues. However, in course of global journey and mammoth revenue growth, Nestlé was adequately supported by its brand building process. It nurtured about 7500 local brands, 140 regional brands, 45 worldwide strategic brands with global spread and above all, 10 worldwide corporate brands bearing the corporate name Nestle. At that point of time the company almost looked like one brand loaded armoured car ready to take up the marketing war at all levels, be it local, regional or global. In fact, the company fought many fierce marketing wars and enjoyed the competitive advantages because of huge number of brands at all levels in its armoury.

There is no doubt that in order to compete internationally, the company requires a well-knit branding strategy. It is always a challenge for companies to determine how a home-grown brand, in the initial phase of internationalisation, can be thrown open for the international consumers. The brand will be almost alien to the new consumers of other countries. The acceptability of the brand image in a new country may be influenced by country culture and tradition. Language differences may distort the meaning of the brand name and hence its acceptance may be challenged. This may also happen when a brand name or logo in a certain culture acquires a negative meaning.

However, the history of many companies testifies that in spite of initial problems, the companies are able to overcome the challenges. They either put pressure on brand building exercises around their home grown brand or acquire a local brand. There are many instances where the company resorted to both these methods simultaneously. In this way some companies, while internationalising, continues to add brand after brand to their kitty while penetrating different country markets. At some stage, the question of maintaining an optimum size of international brand architecture arises since there is a need to manage a favourable balance between the cost of nurturing brands and company profitability.

This chapter, therefore, deals with the branding issues discussed above, in the context of marketing internationally. It starts with a basic understanding of the brand vocabulary and then discusses issues such as problems associated with brand building in the international context, managing brands in international markets, and timing of brand building in foreign countries.

DEFINING A BRAND

According to Aaker[1], a brand is a distinguishing name and/or symbol (such as logo, trademark, or package design) intended to identify the goods or services of either one seller or a group of sellers, and to differentiate those goods or services from those of the competitors. A brand, therefore, has the ability to provide impression to the customer about the source of the product, its quality and status against similar competitive products in the market place. In a sense, therefore, customers are benefited by receiving the right information about the product so that they are not deceived by the mischievous information coming from products that appear to be identical but inferior. It is beneficial to the producers as well as it can project the product's distinctiveness to attract the customers.

In a competitive market, producers of similar products desperately try to reach almost the same customer base. One particular producer often gets an edge over the others if the targeted customers are attracted by superior brand status. It may so happen that attraction towards to brand becomes so much that the prospective consumers themselves take the initiative to identify the targeted products in a competitive market place. But how this can possibly be accomplished? There are so many competing products in the market place. How can the prospective consumer isolate the products of his/her choice? It is here that the role of the brand comes in, since effective branding can be used by prospective customers as a selection criterion for a product.

An effective brand, therefore, can be used as a tool through which a producer can pull the customers towards a particular product. Therefore, in a competitive market the producers make all round efforts to develop an effective brand by unleashing all the descriptive and evaluative brand-related information in the public place over a period of time. Thus, from the customer's point of view, a brand is almost the sum total of the experience that the customers had matured over a period of time through interactions

[1] Aaker, D. A. (1991), *Managing Brand Equity*, The Free Press, New York, pp. 7, 39, 61, 110.

with the product and marketing communications released by the producer time to time. The consumers use their previous experience with the product and accumulated brand-knowledge in evaluating the product in the purchase situation. Eventually the same brand knowledge and experience of the consumers act as the much needed pull factor to bring customers close towards the product/products.

Brand Identity

According to Aaker, [2] "Brand identity is a unique set of brand associations a brand strategist aspires to create or maintain". This is the basic requirement of a brand. It is said that brand identity is to brand and personality is to human being. It acts almost in the same manner when a person can be recognised or identified from a mass gathering because of his/her differentiable and identifiable characteristics leading to development of a unique personality. This differentiability factor allows the other concerned people to select a few persons from a mass gathering first and identifiable characteristics allow zooming on the right person thereafter. Similarly, prospective consumers of a product are also helped by the differentiability and identifiable personality of the brand. The uniqueness in terms of personality associated with a man is known as that person's unique identity. Similarly, a unique personality is associated with a brand is known as that brand's unique identity. Brand identity is purposefully created by the producers so that a brand can have a personality unique to itself only. This uniqueness is essential for a brand so that prospective consumers can sense its presence in a competitive market place. Therefore, the producers put deliberate efforts for making a brand identifiable in the market place by the prospective customers. Brand identity can be of two types – core identity and extended identity. Core identity essentially focuses on product attributes, service, user profile, store ambience, product performance, etc., which are likely to remain constant over a period of time irrespective of the market it enters. Core identity is important because it provides uniqueness and credibility and the organisation express its value through it. It could be a unique promise made by the brand and its fulfilment thereof. Therefore, the organisation must professionally and emotionally own the core identity. Extended identity must coexist synergistically around core brand identity elements and rightfully garnish it to provide a correct, desired and competitive meaning to the core identity to complete the differentiation. Since the brand identity is very important for an organisation to install the desired differentiation from the others in a competitive environment, companies strive hard to develop the unique brand identity and nurture them to get the competitive advantage.

Brand Proposition

Why will some consumers prefer one brand over the other brands? The answer is simple. It is because of the reason that the particular brand made better promises to its consumers using its product than the other. Take the

[2] Aaker, D. A. (2002), *Building Strong Brands,* Free Press. New York.

example of the 1929 born Lux soap. Since then the brand Lux has been reiterating its promise that they produce 'the beauty soap of film stars'. Unilever, the producer of Lux soap, in different ways and at different customer touch points has been conveying the brand promise through marketing communication. It is because of such a tall promise or an excellent brand proposition Lux is being preferred by the consumers. Therefore, in order to occupy a clear position in the minds of the consumers and feel attracted towards the concerned product a unique, strong and relevant proposition is a must. When brands travel internationally what would be its proposition to the targeted foreign consumer? Will the company offer the same proposition in the foreign market or change it in accordance with the market scenario, competition, culture, etc.? This question is normally faced by a company intending to develop its brand abroad. The answer depends on several factors. Important amongst them are the type of products being marketed as well as country being explored.

Standardised vs Customised Brand

In international marketing, the question of standardisation or adaptation forms the core of the brand strategy. A major decision a company requires to make in terms of standardisation or adaptation of its branding approach. In a standardised brand scenario, the core and attributes are primarily developed and tailored domestically, i.e., in terms of domestic country requirements and then extended to foreign countries. Therefore, naturally, the brand proposition is originally developed for the domestic country and extended to other countries. If foreign consumers accept the proposition without any difficulty, then the company can avoid the exercise of building a new identity in the foreign market. It is understandable that such approach would save time and money. Virgin airline of USA, for example, made a huge effort to build its core identity based on quality commitment, fun and entertainment, value for money and innovation. The extended identity of Virgin brand was built up effectively around innovativeness, underdog character and flaunts the rule type of attitude. The brand propositions were propagated across its consumer base through the youthfulness of the company staff, sense of humour, logo, tagline, etc. The entire approach to branding was taken up by the company keeping home country, i.e., USA in the forefront. The company, therefore, had to make every effort to retain the uniqueness of its brand identity while operating in another country. Otherwise the strong brand proposition that the company created in home country situation purposefully to maintain its unique appeal will be lost. This perfectly made sense to the company strategist. In another example, American company Mattel took up marketing of Barbie dolls in a number of countries without modification in the brand proposition which was basically developed around American "feminism". The strategy paid result in many countries. However, it had to face the wrath of customers in Arab world whose concept of feminism was different. Therefore, the question of brand customisation arises. When a brand is customised or adapted as per a country requirement, the core and the attributes of a brand are customised or modified to suit the individual country need. Accordingly, these brands, therefore, would have different propositions in different countries.

The basic objective of such customisation would to match country-specific culture or characteristics, requirements and desires. It is expected by a company that the customised brand propositions would be close enough to attracted customers towards the brand leading to desired revenue generation. A company, in general, would try to avoid brand customisation and favour a standardised practice of brand building in new countries as well. The standardisation would decrease the cost associated with the brand building exercise in an adapted line. The brand communication costs would come down drastically as same brand propositions will be repeated irrespective of cultural or economic differences across the different countries where the company has forayed into business. Also, starting from the scratch in regards to brand building would require sufficient time to be elapsed before getting a foothold in the competitive foreign market. Additionally, there would be no requirement of brand proposition transformation in the countries of presence which could be the starting point of global branding. Any step forward towards global branding would be rewarding enough as world is fast becoming a global village due increased mobility of the customers. However, there are demerits of standardised brands also. The most important one being the brand stereotyping when company does marketing with a fixed idea that world is flat and hence no variation in brand identity is required. In the process marketing potential of some countries remain underutilised.

Brands based on Geographical Coverage

A multi brand company may, in a strategic sense, allow its different brands to cover country markets differently. This may happen with a single brand company as well. Its product may be present either in one country market or covering countries of a region and serving very effectively a distinct group of customers living in the region. By strategising brand coverage across countries a company gets huge benefits in terms of marketing. One particular brand may be purposefully placed in the local country market only to take advantage in terms of localness. It works perfectly for culture backed products or if the product has connectedness with the nation's history. For example, L'Oreal maintains Yue Sai cosmetic brand exclusively for China. This local brand is the most favourite cosmetic brand in China for many years. On the other extreme there are brands that are not confined to a particular national territory or one country market but have a global presence. The global brand works well for companies when they are used to serve a selected segment present across the countries of the world. These segments may vary in size from country to country but often are rewarding for a company because of huge market size in totality. For example, Lancôme for the women selective cosmetics adjusted as the most rewarding global brand from L'Oreal in terms of revenue earned from 130 countries. In between these two extremes, there exist the regional brands that act like a bridge between the local and global brands in terms of their enhanced geographic spread more than a single country but less than a global status. For example, Shu Umera cosmetic brand of L'Oreal is present in eight Asian, two North American and European countries only. So, based on the geographic coverage three types of brands, local, regional and global are possible.

Local brand

Shuiling and Kepferer (2004)[3] define local brands as brands that exist in one country or in a limited geographical region. Global companies are interested in nurturing a certain number of local brands to fight out local competition created by other local brands from domestic companies as well as other multinationals. A company with an established local brand enjoy certain edge over the competitors. Through this local brand a company successfully push certain products in a country market with emphasis on localness as marketing strategy. Sometimes, a global manufacturer, without a global brand, feels the need of a local brand to fight out localised competition. In such situation, they act in haste and desperately acquire a domestic brand of a domestic manufacturer in a particular country in order to stand up to the competition. A local brand of global company brings the products very close to the ethnocentric local customer who are fond of local brands only. Through creation of local brand a global company creates a level playing field for the intense competition from a local player. A local brand takes on the local competition head on through flexible pricing strategy without disturbing its global image. For example, Nestlé created a strong presence in a 7000-strong local product brands such as Brigadeiro, Rocky, Solis, etc., in order to fight out local competition through flexible pricing and without hurting its global brand image. In a particular case of developing local brand the company acted in haste to create a local brand in Brazilian market. At that time Brigadier Air Marshall Eduardo Gomes was very much famous in Brazil as a politician and military figure and Nestlé, while introducing its new brand of chocolate powder and condensed milk into the country used 'Brigadeiro' as local brand and popularised sweet products under this brand name only in Brazil. In almost a similar situation the company Nestle acted quickly to launch Solis brand to cover a range of tomato-based product in Spain.

Box 8.1 GM's local brand in China

Foreign automobile manufacturers are aware of the requirements of local brands in China and hence collaborate with local Chinese auto companies to attract attention of prospective customers from the different cities of China. Foreign automakers such as Japan's Nissan Motor Co Ltd and Honda Motor Co. Ltd and France's PSA Peugeot Citroen are planning to introduce local brands. BMW, the German automaker, is in talks with a local brand owner for outright purchase. The Chinese partners for Ford Motor Co. and Hyundai Motor Co. also have expressed a desire to join that club. General Motors USA is not an exception to this count. These drives are all to woo the customers more as China is all poised to become the largest automobile market of the world. It is estimated that the demand of low-end automobile in China is more that the combined demand for France and Britain. General Motors, USA, understood the requirement of local brand ahead of others. It understood that in order to capture the hearts and minds of the Chinese under a competitive situation, the company required to launch a local brand. Accordingly, it introduced the 'Baojun' brand as a local brand and it is used for launching of low-cost cars while marketing in Chinese cities targeting first-time and price sensitive buyers. The local brand has been allowed a flexible pricing with prices generally under $10,000. Baojun, so long, has proved to be successful in drawing customers who otherwise would have settled for local automobiles. Chinese rivals such as Chery Automobile, Geely Automobile Holdings Ltd and Warren

[3] Shuiling, L and J. N. Kapferer (2004), "Executive insights: Real differences between local and international brands: Strategic implications for international marketers", *Journal of International Marketing*, Vol. 12, Issue 4, pp. 97–112.

Buffet-backed BYD Co. Ltd were put on the back foot when GM launched this local brand in the market. The market success has also made GM's local partner Wuling Co. Ltd enthusiastic in supporting the aggressive marketing move of the foreign company. It has been jointly planned to bring more models under the local brand umbrella to capture more market share. It will also launch its once popular but now-discontinued version of the Chevy Spark mini car under the Baojun brand but, of course, under a new local name. Lechi, which means "happy driving" in Chinese, will be used to introduce the grand old, 2003 born, Chevy Spark in China. Seeing this marketing extravaganza of GM, observers of the automobile sector are of the view that a strong local brand is good for a company but it should not come at the cost of parent brand. Strong local brands may eat up the parent brand's future possibilities and hence GM, as an experienced global company, must know how to balance the brand portfolio with a right mix of local and global brand to optimise company performance.

Regional brand

As the name suggest the regional brands go beyond one country in terms of geographical coverage but limit their exposure only to the regional markets. It has been observed that companies, generally, find it easy to spread these types of brands in few geographically close countries and hence concentrate on developing regional brands. Companies by possessing strong regional brands enjoy strategic importance in a regional context. Generally, one regional brand originates from a local brand only and then in course of time it spreads to other geographically close countries. The following are the characteristics of regional brands:

(a) The regional brands position themselves to win over the consumers of a particular region and address the unique need of that region.

(b) The regional brand's marketing approach falls between local and global brand. The ongoing momentum of regional economic integration of countries provides good opportunities for regional brand positioning due to harmonisation of environment. For example in European Union (EU), many regional brands are popular. Nestlé has about 140 regional strategic brands, such as Perugina, Stouffer's, Mackintosh, Vittel, Contadina, Herta, Alpo, etc., to take the advantage of Europe and elsewhere. The famous, Nestlé owned Perugina Confectionery Company of Perugia, Italy, and marketed chocolates and food products under the brand name 'Perugina' for EU. Nestlé's Stouffer's brand of frozen food is available in the United States and Canada. Various frozen foods produced in Sweden, under the brand 'Findus' are regionalised especially in countries of EU.

(c) These brands are not absolutely culture neurtral in terms of marketing approach. But rather takes the advantage of commonality of regional culture in marketing products in countries of its presence.

(d) By spreading in to a number of countries the regional brands attempts at least to enjoy economies of scale at least in the regional markets.

Global brands

As the name suggest a global brand is global in terms of geographical coverage. The characteristics of global brands are as under:

(a) It must have enough country coverage to be able to be called global.

(b) These brands are culture neutral and hence do not change their propositions due to country-specific differences. It is expected that the global brand will use same marketing strategy and mix in all target markets covered by them.
(c) These brands confront the local brands of the different country markets by projecting their global image.
(d) They are largely benefited due to scale economics and hence they never succumb to localisation desire in the interest of any specific country.
(e) Many of global brands are with corporate name. In other words, corporate named brand with global spread are expected to be culture neutral in terms of marketing approach. Big corporate brands are more certain to achieve the global reach than the smaller size companies. Brands with corporate name such as Shell, Philips, Apple, Nike are absolutely global in nature.
(f) Global brands with corporate name are expected to provide shelter to many products under the brand umbrella.
(g) Global product brands are also many in numbers. For example, the dehydrated soup brand Knorr of German origin cater to different types of soups and market across many countries of the world.

Brands based on Product Coverage

Brands can also be differentiated based on the number and types of product coverage.

Product brand

In product branding, a company brands each product with a single brand identity. For example, Unilever has taken up a strategy to project Dove as a brand while it is a single soap product line of Unilever. Here, all brand development efforts are directed to give cover to only one product line. Through this product branding, Unilever has been able to project unique a brand image of Dove branded product line. A company may go for product branding in order to bring the focus of the customers directly on to the product. A product brand can work wonders for a company in a competitive situation. It draws the customer's attention to the product and not on the corporate image. Many customers may not even know that Dove is a brand of the company Unilever. Moreover, a company which has introduced a product in the foreign market and considers that the product has all the attributes to attract consumers' attention would like to surround the product with the emotions and associations of a product brand. Handling product brand in a new foreign market is also safer as many customers of that country may not know about a foreign company and its history. McDonald, de Chernatony and Harris[4] (2001) argued that a company using a product dominant brand strategy will experience less damage to its corporate image in case one of its individual brands fails. The following are the distinctions between corporate branding and product branding

[4] McDonald, M., L. de Chernatony, and F. Harris (2001), "Corporate marketing and service brands – Moving beyond the fast-moving consumer goods model", *European Journal of Marketing*, Vol. 35 (3/4), pp. 335–346.

Table 8.1 Differences between corporate, family and product branding

Parameters	Product brand	Corporate brand	Family Brand
Management attention on	The product	The company	Product family
Managed by	Middle manager	CEO	Regional manager
Attract attention and gain support of	Customers	Multiple stakeholders	Segments
Delivered by	Marketing head	Whole company	Regional head
Communication focus	On product	On Corporate	On product family
Importance to the company	Functional	Strategic	Strategic
Time horizon	Short (life of product)	Long (life of company)	Varies
Value	Mainly derived from local inspiration	Exclusively of founding member and country	Mainly derived from regional inspiration

(Adapted from Hatch & Schultz 2003[5] and author's addition).

Family brand

Family branding is a concept of branding where one brand name spreads its umbrella to cover several related products under it. Family branding is cost-effective for a company as it can save cost on marketing communication. It is not required to come up with repeated advertisements for different product brands separately. Rather, when the company publicises for one brand, a family of products kept under that brand gets promoted. However, the company resorting to family brand must maintain consistency of product quality for all products in the family. Otherwise, bad image for one product may lead to distortion of the brand image as a whole. Family branding strategy, therefore, must be looked after by competent people in the organisation so that products are marketed with consistent quality. It is generally suggested that only different product lines with similar types of products and quality should be brought under family branding. In spite of the challenges associated with family branding, it is rewarding for the company. Family branding allows the company to launch similar product lines under the same name and same logo. This will make introduction of a new product line easier because of name familiarity. For example, Nivea body care, Nivea moisturisers, Nivea lip care, and Nivea men's care products are almost like family members under the brand umbrella of Nivea from Beiersdorf, Germany.

Corporate brand

A corporate brand comes with the company name. The company lends its name to act as umbrella over the products to be marketed. Many related or unrelated products may be accommodated under the corporate brand thereby allowing the brand to act as single but powerful banner. Corporate branding can be effected either by deliberate attempt to use the corporate name as an umbrella for covering company produced products or by

[5] Hatch, J. H. and M. Schultz (2003), "Bringing the corporation into corporate branding", *European Journal of Marketing*, Vol. 37(7/8), pp. 1041–1064.

attaching the corporate name with the sub-brands. For example, Sony is a corporate umbrella brand. Philips is also a very successful corporate umbrella brand. Virgin has been using its corporate name as umbrella to cover many related as well as unrelated products. On the other hand, Nestlé lends its corporate name to its sub-brand Maggi to make it Nestlé Maggi. The sub-brand provides the product reputation, whereas the corporate name provides the status and geographical spread. Toyota, the famous corporate house of Japan, is itself a corporate brand for instance. The brand name Toyota, when attached to automobiles, provides the desired edge signifying that they are coming from the stable of Toyota, Japan. This helps the company in developing appeal in the foreign country rapidly. Corporate branding will be beneficial for a domestic company enjoying a huge reputation in the domestic market and desires to get leverage of the company's name across foreign countries as well. For example, consider the case of TATA, which has a huge reputation in the Indian market. It is natural that the company would like to endorse its vehicle with the corporate name in foreign countries as well to pass on its home country reputation to other countries. According to Knox and Bickerton[6], "corporate branding is the visual, verbal, and behavioural expression of an organisation's unique business model". By endorsing automobiles with the TATA brand in different country markets, the company has successfully extended the company's reputation, culture, values, and relationships. Another useful feature of corporate branding is its straightforwardness. It endeavours to develop a single unique identity everywhere. Also, Corporate branding makes the brand architecture very simple and manageable. For example, companies like Microsoft as a corporate brand maintained its relatively narrow brand architecture in the field of information technology. Corporate brand has helped consumer goods companies like Phillips to retain a particular focus in electronic products in every country of its presence. Consistent focus on the image over the years has also helped the company to establish a strong brand identity everywhere. The corporate brands are generally successful in bulldozing the localisation requirements in foreign countries by using their strong reputation. The corporate logo or visual identification of companies in course of time becomes so strong that they penetrate the minds of consumers irrespective of the country, culture, language, etc.

Mixed brand

A mixed brand is a mixture of two brand names, corporate brand as well as product brand. For example Nestle KitKat. KitKat is a chocolate-covered wafer biscuit bar, now produced worldwide by Nestlé. In fact, KitKat of Rowntree, England, was acquired in 1988 by Nestlé, which adopted a mixed branding strategy for the product in the international market. The company uses corporate name Nestlé along with the strong product brand, KitKat, in international marketing of chocolate as 'Nestlé KitKat', where corporate name has the same emphasis as the product brand name. The Hershey Company, which retained license to market KitKat in USA, did not resort to mixed branding while marketing in USA. Hence, in USA, KitKat is marketed as 'KitKat' only. Hershey company never used its corporate name and

[6] Knox, S., and D. Bickerton (2003), "The six conventions of corporate branding", *European Journal of Marketing*, Vol. 37 (7/8), 998–1016.

market it as 'Hershey Kit Kat' to differentiate the brand from other country. Similarly, the top-selling chocolate bar from Cadbury uses the corporate name 'Cadbury' more strongly when using the mixed brand name as 'Cadbury Dairy Milk'. The corporate name 'Cadbury' is made more prominent when it is followed by the product name 'Dairy Milk', which makes this product more easily associated with the other products under the same corporate name. So, the intention in the foreign market for this mixed branding is to allow the consumers to relate them with a corporate name that is more acceptable. On the other hand, KitKat marketed by Hershey Company in USA allowed the product brand name to be more prominent and strived to give the product brand a distinct positioning.

When a new product brand enters a foreign market, it suffers from extrication in the initial years. Companies, therefore, commit more marketing investments and resources so as to make the product brands as prominent as possible. In contrast, if the corporate name is very prominent in the foreign country market, because of the country of origin effect or company culture, then attaching the corporate name with the product brand makes sense. The use of mixed branding strategy saves considerable marketing investment. Another scenario in this respect would be when both the corporate name and the product name are unknown or not heard by the prospective consumer of the foreign market. This is mostly common in case of the smaller size companies entering the foreign market for the first time with a product but surely with long-term ambition. For example, Red Tape brand of shoes from the Indian company Mirza International is now hugely popular in the UK and US market but was totally unknown in the initial years of product launch. The company had to build 'Red Tape' as a brand from the scratch by positioning it to convey the statement of style, good craftsmanship and finesse. The company deliberately did not use the company name

Box 8.2 Single brand or multi brand in foreign market

Hidesign started as a small Indian brand of a small Indian company producing leather products for domestic market. The company made an efficient move in internationalising the brand but, all along, it maintained the single brand status. The leather products of the company are available in 23 countries in over 2000 stores, but under the same brand name. The company did not go for multiple branding or launching a specific brand for a particular country. This strategy of using a single brand internationally suited the company well and it was able to position the product in the world market. But this is not the case for all companies. LVMH (Moët Hennessy Louis Vuitton) sells luxury goods such as wine, clothing, jewellery and cosmetics under its namesake brands as well as using brand names such as Dom Pérignon, Fendi, and Marc Jacobs. In international market, the company sells exclusive leather products using multiple brand names such as Louis Vuitton, Fendi, Donna Karan, Loewe, Marc Jacobs, Celine, Kenzo, Givenchy, Thomas Pink, Pucci, Berluti, Stefanobi, and Rossimoda to maintain its luxury brand positioning and international diversity. In the automobile sector multiple branding is very common. The General Motor of USA used multiple branding strategy to gain marketing advantage in lucrative foreign markets like China. The oversized brand portfolio of GM consisted of about a dozen automotive brands. But the company was not satisfied. GM further announced plans to introduce a new localised single country car brand for the Chinese market. However, this is not the case with Toyota and BMW which appear to act economically by using simple brand architecture while invading foreign country markets.

and resorted to mixed branding because of the target consumers' unfamiliarity with the corporate name.

BRAND INTERNATIONALISATION: PROBLEMS

There are various problems associated with internationalisation of brand. An internationalising company requires taking decision on how it would transfer graphics, names, logos, colours, and symbols, constituting the brand identity, in the foreign country to build up the requisite brand image. It also requires the company to decide how it would communicate to its potential consumers for brand building in the foreign country. These communications are important as the 'persona' of the brand is build up in the minds of the potential consumers through these communications only. Effective communication would help the company to develop the requisite distinguishing characteristics of the brand which emotionally attracts the consumers to the product. In a competitive foreign market, therefore, the entrant company faces a number of problems regarding correct positioning of brand. The various problems encountered by a company in this direction are as follows:

Standardisation or adaptation: This is possibly the first problem the internationalising company faces. Companies spend resources in home country to build brand identity and personality for a long period of time and desire to retain the same brand traits across the countries where it enters for marketing the products. This effort of maintaining a standardised appeal in respect of brand, which forms the fundamental building block of a brand itself, poses the first challenge in cross-cultural marketing situations. Adaptation requirement arises from different elements of country-specific culture such as language, religion, values, attitude, manners/customs, material culture, education, aesthetics, and social institutions. The company requires deciding correctly on the issues regarding standardisation or adaptation of the home-grown brand. Extending Barbie brand of Mattel Inc. of US to Arab countries is an example to this effect. Mattel Inc of USA had to put serious thought on adaptation of Barbie brand for Arab countries in order to capture market there.

Level of adaptation: The required level of adaptation of brand image and personality in different countries is also a concern. If the brand becomes candidate for country-specific total adaptations to suit the requirement of different cultures then it would be difficult for the company to project multiple images for multiple countries or even a global image. However, in certain countries, some cursory adaptation may be required, which the company would not mind much. The level of adaptation problem becomes acute when a company handles multi-brand in multiple countries with different image projections. Therefore, deft handling on deciding the required level of assimilation and standardisation or adaptation thereof becomes extremely crucial in international brand management. It is needless to say that companies going to another country for taking advantage of the outstanding growth opportunities would be desperate for optimum brand positioning. Hence, they would go all out to ensure that the brand adequately lends its support to the products while they are marketed in foreign countries. The higher level of adaptation would entail higher cost as well as risk of spending but not achieving the desired result in foreign market. Adaptation of J.K Rowling's Harry potter brand in China is an example to this effect as the books had to be rewritten to remove 'wizardry' content and replace with 'magic content' to comply with country dictum.

Foreign country awareness: It may so happen that the target consumers in the foreign market/markets are not at all aware of the brand name of the entrant company, and hence, the product may fail to create a brand-led credibility in the minds of the targeted consumers in the new countries. The Scorpio brand of Mahindra and Mahindra faced all unknown situation in US market when introduced and had a tough time in deciding about the exact marketing communication for the target customers. The US consumers found totally in dark about the Indian brand name Scorpio.

Different expectations: The customers' expectations are greatly varying in different countries creating imbalance in the brand standardisation/adaptation approach. This may put the company in difficult position to satisfy different customers differently in different countries.

Emotional connect: Cross-cultural differences across countries may not permit the entrant company to compete with its local competitors along emotional dimensions. The local brands are expected to enjoy better emotional connect with the local consumers. Kinley brand of Coca-Cola had a difficult time while competing with local Bisleri brand in Indian market. The entrant company brand evoking lesser emotions in target country may face customer loyalty issues.

Communication mix effectiveness: The unique positioning enjoyed by a brand in the domestic market may not be easily transferred to the foreign country markets. This may be simply because the elements of the communications mix are not equally effective in all the country markets similarly and hence the home country positioning could not be transferred easily in the new market. For example, Dove brand from Unilever failed to position the theme of 'beauty concept' in African countries because the required elements of communication mixes to build up the concept could not be marshalled there with efficiency. You tube based advertising of Dove could not be run because of poor internet penetration. Personal selling as strategy is not very effective in Japan because of cultural reason as Japanese consumers may consider them as intrusion to the privacy of an individual. Stealth advertising is actively discouraged in many developed countries.

Brand Image Transfer

As per Keller[7], brand image is the perceptions of the potential consumer about a brand as reflected by the brand associations held in consumer memory. Transfer of the right brand image to a target country is an essential requirement associated with internationalisation. If the requisite brand

[7] Keller, K. (2003), "Strategic brand management: Building, measuring, and managing brand equity", Upper Saddle River, NJ: Prentice-Hall

image is transferred to the destination country then it can lend its image to the products offered in the international market for ensuring marketing success. However, the effectiveness of brand image transfer depends on the mental process of the target customer of the destination country to a great extent. An entrant company, therefore, plan brand image transfer process after careful analysis of destination market condition. The case of IKEA, the great Swedish multinational company dealing with ready -to-assemble furniture, can be an example in this direction. IKEA started internationalisation way back in 1963 by adopting an international marketing strategy of presenting itself identical to its Swedish brand image in every country. This involved image transfer to the destination countries in a standardised manner. Proceeding in line with this pre decided strategy, IKEA initiated the process of image transfer actively by disseminating all sorts of standardised information about the company to the target markets. The objective was to build up standardised image of the Swedish company in the minds of the foreign consumers. According to Edvardsson and Edquist[8] this was a big challenge to IKEA in terms of its ability to transfer standardised brand image to destination country and their acceptability by the foreign consumers. The entry to China in the year 1998 and re-entry to Japan during 2006 were the toughest challenge. In both the cases the challenge was huge because of existence of high cultural dissimilates between the countries. IKEA took up the stiff challenge boldly and started actively sharing standardised information on different aspects about the company such as store image, product quality, company service standard, standard pricing system, product delivery ease, country of origin, etc., with the Chinese and Japanese customers. In the process IKEA noticed that in China, a brand name with a nice meaning had a special place in the perceptive domain of the consumers. The company observed that, in the past, brands with good meaning fast occupied the minds of the prospective consumers. Accordingly, IKEA analysed its own brand name and its meaning in local language. The IKEA officials were surprised to know that the Chinese name of IKEA (Yi Jia) meant a suitable or comfortable home with a touch of ancient Chinese culture to it. The company was overjoyed as it would be to the advantage of the company in developing right image in China and exactly in line with the IKEA image build up back home in Sweden. Thus, a brand name acceptable and linked with the country's history gave IKEA a good start in the Chinese market. Further, in a pre entry survey of Chinese market, the IKEA official came to know that historically Chinese consumers accepted a brand if the country of origin had requisite status or experience of producing the product. This also delighted the company official because Sweden as a country of wooden artefacts had always earned respect from Chinese consumers. Therefore, the good image of the country of its origin, i.e., Sweden, also contributed to IKEA's standardised brand image transfer. The image of the country, though cannot be directly equated with the image of the company's products, but can influence the consumers' image building process about the brand. Additionally, IKEA, took care to properly find the names of the

[8] Edvardsson, B. and B. Edquist (2002), "The IKEA saga: How service culture drives service strategy", *The Service Industries Journal*, Vol. 22, Issue 4, pp. 153–186.

products in Chinese as it did in home country market. The founder of IKEA Ingvar Kamprad, was particularly keen in naming products with proper names and words to make them easily remembered by the Swedish. While in China the IKEA officials did the same thing and put extra effort on proper transliteration[9] of the product name in Chinese with a local meaning acceptable to the consumers of the country. All these efforts led to the desired result and the brand image of IKEA was transferred to China in a standardised format successfully.

Brand Logo Transfer

Logo is the much needed visual representation of a brand. Logo is an essential component of brand helping to create the much needed brand identity. Logo is not the brand but without logo brand building will be incomplete. Take the example of a famous logo of a global company commonly known as "the Swoosh" This Nike logo represented by a famous single curved line that goes thicker at one end brings the unique selling proposition of the company. The customers all around the world got to know the character of the Nike company as 'Minimalism at its Finest'. While a company is confined to the domestic market, it is natural that it would devise a brand logo based on the native country advantage. It is equally natural that the logo so chosen would be intensely entrenched in the native culture and would convey a carefully chosen meaning in that language. For example, Hawley & Hazel, a Taiwan based company, had a popular toothpaste brand by the name *Darkie* that used to be sold in Asia quite well in markets such as Taiwan, Hong Kong, Singapore, Malaysia, and Thailand. The package featured an image of a wide-eyed, smiling dark-skinned black male wearing a top hat, monocle and bow-tie. The founder of the company while visiting United States fell in love with Al Jolson, then a very popular black-faced entertainer (i.e., a white person with black makeup on his face). The founder decided to re-create the spirit of this character in the form of a trademark logo for his toothpaste because of the character's big smile and white teeth. He loved the person's face so much that he made a determination to make the 'black face with white teeth' as logo for Hawley & Hazel. Thereafter, on his return to Taiwan he copyrighted the name "Darkie" to go along with the logo. As thought of by the founder, 'black face with white teeth' logo was an instant hit. Many people used to remember the 'Darkey' brand because of the logo. Particularly the Asian segment customer started showing loyalty by repeat purchase behaviour because of the brand logo featuring Al Jolson. It is said that a housewife in Taipei one remarked "The toothpaste featuring a Black man with a toothy smile is an excellent advertisement and we buy it because of the Black man's white teeth." Incidentally, because of huge market success, the US multi-national Colgate-Palmolive was interested to acquire the company. When Hawley &. Hazel was acquired in 1985, Colgate-Palmolive wanted to expand the market for the Darkie brand to USA and Europe as well. However, to their surprise, the company found that the logo was not easily transferable to the

[9] Pan,Y. (2005) Marketing Across Cultures: A case study of IKEA Shanghai. Lund: Lund University. Masters Dissertation, Unpublished

new market segment dominated by the white, English-speaking population as they perceived a mental distance with the product name as Darkie or dark colour man. The company had to change the logo and when the logo was changed then the brand name did not carry any meaning. So the company also changed brand name from "Darkie" to "Darlie" along with the 'logotype' to avoid controversy in the face of changing sensibilities regarding race and racism[10]. However, only the English name was changed without effecting the local Chinese name for "Darkie" (pronounced *hak ye nga goh*) which means "Black Man Toothpaste" because the logo seemed to enhance brand loyalty in Chinese market.

Brand Name Transfer

The brand name transfer with its exact meaning to another country has been a very challenging task for the international marketers. A strong name is essentially developed by a marketer for ensuring marketing success in the domestic market first. The brand names are carefully chosen words which can bring immediate value to the brand. Such a name can be a complex symbol but representing a variety of ideas or attributes. The pronunciation of the name can develop a sound and/or its meaning understandable by the target group due to their acquaintance over a long period of time[11]. As companies expand abroad, the marketers desire to retain the same effectiveness and benefit of the brand name as it lend to the product/products when in the home country. This desire brings the requirements of standardisation/adaptation of brand name. The original brand name may not able to provide the desirable association or meaning because of language differences. In a study of a representative sample of 49 Fortune-500 companies with 209 brand names, it was found that a vast majority of companies had to localise their brand names for the Chinese market because they did not carry the desired meaning[12]. A very well known example in this direction has been adaptation of world's most known brand name Coca-Cola in to ke-kou-ke-le in Mandarin and ho-hau-ho-lohk in Cantonese. To this effect the adaptation of brand name "Oil of Olay" to Oil of Ulan in Chinese was no less interesting.

Considering the compulsive requirement of adaptation in a foreign market and the problem associated with reintroducing it to the target consumers a global brand is much sought after by the companies. A global brand name is considered, metaphorically, as all terrain vehicles which would perform a consistent performance across the countries of the world. Simplistically speaking, a global brand conveys the same meaning everywhere and is pronounced similarly across cultures with common positioning in the world irrespective of country differences by sharing the same customer need in same target segment but located in different countries.

---

10 "Colgate to Rename a Toothpaste's Name", *New York Times*, January Published: January 27, 1989

11 Gardner, Burleigh B. and Sidney J. Levy (1955), "The product and the brand", *Harvard Business Review*, Vol. 33, Issue 2, pp. 33–39.

12 Francis, Lam and Walls (2002), "The impact of linguistic differences on international brand name standardisation: A comparison of English and Chinese brand names of Fortune -500 companies". Journal of International Marketing, 10(1), 98 – 116.

There are benefits of such brands through standardisation of brand name, positioning, etc., particularly arising out of economies of scale, consistency and universal company image. This falls perfectly in line with the Professor Ted Levitt's famous observations on standardisation requirements. Therefore, international marketers must first look out for the level of acceptability of the brand name in the target foreign country before thinking of customisation.

Name Customisation: The level of customisation also depends on the level of rejection of the foreign brand name in a target foreign country. How can one understand or assess the level of rejection of foreign brand in a foreign country? The answer is simple. This can be done through developing an understanding of the target customers in the foreign country in relation to the brand name by studying the following four parameters.

(1) **Offensiveness:** A brand name upon translation in to another language may not be acceptable to the people speaking the same language because of vulgarity associated with the translated word. Sometimes the translated name link itself up with a particular image, etc., which generally the potential consumers do not like to recall or remember. Therefore, it is required to assess the possible offensiveness resulting from the word meaning.

(2) **Meaning:** A brand name is likely to be accepted by the target group if the translated meaning of the brand name in the foreign country language finds its suitability with the products. Hence it is required to understand the appropriateness of idiomatic fit of the translated name of the product or company in the foreign country situation.

(3) **Easy to remember:** Some brand names are very easy to remember. For example, brand name Santa Clara University is a memorable name which can be remembered easily by English Speaking people. Hence it is necessary to bring out the difficulty in memorising the brand name in that target country.

(4) **Linguistic ease:** The brand awareness, brand building efforts, ease of pronunciation of the foreign brand name, etc., can be gauged by the level of linguistic ease of the brand name in the language of the other country. Three linguistic components of a brand name facilitate consumers to recognise and create a distinct identity in their minds and if these three components are different then brand name may have to undergo customisation. These three linguistic components are: phonology, morphology, and semantics.

Phonology of brand name: It is important to know how the brand name, when introduced to another country, is pronounced. Does the type of the sound differ and give a different meaning in the foreign language? If the sound differs, is that different sound able to maintain the phonetic features which it had in the original version? This is almost like the care that has to be taken when poems are translated and read in another language. The translator of Spanish poem in Hindi does the job of alliterations to keep the original expressiveness of the Spanish poet and if the translator is successful then the translated poem would attract Hindi speaking listeners.

The translated brand name in the same way may sound odd to the listener. A new sound when pronounced in a foreign language required to convey the same meaning, evokes the same emotions and communicates the underlying essences of the brand. For example, the brand when pronounced in English may convey a pleasing sound but that pleasing effect may be missed when pronounced by a customer of another country. The famous case of English brand name Coca-Cola's pronunciation in Chinese may be referred here as an example. Sensing trouble in phonetic conversion of the brand name Coca-Cola appointed an expert for making the Chinese translation of Coca-Cola. This led to pronunciation of Coca-Cola into "kekoukele" in Mandarin and ho- hou-ho-lohk in Cantonese in order to maintain the phonetic requirements. Peugeot is a major French car brand and the second largest carmaker based in Europe with rare presence in India. In India, general consumers face considerable difficulty in pronouncing the name as 'Poo-zjoe'. It is the same thing with the beverage brand 'Schweppes' in terms of correct pronunciation in India. After a long presence in Indian market, Indian customers had overcome the problem with Korean Hyundai in pronouncing the name with pleasing effect. In contrast, some brand names have easy accessibility in other languages too. For example, a brand name like Nokia has a sonic interaction that is quick and easy to pronounce by Indians too. Dove, the beauty soap brand from P&G, sounds softer to the Indian and hence is easily accepted throughout the country. Therefore, when brands travel to foreign countries, the principles of phonetics provides the much needed clue to understand the standardisation/adaptation issues related to the brand.

Morphology of brand name: In linguistics the morphemes are the smallest meaning-bearing units of a language. If transliterated properly, brand name Coca-Cola in Mandarin will have four morphemes: (1) ke, (2) kou, (3) ke, and (4) le. These morphemes are very simple and easy to write down with only four simple characters[13]. The English name of Coca-Cola also has the four morphemes: (1) co, (2) ca, (3) co, and (4) la. Now, the problem is that none of the four morphemes used in English has meaning. But each of the four morphemes in Mandarin has more than one meaning. 'ke' means 'to permit' or 'be able'; 'kóu' means 'mouth' or 'hole' or 'pass'; 'ké' means 'same as first 'and 'lè' means 'joy', or 'to be happy'. The more the morphological differences across languages, the more would be the difficulty in conveying the same understanding coming out of a word, say, the brand name. Therefore, morphological differences across languages create differences in meaning. In the context of brand name, it is related to the length of the brand name, including issues such as how words are combined, compounded, abbreviated, affixed, or blended[14].

Semantics of brand name: Semantics refers to the collective meaning of all the words in linguistic units, i.e., word, sentences or texts. The underlying meaning of the linguistic units, i.e., word, sentences or texts is very important as a company would like to convey a certain meaning through the

[13] Shiyang Ran (2010), "Chinese translation of Coca-Cola: Analysis and enlightenment", *Asian Culture and History*, Vol. 2, No. 1.

[14] Huang, Yue Yang and Allan K.K. Chan (1997), "Chinese brand naming: From general principles to specific rules", *International Journal of Advertising*, Vol. 16, No. 4, pp. 320–35.

brand name. Research suggests that meaningful brand names are recalled to a greater extent than meaningless ones[15]. It is, therefore, important to understand the collective meaning of the brand name in another language from the marketing point of view. Let us take some examples where companies were lucky. NIKE means "Victory" in Greek; so the name has been used by the company producing running shoes and other athletic wear to indicate victory in athletic events. The semantic translation of Nike in Chinese ('Nai ke' in Chinese) leads to the meaning "Enduring and Persevering." The American company did not dislike the semantic meaning altogether because the new Chinese meaning adjusts well with the product. In the same way Proctor & Gamble (P&G) found to be lucky with semantic meaning of Pantene shampoo. The semantic translation of Pentene in Chinese ('pan-ting' in Chinese) leads to the meaning "slim and graceful woman" The product brand name in Chinese found to be suited well for the marketing purpose of P&G. The same is the case with semantic translation of Rolls-Royce ('Laosi-Laisi' in Chinese) leads to the meaning "labor and plants" that more or less fit with the marketing purpose of the company. But all were not that lucky. The well-known British Johnson Company with popular brand 'Mr Muscle' for surface cleaners was surprised to know that semantic meaning of it brand in Chinese was 'Mr Chicken Meat'. Peugeot, the major French car brand, got the brand name from the family name of the person who founded the car company. This name became the brand name 'Biao zhi' which sounded like the Chinese slang for "prostitute" (biaozi).

Box 8.3 Brand names in China

Internationalising companies are now aware of the problem faced by Coca-Cola in China while trying to find a close phonetic equivalent, "ko-kou-ko-le," which loosely translated as "happiness in the mouth." Microsoft got terribly saddened when they came to know that its 'Bing' search engine name, in Chinese, meant "disease," "defect" and "virus". They quickly understood that with this meaning the search engine would face rough weather and hence considered changing the name of the search engine to 'Bi ying', which roughly means "responds without fail." Many other companies looking to bring their products to China have had to face similar problem. Examples such problems of the internationalising companies related to brand name and their meaning in the new foreign language are many. The problem is somewhat acute in China. This has led Western companies to take a cautious approach while opening their brand in China. Any naming mishap may ruin the market ambition with serious financial consequences, given the fact that China's market for consumer goods is growing by more than double-digit figure annually and luxury-goods sales, by 25%. In competitive Chinese market keeping a weak point open means you are allowing competitors to build advantage. Therefore, to avoid any such naming mishaps, internationalising companies need to do some homework before entry to the market to understand correctly whether their brand name resonates well with the local consumers or not. The Western companies in China take the help of local consultants to carry out linguistic analyses to ensure that the brand name trickles down through Mandarin and Cantonese ear equally well. This is a difficult job on the ground that the internationalising companies do not want their original name should be disturbed. At the same time it must convey the essence of taste and fun in the foreign language in the same way as it did through its original name in the originating country. In China, the level of difficulty is multiplied when the internationalising companies also want to ensure that two major languages of China, Mandarin and Cantonese, are equally taken care off while pronouncing their original brand name. Therefore, to provide an impressive translation of the brand name, the companies or their local consultants need to do

[15] Robertson, Kim (1989), "Strategically desirable brand name characteristics", *Journal of Consumer Marketing*, Vol. 6, No. 4, pp. 61–71.

a lot of research before suggesting for name change or alterations. Here, after a lot of research, the foreign companies operating in China understood that there are three options for them. One, translate the original name to find a suitable Chinese name that convey appropriate thing in Chinese; two, do not disturb highly established brand names whose name are already associated with prestige; and three, be local in China by taking a local name that is very close to the Chinese ear.

Examples of the first alternative are many. Consider the case of Unilever's Tide detergent whose Chinese name Taizi came out well as it literally mean "gets rid of dirt." Reebok, need to be pronounced as 'Rui bu', to mean "quick steps." Colgate got its name as 'Gao lu jie' which translates into "revealing superior cleanliness." Lay's snack food became 'Le shi' to mean "happy things." The English name Nike had to be 'Nai ke' and German abbreviation BMW as 'Bao Ma' to sound nice and clear in the German names.

Example of the second alternative also includes some big names. For example, Cadillac car or Hilton Hotel, having a huge reputation behind their names, did not want to compromise with it. These brands, Cadillac (Ka di la ke), or Hilton (Xi er dun) chose phonetic translations that mean nothing in Chinese. Rolls-Royce or 'Laosi-Laisi' includes two Chinese characters for "labour" and "plants" that have no relation with automobile but allowed the car to retain the prestigious foreign ancestry.

Companies that opted for the third alternative are strong believers of the fact that when you have long-term ambitions in a country market it is better to be localised with the brand name. A local name would communicate the brand image in a better way than a mere collection of homonyms. Consider the example of Citibank or Marriot Hotel. The Citibank's Chinese name 'Hua qi yinhang' carried with it more deserving meaning as it literally means "star-spangled banner bank". Marriott's Chinese name, 'Wan hao', meaning "10,000 wealthy elites" can do a lot of good things for the hotel as it conveys some accurate meaning to the local consumers. Marvel comics of England had to convert the name to "Man wei" with the meaning "comic power" which nicely conveyed to the Chinese about the strength of the comic book publishers who gave the world superhero comic characters such as Hulk, Spider-Man, etc. Mercedes, BMW, and even Kia had to fall in the line of localisation of their brand name in their desire to include reference to a horse in their automobile brand names as it would then provide them an advantage of bringing an automatic reference to strength. Thus, Kia's sedan is named "Qian li ma" conveying a meaning of "thousand-kilometre horse," in Chinese.

Source: The New York Times, November 12, 2011

Brand Portfolio Transfer

Brand portfolio: It is the number of brands the company offers to its customers in a country. A company deploys a number of brands to woo the customers in different segments and maximise market coverage.

Brand architecture: A company strategically decides and constitutes the brand portfolio so that the deployment of brands and management of multiple brands brings best result for the company not only in terms of maximisation of sale but for minimisation of cost as well. It also pays careful attention to ensure that there is minimum brand overlap while deciding number of brands to exist in the portfolio. Brand architecture of a company, therefore, refers to the strategic positioning of the brand portfolio of the company to achieve the best marketing result in a competitive scenario. Brand architecture management refers to the strategic attempt of the company to diminish customer uncertainty by positioning its assortment of brands in a way that makes it easy for customers to look out for their preference and also to understand what the company has to offer for them.

International brand architecture: It is the multi country brand architecture of a company strategically designed to maximise the marketing opportunity in every country in particular and its entire geographical spread as a whole. Simplistically speaking, a company with multi-country presence is required to decide its optimum brand architecture across the countries of its presence to maximise profit and minimise cost of nurturing these brands. A judicious balance of all the different brands, the company had in its kitty, is required to achieve the synergetic marketing result as whole for the company. For example, a company may think of constituting brand architecture for its international operation of 50 countries with 100 brands, 60 being local, 30 regional and 10 global brands. Also out of these 100 brands, 50 may be product brands, 40 family brands and 10 may be corporate brands. At the next level, the company may decide on country-specific brand architecture. It may decide to cover all 50 countries of its presence with the same brand architecture. On the other extreme, the company may strategically decide to have country-specific brand architecture. For example, the company may decide to present a judicious mix of different types of brands based on country attractiveness and acceptances for its brands. The beauty cosmetics company L'Oreal entered the Asian country markets with only four brands in 1997 but its brand architecture was found to be comprised of over 20 brands in 2012. Table 8.2 indicates country specific brand architecture of L'Oreal in respect of three Asian countries.

As it can be seen from the Table 8.2 that the 2012 brand architecture of L'Oreal consisted of 14 brands for India, 17 brands for Thailand and 20 brands for China. The mass-market brands of the company such as Maybelline and Garnier were available in all the three countries. In fact, the company could get maximum benefits of these brands in China. The company made Maybelline available in more than 300 cities of China with the adaptation of the product according to the Chinese condition. At the same time the company reinforced it brand wagon with luxury brand Giorgio Armani and Lancome in these three countries to take advantage of the money power of the neo rich population. In China both the products were made available in more than 70 cities for the niche segment of customers. Local brand Yue-Sai, acquired by the company in 2004, served the requirement of ethnocentric customers in China as well as Thailand but not in India. Yue-Sai brand was build with the tall claim that the company have studied, in depth, the Chinese skin fundamentals and is therefore very close to the locals. Shu Uemura, the Japanese origin brand, was positioned in China and Thailand as new UV protection device for women but not in India. In order to garnish the brand architecture more, L'Oreal

Table 8.2 L'Oréal Brands in three Asian markets as of 2012

S. No.	L'Oréal Brands	Available in		
		India	China	Thailand
1.	L'OréalParis	Yes	Yes	Yes
2.	Garnier	Yes	Yes	Yes
3.	MaybellineNewYork	Yes	Yes	Yes
4.	Lancôme	Yes	Yes	Yes
5.	Kiehl's	Yes	Yes	Yes
6.	RalphLauren	Yes	Yes	Yes

(Continued)

Table 8.2 (*Continued*)

S. No.	L'Oréal Brands	Available in		
		India	China	Thailand
7.	GiorgioArmani	Yes	Yes	Yes
8.	Diesel	Yes	Yes	No
9.	L'OréalProfessional	Yes	Yes	Yes
10.	Matrix	Yes	Yes	Yes
11.	KérastaseKéraskin	Yes	Yes	Yes
12.	Esthetics	Yes	Yes	No
13.	Biotherm	No	Yes	Yes
14.	Helena Rubinstein	No	Yes	No
15.	Vichy	Yes	Yes	Yes
16.	La Roche Posay	Yes	Yes	Yes
17.	Mini Nurse	No	Yes	No
18.	Skinceuticals	No	Yes	No
19.	Shu Uemura	No	Yes	Yes
20.	Yue Sai	No	Yes	Yes
21.	Cacharel	No	No	Yes
22.	Victor and Rolf	No	No	Yes
	Total brand	14 brands	20 brands	17 brands

Source: Author's compilation from Web site

introduced a brash newcomer brand Kiehl's again in China and Thailand but not in India. This created a stir with its move into China as 'American cosmetics' which allowed the company in maximising its benefit. Three other L'Oreal brands, namely L'Oreal Paris, L'Oreal Professional, and Vichy were made available in three countries to serve big segments such as hair salons, dermo-cosmetics, make-up, and facial skincare in all the three country cosmetics market.

It is a challenging task to create the brand architecture for a country by including different types of brands. Experience suggests that companies prefer to maintain an ideal global–local balance as well as product–corporate balance. A company like Unilever has always kept the best-known local brand intact in national markets. Miko in France, Wall's in the United Kingdom, and Agnesi in Italy are the examples to this effect. L'Oreal also pursued the right balance of global – local by adopting double-branding strategy in which Maybelline is the global brand name and another name is the local brand. For example, the company markets Gemey–Maybelline in France, BB–Maybelline in China, and Jade–Maybelline in Germany.

Optimum brand mix

How to decide the optimum brand mix for a multi–brand international company for country market? An international company needs to consider many aspects that can create a real challenge for marketing manager in deciding the exact combination of different types of brands. The objective of achieving optimum level in brand mix would be to reduce the possibilities of not meeting the aspirations of the targeted segments in comparison to the nearest competitors but at a least cost. The following points can guide a company, in general terms, in this direction:

1. **Segment aspiration:** The entrant company needs to think about the ways to satisfy the requirements of the targeted segments in a foreign country market. Mapping of aspiration level in the perceptual domain of different segments to cater would be an important task. This can be done through laddering interview of the segment representatives and linking desired attribute requirements with their value system.
2. **Hierarchical relationship:** How the hierarchical relationships between corporate, family, and products brands are working in the brand architecture of the company? The manager needs to take a close look at this aspect to avoid overlap and clarity in representing them to the customers.
3. **Brand mix:** How many product, family, and corporate brands need to be introduced from time to time? What will be the right mix of local and global type? It may be required to load the market with some exclusive brands carrying corporate names in order to dismiss competition from local players. The company in the foreign market may consider acquiring some local brands from small local players. The objective here is to make an optimum team of brands with a judicious mix of global and local type which will perfectly fit in dealing with the target customers' aspirational requirements.
4. **Rationalisation:** The steps 1, 2, and 3 provides a clear understanding about the requirements at the consumers' front and exactly what the company can offer. At this stage, therefore, company may pull brands of different types to cover the aspirational dimension of the consumers. In addition, the company may be required to phase out brands, reposition some brand as premium or low-cost one, and lend corporate brand to strengthen product or family brand with the intention of establishing itself in the market better that the competitors. However, an important consideration at this juncture would be the cost to be incurred in nurturing the brands in the country market. The optimum brand mix would be a judicious mix of different types of brands which will make a right balance between the marketing requirements and cost of brand nurturing for a country market. For an international company manager, it would be natural desire to have as many brands as possible to achieve the marketing objective. Interestingly, more the uncertainties associated with the market place, the more would be the desire of the manager to pull more brands in country market. However, it should be remembered that every brand maintained in the country market needs nourishment from time to time in order to keep them alive and active in the minds of the consumers. This involves a huge expenditure. Therefore, the brand mix needs to be a rationalised one. It should be consolidate and yet have the versatility of strengthening the role of individual brands.

5. **Consistency check:** Consistency in the brand mix is desired to achieve competitiveness. Too much change of brand positioning in accordance with the requirement difference of different countries reduces the consistency. The international manager may feel for requirements of changing logo, tag line, etc., for the country market to move more close to the customer, but it would lead to inconsistency, resulting in loosing the support of the global image of the company as a whole. This is because brand inconsistency would disturb the process of brand identity formation overtime. The same brand positioned as luxury brand in one country and commodity type in another would hurt the consistency formation and move the whole company away from its global positioning ambition in course of time. The case of Nestle may illustrate the point here. The strategy managers of Switzerland based Nestlé Company was started worrying about the number of brands it amassed during a long global journey. The pressure of maintaining about 8000 brands was huge. Straightway deleting brands would have detrimental effect on the company revenue as well. Nestlé wanted to reorganize its brands based on the principles of consistency. The company put a conscious effort to provide common brand name to similar products, provided corporate endorsement, repositioned of non-consistent ones, etc., in order to consolidate and bring consistency in the identity of the Nestlé brand. Nestlé attempted to connect its products such as infant cereals, baby food and infant formula, powdered, condensed, and refrigerated milk products, chocolate, confectionery, breakfast cereals, and ice-cream with Nestlé brand only when such corporate endorsement of these products enhanced the Nestlé image and not on based on what Nestlé brings to these products. In course of time, the result started pouring in and the company started earning about 40% of its total turnover from products covered by the Nestlé corporate brand, which in a sense indicate that effort of bringing consistency worked for the company. However, some of the products which achieved distinct identity in some country markets were excluded without the corporate endorsement. For example, Nestlé did not combine the Nestlé brand with Buitoni, because it represents the authentic Italian lifestyle for country Italy.
6. **Implementation check:** Surely, an active consideration of possible brand mix in the foreign market would be to reduce the possibility of developing inefficiencies. However, the market complexities and the dynamic nature of competition may make pre-plan ineffective in actual practice and pose a challenge to the managers. Therefore, it is necessary to check practical efficiency of the decided brand mix initially by marshalling them in one of the strategic city or town of the targeted country first.

Factors Affecting Brand Performance for SMEs

The small and medium enterprises (SMEs) suffer the most in foreign countries because of lack of effective brand that can be showcased for the foreign customers. The national level brand of many SMEs performs well within the national market but usually fail to do so in the foreign soil. Initially, in the first phase of internationalisation, the products are first time exposed to foreign consumers. However, the products seem to remain unaccepted by the new target consumers. The brand accompanying the product would also suffers from marketing wilderness and fails to provide distinct identity to the exported product. Therefore, it is logical to decide to export the brand along with the product seems to be a wise decision, but the success of such decision is not assured. Many a time, the exporter cannot gather the necessary courage and establish the domestic brand in foreign market causing distress sale and less profit generation. The various factors affecting brand performance of SMEs are as follows:

Management orientation

This is an internal factor and remains within the company. The SME management's emphasis remains primarily on internationalisation process and ambition to earn increasingly more revenue from foreign market sans the decision of brand building in foreign market. The management places importance on its internationalisation process but not on the brand building process. General perception is that the brand development is related to the large enterprises, and the small enterprises, therefore, remain non-committal towards branding in foreign market. A non-committed company would not believe in developing a long–term strategy towards internationalisation and brand building thereof. Generally, people in the management level of SMEs do not consider the fact that higher profit generation in foreign country can only be possible through sale of branded product only and not through becoming the supplier of unbranded products to the big foreign retailers.

Financial commitment: The management would not try to assess the financial involvement associated with brand creation in the foreign market. Since brand identity and image are to be created in the minds of the foreign consumers, so it has substantial financial involvement. In some cases, the financial involvement becomes bigger than certain self-determined benchmark of a SME manager, which makes proceeding in the forward direction impossible. In some cases, half-hearted efforts are made which again prove to be insufficient to the actual requirements. So, the size of the financial commitment for the brand building should be big, while internationalising dampens the momentum of the branding building effort in the foreign market.

Supports from experts: Availability of experienced in-house managers/ experts for handing foreign branding process, etc., is vital. Most of the time, managers with traditional orientation will look for direct relationship between the financial resources spent and their impact on sales volume in foreign country. But, brand building effort in the initial stage is understandably very sluggish and requires time to occupy the minds of the targeted customers. It is difficult for the SMEs to recruit well-versed international brand manager to drive the entire programme of brand building.

Research on the host market

This relates to the external factors. How is the foreign market structure in the particular sector of entry? What are the consumers' needs and to what extent are they different or similar to the domestic country? What is the level of competition and buyers' intensity and density in the target market? What type of distribution channel is expected on entry? The answer to this factor will help to decide on the brand positioning and the required intensity of its development. The analysis of legal factors of the host country is also a must in order to assess the legal space the brand can enjoy while communicating its identity to the target foreign customers. However, many SMEs do not create necessary research-based understanding about the foreign consumers while internationalising in spite of long-time presence in the country through exporting.

Cultural factors

It is essential to understand the cultural factors of the target foreign country market at this stage correctly. This is required for assessing the adaptation or modification required in the brand attributes. A very dissimilar country in terms of cultural attributes would have cultural distance, which the brand requires to overcome. Therefore, it is important to understand to what extent the cultural factors are strong and differentiated in the target market than the domestic market. What translation or transliteration requirements for the brand name or the product name in the destination country language? SMEs generally are weak in understanding the cultural complexities of doing business in a culturally dissimilar country.

Home country position

It is well documented in the literature of international marketing that the country of origin (COO) or country of manufacturing (COM) affects the brand performance in the foreign country. A well-known COO; for the product under internationalisation would have quick acceptance for the brand name. For technical products, the COM matters much than the COO, hence, for such products, if the home country is different than the COM, then also brand building will be affected in the foreign country. Hence, SMEs of developing countries remain at the disadvantageous position in the developed country market even if they initiate a well-structured brand building effort in foreign land.

Brand Positioning in Foreign Countries

Brand positioning is the most critical part in the international brand creation process. It requires a marketing strategy which allows the entrant brand to occupy a distinct position in the minds of the target consumers in the foreign country. This distinct position must be in relation to the competing brands. The process involves a series of actions stated below.

1. **Segment analysis:** Typically the initiation is made in this direction by critically ascertaining the segment of consumers targeted by the entrant company. The segment variables such as demographic, psychographic, benefit, etc., are required to be clearly understood in the foreign market condition. This is a very critical and important task as the foundation of the entire analysis would be based on the segment analysis carried out at this stage. This stage also allows finding out the need parameters of

the segment in general and as well in particular to the product category offered by the company.

2. **Product attribute analysis:** The product on offer was actually developed considering the requirement of the country of origin. Naturally the product will be expected to have all its attributes developed as per the origin country standards or requirement, both tangible as well as intangible. The product component analysis discussed in the previous chapter would be very handy in listing the product attributes, tangible and intangible, exist in the product/products on offer to the target country customer segment. At this stage the analyst also need to take in to cognizance the product attributes of the nearest competitors in the target country market and understand how they have successfully crafted the products attributes, tangible and intangible, in to the product to make them attractive to the target country consumers. In the intangible part, the product required to provide requisite experience to the foreign customer. For example, if the product is beer and effort is made to capture the intangible component associated with the concerned product. The American will drink beer in open pub. In India, beer may be consumed during party-time but in USA, it can be treated as a regular drink even when there is no party. Beer may be a common drink for dinner for the Swedish. In a way, this indicates that products will have many intangible attributes which required to be captured successfully based on the usage convention. The intangible attributes may be affected by the difference of cultural convention as well. This is also very important because cultural different between the host country and home country may affect the brand appeals to the consumers. For example, the target country consumers may be may sensitive to the uncertainties of life culturally. It is therefore important to bring changes in the outer layers of the product component. The attribute 'warranty period' may be extended suitably to enhance the brand appeal to the targeted customers. The brand may be required to appeal differently to the prospective consumers of different countries involving change in the product attributes both in tangible part as well as intangible part. The product Volkswagen Beetle car is expected to satisfy the need of exclusiveness for the Japanese but not for Americans. The French wine may satisfy the esteem need for Indians but it is a day-to-day drink for the French people. The product attribute analyse must capture these intangible component associated with the product correctly. Brands that are closer to the consumer's need in the host country, both tangible and intangible wise, are likely to succeed and build positive perception in the minds of the prospective consumers.
3. **Gap identification:** In this stage attention is require to be paid to understand of the gap between the target segment requirements and suitability of the existing attributes. It may be noted here that when Mahindra & Mahindra offered its product Scorpio for the targeted American consumers this stage led to the identification of 186 products attribute modification requirements. This quantum of gap is generally considered very high and hence this identification of such high gap helps to understand the level of difficulty in brand positioning in the foreign market.
4. **Depth of adaptation:** Once the gap between the requirements and existing attributes are identified it requires for company to understand the

depth of adaptation required. Here, the most usable benchmark against which the adaptation depth can be judged is the adaptation cost. The more adaptations required, the more would be the cost of transforming the national brand into an international brand. Therefore, at this stage one seeks to identify the needed depth of adaptations and their possible impact on marketing potentiality.

5. **Brand constituents transferability:** The home grown brand will be transferred to the foreign market. Hence, it is important to know the implication of transferring the product name, symbol, logo, manufacturer country, character, slogan, etc., in the targeted foreign country context.
6. **Decide on positioning uniqueness:** At this stage the product required from introduction in the target country is known with all its adaptation requirements. At the same time issues regarding brand constituents transferability are also known. The manufacturing department of the company now will be producing products as per the management accepted possible modifications requirements and would be despatched to the target country. At this juncture the marketing department will come up with the three perceptual maps displaying the perceptions of representative potential customers of target country about product, brand, and company. The perception map of the product allows the marketer to understand how the existing competitive products are perceived by the potential customers. The perceptual map of existing brands will through light on the unique identity of each brand positioned in the market. The third perceptual map allows a great understanding on the existing companies producing the products and their representation in the minds of potential consumers. With the attributes known for the adapted product of the entrant company and perception of the potential consumers, the marketer will be able to identify a unique positioning of the brand on transfer. Based on these understanding the advertising theme and message will be developed.
7. **Deciding on the Media use:** As always, selection of appropriate media plays a big role in brand communication. How conventionally the brands or products under the brand name are exposed to the public in the target country required to be explored. Jewellery brand will try to get in telecast during soap opera time conventionally in India. Legal restrictions are also required to be known at this juncture regarding media use in the target country. For example, alcohol advertisements are not shown in India as per legal restriction. So, it is important to know the legal side as well the convention of media use followed in the target country. The media budget of the entrant company will be another big factor at this juncture and can have influence on actual media use. For example, Mahindra & Mahindra while introducing Scorpio brand in USA decided not to use television commercial and depend mostly on hand out circulations amongst the prospective buyers. The company came to know from the perception mapping of the potential consumers that Americans do not believe that the Indian company possesses updated automobile technology. Hence, the company wanted the potential customers first test drive the automobile by themselves and then buy them out. Also the company had limited budget for media use and hence both the factors together influenced the media use.

Box 8.4 China's local brands preparing for a showdown with global brands

The automobile sector of China is the biggest in the world. In the market there are two types of brands- local automobile brands and foreign global brands. Invariably all the big name of automobile made their presence felt in Chinese market to take the benefit of market size. Over the years the local manufactures such as SAIC Motor, Dongfeng Motor Group, FAW Group, Changan Automobile, Brilliance Automotive, BYD, Geely, Chery, Guangzhou Automobile Group, BAIC Group, etc., remained active in manufacturing automobiles mainly for meeting local demand with home grown brand. Four local manufacturers namely, SAIC, Chang'an Motors, FAW Group, and Dongfeng Motor excelled better than the others and came to known as 'Big Four' in the automobile parlance of China. SAIC or Shanghai Automotive Industry Holding Co, led the 'big four' pack with production of around 4.5 million automobile during 2014. BAIC motors (Beijing Automotive Industry Holding Co) with Beijing brand, though out of 'Big Four' group but still managed to produce around 2.25 million automobile during 2014. Big or small, one of the major characteristics of the Chinese automobile companies was that they remained crazy about foreign manufacturing collaboration throughout. For example, Chang'an currently participates in joint ventures with Suzuki of Japan and Ford of USA. SAIC participates in cooperative efforts with General Motors of USA and Volkswagen of Germany. The state owned FAW group which crossed the production of 2.7 million vehicles during 2014 has manufacturing collaboration with Toyota motor of Japan. BAIC has manufacturing collaboration with both Daimler and Hyundai. Though market size of automobile sector grew leaps and bounds but local manufactures were worried about subdued craze about the home grown Chinese branded automobiles in China. This casted a shadow of doubt on the future propects and hence were looking for a suitable strategy to boost brand image. For example, some Chinese automakers have brought in star designers from abroad. BAIC hired Leonardo Fioravanti, who designed the Ferrari Daytona, as chief design officer. BMW's (BMW) China partner, Brilliance China Automotive Holdings, lured Dimitri Vicedomini from Italian design house Pininfarina. As part of the expansive strategy the BAIC had gone ahead to recruit more dealers across the country to increase sales. But to its surprise there was very lukewarm response even after making a pretty generous offer of about $ 1 million subsidy to the entrepreneur willing to open dealership agency for BAIC. The scenario was not very different for other manufacturers of China. However, there was no dearth of takers for automobile dealership seekers in case of these companies' joint ventures with globally reputed automobile brands. There were many dealership seekers even without the subsidy components. Greatly disturbed by the situation, Mr Liu of BAIC quipped "China's indigenous cars are the lowest in the food chain and many consumers are biased against them." The awkward situation made the policy makers in a difficult situation. Three decades of open arm welcome for the reputed foreign automakers to form ventures with domestic manufacturers to build cars in the country, the strategy appears to be failing in one of its key goals. While the policy has attracted investment and created millions of jobs, it has done little to help China build strong car brands of its own. "We have been trying to exchange market access for technology, but we have barely gotten hold of any key technologies in the past 30 years. As a result the local brands could not make the local enthused" says Liao Xionghui, vice president of car and motorcycle maker Lifan Industry Group. Chinese auto brands have lost a quarter of their market share in the past two years as consumers choose vehicles made by foreigners such as General Motors (GM) and Volkswagen (VOW). As many as half of China's 171 local carmakers may go out of business within three years, the state-backed auto association predicts, as foreign brands push into smaller cities. Foreign and joint-venture brands already have captured 63% of the passenger vehicle market domestic brands witnessing their share declining helplessly. "There is a belief... that international brands have more technology, in some cases better craftsmanship," says Joe Hinrichs, president of Ford Motor's (F) Asia-Pacific and Africa region.

Analysts say that the Chinese manufacturers were busy in making joint venture with the globally established automobile brands only for earning manufacturing profits. They almost became the contact manufacture of the great Western and Japanese automobiles companies. In the process, the Chinese indigenous brands neglected the job of brand building both in the local market as well as in the foreign markets. The foreign reputed partners of the Chinese companies not only successfully guarded their updated technology from partners but also did not allow their brand name and fame to touch the Chinese local brands. Capital Markets analyst Jeff Chung described the situation in his own way, "Foreign partners are not willing to transfer their key technology to local partners, and most state-owned companies don't really care that much. Their focus is more on sales volume and a high utilisation rate."

According great known automotive consultant J.D. Power and Associates although Chinese cars have improved considerably over the years the problems lies with the local nameplates. The global brands are in the minds and souls of Chinese consumers. They feel proud and gain social status after owning a foreign branded car. However, time will only say whether the local brands can take up a successful fight with mighty global brands.

Source: *Bloomberg Business Week*, August 30, 2012 and China automobile website.

CHAPTER SUMMARY

1. In a competitive market, all similar products look out for customers. The producers often feel that customers should also look out for the targeted products just as producers look out for targeted customers. When prospective consumers themselves take the initiative to identify the targeted products in a competitive market place then it becomes a winning situation for the producers. This phenomenon can happen for the producers only through effective branding.
2. Brand standardisation, in the international context, means that the company has been able to retain the uniqueness of its brand identity while operating in another country. The strong brand proposition created by the company in its home country would maintain its unique appeal in the foreign country as well. The standardised brand has the same propositions in different countries. The effort of brand building without the requirement of transformation in the countries of its presence would be a good starting point of global branding.
3. An international company maintains different types of brands. They could be based on geographical coverage or product coverage.
4. While domestic brands open up in the international market, it confronts with many problems in terms of market acceptance. These may be broadly categorised to problem of recognition, problem of consistency, problem of emotion and problem of uniqueness.
5. Transferring the brand image to a country is an essential requirement associated with internationalisation and a company needs to execute it with precision through sharing of standardised information with the prospective customers in the foreign country. Similarly, a brand logo based on the native country advantage should be made able to transfer smoothly across the countries. The brand name transfer in international markets is another critical task for the international marketers, as the original brand name may not able to provide the desirable association or meaning because of language differences.
6. Brand portfolio is the number of brands the company is offering the customers in order to maximise market coverage and minimise brand overlap. The aim of the company is to remain effective so that the deployment of brands and management of multiple brands brings the best result for the company not only in terms of maximisation of sale but minimisation of cost as well. The strategic brand architecture management allows a company to minimise customer confusion by positioning its assortment of brands in a way that makes it easy for customers to find what they are looking for and to understand what the company has to offer.
7. However, in spite of the complexities, the principles of parsimony and consistency set the guideline for designing optimal brand architecture in the global market.
8. For optimal brand positioning in the foreign market, the internationalising company has to assess three conventions, namely, conventions of representation, conventions of product experience, media conventions and needs conventions in the host country market.

QUESTIONS FOR REVIEW

Short Answer Questions

1. What is a standardised brand in international marketing context? Explain with example.
2. What is a customised brand in international marketing context? How does it benefit the company?
3. Differentiate between brand and brand identity.
4. State the reasons why you cannot expect a domestic brand to perform in the international market as it does in its own country.
5. Differentiate between product brand and corporate brand
6. Differentiate between local brand and global brand.

Descriptive Questions

7. 'Dabur' of Dabur India Ltd. is a good corporate brand in the Indian context. Identify the countries where the company has its presence internationally and then describe the benefits the company would enjoy if the corporate brand extended to other countries. Do you think that company should also take its product brand abroad? Why or why not? Justify your answer.
8. Godrej Consumer Products entered the Indonesian market by acquiring the household product major Megasari. Investigate the feasibility of launching Godrej's own brands in the Indonesian market. What are the areas the brand manager needs to look at to for taking the decision of launching its own brand in the Indonesian market?
9. What is brand portfolio rationalisation? Why is it required? Describe a framework, with the help of an example, the brand port folio rationalisation process for an international company.
10. "The company should assess consumer feedback to understand perceived difference in the host and home country market before entry with a new brand in the foreign market." Why is it important for a company? How can this be done? Answer with the help of an example.
11. How brand name analysis can be executed before entering to a new market? Why is it important? Answer with the help of examples
12. Dabur of Dabur India Ltd. brand is entering China with Dabur tooth powder. Execute the name analysis through adequate secondary research and comment on its acceptability in China.
13. What is family branding? What are the merits and demerits of family branding in the international market? Answer with the help of examples.
14. How would an FMCG company with presence in about 100 country markets decide on brand portfolio? What are the key factors the company should consider while deciding on the brand port folio? Answer with the help of an example.
15. Visit the Web site of Proctor and Gamble and categorise their brands in the six groups: corporate brand, family brand, product brand, global brand, regional brand and local brand (one country brand). Can you rationalise the brand architecture of Proctor and Gamble if you are given an offer by the company? How you will proceed with the rationalisation?
16. Multinationals such as Unilever Mashreq, Procter & Gamble Egypt SAE, Lord Precision Industries, and other companies hold majority of the share in the Egypt beauty care market with well-known brands such as Dove, Lux, Fair & Lovely, etc. In 2010, Emami (Indian company with about 30 FMCG brands) bought an Egyptian company for 25 crore and entered in to the country market. Emami is also planning to take on the leading brand with its own domestic brands such as Zandu, Fair and Handsome, Navaratna oil, and Boro plus, which are very popular in India. What are the factors the international marketing manager will look into while extending the domestic brands into the competitive Egypt market?

EXERCISES

1. Install a secondary research to understand the internationalisation process of corporate brand McDonald of USA. How did McDonald brand enter into the different countries in the initial years and subsequently? Highlight the problems the company faced throughout the internationalisation of the brands in different countries. How were the standardisation and adaptation issues handled by the company? List the learning points so that other companies can follow the path while internationalising.
2. Visit the corporate global Web site of Unilever and categorise its brands into corporate, family and product brand. Asses the geographical spread of the brands and re-categorise them into local, regional and global brands. Take 5 countries each from Europe and Asia and find the different categories of brands that are present there. Then, justify their presence from the marketing point of view.
3. Visit a Mandarin language teaching centre in your neighbourhood and interpret the meaning of ten progressive Indian brands such as Godrej, Tata, Narula, Mahindra & Mahindra, Maruti, Bajaj, Adani, Emami, Taj, and Jindal. Assess the possible language-related problems associated with these brand names and tag lines when they internationalise in China. Prepare brand strategy papers individually for each of the brands and submit to the companies as they are preparing for marketing in China.

End Case: Internationalisation of Red Tape Brand[16]

Introduction

In footwear manufacturing, India is an established player where in terms of production value the country is only next to China. India produces over 2 billion pairs of shoes per year, which according to the different estimates, would be around 15% of global footwear production. The country traditionally supports entrepreneurship in the footwear sub-sector through different policy level measures. The sub-sector is competitive both in the local as well as in the international markets. The competitiveness of the industries in the footwear producing subsector is evident from the increasing trend of revenue generated by the producers in the sector. The domestic footwear producers were able to generate 211 billion (INR) in revenue during 2010, which was roughly three times more than that of the 2000 figure. The sub-sector is populated by many small footwear production centres across the length and breadth of the country but the big ones are mainly confined to a few states such as Tamil Nadu, Uttar Pradesh, Punjab, and Delhi. However, the supply chain works very well in the hub-and-spoke model, which eventually helped the country to become the host of many fast-growing footwear industries. While leather shoes and uppers are produced in medium- to large-scale units, sandals and chappals are produced in the household and cottage category. India's footwear industry is majorly dominated by the men's segment, which comprises almost 60% of the local production, although this pattern is changing in these days. Leather-based footwear is the forte of India where its share of global export has increased from 2% in 2004 to 3% in 2008. In the segment of leather footwear parts, its share in global exports was above 4% in 2008.

Footwear – Global Scenario and India's Share

The global import of footwear (made of leather as well as non-leather) increased from US$101.01 billion in 2010 to US$131.74 billion in 2014, growing at a CAGR of 5.45%. During 2014, India's share in the global import was 2.27% which was marked increase from 1.63% during 2010.

Footwear is the engine of growth of the leather industry in India. India's export of leather footwear

[16] The case has been developed by Professor Gautam Dutta solely as a basis for classroom discussion only, on the issues of international branding of Indian companies abroad. This case is not intended to serve as endorsement, source of primary data or illustration of effective or ineffective management.

touched US$2126.78 million in 2014, with a share of 3.67% in global import of leather footwear. Export of leather footwear from India increased manifold over the last four decades. During 2010, India's leather footwear export was valued at US$1341.31 million, constituting 2.76% share in total import of leather footwear (Table 8.3).

Major Markets

During 2014, the main markets for Indian footwear were UK with a share of 16.59%, Germany 13.46%, USA 12.04%, France 6.96%, Italy 6.53%, UAE 5.98%, Spain 4.53%, Netherlands 3.43%, Belgium 2.63%, Poland 2.11%, Somalia 1.44%, and Portugal 1.32%. These 10 countries together accounts for 77.030% share in India's total footwear export. Nearly 90% of India's export of footwear goes to European Countries and the USA. Future growth of Indian footwear in India will continue to be market driven. The European countries and the US are major consumers for the Indian footwear (Table 8.4).

Table 8.3 Export/import of footwear from India in million USD

	2010	2011	2012	2013	2014
Global import of footwear (Leather as well as non-leather)	101,005.98	115,486.68	114,680.77	121,921.45	131,742.08
India's export of footwear(Leather as well as non-leather)	1642.90	2090.54	1958.29	2609.8	2990.73
% Share of India in global import (Leather as well as non-leather)	1.63%	1.81%	1.71%	2.14%	2.27%
Global import of leather footwear	48,557.35	53,950.55	52,569.28	55,404.67	57,918.4
India's export of leather footwear	1341.31	1649.9	1491.84	1964.73	2126.78
% Share of India in global import of leather footwear	2.76	3.06	2.84	3.55	3.67

Source: WITS Data

Table 8.4 India's export of footwear to different countries in USD thousand

Country	2010	2011	2012	2013	2014	% Share (2014)
United Kingdom	320,732	368,341	370,852	451,258	496,044	16.59
Germany	249,415	371,205	271,824	357,391	402,701	13.46
United States of America	137,983	165,637	223,095	305,231	360,173	12.04
France	150,177	165,048	144,555	193,028	208,246	6.96
Italy	216,725	236,110	165,050	192,776	195,173	6.53
United Arab Emirates	40,728	57,237	65,422	106,734	178,840	5.98
Spain	110,031	122,613	97,567	124,141	135,440	4.53
Netherlands	69,086	103,044	94,574	99,127	102,548	3.43

(*Continued*)

Table 8.4 (*Continued*)

Country	2010	2011	2012	2013	2014	% Share (2014)
Belgium	44,507	74,289	64,704	67,454	78,651	2.63
Poland	14,532	27,892	17,983	39,605	63,171	2.11
Somalia	122	165	194	8461	43,060	1.44
Portugal	24,694	31,252	20,898	29,839	39,621	1.32
Slovakia	17,413	27,569	31,353	36,202	38,196	1.28
Saudi Arabia	12,322	20,249	27,624	29,610	32,860	1.10
Sudan (North + South)	22	390	1635	20,510	32,138	1.07
Others	234,406	319,496	360,960	548,437	583,871	19.52
Total	**16,42,895**	**20,90,537**	**19,58,290**	**26,09,804**	**29,90,733**	**100**

Source: WITS Data

Major Players

Bata is the largest player with around 10% volume share and about 60% market-share in the organised segment. The company has a market share of 70% in the canvas shoes segment while it has a share of 60% in leather shoes. The company competes with Liberty Shoes in the popular segment of the organised market and with regional/local players in unorganised market. Other leading organised sector players are Phoenix International, Action Shoes, Red Tape and Lakhani Shoes. In the backdrop of India's advantageous situation, Mr Irshad Mirza, now a well known entrepreneur, made a modest beginning by setting up his own small-scale tannery in the name Mirza Tanners at Kanpur in 1979 with the full support of his father who was renowned leather technologist during at that time. Mr Mirza got the experience and knowledge of the footwear sector when he was Manager in the 'Bata India Limited' factory at Mokama (Bihar). The sheer attractiveness of the sector provoked Mr Mirza to start the tannery with a meagre capital of ₹25,000 and 40 employees. The one-time small tannery grew by leaps and bounds taking advantage of local and international demand. By 2009, Mirza Tanners Pvt. Ltd had finally grown enough big to be incorporated as a private limited company. Another tannery unit of the Mirza Tanners was set up at Magarwara in Unnao in 1981. The company became a deemed public limited company from 1st July, 1993. Mr Irshad Mirza carefully built up today's Mirza International with focus on export and providing direct and indirect employment of 11,000 people. The thrust for intense internationalisation started after entry of the new generation into the business. Rashid Mirza, son of Mr Irshad Mirza, obtained a Diploma in Leather Technology from UK and was soon inducted into the business as the Managing Director of the company. Mr Tauseef Mirza, younger brother of Rashid Mirza, was also inducted as whole-time Director of Mirza International Ltd during 1989 on completion of his education in shoe technology from London. The company tapped the capital market in September 1994 and became a public limited company incorporated in India with the management retaining more than 75% of the equity, while 11% was held by financial institutions and the rest was with the public. To manage its financial resources and to achieve management efficiency, the company appointed Price Waterhouse Coopers (P) Ltd as consultant to examine various restructuring options. Soon, the result of hard work started paying off in terms of increases sales abroad. The Council for Indian Leather Exports, India conferred recognition to Mirza International as 'best exporter of the year' and thereafter consecutively for the next seven years the crown remained with the company because of the sustained outstanding performance in the field of export.

Footwear Exports from India Jumped Further

India's footwear export was about 211 million USD during 2006 which increased to 346 million USD in 2011 registering an increase of about 63% in a span of five years. USA, UK, Germany, France and Italy remained the biggest buyers of the India-made products. Indian producers exported footwear worth 34.3 million USD during 2006 to the UK and increased the figure to 69.4 million USD in 2011, registering a jump of about 102% in a five-year period indicating a preference of British buyers towards India-made products. During the same five years, export to France increased by 114%, followed by Italy 37%, USA 31% and Germany 23%. These increases indicated a competitiveness of Indian products in the Western country markets (Fig. 8.1).

FIGURE 8.1 Indian Footwear exports to other countries

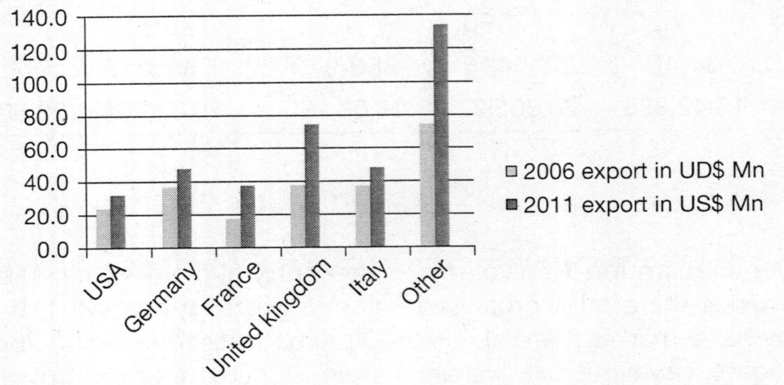

Export from Mirza International

In tandem with the competitiveness attained by the India-made products in foreign markets, Mirza International Limited also emerged as a frontrunner in the manufacturing and marketing of leather and leather footwear. The company, headquartered in the Indian capital of New Delhi, emphasised on export orientation and continued to market its products across the globe to countries such as the UK, Europe, South Africa, and the Middle East, to name a few. The internal efficiency and production +capacity were further strengthened with a fully integrated in-house technology backed shoe production facility linked with tannery and a dedicated design studio in London. The company facility at Shahjani-Unnao, UP, was repositioned to manufacture 6 lakh pairs of shoe uppers and 4.5 lakh pairs of shoes per annum. To support the increased production capacity, the tannery at Magarwara-Unnao started producing 60 lakh sq. ft of finished leather per annum. Subsequently, the company added another facility in the year 1990 at Magarwara, Unnao, for manufacture of 2.25 lakh pairs of shoes per annum. The objective of the company behind setting up these factories was for catering to the quality conscious export markets of United Kingdom, Germany, Italy, Portugal and Australia. After the successful launching of Double Density PU shoes, the company added a second plant at its Noida Factory for doubling the capacity. The company also sources its cowhides from Europe and manufactures leather in stringent adherence to international norms, ensuring that no banned chemicals are used in the production process. Such strategic moves by the company made it really competitive and resulted in a positive impact on its revenue generation. The gross income of the company increased from 70.03 million USD during 2007–08 to 84.40 million USD during 2009–10. However, as with other export-oriented businesses, the export revenue of Mirza International constituted a major part of the company income. Export market dependency of the company, in terms of ratio of revenue earned from export to gross income, increased from 79.69% during 2007–08 to 80.05% during 2008-09. It only reduced marginally to 77.77% during 2009–10 possibly because of the recession which the entire European countries had to face during the year (Table 8.5).

Table 8.5 Export from Mirza International

	2007-08	2008-09	2009-10
Gross Income	70.03	80.26	84.40
Profit after tax	0.80	1.19	4.19
Export revenue	55.81	64.25	65.64
Export as % of total income	79.69	80.05	77.77

Figures are in Million USD
Source: Annual reports of the company.

Branding at Mirza International

Initially, the company was happy with direct sales to leading global footwear retailers in countries such as UK, USA, etc. However, the company soon realised that it needs to create the presence of its own brand in the foreign market for ensuring sustainable growth. The company, thereafter, started building its own brand under the name Red Tape, Oak Tape and Red Tape Gal. The Red Tape brand was introduced in the UK in the mid 1990s as a fashion brand in some of the boutiques — and it became an instant hit. Since the commencement of the brand coincided with the collapse of the Soviet Union and signalled the end of red-tapism and the beginning of a new era, company officials decided to christen their brand based on the 'Red Tape' symbolism. Their first advertising campaign in the UK titled 'Cut Red Tape' had shown a pair of scissors cutting red tape. Like in the UK, the brand positioned itself as a lifestyle product, targeting young and fashion conscious consumers elsewhere including in India and was backed by heavy advertising since its launch. In order to position itself as "category supplier", it launched adult apparel products under the Red Tape brand to attract its targeted teenage customers more intensely. In fact, it is the success of its flagship brand Red Tape in the UK in 1996 that gave Mirzas a foothold in the overseas market. "We realised that the trade margins were much higher when we sold shoes under our own brand. That was the trigger for starting Red Tape brand" remarked Tauseef Mirza, Irshad Mirza's younger son and director of Mirza International. Mr Irshad Mirza recalled that his marketing strategy for projecting Red Tape in the foreign market as a premium brand really paid off. The Mirzas continued to route the selling of their products through the retailers of the West under their own labels but also decided to strengthen the brand image of "Red Tape" to a new level so that company's total sales from Red Tape branded shoes increased to fifteen percent at that time. In order to craft their product as per the latest fashion in the foreign market, Mirza International set up its design units at global fashion centres such as Milan, London, New York, Paris and Tokyo. The company, which claimed to churn out a thousand designs a day, employed 40 people in its design and development wing in India also.

Mirzas in the Home Turf

The company also made attempts to popularise Red Tape brand in its home country, i.e., India. As usual, the domestic market found to be very cost conscious and competitive. Bata was the oldest but leading footwear makers in India with about 5% value share during 2008 followed by international brands Reebok with 2.8 % and Adidas with value shares of 3.8%. Bata led the market both in terms of value and volume and its products were economically priced. It also provided seasonal and festival discounts to grab sales. Since 2008, Bata is maintained the lead but the international brand Reebok had definitely advanced its market share from 2.8% in 2008 to 3.5% in 2011 (Table 8.6).

Table 8.6 Brands in Indian market

Brand	2008	2009	2010	2011
Bata	4.9	3.9	3.8	3.8
Reebok	2.8	3.1	3.6	3.5
Adidas	3.8	3.5	3.3	3.1
Relaxo	1.2	1.4	1.7	1.8
Red Tape	1.5	1.4	1.4	1.3
Paragon	0.9	1	1	1.2
Liberty	1.3	1.2	1.2	1.2
Khadim	0.9	1	1	1.1
Metro M	0.7	0.7	0.8	1
Nike N	0.3	0.4	0.3	0.4
Lakhani	0.3	0.3	0.3	0.3
Action	0.4	0.3	0.3	0.3
Westside T	0.2	0.2	0.2	0.2
Milano	0.2	0.2	0.2	0.2

Figures are in percent of retail value

In terms of market share, Red Tape was in the fourth position in the Indian market during 2008 but another Indian brand Relaxo came up very fast and occupied the fourth position, relegating Red Tape to the sixth position in the subsequent years. However, the Mirzas continued with the objective to position and maintain Red Tape brand as a leading brand in the Indian situation as well. Indian cities, in a short span of time, saw about 40 exclusive stores coming up and selling Red Tape branded footwear. "We will have 200 exclusive Red Tape stores in India by 2011" said Rashid Mirza. The company always believed in having a solid home country foundation to ensure sustained internationalisation. The lack of a true-blue fashionable shoe brand in India provided an ideal launch pad for Red Tape and the company was keen to push it further. Mirzas introduced the RTS-8 model of shoes, India's first square-toed shoe, which instantly caught the fancy of the Indian consumers. In fact, it was so successful that the company had to work overnight to meet demand. "And after that, there was no looking back," remembers Mr Tauseef Mirza. Today, Indian teenagers regard the Red Tape brand as a style statement. The company, which spends 10–15% of sales on advertising, roped in Salman Khan in 2004 to endorse Red Tape. Although Salman's engagement with the brand was for a short time, it served the purpose and branding effort in the home market looked successful to some extent.

Sustenance of International Branding Efforts

Shuja Mirza, Vice President – Marketing, of Red Tape, Mirza International, was presiding over a team meeting for deciding about promoting the company's own brands more aggressively in international markets. At the outset, he narrated the objective of the meeting: "The Company has been selling products in international markets such as the UK, USA, and UAE with its own brand name – Red Tape. For other countries, the products are exported to established brands who, in turn, market the products. So far in many countries, the company acted as suppliers to the leading brands. In fact, though 80% of our business comes from abroad but not all comes through marketing of our own brand. However, if the company sells through its own brand progressively rather than through others' brands, then this would provide the required leverage to enhance revenue from foreign operation further". Then he placed the following issues for discussion in the meeting:

- There are many pros and cons of intensive branding abroad. Issues like country of importance need to be sorted out – such as whether it would like to pursue the UK first followed by USA or whether both markets should be tapped simultaneously.
- There are various countries which may be reached in both ways – selling similar shoes under own brand as well as supplying shoes directly to other brands. Looks interesting, but it involves cannibalisation of one's own brand building exercise. How to resolve this conflict?
- Should the products be positioned in different foreign markets differently based on their taste preferences, etc.? Or, should the company continue with its standardised "fashion and lifestyle" positioning for all the countries?
- Going back to the home country market may be quite unusual for a traditional company. The Mirzas have focussed on being a successful brand in the foreign market first and then put efforts to popularise the brand in the home country market. Is this going to provide any leverage in the international market?
- To succeed in its recent diversification plan to establish Red Tape as a fashion brand, the company is willing to enter all segments of dressing including accessories. Is that strategic to the international market also? Will its efforts pay off in brand building internationally?

CASE QUESTIONS

Q1. How accomplished is Mirza International in the domestic market, particularly in the trendy and stylish footwear segment?

Q2. How did Mirza International attain a respectable position in the target foreign market? Does the foreign sales testify to the respectability?

Q3. What was the marketing strategy of Mirza International in the target country markets? Do you think that Mirza International was more than a normal exporter of finished products to the foreign markets?

Q4. What was the problem for Mirza International to go all out to create and nurture its brands in the UK and EU markets? What are the primary issues the company should take into account before embarking on such a task?

Q5. Comment on the presence of Mirza International in the domestic market. What was the status of 'Red Tape' brand in the Indian market? What is the relationship between the company's domestic brand image and the international brand image?

Q6. What are the factors a domestic company like Mirza International should consider while taking a decision to extend the domestic brand to the international level?

Q7. Do you think that Mirza International should strive for building its brand in the target market? Suggest a framework to assess the brand building eligibility of the company.

FURTHER READINGS

Schuiling, I. and J.N. Kapferer (2004), "Real differences between local and international brands: Strategic implications for international marketers", *Journal of International Marketing*, Vol. 12, No. 4, pp. 97–112.

Barwise, P. and T. Robertson (1992), "Brand portfolios", *European Management Journal*, Vol. 10, No. 3' pp. 277–285.

De Chematony, L., C. Halliburton and R. Bemath (1995), "International branding: Demand or supply driven opportunity?", *International Marketing Review*, Vol. 12, No. 2, pp. 9–21.

Douglas, S.P., C.S. Craig and E.J. Nijssen (2001), "Integrating branding strategy across markets: Building international brand architecture", *Journal of International Marketing*, Vol. 9, No. 2, pp. 97–114.

Kuvykaite, R. and J. Mascinskiene (2010), "Transformation of a national brand into an international brand", *Engineering Economics*, Vol. 21, No. 4, pp. 446–455

Hsieh, M.H. (2002), "Identifying brand image dimensionality and measuring the degree of brand globalisation: A cross-national study", *Journal of International Marketing*, Vol. 10, No. 2, pp. 46–67.

Moore, Christopher M. and John Fernie (2000), "Brands without boundaries: The internationalisation of the designer retailer's brand", *European Journal of Marketing*, Vol. 34, No. 8, pp. 919–937.

This paper deals with the internationalisation of the fashion designer's brand through exploratory research. It indicates that the US and European fashion designers are spending between 20–30% of gross margin for advertising support in developing global campaigns to enhance brand image in foreign markets. The study indicated that increasing tension between the desire to be exclusive and that for becoming involved in product line extensions and widespread distribution, ultimately leads to dilution of the brand's value.

Leclerc, France, Bernd H. Schmitt and Laurette Dubé (1994), "Foreign branding and its effects on product perceptions and attitudes", *Journal of Marketing Research*, Vol. 31, No. 2, May.

The article deals with three important aspects of branding strategy where pronouncing or spelling a brand name in a foreign language is involved. The writer chooses French brands to understand how the French pronunciation of a brand name affects the perceived hedonism of the products, attitudes toward the brand, and attitudes toward the brand name.

Sophonsiri, S and Polyorat, K (2009), "The impact of brand personality dimensions on brand association and brand attractiveness: The case study of KFC in Thailand", *Journal of Global Business and Technology*, Vol. 5, No. 2.

The study was conducted in Thailand to deal with the brand personality dimension of the American fast food brand KFC and its influence on brand association and brand attractiveness on the culturally different Thai consumers. The study revealed that brand personality has an impact on brand association and brand attractiveness.

Alden, D.L. and R. Batra (1999), "Brand positioning through advertising in Asia, North America, and Europe: The role of global consumer culture, *Journal of Marketing*, Vol. 63, No. 1, pp. 75–87.

This article proposes and tests a new construct known as global consumer culture positioning (GCCP), which associates the brand with a widely understood and recognised set of symbols believed to constitute emerging global consumer culture. The study found that the GCCP could explain those advertisements that were not released to position the brand as a member of a local consumer culture or a specific foreign consumer culture. Identification of GCCP as a positioning tool suggests a pathway through which certain brands come to be perceived by consumers as "global" and provides managers with strategic direction in the multinational markets.

Steenkamp, J.B., E.M. Steenkamp, R. Batra and D.L. Alden (2003), "How perceived brand globalness creates brand value", *Journal of International Business Studies*, Vol. 34, No. 1, pp. 53–65.

The authors of this article elaborate on why some consumers prefer global brands to local brands. The articles used a term called perceived brand globalness (PBG) and tested it on consumer data of USA and Korea and found that PBG is positively related to both perceived brand quality and prestige. The authors, therefore, came to the conclusion that PBG increases the purchase likelihood of a global brand. However, the PBG effects are weaker for more ethnocentric consumers.

Zhou, Lianxi, Zhiyong Yang and Michael K. Hui (2010), "Non-local or local brands? A multi-level investigation into confidence in brand origin identification and its strategic implications", *Journal of the Academy of Marketing Science*, Vol. 38, Issue 2, pp. 202 –218.

This article addresses a growing dilemma surrounding the strategic value of perceived brand foreignness (PBF) among consumers in emerging economies. Building on recent research evidence from the brand origin literature, the authors introduce the concept of confidence in brand origin identification (CBO) and theorise its moderat ing impact on the value of PBF in explaining and predicting brand evaluation. Using a multi-level modelling technique, this study provides evidence showing that CBO moderates the effect of PBF on consumer evaluations of brand value. Moreover, the moderating influence of CBO is found to be more profound for local than for foreign brands. It also discusses managerial implications for building both global and local brands in emerging markets.

REFERENCES

Annual reports of Mirza International available on the company Web site at www.mirza.co.in.

Barnes reports: US Shoe Stores, 2009.

Cnbc–TV18, Interview with Rashid Mirza, Md., Mirza Internationals *available at* www.moneycontrol.com.

Data monitor, Industry profile, *Footwear in India*, 2009.

Data monitor, Industry profile, *Global Footwear*, 2009.

"Flourishing on Red Tape, Mirza International leaves global footprint", *The Economic Times*, December 16, 2009.

Ho Yin Wong and Bill Merrilees (2008), "Determinants of SME international marketing communications", *Journal of Global Marketing*, Vol. 21, No. 4.

"Indian footwear market has large potential", One India News, July 13, 2009.

"Mirza international reports ₹95.09 crore turnover for quarter ended June 2010, available at www.moneycontrol.com, August 10, 2010.

Press releases of Mirza international available at http://www.mirza.co.in/announcements.html.

Red tape plans 16 more exclusive outlets, *Business Line*, July 27, 2007.

Successful product differentiation strategies: Examples from Heinz, Snyder's of Hanover and the Fonterra Cooperative Group (2010) Strategic Direction, 26 (1), pp. 17-20.

UK Footwear Retailers 2010, Close-Up Media, Inc., available at www.closeupmedia.com/.

Deciding on Pricing

9

Learning Objectives

After studying this chapter, you should be able to:

- Understand the basic complexities of price fixing in the context of international marketing.
- Understand the different factors that influence pricing decision in the international markets and their role in price fixing.
- Understand the role of company internal factors like transfer pricing in ascertaining the price of a product.
- Understand the different pricing methods used in the exportation process.
- Understand the various factors that affect export pricing.
- Assess the role of non-pricing factors in fixing export pricing for international products.
- Understand the framework for assessing correctness or variability of the international pricing of a company.

Chapter Overview

Pricing decision in the international market is complex because of the involvement of several factors unique to country-specific situations. This chapter first deals with the factors that affect fixing of price in international market in detail and then details out different methods of price fixing in the international markets. At the end, this chapter devices a framework that can come handy for international marketing managers to fix the international price of a product.

Opening Vignette

Toshiba fixing competitive price for its Kirabook

Can any of the world's laptop manufacturers outsmart Apple's 'MacBook Air Pro with Retina display' with price and technology to win over the market share from Apple? This was the question going around in Toshiba during 2012. In fact, ever since MacBook Air ultra-thin laptop series were introduced by Apple it became even the critics' first choice. According to them it is the best of the dozens of others available in the market in terms of their worth in relation to the price. Many of them even went ahead to term the thin and light laptops of Apple as 'gold standard'. The classy light aluminium body MacBook Air came out of the stable of Apple with larger backlit keyboard and responsive track pad to win the hearts of millions of customers. It was almost love at first sight for the customers on introduction of the product. The MacBook Air laptops were made available in two screen sizes, 13.3-inch and 11.6-inch and with solid-state drive (SSD) storage and Intel Core i5 or i7 central processing units (CPUs). The customers also liked the six or seven hours long battery life and glossy resolution of 1600 pixels display of the product. In totality, the product seemed to be complete in itself in all respect. The customers experienced, while using, that such mastery in craftsmanship would not have been possible without 'Apple like' control in design and manufacturing process. Apple launched its first generation MacBook Air during 2008 and subsequently, as expected, the company almost every year kept on modifying the product with improvements. The 2011 version, MacBook Airs were powered by the new Sandy Bridge 1.6 or 1.7 GHz dual-core Intel Core i5 or 1.8 GHz dual-core Intel Core i7 processors with 2 GB of RAM storage. During mid-2012, Apple further technologically improved the product by doubling the RAM and SSD speeds. Then finally Apple, during 2013, released the bigger version, i.e., 13-inch and 15-inch MacBook Pro with Retina display at a price of $1699 and $2199 respectively for the globe with price variation across the countries due to logistic and tax differences. All along, the Japanese giant Toshiba was watching from a distance how Apple was successfully skimming the market with its ultrathin range. During April 2012, Toshiba gave a faint signal of coming up with something in line with ultra thin laptop. Finally, during first part of 2013, the news broke that Toshiba was taking the competition to Apple first in its own home ground, i.e., Japan and then to the home ground of Apple, i.e., USA. Thereafter, the company proudly unearthed its ultra thin laptop range with full knowledge of eminent competition from Apple. The prospective customers for the first time saw the premium product named 'Kirabook' from Toshiba. It was a super-slim 13-inch Ultrabook crafted with a magnesium alloy chassis and featuring a 2560-by-1440 Pixel display. This sleek new machine of Toshiba almost proved to be a showstopper and interfered in the juggernaut of Apple in the luxury notebook market. Toshiba matched up at per with Apple by all accounts. The design of Kirabook was almost looked like premium Apple MacBook Pro with Retina display. Kirabook also had third-generation Intel Core i5 or i7 processors.

According to the experts both the products were of almost equal technology competence. However, distinction came when the question came about pricing of these two products in US market and elsewhere. Both the companies wanted to show their distinctiveness by suitable pricing. If Toshiba proceeded to market the product in the US at a price lower than a comparable MacBook Pro with Retina model then there would have been the problem of image. In fact, this point was very much under the consideration of Toshiba and hence before Toshiba first launched the product in the US, it was shown to sample prospective customers for opinion survey about possible pricing. Not to the surprise of Toshiba, a majority opined that it should be priced at the Apple's range as otherwise it would be difficult to convince customers about its superior quality. The marketing strategist of Toshiba was in a dilemma. They were fully aware of how important it was to win over market from Apple in USA. But how it would come, image with higher price or sacrificing image with lower price? Independent marketing experts advised Toshiba to price it slightly below than Apple, i.e., $1599-to-$1999 range as Apple was a dominant market player in that sector. "Although Kirabook had all the comparable features and was half a pound lighter than the Apple Mac book, people who handle laptops on a daily basis would not think of how much actually the product is worth," opined the experts. Again, Apple had the edge of home country advantage with the huge Steve Jobs legacy not only in US but world over. The puzzled marketing officials were trying to answer the question, how an average consumer in the US, standing in the showroom, was going to decide Kirabook's worth? How this will be done in other countries as well? Toshiba considered all these, and finally decided to launch Kirabook at a standard range of price for the US and other countries. The base model, comparable with MacBook Pro with Retina but at the same time it showed the courage to price another model with the top-end configuration at $2299, higher than that of the comparable MacBook model.

When this pricing story was told to the students of international marketing in the classroom, the students quipped, "fixing price competitively against Apple in its home turf is really difficult but international companies must learn how to do it. Can the Japanese company which has so carefully produced the product really fix the price below Apple's product only because of the existence of a local strong brand? What were the different methods of pricing available to the Japanese company? Should the company extend the American price to the other countries of the world? What are the factors which generally decide the variation of prices in different countries? Is there any framework available to understand the quantum of price adaptation required for a country?"

Pricing is one of the most complicated decisions encountered by international marketers. Pricing in international market place requires a combination of intimate knowledge of the market cost and regulations, infinite patience for details and a shrewd sense of market strategy.

— Keteora (1990)

INTRODUCTION

Price is the amount of money and/or other items with utility needed to acquire a product. Here, one can very well understand that for acquiring a product, the purchaser needs to exchange money for becoming the proud owner of the desired product and the amount of money that one would spend is the price of the product. Now, how much would one be likely to pay for the product if the person purchases the product in his own country of residence? Would the price remain same if the same person purchases the same product in another country? Will the same price attract buyers if that product is offered to the residents of other countries at their own respective market? How much should the company take into account for relative competition and situations of price volatility in the target country markets when deciding the price of its products? These questions complicate decision making, and hence influence the price of a product in international markets. The marketers, on the other hand, must put a price that not only satisfies the producers' need of cost realisation and profit but also has the ability to create demand in the competitive market place. In addition, the manufacturing company is also likely to offer the product at different prices in different countries based on the factors such as affordability, distance from production centre, stage of product cycle, etc. Therefore, in respect of international pricing another question arises: how much should be the variation? On what factors will the variations depend? To what extent will the variations be possible? The answers to these questions appear to be difficult when a product is marketed across many countries of the world simultaneously. This is simply because of the involvement of various country specific factors that have the ability to cause the variation. Therefore, a considerable amount of confusion prevails while a company decides on international pricing for products. As Cateora[1] points out, pricing is one of the most complicated decision areas encountered by the international marketer. Jain[2] adds to that by saying "international marketing becomes more complicated almost daily. Sometimes, the price of the same or comparable products will vary significantly in various parts of the world". For example, Apple may set its iPad at a different price in the US than in UK or in other European countries. On the other hand, some producers may like to keep the price of their products same irrespective of the country where it is marketed to project their global image. In fact, some companies are very straightforward in fixing a global standard price and thereby do good business as well. For example, international watch brands Christian Dior kept the price of its product while launching the product for the Indian market

[1] Cateora, Philip, Mary Gilly and John Graham (2010), *International Marketing* McGraw-Hill/Irwin

[2] Jain S. (1989), "Standardisation of international marketing strategy: Some research hypotheses", *Journal of Marketing* Vol. 53 (January), pp. 70–79.

between ₹18,000 and ₹40,000, which was at par with the international price. "Despite the various odds, we will make sure that the pricing of our brands are on a par with pricing in other countries such as Dubai." remarked the marketing manager of the company knowing the difference of per capita income of India with rich countries of the West[3]. Understandably international marketers do not get surprised if they are required to do the other way round. There are many instances where marketers intentionally kept the price of their products differently in different countries to get a foothold in the market place.

In fact, various factors are required to be considered for fixing product price in the international markets. Various factors that are not related to production also play important roles. For example, in a specific country, the high import duty on the product may be the most important factor for increment in the final pricing; but for another country, this may not be an important factor because of an existing trade relationship like FTA or PTA, which smoothens the impact of import duty. In addition, although grey markets of luxury products are no longer as attractive to cross-country customers as what it used to be some 10–15 years back, in some countries it is still creating havoc and putting pressure on the international marketer to re-work the pricing. Relocation of production centres by the competitors to low-cost countries also disturbs average industry pricing frequently. Shifting of production base of XBox 360 gaming gadget from Guadalajara, Mexico industrial park to Doumen, China is an example to this effect which allowed Microsoft to beat the market competition through pricing advantageously. Moreover, information flow across the international borders are much faster now a days which put, pressure is on companies for price alignment across countries in spite of existence of various valid reasons for differentiating the price. For example, the information of iphone launching price in USA reached very quickly which infuriated the prospective consumers in UK when they observed price variation. Other factors such as currency devaluation and exchange rate volatility can also make a product cheaper or dearer in one country than another. The price in one country may vary substantially than the other if the two countries are in different phases of product life cycle. An LCD TV may cost at least 25–30% less in Dubai than in India or in Bangladesh. The price differential also happens due to differences in distribution structure, country-specific tax system and consumer behaviour. For example, the complexity of the distribution system of Japan continues to give anxiety to the international marketers as it did ten or fifteen years back. Different tax systems in different countries also make the life of international marketers difficult. Say, if Country A imposes tax on companies selling canned cold drinks for disposal of empty cans as well, the price of canned cold drinks is expected to be higher in Country A than in Country B where environmental norms are not so stringent. For example, Japanese prefectures bill the concerned company for realisation of disposal charges of packaging cans on monthly basis. So, in a nutshell, there are various factors affecting the price across countries and these factors are expected to impact different countries to different extents. This ground situation makes it difficult for international marketers to come up with a

[3] *Businessline*, Chennai: Nov 22, 2002. pg. 1.

global or standardised pricing for their products and puts pressure on them to decide on the price of the product based on the country market.

Let us take an example to understand the whole situation practically. The US jeanswear company Levi Strauss & Co decided to market its mid-market brand Denizen, in India. It had already ensured domination in the country's upper market category with another brand. They were deciding on the price tag the product would carry on its launch in the Indian market. The answer was not as simple as deciding on the cost first and then simply adding the allowances for the profit the company would like to keep. It was also not the equilibrium point where demand and supply meet. The company rather acted in the direction of achieving a certain strategic objective at the company level through pricing, i.e., capturing a certain market share in India. From strategy point of view it was important that the company would put due attention to achieve the set objective through pricing. Accordingly, Levi's also considered how much the Indian customers were likely to pay for taking possession of the product by considering the tangible and intangible value of the offer, i.e., the product. The tangible factors are product features such as performance, strength, durability, etc. The intangible factors are prestige, status, newness, timeliness, beauty, brand appeal, etc. Accordingly, the company roped in Imran Khan, an upcoming hero of Bollywood cinema, as its brand ambassador to increase the intangible value of the product. On the tangible front, the company was ensuring that the product quality should be of international standard and satisfy the Indian consumers. Now, in regards to the company marketing objective, it wanted to make inroads to the mid-market category of denim jeans quickly and stop the crossing over of consumers into competitor's brand. By considering all these aspects, the company finally decided to keep the price range of Levi Strauss Denizen between ₹799 and ₹1399 per piece and test market the product in the Indian state of Karnataka.

Box 9.1 Various pricing objectives pursued by companies in international market

- Fight out competition.
- Generation of satisfactory profits above cost of production.
- Profit maximisation by taking advantage of market condition.
- Achievement of satisfactory sales on launch and further.
- Liquidity enough to fight out odd situation.
- Market share increment with time.
- Sales stability in the market.
- Market share leadership through pricing.
- Target rate of return on investment (ROI) as per industry standard at least.
- Discouraging effect on the new entrants.
- Price stability in the market and avoidance of price war with the competitors.
- Maintaining prices in accordance with legal system of the country.
- Developing loyal customer base.
- Attraction of new customers.
- Creation of a prestige image for the brand.
- Survival in the long run.
- Achievement of social goals.
- Price differentiation.

How did the company arrive at the above price? On being asked, one marketing executive of the company indicated the various factors it had to consider for fixing the price. This included the level of competition, economic structure of the market, the target consumer's expectation and behaviour, product variety on offer, communication plan and distribution strategy apart from the company's own marketing objective.

Now suppose the company wants to launch the product in Bangladesh. Due to change in country of target, there would also be a change in the competition level, economic structure, and consumer's expectation from the product, etc. For example, Levi Strauss Denizen is known for its strength in the premium and super premium denim price segment in USA. Would the company try the same in Bangladesh considering the least developed economic status of the country? In fact, only a month before launching the product in India, the company started marketing it in China by maintaining its US positioning type of premium and super premium products and priced the products accordingly. But in India, the company had chosen a different positioning with pricing as an indicator of product quality.

The above discussion clearly makes us understand that pricing decision in the international market is complex because of the involvement of several factors unique to country-specific situations. This chapter, therefore, first deals with the factors that affect fixing of the price in the international market in detail and then devices a framework which can come handy for international marketing managers in fixing the international price of a product.

DETERMINANTS OF INTERNATIONAL PRICE

Various factors affect international pricing, which the marketers need to consider while fixing price in a particular country. Some of the factors are conventional such as demand in the market, cost of the product and nature of competitions (Figure 9.1). These factors are interrelated and the interplay between them give rise to new situations almost every day on which the companies need to act for retaining marketing supremacy. Consider the case of the Microsoft Xbox gaming gadget that happened in November, 2001 while launching the product in USA. Microsoft spent huge amounts of money to put advance features on its gaming console and was committed to spend $500 million on Xbox marketing to beat the competition from existing Japanese leading players in the gaming console market, i.e., Nintendo and Sony. The Xbox production costs were expected to be unusually high at $375 per machine in spite contract manufacturing because of the rise in input cost. Sony's PlayStation 2, another very popular gaming devise from the Japanese company, was available for $299 per machine during 2001 in USA. As per market news, Nintendo was expected to launch its next-generation GameCube at a much lesser price of $199 per machine in the near future. The presence of Sony's PlayStation 2 and the news of Nintendo's possible launch put real pressure on Microsoft while deciding the market price of Xbox. What would be the price of Microsoft Xbox on launch in USA was a very important question to the Microsoft officials at that juncture? In fact,

FIGURE 9.1 The pricing tripod

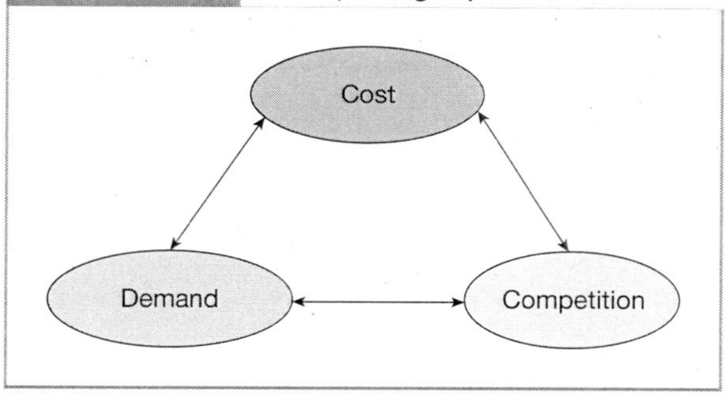

Microsoft seemed to have very few options in deciding on the price, as the company appeared to be trapped by the competition from PlayStation 2 and Nintendo. It was because of cost of product as high as $375 per machine on one side and competition from Sony on the other side who already set the market price for its product at $299. "The interplay between cost and competition would also effect the demand of our product," quipped Peter Moore, the Microsoft vice president and in charge of Xbox marketing.

Market analysts observing the situation, opined "Xbox is definitely not going to be priced above $300 even though there is loss. It cannot also go for cost recovery pricing and set price somewhere around $375 per machine because Microsoft is a new name in the gaming gadget product line. However, if it is going to fix the price at $299 to attract the customers to its product then there is great financial loss to the company". This was a catch twenty situation. A wrong pricing strategy would have affected the demand in the market as the company had the intention of selling 5 million Xbox units in the fiscal year. Business analyst of the company further enlightened the marketing team of Microsoft that if the price for the product was fixed at $279 then the company would take about three years to reach the break-even. On the reality front, to give Sony a grand fight it was required to match up the Sony's play station price and offer Xbox at $299 only. In that scenario, Microsoft would lose about $75 on every Xbox console sold in the market. This loss was without considering the sales, marketing and other administrative costs. So, in a sense, more units are sold in the initial years there will be more loss to the company if $299 price is fixed for the product. In addition to this demand–cost – competition scenario, other marketing factors also disturbed the Microsoft strategist. The brand image of Microsoft should help the company in pushing the demand of the product even if the company maintained a higher price than the competitors. But Microsoft was not an established name in the gaming console sector, unlike its two strong Japanese competitors. Again, peculiars product characteristics of video games consoles where technology obsolescence are very fast leading to peak and valley type of product life cycle would also influence the price setting. This made the strategists at Microsoft to think about launching the product with a market skimming price at one point of time. But it did not suit the company objective of long time market presence. In addition, strategists were considering the ability of Microsoft to render post purchase support, pre-purchase support, its ability to provide the complete range, etc., to arrive at the final price for launching the product. The case of XBox pricing clearly demonstrates that are many factors which act on the interplay between demand and cost competitions, making the situation more dynamic while fixing the price. The following section discusses the factors one by one.

Country of Origin Effect

The country of origin influences price fixing in the international market. "Country of origin" or simply COO of a product is the country where the product is originally produced or where its corporate headquarters are located. If the products are originated other than the home country consumers would like to understand the country of origin and infer the risks or benefits to be derived from the use of the products based on their understanding about the country. While doing so the consumers use many cues which they have accumulated in their mind over the years either by their own experience or by listening about the country. In this way the developed country consumers, in general, retain a biased opinion towards the quality of products produced in developing countries. If the product is produced in developing country the development country consumers automatically infer it to have poor quality and hence will not be willing to pay higher price. This is particularly truer in case of technology oriented products. In a sense, therefore, the least developing countries products would remain disadvantageous in international markets in the matter of fixing price for developed country markets because of the poor COO effect. This psychologically induced pre-conceived notion about poor product quality brings down the consumer's willingness to pay. In these days there has been prevalence of producing products in low cost least developing countries to enjoy least cost manufacturing advantages by the developed country consumers. This gave rise to the concept of Country of Manufacturing or simply COM. Research shows that prospective consumers would be evaluating both COO and COM simultaneously before the purchase of the product and give higher weightage to COO based evaluation that the COM based evaluation while generating their willingness to pay. All these imply that the producers, therefore, before deciding on the price need to ascertain the intensity of COO or COM effect on the consumers' mind in the target country. Because of negative COO effect, China could not charge high price for made-in-China automobiles across many countries of the world. In contrast, Japanese electronic products such as camera, TV, etc., can go for premium pricing because of positive COO effect. The same is the case for the cars originating from Japan. Germany is famous for technological advancement and its application in the products and hence a German company can ask for high price for technology products. Coredell (1991)[4] conducted a study to understand the real problem of price fixing in respect of four products such as colour televisions, microwave ovens, bicycles, and telephones. The study led to development of understanding that when COO effect is active in the positive direction, the producer can charge higher price premium for the product in the target country for the above four products. Drozdenko and Jensen (2009) conducted a study to understand the effect of COO on willingness to pay pricing premiums for the American consumers in respect of 11 different categories of product such as toothpaste, shampoo, toys, TV, etc. One of the questions that were asked is: "Assume you need to purchase a specific type of toy for a favourite youngster. You consider one which costs $10 and see it is made in China. What is the most you would be willing to pay if it was instead made in the United States? They were then asked how much more (if anything) they would be willing to pay if the product was made in Germany, the USA, or India". The result reconfirmed the belief that developed country consumers like the Americans would be highly influenced by positive COO image while paying price for a product. Figure 9.2 was constructed by the aforesaid researchers by taking data from several previous studies to indicate the fact that the highest premium was with toothpaste for

[4] Coredell, V. (1991), "Competitive context and price as moderators of country of origin preference", *Journal of the Academy of Marketing Science*, Vol. 19, Spring, pp. 123–8.

FIGURE 9.2 Price premium and COO effect

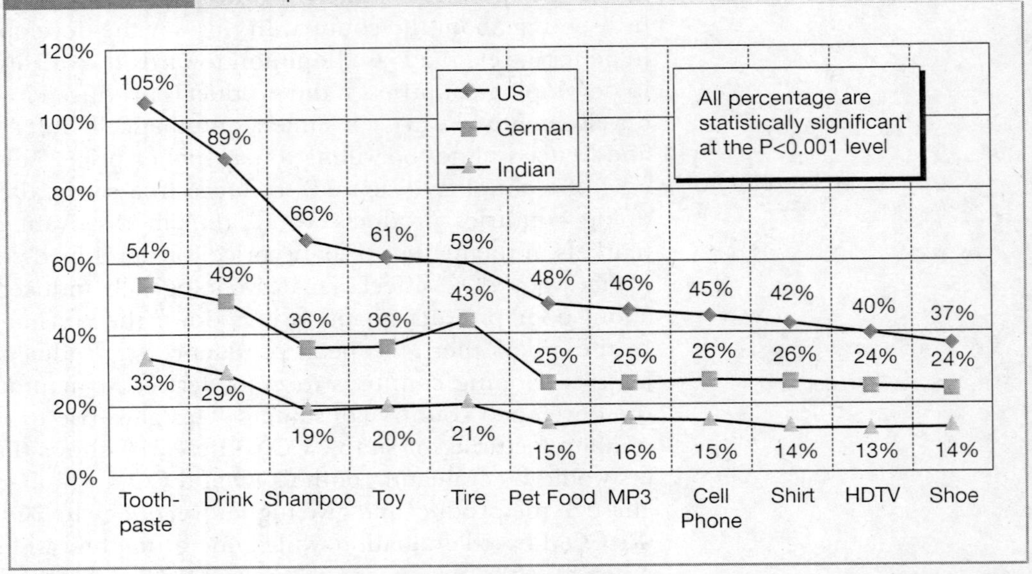

Source: Drozdenko, Ronald and Jensen, Marlene (2009), *The Journal of Product and Brand Management*, Vol. 18, Issue 5, pp. 371–378.

all three countries. The differential was almost two times greater for the US product relative to the German product and three times greater for the US product relative to the Indian product.

Stage of Product Life Cycle

The stages of product life cycle also influence product pricing. As per marketing wisdom products undergo several stages after it is introduced in a market by a company. These stages are broadly introduction, growth, maturity and decline when buyers' sensitivity towards the product changes along with competition in the market. In general, the stages in the product life cycle determine the price of the product. At the decline stage, a product cannot be priced at a premium rate because of the falling demand. Now because of economic differences amongst the countries of the world it may so happen that a particular product is in the decline stage in one country, say USA, but the same product is in the growth stage in another country, say Bangladesh. The producers, therefore, adjust the pricing programme differently for different countries in accordance with the product's stage in its life cycle. The price variation diminishes across countries where there is insignificant difference in the product life cycle stage. In case of technology oriented products the manufactures shows inclination towards deliberate extension of product life cycle in countries of low economic power by using pricing as strategic tool. A combination strategy of regulated product supply along with pricing variations may allow a company to extend the different stages of product life cycle differently in different countries. Short supply with higher price may extent the growth stage in developing countries. The Chinese company Xiaomi has been restricting supply of its Mi series mobile phone handsets in

Table 9.1 Comparative price of ipad in US and India in INR

Model	E bay India price in INR	US price in INR
ipad 2 16 GB Wi-Fi only	34,000	22,492
ipad 2 16 GB Wi-Fi + 3G	45,000	28,352
ipad 2 32 GB Wi-Fi only	42,900	26,999
ipad 2 32 GB Wi-Fi 3S	52,900	32,860
ipad 2 64 GB Wi-Fi only	49,900	31,507
ipad 2 64 GB Wi-Fi + 3G	59,900	37,367

Source: Author's compilation from the internet

Indian market coupled with higher price and thereby extending the introductory phase. Companies also deliberately create different phases of product life cycle differently for different countries and use pricing as tool to reap maximum marketing benefits. Apple iphone version 1 was never released in India while it was in the introductory phase in countries such as USA and UK. Although iphone 3G was released only after one month of official release in USA during July 2008 and marketed through Airtel and Vodafone, at that time India did not have 3G services. For obvious reasons, therefore, the sales was not much but the company was successful in getting good publicity which will be quite useful for marketing products in pipeline. About nine months of its official release in July 2008 in USA iphone 3 GS ("S" stands for speed) was released India. iphone 4 made entry in USA during June 2010 and Indian market saw its after a month only. The same strategy was adapted by Apple is the case of ipad as well. This effect of keeping introductory stage differently in different countries allowed the company to realise higher price in some countries. The Apple's differential price is reflected in the Table 9.1 above.

Competitive Structure

The competitive structure prevailing in a country has the ability to influence pricing. Different country markets have different competitive environments because of interplay between foreign and domestic companies, or between two or more foreign companies depending upon the market condition that exists in a particular country. In addition, a company, when entering a country, pre sets a target of market share to be achieved. However, it is imperative that the company requires attaining the desired market share by fighting out the existing competition where price would be used as an effective tool. Therefore, entry level ground work is required to clearly understand the competitive landscape in regards the whole pricing scenario comprising of company's own product with that of product alternatives in the target country. It involves analysing the product's unique or competitive features/benefits package in relation to the comparable products available in the host country market place. This process would allow to set price of the entrant product after necessary adjustment made in accordance with the possible demand the new product. The more unique the product will be in relation to the competition, the stronger demand will be its position in the foreign market. This will again influence the entrant company's ability to carry a premium price.

This situation varies from country to country as competitive situation varies. Thus, a company is likely to take advantage of the different types of demand and competition situations in different countries by not setting a uniform price across country markets where its products are made available. Similarly, the more the products are of the commodity type, the lesser will be their ability to command a premium price.

Box 9.2 Pricing is important in the game plan

Daikin has a long history on internationalisation. This Japanese company made a modest beginning in the city of Osaka during 1920 with the production of aircraft radiator tubes and other related products. Daikin slowly became a diversified manufacturing company with active interest in air-conditioning, chemicals and oil hydraulics. Now, Daikin Industries Ltd is a global leader in the market of commercial- and industrial-use air conditioning systems, with more than 40% of the market share in Japan and a well-established presence in China, Southeast Asia, Europe and North America. It has now its manufacturing base in eleven countries of the world and thus making it world's second-largest maker of air conditioners. Daikin never lost sight of wining over the lucrative Indian market for air conditioner. But this Japanese electronics maker was completely outsmarted in the battle for the fast-growing Indian market by the aggressive pricing strategy of the Koreans. In air conditioning products market, Daikin understood quickly that unless pricing is competitive it would be difficult to win over the Indian market. "The mandate from the headquarters is to become number one in India", says Daikin India managing director Toshiki Hayashi. All around in Indian market, other Japanese electronic brands such as Panasonic, Sony, Canon and Nikon had to re-jig its price when the Korean manufacturers such as LG Electronics and Samsung Electronics entered the market with comparatively low pricing strategy well supported by a nicely knit distribution network across Indian cities and rural areas. In air conditioning market Dakin understood that, in general, Japanese products were miles ahead of Chinese and Korean electronics products in terms of brand image. But alas! For Samsung, India is the fastest-growing market while LG plans to make the country the second-highest revenue generation centre by 2015. During festivals like Diwali, sales of these companies rise by more than 20% which became a matter of envy for the Japanese electronic companies' present Indian market.

Daikin Industries Ltd globally competes with Carrier, the market leader in the air conditioning business. Daikin commissioned its wholly owned manufacturing plant in Rajasthan during 2009 and gave a loud signal that it wanted to convert the Indian market as its prime market since at that time it was worth around $5 billion. The forecast was that India's market size would further grow at nearly 15% per year. Daikin wanted to capitalise its premium brand image in India as it did elsewhere. But company proposes market reality disposes. The market shares of Daikin rather shrunk in India despite occupying a premium brand image in the consumer mind-set and enjoying an early-mover advantage. The Koreans such as LG and Samsung were quickly entering in Indian's mind. With no time they became the household names in India by capturing about fifty percent market share in air-conditioner business.

During 2011, Daikin sensed revival. Daikin's new pricing strategy started paying off. It actually started lowering prices to make products comparable or even lower than the Koreans. Another brand Sony followed the same path and positioned itself only 3 to 4% costlier than an LG or Samsung compared to nearly 20% during the previous years. To the surprise of the customers even its LCD television models were cheaper than the Koreans. The result was good. Sony sold the highest number of LCD televisions in India during the last quarter of the 20011–12. Similarly, Panasonic positioned its entry-level models to outsmart the Korean through pricing. Daikin cut the price of its 1.5 tonne split air-conditioner by ₹5000 to make them comparable to the Korean premium model. The company also launched a new range of products in this category at ₹32,000 by increasing its efficiency in sourcing components globally. Very soon Daikin, which were about 50% costlier than the Korean brands a year ago, became only about 10–15% dearer through their low-priced models. The result of aggressive pricing started reflecting in the marketing performance parameters also. While LG and Samsung together lost almost 5% of market share between January and May 2011, the three Japanese firms Daikin, Hitachi and Panasonic were among the largest gainers.

How competition influences price can be well understood from the Skoda example. The Czech company Skoda, now a part of Euorpe's top carmaker Volkswagen group, wanted to increase its market share from 3% to 7% in the ever competitive Indian market in the premium hatchback segment. This segment was going strong with an estimated sale of 4.5 lakh units a year. Accordingly, Skoda launched its car Fabia and directly put it in front of Indians as an alternative to Maruti Swift, Hyundai i20, Fiat Grande Punto, and Honda Jazz. The segment leader, Swift, was priced in the range of ₹4.27 lakh–5.52 lakh, while Hyundai i20 is in the ₹4.58 lakh–7.56 lakh range. Skoda was very careful in its game plan and wanted its new pricing mechanism to do the tricks to pump up the sales volumes of Fabia. According to Skoda Auto India director (sales and marketing) Thomas Kuehl,[5] "We have gone on a new pricing for the Fabia that makes the car a compelling proposition and pits it aggressively against rivals. We feel that we can make a good impact in the market if our cars are placed within the 3%–5% price range of that of successful models from Maruti and Hyundai". Fabia's entry-level model, initially priced at ₹5.02 lakh (ex-showroom Delhi), was reduced to ₹4.35 lakh, while the diesel version was reduced to ₹5.4 lakh from the previous price of ₹6.5 lakh. However, Skoda's Fabia model launched in early 2008 in the Indian market, failed to make much impact in terms of sales. The potential customers were still not very convinced with price which was still marginally higher than competing models such as Maruti Swift and Hyundai i20.

Box 9.3 Dr Reddy's generic of Roche's cancer drug to cost 50% less

US companies Genentech and Biogen Idec made an impact in the world when it first came out with the drug MabTheran 1997 duly approved by the US Food and Drug Administration for treatment of B cell non-Hodgkins lymphoma patients who were resistant to other chemotherapy regimens. Genentech and Biogen Idec marketed MabThera under the brand name Rituxan in the United States, Japan and Canada. Genentech and Biogen Idec collaborated with Roche for marketing MabThera in the rest of the world under the brand name Rituximab. India's third-biggest drug maker Dr Reddy's Laboratories Ltd is producing Rituximab in India, under the name Reditux for marketing in India and abroad when it became generic. Interestingly, Reditux has been priced 50% cheaper than the original Rituximab which will allow the company to market the product in low or medium income countries. Interestingly in many such countries Reditux will compete directly with its originator Rituximab and is expected to create a better market than the originator because of the price advantage. The generic-drug maker will also seek to sell the treatment in the US and EU markets at a fraction of the price when the product loses the patent protection (estimated to happen in 2015 and 2018, in US and EU respectively).

These types of complex drugs, known as biologics, are expected to have good market in the future. Dr Reddy's Laboratories Ltd also works on similar lines to develop its capabilities to produce similar biologics when they become generic. In fact, biologics sales are growing at 14 times the pace of traditional chemical compounds and are among the most expensive prescriptions. Rituximab alone generated more than $2 billion (₹8,200 crore) during 2008. Biologics are generally developed and used in rich countries first owing to the high price attached to the products.

Dr Reddy is expected to get good markets in different countries of the world because of the substantial saving it can provide to the customers. For example, a month's supply of Rituxan costs may cost $4,200 in the US but the use of the generic product would straightway save at least $25,200 a year for the customer because Reditux would be available at a price 50% lower than the original product.

---

[5] Skoda cuts Fabia tag, may fuel price war, *The Times of India*, Oct 13, 2010.

When the management was jostling with pricing strategy Skoda received a further jolt when parent German Volkswagen decided to launch its Polo compact hatchback below the price of Fabia. Marketers of Fabia were dumbstruck with the turn of the event because globally VW brand had better acceptance than Czechoslovakian Skoda. Fabia faced further setback when competing cars from the stable of well-known brands Maruti (Ritz, new WagonR), Ford (Figo) and GM (Beat) came out with price below Fabia. This made the Indian journey of Fabia miserable. The model just some managed to sell only 2820 units in a span of six months from the launch. The market observers were not very happy with the strategist of the Czech company and remarked, "The company forgot the basic international marketing lesson that before entry, judge your position against present and eminent competition in terms of pricing. If you are wrong in pricing, it can break your market position to wipe you out of competition".

Income Levels

The economic factors pertaining to a country also influence the price of the entrant product. Consideration of economic factors is increasingly becoming important for companies when deciding on price in the international markets. The purchasing power expressed in terms of disposable income per capita widely varies across the countries of the world. Therefore, maintaining the same price for products across countries would mean that poor countries are likely to find the designated price as high because of affordability factor while the same price would be considered low in rich countries. Therefore, price that can be fixed for the entrant product entails a detail examination of the factors such as disposable income level, per capita income, income inequalities, etc., for the target countries. Companies, in the next level of price fixing, therefore, endeavour to understand the income quotients of the target segment and then set the pricing strategy that can enlarge the market. For example, American auto major General Motors (GM) made collaboration with a local Chinese company to produce and market micro-vans in China. The segment targeted was the Chinese buyers living in the second and third-tier cities of the country. China being the world's largest auto market, the Company General Motor took extra care in fixing price of the China made automobiles for the targeted customers. GM analysed the whole marketing environment and found that against demand sluggishness in many European countries, Chinese car sales continued to grow at a double-digit rate. However, Chinese cities such as Baizing, Shanghai, etc., were overloaded with offers but that did not expand beyond big cities. More than 200 cities with populations of one million residents and above were looking towards big cities to fulfil their individual need. As people living in these cities were usually daily-wage earners with limited spending ability in comparison to those living in other parts of the country the auto marketers traditionally overlooked them. GM wanted to capture this segment by emphasising on producing small, relatively stripped-down cars under its local Baojun brand name. "We aim to surpass customer expectations by creating a brand that combines world-class quality with low ownership costs," said Shen Yang, general manager of GM-SAIC-Wuling[6]. Accordingly, GM produced and positioned its tier II city cars for this segment and used low pricing strategy to woo the consumers of the target segment with comparatively low income.

Grey Marketing

Grey marketing or parallel importing can affect pricing in international markets. Grey marketing is said to have taken place when branded or trademarked goods sneak in a country and make them available to consumers at a lower price without authorisation of the brand or trade mark owner. The low price of the products is the key factor to the marketing success of the products available in the grey market. So, under grey marketing, the consumers get perplexed when they encounter same products are being offered at different prices; one much less costlier available in grey market places and two, higher priced products available in the legal or authorised shops. Grey marketing is also known as parallel importing. Parallel importing happens due to manufacturers' international price discrimination and unofficial importing to other countries. Some of the root causes for price differentiation between countries have been deliberate attempt by producer, growing inventories, sharp changes in exchange rates, and slowing of economic growth in some countries. Sony's historical problem with grey marketing and price fixing for gaming gadget Sony PS3 can be sighted here as an example of grey marketing fall outs. Sony was introducing successive versions of its flagship play station gaming products at different prices in its core markets of Japan, Europe and the USA. For example, the 20 gigabyte version of PS3 had a recommended price of $499 compared to the equivalent of $430 in Japan and almost $640 in EU[7]. Let us explain how the differential pricing can help grey marketing to thrive in countries with the help of an hypothetical example (Figure 9.3) of Apple iPhone 6s and 6s Plus. Let A be the country America where Apple's production centre is located. Now, the 6s mobile phone is exported out to Country B (Bangladesh) and Country I (India) both in authorised and unauthorised way. Apple exports the product to Bangladesh and India legally, and hence, 6s & 6s Plus will be available in the legal shops located at Bangladesh and India at the company determined price of $499 and $640, respectively. It may so happened that some unscrupulous agents purchased the product in USA at the prevailing price $400 at that time and exported it to India and Bangladesh. As a result, the imported 6s phone was available in India and Bangladesh at two different prices, i.e., one at company registered price and other at grey market dictated price. Ironically, in the process, the producer Apple got involved in a price war with products of its own made in a distant markets. To make situation more complex there could also be a lateral import to Country I from Country B as well as there could be export of the product back to USA from India and Bangladesh where also the product would be available at two prices.

---

6 "Foreign Carmakers Try Brands Just for China", *Business Week*, March 3, 2011.

7 Thompson, Steve (2009), "Grey power: An empirical investigation of the impact of parallel imports on market prices", *Journal of Industry, Competition and Trade*, Hingham, September, Volume 9, Issue 3 p. 219.

FIGURE 9.3 Parallel imports

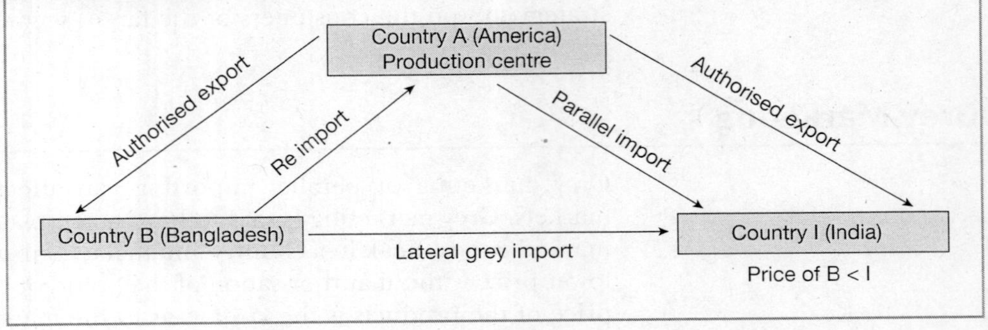

The original producer has to face a lot of difficulty in dealing with parallel importing and the resultant grey market. It affects the profits generation as comparatively low-priced imported versions would be going to the hands of the consumers. Interestingly, there would be some consumers who would prefer to take the risk of buying products from grey market than paying a higher price and buying from company registered shops. These consumers knowingly buy products from grey market without equivalent service from the manufacturing company in terms of warranty, after-sales service, shop décor, salesman support, etc. In the process, a good number of consumers, who otherwise would have been the prospective customer of the producer, drift away to the grey market because of availing low price only. The entire pricing strategy of a company for a country, therefore, gets a jolt when grey marketing is rampant.

Box 9.4 Grey market can affect pricing

International mobile handset manufacturers such as Nokia, Samsung, and LG are the worst sufferer in India due to grey marketing. These companies are not only required to compete with each other for the mobile handset markets across the country but also with their own products available in the grey market. These companies are supposed to draw their marketing strategy independently by keeping each others in the dark. However, the menace of grey marketing brought these three rivals close, arguably for the first time, in the matter of pricing strategy to fight out the grey marketers. These companies saw that the final price of the products sold from authorised shops was hiked steeply when different Indian states revised the value-added tax (VAT) on the mobile handsets. Maharashtra increased VAT on mobile phones from 4% to 12.5%. It was followed by Madhya Pradesh and Chattisgarh where rates were 12.5% and 14%, respectively. The higher price caused the customers to drift towards to the grey market where these products were available at a considerably lesser price. These companies recently met for a discussion on this issue as all of them were disturbed to see that the higher price of the mobile handset due higher VAT had impacted the sales of the products. To counter the grey market challenge, the three companies jointly decided to reduce their prices by up to 8% on the handsets. The meeting saw company executives who were determined to stop grey marketing of their products. They agreed not only on lowering of retail price but also promised to standardise the retail prices across the country in spite of higher tax rates to check grey market growth. "The mobile phone industry has rallied at its own cost to save the legal trade from total capitulation by the grey market," says Pankaj Mohindroo, national president of Indian Cellular Association (ICA), a mobile phone industry body.

Dealing with Grey Marketing

In international marketing, grey marketing menace was rampant in the previous years. The companies have learnt different ways to handle the situation effectively. Some of them are mentioned here below.

Product differentiation

Under this strategy company brings product differentiation so that products exported from one country are not attractive enough for other countries. Simplistically, customisation as per local tastes, preferences, safety rules, packaging requirements, technical standards and income levels for different markets would render the products not transferable from one country to another. This would have a dampening effect on parallel importing efforts. It is expected that developing different versions of a product to suit country-specific requirements would discourage the customers in the grey markets. Nokia, for example, marketed a customised mobile handset in India which may not have it market elsewhere. Sometimes companies also put different names and warranties for different markets to discourage grey marketing. Porsche makes its cars for the US market more powerful and better equipped in order to reflect the higher price. Of course, this type of strategy may back fire as it would lead to sacrificing the economies of scale and increases the production, inventory and marketing costs. Hence companies must weigh such options against the opportunity costs associated with grey market activities.

Strategic pricing

This option deals with strategic pricing strategy. Here, the marketers deliberately attempt to destroy the main attraction for customers in the grey markets, i.e., the lower price of the product. In order to curb grey marketing, therefore, the company needs to ensure standardised price across the countries where the products are available. It is understandable that standardised pricing strategies may have an adverse effect on marketing. Therefore, it is suggested that before opting such a strategy it is required to have a careful trade-off analysis between the costs and benefits of employing the strategy. Again narrowing the pricing and discount structure across countries would mean reducing the incentives for authorised distributors. This may have unwanted discouraging effects on the channel partners.

Relationships management

Under this strategy company lays emphasis on developing good relationship with distributors located in target country and handle the grey marketing menace through them only. Good relationship allows the company to receive immediate information if some disgruntled distributor diverts products to the grey markets. The good relationship also allow the distributors to walk an extra mile in checking grey marketing efforts in the country and build societal or legal pressure to stop selling products under grey market coverage.

Customer communications

In a country of excessive grey marketing sometimes the company seeks the support of the prospective customers. The company, under this strategy, develop a communication process for letting the customers know about the demerits associated with purchasing products from grey markets. An appropriate marketing communications program is developed depicting the negative side of grey market products such as non-availability of warranty period, obsolete or worn-out models not designed to meet the requirements for use in a specific country, buy-back issues, product upgrades, etc., and offloaded to the target customers by using an effective communication medium.

Anti-grey market alliance

Marketers must be aware of aware of issues in different countries to pre-empt grey marketing. Many companies can keep strong vigil on the legal laxity in countries of their interest which ultimately led to the problem of grey marketing and develop appropriate timely measures to outsmart grey marketers. The instantaneously developed anti-grey market alliance by the mobile handset manufacturers such as Nokia, Samsung and LG in India was found to be very effective to reduce grey marketing in the country. The affected companies helped each other and addressed the problem of unauthorised distribution jointly and promised to reduce price differentiation.

Building in-company awareness: The company employees could provide great support to eradicate the grey marketing in a country. For getting their adequate support it is required that employees to recognise the grey market issues of the country correctly and empowered to address the root causes. If required, the employees, especially those in customer service, sales, product marketing and management may be given training so that they can recognise the sign of grey marketing and initiate appropriate action to stop them.

Legal actions: The aggrieved company may also initiate the process of strengthening legal actions against the grey market operators or anybody who helps the leakage of products to the grey market. For this it requires the company management to visit the particular country and create appropriate awareness by organising seminar, press conference, etc., in order to built a right platform to initiate requisite legal processes to defuse the activity of grey marketing through legal intervention.

Countertrade

Countertrade practiced in a country also indirectly effects price fixing of company involved in international marketing. In general, countertrade is a cross border trading practice between a company and the government or companies of two different countries to exchange goods or commodities across international border without the requirement of currency transaction. The countertrade between two parties, be it government or private, materialises only through policy support of the concerned governments. Accordingly, two concerned parties of two different countries get involve in an exchange of a particular type of commodity or products against another type of commodity or products. There are many examples of countertrade in the world. However, one private to government cross border transaction involving Saudi Arabian government and Boeing Company worth mentioning. Saudi Arabia exchanged oil for Boeing aircraft worth $1 billion in the year 1984.

These types of arrangements, of course, are not regular happenings but based on the situational requirements. The need of countertrade arises when involved parties feel that

- One involved country has limited convertible currency. For example, PepsiCo of USA traded billions of dollars-worth of Pepsi in exchange for Stolichnaya vodka when Russian currency roubles were not tradable on the world market.
- Trade balance between two unequal countries is an issue. For example, India – Myanmar border trade agreement also stipulates countertrade between traders of the two countries wherein goods will be exchanged across the land border to ensure trade balance between the involved countries. This kept trade balance between these countries low.

Countertrade is required to get bargaining advantage. For example, Saudi Arabia cracked a good deal when Boeing accepted the offer to supply ten aircrafts in exchange crude oil priced 10% below the prevailing price. GE made an access to Romanian electric generator project in Romania in lieu of agreeing to market Romanian products in other country markets.

Forms of countertrade

Countertrade can take place in several forms:

Barter: In barter trade goods or services are exchanged for goods or services across the border. Since goods are paid by goods so no cash transaction is involved in the process. Mostly in international border areas barter trade can be an effective instrument facilitating products exchange without involvement of currency.

Counter-purchase: As the name suggests it is a combination of a purchase agreement and a reciprocal buying agreement. It has, therefore, two contracts to be executed with the involvement of hard currency at different dates. First, the exporter of a country negotiates with an importer and executes the deal with the involvement of hard currency. Then under the second contract the exporter is obligated to purchase goods from the importer at a specified value over a period of time. The volume of trade may not be equal but mostly depend on contract clause.

Offset: In this type, say company A has executed a cross border contract for company B and expecting to realise X USD from A. Now instead of receiving the sales proceed from B, now A has agreed to purchase goods and services with a specified percentage of its proceeds from its original sale to B. The product may be the same as in the first deal or may be different.

Dumping

In general, the term dumping is used when the price of a product sold in the importing country is less than the price of that product in the market of the exporting country. The interesting point here is how it can be possible and apparently it seems to be the result of discriminatory practice of the exporting company with the intention to destabilise the target country market.

For the first time, this discrimination became a matter of debate when Article VI of General Agreement on Tariffs and Trade (GATT), 1947, introduced international rules and a discipline outlining the dumping activities. GATT rules were in favour of condemning dumping if such imports caused material injury to the domestic industry producing similar type of products and were marketed domestically at a comparatively higher price than the imported one[8]. The basic idea of GATT was to check unfairness in pricing of the products by an exporter so that these foreign products on importation to a country cannot create an unfair competition with the local product because of 'unfair price'. GATT came out with the provision of anti-dumping duties, which may be levied by an aggrieved country if and only if following conditions are satisfied.

---

1. Prices are set at less than the 'normal value' and this has resulted in 'material injury' to the domestic industry.

Example: Dumping occurred when the export price of cycle rickshaws imported into India was found less than the normal value of 'like articles' sold in India. The price of a cycle rickshaw is around ₹10,000 to ₹12,000, depending on extra fittings needed in India, and hence, this value will be referred to as the "Normal Value" of the 'like articles'. The export price of cycle rickshaw imported into India from China was found to be only ₹3000, which was much cheaper that the normal prevailing price in the importing country. However, imports at cheap or low prices do not per se indicate dumping; it is only indicative. Margin of dumping refers to the difference between the normal value of the like article and the export price of the product under consideration. In this example, the margin of dumping was ₹7000. Material injury may be in terms of volume effect or price effect.

2. The domestic industry produces 'like articles'.

Example: The domestic cycle rickshaw industry is actively producing exactly similar types of products. Although it is not exactly a carbon copy, they are characteristically similar. It may not a comparison of an apple with an apple but the imported 'apple' is characteristically similar to the domestically produced apple. The cycle rickshaw imported in India was not exactly what is produced by the Indian small-scale sector, but it has a very close resemblance.

3. Imports are likely to cause material injury to the domestic industry.

Examples: The cycle rickshaws are produced in small-scale industrial sector of India. With the onslaught of auto rickshaws, the cycle rickshaws are nowadays on the back foot. The production process of cycle rickshaw is also very simple but requires significant manpower. With the slowing of demand, most of these workers are lowly paid. If the imported cycle rickshaws are allowed to enter the Indian market, then there will be (a) decline in output of the existing Indian producers, (ii) loss of sales, (iii) loss of market share, (iv) reduced profits, (v) decline in productivity, (vi) decline in

[8] _For a more interesting discussion on dumping, see Kazeki, Jun (2010), 'Anti-dumping negotiations under the WTO and FANs', *Journal of World Trade*, Vol. 44, No. 5, pp. 931–965.

Table 9.2 Share of selected countries in world antidumping initiations: 1995–2000

Country	Incidence
USA	0.03
EC	0.02
Canada	0.06
Korea	0.06
Argentina	0.73
Brazil	0.24
Mexico	0.07
India	0.69
World	0.06

Sources: WTO database; World Economic Outlook.

capacity utilisation, (vii) reduced return on investments, (viii) price effects as the price of the imported product will pull the domestic price down, and (ix) the small-scale producers will be adversely impacted on cash flow, inventories, employment, wages, growth, investments, ability to raise capital, etc. Therefore, one can say that importation of this product will cause material injury to the domestic cycle rickshaw industry. If the above conditions are satisfied, then the importing country may levy anti-dumping duty on a source-specific basis, which can be expressed either ad valorem or on specific basis.

The incidence of dumping, i.e., anti-dumping cases initiated by the importing country per billion dollar of import also varies from country to country. The Table 9.2 given above indicates that incidence of dumping in India stands at 0.69 as compared to 0.06 for the world indicating the higher number of anti-dumping cases initiated by the country than the world average. In fact, India's position in this regard is only second after Argentina in the world.

Company Internal Factors

In the matter of deciding on pricing strategy, it is important that companies consider all pertinent and prevailing internal issues in totality. Consideration of greater corporate goals, long-term perspective, market leadership commitments and commitment on depth internationalisation of the company are extremely important. At any point of time, it should not be felt that strategy decisions in pricing are only pertaining to the factors external to the company. Consideration of the long-term goal of the company is specifically important as it will set the pricing objectives rolling. Let us take an example to understand the case well. Toshiba elevator of Japan was very active in the gulf region during 2010 when recovery after economic slowdown began. The company also had done reasonably well through execution of projects worth more than Dh 300 million. Looking at the upcoming infrastructure development projects in the gulf region, Toshiba elevators decided to set a goal to double its turnover in the region by the end of 2015. Toshiba elevators, accordingly, started bidding aggressively in infrastructure projects.

It opened offices in Saudi Arabia, Oman and Qatar with local partners. The efforts bore fruits and the company started reaping the benefits. It executed large number of projects in Dubai and Abu Dhabi. Abu Dhabi emerged as a key market for Toshiba where the company executed order worth Dh 100 million in Reem Islands' Marina Square involving 126 elevators in 13 Towers[9]. Its president and CEO Sunichi Kimura looked after the developments in the middle-east market personally from the headquarters in Japan. Mr Kimura ensured that the long-term objective of the company in the matter of middle-east market in particular and other country markets in general are considered while deciding on the price for bidding in different projects. The company also considered its corporate goal to have long-term presence in the foreign market pricing as well. As a result, the pricing decided by the company did not reflect any intention to maximise profit in the short-term. The company never quoted abnormally higher price in any contract. Never did it look like that the company is in a hurry to make profit by some short-cut way. The internal control system of the company was also evident from the pricing. Because of headquarter control, the company always quoted price in a uniform way and did not charge different prices for different markets. The company was neither market leader nor in a race to retain its leadership status in the middle-east market. This was also nicely reflected in the pricing. The company never showed a tendency to use pricing as a tool for getting temporary benefits and thereby refrained from varying price with intent to defeat the market rivals.

Transfer pricing

Transfer pricing is a term used to describe inter-company pricing arrangements relating to transactions between related business entities. These can include transfers of intellectual property, tangible goods, services and loans or other financing transactions. International businesses require managing a supply chain that may be spread across countries. In fact, an international supply chain gives more competitive strength to the organisation than one which is restricted to one country only. International businesses work hard to build up a cross-country supply chain that is integrated and interdependent and developed meticulously on the sole ground of efficiency. For Ford motor car, 30% of the car's value originates in Korea, 17.5% in Japan, 7.5% in Germany, 4% in Taiwan and Singapore, 2.5% in the U.K., and 1.5% in Ireland and Barbados. That is, only 37% of the production value is generated in the United States. Nike products are manufactured in more than 700 factories, employing over 500,000 workers in 51 countries. The cross-country spread of supply chain takes the advantage of country-specific market, skilled labour, raw material abundance, etc. Suppose a USA multinational firm has two subsidiaries, one located in India and the other in Mauritius. The Indian subsidiary manufactures its products and sends them to Mauritius, which in turn markets the product. The Mauritius subsidiary must pay a price to the Indian arm for the products it receives from them. Now what would be the transfer price? Who will determine it? How would this be fixed? This continues to

[9] *Khaleej Times*, 28 March 2010.

be a major issue in the context of international business as by this "transfer price" the firm may shift the profit generation in one country to another. Let us take the same example and consider it in more detail: ABC enterprise of the US has two subsidiaries – the Indian firm manufactures the products and transfers it to the Mauritius sales subsidiary. In the year 2012, the Indian firm transferred the products to the sales subsidiary in Mauritius and priced it as ₹10,000. Say, the Indian firm pays tax @ 25% while the Mauritius firm pays tax @ 50%. The Indian firm made a profit of ₹2250 while the Mauritius firm's profit was ₹4500 after deducting the operating expenses and country-specific tax leading to a consolidated company profit of ₹6750. The next year the firm decided to transfer the same quantity of product produced at an inflated price of ₹14,000 to the Mauritius firm so that that profit generation in the high-tax regime is low. As a result, in the year, profit generation in the Indian firm increased to ₹5250, whereas the Mauritius firm's profit reduced to ₹2500 after deducting the operating expenses and country-specific tax leading to enhancement of consolidated company profit to ₹7750 (Table 9.3).

Now the question arises, can the company fix the transfer price (in this case, ₹10,000 in 2012 and ₹14,000 in 2013) and change it? If not, how will this be fixed? The definition of "transfer price" in business economics says that it is: "the price paid for goods and services involved in intra corporate transactions between a subsidiary and other branches of the corporate family." If the transfer price is not set as per some internationally accepted regulations, then international companies will be in trouble ascertaining the correctness of the price in intra company transfer situation where price bargaining does not matter. Possibly, in such situation, companies would be driven by the objective of accumulating more profit in the low-tax countries and hence manipulate the transfer price that increase the consolidated profit as a whole for the concerned company. Furthermore, a company may involve in accumulating profits in it's headquarter country rather than in another country subsidiary formed by minority share holding. In worst cases, the company may use transfer price as a tool to deprive producers located in poor countries by showing less profit generation in such countries and thereby escaping from statutory payments to the workers such as bonus, etc.

Table 9.3 Impact of transfer pricing on net income

Item	Indian subsidiary (mfg)		Mauritius subsidiary (sales)		Consolidated company profit	
	2012	2013	2012	2013	2012	2013
Sales	10,000	14,000	20,000	20,000	20,000	20,000
Less cost of the good sold	6000	6000	10,000	14,000	6000	6000
Gross profit	4000	8000	10,000	6000	14,000	14,000
Operating expenses	1000	1000	1000	1000	2000	2000
Taxable income	3000	7000	9000	5000	12,000	12,000
Tax rate	25%	25%	50%	50%		
Tax	750	1750	4500	2500	5250	3000
Net income	2250	5250	4500	2500	6750	7750

Source: Author

FIGURE 9.4 Arm's length price

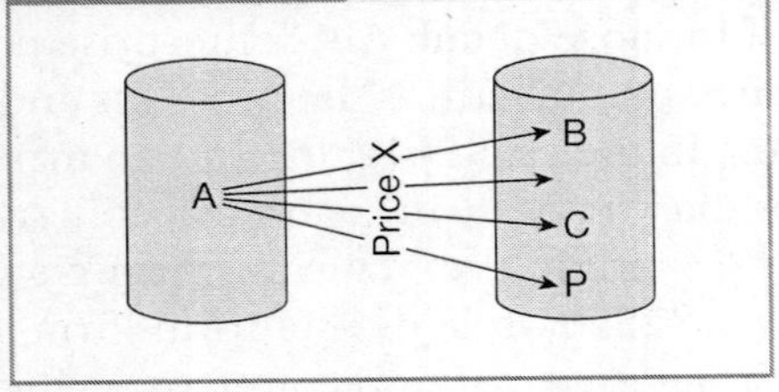

In order to bring uniformity and clarity in determining the transfer price by companies independently when involved in cross country intra-firm transfer of products and commodities, Organisation for Economic Cooperation and Development (OECD) formulated the arm's length principles in arriving at the transfer price. According to the OECD, the "arm's length" principle is active in transaction when company A sets the transaction price X while transacting the product or commodity with its related group entities, i.e., company B, C, etc., and thereafter reflects that same price X while transacting the same product or commodity with unrelated companies P, Q, etc., in similar types of transactions under similar conditions (Figure 9.4).

Interestingly, the onus of proving that company A has transacted with its related subsidiary companies B and C in Mauritius by following arm's length price lies on A only when challenged by any statutory body responsible for ensuring intra company transfer price in accordance with arm's length principle. Therefore, the issue of transfer pricing are also going to affect the price fixing of the final product in the distant market if the product is manufactured in a country and transferred to another country sales subsidiary for marketing purpose.

Box 9.5 Companies are faltering on transfer pricing issues

During the year 2012–13, the transfer pricing department of India had raised doubts on as many as 1600 transactions between corporates in India and their parent companies/associates abroad regarding the transfer price maintained in those transactions. According to them, the prices did not follow the principles of arm's length pricing. Mostly, these intra-company deals were executed by banks, FMCG companies, pharmaceutical companies and diamond companies. The transfer pricing department of Ministry of Finance, therefore, issued tax demand notices to many such companies on the ground of transfer price rules violation. Considering the fact that the country was yet to develop maturity in handling transfer pricing issues like western countries, additional facility was provided to the erring companies to defend their individual cases in front of Dispute Resolution Panel (DRP) created in major cities.

The industry as a whole in India welcomed the formation of DRP, which basically constituted by two commissioner level officers and one director (international taxation). Here, any aggrieved party can freely appeal against transfer pricing rulings. In many cases, the DRP involvement has been beneficial to unveil the actual income of the concerned parties, which is typically concealed by measures such as showing losses, comparing transaction values incorrectly or showing artificial expenses.

The transfer pricing department officers handling cases of transfer pricing narrated a few interesting cases of tax evasion by not following arm's length pricing system. In one such case, a diamond merchant of India was executing contract work of cutting and polishing diamonds entrusted to his firm from time to time. The firm was showing losses continuously in the past years. Surprisingly, the contracted rate remained same at $100 a diamond even the firm was losing money. Also the owner did not asked for revision of the contracted rate in the past years. This behaviors of contract manufacturer raised doubt of the transfer pricing officials about the application of arm's length pricing principle in the instant case. In another case, a major detergent manufacturer justified the transaction price as arm's length price by comparing the same with a cross border deal and transacted price thereon for a shoes manufacturer. The official of transfer pricing department lamented, "They do not even know that arm's length price can only be established by comparing only with the transaction value of similar companies in the industry". Interestingly, when pressed for an explanation, the detergent major said that both shoe and detergent manufacturer belonged to the same FMCG sector.

Source: The Economic Times, 11 December 2009

Export Pricing

Export is the simplest form of internationalisation involving two parties, exporter and importer, separated by an international border. The exporter decides on the price of the products to be exported in advance so that it can be quoted to the importer. Broadly, an exporter is guided by one of the following two methods of product pricing: Cost based pricing and market based pricing.

Cost-based export pricing

This is the most commonly used approach for export pricing. As the name indicates, in this method, the company first calculates the cost of the product and then decides on the margin or profit. The exporter may use the method in the following two ways.

Full cost pricing This is a very simple method of pricing with the objective of ensuring full recovery of cost of production and exportation. It also ensures recovery of a certain amount of pre-determined profit as per industry practice. As shown in the Figure 9.5 below, the total manufacturing cost of flower vase calculated to be ₹5000. The industry standard market up in handicraft sector is about 25-40% on the cost of production. So, this mark up price is added to find out the ex-work or ex factory price of the product. The exporter would quote this price for the products to the importer if the products are expected to deliver at the factory gate of the producer. However, if the importer desires the exporter to load the products on the ship for sea transport to the destination country, then the exporter needs to add up the exportation costs such as export documentation cost, transportation cost to the port and loading cost on the ship, etc., to arrive at the free on board price (FOB). The exporter may further adds the cost of marine insurance and cost of sea freight up to the port of destination to arrive at the cost insurance and freight (CIF) price of the products (₹7250 in the example).

FIGURE 9.5 Full cost pricing

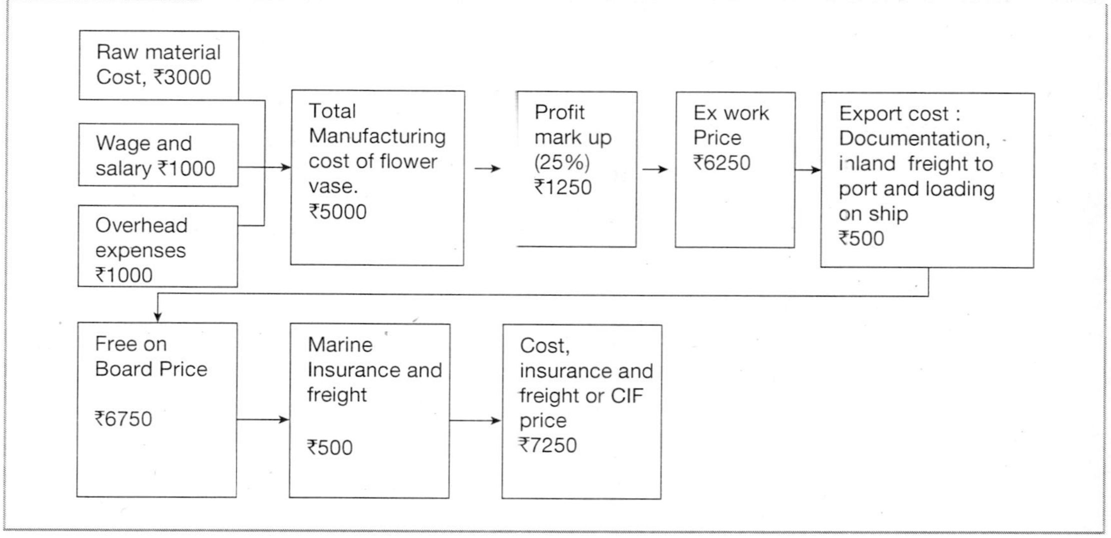

Marginal cost pricing Marginal cost pricing is also based on cost. Therefore, in arriving at marginal cost pricing, it is necessary that the manufacturer cum exporter first understands different types of costs incurred in production and thereafter calculate the break-even volume of production of the product that is contemplated for export. In other words, the manufacturer cum exporter should know the point of production at which total cost (fixed cost and variable cost) is equal to the total revenue. To illustrate the concept of marginal costing, let us use an example:

Assume that the manufacturing cum exporting company received an export order for exporting handcrafted flower vase from India. The company has the factory capacity to produce 120,000 flower vases per year based on the equipment, raw material and skilled labour availability. Now, the company incurs various variable costs pertaining to raw material cost, wage payment, sales commission, production supplies, etc. The variable costs pertaining to a company are those which vary in accordance with production. It also incurs fixed cost estimated to be of ₹12,00,000 per year, which includes permanent portion of salary and wages, factory rent, lease payments on account of machines, electricity, etc. This is the fixed cost to the company as the company has to spend this amount even if there is no production in the factory. Thus, the company calculated that for producing a single flower vase for the domestic market, it had to spend ₹40 towards the variable costs such as direct labour, direct material, and direct expenses, which can be directly attributed to the product and will vary with production. The company, say, sells a single such flower vase at ₹60 in the domestic market. The company, based on the above information, calculated the break-even volume for domestic sales in the following way.

$$\begin{aligned}\text{Breakeven volume} &= \text{Fixed costs/Contribution}\\ &= (\text{Fixed costs/Selling price} - \text{Variable costs})\\ &= (₹12{,}00{,}000/(₹60 - ₹40)\\ &= ₹12{,}00{,}000/₹20\\ &= 60{,}000 \text{ units}\end{aligned}$$

Now, from above it is clear that the company covers the fixed cost of production after selling 60,000 units @ ₹60 in the domestic market. So, each unit sold after 60,000 units, required to covers only the variable cost, i.e., ₹40 only because the fixed cost part has already been covered by 60,000 units already sold in the domestic market. If the company now takes a policy decision of selling the balance 60,000 units in the export market, then it can sell them at a price lower than the domestic market price to tackle the competition there since the fixed cost amount has already been earned through domestic marketing.

Advantage/disadvantage of cost based pricing

1. The cost-based pricing method is frequently used by exporters because it is easy to understand and implement even by first time exporters.
2. The exporter- manufacturer seriously understands and documents various types of costs incurred while producing and exporting a consignment. The exporter drive satisfaction when utilises such costs as basis of

pricing as the price arrived at would lead to the recovery of all sorts of costs incurred during the actual transaction.

3. The cost based pricing makes the exporter very stereotype and inward looking and hence in the process may miss some wonderful opportunities abroad where higher prices could have been charged.
4. The method of marginal cost pricing may allow a firm to fight out some very acute price competition in the foreign market but there is a possibility that it may also be viewed by the importing country government of as dumping.

Market-based export pricing

In cost-based pricing, prices are determined on the basis of costs with little interest in the market or competitive factors in the export market. Cost based pricing are, therefore, termed as inwards looking because of its emphasis on factory rather than to the market and competition while fixing price of a product. Market-based export pricing, on the other hand, takes into account market and competition factors when setting the price. Exporters who matures with time and has gathered in-depth country-specific market knowledge would like to look beyond the factory. At that time the exporter may like to be more market oriented than cost oriented in fixing price of the products. For example, the hand crafted flower vase manufacturer cum exporter may not like to fix the price by looking at the cost of production and various types of cost associated with it but instead, may prefer enhance profit by being speculative on country specific opportunities. This can be done through utilisation of various marketing measures based on respective country-specific marketing environment constituted by consumers' preference, etc. There are various market based pricing methods but three very popular methods such as premium pricing, penetration pricing and market skimming pricing are discussed here.

Premium pricing strategy

In this method, the exporter exploits the market by fixing the price of the product at a considerably higher level. For example, the flower vase manufacturer would not base his pricing calculation on cost of production but by marketing objective. Under premium pricing strategy, the exporter first carefully studies the market segment targeted to exploit and then position the product as premium product through requisite marketing communication. When the product is a premium product then a higher price for the product, i.e., hand-crafted flower vase can be fixed and accordingly marketed. However, care should be taken to ensure that right and desired positioning is achieved for the flower vase in the minds of the consumers. Accordingly, the exporter needs to communicate to the target consumers about the exclusivity of the handcrafted flower vase produced in India. The exclusivity may be due to uniqueness of craft, use of ancient traditional Indian manufacturing process, Indianness in design, involvement of handicraft rather than use of machine, etc. This type of pricing strategy is suitable when the target consumers want to be different than the general people living in the country and hence the positioning, media planning, etc., have to be very strategic.

Penetration pricing strategy

The flower vase manufacturer cum exporter may use penetration pricing when it wants to use price as a tool to gain market position first and then consolidate its position for long-term presence in the foreign market. Therefore, it will first attempt to create a space of its own in the market and then expand. A low price on entry into the foreign market allows them to slowly gain the market share by convincing the target customers about the quality of the product. One precondition for adopting the penetration pricing has been the quality of the product. The exporter, hence, may undergo some losses for some length of time but once the good name associated with superior quality of the product at low price is spread, the market demand increases. It is expected that increased sales volume in future eventually offsets the initially loss made by the exporter.

Market skimming pricing strategy

Market skimming strategy is a proactive strategy for the exporter. It requires the exporter to understand the current competitive situation of the foreign market. When there is a void in the market place and entry of a number of producers producing similar products are expected then market skimming strategy works well. So, there is short period of time available for the exporter to maximise revenue in the foreign market by charging a higher price for the products. However, exporters using this strategy must resort to adequate communication in the foreign market so that more number of customers buy the products within this time limit. If the product is in the introductory phase of the product life cycle in the foreign market and marketing communications are aggressive, the early adopters will be willing to pay higher price. This pricing strategy cannot be practiced when competition becomes pronounced and immense pressure is felt to drop the price of the product to the level of the competitors or below.

Factors Affecting Export Pricing

Currency of transaction

The currency in which the price is quoted by the exporter influences the price setting. Three choices are available to the exporter: to quote the price in the currency of buyer, seller or to quote in another foreign currency. However, if the price quoted is quoted in the USD or Euro, it becomes easier to compare and understand the transaction. Suppose an Indian exporter sells to an American importer a handcrafted carpet worth 10,000 USD in value terms, with an understanding that the importer will pay the contracted amount within 90 days to the exporter. On the date when the contract was executed, the exchange rate was 1 USD = 50 INR on the foreign exchange market. Now, if on the contract executing day, the Indian exporter receives the money from the American as advance payment in full, he can expect to earn 500,000 INR. However, as per the contract the importer may also pay within 90 days. Say, on the 90th day, the exchange rate was 1 USD = 40 INR. Now, although the American importer will pay USD 10,000, the Indian exporter will eventually receive 400,000 INR. In this case, the loss of the Indian exporter does not

Box 9.6 Countries with pegged currency

1. **Euro currency members pegged to the Euro**
   Austria, Germany, Luxembourg, Belgium, Greece, Netherlands, Finland, Ireland, Portugal, France, Italy, Spain.
2. **Non-members pegged to the Euro**
   Bosnia, Bulgaria, Cyprus, Denmark, Estonia, Hungary, Latvia, Lithuania, Malta, Slovakia, Slovenia.
3. **CFA Franc Zone (Central and West African), pegged to the Euro**
   Benin (Africa), Congo-Brazzaville, Mali, Burkina Faso, Côte d'Ivoire, Niger, Cameroon, Equatorial Guinea, Senegal, Central African Rep. Gabon, Togo, Chad, Guinea-Bissau.
4. **Countries with currencies pegged to the USD**
   Dijibouti, Bahamas, Jordan, Panama, Bahrain, Kuwait, Qatar, Barbados, Lebanon, Saudi Arabia, Belize, Maldives, Seychelles, Ecuador, Micronesia, Syria, El Salvador, Netherlands, Antilles Archipelago, UAE, Eritrea, Oman, Venezuela.
5. **Eastern Caribbean Currency Union, pegged to the USD**
   Antigua & Barbuda, Grenada, St Lucia, Dominica, St Kitts & Nevis, St Vincent & the Grenadines.
6. **African country pegged with South African currency Rand**
   Lesotho.

Source: Compilation by author from internet

mean a gain of the American importer either. However, if the reverse thing happens, i.e., the exchange rate became 1 USD = 60 INR on the 90th day there will be gain of the exporter. The exporter will then receive 600,000 INR out of the transaction. Therefore, while fixing the export price, the exporter needs to take in to consideration the expected exchange rate fluctuation. However, some currencies do not fluctuate against another. Such currencies are known as pegged currency, otherwise known as floating currency. Pegged currency can be tied to a particular currency (for example, fixed to the USD) or as a currency union (such as countries in the euro area). Pegging reduces volatility and hence must not impact the export pricing much. A floating currency, on the other hand, impacts the export pricing decision since the exchange rate with another currency is determined by supply and demand of the currency in private market and absolutely not in the hand of exporter.

Type of channel used

The distribution channel used by the exporting company for distribution in the foreign market can also influence the price setting. The exporter has the option of either reaching the customer through own sales subsidiary created for the purpose or through independent distributors. In own distribution situation, the exporter focuses on achieving marketing objectives and hence, the price is expected to vary in accordance with situational requirement. In the case of independent distributors, the exporter has no formal authority to control the marketing programme of the importer cum distributor. Hence, it is expected that once the products are reached to the importer and the landed cost is realised, the exporter has no other monetary commitments. The following Table 9.4 expresses the pricing implication of the exporter in respect of the two cases described above.

Table 9.4 Chanel used and price variation

	Pricing implication (in ₹) to exporter in cases of	
	Own distributors	**Independent distributors**
Cost price at Kolkata factory	90	90
Profit	10	10
Selling price at Kolkata	100	100
Transportation to Kolkata port	20	20
Freight and insurance	20	20
Landed cost at Dubai	140	140
Import tariff (50% on landed cost)	70	70
Importers cost or Exporter quoted price	210	210
Add Importer's margin 20%	42	42
Wholesalers cost	252	–
Wholesaler's margin 20%	50.40	–
Retailers cost	302.40	–
Retailer's margin 20%	60.48	–
Retail price at Dubai	362.88	–

The various factors influencing retail price in case of independent distributors marketing are:

- The choice of intermediaries to deliver the product to the ultimate users.
- The number of intermediaries engaged by the importer to deliver the product to the ultimate users.
- The contractual relationship between the importer and its intermediaries.
- The profit sharing arrangement between the importer and inter-mediaries.

Marketing goal

The exporter's marketing intention influences the pricing pattern. The manufacturer exporter may limit its responsibility in the foreign market by delivering the product to the importer's port. In that case, the exporter is likely to be motivated by cost recovery aspects. However, in certain markets the exporter may be more involved and desires to achieve specific marketing objectives. Thus in these markets the exporting company may even drop price by reducing its own margin to sustain long-time presence.

Level of adaptation

The depth of adaptation required of the product to suit the foreign market and its nature of deviation from the usual shape, colour, characteristics, etc., would influence pricing. In fact, more the adaption is required more will be the cost incurred by the exporter. Although the first casualty in the process would be the economies of scale because the adapted product is expected to be only for a country market, it also has pricing implication. The exporter now will have to incur more production cost and hence the quoted price to the importer or the ultimate price at the market will be escalated.

FIGURE 9.6 Book adaptation may cost less

In terms of product component, the core adaptation would entail huge cost. But support service components or peripheral adaptations may not incur significant cost even if it is adapted to foreign requirements. For example, Warren J. Keegan and Mark C. Green had written the famous book on Global Marketing which was subsequently translated into Chinese, Portuguese and other languages. The language adaptation or putting simply translation of the book in to Chinese language would not increase the price of the product much (Figure 9.6). But consider the more in-depth product adaptation of J.K. Rowling's Harry Potter books in China (Table 9.5).

All the above mentioned adaptations made Harry Potter books close to the Chinese young readers. The huge adaptation efforts made by several translators also were paid off when the first three books of Harry Potter were sold more than 1.3 million copies in China. But very few people would know about the marketing decision took by the British publishers to adapt to books closely in Chinese inspite of huge adaptation costs.

It is apparent from the above Table 9.6 that the T- Shirt manufacturer almost undertaken a complete adaptation of product for making it suitable for American and European markets and appealing to the targeted segments. Of course, the size of the segment would be the deciding factor for embarking on such an adaptation programme. However, the cost of such adaptation would have to be absorbed by the producers as otherwise it will affect the customers and impact pricing.

Packaging/Labelling Requirements

Countries recommend certain norms of packaging/labelling before products are marketed in a country. These norms are mostly guided by country-specific legal regulations or for ensuring safety during transportation, storage, and handling. For example, fish products exported from the Indian subcontinent to EU or USA need to be transported in sub-zero packaging condition throughout for maintaining its freshness. Labelling requirements, such

Table 9.5 Book adaptation may cost more

Adaptation component	Adapted component	Reason for adaptation
Name of characters: (1) Harry Potter, (2) Hermione Granger, (3) Ron Weasley, (4) Albus Dumbledore, (5) Voldemort	Adapted names: (1) Hali Bote, (2) Hemin Gelanjie, (3) Luo'en Weisilai, (4) Abusi Dengbuliduo, (5) Fudimo	Transliterations to suit Chinese pronunciation. British name carried semantic load. Their structure and sound were needed to be adapted.
Cultural environment in the storyline which was decidedly British.	Back drop of the storyline with as much as possible with Chinese touch. Hogwarts type of wizardry school was never heard by Chinese youngsters. Hogwarts inmates like boy wizard are transformed into a fat hairy dwarf.	To suit to the imagination of young readers not knowing British culture.
Food Items refereed in the story like Cornflakes.	Had to use a footnote in the Chinese translation, to indicate that these are consumed immersed in milk for breakfast.	To allow readers to understand the English food.
Themes which the story used like Wizardry, superstitious belief.	Had to change with touch of magic as per Chinese standard.	China does not allow wizardry, superstitions to spread in society.
Rhymes, anagrams or invented words, acronyms used by different characters of the story.	House names (Raven claw), or Voldemort's name. Acronyms such as O.W.L.s (Ordinary Wizarding Levels) and N.E.W.T.s (Nastily Exhausting Wizarding Tests) had undergone change. Invented words such as quidditch, quaffles, and muggles were difficult to translate by keeping only the theme.	Unless grown up in British environment these words would be alien.

Table 9.6 Product complete adaptation for T-Shirts

Adaptation component	For India	For USA and Europe
Fabrics modification	Fabric is finer and stronger	American and the European markets require finer and stronger fabric so that they reflect quality.
Stitching modification	Thicker stitch	Americans like finer stitching.
Inside lining	Lining provided	American like without lining.
Sizing of the T-Shirts	Indian sizing standards	Americans- European-standards.
Tags	Provided in English or in local language	In English as well as languages of European countries.
Design	Usually with some design	Latest design from Paris fashion show.

as for foodstuffs, may be particularly stringent in some rich countries such as EU and US, thereby affecting the pricing structure. For example, packaged food products exported to EU require different labelling with following information:

- Product name.
- Form (for example, smoked or frozen).
- Coding of additives, colourings and flavour enhancers.
- Name and address of importer.
- Country of origin, and name and address of manufacturer.
- Date of manufacture, or date by which product must be consumed.
- Storage requirements.

- Ingredients in order of relative importance, often by weight.
- Instructions for preparation or use, including precautions, if any, that may be required.
- Net weight shown in measurements used by the importing country.
- Translated information in the relevant language of the importing country.

When exporter's marketing responsibility ends at the port of the importer and the importer takes on the responsibility of labelling and packaging modification, the price is not expected to vary much. However, pricing decision will be impacted proportionally to value chain members if the responsibility of reaching the customer segment is on the exporter.

Transport infrastructure and delay in export/import clearance

When the distant market is difficult to be reached, it will increase the transportation cost and hence price of the product. In addition, poor customs and shipping infrastructure in terms of road, rail, port handling, etc., will put extra pressure on the price for upward revision. It can be further aggravated if the law and order problem requires the exporter to resort to some extra insurance coverage. In some countries trade facilitation services in the seaports takes a long time. For example, as per the doing business report of World Bank 2013, import clearance in the African country Chad takes a total of 98 days. An exporter while fixing price, therefore, need to look in to the doing business report of World Bank 2013 to understand the level of trading difficulties with the country. The exporter may not like to absorb these additional costs but prefer to enhance the price if the products are required to be delivered at the importer's place. In addition, to understand the customs and shipping infrastructure of the country the exporter needs to consult the logistics performance index (LP1) and ranking of the destination countries. The Table 9.7 below depicts the ranking of the bottom fifteen countries of World Bank's as per logistics performance report of 2015. Understandably, the higher the overall LPI ranking of export destination country, the more will be transport cost and effect on product pricing.

Customs duty

Export price is greatly affected by the applicable customs duty or import duty of the concerned importing country. Every country sets customs duty according to its own requirements. Therefore, import duties of products reflect the priorities and preferences of the country. For example, India may impose import duty on 22 carat of jewellery when imported from Thailand at a rate which is as low as zero percent but the same would be about 10% when imported from USA. In addition, country-specific trade agreements like RTA, FTA, or CECA also influence tariff rate. For example, South African Customs Union (SACU) member country South Africa will allow import of product from another member country like Namibia at zero import duty but may charge a high tariff rate for products imported from a non-member country like India. France would charge import duty on fresh or dried pineapple at the rate 5.8% when it imports from New Zealand but the same product entering

Table 9.7 Logistics difficulties to cost more for the exporter

Country	Overall LPI rank	Ease of shipment rank	Logistics services rank	Ease of tracking rank	Domestic logistics costs rank	Timeliness rank
Mongolia	136	91	144	136	70	142
Tanzania	137	132	138	120	15	140
Solomon Islands	138	104	123	131	111	139
Albania	139	109	130	145	105	144
Algeria	140	139	139	108	33	103
Guyana	141	144	137	98	4	129
Chad	142	142	143	138	1	127
Niger	143	145	134	133	150	85
Sierra Leone	144	143	140	135	69	121
Djibouti	145	137	133	143	99	138
Tajikistan	146	136	141	146	138	146
Myanmar	147	146	135	149	76	147
Rwanda	148	148	148	148	52	135
Timor-Leste	149	149	149	147	16	141
Afghanistan	150	150	150	150	40	150

Source: World Bank's logistics performance report of 2015

from Ghana would face 2.3% as reduced tariff rate under Generalised System of Preference (GSP) offered to underdeveloped countries.

Hence exporters' pricing decisions are greatly affected by the import duty structure of the importing countries as customs duty is calculated on the 'assessable *v*alue', which is often the transaction value determined by the exporter and importer for a particular product being exported. The duty is levied *ad valorem,* i.e., on percentage term. However, for certain items such as petroleum and alcohol, customs duty is based on a *specific rate* applicable to the volume of the import or export consignments.

The exporter may start assessing the impact of customs duty on the proposed export price to be quoted to the importer by first finding the exact HS codes (Harmonised Commodity Description and Coding System) of the product. The World Customs Organisation (WCO) which is the apex body of all the customs organisations of the respective countries provides and maintains the internationally standardised HS codes. The WCO, based in Brussels, Belgium, is an independent intergovernmental organisation with over 170 member country membership. The simplified HS nomenclature allows developing a common understanding amongst the involved parties in trade – the exporter, the importer and customs officials of both the countries. As the usual names of products on transit are represented by universally accepted numbers, so no misunderstanding is allowed to be created on the nature and characteristics of the products amongst the involved parties. Each product's name has an allotted number which is universally the same. Countries fix their import duties in those numbers and hence they are also known as a tariff line. 'Tariff line' defines a product at a detailed level for the purposes of setting a customs tariff. HS codes are also easy to follow as they are nicely arranged in

96 chapters and each chapter begins with general rules of interpretation and explanatory notes. The HS system begins with two-digit codes that designate the sector to which the product belongs. With the increase of digits to four, referred to as headings, the products of different complexities are described. The addition of subsequent digits, therefore, describes further subdivisions or level of value addition of the products. The four digits product codes are commodities in nature followed by product codes of 6 digits. The HS product codes up to 6-digit level are the same throughout the world and hence termed as harmonised. However beyond six digits, they may differ in each country or group of countries (Table 9.8). For example, European Union the 6-digit HS codes are further extended to 8 digits or to 10 digits for further discrimination of customs duty and levels of value addition in products. EU felt the need to have common product code for coming out with common tariff for the union. Accordingly, EU created common nomenclature (CN) using 8-digit codes where seventh and eighth digits identify the CN subheadings. Then again the EU felt that all the import measures such as tariff measures (duty rates, tariff quota rates, etc.), commercial measure (initiating dumping action, prohibitions, etc., were required to be applied in an identical way by all the member countries of EU and hence it came out with 10-digit TARIC (Integrated Tariff of the European Communities) codes. It uses international HS code system, European Union's CN, and further addition of an unique 2-digit TARIC component as well (in some instances four digits) as shown in the Table 9.8 below.

Other than EU, countries such as USA, China, and Canada also use 10-digit subdivisions. Countries such as Japan and Moldova use 9-digit subdivisions. Twelve digits are common in Turkey. The ten ASEAN countries have adopted ASEAN Harmonised Tariff Nomenclature (AHTN), which is an 8-digit commodity nomenclature based on Harmonised System (HS) but each member state has national subheadings.

Table 9.8 HS nomenclature with CN subheading

1	2	3	4	5	6	7	8	9	10
HS chapter									
E.g. 04 – Cotton.		HS heading							
		E.g. 0401– Milk cream not concentrated not sweetened.		HS subheading					
				E.g. 0401 10 – Milk not concentrated and unsweetened exceeding 1% fat not exceeding 6% fat.		CN subheading			
						E.g. 0401 10 10 – Milk and cream of a fat content by weight of <=1% in immediate packing of <=21, not concentrated nor containing added sugar or other sweetening matter.		TARIC Sub heading	
								E.g. 0401 10 10 00	

Table 9.9 Tariff increases with value addition

S. No.	Country	Basic product with HS code		Processed product with HS code	
1.	France	Product	MFN Tariff (Ad velorem equivalent). Year: 2015	Product	MFN Tariff (Ad Velorem equivalent). Year: 2015
		070190 - Potatoes, fresh	0	110520 - Potato flakes	12.2
				200520 - Potatoes, prepared or preserved otherwise than by vinegar or acetic acid (excl. froz)	8.8 + agricultural component
				200599 - Vegetables and mixtures of vegetables, prepared or preserved	6.4
2.	Japan	040110 - Milk and cream, not concentrated or containing added sugar.	21.30	040310190 - Buttermilk, curdled milk and cream, yogurt, containing added fruit, nuts and cocoa: yogurt.	139.39
		080430 - Pineapples, fresh or dried.	17	200941 - Pineapple juice.	23
		Grapes	17	200961 - Grape juice, incl. grape must, unfermented, Brix value <= 30 at 20°C, whether or not containing added sugar or other sweetening matter	23
		520512 - Cotton yarn.	5.6	600191 - Pile knitted or crocheted fabrics of cotton.	9.8
		080810 - Fresh apples	17	200971 - Apple juice,	23
3.	USA	040110 Milk	0.57	040210 - Milk powder	0.88
				040610 - Fresh cheese	10

Source: Trade wizard data base

In general, as value addition possibilities increase in the foreign country, the tariff rate gets reduced proportionately. For example, basic products such as milk attract import tariff of 66% in USA but processed milk in the form of milk powder would attract tariff at the rate 179% (Table 9.9).

Tariff rate quota

As with tariff rate, tariff rate quota (TRQ) may influence pricing to a great extent. TRQ provides a level of a product or commodity, in terms of quantity, beyond which the importing country would levy highly enhanced customs duty. The TRQ rates are fixed by the countries themselves. For example, European Union levies an in-quota tariff for rice at the rate of 0% and out-of-quota tariff at the rate of 87%. Country like USA levies an in-quota tariff for sugar at the rate of 2% while it's out of quota tariff stand at 49%. Exporter suffers from huge uncertainly from TRQ because they usually come to know about the higher tariff to be levied on the products while

Table 9.10 Tariff rate quota

Market	Product	In-quota ad valorem tariff, %	Out of quota ad valorem tariff, %
EU	Wheat	0%	87%
USA	Sugar	2%	49%
Canada	Wheat	1%	100%
Japan	Wheat	0%	234%
Korea	Rice	5%	89%

Source: http://commerce.nic.in/trade/international_trade_papers_agriculture_19.asp

clearing the imports. The following Table 9.10 shows the in-quota and out quota tariff rate for certain agricultural commodities for a few countries.

Internal tax structure

Every country has its own internal tax structure which will be loaded on the product price. These country-specific internal tax structures of a country, therefore, influence the pricing arrangement of the exporters. In some situation, like in case of Europe, when an exporter exports the product the Value added tax (VAT) is required to be paid at the time of imports so that the imported goods are made equivalent to the similar types of goods available with the EU. However, if the value added tax is paid latter in the market then also the pricing of the product would be affected. Although an exporter can avoid the botheration by selecting transaction term with the importer conveniently so that the payment of internal taxes are offloaded to the importer of the product but then again concern will be there for the retail market price. The exporter, hence, requires having careful watch on the ultimate price based on the prevailing competition in the market which varies across countries. Even in Europe different member countries also have different VAT rates. For example, Luxembourg levies at the rate 17% while Hungary levies at the rate 27% for the year 2015. The Indian exporter exporting Apple to these countries,

Box 9.7 Some terms are important

Ad valorem (AV): A tariff rate charged as percentage of the price.

Applied rates: Duties that are actually charged on imports. These can be below the bound rates.

Bound rates (tariff binding): Commitment not to increase the rate of duty beyond an agreed level. Once a rate of duty is bound, it may not be raised without compensating the affected parties.

Consolidated tariff schedules (CTS): WTO database of member countries' legally binding commitments on tariffs, tariff quotas and agricultural subsidies.

Digits, digit-level (tariffs): A reference to the codes used to identify products. Categories of products are subdivided by adding digits.

Integrated database (IDB): WTO database of countries' bound and applied tariffs and imports.

MFN (most-favoured-nation) tariff: Normal non-discriminatory tariff charged on imports (excludes preferential tariffs under free trade agreements and other schemes or tariffs charged inside quotas).

Source: WTO Web sites

therefore, would be able to bring its product in two different prices. The 15 GB ipod had a retail market price $429 in Luxembourg while the US price was merely $399 because of internal tax structure differences between the countries.

Non Price Factors

The price a customer eventually pays for a product is also influenced by many other factors which are not related to the cost of production. These factors include commercial terms used, customers' prejudice against products manufactured in developing countries, brand image, availability of after-sales services, prompt delivery and availability of complete range of products under the same brand.

INCO term used

The International Commercial Terms or INCO terms are widely used in international commercial transactions. These terms were first published in 1936 by the International Chamber of Commerce (ICC) and subsequently revised several times to reflect the need of the time. Since INCO terms are used to indicate and communicate clearly the tasks, costs and risks associated with the transportation and delivery of goods, the pricing decisions are also affected by the specific terms used. The recent revision by ICC, effective from January 1, 2011, superseded the previous one and is popularly known as INCOTERMS 2010. INCOTERMS 2010 introduced two new terms while dropping four existing terms, thus reducing the total number of terms to 11 from 13 terms.

The INCOTERMS 2010 are as follows:

Group A: Terms for any transport mode

1. EXW – EX WORKS (... named place of delivery)

Description: The seller's only responsibility is to make the goods available at the seller's premises. The buyer bears full costs and risks of moving the goods from there to the destination.

2. FCA – FREE CARRIER (... named place of delivery)

Description: The seller delivers the goods cleared for export, to the carrier selected by the buyer. The seller loads the goods if the carrier pickup is at the seller's premises. From that point, the buyer bears the costs and risks associated with moving the goods to destination.

3. CPT – CARRIAGE PAID TO (... named place of destination)

Description: The seller pays for moving the goods to destination. From the time the goods are transferred to the first carrier, the buyer bears the risks of loss or damage.

4. CIP – CARRIAGE AND INSURANCE PAID TO (... named place of destination)

Description: The seller pays for moving the goods to destination. From the time the goods are transferred to the first carrier, the buyer bears the risks of loss or damage. The seller, however, purchases the cargo insurance.

5. DAT[10] – DELIVERED AT TERMINAL (... named terminal at port or place of destination)

Description: The seller delivers when the goods, once unloaded from the arriving means of transport, are placed at the buyer's disposal at a named terminal at the named port or place of destination. "Terminal" includes any place, whether covered or not, such as a quay, warehouse, container yard or road, rail or air cargo terminal. The seller bears all risks involved in bringing the goods to and unloading them at the terminal at the named port or place of destination.

6. DAP – DELIVERED AT PLACE (... named place of destination)

Description: The seller delivers when the goods are placed at the buyer's disposal on the arriving means of transport ready for unloading at the named place of destination. The seller bears all risks involved in bringing the goods to the named place.

7. DDP – DELIVERED DUTY PAID (... named place)

Description: The seller delivers the goods – cleared for import – to the buyer at destination. The seller bears all costs and risks of moving the goods, including the payment of customs duties and taxes.

B. Maritime-only terms

8. FAS – FREE ALONGSIDE SHIP (... named port of shipment)

Description: The seller delivers the goods to the origin port. From that point, the buyer bears all costs and risks of loss or damage.

9. FOB – FREE ON BOARD (... named port of shipment)

Description: The seller delivers the goods on board the ship and clears the goods for export. From that point, the buyer bears all costs and risks of loss or damage.

10. CFR – COST AND FREIGHT (... named port of destination)

Description: The seller clears the goods for export and pays the costs of moving the goods to destination. The buyer bears all risks of loss or damage.

11. CIF – COST INSURANCE AND FREIGHT (... named port of destination)

Description: The seller clears the goods for export and pays the costs of moving the goods to the port of destination. The buyer bears all risks of loss or damage. The seller, however, purchases the cargo insurance.

[10] Delivered at Terminal (DAT) and Delivered at Place (DAP) have been newly added in INCOTERMS 2010. DAF, DES, DEQ, and DDU designations have been eliminated.

How pricing is affected by INCOTERMS used by exporter

The importer's inquiries received from potential importers often request a quotation based on a specific INCOTERM, i.e., the importer shall want to understand his risk and responsibility. In other words, the importer would want to understand clearly, the following:

1. Mode of transport (sea/air/road/multi-modal) to be used in conveying the goods to destination.
2. Who will bear the transportation cost – exporter or importer.
3. Who will bear the insurance cost – exporter or importer.
4. Who will bear the loading and unloading cost – exporter or importer.

Each of the INCO terms relate to certain ways of cost sharing process between the exporter and the importer.

Transfer of risk and pricing: In addition to indicating the seller's and buyer's obligation in terms of responsibilities for the transportation costs while transferring goods, the INCOTERMS also specify the point when the risks associated with transportation transfers from the seller to the buyer which clearly depicted in Figure 9.7. It can be seen from Figure 9.7 that in EXW, the risks get transferred when the goods are at the disposal of the buyer.

FIGURE 9.7 INCOTERMS and cost implication

	Export packaging	Customs clearance	Inspection	Loading	Carriage	Insurance	Import clearance	Unloading
TERMS FOR ANY TRANSPORT MODE								
Ex work	⇨		NO OBLIGATION, BUT BUYER'S COSTS, IF REQURED					
FCA					⇨			
CPT					⇨			
CIP					⇨			
DAT					⇨			
DAP							⇨	
DDP								⇨
MARITIME-ONLY TERMS								
FAS			NO OBLIGATION, BUT BUYER'S COSTS,IF REQURED	⇨				
FOB					⇨			
CFR					⇨			
CIF					⇨			

Shaded parts are seller's cost
Un-shaded parts are buyer's cost

⇨ Transfer of risk from buyer to seller

Since the seller delivers (without loading) the goods to the buyer at the seller's premises, there is not much cost implication for the seller and hence it is the most preferable term for new entrants to the export business. In FCA, the risk is transferred when the goods have been delivered to the carrier at the named place. This term is used more frequently than EXW because it includes loading at pick-up, which is commonly expected by the importers. The quoted price of export will be more under this term than in EXW. Under FAS term, the risk is transferred when the goods have been placed alongside the ship. Hence, the buyer makes payment for all further transportation and insurance costs after delivery of products alongside the ship by the seller (realistically, at the named port terminal). Under FCA, the export clearance obligation rests with the seller, which the seller need to consider when pricing the product. In most commonly used terms of FOB, it is the ship's rail at the port of export (origin) that risk transfer takes place. So, the seller needs to consider loading charge (both at factory and port of origin) and internal transportation while fixing the price. It is the same with the terms CFR and CIF. In CIP and CPT, the risk is extended and ends when the goods have been delivered to the main carrier at the port of export (origin). In CPT, the seller pays for the cost of carriage to the named place of destination while in CIP it includes the insurance cost also. Hence, the exporter needs to take care of this difference while pricing. However, in DDP, risk transfer takes place only when the goods are placed at the disposal of the buyer at the destination port. It is the exporter's responsibility to arrange and pay for all transit costs, including delivery to a designated facility of the importer. Since under this term the seller takes all responsibilities to deliver the product to the importer's place, the exporter must be prepared to pay for insurance coverage and duties/tariff charges, demurrage or detention, inland or ocean transportation costs, currency exchange fees, etc. Shipping with DDP should be undertaken only by experienced exporters since product transfer to the buyer takes a long time owing to delays at customs and the added logistics costs that may be consequently be anticipated. In DAT, the seller bears all risk until the goods are unloaded (delivered) at the named quay, warehouse, yard, or terminal at destination, which may include demurrage or detention charges as and when applicable.

Government regulations

The government regulations of respective countries also distantly influence the export pricing. In fact, every country government keeps a watch full eye on international companies' pricing practices. Basic intention behind such move would be to protect consumers against exploitation from company's deceptive pricing, price discrimination, predatory pricing with or without connivance other players. The governments also set up different surveillance agencies to check price cartel type of attempt and save local consumers. It is important that international businesses are aware of such country policy and use them as clues in setting price for the product. Any violation to these regulations would usually attract heavy penalty on the offenders so that such efforts can be heavily be discouraged. American company Eli Lilly could not increase the prices of its imported insulin brands in the Indian market as the pharmaceutical regulator National Pharmaceutical Pricing Authority (NPPA) had regulation on the upper limit on the price. NPPA, in India, has the mandate to fix the MRP of imported medicines using one of the 74 bulk drugs that fall within price control. The Danish pharmaceuticals company Novo Nordisk disputed with NPPA when they found that they were not allowed to increase the price of their own insulin brand. It was disturbing for them further when Indian companies such as Biocon and Wockhardt were allowed to raise the price of their brands. The world's largest drug maker Pfizer could not increase the price of imported brand Medrol, used to treat allergic disorders and arthritis, for the Indian market because NNPA rejected the companies pricing arguments.

Frame Work for Global Pricing

Price decision in the international market is crucial for a company and decision making is often complicated because of the different intervening factors that have been discussed so far. However, a practising manager is loaded with different business-related tasks and, in practical terms, he has less time to execute extensive international pricing research. Therefore, a readymade framework of pricing would of great help to such managers to help them to decide on the pricing in the international market. A. Coskun Samli, Professor of Marketing and International Business at the University of North Florida suggested a framework for international pricing. This framework uses external and internal variables. External variables are related to the environment external to the company in the foreign country and include parameters such as competitive pressure, demand level, legal and governmental restrictions, general economic conditions, foreign exchange supply, etc. Internal variables are internal to the internationalising company and include parameters such as corporate goals, centralised control system, long range commitment of the company in the target country, and degree of internationalisation, etc. The commentary stated first provides a brief description a German company during its entry in India and then demonstrate the significance of external and internal variables surrounding the company in fixing international prices for a new market.

The Krüger GmbH & Co is a famous German company engaged in producing instant food products through its 17 production facilities worldwide to market its product globally. The company was founded way back in 1971 by Willibert Krüger of Germany and became a highly recognised brand with the passage of time. Mr Krüger had the desire and passion for internationalisation of the company and soon the company became a leading name in manufacturing a wide assortment of branded beverages, foodstuffs and pharmaceutical products in instant form, as well as ready-to-drink products and coffee flavours and aromas under the brand name 'Krüger'. It is now an established market player in the industry. It employed over 4,000 people in different parts of the world and clocked a record annual sale of about 1.6 billion Euros during 2011. The huge market success to the company came from its ability to produce and market quality products at a standard price which gives the customers a feeling of 'value for money'. The company's key competitive advantage is derived not only from the successful merging of technical expertise, production performance and site-related cost benefits, but also from its deep-seated business relations in the producer countries, the proximity to its customers and clients, and the close cooperation with leading local enterprises. In its endeavour of market penetration in the emerging economics, Krüger entered the Indian market through direct exports and launched three products in June 2009. These were Ice Tea, Pure Cappuccino and Chai Latte. However, the company had to face the challenge of correctly assessing the market and fixing the price of the product strategically. The Indian market was very competitive during 2009 and a number of intervening variables, both internal and external to the company, kept disturbing the company management about fixing the entry prices for the products for Indian market. Mr James Milner, the country manager, deputed for the purpose, was wondering how the company would attempt execute the task. "You see, we cannot straightway export the European price for the Indian market considering the economic difference between the countries. But what would be the price for products? Does anybody know any methodology for price fixing in distant market which can bring good marketing result? What factors the company would consider for understanding the price of its products in India and variation it required from other countries?" said Mr Milner impatiently in a meeting organised in its office in Mumbai.

Krüger's management always believed in winning the trust and confidence of its customers through quality and performance – not only in Germany, but also in its business relations in over 90 countries of the world. Krüger believed that emerging countries required to be explored more intensely through exportation of products from the nearest production centre or directly from Germany. In fact, its logistics planning centre in Bergisch Gladbach, in the Cologne/Bonn Region of Germany, has been successfully managing Krüger's product distribution to the various country markets efficiently. Being a company that claims to contribute to the quality of life on an everyday basis, Krüger has a self-imposed commitment to comply with certain values and guidelines. This includes, for example, manufacturing according to the strictest hygiene regulations, carefully selecting the raw materials it uses to make its products, acting in accordance with proper commercial principles, and taking account of ecological aspects and the interests of the world. With regard to hygiene and cleanliness, it has developed its own standards that far exceed the legal regulations imposed by different countries. State-of-the-art manufacturing facilities give the company a decisive production lead. For example, the 12 spray towers at the Krüger milk plant at Mittelelbe in Stendal, which produce Europe's largest range and volume of baby milk powder and skimmed milk powder for further industrial processing has been rated the best in the world. The production facilities are subjected to continuous upgradation to produce leaven, maltodextrin, coffee creamer, sweetener powder, dispenser cocoa, cappuccino, fruit powder and high-quality powder products. As per market survey, Krüger was expected to face both direct and indirect price competition from competitors in the Indian market. The competitors were also very aggressive in their behaviour to retain their market share and Krüger required to price products keeping this in mind. Too much localisation of price as per Indian requirement was not possible as Krüger had major global aspirations as a company exporting products to 90 countries. Moreover, it was required to meet all major legal regulations (such as WHO, IFS, and BRC standards) in production and packaging of the products adding further strain on the cost of production. Of course, global strategic sourcing has been providing some advantage on the matter of product cost than the Indian local players. With long-term marketing intention in India, it not only desired to maximise its short-run profit through price skimming, but also focussed on stability and long-term growth in the Indian market and elsewhere with emphasis on social responsiveness and market leadership. Although the company wanted to address country-specific interest it was still not decentralised and hence all major decisions originated from the headquarters. There were no efforts for major product modifications for Indian market. The company also did not want to go with local positioning strategy for India and considered that retention of global image would support the company's objective for long-term presence in Indian market.

Based on the above understanding of the major internal and external factors, the company's pricing situation was re-evaluated using the Samli's frame work. In this framework, all the relevant external and internal factors were first identified and then scored (yes, no and not applicable) through the responses gathered from a cross-section of the company policy makers who had an in-depth understanding of the company as well as country of entry.

FIGURE 9.8 Samli's framework score

	Samli's Pricing Framework	r (Response)			s (Significance)		
		Yes	No	NA	Some	Major	
		1	-1	0	1	2	
EXTERNAL	Is there direct Price competition?	•				•	2
	Is there indirect Price competition?	•			•		1
	Is there promotional competition?		•		•		-1
	Is there global aspiration for the firm?	•				•	2
	Is there aggressiveness of competitors?	•				•	2
	Is there demand variability?		•		•		-1
	Is there a need for enforcing regulations?	•			•		1
	Is there a possibility of global sourcing?	•			•		1
INTERNAL	Is there emphasis on maximizing on short run profit?		•		•		-1
	Is there emphasis on social responsiveness?	•			•		1
	Is there emphasis on market leadership?	•			•		1
	Are most decisions made at local level?		•			•	-2
	What there frequent product modifications?		•			•	-2
	Is there a large geographical market coverage?	•			•		1
	Is there a local positioning strategy?		•		•		-1
	Does the company engage in sales internationally for off load short term overcapacity?		•			•	-2

$$\sum_{i=1}^{8} r_i s_i + 16 = 23$$

$$\sum_{j=1}^{8} r_j s_j + 16 = 11$$

$$C_{A,B} = \sum_{i=1}^{8} r_i s_i + 16, \sum_{j=1}^{8} r_j s_j + 16 = \mathbf{23\ ,\ 11}$$

The depth of impact of these factors was also understood through rating of their significance to the company. Then, the coordinate C (A, B) is found out using the formula shown in the Figure 9.8. Here, the calculated score was A = 23 and B = 11, where A and B stand for the external and internal variables respectively. The scores were then matched with the template.

In the template, the external and internal score C (A, B) fitted well in the particular quadrant which was suggesting that the company should proceed with 'mild tendency for fixed global price'. It indicated towards possible pricing in line with its global standard but with possible 'mild' relaxation in some situations.

CHAPTER SUMMARY

1. Various factors affect international pricing, which the marketers need to consider while fixing price in a particular country. Some of the factors are conventional such as demand in the market, cost of the product, and nature of competitions. These factors are interrelated and the interplay between them gives rise to new situations on which the companies need to act smartly and promptly. In addition, there are many other factors which act on the interplay among demand, cost and competitions, making the pricing situation a dynamic one.
2. Country of origin, stages of product life cycle, competitive structure, income level, grey marketing counter trade and dumping are the external factors influencing the price fixation in the international market.
3. Company internal factors like transfer pricing also have an effect on the product price
4. Export is the simplest form of internationalisation involving two parties separated by an international border. Broadly, exporters follow the following two methods of pricing depending on their ability to address the core issue of marketing, i.e., customer satisfaction.
5. There are various factors such as currency adopted for transaction, type of distribution channel used, marketing goal, level of product adaptation required, packaging/labelling requirements, customs duty, etc., that influence the export pricing of an exporter.
6. Some non-pricing factors such as prejudice against products manufactured in developing countries, brand image, ability to provide after-sales services, prompt delivery, ability to supply complete range of products and brand image have indirect effects on pricing decision.
7. Price decisions in the international market are crucial for the company and decision making is often complicated because of difficulty of assessing the impact of the different intervening factors on the purpose at hand. Therefore, a readymade framework of pricing comes very handy to practicing managers as a tool that helps them to decide on pricing their products in the international market.

QUESTIONS FOR REVIEW

Short Answer Questions

1. What do you mean by 'price' of a product?
2. What do you understand by country of origin and its effect on international pricing?
3. What is parallel import?
4. What is 'dumping' in the context of international trade?
5. What is full cost pricing in exportation process?
6. What do you understand by the term 'countries with pegged currency'?

Descriptive Questions

1. Suppose you are the marketing manager of a major international food company and are interested in introducing a consumer product into an Asian market. Pick up the country of your

choice, appraise the pricing situation there using Samli's pricing framework and comment on the pricing policy that can be adopted.

2. Select a company which has its presence in at least 25 country markets. Visit their Web site and other possible information sources to assess the standardisation effort of the company in respect of international pricing decision.
3. "The mobile phone industry has rallied at its own cost to save the legal trade from total capitulation by the grey market. Almost 60% of legitimate sales in Maharashtra have gone to the grey market since the state increased value-added tax a year ago" says a Nokia India spokeswoman.
   What is grey marketing? How does it create an impact on international pricing? What can a company do to check grey marketing?
4. What do you understand by 'arm's length price'? How is transfer price determined? Explain with the help of an example.
5. Conduct an historical analysis of transfer pricing practices in India. Identify a company having multi-country operation and assess the most dominant current approaches of transfer pricing practice.
6. What are the different methods of pricing? Explain, with example, the process of marginal cost pricing.
7. ABC International is in receipt of a query from a prospective buyer from USA about purchase of Indian bamboo-based handcrafted flower vase. The Indian seller wanted to assess the implication of price quoting based on different INCO terms. Given that ₹1000 is the cost of production for each unit of flower vase, indicate the impact on its price if different INCO terms are used. Assume the following: the exporter wants to make a profit of 20% on the cost, only multi-modal INCO terms to be utilised.
8. Why is it so difficult to set and control uniform standard prices in global markets? Explain with examples you are familiar with.
9. Nike spent a lot of money to promote their brand as top of the range in international markets. Customers buy the product for the Nike symbol and are willing to pay high prices regardless of the product's actual value. As a result, Nike sports shoes are priced between 500 to 1500 Yuan in Chinese cities. On the other hand, in Europe, Nike shoes cost the equivalent of between 400 and 600 Yuan, making them more accessible to ordinary consumers as a leisure brand. The domestic rivals Li Ning and Anta are coming up very fast to place themselves as key players in the sports shoes market of worth 69 billion Yuan and projected to be 297 billion Yuan by 2020. Li-Ning sells the majority of its sports shoes for only 300 Yuan, hence dominating China's rural markets primarily due to the lower price. Li Ning is also getting ready to take on its rival Nike with branding and changed its slogan to "Make the Change" from "Anything is Possible" to attract younger consumers.
   Why is Nike differentiating its price between Europe and China? Would you support the premium pricing strategy of Nike in China? Why or why not? Can Nike go with a global pricing strategy? What are the factors Nike needs to consider before deciding on the new pricing strategy for China to counter its rival? As marketing manager of Nike, prepare a strategic pricing plan to gain market supremacy in China.

EXERCISES

1. UK was the world's costliest place to buy Apple's iPad with prices around a quarter higher than in the US. The company also set inflated pricing for other European countries. In Germany, France and Italy an iPad costs 20–25% more than in the US. It was believed that the premium pricing strategy worked even in recession (as evident from record profits without much price cut). Would it be possible for Apple to have a standard price across US, UK and China? Imagine that you are the pricing strategist in Apple and hence develop a pricing road map for these three countries by considering different cost components such as VAT, duty, etc., and then loading appropriate market based pricing strategy for the company.
2. Ford Motor Company made a strategic move with their pricing by holding the prices of their entry-level cars such as Escorts as low as possible. Low prices represented an attempt to attract young buyers, with the hope that as they grew older and need bigger vehicles they would remain loyal to the brand and trade up. The problem was that while Ford sold a lot of inexpensive cars, their profit margins on these models were non-existent. To earn profits, Ford relied on the higher margins on bigger cars, like the Explorer

or Crown Victoria. However, this strategy did not run well as Ford sold fewer of the expensive luxury cars as compared to the economy ones. Research the entry and presence of Ford Motor in India and the pricing strategy the company has adopted for Indian market. How different is that pricing strategy from its pricing of automobiles in China and USA? Justify the strategy from the marketing point of view.

3. AKZ leather limited produces leather products (leather purse, wallet, passport holders for men) in Kolkata and markets them across the different countries of EU and the USA through its own brand 'Leatherland'. It exports the products from its Kolkata factory to its own sales subsidiary in New York and Bonn, Germany. Develop a cost sheet of these products by visiting them in Kasba Industrial Estate or a similar company in your neighbourhood and calculate the DDP (delivery duty paid) price for the company for the consignment now ready for export for US as well as Germany.

End case: Think Local and Price Local Strategy Worked Wonder for Micromax [11]

By now, the Indian mobile handset manufacturing company 'Micromax' needs no introduction even in the international level. The experts in this field, at least to those who are familiar with the Indian mobile handset business situation, always regarded this Indian company as 'giant killer'. The brand name of the mobile handset is now uttered by the consumers along with the 'bigs' in the field such as Nokia, Samsung, Apple, Sony, etc. However, very few will be remembering those days when the company was looking for some open space in the super competitive Indian market. However, there was no respite for the company as the big international brands surrounded this comparatively small local player with the motive of strangulating it immature death. The story of Micromax's first survival on entry, then building brand in Indian market followed by internationalisation in neighbouring countries, were like Hollywood movies. The more these big brands tried to corner the Indian manufacturer, the more strategic determination the company Micromax had shown to remain active in the Indian market. It was great global versus local episode played in the backdrop of Indian market.

Micromax was founded by Rajesh Agarwal during 1991 without any funfair. It was initially a small distributing company of computer hardware. Mr Agarwal had deep ambition in his mind to turn the company from mere distributor to a marketer of telecommunication equipments. But as every successful entrepreneur said, you have to form a suitable team during the start up phase for the big leap. An all-important team comprising of Sumit Arora, Rahul Sharma and Vikas Jain was formed during 1998 to completely change the company's landscape. It took little bit more time than what Rajesh had expected but it never looked impossible to him. Micromax finally ventured into the mobile handset market during 2008 successfully and never looked back.

By 2011 Micromax managed to grab about 6% share of Indian GSM mobile handsets after Nokia (62%) and Samsung (8%). Becoming third largest market share holder only after global giants Nokia and Samsung and that too in a very short period of time was very satisfying. It was really a difficult war to fight with global icons in the industry such as Nokia and Samsung in a growing market like India. When Micromax entered the market, products from LG, Samsung, Nokia and Motorola were doing well in the market (Table 9.11). The leader was Nokia with its accepted brand image, quality and high awareness level amongst Indian consumers. Every other manufactures took it for granted that the leader–follower relationship was to be obeyed and respected. But the Micromax team thought it in other way round. It openly challenged the market leaders with the successive launch different Micromax mobile handsets to suit Indian customers. A ripple in the otherwise calm market started taking the shape of wave.

[11] The case 'Think local and price local strategy worked wonder for Micromax' has been developed by case writer Dr Gautam Dutta of Indian Institute of Foreign Trade as a basis for class room discussion rather than to illustrate the effective or ineffective handling of a business situation.

Table 9.11 Market share positions of the different companies in India during 2009

Mobile handsets	Market share in percent			Remark
	2008-09	2009-10	2013-14	
Nokia	64	52.2		Lost
Samsung	10	17.4		Increased
LG	4.5	5.9		Increased
Sony Ericson	6	3		Lost
Motorola	3.5	1		Lost
ZTE	5.6	1.9		Lost
Karbonn	0	3		Increased
Micromax	0	6		Increased

Source: different website, compiled by author.

Many market observers who saw rise and fall of a number of Indian mobile handset manufactures thought of Micromax as a fly-by-night operator who joined the market to make some quick money and wind up the operation very quickly. In fact, prior to Micromax Indians customers also did not have good experience with a couple of Indian mobile handsets launched before Micromax. Hence, it was not difficult to understand the perception of Indian target customers about an upcoming Indian brand and market observers too that Micromax would start its operations with a bang but wind it up with a whimper. But thanks to the marketing strategies of Micromax, the company was able to not only persist in the market but also give the market leaders a run for their market share.

The market observers initially termed it as 'miracle'. But how the Indian company did the so called 'miracle'? What marketing strategy it adapted to get in to the market by out witting the powerful competitors? How successfully it occupied the customers' mind? These were the few questions going around in the expert circle. A number of case or caselets were written and discussed in the B-Schools in India to unfold the real mystery behind upsetting the global giant like Nokia. No doubt that the company successfully carried pursued different brand awareness programmes and was successful in creating sustained brand awareness among the target audience. They even signed up Bollywood actors Akshay Kumar and Twinkle Khanna for their advertisement. Sales promotion and advertisement continued in full swing in tandem with the company's effort to develop each successive models loaded with features comparable to the international competitors. Then came a good opportunity in the form of Indian Premiere Cricket League (IPL) cricket to get closer to the customer and Micromax used it to the best to build up a pan Indian image. IPL 2010 created all-round awareness about the company handsets. The company also understood it clearly that in order to be a long time player by beating the competition it had to come close to the Indian customer in addition to creating brand awareness. For this it required product adaptation as per Indian customers' requirement otherwise the customer would be drifted away to the more appealing international brands. At the same time the product features required being comparable or even more than the leading products. Backed by this idea, the company took market leader Nokia head on in a very competitive but growing market. Micromax put all effort to make its technology front stronger and started producing products, i.e., handset equipment in an advanced technology platform. The rolled out products had the matching core product platform and attributes at par with the mobile handsets from the international players, Micromax kept on introducing new products with new features at regular intervals. The speed even puzzled the global rivals and interstinglly the competitors took could not effort to match up the speed possibly because of cumbersome decision making hierarchy associated with company global structure. Every time it brought out new models, they began creating excitement in the target customer segment as the customers' expectation seemed to have been crossed and that too with comparatively low price. These product variants and features were just what customers were looking for. In addition to product features, the company came out with an excellent pricing strategy. Purposefully the company kept the price of the products comparatively lower that the competitors. Product customisation couple with lower price worked well. Results were noticed when the models such as Ezpad and Q7 did good business for the company. The sensitised customers thronged to the retail stores to have a look at the products and low pricing strategy did the rest. The company was further delight when as a result of the wonderful marketing strategy there were visible changes in the market share positions of the different companies as presented below.

The mobile models of initial periods of Micromax, illustrated below, demonstrates the product –pricing combination marketing strategy of Micromax that really created havoc on its rival and market leader Nokia for the Indian market.

Micromax Q7 Mobile with Product Description

Micromax Q7 is equipped with an internal memory of 78 MB and it has a micro SD memory card which can be extended to 4 GB. The lithium ion battery provides a talk time of about 4.5 hours and has a standby life of up to 144 hours. The network connectivity options of the phone include Bluetooth, WiFi, WAP and GPRS. The phone has a USB connectivity slot as well. Micromax Q7 is equipped with other features such as a QWERTY keypad, FM radio, a music player and a video player. It can also be connected to external speaker/headphones using the in-built 3.5 mm audio jack. The phone also features a basic 2MP camera. It supports music formats such as MP3, WAV, MIDI and AMR and comes with one-year manufacturer warranty. Two SIM cards can be inserted into the phone and a single handset for two numbers. The phone is pre-loaded with features such as Facebook for social networking needs, an Opera mini browser and Nimbooz messenger.

- Micromax Price Range: ₹3799. Announced in 2010, May. Available and released in 2010, July.
- Comparable Nokia phone: Nokia E-63; Price Range: ₹7790.; Released in 2011, January.

MICROMAX Q5 Mobile with Product Description

Micromax Q5 is a business mobile phone with QWERTY keypad and a track ball. It is a dual SIM GSM mobile phone. Q5 mobile phone is Facebook ready, has Instant Messenger, Music Player, Pre-loaded Opera Mini Browser, and 2MP Camera. Display: QVGA. Number of Colours: 262K Display Resolution: 240 × 320. Standard battery type.

- Micromax price range: ₹2690.
- Comparable Nokia phone: Nokia C-3; Price Range: ₹5770.

MICROMAX X360 with Product Description

The Micromax X360 is a dual-SIM GSM music-centric mobile phone. The key features of Micromax X360 are: Dual GSM-Dual Standby, Multi-format music player with Yamaha & Wolfsan Amplifiers, Stereo FM Radio/Recorder, 1.3 Mega CMOS Camera, Bluetooth (A2DP), Expandable memory (up to 8GB),Video recorder/Player.

- Miromax price range: ₹2392
- Comparable Nokia phone: Nokia C2-02 Price Range: ₹3799.

MICROMAX X 310 MODELS

Micromax X310 mobile phone is Dual SIM, GSM Tri-band handset with a weight of 74 grams. It supports multi-format music player, expandable memory up to 8GB, Stereo FM Radio/Recorder, 1.3MP Camera, Bluetooth (A2DP), GPRS/WAP/MMS, Video recorder/Player and Large PHB/SMS memory. Bar input type: Keypad display; Number of Colours: 65K; Display resolution: 176 × 220; Secondary display: Non-standard; Battery features: Standard.

- Micromax price range: ₹3807. Announced September 2009
- Comparable Nokia phone X3-02 Touch and Type. Announced August 2010; Price range ₹7500

Market Entry Strategies: Think Local Price Local

Micromax understood correctly that the company could be victorious in an uneven competitive situation like that with international giant brands only when it customised the products as per local requirements better than others. The company's first phone, the X1i, was a reflection to that which was born from its basic understanding of the requirements of Indian villages and towns. By increasing the size of the battery to 1800 mAh, Micromax was able to push the standby time to 30 days for the X1i model and offered it at a very affordable price of ₹2150. The phone immediately was a big success in rural India as Indian villages had chronic shortage of electricity. The company maintained this strategy 'think local act local' throughout. Micromax, being a local company, had the advantage of understanding certain local needs faster which could not be understood or explored by the international players at that pace. In course of time Micromax achieved mastery in identify the unmet latent needs of local people and come up with a product which no one else had fulfilled so far. The products so crafted for satisfying local needs were offered at comparatively low price to do wonder for the company. "When Nokia or Samsung roll out a new model they do so from its global portfolio rather than launching something specifically for India, we will have lot of 'firsts' in our product portfolio" said the company official in an official meeting to make the marketing strategy of the company in clear terms. As strategised by the company things also happened in accordance with that in the market place. The more success it tasted the more the company practiced 'think local price local strategy' which was evident in their handsets with 30 days battery backup (Micromax X1i). The company subsequently came up with handsets with with dual SIM/dual standby, handsets for switching networks (GSM – CDMA) using gravity sensors, aspirational QWERTY keypad handsets, operator branded 3G handsets, open market handset (OMH) CDMA handsets, etc. Through its gaming phone Gameolution it tried to capture a new segment in terms of youngsters and demonstrate its technology advancement. This phone brought in technology like wireless 'wii' of Nintendo, which worked on motion sensor technology and could convert PC/Laptop in gaming device. Micromax also came up with MTV music phone MTV X360 with Yamaha amplifiers targeted at music loving youth to match up with Samsung. The global players failed to notice that a vast section of Indian consumers initially subscribed to the state-owned BSNL mobile networks were trying to have another connection with updated private service providers such as Airtel, Vodaphone, etc. Micromax correctly observed that though state owned BSNL took the lead in telecommunication infrastructure development and a large section of the population subscribed to its network throughout India but connectivity used to have huge uncertainty. Call drops were very common feature of the BSNL service. Subsequently, private telecom operators joined sector as service provider across India and started providing better services but of course at higher cost in comparative terms. As a result, there was a growing group of customers who wanted to have a mobile handset with dual SIM. – One to retain BSNL connection which would be pan India including rural area another for efficient and faster connectivity in cities.

As usual, Micromax understood the need of the market first and focussed on dual SIM phones manufacturing. Hence, most of its phones were of dual SIM, allowing Micromax to take full advantage of the situation. Micromax availed this product-based local opportunity which the market leader Nokia failed to capitalise on. The global companies were more on believing in its global strategy and lacked the urge for country-specific manoeuvring required at that time to take on the 'locals' through product advantage. As a result, the dual SIM phones and Micromax grabbed substantial market in this category. To make best use of situation, the Indian company maintained an aggressive pricing strategy for its products in comparison to the competitors.

It understood the local middle class consumers' sentiment very correctly that this price-sensitive class aspire to belong feature-rich products but at lower price. A vast majority of people living in the B and C category of towns were also looking for different modern features of mobile handsets released by the global players but could not buy them out because of higher price only. Micromax just put their low priced feature rich handsets in front of them with the help of a well designed distribution network to take full advantage of the situation. For example, its QWERTY phones were released at a price below ₹5000. The features of the model included EDGE/GPRS/WAP/MMS. Another model Q55 was packed with excellent storage capacities to hold 1000 mobile contacts and 300 SMS with a total internal memory of 10 MB extendable to 8 GB. In addition, the company never forgot to load all its phone with enhanced battery power considering the power shortage condition prevailing in rural India. Its refined Q55 Bling model phones were powered it with a battery of strength 850 mAh, which meant that anyone with this model enjoyed a talk time up to 4 hours without recharge and a stand-by time up to 180 hours. Apart from gaming support, this model also supported SMS and MMS facilities. All these features were packed and priced aggressively at ₹5500 to ₹6000.

CASE QUESTIONS

Q1. Assess Micromax's pricing strategy in the Indian market. Can Nokia resort to variable pricing in different countries to counter local companies' low pricing policy? Why or why not?

Q2. Can Micromax extend its strategy while internationalising to Bangladesh or Sri Lanka? Visit Micromax website and compare its pricing strategy in these two countries and justify their relevance.

FURTHER READINGS

Carlos M.P. Sousa and Frank Bradley (2009), "Price adaptation in export markets", *European Journal of Marketing*, Vol. 43, No. 3/4.

The article delve on to identify the factors that influence pricing in export markets. The results of the study demonstrate that there is a relationship between the size of the firm and degree of price adaptation. Apart from firm size factors such as degree of product promotion, distribution adaptation as well as by the differences that exist between the home and the foreign market also exert pressure on pricing adaptation.

Samli, A.C. and Jacobs, L.W. (1993), "International pricing decisions: A diagnostic approach", *Journal of Marketing Theory and Practice*, Vol. 1, No. 4.

This paper is simple but suggest a method for price fixation by considering different external and internal factors such as government regulations, communications infrastructure, market competitiveness, and technical requirements prevailing in target country market. The suggested framework would be very useful to the practicing managers for understanding and linking market difference to the degree of price adaptation.

Stottinger, Barbara (2001), "Strategic export pricing: A long and winding road", *Journal of International Marketing*, Vol. 9, No. 1.

In this paper, the author sheds light on the process of industrial exporters' international pricing practices. On the basis of a series of 45 qualitative interviews with seasoned international business executives from five different industries, the author describes common "best practices". Along with insights gained from the available literature, these linkages are tied to a conceptual framework. As the information comes from experienced, internationally active firms from a European Union country, the findings are indicative for other European Union countries also.

Myers, Matthew B., Cavusgil, S. Tamer, Diamantopoulos, Adamantios (2002), "Antecedents and actions of export pricing strategy: A conceptual framework and research propositions," *European Journal of Marketing*, Vol. 36, No. 1/2.

This article brings out empirically the relationship between an export-pricing strategy and the factors that influence this strategy. It also shows the relationship between strategy and the performance of an export venture. A multidimensional conceptualisation of export-pricing is proposed to integrate the various components of an adopted strategy to that of its antecedents.

Gullstrand, J., Olofsdotter, K. and Thede, S. (2014), "Markups and export-pricing strategies", *Review of World Economics*, Vol 150.

This paper provides understanding in respect of a large number of Swedish firms operating in food sector, both manufacturing as well as trading, in terms of their pricing strategies. The paper documents how the firms in two sub-sectors used differential mark-ups as a part of their marketing strategy. The results of the study offer information that markups practiced by firms are a complex function of respective firms and destination characteristics and this relationship is exclusively sector specific and, hence, cannot be generalised.

Samli, Coskun and Jacobs, Laurence (1994), "Pricing practices of American multinational firms: Standardisation vs localisation dichotomy", *Journal of Global Marketing*, Vol. 8, No. 2.

This article discusses the international pricing practices of a sample of Fortune 500 companies with the intention of determining the manner in which the global and multi-local handle pricing issues. The authors also explore some of the specific international pricing imperatives with regards to standardisation and adaptation activities of these firms and establishes some implicit connection between them.

Hofer, K.M., Niehoff, L.M. and Wuehrer, G.A. (2015), "A taxonomy of export-pricing strategies and their performance in international markets", *Advances in International Marketing*, Vol 26.

This paper explores the elements of pricing approaches in export businesses and relates them with performance. This paper deals with how different pricing approaches such as cost-based, competitor-based, and value-based influenced export performance of the firms. This paper broadly covered 172 different types of export firms to understand how export pricing approaches are related to firm performance. At the end, the paper identifies that export performances are significantly influenced by the type of pricing strategy used by firms.

Deciding on Distribution

10

Learning Objectives

After studying this chapter, you should be able to:

- Understand the basic distribution channel structure through which consumer goods can be transferred to the ultimate consumers internationally.
- Understand the various distribution alternatives available to international manufacturers, along with their merits and demerits.
- Assess the basic features of the distribution channels such as controllability, resource requirements flexibilities, marketing efforts, etc.
- Understand the various difficulties associated with international distribution systems that cause problems not only at the planning stage but also at the implementation stage.
- Assess the channel structure differences of various countries.
- Understand the concept of international channel performance and the various components involved in channel performance management at the international level.
- Understand the steps involved in the designing an international distribution channel.

Chapter Overview

Marketing globally involves production at advantage-specific decentralised locations and distribution of products across the countries. For that to happen efficiently, a company would require efficient channels and distribution systems built up in different countries through which products reach the ultimate consumers. This is a very challenging task and requires a sound understanding of the issues such as physical distribution planning, designing channel structure, etc., in a cross-country market environment with adequate emphasis on channel relationship management. Therefore, this chapter deals with the different aspects of international distribution management.

Opening Vignette

Revlon faltered in designing its distribution system in China

Way back in 1931, two Americans Revsan and Lachman founded the Revlon Company to produce and market a special nail enamel product across USA. The company grew bigger and bigger over the years and as of December 31, 2014 it clocked a consolidated net worldwide sales of $1941 million. During these years the company came out of USA and extended its operation to 14 foreign countries. Its products were also made available for purchase almost throughout the world through different distribution networks. While internationalising, the company confronted the global as well as local established brands without wincing a bit while facing competition in countries of Asia, Eastern Europe, Latin America (including Venezuela) and South Africa. The result sometimes went in favour of the company and sometimes not. It lost the battle with Estee Lauder and then performed a miss adventure while taking over Gillette during 1980s. The company learnt lesson from mistakes and went on through the path of internationalisation. Some visible and encouraging results were also reported for the company from different countries. For example, higher sales of Revlon products such as Revlon colour cosmetics, Revlon Colour Silk hair colour and Sinful Colours cosmetics, Pure Ice colour cosmetics, etc. The company management was happy to note that net global sales of the company were overall showing an increasing trend. The company management during 1995 could see a huge potential in Chinese market and entered the country during 1996 to bolster its revenue growth momentum. The global brand immediately attracted the China's rapidly increasing middle class who were busy in enjoying the fruits of economic development of the country. Revlon also clearly understood the importance of doing well in super competitive China market and was hastily unleashing the entire usual marketing weapon to entice the target customers. Quickly the company made its products available in more than 50 cities. However, all of a sudden there was unusual news from China during 2011 for the company. It was all about losing market share to the competitors due to failure of its products to create customer value for Chinese women in China. Initially, the company had no clue for decline in sales but in general attributed the fall in revenue to declining consumption linked to a slowdown in Chinese economic growth. But the trend continued in spite of the best effort by the company strategist to put a halt in the downfall. The company management's high hope of enthralling the large customer segment with brand image and product variety seemed to be have receded fast. Finally, during December 2013 the company declared that it would exit China to save about $11 million a year, which the company had to spend for doing business there. It was a painful decision to make as the Chinese market has always been referred to as being 'full of potential' for Western cosmetic brands. In addition, the Chinese cosmetics market size also grew to $22.8 billion during 2012, more than double the 2008 market size. Even Estee Lauder Cos Inc. grew along with the market to register an increase of 7% sales during 2012. So, what went wrong with Revlon? Not only the company experts but also business consultants as well took interest in understanding the reason behind downfall of Revlon in China. They noted a few key reasons. Firstly, when Estee Lauder expanded its distribution network to the second-tier cities, Revlon confined only to the Tier-1 cities. Knowing well that distribution planning in beauty and cosmetics marketing plays a major role, Revlon maintained a single distribution channel – mostly at makeup counters of large department stores – in China making the consumers believe that the products of the company were not made for up-market beauty-conscious Chinese women. Revlon was hardly seen occupying the shopping windows of supermarkets or online retailing, thus limiting the width of retailing. In the pricing front the company adopted strategy of satisfying the requirements of average consumers also misfired. A general perception was built up that the product was 'not of high standard' which was further fuelled by products' availability in the departmental stores retail formats. The company failed to take the advantage of a well-known fact that the middle-income Chinese women usually get psychologically charged up when purchasing western cosmetic products at a considerable higher price from exclusive shops. The company officials at the end of their stay in China started realising the importance of being present in required types of retail formats in China to allure target customers. But, it was too late. Business experts felt that the company simply did not have the expertise to handle distribution management in China.

When this distribution planning mishap of Revlon was told to the students of international marketing in the classroom the students quipped, "Why was the American company not aware of the distribution requirements of China? Is it required that a company has to plan its distribution system according to the requirement of the country in which it plans to conduct business? Can it not be possible to have a standardised and global distribution system for a global company? If not, then to what extent is country-wise planning different? How does a company plan distribution for a specific country? Is there any framework available to understand the difference and plan distribution accordingly?"

"We know about physical distribution just as much as Napoleon's contemporaries new about the interior of Africa. We know it is there, it is big, and that's all"

—Peter F Drucker (1962)

INTRODUCTION

Current overseas market distribution channel structures can be extremely difficult to change to other structures. Wrong decisions may lead to poor results and low satisfaction because of low operation performance in the initial entry market.— Yongkyu Kim (1998).

Successful international marketing involves production at advantageous decentralised locations and distribution of products to the countries where consumers exist. For that to happen efficiently, a company would require channel and distribution systems built up at different countries through which its products would reach the ultimate consumers. These strategic productions - channels combinations are extremely important for a company to make product available and showcase them in different country markets. An excellent example to this effect is demonstrated by the American athletic shoe manufacturer Nike. Nike successfully produces its products in more than 700 factories with low cost advantage, employing over 500,000 workers in 51 countries. It has also engaged factories through subcontracting in locations such as Thailand, Indonesia, Cambodia, and Vietnam to produce Nike products. The products so produced are fed through efficient distribution channels for marketing across different countries. US company Mattel's Barbie doll is manufactured in Hong Kong through importation of materials from countries such as Taiwan, Japan, and the US and then marketed through well crafted distribution channels in other countries of the world. Another famous American company Microsoft manufactures its gaming gadget XBOX in China through contact manufacturing and itself take the responsibility of distribution by creating a well knitted distribution network in most of the countries of the world. So, after manufacturing successfully at the location of production interest, the product needs to travel to the countries of marketing interest and win over consumers there. The last part is the most challenging and difficult task, in most cases, for the marketers. Let us take some examples to illustrate this point. The rapid increase of the market for electronic goods saw the rise of demand for semiconductors as key input in electronic goods manufacturing. Motorola, one of the world's leading manufacturers of advanced telecommunications and electronics equipment, located the semiconductor production facilities in countries such as Malaysia, Philippines, Hong Kong, Taiwan, South Korea, China, and Japan because of locational advantage. However, the largest markets for semiconductors were the US (33% of the global market) followed by Japan (26%), Europe (19%) and South-east Asia (22%). The downstream assembling plants and marketing offices, therefore, were located close to the markets, i.e., USA, Canada and Europe. The product, i.e., semiconductor, being of high value/weight ratio, can be manufactured at a distant place where cost of production is less. However, Motorola not only required to produce them at low cost but also to transport them to the marketing/assembling locations as quickly as possible. The physical dispatch of the produce from production location to marketing/assembly location, in this particular case, would require minimum fifteen days involving multi-modal transportation through sea, road transport by truck with requisite haulage at transit locations, time for customs clearance, etc.

This transit time can be reduced to as much as 111 hours if the products are transported largely by air and road transportation in some locations. This time could be further reduced to 48 hours with the dedicated use of a special chartered aircraft. The problem with sea transport was the long delay in reaching the ultimate customers; on the other hand, if the entire distance is covered by air transport the cost would be prohibitive for the company. So, the difficulty of optimally balancing the two – cost of transportation and time to reach the customer often becomes the most challenging job in distribution management. Another difficult area is channel selection and management. In the earlier example, Motorola could avoid it partly because of B2B type of marketing practice of semiconductor and use of the produce for own consumption. However, every other company may not be that lucky. L'Occitane, the high-end boutique-cum-cosmetic company from southern France wanted to market a line of high-quality body care, skincare and fragrance products in India. The company is known for using ingredients like 'Shea butter,' a nourishing agent naturally cultivated in Africa that repairs and renews skin. L'Occitane, therefore, decided to reach the Indian customer by exporting the products directly from France to India. It also looked beneficial to the company as this arrangement would ensure retention of the original 'French' quality. However, to set the plan into action, the company required a good and efficient channel partner in India who not only understood L'Occitane's way of doing business but also had the capacity to market products to the Indian target consumers. In the process, the company entered into an agreement with Delhi based luxury and lifestyle business house Ravissant as their channel partner during 2001 following a general distributorship model. In fact, Ravissant was one of India's best known luxury product houses having luxury stores in Delhi, Mumbai and Agra, and this was the driving cause for L'Occitane to select the company as its channel partner. According to a well-set marketing plan L'Occitane was targeting the consumers living in class A and B-1 in cities with pricing suitable for positioning the products as affordable luxury brands. However, all these efforts proved futile as the channel partner Ravissant acted in a different way than expected by the parent company. Ravissant had many other luxury products' marketing rights exclusively for India. Some of them were world's best-known luxury European brands such as Cartier, Rosenthal, Bvlgari, Versace Tableware, Wedgewood, and Royal Doulton. L'Occitane, in course of time, realised that Ravissant was not paying due attention to its products and, as a result, prospective consumers were not sufficiently aware of their products. This led to the development of troubled relationship between L'Occitane and Ravvissant and ultimately severance of the distribution tie-up. The effect of this debacle was enormous. Primarily, it made the French company move out of Indian market for three long years before re-entering the country with a new distribution strategy. In addition, there was a loss of opportunity for the French company to earn huge revenue, had there been a perfectly matched distribution channel partners for Indian market.

Another problem international businesses face is due the structural differences between home country distribution channels and that of another country. Toys "R"Us, the largest toy manufacturer of the United States, is highly international almost since its start up. The company now operates approximately 875 Toys “R”Us and Babies “R”Us stores in the United States with more than 600 international stores and over 140 licensed stores in 35 countries of the world. It would be highly unnatural if the Toys “R”Us had not penetrated so far across all the developed country markets. But when it tried to enter Japan, the company faced a major problem because of huge structural differences between distribution channel of Japan and that of USA. The company found that Japanese toy retailing was dominated by many small speciality stores, small general retailers and many large retailers. A unique hierarchical relationship between these retailers was also maintained without much emphasis on profit sharing. In addition, these retailers blindly obeyed Japanese big manufacturers only. Thus, entering into the channel was difficult because of the lengthiness of the channel which would have curtailed the profit margin below industry average. Also Toys “R”Us had a policy that none of their stores would be less than 3000 square feet in size but Japanese law did not support big stores. To make the situation worse for the American company, Japanese small-toy retailers declined to be the retailers under Toys “R” Us unless a big Japanese manufacturer leading the channel permitted it.

The above instances point towards a pivotal requirement of paying a great amount of attention to distribution planning and channel design while entering a new country market by any international marketer. There are various critical aspects a company needs to look into when selecting the international channel and designing its product distribution. First, it requires close understanding of the structure of the distribution system of the targeted country. It also needs to gain an insight into channel members' behaviour and style, the transaction mechanism and above all, the variability of the distribution structure by comparing the distribution structure of the target country with the channel structure earlier successfully used by the company. The structure of the distribution system of a specific country refers to the types and number of distribution related agencies engaged and functioned with a specific set of marketing relationships to carry out marketing tasks on collective basis. The channel members' behaviour and style relates to the specific set of behaviours of the participating agencies involved in the channel. These behaviours are generalised reflections and not recorded on one to one basis which can easily be attributed towards the cultural situations existing in a particular country. The aspect, i.e., the variability of the distribution structure refers to degree to which the structure of the distribution system of the target country is different from the structure the home country of the internationalising country or the country to which the company is highly familiar with. If the structural variation is too high in the targeted country, then it may require adjusting other components of the marketing mix to suit the situation. Hence, a prior understanding of the level of variability of distribution channel structure is of utmost importance for successful international marketing.

Therefore, this chapter focuses on issues such as physical distribution planning and designing channel structure in a foreign country market with adequate emphasis on channel relationship management. It also endeavours to develop an understanding about the distribution channel structure differences that exist in different countries.

DISTRIBUTION CHANNELS

Distribution channel refers the conduit through which the merchandises pass to reach the ultimate consumers. Different types of channel members such as wholesalers, retailers, etc., are located inside the conduit to facilitate and accelerate the movement of products. Distribution channel is also known as marketing channel it performs one of the most important marketing tasks, i.e., delivery of merchandises to the consumers. Distribution of merchandise and services in the market place for consumption is a very important task for the producers to achieve business objectives. In fact, many marketing gurus opined that this P (place or distribution) is the most difficult amongst 4Ps (product, price, place, promotion) in terms of strategy formation and execution. However, the marketers try their level best to execute this P by using a combination of utilities and functions arranged in successive stages for ensuring smooth transfer of merchandises as well as the property right from origin to the ultimate users. These utilities, present between the producer and the consumer for movement of product or service, are also known as channel intermediaries. These channel intermediaries such as wholesalers, retailers, distributors, etc., perform different purposeful functions to facilitate the flow of merchandises to the distant consumers. The distribution channel, thus built up with the support of various utilities, acts like a conduit through which not only merchandise flows but it also accommodates information flows, financial flows, monetary and other associated risk flows to support the transfer efficiency. An effective distribution channel is one which allows smooth, economical and optimal flow of goods and merchandise from producers to the ultimate users. In practical situation designing an effective distribution channel is very much a challenging task. The channel designed and used for a specific purpose may be allowing smooth flow of products but may not be economical for the producers. When it is both economical and smooth then it may not depict an optimal solution for the company. Therefore, in all practical purposes the designing of an effective marketing (distribution) channel is a very challenging task for the producer or marketers. The contradictory nature of various objectives set while designing a channel makes it a very difficult task. The management guru Peter Drucker, therefore, compared the distribution domain of marketing as 'dark continent' where still many things remain unknown but the marketer requires moving forward in search of bringing efficiency in marketing. However, even in the 'dark situation' it is important for the marketing or distribution manager to take important distribution related decisions which would allow the goods or products to travel to the consumers in the optimum way possible through the pre designed distribution channel. The different channel members or intermediaries such as wholesalers, retailers, distributors, etc., are required to play their respective roles in the designed distribution set up to bring efficiency in the system. The transportation and logistics part also play an important role in ensuring performance of the distribution channel. A well knitted logistics measure is a must to ensure optimum channel performance. High performance of the channel members in conjunction with an efficient logistics arrangement can ensure high channel performance measured in terms of the ability to make products available to the consumers just in time, when required, with minimum financial involvement.

Distribution Channel Structure

Distribution channel structure refers to the basic fabric of a particular distribution channel where a unique configuration of channel members such as wholesalers, retailers, etc., has been worked out to facilitate flow of certain merchandise from producers to the consumers with the involvement requisite logistic supports. This particular channel structure has the mandate of functioning as per expectation of the stake holders in the channel. Therefore, a distribution channel structure may vary from market to market, product to product and country to country depending upon the requirements of the stakeholders. The structural differences may occur in the following way.

1. **Configuration wise:** The basic configuration (both vertical and horizontal) of utilities and functions in the channel may be different. Vertical configuration refers to number of linking intermediaries participating for successive products and property transfers towards the ultimate consumers by maintaining an alignment from producer to customer. Horizontal configuration refers to the number of vertical configuration crafted out from the producers using same or different medium to reach ultimate consumers. Horizontal configuration or drifted out vertical configuration is required to cater to the different needs of the customer in a highly competitive environment when the producer deems it fit to maintain multiple vertical channels. Therefore, based on the situational requirements the producer may design the channel configuration differently for achieving the marketing objectives.
2. **Length wise:** There may be difference in number of intermediaries connected in the configured channel structure to successively transfer of products and property rights from producer to the ultimate consumers. For example, one channel structure may require a particular vertical configuration with the participation of two successive wholesalers followed by two successive retailers to transfer the particular products from manufacturer to the ultimate consumers while other may require differently.
3. **Width wise:** Horizontal configuration of a particular channel structure may be different from another. For example, in one particular situation a producer may have two wholesalers, one e- wholesalers and another physical wholesaler, created for the purpose of achieving the configuration of twin parallel channels to reach the customers intensively. In another situation this twin channel configuration may not be used and replaced by a single channel.
4. **Depth wise:** The channel structure may vary depth wise also. For example, one producer may like to go to the market directly without the involvement of any intermediary by acting as its own retailer while the other one may like to reach out consumers with the involvement of one retailer only, i.e., bypassing the wholesalers[1].

Designing Distribution Channel Structure: Problems

The new competitive order of the world market coupled with ever demanding customers in the market place have forced business entities to place products

[1] Stern, Louis W. and Adel I. El-Ansary (1996), *Marketing Channels*, 5th ed. Prentice-Hall, Upper Saddle River, NJ.

as close as possible to the customers so that they can easily be accessed by the consumers at the time of requirement. This has put huge pressure on the producers/marketers as it requires a very delicate distribution planning to put a strategically designed distribution structure in place which perfectly suits the requirement. The aim of the distribution structure is to move forward the product at the right place, at the right time and at the lowest cost. The following points illustrate the problems associated with designing a well knit distribution channel structure of a company.

Cost minimisation: This refers to minimisation of product distribution related costs which include transport cost, warehouse cost, stocks and inventory costs, packaging cost, etc. The severity of competition in every country market has forced the producers to think of minimising these costs involved in transferring the products to the ultimate consumers. Higher distribution cost would put pressure on competitiveness of product cost. At the same time, producers require to be present with sufficient products at the right time and at the right place. Which again brings cost escalation and hence market price.

Role optimisation: Producers require entering into partnership with different channel intermediaries to increase exposure of the products to the prospective customers. This calls for putting efforts on optimising the respective roles of all the involved channel intermediaries so that the products can reach to the customers in the best possible way. Sometimes the size of the intermediaries is bigger than the producers themselves. Hence, any effort put by the producers in moulding the role of the intermediaries in the desired direction often becomes futile.

Achieving synergy: A distribution channel structure becomes efficient when all the intermediaries and the producer involved in the channel work synergistically to achieve the marketing objective. However, for achieving synergy it requires that all the intermediaries perform as a team. In practice, the producer fails to get cooperation and co-ordination from the intermediaries because all the involved channel members have their own respective business agenda. It is not surprising then that when everybody works in accordance with their respective interest achieving synergy becomes too difficult.

Logistic time optimisation: Designing distribution channel structure also requires decision making in the matter of on transportation and logistics issues as they can highly influence the cost and efficiency of the distribution structure. The product may reach the customers faster if the mode of transport is aeroplane. But this time minimisation effort entails higher cost. At the same time low cost mode of transport increases the time to reach the target customers. At this juncture, often it is difficult to strike a right balance between the logistic cost and time.

Distribution Channels for International Marketing

In international marketing, a company looks to penetrate the host country market seamlessly. It desires to make the products available to the target customers in a more efficient way than the competitors. In the quest for efficiency, the company can have two options. It can reach the ultimate customers either by developing its own distribution channel in the host country or by using the existing independent intermediaries for transfer of its products to the ultimate customers. In the former case, the company requires to make a sizable investment in the host country for setting up wholly owned distribution outlets. In the latter case, the company requires to make strategic use of already existing distribution channel of the host country with participating intermediaries such as wholesalers, retailers, distributors, etc. In this second alternative, the upfront investment is comparatively much less. However, in both the cases, it is important that the company makes advance decision on the depth, length and width of the proposed the international distribution channel structure. This decision making is influenced by the marketing objective of the company. Further, decision on host country distribution channel structures is also greatly influenced and refined by factors such as its own preference, experience, marketing impact and cost considerations. However, in practice, the company can often expect a mismatch between its pre-entry planned distribution channel structure and the existing or available one.

Let us take a look, at this juncture, towards the five basic ways which can be used by international marketers to send consumer goods to the ultimate consumers in the target country market (Figure 10.1).

Producer–consumer relationship

This is a direct channel from producer to the consumers. The obvious benefit will be in terms of saving the profit margin of the middleman and appears to be an attractive option to producers. Nowadays, with the extensive use information and communication technology, direct selling has become popular. A few companies like Avon opt for direct selling of its cosmetics products. Nu Skin, an internationally networked marketing company, is selling its skin care and personal care products around the world through a multi-marketing system. Direct marketing is of growing importance in developed countries of the world. Companies are also using direct mail, tele-marketing, etc., to get close to the customers.

Producer-retailer–consumer

Retailers have grown in size in many countries and gained command over the country market. Big Bazaar is a big retailer with about 214 stores across

FIGURE 10.1 Basic channel structures

Producers → Consumers

Producers → Retailers → Consumers

Producers Wholesaler → Retailer → Consumers

Producers → Agent /Distributor → Retailer → Consumers

Producers → Agent /Distributor → Wholesaler → Retailer → Consumers

90 cities and towns in India covering around 16 million sq. ft. of retail space as of June 2, 2012. It means that producers will be inclined to park their produce with one such retailer and avoid bringing wholesalers in between. The presence of global retailers such as Carrefour, Walmart, Ahold, etc., opened avenues to producers to put their product directly to the retailers without going through wholesalers for international sales. Carrefour, which is the second largest retailer in the world after Walmart, operates hypermarkets, supermarkets, and hard discount stores in thirty countries across Europe, Latin America, and Asia. So a producer will feel good to avoid wholesalers or distributors while going to these kinds of markets.

Producer-wholesaler-retailer-consumer

If the retailer is small in size, it would need assortment breaking and therefore the use of wholesalers makes economic sense. Wholesalers can buy in bulk from producers, and sell smaller quantities to numerous retailers. This used to be the traditional and stable distribution system in many country markets. The presence of large retailers in the market place seems to have disturbed the system stability. Since the large retailers do not require the bulk breaking provided by the wholesalers, so they could sell the same product comparatively cheaper. However, in many country markets small retailers continue to dominate the show. In many cases there have been be a clash of power between large retailers and producers. In the Indian market, Cadbury made bad blood with Big Bazar over margin issues and hence dissociated itself with the big retailer. Again many small retailers can be reached with the help of one wholesaler. In fact, when Cadbury dissociated itself from Big Bazaar, the producer used to get sales of only one percent of its total revenue through this big retailer[2]. Therefore, many producers depend on the lengthy channel by involving wholesalers between them and retailers. In Europe long channels involving wholesalers are common in France and Italy.

Producer-agent/distributor-retailer-consumer / Producer-agent/distributor-wholesaler-retailer-consumer

Many international marketers prefer to create this type of channel while entering into the other country markets. It serves them two purposes. One, the agent/distributors are all equipped to take the stock transfer from international marketers with a set downwards channel in the foreign country. Second, it saves investment on the part of the producer as there is no need for to create the distribution channel from the scratch in the foreign country. Exporting companies mostly use this type of channel since they can feel relieved if the task of selling rests with the agent/distributor. Agents also constantly look out for foreign producers which make contacting them easy for the producers. In case of small produce exporters, the distributor purchases the product and even use its own brand name to market the product. However, in case of a big producer with existing brand image, the distributor would use the producer's brand name. The distributor would then take over the responsibility of the rest of the distribution channel such as choice of

[2] No celebration for Cadbury; Big Bazaar takes it off shelves, (www.money control.com).

intermediaries, storage and marketing and will have various responsibilities depending on the agreement with the producer.

Choice of Channels: Control and Responsibilities

A manufacturer has various options for reaching foreign country markets. The responsibility pattern of the producers and marketing control vary across each alternative of distribution channel possibilities.

Alternative 1: The Company can reach the customer through its own distribution activities. For this, the manufacturing company is required to set up its own sales subsidiary in the foreign countries where it tries to sell its product. The benefits of such channel structure would be huge in terms of marketing as the company would have control on the marketing operations and hence it will be closer to the customers' requirements. However, this entails setting up of own subsidiary operations in the foreign country with resource commitment which is almost of irreversible nature. Figure 10.2 below shows the possible channel alternatives from which a company has to select one that best suits them.

Alternative 2: The manufacturing company can directly send its products to the appointed retailers in the target country. Here, as with Alternative 1, the company may require to operate through its own sales subsidiary and import products from the parent company in the home country and break the bulk to distribute the product amongst the appointed local retailers. Since the producer has the reach up to the retailers, it can control the marketing activities better using this alternative.

Alternative 3: The manufacturer exports the products from home country to a middleman or agent in the target country. The agent or middleman

FIGURE 10.2 Channel alternatives

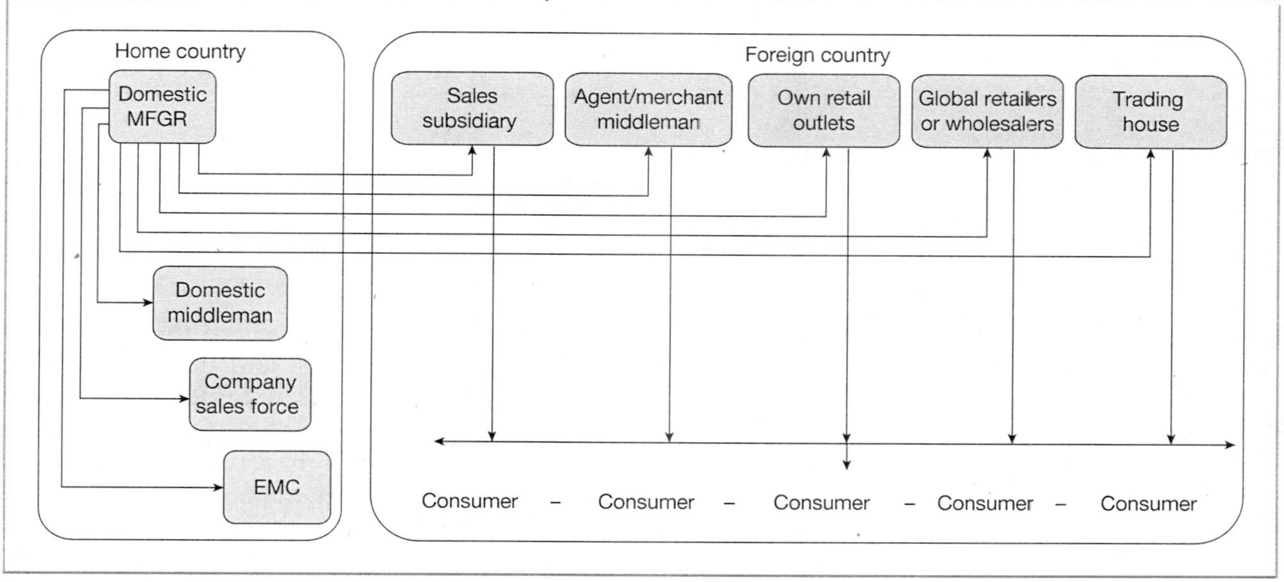

does not take the title of the products but helps the producer to channelise the products to the ultimate consumers through retailers on commission basis. The merchant middlemen, on the other hand, would take the title of the goods through buying and thereafter sell them from their own account. Understandably, in this process, the merchant middleman becomes a powerful controller of the marketing operation. The producer gets the benefits of realisation of the sales before the ultimate consumers purchase the products but at the cost of losing the control of marketing to the new title owner. For practical purposes, the merchant middlemen source products from various producers. Hence, they will not show special considerations to any particular manufacturer unless the producer has a very respectful brand.

Alternative 4: The manufacturer sends the products to a middleman located in the home country itself. Here the producer, interested in sending products abroad, selects a suitable home country middleman and offloads the responsibilities of exporting and distributing the products in the foreign country market. This particularly suits small- and medium-scale producers with small international sales volumes and limited exposure to the nitty-gritty of foreign distribution system. Since the producer handles no international marketing but simply depends on the ability of the middleman to do so, the possibilities of the producer learning or building capabilities of international marketing is less.

Alternative 5: The manufacturer may send its products to own retail outlets located in a foreign country. Many big producers with multi-country operations like Benetton exercise this option. The foreign retail outlets either can be owned or given on franchisee basis. However, to tie up with a franchisee in a foreign market requires the producers to have sufficient brand fame.

Alternative 6: The manufacturer may send the products to global retailers or wholesalers. There are many multiband retailers in the different markets such as Walmart, Carrefour, Costco, Tesco, etc., who look out for sourcing the products from producers across the world. Also, there are multi-brand wholesalers such as German Metro Cash and Carry who absorb the products from different producers by way of continuous sourcing from different countries.

Alternative 7: The manufacturer may send the products to the export management company (EMC) located in the home country. In India, star category export houses provide good opportunities for the domestic manufacturers to send their products to foreign countries. The EMCs will collect exportable products from the home country and develop bulk for exportation.

Alternative 8: The manufacturer may send products to the export management company located in the foreign market and that, in turn, may take care of promotion and distribution. For example, Ravissant General Trading is an export management company which imports and distributes many American and European brands in health products, beauty products, stationary, toys, gifts, greeting cards, etc., to market them in the Middle-east and in India.

Alternative 9: The manufacturer, in order to send products abroad, may come in touch with brokers of foreign companies located in the home country. These brokers are commission agents who source products on behalf of foreign companies. The job of the broker is to bring the buyer and seller close to each other so that a deal takes place and the agent earn a commission on the deal. A number of big retailers like J.C Penny USA take the help of brokers for sourcing handicraft products from India. In fact, the brokers are generally get specialised in dealing with a specific type of commodity. In many cases the foreign companies set up buying offices in countries of sourcing possibilities. The task of the buying office is to look out for the right kind of products in the sourcing country, support the sourcing company with product information and export the product to the principal. Small- and medium-size companies find a good way of getting their products exposed to other countries through this channel. However, there is almost no marketing control for the manufacturer in this channel alternative primarily because of the size difference between the manufacturer and the principal buyer.

Problem of International Distribution

What type of intermediates will be used in the foreign country? How many tiers will be created there for successive transfer of products to the ultimate consumers? What should be the roles and responsibilities to be assigned to the involved intermediaries? What type of logistics would be cost-effective in transferring products from manufacturing locations to the intermediaries? What would be the profit sharing equation with the intermediaries? What would the strategy to maintain good relationship with the intermediaries? Answering these questions advance constitute international distribution planning. International distribution planning is far more difficult than domestic planning for the reasons described below. Many big companies have faltered in the matter of distribution planning in foreign countries. The Italian automobile major Fiat planned its distribution in India and accordingly made a tie-up arrangement with Tata Motors of India. The plan was to use the country-wide distribution network of Tata Motors and to sell its cars through Tata's dealers. But the plan did not work out in practice. Despite the alliance, the Italian car maker failed to push its sagging sales in the country. It had only 0.6% share of the domestic car market and finally, after six years, the Italian car company broke the tie-up and decided to go alone.

Varying distribution system: The distribution structure and system of a country traditionally develops over the years reflecting the culture, government interventions, etc., of that particular country. Therefore, the distribution system varies from country to country. For example, Japan has a multi-tier distribution system where similar types of intermediaries are placed in a hierarchical fashion to send products from producer to the consumer. Such system usually takes longer time to send product from producer to ultimate consumers and involves higher distribution cost. However, in countries like USA, the distribution channel structure is much more flat and rational, where duplicity of same type of intermediary in one vertical channel system is strictly not practiced. Korea has its own 'Chaebol' type of distribution system that traditionally got developed in that country over the years.

Distribution channel selection: This is a big problem for many companies entering a distant country market for the first time. A company, for example, may be comfortable in operating in a hyper-market type of shopping mall only, but while entering a new country, it may not get that kind of an environment because of unavailability of such retailer or pricing reasons. For example, Body Shop, the UK-based cosmetic company that is now a part of L'Oreal corporate group, was forced to open shops in malls when it entered USA, while it was comfortable in boutique type of exclusive shops.

Distance between manufacturing and POS: The geographical distance between the place of manufacturing and the point of sale (POS) in another country surely matters for ensuring customer satisfaction. Lack of supply, delivery delay, lost shipment, access to spare parts, etc., are the inherent problems associated with many international marketers. For example, Sony could not make available its Play Station 2 in USA in time due to logistical problems, which allowed its rival XBOX 360 from local company Microsoft to take marketing advantage and dominate the market.

Information about the channel: The structure of a distribution channel of a foreign country, the behind-the-scene movers and shakers of the business, etc., are difficult to be known before entering the market. It has caused many companies to change channel afterwards. For example, L'Occitone, a French cosmetic company, had to change its distribution channel in India after incurring huge loss of sales. (See the end-case study.)

Organising human resources: Many a time, it becomes difficult for a company to get a suitable person to head the distribution system of the company in a foreign country market. The distance, cultural differences, language differences, etc., may force a company to select a local person and rely solely on his or her knowledge of the local culture and demography when much better talent refuses to take up the job in the foreign country. Volkswagen deputed its one of the best German executives to India to look after the booming Indian operation. However, the same executive, posted in Bangalore, rushed back to Germany by showing reasons that domestic cows and buffalo freely seating in streets of the city causing huge problem in driving vehicle.

Pricing factors: The home country type pricing is generally preferred by an ethnocentric company in the foreign market. However, the margin of the distributors of the foreign country sometimes becomes unexpectedly high and this makes the pricing difficult.

Commitment: The selected foreign distributors may not be always as serious as the producers. This difference between manufacturer and distributor creates a rift leading to fall in sales. For example, when there is an urgent need of releasing aggressive or multiple advertisements to check downward trend of sales, the drive seen among the producers may not be matched by equal seriousness in the foreign country distributors. The difference in commitment level would bring discontentment between the producer and the intermediaries.

Imbalance in channel power: Channel power is the ability of a channel member to control or influence the marketing strategy of an independent channel member at another level in the channel[3]. In other words, channel power provides the requisite strength to one channel member to spell out its own terms to another channel member on marketing issues and the later follow them with all sincerity which otherwise would have been left unattended. It is obvious, therefore, that a manufacturer would desires to gain and retain channel power so that it can easily dictate the roles of the intermediaries to be performed. The following are the advantages of channel power:

(a) A manufacturer equipped with channel power, therefore, would be in a comfortable position to set different supplementary or complementary roles to the intermediaries which enhance the channel efficiency as a whole.
(b) The channel power can also be utilised to gain effective cooperation from intermediaries and nullify conflicts in order to attain marketing objectives.
(c) The channel power can be used to castigate the erring intermediaries in case of requirement but still keeping channel conflict within control. The producer finds it easy even to formally enforce some punishment to the erring intermediaries for the sake of making the whole channel work harmoniously.
(d) The channel power helps the producers to effect changes to the allotted roles of the intermediaries in accordance with the market requirements.
(e) To share the profit from business operation or incentivising intermediaries in accordance with market position of the company.
(f) Inter channel conflict resolution becomes easy for the producer.

But, where from this channel power can come to the producers and marketers which can be effectively used to influence foreign country intermediaries? Usually channel power can be gained in the following ways:

(a) It can be gained through legal agreement executed between producers and marketers which can be effectively used to influence foreign country intermediaries? and different intermediaries. The legal clauses contained in the agreement provide the requisite power to the producers to put restrictions on sharing of information, approval of further territory rights, etc., as per the situational demand. However, many a times such legal agreements have different respectability in different countries.
(b) The channel power can also be gained by producer by using its business size superiority in comparison to that of channel members. Technological excellence or marketing excellence can also provide channel power. The SMEs, in general, do not have this size advantage and, hence, may suffer a lot in foreign markets for not having the channel power.

Now, think of a situation when an international marketing company 'A' failed to gain requisite channel power in a particular country. It also experienced that fundamental of the legal system in that country was very weak. The legal powers were not at all enforceable because of laxity in the system. Even in previous cases, some companies had to leave the country who simply failed to exercise legal power and get leverage out of it. In some cases,

[3] Berman, B. (1996), *Marketing Channels*, John Wiley and Sons, USA, p. 663.

Box 10.1 India slipped in the retailing race of the emerging markets

The availability of good and efficient retailing infrastructure is an important consideration for international marketers. An efficient retailing system allows products to flow into a market and exposes them to the consumers for selection and purchase. It is not possible for a company to develop exclusive company owned retailers in every country market. Hence, in most countries, the international marketers have to use the services of local retailers. A strong retailing strength in such country market would be helpful for international marketers to showcase product variety, render promotional activities and receive consumer feedback to better their market performance. Information about the type of retailers available in a country, structure of the retailing system and the retail development status of the country would, therefore, be highly essential for devising a foreign country distribution plan. The Global Retail Development Index (GRD Index), first published by A.T. Kearney during 2002, has been an important tool in the hands of international marketers to understand the retailing situation of a country. The GRD Index helps international marketers to understand the retailing status and its expansion trend, and then to prioritise their market development strategies. The index ranks emerging countries based on more than 25 macroeconomic and retail-specific variables. The variables included in the calculation of the GRD index are economic and political risk, retail market attractiveness, retail saturation levels, and modern retailing sales area and sales growth of the countries.

As per the GRD index shown in Table 10.1, India did not figure in the top ten countries during 1995. This can be attributed to poor scoring of marks on macroeconomic parameters. However, things changed with the advent of globalisation and liberalisation during 1991 and the macroeconomic situation in India started improving. The economic situation also improved

as a result of the fallout with the foreign producers, the defiant intermediaries in the host country did not even hesitate to divulge important market information to the local competitors. Also, the home country business superiority of 'A' was not respected by the host country intermediaries deliberately. The home country brand image of 'A' could not retain its brilliance on transfer, thereby causing huge problem in regaining channel power in the foreign country. The company 'A' was experiencing total imbalance in power and helplessly observed the malfunctioning of the channel structure. Some intermediaries became unduly more powerful in the channel. This situation was dangerous and detrimental to the cause of international marketing ambition of the foreign company 'A'. The total doldrums in the channel structure provided undue advantage for a local competitor in the following way. Suppose that the foreign company 'A' in country X lost channel power and a channel member unduly assumed the power because of a relaxed legal enforcement system in Country X and 'A' had no other way than to accept it. However, the domestic producer B in its own country X could somehow prevail on the channel members which allowed it to use fully the specialisation of channel members leading to generation of channel efficiency. In that situation, what the company 'A' lost was gained by domestic producer B.

Higher logistic cost: The logistic system in different countries has different efficiencies. A producer from Country A may be very cost effective in Country X but not in Country Y because of higher logistic cost. So, a standardised distribution plan may not be very effective in some countries in attaining the marketing objectives. The simple reason for this is 'world is not flat', and hence, efficiency of the channel structure would be different in different countries.

Table 10.1 Global retail development index

Rank 1995	GRDI 1995	Rank 2006	GRDI 2006	Rank 2011	GRDI 2011
1	South Korea	1	India	1	Brazil
2	Poland	2	Russia	2	Uruguay
3	Brazil	3	Vietnam	3	Chile
4	Chile Americas	4	Ukraine	4	India
5	Taiwan	5	China	5	Kuwait
6	Indonesia	6	Chile	6	China
7	Malaysia	7	Latvia	7	Saudi Arabia
8	Argentina	8	Slovenia	8	Peru
9	Thailand	9	Croatia	9	U.A.E.
10	Czech Republic Eastern	10	Turkey	10	Turkey

Source: www.atkearney.com

and the country started growing at a rate of about 8% of GDP. The famous middle-income segment of the Indian economy started surfacing and attracting leading consumer goods companies of the world due to their huge buying power. The result was visible as many leading companies in the retail sector started applying for market entry in India. The Indian government also proved to be proactive when it allowed removal of the clause of foreign companies owning up to 51% share in case of single-brand retailing. Renowned company such as Gap, Zara, Metro, Timex, and United Colors of Benetton entered the Indian market at the time of liberalisation. Local companies such as Reliance, K Raheja Corp Group, Spencer and Future retail did not also want to miss the market opportunity and hence came out with ambitious plans of investment in the retail sector. However, from 2009 onwards India seemed to have become distracted from the growth path. During 2011, India slipped to the fourth position in the GRD Index rating. The retail king tag passed on to Brazil, another emerging country in Latin America. Three fellow Latin American countries – Chile, Peru and Uruguay – also improved and figured in the top 10 countries showing favourable GRD index during 2011.

Designing the Distribution Channel

Designing a distribution channel in a foreign country is a complex process because of the large number of variables involved. Often these variables are not much definable. The complexity increases more when the foreign country channel environment is significantly different than that in the home country to which the company is used to. However, to begin with the distribution planning process, an internationalising company may look into the following factors pertaining to the target country:

- Different kinds of marketing channels available in the target country.
- Macroeconomic parameters (political-legal, cultural, economic and technological) prevailing in the target country.
- Level of competition in the target country in that particular product category.

- Channel choice of the close competitors.
- Channel length, i.e., flow of product from importer/wholesalers/sales office to the ultimate customers, available and preferred by the competitors.
- Channel spread, i.e., use of multiple channel to reach more customers.
- Controllability of the channel members.
- Investment–return expectations both in terms of channel development and profit sharing.
- Volume of product expected to flow through the channel/channels.
- Channel continuity and events of disruption.
- Channel members' behavioural pattern and effect of country culture.
- Usual channel members allegiance pattern to the foreign company.
- Channel power origin and trend in channel dependency system.
- Legal enforcement of contracts and their enforceability in maintaining channel harmony.

At the planning level it is required that the internationalising company collects data, information, facts, etc., about the above factors pertaining to the targeted country. A short cut approach in synthesising the data would not lead the desired accuracy in distribution structure designing for the company. With requisite data and information in place the company can proceed for a suitable distribution structure to be followed while entering a particular country. One of the main objectives behind information gathering about the target country would be to understand the depth of differences between channel environment in the host and home country. However, the size of the company and internationalisation experience would play a critical role in confronting with the differences and in reducing the channel design complexities. A company like L'Oreal would take on the differences in channel environment more confidently than a small company with limited years of international experience. It has been well documented in the international marketing literature that distribution environment of a particular country grows with time through taking inputs heavily from country culture, history, etc. Hence, one international marketer can hardly do anything to effect change there. For example, Japanese orthodox distribution system retained its Japanese nature even today in spite to best efforts put by western marketers to change the system. The Korean Chaebol[4] system is still continuing in South Korea. So, in the backdrop of unchangeable traditionalist distribution structure of a foreign country, it is a continuous struggle for a small internationalising company to retain control on the foreign intermediaries in the host country and 'making a refrigerator a refrigerator at the earliest possible time and better than that of the competitor'.[5]

Channel Structure Differences Across Countries

The distribution structure of any country has evolved to its present form through a long drawn process. Various country specific environmental factors

[4] Chaebol refers to a South Korean form of business conglomerate and the Korean channel members have total allegiance to the Chaebol induced system of producer-intermediary relationship.

[5] Johansson, Johny, K in his book *Marketing: Foreign Entry, Local Marketing, and Global Management*, published by McGraw-Hill/Irwin, 2005, used refrigerator as metaphor to indicate the urgency of transferring the product from factory to its practical use by the ultimate customer. A refrigerator remains only a box until it is sold to the customer.

supported the evolution process. At the beginning of evolution, the channel structure was totally non –specialised and without any clear role demarcation. With the passage of time as competition intensified the business organisations learnt the art of doing business through specialisation. Accordingly channel structures evolved in countries where different specialised agencies such as distributors, wholesalers, agents, and retailers started performing their distinctive functions to facilitate seamless transfer of products from the manufacturer's place to the ultimate consumers. According to Mallen[6], the structure of distribution channels in a country is a reflection of the economy's level of development in that country. Mueller et.al.[7] argued that generalisations theory about distribution systems actually challenged the impact of many contextual variables ranging from the economic, social and political spheres that expected to have created influence on the distribution system development. Going by these theories, therefore, each country has a distribution system and structure which is country-specific. Internationalising companies, while entering new foreign country markets, would prefer a distribution channel structure similar to the one in which they have demonstrated proficiency of attaining marketing objective efficiently. However, when confronted with differences, they first take an ethnocentric outlook and actively endeavour to change the system to their likings. But soon get back to track by realising the stubbornness to change and then make sincere attempt to adapt to the new system of distribution structure, but with a desperate desire to enjoy a globally standardised distribution channel structure. Many companies make mistakes in adaptations to new distribution structures in a new country. Hence, it is of utmost importance at this stage that a company before entering a foreign country must understands the distribution structure and system of the host country and assesses the difference correctly.

Japanese distribution channels

Japan has a significantly different and complicated distribution structure which had created colossal problem for many foreign manufacturers in the past. As a consequence to that many reputed western companies had to leave Japan altogether. These companies could not adjust with the peculiar Japanese ways of distribution. The traditional Japanese ways of merchandise distribution system were perceived by the entrant foreign companies as clumsy and highly inefficient. They termed the system as 'distribution barrier' rather than as 'distribution facilitator'. The primary reason was the excessive length of the distribution channels which according to the foreign producers absolutely unbecoming of an efficient system. However, the system was very stubborn to change as it took years to evolve. The distribution channels in Japan used to be consisting of more than one layer of similar type of intermediaries and manufactured goods were required to pass through these layers before reaching the ultimate consumers.

[6] Mallen, B. (1975), "Marketing channels and economic development: A literature review", *International Journal of Physical Distribution*, Vol. 5, No. 5, pp. 230–7.

[7] Mueller, R.D., Wenthe, J. and Baron, P. (1993), "Case note: The evolution of distribution systems – A framework for analysing market changes in Eastern Europe: The case of Hungary", *International Marketing Review*, Vol. 10, No.4, pp. 36–52.

Many such long chains of distribution were prominent in different category of products. The Sogo Shosha or the big traders used to have full control on the chains. Even a number of wholesaler or retailer will not dare to participate in any other chain without due authorisation from controlling Sogo Shosha. In local language, this type of allegiance based network is known as "Keiretsu" networks. This so called "Keiretsu" network consists of manufacturers, big traders, wholesalers and retailers. Businesses will be conducted within the Keiretsu network through the unquestioned leadership of manufacturer and with reciprocal trade obligations from all the Keiretsu members. The manufacturer's supremacy would not be questioned by any member. However, manufacturers from its own side obligated to look after the business interests of the channel members on voluntary basis. Naturally, the foreign companies who were attracted by the economic progress of Japan wanted to enter the country to market products. But on entry they got major jolt; first, by knowing the inefficient system of distribution and second, by experiencing the difficulty of entering the Keiretsu network. As a result, the Americans manufacturers faced huge problem in reaching the ultimate Japanese consumers with their products. The fate and experience of the famous US toy producer Toys 'R' Us in Japan and US automobile companies are well documented. Interestingly, the government actively supported the 'keiretsu' network system as this system used to create more channel intermediaries which, in turn, generated opportunities for employment. Further, the Japanese government enacted laws that did not allow large-scale retail stores to open or flourish in Japan. So, in course of time, many small retailers crowded the Japanese distribution system. Data shows that only 11 large retail stores were permitted to open in the whole of Japan during the period 1985–88[8]. All these made Japan to achieve a lowest figure in terms of consumer to retail store ratio. Figure 10.3 shows a broad outline of the Japanese distribution structure.

Manufacturers from other countries had a problem with the long Japanese channel as product transfer time became unduly lengthy and impacted the price of the products. They found that the products were travelling through many retailers and wholesalers, vertically connected, and each of them was claiming their share of profit. The Japanese government, on facing constant pressure from the US government, announced deregulation of the retail sector and brought about a reform of the 'Large Scale Retail Store Law' only during 1989–90.

Details of opening up of the distribution channel process and its impact on the retail and wholesale outlets are given in Table 10.2. There were about 1.62 million retail outlets in Japan during 1988 responsible for 115 trillion yen of sales volume and employing about 6.9 million persons. During the same time there was 0.4 million wholesale outlets responsible for 446 trillion yen of sales volume and employing about 4.3 million persons. Interestingly 54% of the total retail establishment employed only one to two persons indicating the

[8] Hokey Min, (1996),"Distribution channels in Japan", International Journal of Physical Distribution & Logistics Management, Vol. 26 Iss: 10, pp. 22 – 35.

FIGURE 10.3 Japanese distribution channel structure

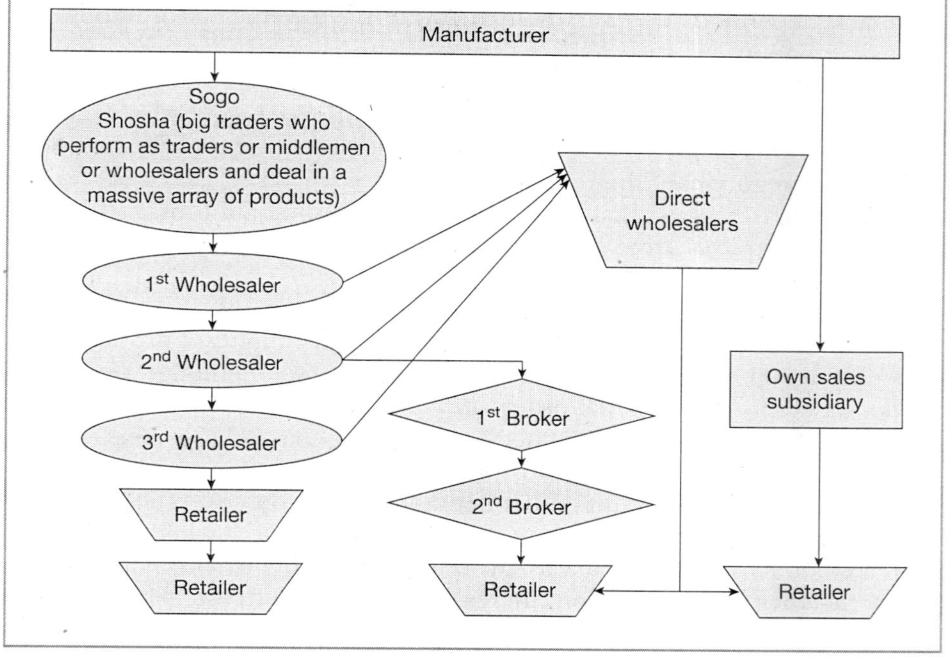

Table 10.2 Japanese wholesalers to retailer ratio

Parameters	Year				
	1982	**1985**	**1988**	**1999**	**2002**
No of retail outlets	17,21,500	16,28,600	16,19,800	12,08,000	13,00,000
No of wholesalers	428,900	413,000	436,400	342,000	379,000
Ratio of retailers to wholesalers	4.0	3.9	3.71	3.5	3.4
No of employees: Retail	63,69,000	63,27,000	68,51,300	83,57,004	84,40,574
No of employees: Wholesale	40,90,900	39,98,400	43,31,700	41,39,579	41,72,696
Sales volume: Retail (Million Yen)	939,71,000	10,17,19,000	11,48,40,000	12,73,41,465	13,51,09,295
Sales volume: Wholesale (Million Yen)	39,85,36,000	42,82,91,000	44,64,84,000	35,45,05,716	41,33,54,831

Source: 1. Ministry of Economy, Trade and Industry (2002).
2. A study of Japanese distribution system by M Maruyama, Organisation for Economic Cooperation and Development (1993).

dominance of the small-scale retailers.[9] The table also indicates that, over the years, the ratio of retailers to wholesalers has reduced from 4 during 1982 to 3.4 in 2002.

[9] Maruyama, M (1993), "A study of Japanese distribution system" Working paper, *Organisation for Economic Cooperation and Development.*

Characteristics of Japanese channel structure:

- There are many small retailers and small wholesalers. Retailers are totally dependent on the wholesalers for the product information and procurements.
- Small retailers are dependent on the wholesalers.
- Small wholesalers who are again connected with the bigger wholesalers.
- Distribution channels have a vertically segregated structure and are specialised in category handling.
- A diversified business house with business interest in different categories of products requires using different channels.
- The tasks to be performed by the channel partners are well-defined and traditional without consideration of efficiency.
- Initiation of orders, transfer of products, replenishments of products, etc., within the channel takes place without proper documentation or formalities based mostly on verbal orders and faith on each other.
- Channel members feels obligated to help other channel members and preserve their dignity. Monetary loss may not matter there.
- Works such as unitisation and palletisation based on cost efficiency, elimination of small orders to reduce transport cost, etc., would not be preferred or actively supported by any one participating in the channel.
- Inefficiency in distribution increased distribution cost. This becomes evident when Japanese distribution costs are compared with the corresponding costs in USA. A study comparing the distribution costs in the two countries revealed that Japan's total distribution costs were relatively higher for apparel products, leather products, chemical products, petroleum products, and transportation vehicles.

Chinese Distribution Channels

Traditional Chinese distribution channels

China had a traditional distribution system for a longtime for consumer goods, which was orientated more towards allocation of product and commodities across the country rather than distribution (Figure 10.4). Out of the three-tier Chinese distribution system, the first tier wholesalers, monopolised by the state owned enterprises, had the dual role of allocation and distribution. These exclusive wholesale enterprises were strategically located in major cities and industrial hubs to control the entire process of receiving goods and products from the producers and then allocate them amongst the tier 2 wholesalers located in the tier 2 cities for further distribution. These second level of wholesalers were scattered in different smaller cities and towns for off loading the products and commodities to the different retailers who, in turn, used to pass on the products/commodities to the consumers within their areas. This entire three-tier distribution process was highly system driven and none of the participating members were allowed to create any disturbance to the system either by passing or not obeying the designated role. This is reason why the distribution process used to be known 'Xitong', which means system driven. This traditional closed type of distribution system continued till 1994. But, thereafter, with the rise of economic activities, the 'Xitong' started malfunctioning. The 1994 reform first freed the tier 1 wholesalers from the domination of government and privately controlled enterprises

FIGURE 10.4 Traditional Chinese distribution structure

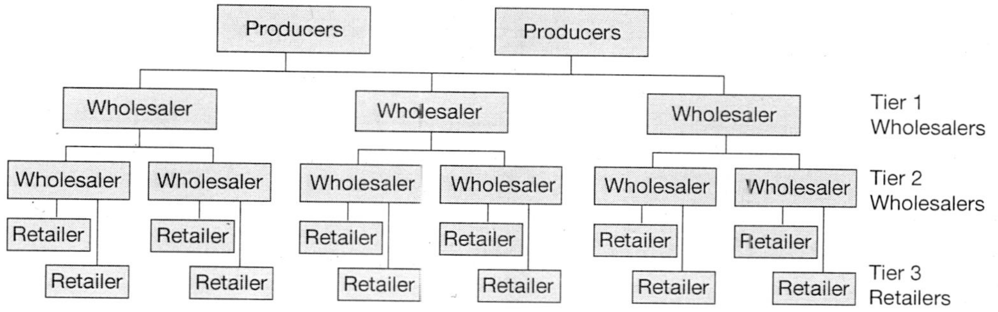

started replacing the old ones. The newly formed private wholesalers not only started competing against each other but also became market driven.

Advent of modern retailing formats

The distribution reform started with the wholesale sector but very soon started reflecting in the retailing sector as well. The retail sector saw advent in the form of different types of modern retail formats taking shape to match the rapid economic progress of the country. This sector grew very fast in China to accommodate people's aspirations, which generally come up with economic progress. The total retail sale was merely around RMB 940 billion in the early 1990, which went up RMB 4.33 trillion during 2009 and further to RMB 9.85 trillion during 2013 (Table 10.3). The growth in size was possible due to openness in the retail environment and economic prosperity of the country as a whole. There was participation of different types of modern retail outlets such as large super market, chain stores, and hypermarkets, which coexisted with traditional mom and pop stores or convenient stores.

Convenience store: Convenience stores or C stores have increased its presence in China over the years. Many locally owned C stores brand dominate the market. Easy Joy brand stores have the largest presence with around 24,000 (during 2013) retail stores throughout China. USmile (14,000 units, 2013), Meiyijia (5580 units, 2013), Tianfu (2300 units, 2013), and Gongxiao (2123 units, 2013) are the some other Chinese origin C sores brand operational in and around China. The Japanese C stores brand 7-11 is not also far behind with 1925 units (during 2013) in China. The C stores are also increasingly entering in online retailing format as well to make them more convenient and popular for the consumers.

Table 10.3 Retail trade in China

Items	Year				
	09	10	11	12	13
No of retail enterprises in million	42.62	52.3	58.47	65.92	80.37
Total sales in trillion RMB	4.3	5.75	7.13	8.3	9.8
Employment no of person (in 000)	4367	5013	5276	5752	6553

Source: National Bureau of Statistics of China (NBS)

Mom and pop stores: These are individually owned most densely located retail format operational in China and very popular amongst the consumers. Characteristically these stores are very small and are engaged in selling of various essential consumer goods such as snacks, fruits, drinks, shampoo, soaps, etc.

Super markets and Hypermarkets: The journey of super market in China started during the end of 1990s, but grew very fast with the participation of local as well as foreign operators. Mostly started in tier 1 cities and then opened branches in other small cities in China. Hypermarkets began their journey in China with a bang that attracted the affluent Chinese population. These hyper markets are substantially bigger in size and combined supermarkets and departmental stores. During 2010, the country had around 2400 hypermarkets of both Chinese and foreign origin located in the Tier 1 and Tier 2 cities. China Resources Vanguard Co. Ltd., of Chinese origin is the largest operator in terms of number of market stores as well as sales revenue (2013) in China with about 4337 outlets. RT-Mart, Shanghai is the second largest super market chain in terms of revenue with 264 outlets across China. Global hyper market chains such as Wal-Mart, Carrefour, Tesco, etc., also have their gracious presence in China with about 407, 236, and 147 retail outlets during 2013, respectively.

Departmental stores: This retail format dealing with a wide range of consumer goods in different product categories made a humble beginning in China. They grew up in numbers very fast to spread in different parts of the country but had to slow the pace as the landscape became very competitive with the inroad of supermarkets, hypermarkets, and increasing online shopping habit of the consumers.

Channel structure design in China

Foreign company could not enter China through setting up of own nationwide wholesale distribution set up prior to 2004. The products and commodities used to route through the Chinese foreign trade corporations who ensured timely delivery of the products through requisite retailers. This was favourable to the companies who did not want to handle the problems related to distributions such as logistics, execution of distribution contracts, etc. However, with the liberalisation in the system initiated by the government time to time, it is made possible for setting up a wholly owned trading company for handling import and export activities, domestic wholesaling, retailing, and franchising trade activities in China. Such trading companies are is popularly known as FICE, i.e., Foreign-Invested Commercial Enterprise. A FICE can also involve it in various other business activities related to assembling, commission agency, after-sales services, technology transfer, technology consulting, technology development, and other business consulting services in China. A channel design for China, therefore, can take many shapes in the following ways (Figure 10.4 a):

Foreign company-FICE combination: China's logistics infrastructure is one of the best in the world. Many foreign companies, therefore, are inclined to use this infrastructure to send their products to the Chinese consumer

FIGURE 10.4a Possible distribution channel in China

Foreign company	⟹	Own FICE	⟹	Own wholesaler	⟹	Retailer	⟹	Consumers
Foreign company	⟹	Agent or Distributor	⟹	Wholesaler	⟹	Retailer	⟹	Consumers
Foreign company	⟹				⟹	Retailer	⟹	Consumers
Foreign company	⟹		⟹		⟹		⟹	Consumers

by themselves. This saves them from paying high rate of commissions to the agents or distributors. Reputed companies like Procter & Gamble and others found this system of direct selling through own managed channel advantageous to them. This also allows them to estimate the market sentiment correctly and promptly.

Foreign company–agent/distributor combination: The foreign company can approach contracted distributors or agents in China and authorise them to distribute the products across China. This is a good arrangement for the companies who do not want to involve in manufacturing in China or take the pain of dealing with retailing of products to be distributed. On the foreign manufacture's behalf, the contracted agent would take the possession of the products, carrying inventory and deliver them to the retailers for distribution. The agent may not buy out the products but will do the job on commissions basis decided on mutual basis. The agent has full knowledge of the distribution system in China and can also enjoy the advantage of owning a full-fledged infrastructure to handle such activities with efficiency. In addition, these types of agents are well networked with the local-related agencies, and hence, they are expected to execute the job of distribution with perfection.

Foreign company–Retailer combination: Many established supermarkets type of retailers perform both the job of importation as well as distribution of the products directly to the consumers. Such supermarket type of retailers with warehousing facilities performs as effective channel to distribute products to the consumers. They do it effectively because of their long presence in the Chinese soil. The foreign company also gets the benefit out of excellent understanding of the Supermarket retailers about the local consumers.

Foreign company–Consumer combination: China with increasing internet connectivity is embracing online distribution very fast. This provided an excellent opportunity to the foreign companies to open online shops on B2C platforms such as Tmall (formerly Taobao Mall from the stable of famous Alibaba group of China) and JD.com (a big ecommerce company with base in the capital city of Beijing providing very effective B2C online platform). This channel is advantageous because of possible instantaneous entry into the consumers' base and showcasing of the products. The main disadvantage is that they only facilitate but do not take the responsibility of logistics, warehousing, and actual distribution to the consumers.

Vietnamese distribution channel

Vietnam became good market for many foreign FMCG companies after the government initiated 'Doi Moi' (open door policy) in the country, and, as a result, the country progressed on the economic front and its retail sector also grew accordingly (Table 10.4). Many companies from countries such as France, Japan, and Korea were quick to set up establishments in the country to take advantage of its openness and economic progress. However, the success of the international marketers would largely depend on efficient functioning of channels of distribution in the country. A snapshot view of the three–tier distribution structure of the country can be seen in Figure 10.5.

Tier 1:

- In this tier, there exist two types of trading companies, government trading companies (GTC) and private trading companies (PTC). GTC imports goods with valid import licences for certain particular products. There are specific GTCs for every type of industry and sector.

Table 10.4 Development of retail sector in Vietnams

Type/Year	2004	2007	2010
Supermarkets and hyper markets	210	400	750
Shopping centre and department stores	18	17	150
Independent stores	619	900	-

Source: Ministry of Trade & Kobe University unpublished draft discussion paper no DP 2011-08[10]

FIGURE 10.5 Vietnam's distribution structure

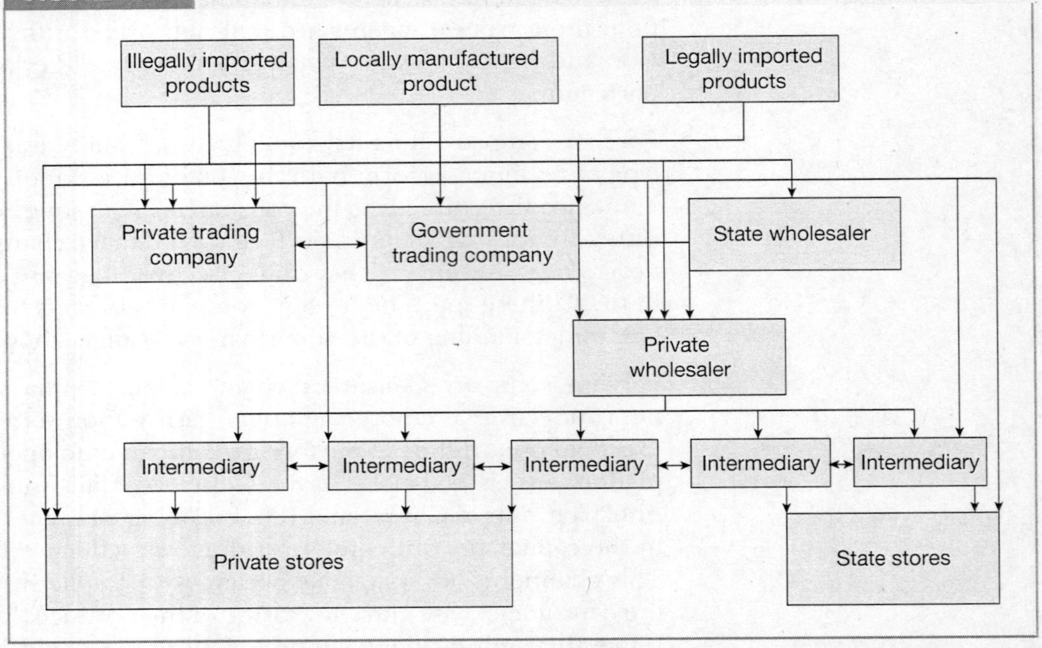

Source: Venard, Bertrand, "Vietnamese distribution channels", International Journal of Retail and Distribution Management, Vol. 24 Iss: 4, pp. 29–40

[10] Maruyama, M. and Le Viet Trung (2011), "Modern retailers in transition economics – The case of Vietnam" available at http://www.rieb.kobe-u.ac.jp/academic/ra/dp/English/DP2011-08.pdf

- The PTC imports goods for which import license is not required. They also handle illegal imports. In addition, they also source locally produced goods.
- The GTCs are linked directly with retailers but this access is very limited in terms of number of retailers and also area covered.

Tier 2:

- There are state wholesalers (SW) as well as private wholesalers (PW) in Tier 2 of the Vietnamese distribution channel. The SWs are at liberty to collect products, both from GTCs and PTCs. Under the patronage of the government they are also allowed to import products whenever required.
- The PWs are not allowed to import products. They depend on the GTCs to source products. If need be, the PWs may also source goods from SWs. The SWs also connect themselves to the PTCs as well as GTCs to source legally imported goods as well as illegally imported goods.

Tier 3:

- Tier 3 is booming with retailers of different formats of different origins. There were around 400 super markets and 2000 convenience stores during 2008. During 2010, the country had around 750 supermarkets and hyper markets to cater to the high degree of preference of urban people for shopping in the modern retail stores than the traditional markets. These bigger retail formats occupy 20% space out of the total retailing formats present in the country.
- During 2007, foreign retailers were allowed to form joint ventures with local companies to the extent of up to 49% participation. During 2008, the participation limit was removed, and finally in 2009, 100% foreign-owned retailing was allowed. However, foreign retailers are required to obtain permission while opening of subsequent retail outlets from the Vietnam's local departments of industry and trade, which has been considered by foreign retailers as trade barrier.
- Many giant global retailers such as Lotte of South Korea, Seiyu and AEON of Japan, Big C of France, Parkson of Malaysia, Diary Farm of Hong Kong, Robinsons department stores under Thailand's Central Group, and Germany's Metro are present in the country. However, still about 80% of retailing is carried out by the Mom and pop type of store outlets.

Russian distribution channel

Russia literally came in the radar of international marketers only after dissolution of the Soviet Union during 1991. As the country started opening up to the foreign marketers, the distribution system also got unshackled from government control. The absolute dominance of centrally administered government owned stores were also diminished drastically after 1991. USSR was a difficult place for international marketers especially because of its closed product distribution system characterised by the following features.

- Retail prices of products and locations of the distribution outlets were to be fixed by the government.
- Government owned specialty stores were meant to cater to the requirements of special groups such as invalids, war veterans, and ruling party officials. Products there were of higher quality.

- 'Biriozka' types of retail outlets were meant for distribution of imported goods or luxury items to which general consumers did not have access.
- Many co-operatives type of retail outlets were meant for carrying a wide variety of consumer goods for general consumers but at a higher price.
- Retailing of agricultural products was the domain of the collective farm (kolkhoz) only.

Immediate to the collapse of Soviet Union, the retail trade structure was disrupted and fragmented, but soon it started to take a new modern shape in order to cater to increasing market demand. The following is a description of how things changed.

- The location of retail outlets and pricing of the products became the outcome of market requirements. Organised and modern retail chains increasingly replaced centralised distribution centres.
- Discount stores came into being emphasising on low prices with relatively small assortment and quality. A typical store size is below 400 m^2. Examples of these in Russia are Diksi, Pjaterochka, Kopeika and Magnit.
- Convenience stores emphasising on location, with relatively higher prices but closer to the customer, with flexible opening hours, were common. Examples of these in Russia are Petrovskij and Spar.
- Supermarkets emphasising on wide assortment, good service and quality of products positioned as one-stop shopping for products of various country origin came up. Examples of these in Russia include Paterson, Sedmoj Kontinent and Perekrestok.
- Hypermarkets emphasising on the combined features of discounters, supermarkets and warehouse operations in one place with low prices and wide assortment started spreading in the cities. Examples of these in Russia include Auchan, Marktkauf, Ramstor, Mosmart/Rosmart and OKei.
- Department stores emphasising on good service, high quality and specialisation in certain products were common feature in Tier-2 cities. Example of a general type of department store selling also food in Russia is Stockmann.
- In addition, the retail tier consisted of numerous entities from street vendors to multinational retail chains. Unorganised retail outlets included kiosks, outdoor markets, Soviet-style general stores (universam) and specialty stores that invaded the roads in the city.

Channel Performance Management

It is true that international marketers try hard to achieve a certain level of channel performance. However, managing channel performance in a cross-country situation is more complex than managing a domestic marketing situation primarily because of the geographic distance between the producers and the channel partner, difference in channel structure and involvement of cross-cultural issues. International marketers forge ties and develop business relationships with different channel partners who may be located anywhere in the world in order to keep their marketing going on globally. If creating customer value is the marketing objective, then distribution channels must contribute and perform efficiently in the cross-country situation. The intense desire for building up competitive ability in the distant markets through creation of customer value better than that of the competitors has made companies dependent on the their channel partners to a great extent. Effective channel performance management, therefore, aims at achieving the following twin objectives:

1. **Cost objective:** Establishing a cross-country channel of distribution to reduce the total distribution cost and increase profit margin without disturbing the level of customer satisfaction in the foreign country. Mathematically stated.

$$D = T + W + I + P + O + S$$

where D – Total distribution cost of system; T – Transport cost (domestic plus international); W – Warehouse cost; I – Stocks and inventory costs; P – Packaging cost; O – Order processing and documentation cost; and S – Total cost of lost sales due to not meeting service standards set or stock out.

2. **Harmonisation objective:** Ensuring that the cross-country distribution channel achieves a high degree of harmonisation where the producers and the independent channel members are effectively and efficiently collaborate with each other for achieving each other's objective individually and the producer's objective collectively.

Efficient delivery of products to foreign country customers requires effective management of five categories of channel performance variables given below and shown in Figure 10.6.

Channel alignment: This refers to a system when the entrant company is in a position to orchestrate the all the channel participants' actions in the international arena in the desired way set by the marketing objectives of the entrant company. The aligned channel, so achieved, would allow achieving the international marketing ambition of the entrant company in an efficient way in the foreign land. This involves tuning of the channel participants'

FIGURE 10.6 Measure of international channel performance

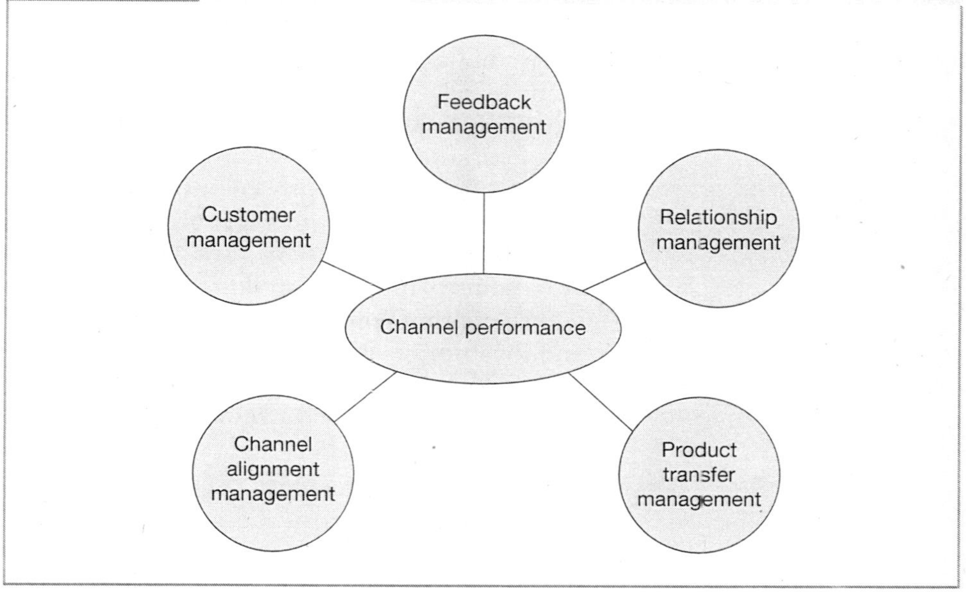

objectives such as the wholesalers, foreign dealership, import agents, and retailers in line with the marketer's own objective. Surely, this not an easy task to achieve that to in a foreign country. The traditional country specific behaviour and functioning of distribution channel partners have to show a clear sign of change and optimally adapt in line with the company's marketing philosophy. The adaption has to be free from conflict and channel partners must voluntarily contribute to the growth of the company by allowing the company-specific competitive advantage to be flourished in the target country. KFC has successfully managed to achieve channel alignment in foreign countries. The channel partners, i.e., its franchises in different countries are so rightly adapted by the company that none of the franchise has reasons to disturb the company's fundamental marketing objective. KFC has made the Swedish, Japanese, Chinese, Thai and other country channel partners behave and function in a standardised way without reflecting any country-specific differences which actually this American company wanted. This is also reflected in KFC's in-store standardised performance across the different countries of the world. The niche international customers of KFC all along liked this standardisation and felt at home in the foreign country as well. This also helped to show case the company's thorough professional and global brand image to the customers. So, this variable is very important measure of channel structure formation and hence requires careful attention from the company in order to achieve higher channel performance in the distant markets.

Customer management: This second variable is a measure of customer retention ability of the designed channel in the foreign land. The channel members' overall performance in the foreign country has to be aimed at reducing the customers' perceived cost of getting the products. The channel member's performance must lead to higher degree of customers' satisfaction. The stock-outs or lost sales have to be minimised. After sales or post sales services also have to be performed to the satisfaction of the customers and hence improve customer retention or customer loyalty levels.

Product transfer management: The third variable measures the supply chain efficiency crafted with the designed channel structure. Managing international supply chain between the strategic warehouses locations up to point of sale is very important. The channel partner networks have to be effectively crafted so that at the operational level parameters such as in-time port operation and maintaining of optimum storage level are duly taken care of with continuous improvement. The channel partners have to understand the costs associated with over stocking or stock-out cost and their effect on the parent company. This variable works in favour of the company when cross-country information flow across the managers of the channel members and the parent company becomes smooth and adequately supports logistics and inventory management planning. Supply chain inefficiency parameters such as delivery schedule mismatch, undue delay in transportation and port demurrage charges, etc., have to be reduced to a large extent in order to score on this variable.

Relationship management: This fourth variable is a measure of channel conflict resolution ability of the entrant company. It is extremely essential that the home country managers get excellent cooperation from the representatives of the channel members located in the foreign country and vice versa.

Any flip flop in this account lead to beginning of channel conflict. The level of coordination between the producer and the foreign dealership largely depends on the relationship status. A healthy relationship keeps the commitment of the channel partners in the same level as that of the producer. For this to happen, it is necessary that both the involved parties understand each other's culture when deliberating on conflicting matters such as profit sharing, investment sharing, etc.

Feedback management: This fifth variable measures the usefulness of the channel partners in providing marketing information from foreign countries back to the producers. It is important in today's context that the foreign channel partners are active in collection of market information and pass it on to the producers as and when required. The information of product demand must reach the producers in time and at regular intervals for assessing the demand condition and inventory replenishment. The channel partners, particularly those in the front end like distributors, being close to the customers, must be in a position to collect and analyse important marketing related information such as change in taste, choice and preference, pricing aspects, etc., from the customers and communicate their analysis to the producers so that timely action can be initiated. So, foreign channel performance can be equated with all the above five intervening variables as shown below.

Foreign channel performance = Channel alignment + Customer management + Product transfer management + Relationship management + Feedback management.

International Channel Structure Design

When deciding on a foreign market entry strategy, the international business must also consider a suitable distribution channel structure to market its products in the foreign country. Generally, the producer will desire to retain its domestic marketing advantages in the foreign marketing situation also. For example, companies like Tata automobiles would like to retain its huge distribution channel advantage in India while marketing in the foreign country market as well. Replicating successful marketing mix strategy in the foreign country situation provides confidence to the domestic company on internationalisation. However, the transferability of these firm-specific domestic advantages to the foreign country is generally not possible. Mahindra and Mahindra, while marketing its SUV in USA had to design its distribution strategy differently than what it practiced in India. Avon had a problem in retaining its chain marketing system in China and Japan. Therefore, a careful analysis of transferability of home country distribution advantages to the foreign market situation is required to be made in order to understand the gap and to cover the gap efficiently. The gap need not necessarily arise because of a difference between the requirement of the company in terms of product distribution and the kind of set up available in the target market. So, the next consideration will be to research the marketing channel structure of the target country and find a reasonably suitable structure for entering into the target country with details of a channel partners' involvement in it.

The nitty-gritty of the partners in terms of margins expected, general involvement and commitment, payment terms, geographical reach of the involved channel members, their already executed deals with other foreign and domestic producers, etc., are important considerations at this stage. A distant country channel requires frequent exchange communication and hence the possible communication channels and distortions expected are also to be noted for strategic considerations. An international business, therefore, requires a process to consider all the above points and arrive at a suitable and efficient channel structure for the company.

Step 1: Understand the foreign country target customer

The channel design should start from a clear understanding of the targeted customers in the foreign country and not from the distribution intermediaries. It is ultimately the end users whose requirements are needed to be served efficiently and better than by the competitors. In many cases, at the designing stage, companies put too much emphasis on understanding the intermediaries first but they should keep in mind that intermediaries are not the ultimate aim of the company. The ultimate target should be to fulfil the customers' requirements. In understanding the foreign customer correctly the following three aspects matter most.

Product related requirements: What are requirements of the target customer in terms of the company's products? How frequently is the product information is required? How much sophistication would the company require in delivering the product information? Different distribution channels have different capacity for off-loading product related information. Similarly, a company may have limitations in delivering the desired level of information to the customer. It depends on the segment of the industry as well. A company dealing with cosmetic products would require delivering product information frequently and in a sophisticated manner. The constituents of the product would matter much for the targeted consumers and will bring about product differentiation in the market. For example, in case of a cosmetics company for women it was found that one of the constituents of the product, 'Shea butter', is considered by the customer to be "more natural" than other similar products. The company was using this information to differentiate the product from the competition. The company took all care to inform the targeted customers from time to time about how much care it was taking to produce the particular constituent in its backyard to maintain the naturalness. In the international market, the different country consumers are differently placed in terms of their requirements not only for products but also for the constituents of the products. For example, the Chinese women welcome the product more aggressively because of the presence of 'more natural Shea butter' as they liked to keep their beautiful skin more natural. To achieve this they were willing to pay a higher price for the cosmetics. But in India, the same may not be the requirement. The skin, which is not that 'god gifted' as compared to that of Chinese women, may require a combination of different ingredients, and emphasising on the naturalness of 'Shea butter' would not bring the preferred result.

Hence, companies with international marketing ambition are required, at the first step of distribution designing, to understand the extent of product adaptation and information dissemination needed in a specific country.

Buying habits: Another important understanding about the product is about how much (volume) or how many (number) the prospective customers of the target country would buy at a time. The buying habit again differs from country to country. For example, Japanese women would not like to buy a big container of cosmetics or several small containers at a time to save the trouble of going to the market frequently or save money due to bulk purchase. However, this may not be the buying pattern in USA or in India. So, the question is how the consumers naturally buy the product? What is the lot size? How different is it from the standard practice for similar products?

Service performance: Culturally, the consumers are differently placed in different countries about the uncertainty of the product performance. Some may require more assurance from the producers than the others. What is the level of assurance the target customers are naturally inclined for? A company may choose to provide more warranty/guaranty for its products in the target country, if need be. The level of pre- and post-purchase services may also be required to be varied based on country-wise requirements. Requirement of the intensity of after-sales service would be good information for a producer at this juncture, as this can be of great help in designing the distribution channel for the country.

Step 2: Understanding channel performance requirements for the target customer

Different channel structures provide different capabilities to the producers in serving the specific requirements of the customers. The data collected in Step 1 will therefore be the benchmark for understanding the channel performance requirement. If the producer is in one country and the next level importer cum distributor is in the host country, this type of distribution structure will not be able to serve the target consumers if they require frequently updated information about the product. Possibly in those circumstances, the producers may require a few company-owned establishments, if not more, in the foreign country for educating the target customers. So in this step, the information gathered on the customers will be used to understand the requisite level of channel performance expected. The list of requirements or expectation from the desired channel will be brought out at this stage in the following manner.

- The channel must be capable of providing updated information to the customers frequently.
- The channel must be capable of providing high level of satisfactory environment/ambience in the actual purchase situation.
- The channel must be capable of providing updated customers' feedback to the producers frequently.
- The channel must be capable of maintaining close touch with the producers/agents/distributors located in different countries for sourcing products or importing them at regular intervals.

- The channel must be capable of reaching to the target customers at many desired places (selling points) for ease of purchase by the customers.
- The channel must be capable of providing satisfaction with, after and before sales services as set by the producer's policy.
- The channel must be capable of effecting necessary peripheral adaptations such as change of warranty clause, product pricing tags, etc., as and when directed by the producer.
- The channel must be capable of organising trade events such as trade shows etc., from time to time in order to provide a good launching pad for new products in that country.
- The channel must not have more than three levels, including the producers, in the target country before the product finally reaches to the end users.
- The channel width must cover the frills offered along with the products as well as the requirements of online customers.

Step 3: Understanding channel structure availability in the target country

After Step 2, which helps in setting the channel performance requirement for the product in the host country, the next task will be to understand the target country channel structure more closely. The following questions will be sought to be answered at this Step 3.

- How the channel system has been built traditionally in the target country over the years?
- What modernisation was effected in the channel structure over the years?
- Who control the channel structure? What role the government plays in enforcing the channel regulations?
- What role the country's culture plays in maintaining the hierarchy in the channel structure or sharing information at all levels of channel?
- What is the level of access of modern retailing system such as hyper markets, etc., in the country? How much can the modern trend of retailing change the buying habits of the target customers or customers in general?
- How much product information can be offloaded through the internet?
- What type distribution channel structure does the competitors in the similar product category use for reaching the customers of that country?
- How is profit shared in the distribution channel?

Step 4: Matchmaking between Step 2 and Step 3

This stage requires creative interpretation of the outputs generated in the first two stages and adjusting the requirements based on availability (Step 3) to arrive at the acceptable level of requirements which can be safely adopted in the company. So, this step will develop a refined requirement for the target country. There are many countries where the requisite retail infrastructure is not available that the internationalising company are accustomed to while marketing their product in home or other countries. For example, there are some countries where the hyper market retail format is yet to make an entry. However, the company may be more comfortable in distributing products through hyper markets only. What the company would do in the new country situation? So, while entering the selected market the requirements are revisited in this stage to arrive at a new or somewhat adjusted set of requirements.

Step 5: Developing channel structure options for the company

This is a simulation stage for the retail strategy practitioners of the company, in which the internationalising company introduces a variety of possible channel structure design with their merits and demerits. Suppose a company intends to market its ladies cosmetics range, the possible channel structure can be devised, for example, in the following ways.

Option 1: Producers – importer cum distributor – wholesaler – retailer (hyper market and super market combination) – customers

Option 2: Producers – buying agent – distributor – wholesaler – retailer (hyper market and company owned retail outlet combination) – customers

Option 3: Producers – company owned distribution set up as importer – wholesaler – retailer (super market and convenience store combination) – customers

Option 4: Producers – independent importing agency – independent distributors – convenience stores combination – customers

Option 5: Producers – Super market and hyper market as importer cum retailer – customers

Option 6: Producer-independent importing agent-distributor–e retailers

This stage allows the internationalising company to develop various options for reaching out to the customers based on actual product availability in the target country market. The channel depth and extent of coverage should be used as the differentiating factors to weigh the various options without considering the cost associated with them.

Step 6: Evaluating the option from the cost and benefit angle

Any option developed in the previous stage requires to be passed through a cost–benefit analysis. The possible revenue expected, market share desired, market penetration gained, transaction costs associated with monitoring and evaluation of channel partners performance, possible product transportation costs, start-up cost, opportunity cost, stock-out costs, cooperation benefits with the channel partners, loss due to possible channel conflicts, warehousing costs, etc., associated with each of the options are to be evaluated. The option which optimises benefits with reduced cost will be the preferred outcome of this analysis. Attempt should be made to make this analysis as quantitative as possible so the net benefit of the best option can easily be understood.

Step 7: Developing the channel strategy

The selected channel structure is given a practical shape by elaborating and detailing the roles and responsibilities of each channel members. Requirement gaps that could not be covered because of lack of infrastructure availability, government control or other such factors are revisited again to determine a suitable strategy to overcome the weak points. The key performance indicators are ascertained to monitor channel performance when practically employed.

Detail Logistics planning: Logistics management is one of the difficult areas in entire channel planning because of the presence of tremendous uncertainties and various trades-off. So, once the channel structure is decided for the entry, the next task is to understand the required logistics so that the products can reach the foreign country warehouse in the shortest possible time and at minimum cost. Various possibilities are created – shortest time scenario, longest time scenario and medium time scenario – and the cost associated with each of the scenario is ascertained. While the best option should be to go with the principle of 'just in time' in terms of inventory pile up and 'shortest time scenario' in terms of reaching target customers, the cost involvement in these modes of distribution should also be considered.

Developing conflicts resolution techniques: International channel structure would have participation of independent business entities of different nationalities. They must be encouraged to participate to carry out certain assigned tasks for the greater marketing interest of the producer. The outcome not only should satisfy the producer's business objectives but also for channel members' respective business objectives. Thus, working for satisfying multiple business interests requires a number of checks and balances to be in place. Any small gap in this direction may lead to conflict in the system. In a multicultural situation the channel members represent different nationalities and therefore it takes time to recognise any hitch in the inter-firm relationship development process, at least, in the initial period. The inability to understand each other's culture based behaviour correctly simply make situation further difficult. The channel conflict at the deeper level may even jeopardise the channel objective altogether. International marketing literature has been very vocal about such situation and advocated that national culture-based behaviour of human beings are hugely predictable. Therefore, it can be said that if the channel members' behavioural dimensions, rooted in their national norms and value system, can be mapped well in advance then conflicting situations can be avoided to a great extent. International marketers who well understand the expected behaviours of channel members in advance can avoid conflicting situation to creep in. In a cross-country situation, therefore, a clear understanding of the cultural norms and value system of the channel members can ensure better preparedness on the part of the producers to handle its channel member with minimum conflict.

Box 10.2 Pricing, margins and discrimination as source of conflict

During 2008, Cadbury of UK developed a conflict with an Indian retailer who was supposed to be one of the most important pillars of the UK Company's Indian ambition. Kishore Biyani, chief executive of Future Group, which owns Pantaloon (now owned by Aditya Birla Nuvo Limited) outlets and Big Bazaar stores across 100 cities and towns in India blamed Cadbury of discriminating against its rival retailers including Germany's Metro and Shoprite from South Africa over pricing issues. The issue was blown out proportion and eventually both the companies stopped business transaction any further. In many international marketing contexts, the conflict between manufacturers and the retailers revolves around "pricing, margins and discrimination". Kishore Biyani had picked up conflict with another US company and, this time, it was Kellogg's from US Again the issue was "'pricing, margins and discrimination" which led India's largest retailer to boycott the breakfast cereal brand across its various retail formats. The retailer was demanding 15–16% margin from Kellogg's but the US Company was not agreeing for more than 12%. In such conflicting situations the loss occurs to both sides. The international marketers like Cadbury lost its most potential intermediary whose access to the vast Indian markets has been enviable. For Kellogg's also, the detachment from Future group would spell a disaster for the company's strategic plan for a country like India. The company, after its debacle on the entry to Indian market with corn flakes positioned as breakfast, has been witnessing a healthy growth in smaller towns and cities of India for its cereal products. Kelloggs too was eager to reach the tier-two and tier-three towns and cities with localised cereal variants palatable for Indian taste. The company also had come out with low-priced packs, especially the ₹10 packs that account for more than 10% of its overall volumes for the smaller towns. The company also launched breakfast cereal products for children, Honey Loops, nationally and had already done a high-dose advertisement to make people aware of the benefits of taking mineral fortified cereal for breakfast. At this juncture, the conflict with the distribution partner was extremely disturbing and had effect on the planned marketing recipe for the Indian market.

How much is the loss to the retailers? Future group was complaining to the manufacturer of the cereal about the loss it apparently incurred by stocking the large-sized packages occupying significant shelf space in the stores. Since many variants of such cereals also took sufficient time to materialise in sales, the cost of holding Kellogg's stocks was high causing efficiency loss to the retailer. According the retailer Future Group's own labels Tasty Treat range of cereals would have given better revenue had those shelf spaces been occupied by them instead of Kellogg's. However, some of the variants of Kellogg's cereal have been doing well and hence the company commands more than 70% share in the country's breakfast cereal market estimated at close to ₹400 crore. For Future group, the conflict leading to total snap in the relationship may prove to be costly in the present situation where other Indian super retailers are also coming up at a fast pace. The loss of Future group today could be the gain of the other retail formats such as Spencer's, etc., tomorrow.

What will be the solution? Will the Future Group aggressively pursue the issue and snap the relation unless the demand of higher margin is not met by the Kellogg's? Kellogg's has been present in the other forms of retailing as well. The company is also allowing traditional retail formats to woo the consumers through discounts and promotions. So, the company will not be immediately bankrupt even if the Future group unilaterally decides to break the retailing tie up. On the other hand, Future group is slashing manpower and freezing expansions to cut costs as part of a series of measures to combat the slowdown. They are seeking concessions from developers, including moving to a revenue-sharing model to cut expenses on real estate as occupancy costs account for 5 to 10%of the turnover. In the midst of all-round effort to cut cost and increase revenue it is not easy to leave aside the demand for higher margins when you have sold ground to fight for it.

Source: The Economic Times, Nov 12, 2009.

CHAPTER SUMMARY

1. International marketers must decide on the depth, length and width of the proposed the international distribution channel structure in advance. The marketing objective of the company becomes the influencing factors in the decision making. While deciding on the distribution channel structures, the company has to keep in mind factors such as its own preference, experience, marketing impact, cost considerations, etc., apart from the marketing objectives. Here, any wrong decisions in setting the structure would lead to poor results.
2. There are various ways through which consumer goods can be transferred to the ultimate consumers internationally with their respective marketing implications.
3. International distribution structure planning is more difficult than planning domestic distribution.

Many big companies have faltered in the matter of distribution in foreign countries. The problems include different channel operating system, optimum structure selection, distance between the country of production and country of sale, lack of information about the channel, commitment imbalance, power imbalance, etc.

4. The evolution of distribution structure in a country is a process that depends on various environmental factors that prevail in the country. The channel structures evolve from initial stage of almost non-specialisation to a sophisticated stage where different specialised agencies such as distributors, wholesalers, agents, and retailers perform their distinctive functions to facilitate seamless transfer of products from the manufacturer's place to the ultimate consumers.
5. If creating customer value is the total marketing objective, then at the channel management level, the objective of the company is to excel in the direction of achieving channel performance in the cross-country situation. Channel performance can be measured by assessing five strategic categories of performance of the company. They are adaptation management, foreign customer management, product transfer management, relationship management and profit management.
6. Designing the channel stricture is an important consideration for international business to ponder with while deciding on the foreign market entry. Generally, the producer will desire to retain its domestic marketing advantages in the foreign marketing situation also.
7. There are various factors which the internationalising company has to consider while designing the international marketing channel. The nitty-gritty of the partners in terms of margins expected, general involvement and commitment, payment terms, geographical reach of the involved channel members, their already executed deals with other foreign and domestic producers, etc., are important at this stage. The channel requires frequent communication and hence, the possible communication channels and distortions expected are also to be noted for final considerations.

QUESTIONS FOR REVIEW

Short Answer Questions

1. Define a distribution channel. What are the basic objectives of a distribution channel?
2. Describe the basic distribution channel structure possible for a company.
3. What are the basic functions of distribution channel members?

Descriptive Questions

1. Italian lifestyle brand Diesel is finally set to make an entry in the Indian market with two stores in Mumbai. Investigate the distribution strategy for Indian market. Does it commensurate with the channel the company used for USA? How is it different in Japan?
2. What are the problems of international distribution channel design when a company decides to enter another country market? Answer with the help of an example.
3. In 1998, when China banned all forms of direct marketing, Avon was forced to turn its direct marketing agents into 6000 licensed distributors. How did that decision affect the entire marketing strategy of the company? Do you think that changing international distribution strategy for a country suited the company? Why or why not? Justify your answer.
4. What are the causes of conflicts in international channels? How should an international company handle a situation in order to resolve the conflict?
5. What are the differences between the Japanese distribution system and that of China? What are the peculiarities of Japanese channels? What implication do they have on an international company entering Japan for the first time?

6. An Indian apparel company with presence in the Indian market for the last 20 years wants to enter Japan to market its lifestyle apparel such as jeans, shirts, and knitted garments for teenagers. In India, the company operates with its exclusive store in metro cities. Given the real estate cost of Japanese cities and newness of the brand in the Japanese market, the company has reservation on opening exclusive stores in Japan initially. You are retained as consultant to look into the matter and suggest a distribution channel to reach customers. Prepare a report for the company suggesting a distribution strategy to be followed.
7. What different alternative marketing channels does a company have while entering in a new country market? Identify the pros and cons of each of them.
8. What is channel power and channel dependence? How it effect the international distribution system?
9. Compare and contrast the electronic goods distribution system of two countries you are familiar with.
10. What do you understand by international marketing channel performance? How can it be measured? How you would design an international marketing channel that can be expected to give high performance?
11. Detail the different steps required for designing an international distribution structure.

EXERCISES

1. Identify a company in your locality involved in export marketing of FMCG products. Study the company to gain a deeper understanding international distribution channels used by this company in terms of distribution cost minimisation and optimisation of marketing control.
2. Approach an international company having business interest in different countries of the world. Interview the management to understand the point of conflicts with their channel intermediaries of different nationalities so far. List the measures which the company used for resolution of conflicts. Use Hofstede country cultural index scores to develop a conflict resolution strategy for the company.
3. Identify a distributor cum importing company hosting foreign FMCG companies in India. Pick up one category of product, say cosmetics products, to critically analyse the distribution efficiency achieved and role of the distributors cum importing company in it. Suggest improvement measures, if any are required, clearly underlining the role of exporting foreign company and importing Indian company for further efficiency improvement.
4. Indian home-grown FMCG major Emami has been focussing on international expansion, especially to neighbouring markets such as Russia and CIS regions with key brands Boroplus, Navratna, Fair and Handsome and Zandu. Develop a blue print of the possible distribution channel for the company in Russia and CIS countries.

End Case: L'Occitane Structures Its Distribution Channel For Indian Market[11]

Introduction

L'Occitane en Provence is an international retailer of beauty and life style products based in Manosque, France. The company was founded in 1976 by Olivier Baussan with the purpose of creating a company that celebrates and preserves the traditions of his native place, Provence. L'Occitane designed,

[11] The case 'The French Company structures its distribution channel for Indian market ' has been created by the case writer Dr Gautam Dutta of Indian Institute of Foreign Trade as a basis for class room discussion rather than to illustrate either effective or ineffective handling of a business situation.

Table 10.5 L'Occitane financial performance

Country	Net sales for FY 2007–8 in (€'000)	% Growth*	Contribution to overall growth in %
Japan	28,773	66.6	32.7
Hong Kong	11,192	62.4	14.8
Taiwan	(496)	8.5	2.1
France	7468	16.1	7.3
United Kingdom	4927	28.7	6.0
United States	882	11.8	10.2
Brazil	3214	20.3	2.2
Other countries	24,556	38.2	24.8

* Growth from all segment including growth from own retail stores

manufactured and marketed a wide range of cosmetics and well-being products based on natural and organic ingredients sourced principally from or near Provence. L'Occitane's products include body care, face care, fragrances, hair care, toiletries, women, men's grooming products such as shaving creams, etc., and home fragrances. All of L'Occitane's products are developed and produced from its base in Manosque. The company sources the majority of its production from local producers who rely exclusively on traditional production methods. In addition to products sourced from Provence, other important constituents, like Shea butter, are even facilitated to be grown in faraway places in Burkina Faso and directly procured for utilisation of finished products of high 'natural' appeal[12].

Mr Baussan, the founder of the company, is still involved in the Company activities but from 1996, Mr Reinold Geiger took control of the business and is now leading its internationalisation process. Presently, L'Occitane products are sold in over 80 countries including Britain, China, France, Japan, South Korea and the United States through over 1500 retail locations. Of them, 753 are owned by company which sell exclusively L'Occitane products, 470 are stores operated by third party distributors and 294 are operated by airport duty-free stores in different countries[13]. The three largest markets in terms of sales are Japan, United States and France. The company had a strategic expansion plan directed towards Asia keeping in view its fast economic progress which suited a luxury brand like L'Occitane as evidenced from the fact that company became the first French company to be listed in Hong Kong stock exchange[14]. The above Table 10.5 reflects the wisdom of the Asian expansion plan by indicating the financial performance of the company in countries such as Japan and Hong Kong. Both the countries contributed handsomely to the overall growth of the company.

Indian Entry

The Company was present in all BRIC countries except India. Indian economy and its possible size in the luxury skin care market attracted the company for a long time. During 2002, the company finally decided to enter in to the Indian market and started rolling the international marketing plan for the country. It was decided that the new range of "Immortelle Collection" would be launched in India on entry targeting consumers of all ages[15]. The company would like to continue with product positioning, i.e., 'natural products' as it had done in other countries. The prices in India would be around 15% lower than that in the US market to make the brand a premium but affordable. The Company wanted to retain the exclusiveness by claiming that all the products are 'made in France' as it has done in the other country markets successfully. The company decided that the entry choice

12 http://usa.loccitane.com
13 http://img.loccitane.com
14 http://www.jingdaily.com
15 Natural cosmetic products unveiled, The Tribune, September 28, 2002, Chandigarh, India.

would be through export only for Indian market, which not only limited their initial investment but also helped in projecting the image of 'original and pure' from France . The company expected that the brand would create an extra appeal for the luxury segment of the Indian consumers and hence would not hesitate to pay little more.

Product Distribution Policy

The Company develops or manufactures almost all its products at two locations in Manosque and Lagorce, France. The products are then sold directly to end customers through 'Sell-out Segment', which principally comprises own L'Occitane Stores such as L'Occitane boutiques and department store corners that are directly managed and operated by the company. Some of the products booked were through own internet-shopping Web sites; mails were also dispatched from the factory's central warehouse located at Manosque and Lagorce which was approximately of 31,984 square meters area. During 2009, about 73.5% of total sales were derived from sales made through their Sell-out Segment. Approximately 23.1% of sales for the same period were made through their Sell-in Segment, which comprised sales of products to the resellers, including those at locations not managed and operated by the company such as distributors, wholesalers, airports and duty free stores, department stores and home-shopping television networks. This segment also included sales of products to corporate customers that use the products as gifts, for instance, to employees or customers. The remaining portion of sales got materialised through B-to-B Segment, i.e., through sale of products to intermediates such as hotels and airlines who use them as free amenities to their customers.

To ensure product availability in different countries in time, the company has strategically owned rented warehousing facilities at Austria, Brazil, Czech Republic, Taiwan, UK and the United States to feed the sell in segment. It stores inventory of finished products at third party warehousing facility providers at different countries or regions where L'Occitane products are sold through own L'Occitane Stores. However, instead of generalisation, the decision to whether maintain their own warehousing facilities or to use warehousing facilities provided by third parties, was taken by the company based on factors such as cost, sophistication of systems provided by professional third party warehousing providers, and amount of management time saved. The Sell-in Segment distributors who purchase products on a wholesale basis are actively encouraged to have their own warehousing for storing products. The products generally have an average shelf life of approximately three years. A batch code is printed on each product, which specifies its month of production. Products that are approaching their expiry date are closely monitored and disposed of through semi-annual discount sales. Any such products which are not sold are usually destroyed.

The company adjusts overall inventory levels based on seasonal changes in demand, sales information from retail management system, timing of any new product launches, sales performance by products and production volume. Shipments to appointed distributors in Asia are made directly from the company's manufacturing plants in Manosque and Lagorce at the distributors' cost. Shipments to the US UK, Brazil and Europe, where company has own distribution centres, are made regularly from the manufacturing plants in Manosque and Lagorce to the relevant regional distribution centre's according to the stock management policy.

The total personal care market in India was estimated at 2.3 billion Euros in 2008. Of this, almost two thirds constituted daily hygiene product categories, namely, personal wash (soaps etc.), oral care (toothpaste and powders) and shampoos. Excluding these three categories from the personal care market, the size of Indian cosmetics market is estimated at 750–800 million euros. Skin care is the most important category in value terms, followed by hair dyes/colours and colour cosmetics. Men's grooming products, which includes skin care, hair grooming and deodorants/perfumes for men, is also emerging as a significant segment in the Indian cosmetics market. The sector is highly dispersed, with close to 100 organised players, including multinationals. There are three principal types of companies in the organised sector – foreign-owned/international companies, large indigenous companies and small/medium companies.

In addition, there is a very large unorganised sector comprising of hundreds of micro/cottage scale enterprises, spread across the country, thriving on products based on traditional and local recipes. Stiff competition has resulted in an increase in the range of new products being introduced for newer application concepts in the last few years. However, low- and medium-priced categories/variants account for almost 85%–90% of the cosmetics market in terms of volume. International players dominate the Indian personal care and cosmetics market. Some of the important international players in the Indian cosmetic market are Unilever (Hindustan Unilever Limited), L'Oreal India, Revlon, La Prairie Switzerland and Sheseido Japan. Oriflame and Amway are the leading international companies in the space of direct marketing. Recently Los Angeles-based Jordana has tied up with North India-based Glanor to launch its products in India. L' Oreal has added a new division to take on the skin care category with its Vichy range of products. Estée Lauder too has started making their presence felt in the Indian market, by taking a minority stake in Forest Essentials, which specialises in Ayurvedic products and is the leading spa brand in India. Some of the popular Italian brands in India are Ferrari, Canali, Versace, Salvatore Ferragamo, Bvlgari, Pupa, Dolce & Gabbana, Max Mara, Clarins Paris, Patricia Milton and Deborah. Leading Indian brands which have created their own niches include CavinKare, Emami Ltd, Ayur Herbal Cosmetics and Biotique. Others such as Himalaya, Shahnaz Hussain, Godrej, Paras, Dabur and Marico also have national presence in their respective categories.

Structuring Distribution System for India

The traditional distribution model in cosmetics is a multi-tiered structure consisting of regional or zonal distributors, C&F agents, stockists and retailers. Of late, new distribution models, especially multilevel marketing, direct selling and on-line marketing have been introduced in several personal care segments. Increasingly, companies are adopting different distribution networks for rural and urban areas, given the stark difference in logistic needs and the off take levels. However, the three principal players in the distribution structure for cosmetics and personal care products are distributors, retailers and import agents. Distributors are the principal link between retail outlets and the brand within the city/region. On an average, a distributor services 400 to 450 retailers. The distributors' sales staffs are responsible for managing supplies to retail outlets. Retailers generally receive supplies from distributors or sub-distributors appointed by companies. Retailers often carry more than one brand. On an average, they stock 3–4 brands of each product category, except in the case of single brand outlets. Import agents are created as a tier in the distribution channel on account of regulations that prohibit foreign investment in India in domestic or retail distribution. The role of importers includes obtaining government approvals, handling customs clearance procedures, appointment of distributors, stockists and retailers; influencing pricing decisions; training sales staff, handling promotion campaigns, etc. The role depends to a great extent on the category and product in consideration.

Having understood the distribution system in India and its competitive landscape the Company decided to look in to the macro environment of the country, the competitors' distribution choices, channel length and breadth expected and controllability of the channel member for finally deciding on the channel structure for the Indian market.

Macro Environment

- The macro environment seemingly was very good for luxury cosmetic products. Despite the huge size of market potential only 8% of the country's population was engaged in retailing while in United States of America it was 20%. The market was poised for definite growth with factors such as increased purchasing power, rise in number of double income families and demanding customers, and due to change in life style. The economic environment had not been tremendously bogged down by the recession. The country had a luxury upper class that can spend more on cosmetics if it is pure and original. This segment had a tremendous liking for 'made in France' products.

- Foreign Direct Investment (FDI), including up to 100% equity holding, was allowed in cosmetics and personal care products. Legally, the country had not allowed majority stake in single brand retailing but there were many multiband retailers flourishing in the country. The approval was automatic and required only a filing of the investment details with the Reserve Bank of India. The Government of India was reviewing the policy on franchisee arrangements between Indian and overseas companies. All foreign investments were fully repatriable for both profit as well as principal, subject to payment of applicable Indian taxes and obtaining due clearances from the Reserve Bank of India.
- The specific regulations for imports of cosmetics products into India were laid down in The Drugs and Cosmetics Act and Rules issued by the Department of Health, Ministry of Health and Family Welfare, Govt. of India. The key features are summarised below. All consignments of cosmetics to be imported have to be accompanied by an invoice or statement showing the name and quantities of each article of cosmetic included in the consignment, name and address of the manufacturer, name and address of the consignee/importer in India along with the Importer Exporter Code (IEC) number. A declaration by the manufacturer or importer that the cosmetics comply with Cosmetic products rules was needed. Products containing dyes, colours and pigments other than those specified by the Bureau of Indian Standards (IS: 4707 Part 1) and Schedule Q, are not permitted to be imported. Also, imports of cosmetics containing hexachlorophene, lead or arsenic compounds, or mercury compounds are not allowed.
- The retailing environment showed good prospect in the country. Future Retail, an Indian retailer was doing well with different formats such as Pantaloons, Big Bazaar, Food Bazaar, and Gold Bazaar. In the luxury segment, Pantaloon was well set and carried brand names such as Bare Denims, Springboard, Lombard and John Miller. It also stocked garments, accessories and life style products. The target audience for pantaloons was the upper and middle class population of urban India. The RPG Group, another upcoming retailer in India with 'FOOD WORLD' chain of grocery stores also stocked cosmetic products. RPG also owned Spencer's hyper market with a wide range of products ranging from groceries, food items, home needs, fresh food, garments and consumer durables. The 'Shopper's Stop' chain of retailers, promoted by K. Raheja Group of Companies, positioned for upper middle class also stocked cosmetics along with apparel, accessories and household items, with presence in many Indian cities. Calvin Klein, the clothing design and marketing outlet in collaboration with Murjani group was coming up with a plan of setting dozens of up-market retail shops in cities. But it was likely that they may not host products from other names. Vishal's Mega mart was also a hyper market but the company was not interested to include their name in the consideration because of the positioning of these retail stores for lower middle class segment.

Competitor's Distribution Choice

- Revlon entered India through 76:24 JV with Modi Mundi pharma by forming Modi Revlon Pvt. Ltd in 1995 and distributing its wide range of cosmetics and beauty care products through exclusive outlets; the one in Delhi is company-owned and the ones in Lucknow and South India are franchised.
- L'Oreal, another French company, exported most of its products from abroad but also depended on its own facilities in Pune. The L'Oreal acquired Body Shop, a brand known for its naturally inspired, ethically produced beauty and cosmetics products and distributed it through a distribution franchisee agreement with Quest Retail Pvt. Ltd, which is the wholly-owned subsidiary of Planet Retail. Presently, there are 21 exclusive outlets in the country including in Tier-2 cities such as Jaipur, Ludhiana, and Pune.
- Toni & Guy, the UK based hair dressing brand was launched in India through distribution agreement with Brushman India.
- World's best-known Luxury European brands such as Cartier, Rosenthal, Bvlgari, Versace Tableware, Wedgewood and Royal Doulton entered into distribution agreement with Ravissant Pvt. Ltd, which had luxury retail outlets in India.
- Cosmetic brands such as Christian Breton and Art Deco entered into agreement with distribution

agent MKP Distributors, who have counters in prominent large format departmental stores. MKP was also increasing its distribution network, with the launch of SH Departmental Stores in eight metros. MKP planned to expand its reach in the retail sector by adding another 10 outlets. MKP Distributors, over the years, have successfully introduced over 50 prestigious international brands including Hugo Boss, Mont Blanc, Dunhill, Austin Reed, Van Gills and Nike fragrances in India. To supplement their retail efforts in a previously untapped market, MKP Distributors recently launched a revolutionary retail approach for its international range of fragrances. MKP Distributors' **new retail** initiative included collaborating with specialty lifestyle boutiques in each city, thereby catering to the upper crust of society. The initiative enabled MKP to reach out to the entire spectrum of its target audience.

- Chicago-based H2O entered into distribution agreement with Sports Station India Pvt. Ltd. and positioned itself in the niche premium segment for the high income group. Presently the brand has an exclusive outlet at the select Citywalk Mall in New Delhi, which is company-owned. It has a franchised outlet at Kanpur. The brand has counters in the MBOs such as Reliance Wellness, Dabur 'New U', Lifestyle International, Central's, and Fortis Healthcare. This brand's USP is using seawater as a base for most of its products.
- French label Thal'ion Laboratories entered into a tie-up with domestic distributor Uttam Biotech for distribution of its marine-based skin-care cosmetics while the products were to be imported from France only.
- Alfaparf Milano, a well-known professional hair care brand from Italy, came to Indian market through franchise and distribution agreement with Delhi-based Yerazig Impex Pvt. Ltd, while retaining the exclusive importation rights of the products with them

Channel Length and Channel Breadth

- Channel design requires the company to dwell on the issues of "length" and "breadth" of a marketing channel in a foreign country. Channel length refers to the number of intermediaries it requires to reach to the ultimate customers. This dimension is given by the number of links and not by the distance in space crossed. If the distribution is "direct", then the channel length will be reduced; but in case of "indirect" channel, the company increases its distribution process. Channel breadth refers to how intensely or selectively the firm wants to distribute its product. L'Occitane decided that ideally the length should be as short as possible. The product was exclusive and belonged to the luxury category; so it would only be proper if it did not travel from one channel member to another before being used by the consumer. Ideally, the company wanted that the product to have only one layer of intermediary before reaching the customer. Regarding the breadth, the company followed the policy of selective distribution so as to satisfy the niece segment who prefers to use the exclusive brand.

Controllability of the Channel Member

- When L'Occitane entered other countries, it always sought cooperation from intermediaries and wanted the channel member to be able to leverage the marketing knowledge and competencies of the principal. The company claims that because of their long drawn experience from different markets of the world it had a huge knowledge base which would allow the intermediary to market the products better than the competitors provided the knowledge and skill is transferred and accepted by the intermediary. A non-cooperation may limit knowledge and skill transfer between the principal and intermediary as well as stall the joint efforts and synergies needed to undertake successful marketing in the competitive space. In short, L'Occitane sought to select the channel partners who will not be confined to their own capabilities but were willing to learn and adapt to the marketing practice of the principal. In this respect, the Company found from its own experience that big multi-brand retailers are not easily amenable to accept learning from principal and adapt thereafter. While this route promises scale and reach, the margins tend to be comparatively lower. The company had already decided not to enter the Indian market either by setting up a joint venture or subsidiary in India, or to appoint an Indian agent for its operations in India. From this point of view, L'Occitane primarily decided to look out for tying up with an Indian importer–distributor who will be handling all import related formalities as well as logistics, retail network and promotion to some extent. The company planned to send the finished products to India since it has no plans to outsource or manufacture locally. "In any case, India is way too complicated to have a subsidiary," Mr Hoffman, Managing Director, L'Occitane (Far East) Ltd, opined[16].

The Distribution Structure Selection

The Company, as a new player in the Indian market, planned its Indian entry through an agreement with Delhi based distribution company Ravissant. The Indian company Ravissant made a modest beginning during 1991 but later expanded to have its own retail stores in Delhi and Mumbai with presence in Luxury hotels like in Oberoi Group's Amarvilas Hotel in Agra. Ravissant is also the exclusive franchisees for Jacques Dessange salons in India and hence was naturally amenable to luxury hotel tie-ups. Ravissant is credited with hosting several other luxury Western brands by providing distribution support for reaching the target customer in India. Ravissant, apart from opening a number of exclusive stores in cities such as Kolkata, Jaipur, Udaipur, Chennai, etc., was also looking to extend its spread to smaller cities in course of time. For L'Occitane, it was an attractive proposition for having importation and distribution tie up with Ravissant because it also had a plan to fully cover the Indian markets slowly, not confining to the metro cities only. Therefore, the tie-up with Ravissant widenec the possibilities to grow with the distributor from time to time. Delhi and Mumbai were considered to be an excellent start because the latter city was the trend leader in the beauty/fashion segments with highest the spenders on personal care while the former was the national capital. Also the role models for the Indian masses live in both this cities which helps new brand adaptation fast.

Restructuring of Distribution Channel

L'Occitane re-entered Indian retail market June 2009 through a 51:49 joint venture[17] with Kolkata-based Beauty Concepts, after ending an eight-year-old distribution deal with Ravissant. The earlier distributorship model with Ravissant did not work well and the company took the key decision to buy 51% stake in its India subsidiary and get into single brand retailing in the country. At present, there are three L'Occitane boutiques in the country, all located in Delhi. Their venture, L'Occitane India, began Indian journey with eight stores: three in Delhi, two in Mumbai and one each in Bangalore, Ludhiana and Kolkata. New initiative included opening of additional stores in cities such as Pune, Chandigarh, and other prominent cities. "Our first few years in India were really like not being here. The company that represented us was nice gentlemen (Ravissant). I even met them in Paris twice. But they did not understand the skincare business." says Guillaume Geslin, India country manager, L'Occitane.

[16] The Financial Express, October 01, 2002.
[17] The Economic Times, July 15, 2010.

CASE QUESTIONS

Q1. What are the factors L'Occitane considered for the channel structure selection for Indian entry?
Q2. What are the reasons that prompted L'Occitane to select Ravissant as its distributor in India?
Q3. What are the possible causes of fall out with its distributor Ravissant?
Q4. Suppose you are the marketing director of L'Occitane and have been given a free hand to decide the marketing channel for India, would you enter India with a distribution model? Why or why not? What are the factors you would have considered in designing the marketing channel for L'Occitane's Indian market entry?

FURTHER READINGS

Mehta, Rajiv, Rolph E. Anderson, Alan J. Dubinsky, Jolanta Mazur, and Pia (2011), "Managing channel partner relationships: A cross-national study", *Journal of Global Marketing,* Vol. 24, Issue 2.

This article nicely captures distribution practices in three different countries and endeavoured to link the effect of national culture in possible channel partner conflict situation. This article also captures the impact of conflict on overall channel performance. The study came out with sugession that businesses need to deal with conflict management in international channels differently for different countries is unlikely to be successful.

Bertrand Venard, (1996),"Vietnamese distribution channels", International Journal of Retail & Distribution Management, Vol. 24, Issue 4, pp. 29–40.

The article describes the Vietnamese wholesaling and retailing situation for consumer products by depicting the distribution characteristics associated with classical less developed country scenario. It allows the readers to understand how inadequacy in banking, import openness, skill of the intermediaries, and economic strength of the target population can affect channel performance. The article is an eye opener for the international marketers who want to enter in the least developing country but not aware of the unexpected and unstable situations they will have to face in the distribution field.

Matthyssens, Paul and Wouter Faes (2006), "Managing channel relations in China: An exploratory study", *Advances in International Marketing,* Vol. 16.

This article deals with the channel relationship management in China by highlighting a number of factors, both contextual and historical, which simultaneously affect the exchange modes and their operation.

Jain, Megha, Shadab Khalil, Angelina Le, Cheng Nhat-Hanh and Julian Ming-Sung (2012), "The glocalisation of channels of distribution: A case study", *Management Decision*, Vol. 50, No. 3.

This article is an wonderful case study which provides insights into understanding of global–local combination behaviour in international channels of distribution. This article is an outcome of interview of senior executives of an international company and information collected through putting purposeful questions related to patterns of glocalisation in channel management, in general. The paper brings an understanding of two types of glocalisation: inter-decision and intra-decision.

Hokey, Min (2004) "The Korean Distribution System: An Overview with Implications for Korean Market Entry", Journal of Marketing Channels, Vol. 12, Issue 2.

This article portrays how an array of invisible market barriers can make situation difficult for international marketers who want to enter a country like Korea and sell their products. Readers understand how a combination of manufacturer-controlled distributors and an excessively large number of small-scale "mom-and-pop" retail stores can play spoil sport in distribution planning of a foreign company in Korea.

Beverland, Michael (2005), "Creating value for channel partners: The Cervena case", *Journal of Business & Industrial Marketing*, Vol. 20, Issue 3.

This article follows the New Zealand Game Industry Board's attempt to create a competitive advantage with channel buyers in the USA and provides a rare glimpse into international strategy implementation in industrial networks. The article suggests that success in channel designing in distant country market will be contingent on initial strategic choices, adaptability, and supportive policies that reinforce market-oriented values. Managers need to ensure adaptability within a relationship or network structure in order to consolidate initial competitive advantages and ensure on-going buyer commitment.

Murphy, Paul R., James M. Daley and Douglas R. Dalenberg (1993), "Doing business in global markets: Perspectives of international freight forwarders", *Journal of Global Marketing*, Vol. 6, No. 4.

This article throws light on functioning and role of one of the important international trade facilitators for efficient distribution of products, i.e., in the international market. The article focuses on international freight forwarders' perceptions of the situations in terms of easiness and difficulties faced in different countries while handling international freight operations. This article as well as throws light on international logistics issues experienced by the freight forwarders. According to this article, Great Britain was the easiest country for arranging international freight operations, while China was identified as the most difficult.

Gabriel Sperandio Milan Eric Dorion José Alberto da Rosa Matos, (2012),"Distribution channel conflict management: a Brazilian experience", Benchmarking: An International Journal, Vol. 19, Issue 1, pp. 32–51.

This paper deals with distribution channel conflict management mechanism of a leading Brazilian truck manufacturing company by indicating various sources of conflicts. The study allows the international marketers to understand the Brazilian distribution channel scenario and provides clues to handle channel conflicts there for bringing efficiency in the system.

Deciding on Global Promotion

11

Learning Objectives

After studying this chapter, you should be able to:

- Understand the model of basic marketing communication and its desired effectiveness as perceived by the marketers.
- Assess the different problems encountered by international marketers while communicating internationally.
- Understand the regulatory control system administered by different countries and their effect on international communication.
- Understand the basic causes of communication prohibitions that lead to communication disruptions.
- Understand the role of media availability for effective communication in different countries.
- Assess the effect of local norms and customs of communication.
- Understand the techniques of analysing communication adaptations in TV and print media advertising.

Chapter Overview

Products or services of an international company will not be sold if the prospective consumers in that country are not aware of it. Therefore, the company needs to communicate the product features, its benefits and brand name to the prospective consumers of that country. This is all the more important for new entrants who want to popularise their product or service to consumers of a different country. The companies naturally prefer to communicate to the consumers of different countries in a standardised way irrespective of country-specific differences in terms of their economic, political, or cultural background. However, country-specific differences always pose challenges by reducing the impact of the communication. This chapter, therefore, discusses about the nitty-gritty of product/service promotion strategy of international marketers for entering country after country and communicating their product or service features effectively in all country markets.

Opening Vignette

Häagen Dazs could not reach to prospective customers due communication mishap

"I wonder if this was an unintentional mistake or rather deliberate. I have heard many cases of multinationals operating in India who hire poorly educated managers rather than skilled staff from India. Isn't that a way of keeping the Indians "out"? It is high time that our lawmakers make the discrimination law a little stronger and implement it effectively. All such incidents should be fined.[1]" This was a kneejerk reaction of an

---

1 ://httptimesofindia.indiatimes.com/india/No-Indians-allowed-Haagen-Dazs-says-wrong-choice-of-words/articleshow/5346805.cms?referral=PM

anonymous blogger against Häagen-Dazs, the American premium ice cream company, on its entry in the Indian market. Why did the company which enjoys the maxim "What Rolls-Royce is to cars, and Cartier is to jewellery, Häagen-Dazs is to ice cream" in 49 countries of its presence have to face such harsh reaction in the 50th country, i.e., India? Certainly the blogger was not questioning the quality of the products. The reason was a faulty international marketing communication released in India while entering the market. Ironically, this communication was designed and released in India for attracting the Indians prospective customers towards the company's premium quality product by making them aware about the 'international-quality' standard it maintained all throughout irrespective of the country it marketed.

It actually happened in this way. Just before the day of opening its first outlet in a mall, in the southern part of India, it planned one innovative way to get in the minds of Indians. It put up sign boards around that locality which read in the following way.

French Riviera?
Welcome.
Haagen-Dazs.
Preview for international travellers.
Entry restricted only to holders of international passports.

At first, the people who saw it could not understand the meaning. Also, Häagen-Dazs was difficult name to pronounce in Indian language and has no local meaning at all. No photograph of ice cream was displayed in the advertisement. Most of the people did not understand what actually the advertisement wanted to convey. Those who knew Haagen-Dazs to be an ice cream brand got annoyed. They questioned to themselves why only foreigners living in India are allowed to get in and taste the American brand ice cream. What actually the words "international travellers" meant? Again there could not be such thing like "international passport" because every passport had the international use only. The advertisement caught the people's imagination and everybody interpreted in their own way since meaning was not clear to them. Some people thought that Indians were not allowed to get the premium ice cream. To make the situation worse, one passer-by took a photograph of the advertisement and e-mailed it to the country's leading daily newspaper. The next day morning it almost became national news and every corner of the country came to know about it because of wide circulation of the newspaper and the front-page coloured photograph of the faulty advertisement. The red-faced management had to douse the fire by blaming the adverting agency. The explanation was that the message was intended to create sensation by suggesting that one can enjoy a taste of the French Riviera (the beautiful coastal strip along the Mediterranean) without travelling to France by taking the mouth-watering Häagen-Dazs ice cream. But the unnecessary reference to the international passport holder played the spoil sport to the entire episode planned during the entry to a potential country like India.

Haagen-Dazs made Indian entry during the end of 2009, almost 15 years after it made its presence felt in the culturally dissimilar but very lucrative China market. The same brand made the Chinese literally dance. The fruit-loving tongues of average Chinese people and latent craze of American brand made dairy product brand instantly famous. It was an example for the international marketers how purposeful communication from the company positioned the American brand in the Chinese situation successfully. Such was the huge market demand that the company even raised the product price five times more than that of USA without affecting the sales volume. The communication strategy right fully targeted luxury loving population and successfully positioned it as luxury product which naturally could then be priced much higher than USA. The pre entry strategy of the American company for India was designed in the same way and wanted to replicate its China story in the Indian market. The brand wanted almost the same premium positioning in the Indian market by mentioning the product to be of international quality by using sentences like, "Now get a taste of abroad right here in India", or " need not to travel to France to enjoy French Riviera" but use of language goofed-up everything. The creativeness in the advertisement was totally missed out. No adaptation was attempted to make the advertisement intelligible to greater Indian audiences. French Riviera was not at all sought after places to travel for many Indian travellers. However, the company did practiced adaptation in full swing elsewhere. In China, the company altered their original American tag line 'dedicated to pleasure', to fit the Chinese circumstance and came up with 'if you love her, bring her to Häagen-Dazs'. The company got the desired benefit from the tag line adaptation and went on increasing outlets with addition of more ice cream variety. It also introduced locally adapted products to suit Chinese tastes. The experts questioned that why then it did not do it for India in a more cautious way? At least it appeared from the opening miscommunication that the company might have thought to proceed in Indian market with partly adaptation strategy, at least, in the marketing communication domain.

When this story of communication mishap of Haagen-Dazs was told to the students of international marketing in the classroom, the students quipped, "Why the American Company did not use the same American tag line in the advertisement in India? Is it required that for every country a company has to plan its communication strategy differently? Will it not be possible to have a standardised and global communication strategy for a company like Haagen-Dazs? If not, to what extent would be the adaptation/standardisation requirement in countries? What are the different factors governing them? Is there any framework available to understand the difference and plan accordingly?"

There is, in fact, little research of any kind of international communication. There is a great deal of essay writing on it. But by research I mean studies in which data is collected to establish or refute some general proposition.

— Ithiel de Sola Pool (1982)

INTRODUCTION

Products or services will not be sold unless the prospective consumers are aware of it. Therefore, the company needs to communicate the product features, its benefits and brand name to the prospective consumers. It is all the more important for new entrants who want to popularise their product or service to different country consumers. Take the case of Indian-made mobile handsets like Micromax, Lava, Karbonn, Spice, Maxx, Olive and Zen who were eyeing for African markets during the early part of 2011 after giving multinational majors such as Nokia a run for their money in India. These companies were sure of the future potential of African country markets as these markets were showing all possibilities of growth in the mobile telephony sector. They also knew that companies entering African countries now will enjoy the first-mover advantage at a later period. The International Telecommunication Union (ITU), a specialised agency of the United Nations responsible for issues that concern information and communication technologies, also came out with some encouraging statistics on the telecom sector in Africa to support the belief of Indian companies. Simply speaking, the ITU had termed Africa as the most promising mobile phone market of the world in terms of the pace of its growth. In Africa overall, the subscriber base of cellular mobile had increased by a wide margin between 2000 and 2009. Mobile cellular access rate, which was merely 32.1% during 2008, encouragingly reached 41% by the end of 2010. This was, indeed, good news for Indian mobile handset manufacturers with internationalisation acumen. The companies felt that although global brands and Chinese brands were very active in the African market, a huge demand gap could be filled up by the Indian manufacturers. Micromax, famed for posing a challenge to Nokia in Indian market, was found to be very proactive in grabbing the opportunity. It took internationalisation seriously and opened a sales office in Nigeria to kick-start business in Africa. It also started releasing formal public communication to let prospective customers know about its presence. Zen Mobile, another newly born mobile handset manufacturer of India, also followed Micromax's trail. It entered the progressive Nigerian market subsequently and started capturing the customers' attention to sell its mobile handsets at a competitive price of $25-$50.

Lava, another company of Indian origin, also entered the market little bit cautiously and wanted to be confined in the limited African country markets only to begin with and then expand its base with the experience gathered. On the other hand, Karbonn Mobiles was very aggressive in its approach. It ambitiously entered in 11 African countries almost simultaneously with various marketing strategies such as offering bundled and non-bundled handsets. The enthusiasm of the Indian companies further went up when prediction came up from marketing gurus that African markets will be consuming at least 100,000 mobile handsets a month in the near future. The Indian companies, because of their exposure and experience in handling of the home market, had a better understanding of the feature requirements of African users. This was visible in their marketing strategy when various tempting bundled offers at affordable prices continued to come out and outsmart even the big global names. Of course, a well-knitted distribution networks and after-sales service helped these companies a lot to replicate their Indian success in the African soil. At that stage the most important thing these companies wanted to happen for them was that of rightfully communicating the prospective consumer about the offer, company, brand, etc. The global brands like Nokia almost mesmerised the Africans with their brand images and the Indian companies would not be able to get in to the market unless the shackles of powerful brands were not broken. The Indian companies were desperate to make the potential consumers know more about the comparative offerings from the Indian mobile phone houses than about the existing global handset makers such as Nokia and Samsung.

In developing communication strategy, these companies dwelled on their Indian experiences to analyse if anything can be replicated in Africa. Micromax, besides focusing on product development, invested heavily in brand building in India upon their entry. They spent a lot towards popularising their brand name and eventually became the lead sponsor of the very popular mega event like Indian Premiere League cricket tournament. It provided the company a giant leap in the Indian market. It continued with the strategy and allowed brand building efforts to revolve around cricket only. Accordingly, apart from Indian Premiere League the company also sponsored several one day international cricket tournaments played by the Indian team in home turf with other cricket-playing nations. They released communications which depicted the uniqueness of the product features in their advertising and relative advantage they could provide to the consumers. The advertising messages highlighted the product features and their unique selling propositions. They used a tagline "nothing like anything" to convey that every product from Micromax had something uniqueness and it was not just like any other products available in the Indian market. Other than traditional media, the company cleverly used other forms of media as well like online blogs, mailers and social media routes for pushing its advertising message in to the minds of the consumers. It also launched a 'design the logo' contest allowing the consumers, artists all across the country to participate and win gifts and prizes.

Micromax also co-branded some of their mobile handsets with music channel MTV and took the advantage of launching new products through MTV. The co-branded mobile handsets were music-oriented handsets with contents from various MTV programmes.

In a big brand image building move Micromax tied its name with Bollywood also to enjoy celebrity power. They roped in the Bollywood Action hero Akshay Kumar as the brand ambassador to take advantage of Akshay Kumar's strong popularity in both urban and rural markets. This helped the company to overcome the perception of a low priced product.

The above discussion shows that there were tremendous marketing opportunities in Africa and Indian mobile handset manufacturers were required to effectively communicate to its Africa consumers in order to replicate their Indian performance in foreign soil. The companies like Micromax successfully communicated to its home country consumers and managed to reap marketing benefits. This simultaneously indicates that these companies must come out with some specific marketing communication strategy for African markets in order to achieve their marketing ambition in Africa. Naturally, the question will be asked at this stage whether the company can communicate the target customers in the African situation like the way it did for home country market. First, there was no such cricket like pan African tournament riding on which Micromax would popularise its products in many countries of the continent. Brand communication using Bollywood hero in Africa surely would not lead to much penetration except amongst the Indian population living in African countries. A market survey report pertaining to Africa had shown that the growth of mobiles phones in Africa was driven by the comparatively young people of the age group 18–34 years and its users were predominantly (67%) male. The unreliability of networks was very common in many parts of Africa and they were keeping two or more handsets for different networks. But how Micromax would take advantage of such situations in Africa when African media was not as strong as that of Indian? In some African countries the television and newspapers were almost ineffective. The local people in such countries were using mobiles to keep themselves ahead of what was happening in their world. Micromax found this situation was quite different than their Indian experience. In addition, the African markets were more price sensitive than in India. So, the home country promotion strategy of the Indian mobile handset makers might not be very useful in foreign country situation. These might undergo changes to suit the new target market requirement. Moreover, fighting with existing global handset marketers such as Nokia and Samsung in the distant markets would not be the same ball game it played in the home country. The Indian companies, therefore, might require planning differently to win over the African market and so to say other countries as well. It involved strategic media planning, deciding on the content of advertising message, content, frequency, coverage, etc. They were also requiring to decide on the vital international marketing communication issues such as the extent to which they would differentiate their campaign plan in Africa from that for India, the depth and coverage of internet based campaign to be adopted, use of celebrities in developing brand image, etc. Companies like Lava realised the need and allocated budget of $15 million so that it could effectively unleash its suitable communication plan for 12 African countries including South and East regions of the continent. Spice mobile wanted to overhaul its communication plan and allocated a budget of $11 million for the purpose which could take its products across the countries like Nigeria, Kenya, Tanzania, South Africa, Uganda and Congo.

Resolving all of these issues is important not only for companies like Micromax, Lava, etc., but also for anyone who would be venturing into international markets. Marketing success abroad would depend on the effectiveness of the communication planned and executed by taking in to account the country specific requirements. This chapter, therefore, discusses issues which the international marketers required to keep in mind while deciding the product promotion strategy in the international markets.

MODEL OF COMMUNICATION

Marketing communication or promotion is one of the four important elements of marketing mix, i.e., 4P and is responsible for channelising the marketing offer to the target market. With the support of this P, i.e., promotion, a company establishes communication with its target market. This is valid in case of beyond domestic, i.e., international marketing as well. Hence it is carefully planned and integrated into the company's activities when internationalising. The objective is to communicate the target consumers in the foreign country in such a way that an all-round awareness is created amongst the consumers about the company, products, etc., which would be used by the company to reap synergistic benefits from the target customers effectively and efficiently. The basic marketing communication process model was built up in line with Shannon and Weaver's (1947) linear model[2] of information transmission. This model depicted four basic stages of the communication. The model was found to be extremely useful in interpersonal communication that almost every marketing book referred to it as the base model for marketing communication as well. In the original model, Shannon and Weaver proposed that all communication must have six elements: a source, an encoder, a massage, a channel, a decoder and a receiver.

Source: The source is the originator in the model. It is the information source which produces the desired message or a chain of messages to be communicated. The originator initiates the message for a particular purpose. There must be some pre-decided recipient for whom the originator starts the communication process. In the marketing sense, the source is the business entity that has a marketing purpose in the marketing place.

Encoder: In the next step, as per Shannon and Weaver, the source takes the help of a transmitter to convert the message into signals. The signals should be easy or distinct enough so that it can be used by the channel and at the same time receivers must know how to decode the massage. So, the transmitter must do the encoding process carefully so that it can be transmitted efficiently and decoded effectively. In the marketing sense, the encoder

[2] Shannon, C. E. and Weaver, W. (1949), *The Mathematical Theory of Communication*, Urbana, University of Illinois Press.

may be that part of the business entity that generates the message with all its creative part for communicating and enticing the prospective customers in a marketing place.

Message: The message is the exact content which is under transmission for the purpose of decoding at the end stage by the receiver. In the marketing sense, this message could be simple statement comprise of the uniqueness of the products, company, brand, etc., which is intended to be communicated from one end of the model, i.e., the source to the receiver. Before the encoding stage, the message may look like a precise description of product benefits but after encoding it can become complex but easy enough for transmission through TV, newspaper advertisement or internet.

Channel: The channel is very important because this is the route through which the message will travel to the destination. The channel must be compatible so that the message can easy be accommodated. In the marketing sense, the channel could be any medium such as a magazine, radio, film, internet, you tube, etc., but compatible enough to create synergistic effect both for the source as well as the receiver. In the entire process the selection of the right channel for the purpose in hand is a critical task. It should be decided in a judicious way so that the transmitted message can travel fast and without distortion.

Decoder: The decoder plays a role that is opposite to that of the encoder. The decoder, as per Shannon and Weaver model, uses its technology to receive the coded message and de-codes them with efficiency. It must take enough care to see that the decoded messages are not distorted much and arrange them in such a way that the receiver understands them correctly. This is the efficiency of the decoding system. An achievement of higher efficiency indicates no distortion in the system. The same thing happened in the marketing sense. If is the target customers could decode the encoded message of the advertisers by using their own intelligence and understand the inner meaning of the message then it will be termed as efficient decoding system.

Receiver: The job of the receiver is to provide feedback to the source and allow it to understand the efficiency of the system. In the marketing sense, the source, i.e., the business entity having the necessity to communicate always will be eager to know if there is any communication gap. In other words, whether the communicated message has achieved its purpose in making the target consumer understood what it actually wanted to communicate. The difference between what was intended to be sent to the target consumer and what the consumers actually received is the gap of communication. Therefore, the feedback send by the consumer is important for the business organisation to analyse so that corrective measures can be taken up in reducing the gap of communication as much as possible.

Model of International Communication

Any marketing communication system, be it domestic or international, is required to be free from noise so that the messages can be transferred to the receiver or target audiences without any distortion. Noise, here in the parlance of marketing, means anything that interferes with the transmission of the message and reduce it efficiency. It is inevitable that there will be some noise or disturbance in the system threatening the possibilities of seamless transmission. It is expected that when a domestic company communicates to the domestic target consumers, the effect of noise will be less because of the acquaintances and expertise of the advertiser with the domestic environment. Then again when the system performs in domestic country environment, the advertiser has the liberty of coding of messages in the native language with more confidence about its correctness. In-depth understanding of the target consumers' process of acceptance of the encoded message and ability of decoding of message helps the advertisers to achieve an enviable level of efficiency in communication.Therefore, in a way, it can be said that when a domestic company communicates with the domestic consumers the efficiency is expected to be very high. However, it may not be the same in the international situation when the country of encoder and decoder will be distanced by international border. Consider the case of an international marketer entering into a distant country market for the first time with its products that were successfully marketed in their home country through a very much effective marketing communication. This marketer may not be fully aware of decoding ability of the target country consumers. The language used in the foreign country could have distorted the theme of the communication on translation which was originally devised in the home country language. In this way so many barriers interfered in the system of communication. Thus the intensity of noise would be increased by different barriers and would be active between the coded message and the decoded message reducing the efficiency of the communication process. The marketer may want to convey a certain proposition about the product to the foreign country consumers but the same proposition may get distorted because of the noise present in the system.

The barriers creating noise may be many in the international marketing situation. Some of them are in the form of language or cultural differences,

FIGURE 11.1 Model for international communication

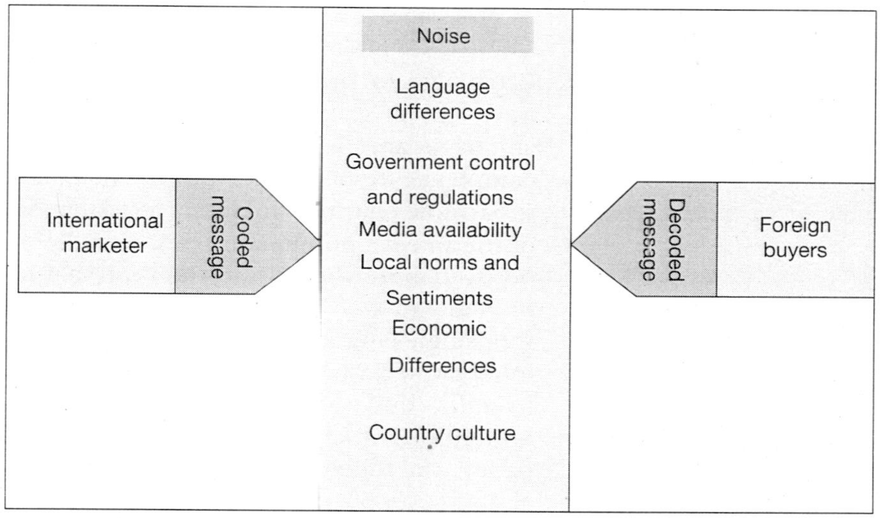

host country government policies on advertising and promotion, difference of media availability, economic differences between home and host country, local distributors' attitude, local sentiments or any other such barrier that prevents dissemination of the message intended to be transmitted by the marketer (Figure 11.1). These barriers intervene in the system and create problems in execution of a pre-determined promotion plan. Interestingly, the barriers could be different in different country situations creating different intensity of noise in the communication process. Let us look at some of the common type of barriers in detail.

Language Differences in Communication

Language differences across countries pose a huge problem for international marketers in accurately communicating to foreign country consumers. The language related problems originate mainly from the following situation:

(a) **Wrong translation:** Sometimes the problem arises from wrong translation of the original message. The translated message did not carry the intended meaning.

(b) **Less vocabulary:** All the languages do not have extensive vocabulary for each word like English. So, conveying a particular message may be difficult in a particular message.

(c) **Phonological difficulty:** Advertising message often uses techniques like rhyme, rhythm, alliteration and assonance to make receiver to remember them easily. This makes translating message developed in one language to another one highly difficult.

(d) **Emotive power of words:** Every word used in a message has an emotion attached to it. The marketers nicely use them to influence customers. These emotive powers of words which strongly influences ones action are different in different languages.

(e) **Adaptability:** Some languages allow to use word puns (multiple meaning), figurative language (words or expressions with a meaning that is different from the literal interpretation), etc., while others lack in this respect making creative parts of message difficult to unfold with original flavour.

There are many languages spoken in the world. As per 'Ethnologue: Languages of the World', there are about 6909 languages. However, one international can have some sigh of relief when it is known that 94% of these languages are spoken by only 6% of the world's population. This reduces the complexity to some extent for the international marketers as language diversity is now confined to about 389 languages (6%) that are spoken by 94% of the world's population. However, 389 languages is still not a small number to handle with for an international marketer. The marketer who finds difficulty in transferring advertising from country to country can go ahead with single-language marketing communication, say in English, and wait for others who do not understand the language to pick up the communication later. But this is simply not possible in practice and hence multiple-language option for marketing communication required to be kept open. In such situation, the following Table 11.1 indicates that twenty languages of the world almost cover 50.4% of the world population considering world population at 7.3 billion.

Table 11.1 Top 20 languages of the world by number of speakers

Rank	Language	Primary country	Total countries	Speakers (millions)
1	Chinese	China	31	1213
2	Spanish	Spain	44	329
3	English	United Kingdom	112	328
4	Arabic	Saudi Arabia	57	221
5	Hindi	India	20	182
6	Bengali	Bangladesh	10	181
7	Portuguese	Portugal	37	178
8	Russian	Russian Federation	33	144
9	Japanese	Japan	25	122
10	German	Germany	43	90.3
11	Javanese	Indonesia	5	84.6
12	Lahnda	Pakistan	8	*78.3*
13	Telugu	India	10	69.8
14	Vietnamese	Viet Nam	23	68.6
15	Marathi	India	5	68.1
16	French	France	60	67.8
17	Korean	Korea, South	33	66.3
18	Tamil	India	17	65.7
19	Italian	Italy	34	61.7
20	Urdu	Pakistan	23	60.6

Source: Ethnologue, 16th Edition

Surely, the international marketers would prefer to develop advertisement campaigns in the language that most of the countries understand while promoting their products. Their natural desire would be to use a common language even if it is different from that spoken in a particular country, with the understanding that slowly people of foreign countries will come to understand its meaning. If the home country language is not at all understandable by the host country people then marketers may also resort to direct translation. But many international marketers make mistakes in the process. The following examples illustrate the language related problems and mistakes of international marketers.

Tag line translation problem: Taglines are brief repeated phrases that are used by the marketers to make customers identify their product or a company amongst many such in the market place. They are expected to wonderful work for promoting company product as well the company in international markets. However, many a time it could not be used effectively because of translation problem. The following examples illustrate the problem.

Pepsi example: In Taiwanese language, the translation of the Pepsi tag line "Come Alive with the Pepsi Generation" was almost devastating for the company. The literal meaning of the tag line came out as "Pepsi will bring your ancestors back from the dead" which did not convey the right message to the target segment and rather kept the consumers confused.

Microsoft example: The famous Microsoft's slogan "We are rolling out the wheels" also met with similar disaster when translated into Russian language. The Russian receiver of the communication could not get any reasonable meaning out of the translated slogan.

Xerox example: Another famous company Xerox's meaningful slogan "We taught the world to copy" did not find any takers in Russia as when literally translated, the meaning was not understood by average Russians.

Volkswagen example: Volkswagen had a very famous 2003 born Germany tagline "Aus Liebe zum Automobil," which provided the company huge marketing advantage in the home market. When internationalising, need was felt to translate the tag line into English[3]. The translated version "For the love of the automobile" not only retained the original flavour but also made the customer feel close to the product. But the magic did not happen when the time came for the company to enter one of the largest automobile markets, i.e., China. When translated in Chinese it got an awkward meaning as "Auto works around the world". The new meaning did not make the Chinese buyer very enthusiastic about the product.

McDonald example: McDonald's, another global company, also demonstrated their wisdom while entering China with its original English iconic tag line "I'm lovin' it!" for the Chinese market. This company also did not go for literal translation. Instead, it opted for of literary translation to avoid mishaps. After an extensive research of the Chinese market, the company found that the Chinese do not use the word 'love' openly, cheaply and publicly. Therefore, the Chinese customer will find it difficult to use the word 'love' in public. So the company effected a change in the tag line for Chinese market and made it sound as "I like you". It was then easy for the average Chinese customer to understand the McDonald tag line with ease without actually using the word 'love'.

In a sense, therefore, the local–global combination worked well for McDonald. The avoidance of literal translation helped them the reach out to the local people with considerable ease. But the company also did not forget to retain some of its global-ness by writing the global tagline "I am lovin' it" in English letters.

Nike example: However, all companies may not have the flair to research on language as MacDonald did in China and hence, they may falter with language differences and their meaning in other languages. Take the case of American Nike Company and the ordeal it faced in the Arab world for advertising and getting involved in the language related implications in different countries. The company spent considerable amount of time and money for developing such shoes, which even when worn for a long time as in the case of the athlete participating in sporting events, would not cause stickiness inside due to sweating. This is because the shoe was manufactured in such a way that it allows air to pass through keeping the insides free from sweating related stickiness. Naturally, the company wanted to communicate this vital quality of the shoe to the consumers by embossing a stylish logo 'Air'. However, the stylish logo resembled 'Allah' when written in Arabic[4].

[3] http://en.wikipedia.org/?title=User:Skyworkeralan/sandboxvw

[4] http://articles.cnn.com/1998-11-21/us/9811_21_nike.islamic_1_nihad-awad-playgrounds-cair?_s=PM:US

This made the Arabic consumers furious and they not only avoided purchase of the shoe totally but also expressed their discontentment openly. The company understood the situation correctly and immediately withdrew all shoes of this type from the market. The entire episode made them lose a huge sum of money they had invested in product development and for developing advertising campaigns.

Slogan translation problem: Slogans are used by marketers to express a company's or product's goal in the market place. Unlike tag line the slogans are comparatively short-lived which company can change rather frequently in case of need. International marketers, like tag line, also faced problem with slogan translation. The following example illustrates translation problem associated with slogan.
Domino's example: Slogans with only three words like "Are you Hungry?" from Domino's Pizza when translated into Hindi became "Hungry Kya?" in India. it was a global–local approach but this peculiar translation in Hindi did not convey the desired meaning.

Nike example: Nike's famous slogan "Just do it" also did not escape from problems in some foreign countries. Consider the case of Nike with their "Just do it" slogan in Russia. Nike, in fact, never wanted to translate its small slogan which consisted of some abstract words joined together without giving a feeling of a complete sentence. They realised that if the three simple words work wonders for the company literally throughout the world, then there is no need of translation. The slogan has been successfully supporting the company's requirement even in those countries where people did not understand its literal meaning but got acquainted with it and enjoyed it. The company headquarter in USA was relishing the fact that many people in a number of countries interpreted the slogan in their own ways and all of them appreciated and got attracted towards the brand. The marketing experts also have time and again advised the company to refrain from translation. But alas! The slogan' unblemished journey across the countries came to a halt in Russia where the prospective customers simply failed to understand it in the absence of a literal translation. As a majority of the Russians did not know English, they failed to be amused by the slogan and could not establish a connection between the company product and the slogan. It was a difficult situation and marketing strategists were undecided on the approach they should pursue whether to push the unknown slogan more forcefully and wait for customers' acceptance or attempt to translate it to Russian at least on an experimental basis. But whatever be the course of action, marketers understood the hard way that in some countries communicating to consumers with incomplete and ambiguous slogans would be difficult.

KFC example: The literal translation of KFC' slogan "It's finger-licking good" in Chinese came out as "eat your fingers off", which was embarrassing for the advertisers. The company faltered knowing well that the almost well-established fact that translation of small slogans or tag line into another language and retaining the same meaning is a big problem.

Volkswagen example: The German automobile manufacturer Volkswagen (VW) felt a need of converting its German language slogan into English as its many target countries were English speaking. However, the new advertising slogan which VW launched during 2006 almost avoided translation requirements when marketed across the world. The slogan was made of just two words "Das Auto" (German for "The Car") and it was introduced with the understanding that it should convey the meaning that whenever you think of a car it is 'VW' or Volkswagen. This slogan was very brief and the company avoided translating it while marketing across the world. But the companies marketing wisdom had a real testing time when it entered China and India using the German language slogan "Das Auto". The company did not put effort on translation aspects in both of these two countries. The Chinese as usual was totally in dark about the meaning of the slogan but appreciated the country of manufacturing (COM) as well as the well-known country of brand (COB), i.e., Germany. Many road side automobile repairing workshops in India also initially thought it to be India made as 'Das' used to be a very popular surname in eastern part of India. However, the company persisted with the decision of not translating the slogan in to Chinese or English. However, the most tempting time in this direction came from the company when popularising its 'think blue' slogan worldwide. The company felt that it was important for the company to make people aware of the philosophy behind the "think blue" slogan. Could the company mete out the same treatment to this slogan? The slogan in itself had no meaning. Would it be worthwhile then to despatch the slogan to other countries without the translated version along with? These questions were creating a big dilemma for the company. VW ultimately decided on retaining the German language slogan everywhere but along with kept a translated English version or in other languages to explain the philosophy behind the slogan.

The explanatory note of the "think blue" was not an exact translation of it in different languages but depended mainly on linguistic requirements in respect of word use, etc. The idea was to make the philosophy behind the 'Think blue' clear to the audience across the countries. For example, in China, VW first studied the target segments correctly and then used the language of the country carefully so that the target segment understands the philosophy of the company with ease.

The Chinese advertisement of VW used Chinese letters, colours and theme to make it understandable to the Chinese clearly that blue colour of 'think blue' slogan actually was indicating the environment around us as the future of everybody living in the planet.[5] The strategy made good sense in making the Chinese and other target country population believe that the VW company was determined to utilise its 'Blue Motion Technology' to build a brighter sustainable future for all. But at the same time they did not forget to use their globalised, standardised component in the campaign, i.e., "Das Auto". This strategy of global–local in avoiding language barriers seems to have worked well with the company as revealed by their increased sales.

Regulatory Control in Communication

Every country has placed some form of regulatory bodies for regulating advertisements in the country. These bodies provides regulations time to

[5] http://www.labbrand.com/brand-source/slogan-analysis-car-slogans-china

time so that advertising environment in the country remains healthy and does not create any harm to the ordinary people living in the country. These regulations are mostly binding on the international advertisers because of legal provisions attached with them. When an international business develops an advertisement for its products or service, the primary intention of the company would be to take the advertisement to other countries where it has its business interest. The country specific regulations would act as barrier in running the standardised advertisement in different countries. These regulations and their implementation also differ from country to country. The country would restrict running of an advertisement if it found to be violating the advertisement regulations of the land. Violation of the regulation may lead to discontinuation or ban, forceful modifications or alterations, etc. On the other hand, international marketers would be tempted to minimise the modifications/alteration of marketing communications so as to keep intact its creative elements and avoid repeat expenditure by developing country specific marketing communication plan. Therefore, companies need to carefully understand rules and regulations and the regulatory bodies of those countries where they have marketing interest.

The main regulatory body or authority almost in every country happens to be a government or government appointed agency which is mandated to play regulatory roles with the help of other supporting bodies like professional (industry) associations, civic groups, advertisers and the media organisations. Their respective roles, in general, are as discussed below.

Government agencies: This organisation acts as main pillar for development of regulations in accordance with the need felt in a country. They are also responsible for enforcement of regulations already passed by the government and has mandate to develop a network of other related organisations so that dubious nature of advertisements, released by domestic as well as international companies under different purposes, cannot create harm to the citizen.

Media associations: These organisations are privately managed associations of broadcasters functioning in a country. These organisations endeavour to develop some codes of conduct for the media agencies and create peer pressure on the association members to behave within the limit set by such code of conducts. These codes of conduct draw heavily from the legal provisions enacted by government of the country. The basic objective of such an organisation is to achieve the goal of self-regulation.

Civic groups: The formations of such groups are comparatively recent phenomenon. Active civic groups are found in many developed countries who frequently voice their opinion about various aspects of media operations. They generally have the status of non-profit organisations having active interest in societal well-being. Though the opinion of such civic groups do not create any binding obligations on the international businesses but they fast gather support from members as well as common public in case of violation of societal norms due to the effect of adverse advertising. Such quick build-up of anti-opinion amongst public could be detrimental to the business interest of the international marketers.

Advertisers' association: This is a privately managed association of the advertising agencies operating in a country. Often such association frame certain written and unwritten codes of conduct for commercial media enterprises. These are important documents for the international marketers as they tend to reveal the basic fabric of the advertising regulations of the country.

Bloggers: General public, in these days of advanced communication medium like the internet, are very active in expressing opinion and framing a general view point about their preferences. In that sense, the bloggers are obvious regulators of media operations, who frequently express their views and opinions on media advertisements. However, acceptability or unacceptability of, say, the advertising content would vary from country to country depending on people's level of awareness.

Country-specific regulations: USA[6]

Federal Trade Commission is the specific agency for media regulation in USA. Media regulation in the United States follows a libertarian outlook that there should be minimal central government involved in the day-to-day operations of media. The following are their advertising guidelines:

Alcoholic beverages: Advertising of alcoholic beverages must adhere to specific guidelines. Advertisers may promote alcoholic beverages, subject to federal, state and local laws, and applicable guidelines from the Federal Communications Commission, Bureau of Alcohol, Tobacco and Firearms, television broadcasters and other entities such as the industry organisation, Distilled Spirits Council of the United States, Inc. Advertisements may not depict the actual consumption of alcoholic beverages, which includes sound effects or visual images of drinking. Advertisements may not encourage excessive alcohol consumption, or any use of alcohol by minors. Advertisements may not be directed or targeted to persons under the legal drinking age of 21.

American flag: Unless the depiction is newsworthy or part of a news event, advertisements depicting the American flag should treat the flag in a dignified and respectful manner.

Availability: The availability of products or services, if limited, must be disclosed. For example, if the products or services are not yet available or not widely available in the advertising market, the advertisement must make this limitation clear.

Children: Advertisements targeting children must comply with federal, state and local laws, Federal Trade Commission, television broadcast and other applicable guidelines, including the Self-Regulatory Guidelines for Children's Advertising of the Children's Advertising Review Unit of the Better Business Bureau.

Cigarettes and tobacco: Cheap TV spots do not accept advertising for cigarettes, cigars, pipe tobacco, tobacco paraphernalia and smokeless tobacco. Advertising for smoking cessation aids, smokeless cigarettes, pipes, and associated paraphernalia will be evaluated on an individual basis.

[6] Based on the **Federal Trade Commission, USA** advertising guidance for business available at www.ftc.gov.

Comparative advertising: Comparative advertising is the presentation of the advertised product or service juxtaposed against a competitor. Advertisements comparing products or services may not distort or exaggerate differences or otherwise create a false, deceptive or misleading impression. Comparative advertisements must comply with federal, state and local laws, Federal Trade Commission, television broadcast and other applicable guidelines.

Contests, lotteries, and sweepstakes: A lottery, gift enterprise or similar scheme generally exists when the following three elements are present: 1.) the distribution of a prize, 2.) dependence on chance, and 3.) consideration such as money or the purchase of a product.

Contraceptives/birth control methods and devices: Advertisements for condoms, contraceptive methods, or devices are must comply with all federal, state and local laws, as well as Federal Trade Commission, Federal Communications Commission, television broadcast and other applicable guidelines.

Demonstrations, dramatisations, re-enactments, simulations and exhibitions: Advertisements that include demonstrations, dramatisations, re-enactments, simulations, tests, experiments or other technical, mechanical, electronic or chemical exhibitions, must comply with all federal, state and local laws and other applicable guidelines. The advertiser must accurately depict the product or service involved, and must disclose when actors are used to portray actual persons.

Dietary supplements and nutritional products: Advertisements related to dietary supplements or nutritional products must comply with federal, state and local laws and other applicable guidelines. Any consumable product making product claims may require disclaimers shown legibly in the advertisement, as well as documentation for any claims, which may be required by networks where the commercial is submitted to air.

Endorsements and testimonials: An endorsement is a statement of public approval or support by a real individual or enterprise. A testimonial is a statement of in-person experience by a real party, such as a consumer or expert who has personally used the product or service. Endorsements and testimonials must always reflect the honest opinions, findings, beliefs, or experience of the endorser. Endorsements and testimonials may not contain claims that could not be substantiated if made by the advertiser directly. All endorsements and testimonials must comply with federal, state and local laws and other applicable guidelines.

Financial and investment: Advertising for banks, funds, stocks, bonds, commodities, insurance, real estate, and other investments must disclose all material restrictions, risk factors and qualifications. Such advertising must comply with federal, state and local laws, the Securities and Exchange Commission, television broadcast and other applicable guidelines, including regulations publicly promoted by the applicable professional or trade groups.

Food and nutrition: Advertisements may not exaggerate the nutritional value of consumables (food, beverages, etc.). Health claims, including claims of food being "nutritious" or "healthy" must be substantiated and in the context of a total diet. All food advertisements must comply with federal, state and local laws and other applicable guidelines.

Guarantees: When using the terms "guarantee," "warranty" or similar words that signify a promise or assurance, advertisers may be required to provide specific information as to the actual terms and conditions. Advertisers should generally disclose whether an advertised warranty is "limited" or "full," its duration, and any major limitations of the warranty. Advertisers should also provide information on where to find the full details of the warranty. All guarantees and warranties must comply with federal, state and local laws, Federal Trade Commission, television broadcast and other applicable guidelines.

Medical and health-related products: Advertisements related to health and medical products and services (including prescription and non-prescription drugs) must comply with federal, state, and local laws, Food and Drug Administration, Federal Trade Commission and other applicable guidelines.

Mail order, telephone, internet, and direct response advertising: All mail orders, telephone, internet and direct response advertising must comply with federal, state and local laws and other applicable guidelines. A few examples of direct response, telephone, internet, and mail order considerations: Any charges beyond the advertised purchase price (postage, handling, etc.) must also be disclosed. The time necessary for the consumer to receive the merchandise must be reasonable. For example, if time for delivery will exceed 30 days, commercials must indicate the actual anticipated time for such delivery.

"New" used to describe products and services: Advertisers should use the term "new" only for a period of six months from the time a product or service is introduced.

Obscenity, indecency, profanity, abusiveness, vulgarity: Advertising may not, directly or by implication, be obscene, indecent, profane or vulgar. Nor may advertising be threatening, abusive, harassing or hateful (racially, ethnically, religiously, or by creed), or otherwise objectionable in light of community norms and standards.

Personal products: Advertisements for personal products (such as feminine hygiene products, home pregnancy tests, home HIV tests, adult diapers, STD medications) must follow television network content guidelines.

Premiums and offers: Advertisers must ensure that the value of any premium is no less than what is stated and that no premiums or offers are unsafe or detrimental to the consumer. The advertiser's responsibilities include, but may not be limited to, the following: Provide all offer details, including rules, eligibility requirements, beginning and end dates, and requirements for fulfilment.

Safety: Advertisers must assure compliance with depictions of normal safety precautions (for example, avoiding depictions of drinking and driving, and other unsafe and illegal activity).

Substantiation of claims: Advertising claims must be substantiated in advance of airing the advertisement, with valid and reliable research or support. Acceptable claim substantiation complies with federal, state and local laws, Federal Trade Commission, and other applicable guidelines.

Superimposed text, "supers": When superimposed copy is used, it must be displayed clearly and conspicuously.

Country-specific regulations: India[7]

Advertising minutes per hour: 12 minutes including 2 minutes of programme promos.

Tobacco, alcohol: Advertisements which promote the production, sale or consumption of the following products are explicitly forbidden.

Advertising revenue restrictions: No limitations.

Contraception: Not to be mentioned explicitly.

Food and beverage: All nutritional claims in food and beverage advertisements need to be substantiated scientifically. Unless a food product has been nutritionally designed as a meal replacement, it should not be portrayed as such. The most explicit guidelines relate to food and beverage advertising targeting children.

Children: Any advertisement which endangers the safety of children or creates in them any interest in unhealthy practices or shows them begging or in an undignified or indecent manner shall not be carried in the cable service. Advertising to children should portray accurately the products in a way that is in keeping with their ability to understand. Advertisements for food should not show or encourage over-consumption. Parental guidance in ensuring proper food choices for children should not be undermined. Visual representation of foods and beverages should be true to fact. Care needs to be taken in the advertising of food and beverages to children under 13, especially ones containing relatively high levels of fat, sugar and salt. Advertisements should not encourage pester power nor imply duty or obligation.

Women: No advertisement will be allowed, which, in its depiction of women, violates the constitutional guarantees to all citizens. No advertisement shall be permitted, which projects a derogatory image of women. Women must not be portrayed in a manner that emphasises passive, submissive qualities and encourages them to play a subordinate, secondary role in the family and society.

Product placement: All advertisements should be clearly distinguishable from the programme and should not in any manner interfere with the programme such as by using of lower part of the screen to carry captions, static or moving alongside the programme.

Motoring advertising: Advertisers are encouraged to depict advertisements in a manner which promotes safe practices. No portrayal of traffic rule violations must be made. Safe practices such as the wearing of helmets and

[7] As per standards of practice for advertising agencies, approved by the Advertising Agencies Association of India, based in Mumbai.

fastening of seatbelts and not using mobiles/cell phones when driving should be depicted.

Country-specific regulations: Malaysia[8]

One distinctive aspect of TV advertising in Malaysia is the stipulation that commercials aired in Malaysia must be produced in Malaysia and feature Malaysian citizens. Eighty percent of production costs must also be spent domestically. Only 20% of footage can be of foreign origin. Localised production is assessed by the National Film Development Corporation of Malaysia (NFDCM), which issues the MIM (Made in Malaysia) certificate that all advertisements must have, or proved as exempt before being aired. Foreign advertisements have to be approved by the NFDCM. Even advertising for overseas tourist destinations is subject to pre-approval by the NFDCM. Indecent content cannot be shown under any circumstances unless approved by the film censorship board. Violence should be portrayed responsibly, not exploitatively, and any menacing content, bad language or content making false claims is banned. Care must be taken with regard to children's content and those representing persons with special needs. Family values need to be safeguarded. The other regulations are as under:

Advertising minutes per hour: Ten minutes per broadcast hour per channel.

Advertising revenue restrictions: None.

Tobacco: Cigarettes, tobacco and its accessories are prohibited in advertising.

Alcohol: Prohibited. If an alcoholic drinks company is sponsoring an event in Malaysia, it is only allowed to promote the event and not its products directly. Permitted in hotel in-house systems.

Pharmaceuticals: Commercials for medical products, treatments and facilities, medicines, remedies, appliances, skills and services relating to diagnosis, prevention and treatment of diseases or conditions affecting the human body are under the authority of the Medicine Advertisements Board, Ministry of Health Malaysia (K.K.L.I.U.).

Gambling: Prohibited in all forms, including betting and gambling tips.

Contraception: Not mentioned explicitly. See Pharmaceutical and Personal Products for guidance on sensible protocols.

Medical: Commercials for medical products, treatments and facilities, medicines, remedies, appliances, skills and services relating to diagnosis, prevention and treatment of diseases or conditions affecting the human body are under the authority of the Medicine Advertisements Board, Ministry of Health, Malaysia (K.K.L.I.U.).

Food and beverage: All advertisements must comply with the requirement of the Food Act, 1983, and Food Regulations, 1985. Advertisements of food and drink products that claim therapeutic or prophylactic qualities will be subject to prior screening; however, food and drink products that

[8] As per the Communications and Multimedia Content Forum of Malaysia.

help improve, restore or maintain the consumers' general health, physical or mental condition will not be subject to prior screening.

Personal: Advertisements for sanitary protection products and incontinence pads are subject to restriction on times of transmission and utmost care must be taken to avoid causing offense or embarrassment when deciding on visual treatments and product descriptions. Good taste and decency as well as human dignity are paramount.

Financial: Any form of financial speculation intended to promote or attract interest in stocks and shares is prohibited. Advertisements applicable to newly approved Initial Public Offering (IPO) are allowed subject to relevant applicable Acts.

Children: Special care and attention needs to be paid on how children are represented and addressed in advertising. Children should only be used in advertising where the products advertised are relevant to them. Issues relating to exploitation, security and hazardous situations should be carefully addressed. Children must be shown to be adequately supervised in their activities.

Women: Advertisements must portray positive images of women and not project women as sex objects.

Claims: Documentary evidence to prove all claims made must be held by the advertiser. Care needs to be taken to not exaggerate the value, accuracy, scientific validity or practical usefulness of the product advertised. Endorsements need to be validated and should not be misleading. Testimonials (medical or otherwise) must be genuine and related to personal experience over a reasonable period of time of the person giving it.

Product placement: It is allowed provided there is relevance to the context of the situation. Products and services that are specifically banned are not allowed. It must be ensured that advertisements are designed and presented in such a way that they are clearly distinguishable from the regular programmes.

Public service: Two minutes per broadcast hour per channel.

Government levy: A 5% government tax applies to all products, media and other agency services.

Communication Prohibitions

Different countries enforce different types of communication prohibitions. The agencies in charge of enforcing advertising regulations generally act on the basis of information collected by them directly or depend on public complaints or a combination of the two. Enforcement of prohibitions varies from country to country. The violations, on the part of the advertisers, could be rated minor in one country but major in another country. For example, a children's food commercial featuring Santa Claus for Christmas greetings came under prohibition in China on the ground that Christmas was not an official holiday in China and the commercial would give wrong information to the children. The same commercial advertisement did not have any problem in USA or UK or in any Anglophone countries. As a result, the company failed to communicate to its target consumer in its usual way. There are many other cases where prohibitions acted as barriers of communication in one country but not in other countries. Marlboro cigarette used to put advertising in television Channel Nine in Australia by showing actor Russell Crowe (famous for his role in epic movie Gladiator) smoking and displaying a package of cigarettes. But the same cannot be done in India. So, international marketers need to understand the communication prohibition barriers historically practiced and imposed on commercial advertisements in target countries before releasing any communications. The following are some other cases where international advertisers were pulled up for violating different codes of conduct in different countries for different reasons.

Against sport (India): Groupe Pernod Ricard is a French liquor company marketing its products in India with intense determination of increasing its market share. Royal Stag, a semi-premium blended Indian whisky, is its largest selling brand in its portfolio of alcoholic beverages in Indian market. During 2011, the company came in to limelight for beating an iconic vodka brand 'Absolut vodka' in terms of sales. However, the company was pulled up by Indian authority for violating advertising standards. In one of its surrogated advertisements featuring its brand ambassador cricketer Harbhajan Singh, it was shown that Mr Singh was enjoying the drink. The commercial was run several times in TV during cricket matches. This led to clamping of prohibition on the advertisement. Similarly Sab Miller India's (Hayward & Hayward 5000) and United Spirits' (McDowell's) surrogated advertisements of their alcoholic products were also declared banned in India. In fact, India does not allow advertisement of alcoholic products during sports events even in its surrogated format.

Against safety standard (India): TVS Motors, a popular motor cycle manufacturer in India, ran a television commercial highlighting the 'body balance' advantage. In the commercial of their gearless two-wheeler, ego, two women were seen pulling off dance-inspired stunts on the back seat of their respective vehicles while driving in the busy street. The Indian authority banned the commercial for violating the advertising law of the country. The reason for pull down was absolute display of stunts in regular traffic environments which is, according to the regulators, detrimental to traffic safety if imitated by others.

False claim (India): French company L'Oréal led one aggressive advertising campaign in India for its Garnier Light Fairness and Dark Spots Prevention moisturiser. The company claimed that the users would "get up to two tones fairer in just seven days". However, the company could not substantiate the claim when confronted with consumer complaints leading to clamping of ban in airing such false claim.

False claim (UK): Time and again, international companies have faced with regulatory provisions either for exaggerating the benefits of product use or making false claim in different countries. For example, the internationally famous advertising agency Saatchi & Saatchi created a commercial for Proctor & Gamble's Olay anti-ageing skin cream particularly to promote the product in UK. Eve Cameron, the beauty director of the famous

'She' magazine was roped in for the commercial by the advertisement agency. In the advertisement, she cites a study which claims that pentapeptides, a constituent of the product, reduce the appearance of lines and wrinkles of face. This fact was claimed to be presented at the World Congress of Dermatology, as shown in the advertisement. In the advertisement Cameron says: "So if you're not ready for cosmetic injections, but want dramatically younger-looking skin, try Olay Regenerist with pentapeptides. Women who aren't ready for cosmetic injections constantly ask me to recommend a skin cream that really works". Also Eve Cameron claimed in the advertisement that the benefits accrued by using the cream were duly vetted by World Congress of Dermatology. The UK regulators were not convinced by the claim and asked for documents substantiating the claim. These claim latter could not be substantiated by the advertiser and hence faced the inevitable ban in airing the advertisement in UK.

Exaggeration (UK): The French company L'Oréal earned the wrath of advertisement regulators of UK for exaggeration and false claim. It ran a magazine advertisement for its product, Revitalift Repair 10, which claimed that the product could make women look substantially younger. In the advertisement it used the 'The Mummy' famous star Rachel Weisz to look at least 10 years younger than her original age 41 and with a smoother skin. The advertising regulators of UK claimed that the image was altered substantially to make her complexion smoother and hence rated the image in the advertisement as "misleading and exaggerated". When subjected to investigation, L'Oréal admitted that they used airbrush to represent Rachel Weisz as favourably as possible and possibly in reality that may not happen. Thereafter, the company had to clear the misunderstanding created and withdrew the advertisement.

Aggressive comparison (India): Another direction in which international advertising has to be careful in most of the countries is comparative claims that could not be justified later. In order to beat the competition, companies compare its own product benefits with that of the competitors' and releases advertisements to communicate the result of such comparison to the prospective customers. Reckitt Benckiser, a multinational consumer goods company headquartered in UK, came out with an advertisement in India claiming that its acid-based toilet bowl cleaner 'Harpic Plus' is five times better than other toilet cleaners. Hindustan Lever was irked by the claim as its bleach-based translucent/white cleaner DOMEX was trying hard to outperform the market leader and arch rival Harpic. Hindustan Lever approached the Advertising Standards Council of India immediately and challenged the claim.

False claim of facts (UK): The H.J. Heinz Company, commonly known as Heinz and famous for its ketchup with presence in 200 countries, also markets baby milks under the brand name Heinz Nurture in UK. The company promoted Heinz Nurture infant formula and milk in UK during 2008 by stating that a baby needed a "special combination of nutrients to sustain the incredible growth in its brain, body and immune system". The regulator of advertisements in that country immediately asked to relate their claim with the new European regulations relating to nutrition and health claims for foods.

However, the company could not submit evidence to support the product's claims in relation to children's immunity and development and hence had to stop the advertisement.

Obscenity and Vulgarity (India): Axe deodorant was first launched in France in 1983 by Unilever as male product targeting young men. Unilever, right from the word go, made all efforts to position the product by dramatising 'Boy gets Girl by use of Axe deodorant' type of scenario so that young boys are attracted to the product and start using them. The advertisement agency working for Unilever used all sorts of creative scenarios to dramatise these benefits to reach out to the brand's 18- to 24-year-old target audience utilising different media including Websites, instant messaging, blogs and games. The different campaigns used to popularise the product in different countries attracted extra attention of prospective buyers and the advertisement regulators because of explicit use of sexual references in order to remind young men that using the product will help them to receive attention from the girls. Regulators kept an eye to see that the advertisements do not cross a level of vulgarity. In one advertisement for Axe deodorant (known as Lynx in Britain), a few scantily-clad attractive women are seen crashing to earth and rushing towards a seemingly unremarkable man preparing to get on a moped. The regulators in UK did not raise any hue and cry in the matter of obscenity or vulgarity and allowed to run the commercial. However, in India, the things were different. The company was pulled up for the reason of vulgarity in one of the advertisements run in several TV channels which showed a man turning into a chocolate boy after spraying the deodorant and few woman followers could not resist the dark temptation of chocolate and flocked to get a chunk of the chocolate boy.

The Indian regulator asked the company to stop running of the Axe Dark Temptation deodorant advertisement, as it was known, in TV by terming it as indecent, vulgar and repulsive. It was interesting to note that the advertisement played on the Indian screens was an edited version of the original which was aired in several European countries without any infringement attracting ban. The famous "give men the edge in the mating game" campaign of Unilever in promotion Axe deodorant's brand image never attracted more than a raise of eyebrow in many western countries but the company never even dared to use it in India for fear of highly possible ban on the count of vulgarity.

However, when the company came up with another advertisement for Lynx deodorant featuring glamour model Lucy Pinder, the UK regulator had to jump in to action and stopped airing of the video by terming it vulgar and obscene. The model was seen promoting the product in a series of provocative video advertisements. The regulators banned the commercial in UK for degrading women and treating them as sex objects.

Use of 'dangerous' image (UK): Prada, one of the most well-known Italian luxury fashion house specialising in ready-to-wear leather and fashion accessories, shoes, luggage, perfumes, watches, etc., was pulled up by the regulator in UK for the use of 'dangerous' images in advertisements. The company casted the famous Oscar nominated child actress Hailee Steinfeld in an advertisement for promoting its "Miu Miu" range products. In the advertisement it was shown that the 14-year-old child actress Hailee Steinfeld sitting alone and apparently upset and crying on a railway track. The advertisement regulator in UK was horrified by the image of a young dejected girl sitting on a railway track and sensed the possible danger of a railway accident arising out of it. The regulator in UK immediately termed the advertisement as 'potentially hazardous' and 'irresponsible act from a responsible company' considering the age of the model and hence banned the advertisement. Prada suggested that the particular campaign was directed to promote a serious, high-fashion apparel brand and that imaginary shot was required to set the brand image but it did not yield any result.

Role of Media Availability in Communication

Availability of right type of medium in target country is important because it is the vehicle through which advertising reaches the audience and create desired impact. More specifically, media here refers to the various mediums like print, broadcast, online, etc., through which information and visuals are relayed to the mass public for their consumption. Traditional media types include TV, radio, newspapers and magazines and now, the more modern like internet. Online advertising of different types are now possible because of access to the internet by a large section people living in the globe. However, the level of media availability is not the same in countries affecting the communication plan of an internationalising company.

Media limitations in one country may ruin an effective advertising campaign which proved successful in other countries where media availability is high. As competition grows, companies may want to get closer to the target consumers by using various marketing communication tools. So naturally, they would attempt to test these well devised and time tested communication tools in other countries as well. KFC markets its products in 118 countries by using almost all the different advertising media and enthralled the consumers over the years (Table 11.2).

However, for communication tools like advertising to be effective it requires the countries to be equipped with the requisite media base. But ironically, countries differ in terms of media availability. For example, the

Table 11.2 KFC's advertisements and use of media

Advertising media	How KFC uses different media	Impact
Social (Facebook, Twitter, Instagram, Pinterest, etc.)	KFC uses Facebook and Tweeters to allot gift coupons to the followers. @kfc_colonel and Face book posts of KFC contains link to a secret page on KFC.com. KFC also uses Instagram to popularise its menu. It also shares images of KFC through image sharing website like Pinterest.	Huge Tweeter and Facebook followers. KFC keeps interaction going with the loyal customers.
Television	Television campaign, Advertisements.	Primarily used to get advertising message out through TV advertisements.
Radio (AM, FM, XM, Pandora, Spotify)	Radio advertisements, Automated music recommendation.	Reach larger audience.
Newspapers	Advertisement, Article about KFC, etc.	In all the countries KFC used this media.

(Continued)

Table 11.2 (*Continued*)

Advertising media	How KFC uses different media	Impact
Consumer magazines	Regular advertisements in different magazines.	To reach larger audience.
Outdoor billboards	KFC billboards are very common in different countries.	It used billboard extensively to specify outlet location and awareness.
Ambient experiential	Used "ambient" campaign to make consumers to think about KFC product differently.	Kellogg's Crunchy Nut Corn Flakes benefited from ambient advertisement.
Public transportation like bus wall	Used for new product launching.	Increased awareness.
Direct mail (DM)	Used to get customer feedback. Social sharing buttons in a KFC email.	Spread product information. Email Marketing to Drive Social Sharing.
Advertising using mobile and mobile applications	KFC is making sure consumers know about its product and are able to find the nearest location to get them by mobile advertising.	Spread product information.
Specialty advertising (on items such as matchbooks, pencils, calendars, telephone pads, shopping bags and so on)	Handbag with fried chicken logo on it.	To remain on the top of customers' mind.

evolution commercial was launched by Unilever in 2006 as a part of its on-going marketing programme for popularising its Dove brand. The commercial was a part of the strategic marketing programme directed to promote the concept that 'every woman is beautiful and it is the source of confidence that counts.' The company termed it as 'Evolution campaign video' and was desperate to spread it across the countries of the world during October 2006. The video was launched mainly as an internet-based campaign. To have broader audience in the world, it was purposefully uploaded to the video sharing Website YouTube. The result was astounding and as desired by the company. It reached the homes of an enviable number of target customers crossing the country barriers which traditional media campaign cannot even imagine. As per statistics, the advertisement was viewed over 40,000 times on its first day, 17,00,000 times within a month of its upload, and 120,00,000 times within its first year[9]. This huge exposure of the brand was possible because of the right medium selected for expressing the creative content of the advertisement. However, expectedly, in countries where internet access is low the 'Real Beauty' marketing campaign did not click for the company. The company was not fully aware of this possibility but came to sense when sales of the Dove branded product did not pick up in countries where internet was not available or slow speed did not allow the You Tube video to create any impact.

The consequence of media effectiveness on advertising effectiveness clearly reflected in the country wise sales figure of the Dove brand. The countries where internet effectiveness was high Dove did wonderfully well. This lesson of Dove made the other international businesses to have a relook on the media use strategy and made them to plan advertising with a right dose of media mix based on country specific effectiveness.

[9] "Real or insincere?" *Brand Republic* at http://www.brandrepublic.com

Box 11.1 Dove broke country barrier

It was a shock for personal care brand Dove, owned by Unilever, to know that only 2% of women considered themselves beautiful in the world. This revelation after market research made the company active and during 2004, it launched a unique marketing communication campaign popularly known as "Dove Campaign for Real Beauty." The campaign's mission was "to create a world where beauty is a source of confidence and not anxiety". The first stage of the campaign centred on a series of billboard advertisements, initially put up in the United Kingdom, and later worldwide. The company used regular women in place of professional models in those advertisements. Regularly, the general people on the road were involved to rate the women who appeared in the advertisements and the results were posted on billboards and on their Website to showcase that all of them were rated beautiful by the voters. The company intended to create a new definition of beauty which will free women from self-doubt and encourage them to embrace their real beauty. This innovative way of appreciating beauty caught the attraction of talk shows, women's magazines and mainstream news broadcasts and publications, which in turn increased the media exposure for the brand 30 times more than the usual. In 2006, the company used another innovative approach when it launched 'Evolution' in an advertising campaign that was broadcasted as a television and cinema spot in the Netherlands and the Middle East. The advertisement was a grand success and won a number of awards in the advertising industry. In order to send "Evolution" quickly to other countries of the world, it was uploaded on the YouTube video sharing Website. The result was one of pure delight to the company as exposure for the brand went up by leaps and bounds. It was viewed by people from different countries of the world in large numbers. The company was very happy because one standardised communication could reach different countries without having to bother about country-specific norms, regulations, etc.

Source: http://en.wikipedia.org/wiki/Evolution_(advertisement)

The statistics of internet penetration shows that different regions of the world are at different levels of its presence and usage even in the present days (Figure 11.2) and hence putting a question mark on the use of digital medium in many such countries with internet deficiency.

The regions like Middle-east, Africa, Oceania/Australia are at the low end of the band of internet users. Therefore, the most successful advertising campaign of Unilever had a localised taste of success in regions like Europe but not in Africa. So the variation of penetration of advertising campaign

FIGURE 11.2 Internet users in the world

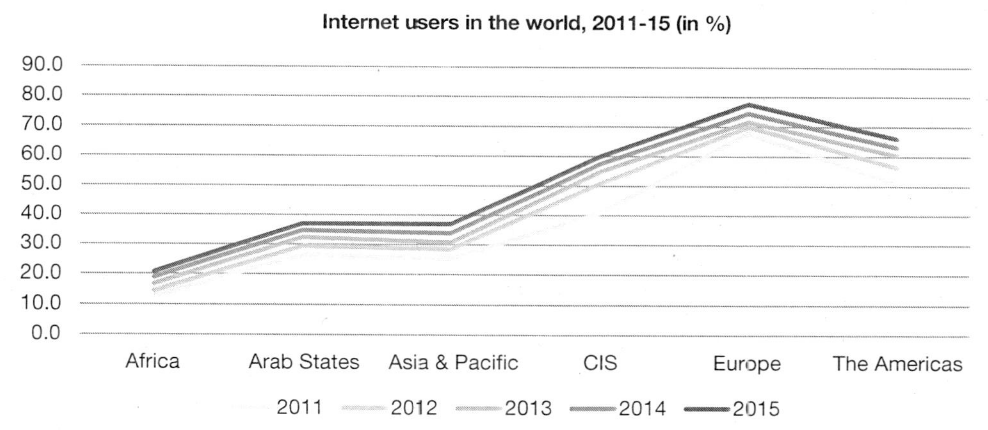

Source: http://www.itu.int/ITU-D/ict/statistics/

in country markets again depended on the media and its availability in that country. In other words, advertising campaigns can be successful in one country riding on the right medium but fall flat in another country because of the absence or scarcity of that medium in another country. Table 11.3 shows the variation of internet population in top 20 countries of the world, which indicates the possible variation of Unilever campaign in different countries.

A good understanding of media availability in the target market country is a must, therefore, in designing the marketing programme effectively. It will give a fair idea to the international marketers about the possible trade-off between media availability and advertising impact and coverage demanded for the country. For example, for African countries like Tanzania or Gabon, what would be the best medium for advertising to reach more number of prospective consumers cutting across the rural urban divide? The international marketers are really required to think about it and put right strategy at right place at right time. Airtel, the Indian multinational, even using office building walls as billboardsin African countries but the same company otherwise is very active in using digital platform extensively in its home country India for communicating target customers.

Table 11.3 Internet population of top 20 countries

S. No.	Country or region	Population	Internet users	Penetration (% Population)	
		2014	2014	2000	2014
1.	China	135,56,92,576	64,22,61,240	36	47.4
2.	United States	31,88,92,103	27,72,03,319	78.2	86.9
3.	India	123,63,44,631	24,30,00,000	8.4	19.7
4.	Japan	12,71,03,388	10,96,26,672	78.4	86.2
5.	Brazil	20,26,56,788	10,97,73,650	37.4	54.2
6.	Germany	809,96,685	717,27,551	79.9	88.6
7.	Russia	14,24,70,272	874,76,747	43	61.4
8.	United Kingdom	31,88,92,103	27,72,03,319	82	86.9
9.	France	662,59,012	552,21,000	-	83.3
10.	Nigeria	17,71,55,754	703,00,000	28.3	39.70
11.	Indonesia	25,36,09,643	57,51,357	16.1	28.1
12.	Korea	490,39,986	453,14,248	80.9	92.4
13.	Iran	818,24,270	468,00,000	46.9	57.2
14.	Turkey	816,19,392	462,82,850	-	56.7
15.	Mexico	12,02,86,655	592,00,000	30.7	49.2
16.	Italy	616,80,122	360,58,199	-	58.5
17.	Philippines	55,67,301	442,00,540	29.2	41.1
18.	Spain	477,37,941	357,05,960	-	74.8
19.	Vietnam	934,21,835	410,12,186	32.3	43.9
20.	Argentina	430,24,374	322,68,280	66	75

Source: http://www.itu.int/ITU-D/ict/statistics/

The successful brands like 'Dove' of Unilever are habitually more internet savvy because of western origin and has long experience of extensive use of modern media such as internet, internet based YouTube, Facebook, etc., which almost set a marketing trend of optimal use of the Internet for brand propagation. However, the company cannot do the same thing in many countries of the world. Take the case of Tanzania with a population of around 46 million, which has 705,460 Facebook users while its neighbour Kenya, with a population of just over 43 million, has nearly three times as many Facebook users[10].

Hence, Dove campaign could not get much response in Tanzania or in other African countries like Gabon, etc. In that sense, Dove's internet-based communication will not be that successful in Asian countries like India as well where the statistics on Facebook users (as dummy variable for internet affinity of population) shows only 0.05% of population penetration in India (Table 11.4). However, newspapers would be a better medium than the internet in these countries. For countries like Tanzania in Africa or India in Asia, because of their relatively good literacy rate, newspapers may be more useful medium for brands like Dove. Even some newspapers in Africa have multi-country spread like 'The East African' which covers four countries like Tanzania, Rwanda, Kenya, and Uganda. Therefore, companies interested in internet starved country markets should be inclined to use newspapers as the medium of marketing communication. But this would result in a compromise between advertising visual effects and media reach. Surely the advertising effect created by Unilever's 'Campaign for Real Beauty' using internet as medium would not be there when the company uses newspaper as its medium. This is a direct fallout of the fact that all the countries of the world are not equal users of a particular medium like internet. Other forms of media like billboards, etc., are also very popular in these countries. Although television usage in a few African countries like Tanzania is increasing fast, the speed of penetration is not the same in other poorer countries of the continent. Interestingly, radio has nearly 100% penetration in countries like Tanzania, which is totally a reverse trend from developed countries. However, if the company wants to quickly penetrate the rural markets in poor countries then organising events and activation may be the best way out. Some large brands spend up to 70% of their marketing budgets on this account rather than on traditional television, radio or print campaigns. A local professor of marketing in Dar-E-Salaam University School of Business noted "A lot of marketing communication can be done with a

Table 11.4 Difference in internet penetration

Countries	Population (2012)	Facebook users as on Dec 31, 2012,
Tanzania	469,12,768	705,460 (1.5% of the population)
Kenya	430,13,341	20,45,900 (4.8% of the population)
Gabon	16,08,321	132,000 (8.2% of the population)
USA	31,38,47,465	16,60,29,240 (53% of population
India	120,50,73,612	6,27,13,680 (5.2% of population)

Source: Internet world stats available at http://www.internetworldstats.com/stats3.htm and the author's calculation.

[10] http://www.socialbakers.com/facebook-statistics/?interval=last-month#chart-intervals

public address system in a truck accompanied by loud music or during local assemblage during Saba Saba Day". This remark is not a surprising one. Data shows that roughly 15.6% of Africans were online against 63.2% in Europe and 78.6% in North America in 2012 and the situation is changing very slowly. Hence, international marketers need to be very careful to about the differential nature of media availability and its impact on marketing communications.

Effect of Local Norms and Sentiments in Communication

The local norms and sentiments also create barriers of communications. Take the case of Japan where Sumo wrestling is one of the oldest and most respected sports. Sumo wrestling is seen as the reflection of Japanese spirit. Can an international marketer take advantage of this popularity in marketing communication? HSBC Holdings, the British multinational banking and financial services company headquartered in London, wanted to use Sumo wrestlers in advertising campaign without understanding the Japanese sentiments associated with this old sport.

In one of the bank's commercial communication, a cosmetically enhanced male model with a wig on his head was used to portray a traditional sumo wrestlers to communicate the message that "fixed savings rate of the bank is not going to budge or vary with time and it is as strong as the sumo wrestler" The Japanese people, however, could not take the advertisement lightly as their sentiment was hurt and they accused the bank of being 'culturally insensitive' towards the people of the country.

Another similar case was reported when Japanese Toyota motor misjudged the Chinese sentiments in respect of their 'Chinese dragon'. The Chinese think, because of old belief, that the dragon gives life and hence consider them to be very sacred. They believe that its breath, called sheng qi, is the divine energy. The dragon is considered essentially friendly to the local people, caring and wise, and associated with abundance and blessing[11]. Hence, it will be beneficial for every Chinese to pray for its blessings. The Japanese car maker Toyota did not understand that and came confronting with the Chinese sentiment. The route cause was the 2003 released advertisements for their almost world conquered car Prado GX and Land Cruiser. The Toyota motor company was almost obsessed with the power of its car and the robust build-up of its two SUVs, i.e., Prado and Land Cruiser. In fact, these SUVs broke all records in terms of sales worldwide, as a section of consumers worldwide were too desperate to own such two marvellous machines with proven robustness and power. Now, when its turn came for entry into the vast and lucrative Chinese market, the company did not want to abandon the image of 'robustness and power.' The task of designing a new local advertisement by depicting that very image was entrusted to the big advertising company Saatchi and Saatchi headquartered in New York, with 140 offices in 76 countries.

Saatchi and Saatchi used its creative mind a developed an advertisement which depicted that a traditional Chinese-style stone-carved lion saluting a moving Prado GX with a headline "badao (The rule by force), you cannot

[11] Much ado about new stamps and dragons, The China Daily, January 7, 2012.

but respect." Later on the experts interpreted its meaning in three different ways: "You can't help but be ruled by Prado's power," "The Prado's power will take you over," or "You have to admire and respect Prado's supreme quality."[12] The other advertisement, Saatchi and Saatchi developed, depicted a Land Cruiser pulling a cumbersome Chinese-made war truck on a bumpy road on a plateau. These two advertisements, when released in the leading car magazine, Friends of Cars, made public in general very angry. Many even equated these two advertisements as 1937 Japanese invasion of China now re-enacted in a new form. The sentiments of the Chinese people were hurt badly[13]. The antagonism was such that the Toyota had to tender an apology to the Chinese people and stop marketing of these two cars in China. Toyota expressed its anger and snapped its long-term tie with the famous advertisement agency Saatchi and Saatchi. However, this episode made international marketer learn a lesson of not muddling with the sentiment of local people.

The famous American sports shoe manufacturer Nike also committed a similar mistake by not understanding the local sentiments of a country like China when they came out with a TV commercial in November 2004, depicting how American NBA player LeBron James defeated an elderly Chinese martial arts specialist monk. The company wanted to emphasise the role of Nike sports shoe which LeBron James was wearing. But the very thought of defeat of the Chinese monk irked the Chinese. The creator of the commercial, J. Walter Thompson (JWT), Shanghai, used this type of Nike TV commercial for other countries as well but those ran without any protest from the local population. JWT understood in a bitter way about the role of local norms and sentiments acting as the barriers of international marketing communications[14].

However, some companies continue to do these types of mistakes in spite of mishaps experienced by some well-known international business establishments. More recent example was seen when the Italian automobile company Fiat launched Lancia Delta model of car in China with a TV advertisement which antagonised the Chinese population. Fiat used Hollywood film star Richard Gere in one 45-second TV advertisement showing the film star getting into a Lancia Delta and driving on a long mountain path to reach a snow-filled valley in the Himalayas. On reaching the Himalayas, he was greeted by a group of young Buddhist monks with whom he chatted with. Then the tagline came up which read: "The power to be Different." The advisement, in fact, had nothing controversial unless one relates it to the personal life of the Hollywood actor who used to be a staunch advocator of Tibetan independence. Fiat ran this advertisement in Italy and in other European countries and got appreciation of the people there for being different than the usual. However, the advertisement was blocked in China since the popular sentiment in the country was against Gere's actions regarding Tibetan independence.

---

[12] Li, Fengru and Nader H. Shooshtari (2007), "Multinational corporations' controversial advertisement campaigns in China—Lessons from Nike and Toyota", *The Advertising Educational Foundation, Inc.*

[13] Toyota apologises for 'humiliating' advertisements, The China Daily, May 12, 2003 (HK Edition).

[14] Normandy Madden, "Nike talks to Chinese kids on their terms: First creative by Wieden drops celebrity athletes," *Ad Age China*, September 3, 2003.

Box 11.2 Nike apologises for footwear advertisement in China

Martial arts and related heroes are very close to the Chinese hearts. Nike wanted to take advantage of the fact when it used Hong Kong martial arts movie heroes of the 1970s in a commercial run in Radio, Film and Television in China. LeBron Raymone James, nicknamed "King James", was an American professional basketball player for the Miami Heat of the National Basketball Association (NBA). King James shot into fames very quickly because of his extraordinary skill as basketball player and won the heart of many Americans who loved the game. King James was nine-time NBA All-Star winner and acclaimed with the crown 'Cleveland Cavaliers' all-time leading scorer'. Nike used this basketball star in its advertisement famously known as "LeBron James in Chamber of Fear".

In the advertisement, King James was shown to make easy work of animated enemies which included a white-haired Kung Fu master, two women in traditional Chinese garb and the pair of dragons while ascending the levels of the "Chamber". The company Nike wanted to demonstrate the power of their Nike athletic shoes in manoeuvring difficult situations as those when confronted with Chinese Kung Fu masters. But the company very soon found that China's State Administration was imposing a ban on the circulation of the advertisement in radio, film and television nationwide and blaming the company of offending the "national feelings". According to the Chinese authority, the Chamber advertisement had violated the regulations that mandated that all advertisements in China should uphold national dignity and interest and respect the motherland's culture. The American company apologised for a footwear advert featuring an attack on a Kung Fu master in public and issued a statement in the newspapers categorically mentioning that the mistake had happened in the 'Chamber of Fear' advertisements' because of their ignorance only but without any deceptive intention to disturb or disgrace any Chinese hero.

Source: http://www.chinadaily.com.cn/english/doc/2004-12/09/content_398845.htm, accessed on May 4, 2011.

Economic Differences Effecting Communication

Burkina Faso is one of the poorest countries in the world with an average income per capita of US$300. Subsistence agriculture is the only option in which more than 80% of the population is engaged. Dependency on highly variable rainfall for agriculture, highly inadequate communication and other infrastructure, a low literacy rate, and above all a stagnant economy are the features of this landlocked country. Can the world's biggest brand Coca Cola be there and if the company is to make its presence felt, then what type of marketing communications are to be put to use? Let us take another contrasting situation. Luxembourg in Europe is one of the richest countries of the world with per capita income of $81,800[15]. Unlike Burkina Faso, in this landlocked country only 2.2% of the population are depending on agriculture. Luxembourg was one of the three countries[16] in Europe where the American Coca Cola established its bottling plant way back in 1947. Understandably, when there is such stark difference of economic situation between these two countries the marketing communication from a company like Coca Cola would be different. It is most likely that the nature and depth the communication would be different because economic differences not only affect the buying power but also how the product is perceived by the target population. In practice, Coca Cola limited its marketing campaign to the level of sales promotion only in Burkina Faso and people perceived the product as any other soft drinks to quench thrust in hot and humid weather.

[15] Source: 2011 CIA World Fact book.

[16] Other two countries are Netherlands, Belgium.

However, the advertisement for Coca Cola in Luxembourg appeared more sophisticated and mature without direct appeal to the customers to use the product. Rather in Luxembourg, Coca Cola focused on the finer aspects like sustainability of environment and role of people in building awareness against global warming.

Advertising Appeal and Culture

All the above stated examples of communication mishaps led to understanding of a very vital point that every country has an exclusive culture which sets the general norms, behaviours, beliefs and customs of the population of the country and international marketers must obey those. The international marketers has to be careful enough that the marketing communications are not antagonising the people of the country by depicting the country's culture in poor light but at the same time the effectiveness of the communication is at the maximum level. Therefore, international marketers endeavour to learn country specificity in respect of culture driven individual's attitude, behaviour, life style, exposure, etc., before releasing marketing communications.

Fortunately, Hofstede's[17] rigorous work on country culture found to be very much useful in this respect. Hofstede's four indices for the countries like power distance index, individualism index, uncertainty avoidance index and masculinity index can be used in deciding on the cultural stereotypes and their variations across the countries on comparative basis. Once it became possible for international marketers to understand the psychological and behavioural characteristics of the population of a country on the basis of Hofstede indices, a need was felt to relate them with the schemes of advertising appeals. Every marketing communication is designed to create some sort of appeal to be rightly conceived by the target customers. Kotler and Armstrong[18] (1991) defined an appeal as the basic idea that advertisers want to communicate to the audience. The purpose would be to let the consumers know the basic reason of initiating action for its possession. If the advertising appeals can be related to the Hofstede indices, then it would be possible for the international marketers to understand the validity of the appeals, their usefulness or otherwise, in a particular country context. Although various researchers in international marketing area are in disagreement with the exact number of advertising appeals possible and their constituents, the following 22 advertising appeals emerged as a much possible set.

1. Safety
2. Technology
3. Tradition
4. Adventure
5. Magic
6. Youth
7. Competition
8. Wealth
9. Effectiveness
10. Work
11. Courtesy
12. Family
13. Nurturance
14. Individualism
15. Uniqueness
16. Beauty

[17] Hofstede, G. (1980), *Culture's Consequences: International Differences in Work-Related Values*, Sage, Beverly Hills, CA.
[18] Kotler, P. and Armstrong, G. (1991), *Principles of Marketing 5th ed.*, Engelwood Cliffs, NJ: Prentice Hall.

17. Health
18. Collectivism
19. Popularity
20. Patriotism
21. Social status
22. Respect for elderly people

Moon & Chan (2005)[19] came out with a very useful classification of these 22 advertising appeals in accordance with the four dimensions of culture given by Hofstede (Tables 11.5 and 11.6). The relationships between cultural indices and advertising appeals may be useful for international marketers while deciding on the suitability of some specific types of appeal for a particular country based on its cultural stereotype.

Table 11.5 Hofstede's indices (Uncertainty avoidance, Masculinity) and suitable advertising appeals

Uncertainty avoidance		**Masculinity**	
This index of Hofstede refers to anxiety, need for security, dependence on expert and application of information.		The masculinity index of Hofstede refers to heroism, material success while femininity index refers to family and personal relationship, caring for the weak, modesty.	
High UA	**Low UA**	**Masculinity**	**Femininity**
1. Safety 2. Technology 3. Tradition	4. Adventure 5. Magic 6. Youth	7. Competition 8. Wealth 9. Effectiveness 10. Work	11. Courtesy 12. Family 13. Nurturance

Table 11.6 Hofstede's indices (individual, power distance) and suitable advertising appeals

Individualism–Collectivism		**Power distance**
The individualism index of Hofstede refers self-sufficiency, distinctiveness, product's benefit to one's own appearance, or robustness of the body while collectivism refers to group decision making.		The power distance index refers to the status of basic human inequalities in society, prestige, wealth, source of power.
Individualism	**Collectivism**	**High PD**
14. Individualism 15. Uniqueness 16. Beauty 17. Health	18. Collectivism 19. Popularity 20. Patriotism	21. Social status 22. Respect for elderly

Advertising appeal in a country: Case of China

As per Hofstede ranking, China has the flowing scores indicating culture based preference of the people living in the country and suitable advertising appeal:

Country: China

Hofstede dimension	Score*	Interpretation	Right advertising appeal**
Power distance index	80	China has comparatively higher rankings of power distance index. The index score 80 indicates that the society believes in inequalities amongst people and are acceptable to the people. They believe that some people in the society have the right to lead and others to follow.	21. Social status 22. Respect for elderly

[19] Moon Y.S. and Chan, K. (2005), "Advertising appeals and cultural values in television commercials: A comparison of Hong Kong and Korea", *International Marketing Review*, Vol. 22, Issue 1, pp. 48-66.

(*Continued*)

Hofstede dimension	Score*	Interpretation	Right advertising appeal**
Individualism	20	Low individualism score 20 in China speaks of a highly collectivist culture where people act in the interests of the group and not necessarily of themselves.	18. Collectivism 19. Popularity 20. Patriotism
Masculinity	66	Fairly high score at 66 in China ndicates that the society is success oriented. This has reflected in the society and been exemplified by the fact that many Chinese will give priority to work than family and leisure.	7. Competition 8. Wealth 9. Effectiveness 10. Work
Uncertainty avoidance	30	Low index score in China indicates that they do not get unsettled by ambiguous or unknown situations. In fact, they accept the unstructured situation as a part of life rather than being bogged down by them.	4. Adventure 5. Magic 6. Youth

*Scores are obtained from Hofstede cultural index table.
**Here the numbers are the serial numbers of the 22 advertising appeals discussed in page 30.

The above interpretation of cultural index scores and matching advertising appeal in the Chinese context shows the right direction for devising flawless marketing communications for the concerned country. As per the above interpretation the Chinese would like patriotic appeals very much and hence international marketers must attune advertising appeals in line with the Chinese cultural stereotypes. Ironically the advertising appeal created by Toyota and subsequently by Fiat during popularising Prado and Lancia automobiles, respectively, was totally against the preferred direction. If the communication material is not adequately adapted in terms of picture, text, colours, layout, logos, tag lines, etc., in line with the acceptable appeal of the target country the chances of success in a culturally dissimilar country will be remote. In fact, many companies in the past have demonstrated success by attuning advertising appeals close to the country culture and culturally acceptable appeal while entering culturally dissimilar markets.

Coca Cola example: Right from the word go, Coca Cola practised its much talked about marketing communication policy of 'think local, act local' to penetrate the Chinese market by breaking the cultural barrier. They did not forget to take clue from Hofstede that high power distance score of the country requires advertising appeals loaded with 'social status' and 'respect for elderly' theme. To bank on this, Coca Cola extensively used celebrity figures and their high degree of influence in the society. The company used Taiwanese and Hong Kong pop stars, personality like Liu Xiang, gold medallist of men's 100 metres at the 2004 Olympics, and many others in the Coca Cola billboards keeping in mind their star figure status and acceptance in the society.

Adidas example: The famous German company Adidas wanted to take advantage the Chinese cultural stereotypes to market its products during the 2008 Beijing Olympic Games. Keeping in mind the culture based advertising, suitable appeals like competition, wealth, effectiveness and work associated with high masculine score of China, the company came up with an advertisement for promoting its shoes featuring world famous soccer stars like Germany's Ballack, England's Jermaine Defoe, Brazilian Kaka, England's David Beckham, Raul from Spain and Argentina's Saviola with a tagline "impossible is nothing". This advertisement was developed for many other countries of the world but when it matched up with the China requirements, it was dubbed in Chinese language and used extensively. In China, the intention of the company was to take advantage of not only the social appeal of the world famous soccer stars but also the appeals emanating from the "success and effectiveness" achieved by these soccer players in their respective arena. The billboard advertisement in China retained the English tagline 'nothing is impossible' with Chinese translation also in order to convey the universal appeal of the brand as well as the featured soccer stars. Adidas rightly assumed that these sports celebrities are familiar to young Chinese audiences because of their closeness with football as a sport. Content-wise the advertisement perfectly suited to the Chinese audience in the global–local dimension and advertising appeal-wise, it was nicely pitched to suit the Chinese power distance and masculinity.

PepsiCo example: PepsiCo casted Chinese actor, singer, and model Huang Xiaoming often referred to as China's "number one heartthrob" and Ethan Ruan, the Taiwanese actor and model, in the Pepsi advertisement for its brands, Pepsi and Lays. Lee Hom Wang, the winner of the best director award of the 2011 Harbin Film Festival and Pop-star Angela Cheung were used in another Lays commercial. They all have been fairly successful in creating advertising appeals that suited the country's culture dominated by high power distance index. The local Chinese advertisers also involve Chinese stars and celebrities in their advertisement campaigns for a range of products.

Motorola example: Motorola used famous Taiwanese singer and actor Jay Chou for popularising their mobile phones in China. To bank on the high power distance index of the country, Chinese companies are also extensively using celebrity figures. "Taiwanese Britney Spears" actress/singer Jolin Tsai, apart from featuring in McDonald's, Levi's, and BMW extended cars advertisement also endorses the China Life Insurance, which is the only Chinese insurance company on the Fortune Global 500 list and the World Brand 500 list.

Box 11.3 Adidas China Launches Campaign - "Together in 2008, Impossible is Nothing"

Adidas China, the Official Sportswear Partner of the Beijing 2008 Olympic Games, kicked off its Olympic Games campaign with a spectacular light show in front of thousands of people at Beijing's Yongdingmen Gate, the historic former front entrance of Beijing's old city walls. "Together in 2008, Impossible is Nothing" is the largest Adidas brand campaign ever created by a single market.

The campaign is about rallying the nation and showing how the entire Chinese nation is supporting their athletes and the Games themselves. Famous Chinese Olympians such as key members of the Chinese women's volleyball team, diving sensation Hu Jia, basketball superstar Sui Feifei and football legend Zheng Zhi are featured in the campaign.

A blend of action photography and computer graphics, the series was released in phases in the run-up to the Beijing 2008 Olympic Games. "Together in 2008, Impossible is Nothing" was an integrated marketing campaign. Through a combination of TV, print, outdoor, PR, digital, point-of-sale and road shows across the country, the campaign provided various platforms enabling consumers to get closer to the athletes and the Olympic Games.

"Adidas believes that Olympic success means more than winning medals and that the Olympic spirit is not just for the athletes. The passion that all Chinese are feeling about the Beijing 2008 Olympic Games will make China a true Sports Nation and Adidas will play an active role in this development," said Wolfgang Bentheimer, Managing Director of Adidas, Greater China. "This is the largest campaign we have ever done in China and it showcases the power of the nation: when 1.3 billion people come together, Impossible is Nothing at the Beijing 2008 Olympic Games." "Adidas really carries the Olympic spirit in their DNA," said Wang Wei, Executive Vice-President and Secretary General of the Beijing Organising Committee for the Games of the XXIX Olympiad (BOCOG). "As the Official Sportswear Partner of the Beijing 2008 Olympic Games, we are confident Adidas will help bring China's appreciation of the Games—and overall popularity of sports—to a new high." "This campaign is inspirational," said Wang Jun, Vice Minister of the State's General Administration of Sports and Vice President of the Chinese Olympic Committee. "Having the Chinese people behind them inspires our athletes and in turn the athletes are great examples to inspire the Chinese people to overcome their own Olympic-like challenges."

As the Official Sportswear Partner, Adidas will supply sportswear for all staff, volunteers and technical officials of the Beijing 2008 Olympic Games and the Beijing 2008 Paralympic Games. Under its agreement with BOCOG, Adidas will also outfit the Chinese Olympic team for the 2008 Games in Beijing. In addition, Adidas will outfit athletes from all over the world competing in 27 out of the 28 sports.

Source: Adidas media release available at http://www.adidas-group.com/en/media/news-archive/press-releases/2007/adidas-china-launches-its-olympic-games-campaign-together-2008-i/

Benefits of Standardisation in Advertising

Though several intervening variables like culture, norms, regulations, etc., push a company for adaptation of communication as per requirements of the respective country markets but there could be several benefits associated with standardisation approach. These benefits are detailed below.

Economy of scale

Achieving economy of scale is a major benefit expected out of standardisation approach in advertisement. Literally, the economy of scale will prevail when a company develops and implements advertisements in a standardised manner without taking in to consideration the differential requirements of different countries of its present. A globally spread company spends huge amount of money in advertisement in quest of establishing superiority in the market place. As competition brews up and becomes intense the company wants to be accurate in positioning of products or services by exactly focusing on the consumers' requirements living in a particular country. In practice, the international marketers broadly agree that these requirements are vastly different in different countries. In a growing competitive international business environment the companies, therefore, continuously search for new and better opportunities around the world. It is almost an established fact that by adapting advertising to country specific requirements the companies gain some differential advantage which in turn allows them to maximise effectiveness in terms of local response and sales. Hence, in practice, these companies use different creative presentations of same or different advertising themes, different colours, layouts, models, etc., to entice the customers of different countries differently

Table 11.7 Spending on advertisement by top multinationals during 2013

Company name	Spending on advertisement during 2013 in US billion						Increase from last year (2012) in %
	TV	Magazines	Newspapers	Internet	Others	Total	
Toyota	0.959	0.152	0.013	0.112	0.815	2.051	12
L'Oréal	0.662	0.873	0.045	0.023	0.73	2.333	4.3
Ford	0.797	0.128	0.013	0.139	1.4	2.477	12.4
Proctor & Gamble	1.9	1.1	0.28	0.234	1.5	5.014	3.3

Source: Ad Age 100 Leading National Advertisers Index

to enjoy greater marketing benefits. Such adaption to the local requirements distorts the economy of scale on account of advertisement production and implementation. This continuously keeps on increasing the expenditure on advertisements for the international companies.

For example, Toyota spent about 5 billion USD during 2013 which was about 3.3% more than their spending during 2012. Similarly, the other global companies are showing yearly increase in expenditure on the account of advertising (Table 11.7).

Better management and specialisation

Standardised approach can lead to better management control on production of advisements and implementation of the same in different markets. Since development and implementation are standardised so a centralised advertisement production facility can function from a strategically located in place. The centrality of management can also take care of execution of advertisements in a timely manner. Customer feedback management system can improve a lot. More delicate analysis of customer feedback can be possible under centralised practice. An efficient centralised advertising management practice, therefore, can lead to better result. Less duplication of efforts in production of advertisement and execution can lead to development of specialisation within the company.

Global image

The major advantage with the standardisation approach is development of a global brand image. The target audiences of different countries are not differently exposed to the brand identity and personality. The centralised advertising department can very well work on developing a consistent image of the company brand in a better way to provide edge over the localised brands present in every country market.

LOCALNESS OR GLOBALNESS OF TV COMMERCIAL: ANALYSIS

Different companies, at different points of time, have shown their inclination to become global or local in advertising. The dilemma of the company is understandable. They possibly want to retain their globalness for enjoying economies of scale as well as economy of scope. But at the same time, when faced with acute local competition in the local market, they may want to compromise with the circumstances and rollover to the localisation aspects. For example, the global company Coca Cola, known for being the dominant force of globalisation, may also compromise with the localisation forces in the matter of advertisements. For example, consider the 'Happiness Factory' commercial run across the globe by the company during 2006 to promote the values of "optimism" and "positivity" that are essential parts of the Coca-Cola brand. The 'Happiness Factory' commercial was aired in over 100 countries and it received global appreciation, awards and accolades. The following is a description of the worldwide popular 'Happiness Factory' commercial that ran in carefully picked up six countries—France, England, Japan, Taiwan, Thailand and India to understand the localness–globalness parameters of the company released TV advertisement and to analyse their status regarding localness or globalness using Whitelock and Rey's model. This understanding is important for an international marketing manager as the same model can be applied to understand localness quantum of any TV based advertisement and its possible trade off with economies of scale.

Analysis of 'Happiness Factory' Commercial—France

The commercial involves a young man, a young woman (both Westerners) and imaginary creatures. The man and the woman are walking towards a cinema hall for watching a movie. The young man suddenly notices a Coco Cola vending machine and gets attracted to it. He puts a coin in the vending machine to buy Coca Cola. Then, inside a Coca Cola vending machine it is revealed how a bottle of Coke is delivered. A magical world is shown, where imaginary creatures transport the empty bottle, which is then filled up and capped by other creatures and then cleaned by fluffy white animals. The bottle is then chilled in a white snowy world before going through a parade to be delivered back to the man waiting outside, who is oblivious to this magical world. After this scene, the man who gets the Coca Cola is shown to drink a sip of it only to find that the young girl has already left for the cinema hall. Then, he also enters into to the cinema hall and both of them enjoy the cola. Duration of the video is 3.27 minutes and the language used is French.

Analysis of 'Happiness Factory' Commercial—England

Two young men are shown to be sleeping in a big vehicle moving along a highway while the third one was driving the vehicle. The vehicle stops and the three young men come out of the vehicle. One of them notices the vending machine and puts a coin in it. Then, inside the Coca Cola vending machine it is revealed how a bottle of Coke is delivered. A magical world is unfolded where some imaginary creatures put the liquid inside the coke bottle. The bottle is then chilled in a white snowy world and it eventually comes out of the vending machine. The young man takes the bottle and tastes its contents and he looks surprised by the taste. Thereafter, all three men get into the vehicle and this time, the mood of the three is completely changed. They are shown singing, whistling and to be in a generally joyous mood. The duration of this video in English is 1.01 minutes.

Analysis of 'Happiness Factory' Commercial–Japan

A young Japanese boy and girl are standing in front of a coke vending machine. A third boy approaches the vending machine with a smile and drops a coin in the machine. The coin comes down from the hill top of the magical world inside the vending machine; then, a few magical characters take one empty bottle to a certain distance before a funny crane fills the bottle with Coca Cola. The bottle is then pushed by certain white puffy characters to a white snowy world where it gets chilled. Seeing that the bottle is ready for delivery, the magical characters started dancing, celebrating and enjoying. After the bottle comes out, the three young friends start walking away from the vending machine. However, after sipping the coke the boy looks back at the vending machine with disbelief. The video runs for 1.31 minutes and it is in the Japanese language.

Analysis of 'Happiness Factory' Commercial–Taiwan

A young boy walks to a vending machine and drops a coin into it. The coin comes down from the hill-top of the magical world inside the vending machine. Then, a few magical characters take one empty bottle to a certain distance before a funny crane fills the bottle with Coca Cola. The bottle is then pushed by certain white puffy characters to a white snowy world. Then the bottle gets chilled. Seeing that the bottle is ready for delivery, the magical characters start dancing, celebrating and enjoying. The video duration is for 32 seconds; the language used is Taiwanese.

Analysis of 'Happiness Factory' Commercial–Thailand

Four young boys are seen in front of a coke vending machine. Two of them are standing and another two, sitting on a bench. One boy looks very sleepy and possibly because of that he asks for coins from the other one. As he approaches the vending machine, a magical character from inside the machine jokingly yawns at the boy without the boy noticed it. Then some magical characters inside the vending machine start agitating its contents and suddenly one cap of the bottle drops down from the top, on one magical character. By getting hit by the cap of the bottle the magical characters are all start rejoicing by sipping coke from small bottles. In the meantime a big coke bottle is seen travelling in from another direction and quickly moving to the delivery slot of the vending machine. The boy then sips from the bottle with satisfaction. The other three boys also start celebrating. Duration of the video is 45 seconds and the language used was Thai.

Analysis of 'Happiness Factory' Commercial–India

A casually dressed young man is seen approaching the vending machine. He drops the coin and some magical activities start happening inside the vending machine. One empty bottle is moving from one direction to another. Some white puffy object appears to take due care of the bottle. Then a peculiar type of crane fills up the empty bottle with coke. The bottle is then pushed by certain white puffy characters to a white snowy world. Then the bottle gets chilled. Seeing that the bottle is ready for delivery, the magical characters start dancing, celebrating and enjoying.

When the bottle comes out, the young man takes it and sips. After sipping the coke, he looks back at the vending machine in disbelief. Duration of the video is 1.02 minutes and the language used is English.

Whitelock and Rey's Model for TV Commercial Analysis[20]

Whitelock and Rey's model calibrates the TV commercials released by international marketers under the following eight headings to understand their localness or globalness.

1. **Characters:** International marketers may vary central characters involved in the commercials depending upon the country requirement. In a culturally dissimilar country a commercial may uses totally different characters to entice the customers more towards it. On the other extreme, a company may think of using same character in different countries to retain its originality and take the risk of exposing it for diverse viewers. In the same sense, the international marketers may also indulge in differentiating actions of the central character from country to country or keeping the same.
2. **Length:** This pertains to the duration of the commercial. The requirement of time for running the commercial in different countries may vary depending upon the requirement. In some countries, it may be required to extend the video running time to express a certain theme or point to develop more clarity.
3. **Music:** This parameter focuses on the background tune differences. The international marketer may spend lot to device background music and wants that it will be the signature tune or music for the commercial in the global level. The feeling may be that any variation of the background tune would affect the very purpose of creating a unique identity in the market place. On the other hand, some may opt for variation in their quest to be more local.
4. **Screen captions/setting:** This aspect looks at how the subtitles or texts are appearing in the different country specific commercials. In some country it may be required to use translation or transliteration of original texts to express the original meaning otherwise there could be a problem related interpreting the correct meaning of the advertisements. In case

[20] Whitelock, J. and Rey, J. (1998), "Cross-cultural advertising in Europe: An empirical survey of television the UK", *International Marketing Review*, Vol. 15, Issue 4, pp. 257–76.

of standardisation across the countries, then the commercial may have a tendency to globalise. The same logic for standardisation and localisation applies for screen settings also.

5. **Scenic background:** It relates to the creation of television scenery or the scenic background used in TV commercials. The purpose of the devising the correct scenic background is to provide right support for the main content of the advertisement to be more expressive. It could be the same in different country commercials by retaining the original or devise differently to suit the local country environment. If the desire is for standardisation then the commercial will retain the original version; otherwise, it has a tendency to localise.
6. **Slogan:** It relates to the slogan or tag line used in the TV commercial by companies to popularise the brand name. In TV commercial, developed for multi country, a company may desire to retain the original or modify them to suit the local country environment. If it is a direct translation, then the inclination would be towards standardisation. Otherwise, the commercial in inclined to localise.
7. **Story of commercial:** This relates to the story line that the commercial wanted to build up. Companies may like to take a local theme and localise the story further. On the other extreme it may prefer to standardise he story line of the commercial. If it is a direct translation in the country's context, then the intention is for standardisation.
8. **Voice-over or dialogue:** The voice-over or dialogue spoken by the characters is important in the commercial to convey the exact coded meaning of the commercial. There could be a total change of dialogue spoken by the protagonist or change of execution of the dialogue which convey the intention of the advertiser towards localisation. On the other hand if it is original and kept unchanged at global level then intention would be at standardisation. A literary translation of the dialogue is also considered as standardisation.

Characters

France	England	Japan	Taiwan	Thailand	India
One French boy; Imaginary creatures	Three young men. Imaginary creatures	A young Japanese boy and a young girl. Also a third Japanese boy; Imaginary creatures	One young (Taiwanese) boy; Imaginary creatures	Four young boys of Thai origin; Imaginary creatures	One young Indian boy; Imaginary creatures

Overall impression: Customisation of the characters as per country's need.

Length

France	England	Japan	Taiwan	Thailand	India
3.27 minutes	1.01 minutes	1.31 minutes	0.32 minutes	0.45 minutes	1.02 minutes

Overall impression: Customisation of the length as per county's need.

Music

France	England	Japan	Taiwan	Thailand	India
Continuous music	Music of a song	Continuous music	Music stops in the middle	Intermittent music	Continuous music

Overall impression: In between customisation and standardisation.

Screen captions/setting

France	England	Japan	Taiwan	Thailand	India
In a metro station	In a roadside vending machine where the vehicle of the protagonist stopped.	In a roadside vending machine	Shopping centre vending machine	In a cinema hall front	In a small town road

Overall impression: Customisation of the setting.

Scenic background

France	England	Japan	Taiwan	Thailand	India
Different	Different	Different	Different	Different	Different

Overall impression: Customisation of the setting.

Slogan

France	England	Japan	Taiwan	Thailand	India
Prends la vie cote Coca Cola (In French)	Coke side of life (In English)	Refreshing and uplifting, The coke side of life (In English language)	Coca Cola adds happiness to your life (In Taiwanese)	Coke side of life (In Thai language)	The Coke side of life (In English)

Overall impression: Customisation of the slogan.

Story

France	England	Japan	Taiwan	Thailand	India
Different	Different	Different	Different	Different	Different

Overall impression: Total customisation as per local culture.

Voice-over or dialogue

France	England	Japan	Taiwan	Thailand	India
Voice-over in French language	No voice-over.	Different	Voice-over in Taiwanese language	Different in Thai language	Different in Hindi

Overall impression: Total customisation as per local culture.

The above analysis of 'Happiness Factory' commercial using Whitelock and Rey's model clearly indicates the "think local–act local" policy of Coca Cola in the matter of international marketing communication.

LOCALNESS OR GLOBALNESS OF PRINT ADVERTISEMENT: ANALYSIS

Print advertisement plays an important role for internationalising companies while extending product or services abroad. It is comparatively less costlier than TV commercials and very easily penetrates the prospective consumer base irrespective of their status of economic development. As with TV commercials, it remains a point of concern as to how localness or globalness should be carried in the print media while entering a new country market. Some companies may like to develop one standardised print advertisement for all the countries of its presence. For example, if Mahindra & Mahindra's Newspaper advertisements developed for SUVs in Indian context are equally tenable in USA context then the company is likely to save some money which otherwise would have spent to develop a new one exclusively for USA. Obviously, here the company keeps in mind the cost versus effectiveness trade off achieved through standardisation and to some extent projection of company image as global in nature. However, localness of print advertisement in USA may not allow Mahindra & Mahindra's to move closer to the American customers as per demand of market competition. Hence, as the practitioners say, the localisation of advertisement comes as a compulsion in foreign country market. In general, the degree of localness of a print advertisement can also vary based on variation effected on the following four components of advertisement while communicating in different countries:

(a) The central character or the model used: Advertisements may use local or different model/spoke persons to make it more appealing to the target group of a particular country.
(b) Text or description of product used or service and slogan, etc.: The text used in print advertisement to describe the product/service or slogan/tag line may be different for different countries.
(c) Layouts used visual background: A company may affect changes in general layout plan or in the visual back ground or in both while releasing advertisement for a particular country than its home country or another.
(d) Product portrayal, i.e., size difference and colour used: The product may be portrayed differently for different countries in print advertisement including packaging but in accordance with the conventional requirement of the particular country. The colour used may be as per the cultural preference of the particular country where the advertisement is getting released.

A close examination of the above four elements of print advertisement is useful to understand the extension of communication adaptation effected by a company in different country markets to have an optimum impact on the consumers. How, the established companies affected variations in their print advertisements in respect of above four components while marketing in different countries are described below one by one.

Different Central Character for Different Countries

Unilever casts film stars for advertising their 'Lux' brand of soap globally. When the soap was launched in India in 1929, the company roped in the then famous Bollywood star Leela Chitnis to run print advertisements in India. Thereafter, the company changed the model with time and its recent advertisements feature the present Bollywood actress Katrina Kaif. In African countries, Munachi Abii, the most beautiful girl in Nigeria and talented singer, was chosen as the new face of Lux soap.

Lux soap in Nepal featured locally famed model-turned-actress Jharana Bajracharya as Lux Girl during 2003. The famous actress Catherine Zeta-Jones was chosen as brand ambassador for the Lux beauty range in China, Japan and other Western countries. One important consideration for localisation of these advertisements was change of the visual background along with changing of the model/spokesperson in accordance with the countries targeted.

Impression: Companies are inclined for total picture adaptation as per local preference as it has been seen in case of Lux.

Different Texts or Description for Different Countries

According to marketing pundits the text or slogan accompanying the print advertisement should be of limited size, clear and easy to remember so that the prospective consumers can remember it with ease. In that sense, therefore, a standardised text within a country or across countries would be preferred. Let us take the case of Cadbury print media slogans. In India, Cadbury Diary Milk chocolates lived with the classic 'Real Taste of Life' campaign introduced in 1994[21]. In 1998, Cadbury Diary Milk became closer to Indians with a tag line that was more appealing to the masses—'Khane Walon ko Khane Ka Bahana Chahiye'—meaning if one were to look for an excuse for eating the chocolate, he/she could effortlessly find it. The suggestion was that people would love to eat Dairy Milk anywhere, anyway. In 2004, the company took a new approach by comparing Cadbury diary milk chocolate with traditional Indian sweets and to popularise this it launched 'Kuch Meetha Ho Jaye' campaign indicative of the common refrain one hears in India after lunch or dinner—let's have something sweet. During 2010, the company introduced another slogan in the form of 'Shubh Aarambh' reminding Indians to start the day or any event auspiciously with Cadbury chocolates to get good result. Presently, the company seems to have settled with a campaign 'Khane Ke Baad, Meethe Mein Kuch Meetha Ho Jaye', in an attempt to secure its place in the lunch or dinner menu as dessert. However, in UK the product continued to remind the people during 1980s about the benefits associated with a "glass-and-a-half of full-cream dairy milk", the equivalent of which one can get by eating Cadbury Diary Milk chocolates. A change in advertising strategy in the 1990s saw the company zooming on the taste of the chocolate by releasing "Chocolate is Cadbury" campaign. However, the company again made a U-turn and brought back the flavour of its iconic slogan 'glass-and-a-half…'. But this time, it was more specific and almost like a doctor's prescription: 'The equivalent of 426 ml of fresh liquid milk in every 227 g of milk chocolate.' The year 2007 saw the company launching 'Gorilla' campaign in UK to promote Cadbury Dairy Milk chocolate. This campaign came out as billboards, print newspapers and magazines, television and cinema spots advertisement.

The African journey for this chocolate was eventful. It released its Africa-based campaign by highlighting its association with fair trade organisation and a hundred-year partnership with Ghanaian cocoa farmers during 2009.

[21] www.cadburyindia.com/in/en/brands/.../csmkuchmeethahojaaye.aspx

During 2010, it used a campaign "release the joy inside". The year 2011 will be remembered by the company for being embroiled in the controversy overusing the slogan, 'Move over Naomi, there is a new diva in the town' for popularising the Dairy Milk Chocolate. The company had to seek apology from Naomi Campbell after the supermodel claimed that comparing her to one of its chocolate bars was racist.

Impression: Total picture adaptation as per local preference is common as it has been observed in case of Cadbury Diary Milk chocolate.

Different Layouts in Different Countries

Advertisement layout is the systematic design of size, colour, scheme, graphics, object and text placement meant for sending the intended message to the target audience. Do the print advertisements released by the same company vary in terms of their layout across the countries for the same product? Let us take the example of Procter & Gamble's Olay range of products.

Procter & Gamble (P&G), in 2008, invited famous Mexican singer and actress Lucero to be the official celebrity spokesperson for Olay range of products in Mexico. The print advertising campaign contained her picture and was used extensively in the country and in the US to cater to the Hispanic population living there. However, during 2010 when P&G was desperate to grab market share from its rival market leader Nivea in Poland, it released a new print advertisement for the Polish population which was totally different in terms of visual placement, narration/headline, contact information, etc. For the Polish advertisement, P&G roped in the popular 37-year-old Polish actress Joanna Brodzik for executing the advertising campaign of Olay Total Effects product line.

During 2011, P&G released Olay Total Effects product line in India and was very keen to develop its presence in the growing Indian market. It released advertisements by roping in popular Hindi film actress Karisma Kapoor as the new brand ambassador for its anti-ageing skincare product, Olay Total Effects. The print advertisement layout meant for Indian market was substantially different than the previous two advertisements of Mexico and Poland.

Impression: Layout adaptation is frequent to match the local preferences, as it has been observed in case of P&G.

Different Product Portrayal, Size and Colours in Different Countries

Company portray products differently in different markets to make them attractive to the local consumers. The print advertisements can also change its size for a particular country to draw consumers' absolute attention. It is a well-known fact that colour preferences across the countries are not similar. To take advantage of respective colour preference of countries, the international advertisers also change application of colour in accordance with the country specific requirements while designing print advertisements.

So, briefly following reasons are responsible for print advertisement adaptation in terms of product portrayal, size and colour

1. Through portrayal of product in print advertisement and applied colour, consumers evaluate quality and it plays a major role in influencing purchase decisions.
2. Different countries show different inclination for different colours. Country culture is responsible to bring out different meaning for several basic colours. A Cadbury chocolate wrapped in white colour will not be appreciated in India where white is a colour of mourning.
3. In some product categories like cosmetics, deliberate attempt is made to convey the sensory characteristics of the product. The company, therefore, vary portrayal and colour in advertising the products across countries to get optimum result.
4. The convenience of using the product and the method of disposal largely depends on the type of packaging. Different country consumers are differently positioned in terms of convenience and disposal system.
5. The so-called 'out of box' positioning can be influenced by size, colour and product portrayal and international marketers desiring to create different appeal in different countries required to vary this component across different countries.

The German luxury car maker BMW launched its 6 Series Gran Coupe in India as well as England and popularised them through print advertisements in local newspapers. The product portrayal and colour used in respective print advertisements was totally different. In Indian advertisement the product was placed in between a leading Hindi actress and BMW's senior official. A lot of different colours were used to please the Indian consumers of the automobile. In comparison, the print advertisement appeared in the local daily of England portrayed only one prominent picture of the automobile without use of multicolour keeping in mind that consumers would only be interested to see the vehicle and not the company officials .

Impression: Print advertisements are liable for adaptation as companies use product portrayal, size and colours differently for different countries for various reasons.

Overall impression: Print advertisements, like digital ones are candidates for adaptation in accordance with the country preferences for marketing products. The degree of adaptation can be measured through analysis of the four components of print advertisement discussed above, both qualitatively and quantitatively.

CHAPTER SUMMARY

1. Marketing communication or promotion is one of the elements of the marketing mix and is responsible for putting the marketing offer to the target market. It is the planned and integrated activity that communicates with an organisation's stakeholders.
2. It can be said that when a domestic company communicates to domestic consumers, the efficiency is expected to be very high. But the same may not hold true in an international situation. A barrier, in that situation, would be active between the coded message and the decoded message,

which may create distortion in the communication process. The barrier may be caused by language difference, host country government control on advertising and promotion, difference of media availability, economic differences between home and host country, local distributors' attitude, specific taste and preference of local customers, etc., across different countries.

3. International marketers would prefer to develop their advertisement campaign in the language that most of the countries understand while promoting their products in different countries. The natural desire would be, even if language spoken in a particular country is different, to persists on a common language that could slowly be understood by people of foreign countries. However, many international marketers have made mistakes in the process.
4. Every country has some form of regulatory bodies to monitor the attributes of advertisements in the country. These regulations are binding on the international advertisers. When an international business develops an advertisement for its products or service, the primary intention of the company would be to take the advertisement to other countries where it has its business. The main barrier in running the same advertisement in different countries would be the country-specific advertisement regulations and their implementation by the respective control boards.
5. International marketers need to understand the causes of prohibitions imposed by different countries at different points of time. The company that operates in a country needs to have full knowledge of the past instances that have attracted prohibitions and the reasons why such prohibitions were imposed. This helps the company to avoid costly mistakes.
6. Media is important because it is the vehicle through which advertising reaches the audience. Different countries have different status of media availability and hence, international marketers may not be able to expect the same communication effectiveness everywhere.
7. Local norms and sentiments are very strong in many countries. International marketers need to understand them before they embark on communication design for a country.
8. The country's culture and economy are two powerful factors that affect the communication process. International marketers, therefore, should resort to cultural and economic analysis of the countries where they desire to promote their products in order to make the communication effective.
9. A clear understanding of the localness–globalness dimension of the various modes of communications such as TV, print media, etc., in vogue in different markets allows the company to set its global communication strategy.

QUESTIONS FOR REVIEW

Short Answer Questions

1. How do marketers communicate in the market?
2. Why is international marketing more problematic that the domestic one?
3. What is the role of country culture in international marketing communications?
4. How are the Hofstede dimensions of culture connected with communication design inter-nationally?
5. List the main regulatory prohibition in vogue in Malaysia for marketing communications.

Descriptive Questions

1. Describe the model of international communication. What are the different barriers in international communication? Do you think that these barriers can be overcome? Justify your answer with example.
2. What roles do government control and regulations play while deciding on international communications? Who frames these regulations in a country, say, China? Why does the international advertiser repeatedly fall in to a zone that violates

government regulations? Elucidate with an example.

3. What role does media availability play in extending an internet-based commercial in African countries? Do you think that this situation leads to failure in the communication a standardised theme to the audiences in those countries where media availability is poor? Justify your answer.
4. What role does language play in distorting the communication in international advertising? If a tag line cannot possibly be translated to communicate the intended meaning, then what should the advertiser do? Elaborate your answer with the help of a real-life example.
5. How would you ascertain the standardisation or adaptation content in a TV commercial? Answer with the help of a TV commercial you are familiar with that has run in at least 10 countries with known cultural differences.
6. An extensive study by Dentsu, Japan's largest advertising agency, concurred with a thesis that asserted that while Western advertising tended to be more verbally oriented, direct and to-the-point with logical messages, Japanese advertising were emotionally oriented and indirect. Some advertising agency executives believe that Japan's distinctive style of advertising is gaining popularity in the West—however, only incrementally. The effectiveness of emotional appeals such as soft music, beautiful scenery and soft voices on the Japanese has been well documented, as is the emotional tendency of Japanese consumers to choose products and brands based on a manufacturer's good works and favourable image. Foreign products which have succeeded in Japan using Japanese imagery include: Coca Cola, Apple Computer and Johnson & Johnson's baby lotion.
   What are the problems of international communications? Explain in the backdrop of a US firm trying to develop its communication strategy for Japanese market.
7. How would you ascertain the standardisation or adaptation content in a print advertisement? Answer with the help of a Chinese print media advertisement run by a multinational for marketing products in China.
8. You are to launch an advertising campaign for your cosmetic products in BRICS countries. Identify the advertising regulations in these countries.
9. Select two countries with different PDI standing, say, China and UK. Compare the communication strategy of an international company for cosmetic products marketing for the above two markets.
10. Follow Pepsi Cola's digital international marketing communications released for Asian countries in the recent past and use Whitelock and Rey's model for analysis of their localness or globalness.
11. An Indian company wishes to establish its line of fragrances 'Wildstone' (men's range) and 'Secret Temptation' (women's range) in African country markets. Use Hofstede cultural index scores for the African countries and relate the advertising appeals relevant to these indices to decide on the advertising communication strategy for the company.
12. Nokia Lumia series of mobile phones were first launched with introduction of two models—Lumia 710 and 800. Research on the international marketing communication used by the company in countries like USA, Germany, Japan, China, and Brazil to understand its characteristics terms of localness.
13. Ford Motor Company, USA. and Toyota Motors of Japan always regarded China as the most lucrative market for their vehicles. Compare and contrast the marketing communication strategy of these two companies for the Chinese market.

End Case: A Case of L'Oréal's Localness in Advertising[22]

The Beginning

The L'Oréal Group, with its registered head office at Paris, is dominating the world's cosmetics and beauty business. Its product portfolio revolves around hair colour, skin care, sun protection, make-up, perfumes and hair care. The group is very active in penetrating the markets of different countries and retaining them with product innovation as per country requirements. L'Oréal has demonstrated how to build up and

[22] The case 'A case of L'Oreal's Localness in advertising' has been created by the case writer Dr Gautam Dutta of Indian Institute of Foreign Trade as a basis for class room discussion rather than to illustrate either effective or ineffective handling of a business situation.

Table 11.8 International performance of L'Oréal group

Region	Performance in 2008	Performance in 2010	Remark
North America	Euro 3739 million of consolidated cosmetics sales with 18.2% market share and 22.9% of group cosmetics sales, which excludes soaps, toothpaste and razors.	Euro 4291 million sales—23.6% of consolidated cosmetics sales	Brands like Maybelline, New York and Inoa performed well.
Latin America	Euro 1151 million of consolidated sales with 12.1% market share and 7.0% of group cosmetics sales	Euro 1518 million Sales with 8.4% Of group cosmetics sales	Brazil, Argentina and Mexico were in focus for hair care and deodorants.
Western Europe	Euro 7382 million of consolidated sales with 22.7% market share and 45.1% of group cosmetics sales	Euro 7181 million sales 39.6 % of group cosmetics sales	United Kingdom, Germany, Sweden and France recorded positive growth.
Eastern Europe	Euro 1380 million of consolidated sales with 16.6% market share and 8.4% of group cosmetics sales	Euro 1399 million of consolidated sales	
Africa, Orient, Pacific	Euro 862 million of consolidated sales with 14.3% market share and 5.3% of group with cosmetics sales	**Africa/Middle East:** Euro 558 million sales—3.1% of group cosmetics sales	Faced with strong competition in South Africa and Turkey. Lebanon and Morocco recorded strong growth.
Asia	Euro 1844 million of consolidated sales with 10.9% market share excluding Japan (2.7% market share in Japan) with 11.3% of group cosmetics sales	**Asia Pacific:** Euro million 3192 with 17.6% of sales **New markets:** Euro 6667 million with 36.8% of cosmetics sales	New markets include 15 new growth markets specially identified for marketing thrust.

Source: Annual reports of L'Oréal, complied by author

retain leadership positions in all continents, channel by channel and category by category. "Armed with its patiently built-up rich and varied brand portfolio, the group has the answer of all beauty aspirations across the different countries of the world irrespective of richness or poorness of the people who live there', quipped its CEO when asked to comment on the company status in a recent advertising concave in Paris.

The group still explores new country markets, understands the consumers' requirements and then unleashes its products equipped with high brand value. In many countries the company understood the consumer's need so well that the brands created a mesmerising effect on the consumers and thereby increased its market strength. Keeping in mind the local requirements it made all concerned efforts to match to the expectation of local people. At the same time it never forgot to increase its globalness as well. In fact, the company over the years learnt the mastery of mixing localness with globalness.

The company managed to register an enviable global consolidated sales volume of €19.5 billion during 2010 by marshalling of 23 global brands in 130 countries with the help of about 66,600 employees across different countries. In order to be ahead of the pack it continued to innovate new products, as testified by the fact that in 2010 alone, it filed 612 patents. Table 11.8 shows the performance of the group in different strategic regions.

'Target 15' Strategy

During 2010, the company reviewed its worldwide position and to invigorate its global position further. The newly constituted expert group on global competitiveness critically reviewed the competitiveness of the company and set up a new 'Target 15' strategy. Under the 'Target 15' strategy, it identified 15 'growth markets' that have a strong potential to grow in the cosmetics market. The 15 markets identified were Poland, Ukraine, Argentina, Colombia, Indonesia, Thailand, Vietnam, Philippines, Turkey, Egypt, Saudi Arabia, Pakistan, Kazakhstan, South Africa and Nigeria. In addition, the company also did not lose focus of new emerging markets like Brazil, Russia, India, Mexico and China because of their rising population and per capita income. Thus, combing the emerging markets, it was 'Target 15 plus' which would be the point of all strategic attention for the next five years in order to fight the odds and welcome positives. Although the expert group developed its vision plan in a highly ambitious manner for the 'Target 15 plus' countries, the CEO of the company was fully aware of the high levels of competition in these markets which it would have to face in order to achieve the objectives set in the vision documents.

Jean-Paul Agon, CEO, L'Oréal, met with high-level officials in the company's headquarter for strategising action plan for the 'Target 15 plus' countries and emphasised on the role of marketing communication in extending products and increasing market share. "Overall, our firepower should thus clearly increase, helping us to develop the relevant positions of our brands and our products." He quipped. "The advertising power of the company has to adequately support its brands so as to elevate them and be remembered by the target consumers in different countries. The company recently has also increased budget for advertising. In fact, L'Oréal is the third-largest global advertiser now (2010), behind only Procter & Gamble Co. and Unilever. It took huge effort inside the company to bring it to this level from 12th position during 2000. However, there is no short cut to developing an international marketing communication strategy and it must act in a holistic manner," Mr Jeans Paul reminded the officials in charge of developing and unleashing the marketing programme for newly targeted countries. He advised them to tread with caution.He then narrated how, until now, the international communication strategy was developed and marshalled in different countries:

Change in model or spokesperson: The portfolio of L'Oréal's 'spokes models' is as diverse as the brands themselves. We have never sought to impose a single model of beauty—our product lines can include many items that are deliberately different from one country to another in order that they reflect the local forms of beauty, culture and tradition. Beauty is not perceived in the same way in India as it is in Asia, the Middle East, northern or southern Europe or America. Up till now the company is successful in delivering "local model local aspiration" framework with efficiency. This may be required to followed more extensively in target 15 plus countries as well.

Decide on slogan: The company's well-known slogan "Because you're worth it" started out as "Because I'm worth it" in 1973 for Preference hair colour and was created by agency McCann-Erickson. Although its roots were distinctly American, in 1996 'Because I'm worth it' became the signature for the L'Oréal Paris brand around the world. The company, thus, never compromised on its globalisation agenda. All along marketing and advertising prowess has been an important factor in the company's growth. When "I'm worth it" was introduced, L'Oréal Paris had less than 20% share of the US hair colour market. By 2007, L'Oréal Paris' share of hair colour in the US stood at 44%. We need to rethink on this aspect particularly from the fact that our target 15 plus countries are culturally different. We may have to compromise on our globalisation drive to a great extent in the matter of developing marketing communication for TV and print media.

Right time acquisition of brands: During 1953, the company entered into Western European countries and the US by forming a licensing arrangement with Cosmair Inc. to sell its hair-care products to beauty salons. Thereafter, it made another two key acquisitions, **Lancôme** in 1964 and **Garnier** in 1965, which strengthened L'Oréal in the mass and luxury segments while forming a strong base for the fragrance and upscale cosmetics businesses. The next major growth spurt came in the 1980s. L'Oréal went on an acquisition spree and, by the beginning of the 21st century, had acquired or established licensee agreements with Ralph Lauren, Giorgio Armani, Redken, Maybelline, SoftSheen, Carson, Kiehl's and Matrix. This was followed by more geographic expansion with gaining of a majority stake in **Shu Uemura** Cosmetics, the namesake of the well-known Japanese makeup artist and acquiring **Yue-Sai** Cosmetics, a leading company in China. Further, it acquired **The Body Shop**, famous for its commitment to natural ingredients and social responsibility. As the competition in the target 15 countries are escalating day by day we need to keep a close watch on the local competitors. It would be very important for the top level management to get the feeler timely on the requirements of acquisition of local brands further from local managers. This is particularly more applicable in case of India and China where a number of local brands are likely to take away the market share.

Managing Balanced growth of product portfolio: Fifteen years ago, L'Oréal depended on Western Europe for 70% of its cosmetics revenue. Today, Western Europe contributes only about 45% and of the remaining, 23% comes from North America and 32% from the rest of the world. Its business has increasingly diversified, with 51% of sales coming from consumer products, 26% from luxury products, 15% from professional products and 8% from specialty dermatological products. Within cosmetics, 26% of sales come from skincare products, 23% from hair care, 21% from makeup, 15% from hair colour and 11% from perfumes. Even so, geographical balance and brand diversity remain high on the to-do list. The company sees a lot more room for its products in new markets, especially for its mass-market brands in emerging countries. For instance, subsidiaries are now being set up in Egypt, Kazakhstan and Pakistan. Now for countries like India, we have to re-assess out product portfolio sufficiency and optimise the same as per practical requirements.

Right cross country balance with brands: Although apparently it may appear that cosmetics, fragrances and hair-care products for women are the only three segments that need to be communicated, a closer look reveals that there are many sub-segments within these three major segments exist in terms of age, ethnicity, prestige, gender. These different sub segments require different marketing approach with required variation to tackle cultural differences across the targeted countries. The company policy throughout the years has been not to leave out even a single consumer out of communication network irrespective of the country he or she belongs. In the mass market situation, L'Oréal's products range from products for 3, 4, 5 year-olds such as shampoo for kids, to anti-aging products for wrinkles and dryness for 65-to 70-year-old women. The company also do not keep men out of the target group. For example, SoftSheen-Carson hair colour directly targets men and women and it is the number one beauty brand in hair care in its segment. The Body Shop, which L'Oréal acquired in 2006, appeals to consumers who want natural ingredients. The company also did not allow the baby boomers to be out of the target net keeping in mind their spending power. The company paid special attention to understand their desire of feeling beautiful and professional. Result is seen in terms of company efforts to contribute to their sense of better life. It was quite a milestone in the marketing strategy of the company to rope in actress Diane Keaton (for L'Oréal Paris), who is fabulous at the age of a little over 60 and thereby enter into the mind of elderly but rich people. At the high end, the company has put together an enviable portfolio of brands aligned with some of the most exclusive names in fashion design, both classic and contemporary. They include Giorgio Armani, Cacharel, Diesel, Guy Laroche, Paloma Picasso, Ralph Lauren, Viktor & Rolf and Yves Saint Laurent, as well as Japanese makeup artist Shu Uemura. Kiehl's since 1851, an exclusive specialty brand, has a particularly personal relationship with a loyal following in the luxury segment. Since its acquisition in 2000, it has been L'Oréal's fastest-growing luxury brand. It can be said that the company was successful in developing three-pronged approaches to cater to the differential need of the varieties of consumers. First, it devised communication programme to reach the target consumers effectively and efficiently. Second, it listened to market continuously to understand the differential needs and wants of different category customers. Third, it played the role of either a beauty expert or a designer while prescribing products for different category consumers. "So, we have to follow our own history to repeat success in the 'Target 15 plus' countries as well" reiterated Jean-Paul Agon, CEO of L'Oréal.

Right amount of localisation in country markets: It may not be a big problem with Chinese consumers as L'Oreal entered the market way back in the 1980s. The entry strategy was to fill each segment with the right brands. For the mass market, the company had its trusted brands like L'Oréal Paris, Maybelline Garnier, and Mini-Nurse. For the rich and exclusive customers, there were exclusive brands Lancome, Biotherm, Shu Uemura, and Kiehl's. For the target market in between the mass and class, brands such as Vichy, Kerastase, and Matrix made up the offerings. The channels of products distribution were also different for these three segments. The class market brands were made available through retail outlets, high-end department stores, and specialised boutiques, while the mass and mid-market products through general stores, beauty salons, etc. All these were complemented with localised advertisement run on TV, print media, billboard, etc. Ziyi Zhang, a famous Chinese actress who also has a stint in Hollywood was cast in Maybelline lipsticks print advertisements. To make the advertisement culturally more appealing, a bunch of red roses with a lot of drops of water on them was purposefully used. The red colour lipsticks in the backdrop of her light yellow skin, dark hair and dark brown eyes really made the advertisement appealing to the Chinese girls. On the right side of this print advertisement we used Chinese characters which meant "Moisture goes deep; colour comes alive." We never forgot to put English words "Moisture Extreme Lipcolor" just at the bottom of the advertisement. The beautiful Chinese lady with gorgeous long silky hair, Zhang Zilin, the first-ever Chinese Miss World, was made brand ambassador in 2008 and she appeared in the advertisement for L'Oreal Repair 5 shampoo. After China, we shifted our attention to the Indian market and made our entry during 1985 and captured the vast market with 1.2 billion consumers, almost on the scale of that of a continent. L'Oreal has already adapted for localisation with the launch of a new fairness cream called Garnier Light Ultra endorsed by Bollywood actress Priyanka Chopra. It is now in the process of launching a locally-developed 'kajal' under the Maybelline umbrella. We have planned to launch about 70% of our products with local flavour only. Right from the word go, we have developed for Indian consumers a marketing communication loaded with local taste. The company have been making of good use of Bollywood beauties like Aishwarya Rai, Slumdog Millionaire star Freida Pinto and Sonam Kapoor to woo Indians, taking advantage of their fondness of Hindi movies. However, a time has come to review its strategy for big market like India. The vision document had sought for additional attention to Indian market because of its enormous potential and competition from many other global players.

The management team responsible for increasing market share listened carefully to what their boss Jean-Paul Agon, CEO, L'Oréal had to say about L'Oréal marketing and communication strategy. Although at the end, the CEO had asked if anyone wanted to know more or had a question, no question came. The management team unanimously decided at the end of the meeting that it was time to act rather than to put more questions. However, they all decided before leaving the place that since the company had good presence in the emerging markets like China, India, etc., they would first review and develop a marketing communication strategy for India and China and place it before the CEO and then take on the other markets based on the feedback received.

CASE QUESTIONS

Q1. Evaluate the strength of international marketing communication strategy of L'Oreal against the prevailing competition that exists in the global scenario in the same product category.

Q2. Do you support the localisation of communication strategy adopted by L'Oreal for China and India?

Q3. How much localisation or standardisation did L'Oreal use in its print and digital media advertisement across the countries of the world?

Q4. Assume that you are a part of the management group responsible for developing marketing communication strategy for India and China. Hence, research on the market requirements and thereafter develop a strategic communication plan for making a presentation to the CEO for approval.

FURTHER READINGS

De Mooij, M. (1998), *Global Marketing and Advertising: Understanding Cultural Paradoxes*, Sage Publications, Thousand Oaks, CA.

This book details out the impact of culture on advertisement that international marketers must understand when they resort to global marketing and advertising in other countries. It throws light on both theory and practical applications in respect of global branding strategies in the backdrop of cultural underpinning of different countries of the world.

Cheng Lu Wang, Allan K.K. Chan, (2001) "A content analysis of connectedness vs separateness themes used in US and PRC print advertisements", International Marketing Review, Vol. 18 Iss: 2, pp. 145–160.

The article provides information about how "connected appeals" and "separated appeals" can be effectively used in print advertising by understanding of the cultural tuning of the population of the target country. The article provides evidences of the understanding developed by using examples of China and USA.

Amitava Chattopadhyay, Tracey Yi, Darren W. Dahl and Gerald J. Gorn (1997), "The effect of color as an executional cue in advertising: They are in shades", *Management Science*, Vol. 43, No. 10, October.

This is of the rare articles that deal with basic information about designing print ads and impact of colours in them. It provides very useful guidelines which can help international marketers to understand the requirements of using colour in country specific situation in order to rouse consumers' feelings and attitudes. It also provides a useful conceptual frame work regarding use of colour in print advertisement.

Harris, Greg and Suleiman Attour (2003), "The international advertising practices of multinational companies", *European Journal of Marketing*, Vol. 37(1/2), pp. 154–68.

This article present a unique model for understanding the localness or globalness of print media advertising. This model is useful to understand the standardisation components and to draw precise comparisons between advertisements deployed in different national markets.

Pollay, R. and Gallagher, K. (1990), "Advertising and cultural values: Reflections in the distorted mirror", *International Journal of Advertising*, Vol. 9.

This paper first reviews the use of culture in advertisement and then presents a method for measuring the cultural character of advertising in countries.

Nelson M.R. and Paek, H. (2007), "A content analysis of advertising in a global magazine across seven countries: Implications for global advertising strategies", *International Marketing Review*, Vol. 24, Issue 1.

This research oriented paper examines global advertising strategies of global brands across seven countries of the world like Brazil, China, France, India, South Korea, Thailand and USA. It then throws light on the contents of local advertisements and compares the extent of standardisation in the matter of different elements of advertisements like advertising copy, models across product nationality and category.

Research Agenda in Cross-border Marketing

12

Learning Objectives

After studying this chapter, you should be able to:

- Recognise the requirement of research by a company before it makes a commitment or progresses further in the mission of profiteering in a foreign market.
- Explain the mechanism of conducting international marketing research.
- Analyse marketing research tools and learn how researchers utilise tools in the context international marketing research.
- Understand the problems of associated with foreign country researches along with their possible solutions.
- Identify the various sources of secondary research already available and their utility in conducting research.
- Assess the various factors affecting the quality of marketing research in the international context.

Chapter Overview

Internationalising companies require definite information on foreign markets to answer vital questions related to their possible competitiveness in the new markets. A company's search for information and arranging them in the most meaningful way through marketing research has to continue even after it establishes itself in the foreign market to reap maximum benefits of presence. Pertinent questions that arise in this context are: What are the research requirements for a company before making a commitment or progressing further in the mission of profiteering in a foreign market? How can international marketing research be installed? What are the problems of conducting those researches? What research tool can the researchers possibly utilise? What types of secondary researches are available? Interestingly, these questions never recede; rather, their numbers increase with the increase of marketing complexities and more intense internationalisation at a later period after entry because of market dynamism. This chapter, therefore, deals with the above issues related to research in the context of international marketing.

Opening Vignette

Goldwin Consumer Products Dumped Internationalisation Plan

Goldwin Consumer Products Private Ltd is an FMCG company based in Delhi that owns the 'Fresh N Fresh' and 'Virgin Beach' deodorant brands. The company was established during 2007 by a young entrepreneur to encourage Indian teenagers coming from the middleclass families but has spare income to spend liberally on deodorant. In a quick move to woo the Indian target consumers, the company successfully introduced separate men's range and women's range with the support of renowned perfumeries in France. Its men's range Fresh N Fresh is continuing to manage good performance for the company and is now only second to Unilever's market leader and global brand 'Axe' in the Indian market. Its women's range brand 'Virgin Beach' is consistently featured amongst the top five deodorants in the country. The products from Virgin Beach have been developed to appeal to young college girls. It enjoys one of the highest consumer loyalty and repeat purchase in the category and its market is predicted to increase to 38.8 billion rupees in 2017 from 15.2 billion rupees during 2012. Both the brands have demonstrated their capability to enthral Indian consumers with contemporary fragrances and offering their products in vibrant and attractive packaging. Having done exceedingly well in the Indian deodorant market over the last 5 years, the company felt that they need to go international and establish 'Fresh N Fresh' and 'Virgin Beach' line of products as high quality brands in the African country markets. The move was primarily because of two reasons: one, the home country market was becoming very competitive with entry of more national and international brands, creating pressure on pricing; two, the conditions of African country markets are perceived to be similar to Indian conditions which could possibly be explored successfully without much problems, while generating additional revenue.

However, in the course of its efforts towards internationalisation, the company was confronted with various questions, as noted below, before allocating budget for taking the mission forward. The questions can be grouped under three broad headings:

Which country markets in Africa to enter first?

The answer to this question involves screening of the quantity of imports of the product (i.e., deodorants) by country, local production, competitiveness parameters, trade intensity, trade openness of shortlisted countries, tariff structure, economic partnership status of the target countries and non-tariff measures.

How to enter the selected country markets?

The answer involves analysis of various host country factors, industry specific factors, and sectors specific factors.

How to market and build the brand?

Brand building may be done by taking count of leading brands of deodorant (national and international) in the host country, mapping competition in the selected countries, identifying distribution channels and making provisions for the country's retailing system, pricing structure, media and agency availability, consumer preferences for deodorant, purchase intention initiator, mode of purchase, frequency of purchase and culture based-commonalities.

In order to get answer to the above questions, Goldwin Consumer Products first tried its expertise within the organisation but no breakthrough could be recorded. Then, the company entrusted the work to a professional consultant but the consultant kept the company waiting for six more months without any fruitful result.

When this story of international marketing research requirements and dillydallying was told to the students of international marketing in the classroom, the students quipped, "What are the problems associated with international marketing research? How can exact research requirement be understood? How is international marketing research conducted? What are the different research tools that can be utilised in the context international marketing research? What are the different sources and availability status of secondary data for conducting the research? What are the various factors affecting the quality of marketing research?"

> *"In the twenty-first century, the role of cross-cultural marketing research has become increasingly critical in guiding business decision making"*
>
> —Stephanie Slater and Mirella Yani-de-Soriano (2010)

INTRODUCTION

Countries of the world are getting closer day by day in terms of their reach and accessibility, thanks to the rapid development of information and communication technology. This closeness is allowing quick spread of information about business opportunities from one country to another. It is not only the big multinationals that gain advantage out of it but it also allows small- and medium-sizes companies, to go from one country to another to set up business and market their products or services. In this way, emerging countries are fast becoming attractive destinations for companies of different sizes from different parts of the world. India, Brazil, Indonesia, Korea, Taiwan, Thailand, etc., have hosted many foreign companies even though these companies had no idea of the business environment while entering these countries. These entries were driven by sheer opportunities perceived to be existed by these companies. Consider the case of Days Inn, the US-based budget hotel chain, which was hardly known in China during 2003. It sensed some business opportunities in China arising out of economic progress in the country and made its journey to China from USA with limited resource and capacity to do business in China. Now, the same US hotel chain is well known in China and has more than 100 properties in various cities and regions in China[1]. Operating under various names such as Days Inn, Days Hotel or Days Hotel and Suites and providing a wide range of amenities. The chain is no longer synonymous with budget hotels as it was in USA, but represents higher-end hotel in China. How the business could make this make over from budget hotel to luxurious one? The answer to this question is very interesting to note. The company while looking for internationalising observed one peculiar tendency of the Chinese customers. In general, the Chinese customers may not stay in big hotel but have a tendency to show off their wealth. The company also noted that in China using expensive hotels is considered a status symbol. The company further noticed that this perception of Chinese consumers was crystallising more with the upward swing of economic conditions of the country. The company consulted some experts on China affairs and came to know that Chinese have a tendency to show off and it has been basically a cultural thing. The US hotel chain, through a primary market research, found that different business hubs of China were regularly visited by business travellers, both Chinese and the foreigners. It also recorded the demand and supply gap prevailing in the major cities of China in terms of hotel accommodation. The research also revealed that there would be more and more requirement of hotels at strategic business locations. The change from budget category to luxury category was felt necessary by the company management as the customer satisfaction registers, maintained in every hotel of the company, showed indications of a need towards status enhancement with more comforts. Accordingly, the management of the hotel chain, while opening up new hotels in China, undertook a major re-branding exercise with considerable financial commitments towards enhancing the standards of its hotels and brand building accordingly. However, the makeover branding was not easy, especially in a different country. First, the financial commitment for brand building must be supported by well-researched findings that the exercise would bring better result for the company. Second, exact materialistic and psychological requirements of Chinese customers must be well understood in advance. Thanks to the quality of research executed by the company and information gathered from there. The company was able to take bold steps. Just as the research-based knowledge wonderfully encouraged US hotel chain to work towards higher positioning of its brand and

[1] http://usa.chinadaily.com.cn/weekly/2012-08/17/content_15682603.htm

reap benefits, so a pre-entry research did save the Swedish furniture retailer IKEA from spending resource for higher branding. The Swedish furniture retailer IKEA could take a conscious decision of not going for upper class branding in China basically because of the research findings about China market executed before entering the country. The company gathered understanding that in China, IKEA is still considered a novelty by most of the consumers because of its strong "foreign" aura[2]. The passive rebranding nicely worked for IKEA. One common thing in the above two cases is that the information collected from the market through formal research helped them to take the correct decision at the correct time and got the taste of success in foreign country.

Large multinational companies have always shown active interest for pre-entry research for understanding the foreign country well for taking full benefits of their presence in that country. In fact, a clear understanding could provide them a real return in terms of revenue. Western clothing brands such as Zara and H&M were able to target the younger Chinese customers correctly who wanted to feel and dress like Americans but could not afford to spend a lot of money to do so, because of sound market research they executed. Both the European brands positioned their retail outlets with 'foreign but affordable one' image as per requirements of the targeted young Chinese consumers. They effectively communicated the target consumers that whether their outlets are located in Hangzhou, Shanghai, London, New York, or Paris, they were all standardised. American KFC, the fast food retailer, researched on the requirements of the vegetarian customers in India at length to understand them correctly before opening its vegetarian retail outlets India. Indian telecom giant Airtel is continuously being fed with market researched data from countries of its presence in Africa, which eventually helped it to increase its market share by beating the strong local/regional competitors. Therefore, understanding of the requirements of the foreign market is a must for a company operating in foreign market. A good understanding will allow the company to decide on the market segmentation, targeting and positioning of its product in a correct way. Without a good amount of knowledge about the distant country customers there could be a huge gap in the communication process and, as a result, the brands may stumble. In many cases, the international companies require updated research based information on different business aspects continuously to take vital decisions to hold market share from the aggression of the competitors.

Whether the strategy of a company is to standardise internationally or customise locally is often decided by consumers' insight generated by research-based information from the respective countries where the company is present. Localising products in line with country-specific requirements is a difficult strategic decision as it involves moving away from global appeal or home-country appeal. All these decisions are heavily depend ent on research-based market knowledge of the foreign country markets and not on a hunch feeling of the country manager of a company. Some of the companies failed because they did not resort to gathering enough research based knowledge of the foreign country. For example, the localisation attempt of a well-known American clothing brand Gap fell flat in

[2] http://news.xinhuanet.com/english/china/2012-08/19/c_131794458_3.htm

China when the company came out with the design of a printed skull on a children's product line, which went against the traditional Chinese culture of peace and love. The company did not have enough information on the impact of culture on the buying behaviour of Chinese consumers.

To support the international companies in their quest for research-based knowledge, many reputed professional market research agencies such as Sofres FSA, Research International, Nielson SRG, etc., regularly churning out research-based market intelligence in a customised way. However, many new emerging country markets such as Vietnam, Indonesian, some countries in Latin America, etc., though are fast becoming attractions for international companies but extensive market researched information/data-bases are yet to be built up by these professional research companies. Again, for smaller companies getting access to foreign market research data of the professional research companies seems to be a bit of luxury, particularly because of the high cost associated with them. Then, again sending research team and executing a foreign market research on their own, hit the hurdles of inexperience and high cost involvement. The result is felt when these companies operating fairly well in the domestic market but failed to reflect the same in the foreign country markets. Shortage of readymade affordable research-based information in the secondary level often puts them in the difficult situation of taking decisions based on their home country understanding only.

What are the research requirements for a company before it makes a commitment for progressing further in the mission of profiteering in a foreign market? How international marketing research can be installed? What are the problems of conducting these researches? What research tools can the researchers possibly utilise? What types of readymade secondary research are available? These are the general questions that frequently haunt a company before it takes a decision on internationalisation. Interestingly, these requirements even continue at a later period after the company enters the country market because of market dynamism. This chapter, therefore, seeks to answer the above questions, which are important for an international company irrespective of its size or the country it has targeted for entry.

RESEARCH REQUIREMENTS

An internationalising company has multidimensional requirements of doing research on various issues pertaining to doing business in foreign country. It involves collecting different types of information/data about the destination country and using that information/data through a right research framework in order to make conscious business decisions. These researchable issues, confronted by an internationalising company, are many ranging from trivial to some of very substantial nature. However, based on commonality in terms of their position in business areas, they essentially can be grouped under five broad groups. They are (1) market entry group, (2) mandatory requirements group, (3) country culture group, (4) marketing mix decision group and (5) multinationality-performance (mp) relationship group. We will discuss them one by one indicating different research issues under each group.

INTERNATIONAL MARKETING: RESEARCH ISSUES

The arena of international business has been hugely competitive where the competitive edge can only come through right business marketing decisions at the right time backed by well-founded research-based understanding. However, executing cross-country research is also very challenging in nature. Companies must understand different research issues related to international marketing before embarking on conducting actual research. The following are the various research issues systematically presented.

Market Entry Group

Market entry research helps the internationalising company to understand the business opportunities in the foreign countries and precise mode of entry (export, joint venture, wholly owned subsidiary, etc.) to be followed while actually entering in the selected country market. This area is a pivotal area in international marketing research in which international market selection based on opportunities and entry mode- related research are executed. Market selection and entry decisions are very crucial for a company, and hence, the company is likely to take these decisions based on adequate research-based understanding before entering the targeted foreign country. This is particularly true for first-time entrants in the international market who wants to be sure about market potential and want to know the impact of different entry methods on profitability aspects generated in the target market. Every entry decision needs to be backed by different financial commitments from the company, and hence, information helps them to justify actions. Also, different entry modes opted for entering a foreign country affect profit generation differently. At this juncture, therefore, the internationalising company may realise that many unknowns are required to be known about the targeted country before arriving at a conscious decision about the exact entry mode to be followed. The standard approach, in international business, on decision making about market selection and entry mode involves researching on host of the issues related to host country market factors, host country macro level factors, and effectiveness of various company-specific factors in the host country environment. The research focus and various research questions handled under the market entry research group are stated in Table 12.1.

Research focus: Host country market opportunities and competition

Internationalising company undertakes research to understand the overall market environment in the target foreign country and level of competition. These are very important aspects that every internationalising country would be interested to understand before deciding the entry and entry mode. In the backdrop of competition, how much market share the company can expect to achieve is another important area on which research- based understanding is required. Surely, a low level of market potential would not encourage the internationalising company to opt for hierarchical entry mode. Here, with this research focus, the researcher/manager of an internationalising

Table 12.1 Research issues: Market entry group

Research focus	Research questions
Host country market opportunities and competition	• What will be the market potential of the products offered to the host country consumers? Which country has the best marketing potential? • What level of market competition the products on offer would face?
Host country macro environment	• What would be the doing business risk in terms of political, economical, etc., in the host country? • How culturally the product is similar to the requirements of the host country consumers? • What government restrictions the company can expect while doing business in the target country?
Compatibility of internationalising company in foreign environment	• What will be the effect of specialised assets/unique capabilities, possessed by the internationalising company, on the host country market competiveness? • What will be effect of existing brand image of the internationalising company on the host country consumers? • What level of financial resources makes it adequate to start foreign operation? • How the international experience of the internationalising company managers would fair in host country market?

company basically tries to establish relationship between host company market condition and its preferred entry mode.

Research focus: Host country market environment

Uncertainty in the political and economic environment also greatly influences the entry mode of a company. Generally, when uncertainty in the foreign environment would be more then there would be a tendency of a company to restrict resource commitment while entering the foreign country. Turmoil in the economic and political environment may drastically effect profit generation in the foreign country and hence the entrant company avoid higher control entry mode. Internationalising company undertakes research to understand hostility exist the foreign market and relates that with the preferred entry mode. The result will indicate towards validity of a pre decided entry mode against prevailing market environment of the targeted foreign country.

Research focus: Compatibility of internationalising company

Internationalising company undertakes research to understand the compatibility of the internationalising company to influence the market competition. Specifically, a researcher desires to establish a relationship between the internationalising company's asset specificity and their ability to influence the existing competition of the target market. Asset specificity refers to the various specialised and unique assets which can provide competitive edge over the competitors. For example, Wal-Mart uses its asset specificity in terms of its unique inventory management system practiced in the company to influence competition in foreign markets. Researcher or manager, with this focus of research, first endeavours to measure the unique competences of the internationalising company in terms of product innovation, product distribution, inventory or supply chain management, etc., and then relate them with its ability to transfer those assets to the foreign country environment. Possession of specialised and unique assets implies that the company may undertake foreign market entry through higher control mode. Understanding the performance of home country grown brand in the foreign country environment is also a very important research area. As a new brand unfolds in the foreign market it may not retain the same attraction as it has in home country market. For example, Scorpio is a very reputed brand for SUV automobile in India with an excellent brand image but the same brand is almost unknown in USA or in Japan. Therefore, an internationalising company must perform research on probable brand effect in the destination country and relate the same with entry mode. When a subdued brand image is expected in foreign country the company may not be interested for opting hierarchical entry mode.

Mandatory Requirements Group

Different countries are prescribing various mandatory requirements differently which a company is required to be followed while doing business in those countries. In some emerging countries there may be some mandatory regulations which foreign companies exclusively need to follow. Developed countries are very strict with their prescribed mandatory requirements that are adequately backed by legal system to penalise the violators. European Union has prescribed various types of strict mandatory requirements for different products, which are required to be complied with while doing business there. Various in-process material standard, process adaptations, environment standard, packaging and labelling standards are required compulsorily by the developed countries. It is required that an internationalising company understands the requirements before entering the foreign market. The research focus and various research questions handled under the mandatory requirements group are stated in Table 12.2.

So, failure to abide by these regulations may attract penalty and expulsion from the country depending on the seriousness of the violation. As per the established trend, a developed country may show almost zero tolerance to violation of the laid-down norms of mandatory nature.

Table 12.2 Research issues: Mandatory requirements group

Research focus	Research questions
Host country mandatory requirements	• What are the laws/regulations of the target country regarding mandatory product modification? • What are the country specific product standards? • What quality norms and certification adherence are to be followed in target country? • What packaging norms are to be followed in the destination country? • What type of environment regulations are practiced in the destination country? • What are the labelling requirements for the products? • What is the production process standard in the destination country. • What the advertising regulations/ legal restrictions and how they can have impact on the marketing communications of the company?

Country Culture Group

Barring industrial products, possibly all other types of products are pervasively touched by the culture of the country in terms of market acceptance. The acceptance of product, marketing communications acceptance, smooth functioning of distribution channel, consumer buying behaviour, etc., are also heavily dictated by country culture. Again, there are reasons to believe that culture-related information is difficult to get because of invisible nature of country culture where the causes cannot be seem but the effects are visible. But if the culture of the host country and its effect on doing business are not understood properly then it may create problems for the company in respect of running a profitable business. By installing research on the country culture, the internationalising company may understand in advance how the prospective consumers of the target country will be forming buying intention, behave in an actual buying situation, product information searching, etc. Therefore, the company will naturally want to know the nuances of country-specific culture and get ready with the requisite marketing programme. The research focus and various research questions handled under the mandatory requirements group are stated below in Table 12.3.

Marketing Mix Decision Group

An internationalising company needs to frame its marketing strategy in accordance with the actual requirements of the target customer in the foreign country. This requires complete research based understanding about the customers in the foreign country in general and targeted segment in particular. A complete understanding through well-structured research would help in deciding the correct segment to target in the foreign country as well as positioning of the product as per requirements. The pricing strategy must be set as per the buying intention of the target consumers. The pricing strategy must also reflect the disposable income and spending pattern of the target consumers. The product component adaptation must be as per the consumer's requirements as unearthed by quality research undertaken in the destination country. In short, for developing an appropriate marketing mix, the company requires primary and fresh data from

Table 12.3 Research issues: Country culture group

Research focus	Research questions
Host country culture	• What is the basic cultural attuning of the target country consumers? • How the consumer will behave in a buying situation and how much of the can be attributed to the culture? • How the society influence the consumers in buying decision making? • What is the material culture of the foreign country population? • What effect of culture has on keeping distribution channel free from channel conflict? • What are the effects of culture on acceptability of advanced technology oriented products? • What are the cultural distances from home country to the destination countries and impact of those distances on marketing? • What are the cultural norms that the advertisements must follow while releasing marketing communication in the target country?

Table 12.4 Research issues: marketing mix decision group

Research focus	Research questions
Host country marketing mix decision making	• What are the profile of the consumers and which consumer segment can be targeted? • What product adaptation best suit the selected consumer segment in the foreign country? • What is the perception of the target segment about the product to be marketed and about the competitors' products already present in the country? • What are the different distribution options in the target country and channel structure? • What are the nature of media availability in the target country and their effectiveness in reaching the target consumers? • What are the pricing strategy of the competitors and impact of price on the demand of the product marketing? • What sales and merchandising strategy would be effective in the foreign market?

the market that could be analysed further to have a meaningful outcome. This should be supplemented by secondary data and knowledge to decide on the marketing strategy to be adopted on entry. The decision on marketing mix, which the company would follow on entry, is very crucial for ensuring early success in foreign market. The research focus and various research questions handled under the marketing mix group are stated in Table 12.4.

Multinationality- Performance (MP) Group

Companies worldwide have continuously expanded their international operations to different countries by taking advantage of globalisation and opening up of different country markets. Indian companies are also not way behind. Reserve Bank India (RBI) data shows that around 3243 Indian companies made commitment for foreign direct investment commitment to the tune of around 23.04 USD billion during the eight month period October 2010 to May 2011 as shown in the Table 12.5.

Many international business managers and scholars of international business have long been arguing that the benefits of multinationality are more than the costs associated with multinationality. In fact, this is the

Table 12.5 Outward FDI from India

Outward FDI from India			
S. No.	Month/Year	No of Indian company	Financial commitment (in USD Million)
1.	October, 2010	399	2934.22
2.	November, 2010	342	2921.62
3.	December, 2010	435	3443.81
4.	January, 2011	414	3074.70
5.	February, 2011	420	3221.49
6.	March, 2011	426	2358.09
7.	April, 2011	379	1390.24
8.	May, 2011	428	3700.64
	Total	3243	23,044.82

Source: Reserve Bank of India

fundamental requirement for making the companies' internationalisation meaningful and attractive. However, the argument took a new dimension when the research scholars wanted to understand the relationship between multinationality and performance empirically. Researchers of different countries at different point of time embarked on collecting specific data on internationalisation of companies and impact of that on their financial performance in a longitudinal manner. Interestingly, the researchers came out with different findings on the exact effect of multinationality on company performance. Some researchers empirically established, with data from companies, that there exist positive linear relationship between internationalisation and performance. This implied that as the companies went on internationalising more and more, the benefits also increased in a linear fashion. This finding was heartening as companies do the border crossing primarily in search of better financial performance. Some other researchers found a U-shaped curvilinear relationship between internationalisation and company performance. Interestingly, some researchers have even found evidence for a cubic association between internationalisation and performance by arriving at a horizontal S-shaped relationship. The U-shaped curvilinear relationship implied that as the companies become more and more multinational the expected performance benefits would be achieved only after elapse of some time. To support this finding, the researcher argued that in the initial year there would be investment only but the real performance benefits would fructify only after crossing of some threshold point. The horizontal S-shaped relationship implied that internationalisation differently impacted the performance of company differently at different point of time. These three types of the multinationality-performance (MP) relationships are depicted in the Figure 12.1.

The above discussion calls for internationalising company to undertake research to understand the exact mp relationship of the companies operating in the same sector of that country. For example, an internationalising company in food processing sector may like to understand the exact pattern of mp relationship of the contemporary Indian multinational companies. This would help the internationalising company to put requisite strategy in place while internationalising. Generally these types of research use yearly financial data of the companies under study. The percent of foreign sales to total sales (FSTS) or foreign assets to total assets (FATA), etc., are taken as dummy for multinationality and other accounting measures such as return on net assets (ROA), return on equity (ROE), as well as the return on sales (ROS) are taken as indicators for performance.

FIGURE 12.1 Multinationality-performance (MP) relationships

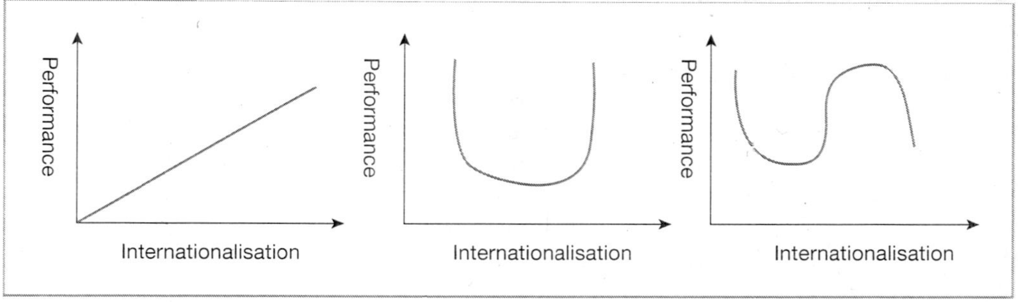

Table 12.6 Research issues: Multinationality-profitability group

Research focus	Research question
Multinationality-performance relationship	• What will be the effect of multinationality on company performance?

Researchers establish relationship between the multinationality and performance with the use of multivariate analysis in order to get suitable answer to the research question mentioned in Table 12.6.

International marketing research: Problems

Conducting cross country research encounters many problems. Comparatively speaking, the smaller companies experience more problems than the bigger one. This is primarily because of inadequacy in in-house research capacity of the smaller companies to handle them effectively. Second, there are problems associated with information/data collection pertaining to a foreign country to conduct a meaningful research. Third, framing right research framework, methodology, etc., again create problem for the managers of internationalising company which can create a major problem in arriving at meaningful and actionable result. Again, all the above problems may vary in accordance with different factors such as type of countries involved, entry method planned, competitive situation prevailing in the target country, type of product dealt with, level of dissimilarity with the home country, geographical distance between home and host country, etc. These problems are elaborated more in details below.

Type of destination country: Countries could be considered open or close in terms of conducting cross country research by an internationalising company. For example, USA could be considered more open and transparent than China. It is far easier to get the required information from both primary and secondary sources in USA than in China or smaller African countries such as Burundi, Gabon, etc. Since USA is a more transparent country, the depth of information/data required by a company would be easily available. This factor mostly affects the second problem, i.e., data inadequacy for conducting a research.

Entry method planned: Comparatively much less information would be required if the planned entry mode into the foreign country is through export only rather than wholly owned subsidiary. A company looking information before entering the target country after deciding the entry mode as wholly owned subsidiary would require more detailed information because of higher risk associated with the mode of entry. So, in investment mode of entry company requires quite a large data set pertaining to various issues which may not easily available to the internationalising company.

Competitive situation: When competition is acute in countries where a company wants to its increase market share, the marketing strategy formulation would require more information back up followed by use of those data through a rightfully framed research framework. In fact, this kind of research requires to be updated with time and hence, it requires constant research support which may not be possible to be handled in a smaller company.

Type of products: Companies dealing with FMCG products would require having more frequent information on the market development than industrial products. FMCG products require to be marketed for a cross section of a target population in the destination country which means more continuous involvement in research in foreign country. For example, research in white goods would be required to be a continuous process while research in handicraft products may be intermittent. In case of industrial products, the target buyers are a few and hence less complexity is involved in the research process.

Level of dissimilarity with the home country: A British company will have to do less marketing research while entering USA because of language similarity in both the countries. The same British company will have to do considerably more marketing research while entering China because of language, culture, and political differences between the two countries. An Indian small-scale exporting company would find the level of dissimilarities between home country and Germany to be much more than between home country and Sri Lanka. Hence, the company would be facing more problems when researching about Germany than Sri Lanka because of higher degree of dissimilarities of business environment of Germany with respect to India. While doing research in Germany, the company would find many business situations that are totally different than in the home country and for correctly framing research agenda prior understanding foreign country business environment is extremely essential. However, it may be possible for the company to proceed with the research for Sri Lanka and manage the Sri Lankan situation through experience of doing business in the home country. This effect increases the requirement of information and complexities of researching process.

Geographical distance: The distance between the home country and destination country also influences research complexity. Many Latin American countries are still unknown to Indian exporting companies mainly because of the long geographical distance involved. The general flow of information about socio-economic situation, business situation, or customer preference climate prevailing in those countries, etc., is not usual. Hence, any Indian company intending to do business in these countries would look for developing extensive research based understanding before investing financial resource there. This entails gathering of relevant and authentic information from distant market through primary and secondary sources. Here, the long geographical distance acts as barrier to primary data collection because of higher cost, time and effort requirement. Data available in the secondary sources also becomes too general to be used in a specific purpose study. This, in turn, increases the depth and width of the research complexities.

RESEARCH PLAN

It is important for a company to develop relevant international marketing research plan before it starts actual research and internationalisation. A well-developed research plan sets the ball rolling by planning about different aspects of conducting the research in hand. The research plan essentially starts with research question/questions that the researcher is pursuing to get answered through the installed research. It also depicts the methodology to be adopted to get answer to the research questions posed in the research. In a simple sense it is the blue print of the research undertaken.

During the internationalisation process, various business decisions are to be taken by the managers which required to be backed by correct research-based knowledge. The manager keeps on looking for data/ready-made information pertaining to the targeted country to facilitate the decision making process. Information deficit areas become the candidates for installing in-house research for the internationalising company. Once entering in the targeted country the research requirements do not come to an end. Companies have to continue researching on various business related issues even after entry into the country market to keep itself updated and to face competition. Since types of information requirement in the context of host country are many, there could be various research agenda for a company. The precise areas of research to be undertaken depend on the actual requirement of the company and the priority level fixed by the managers. Therefore, it is extremely important that the internationalising company managers to list out the priority areas of research first and then assess the quantum of information deficit clearly. Based on the severity of requirement and information gap a marketing research would be installed to know the unknowns. Interestingly, the severity of information deficit generally varies directly in accordance with the depth of expected involvement of the company with the foreign market and level of significance of a particular business decision to the company. In case of a wholly owned subsidiary set up by foreign direct investment, the company will have a more extensive agenda than one planning to export only. In a general sense, the more the company is uncomfortable about its entry and performance in the foreign market, the more will be its research requirements.

Once the research requirements to reduce the level of discomfort in conducting business in the foreign market of the company are understood, the manager/researcher may write down the research plan to proceed further. The research plan should contain a brief introduction of the background, well-articulated problem statements indicating the gaps in terms of present level of understanding, objectives of the research, methodology to be adopted for the research, information requirements and sources, outcome to be achieved, limitations, etc.

Format for Developing Research Plan for International Marketing

There is no specific format recommended for developing a research plan for entry into international marketing because the format may vary depending upon the given differences in products/services and/or countries. However, a basic format is present below which can be altered or modified according to the actual requirements of the researcher. This following is a generic format for presenting an international marketing research plan for a dummy research problem faced by an Indian company in terms of international marketing.

Introduction

Golden Products Private Ltd. is an FMCG firm based in Delhi that owns the brands 'Fresh N Fresh' and 'Virgin Beach' deodorant brands. This Indian company is continuously managing to show good performance in a reasonably competitive Indian market and is right now only second to Reckitt Benckiser's market leader and global brand, 'Axe'. Backed by its impressive sales figures in the domestic market, it now wants to expand its products to five African markets during 2016.

Key questions

The management of the Goldwin Products Private Ltd was in a dilemma about internationalising its deodorant brands in African countries. It felt the need to internationalise its best-known male and female brands and introduce them to a few selected African country markets.

In the words of the firm's management, "Our research problem is: which are the top five potential African markets for the products and to what extent would our brands be acceptable there?"

The critical research questions are:

- Who are our top five target country markets in Africa?
- Who are our competitors in the target markets?
- What is the prevailing attitude of the prospective consumers about deodorant products?
- To what extent are the socio-cultural and political-legal situations of the target countries supportive of a foreign business like ours?
- What should be the unique value propositions emanating from our brands to entice the target consumers?

Research objectives

Based on the above research questions the following are the objectives of the research:

- To find out the best five countries in Africa based on comparative market demand trend for our product, i.e., deodorant.
- To understand the market size for deodorants, its growth potential, ease of entry, competitive factors, distribution possibilities, cultural distance, technological development and receptivity to fashion change.
- To understand the factors responsible for prospective consumers' preferences and choices while selecting the deodorant in top five country markets.
- To find out a suitable marketing mix recipe for launching the products in the selected market.

Methodology

- Understand the comparative market demand trend of the product, i.e., deodorant in all the African countries and find out the top five countries.
- Understand the size of GNP, population, demography, and infrastructure, level of industrial activity, political risk factors, ethnic diversity, disposable income, entry tariff and cultural problems from secondary data.

- Identify the top ten countries based on the above analysis in accordance with country attractiveness.
- Understand the market size for deodorants, its growth potential, ease of entry, competitive factors, distribution possibilities, cultural distance, technological development, receptivity to fashion change.
- Find out the attractiveness score of the top ten countries based on the above criteria.
- Simulate the attractiveness score by weighing each criterion against the company preference to find out the top five countries attractive to our company. Cultural similarity, entry and regulations for doing business need to be judged as these factors are of particular importance. Size of the market is also an important factor. Ease of entry to these countries is the most important factor.
- Understand the factors responsible for prospective consumers' preferences and choices while selecting the deodorant through primary survey in the selected top five country markets.
- Find out a suitable marketing mix recipe for launching the products in the selected markets based on the knowledge based gathered through primary and secondary survey.

Data sources

Both secondary and primary data will be utilised for carrying out the research.

Outcome of the research

- Entry strategy(ies), Decision and rationale (for entry to the country)
- Market-entry plan: Among items to consider for inclusion in this section of the report are a competitive analysis, an analysis of country demand, a marketing plan, a human resource/management plan, a discussion of organisational structure, a manufacturing and/or distribution plan, a discussion of plans for financing the entry strategy, plans for selection of host-country partners (if partners are anticipated), a timetable for the market entry, a plan for evaluating the success of an entry, and any other analyses that may be appropriate.
- Managerial implications
- Caveats and limitations
- Future directions

Conclusion

The study would provide the company a research-based understanding which will allow smooth entry of its product into five African country markets.

Contemporary Research and Benefits

Right from the beginning of internationalisation of businesses, various research-based articles, pertaining to international marketing, have been published in different international journals. They have created a useful knowledge base that is very handy for international marketers. These research articles not only highlighted the various problems encountered by international businesses across the world but also helped to develop quite a good understanding for the existing players. This knowledge base, in fact, provides the following benefits to an international business manager:

1. A thorough understanding of the different critical points in internationalisation of businesses and marketing thereof for an existing business manager.
2. The business managers can understand about the different research methodologies adopted by different researchers to frame methodologies for conducting research by their own.
3. Data collection for conducting research on international business is difficult and expensive for the basic reason of multi country involvement. These articles allow the business manager to comprehend data requirements for conducting research in different areas. This would increase ease of data collection with reduced cost.
4. These articles are pouring knowledge from all over the world as the geographical coverage considered under the existing research base is worldwide. So these articles allow a good understanding of the different categories of research executed by different researchers in different countries. A manager can, therefore, take them as base to solve international marketing problems confronted by the company.

Research categories

There are many scholarly journals pertaining to international business and marketing. The journals vary in terms of geographic spread and media used for publication. It is very much a difficult job to first list out these articles appeared in these journals and then categorise the research articles, published up till now, based on the fundamental areas of international marketing. However, a pioneering attempt, in this direction, came from two well-known writers of international business, Aulakh and Kotabe (1993)[3] in this direction. Another two renowned scholars in international marketing, Tiger Li and S. Tamer Cavusgil (1995)[4], also worked in a similar fashion to understand broad categories of international marketing oriented research studies that were published during the period 1982–1990. More recently, Leonidou et al (2010)[5] made a wonderful contribution to understand the focus of the articles appeared in different journals. These contributions are immensely valuable which, in turn, allowed new researchers and business managers to follow the articles by taking the cue from the broad category they belong. These following are the seven broad categories of research articles published over a period of time and directions of articles contained under these categories are described below:

[3] Aulakh Preet S. and Kotabe Masaaki (1993). An assessment of theoretical and methodological development in international marketing: 1980-1990, Journal of international marketing, Vol. 1 (2), pp. 5-28.

[4] Li Tiger and Cavusgil S. Tamer (1995). A classification and assessment of research streams in international marketing, International business review, Vol. 4 (3), pp. 251 - 277.

[5] Leonidou Leonidas C., Barnes Bradley R., Spyropoulou Stavroula and Katsikeas Constantine S. (2010). Assessing the contribution of leading mainstream marketing journals to the international marketing discipline, International marketing review, Vol. 27 (5), pp. 491 - 518.

Environmental studies

This category is a very important and fundamental area of international marketing which continued to be flourished from a very long time by various research based articles. These articles basically dealt with the impact of environmental differences on companies and their marketing. It captured the difficulties of internationalising companies and doing business in foreign country environment which could be extremely dissimilar to home country. Simply speaking, the abrupt change in the components of environment such as economic, cultural, political, and legal variables, as experienced by the entrant company, had put huge pressure on doing business and carrying out marketing in the foreign country. The articles under this category actually depicted those realities and how the entrant companies handled these issues. These articles indicated that companies found change of environment was different for different countries. These created various problems for the companies. These articles testify success or failure of marketing of companies under study when confronted with new environmental situation. Many companies had to design new marketing mix suitable for new situation where as many continued without effecting any change of their home country strategy. In this category, a dominant area is occupied by studies concerning political environment. However, cross-cultural studies appear to be all time favourite areas where the several researchers unearthed the effect of country culture on businesses. The Western researcher found it very interesting to crack the mystery of culture concerning countries such as China, Japan, and Korea and their impact on businesses as observed from the volume of such articles published.

Comparative studies

The studies, under this category, were comparative in nature. They went on comparing a country's particular system of doing business and marketing with that of another. A number such studies initially compared the 'US system' with 'Japanese system'. Later, many other countries were brought in to its ambit to understand their respective marketing system on a comparative scale. At some point of time, China became focus of such studies when the country became target country of doing business for the US companies. Under this category of study, the main objective of the researchers was to draw a comparative profile between two or more countries and understand how the business and marketing system of companies got changed or modified in accordance with country specific requirements.

Marketing mix studies

This category was an all-time favourite area of research for the researchers with exclusive marketing orientation. The inflow of marketing mix decision oriented studies continued from post-world war period and continued till date. It proved to be an obsessed area of the international business researchers. Theodore Levitt's article in Harvard Business Review, during early part of 1980s, and subsequent debate over standardisation vs adaptation of marketing mix further opened a new vista of research in this direction. Researchers not only embarked on studies related to standardisation/adaptation of various aspects of doing business, in general, but also in the specific product class in specific countries. Further, many researchers researched on standardisation or adaptation of media, advertising massage, brand name, logo, slogan, etc., in accordance with a specific country requirement. Once again, when US or European companies had shown great interest in doing business in China, a huge number of studies were conducted to describe the plight of Western companies while adapting or not adapting marketing mix in accordance with the Chinese system. Through product and communication were the favourite two Ps for study in this category but the other two Ps, i.e., price and distribution never became central focus of the researchers. Again, amongst these two Ps, distribution attracted least number of studies under this category.

Process studies

These category accommodated studies which dealt with internationalisation process of entrant companies. These studies proceeded with an objective to understand how internationalisation of companies took place and their conformity with different theories of internationalisation. Under this category small and medium size companies (SMEs) got the special attention of the researchers. The management orientations of the SMEs, while internationalising, caught the attention of many researchers. These researches highlighted the effect of ethnocentrism, polycentrism and geocentrism on management during the internationalisation process. Another important area under this group was applicability of the theories of internationalisation in practical purpose. These researchers followed the process of internationalisation of a particular company or a group of companies, longitudinally or otherwise, and indicated deviation or conformity with the relevant theories of internationalisation. These studies came out with important findings concerning SME internationalisation process and provided a clear understanding whether companies followed theory in practice while internationalising and noted the important causes of deviation, if any.

Market entry studies

This category of study concentrated on researching on entry mode of companies. Entry mode studies attracted special attention of the researchers when many companies reported faltering on selecting an appropriate entry mode while entering a new country. Researchers attempted establishing relationship between entry mode of internationalising companies and marketing performance. Many researchers found interest in studying the selected entry mode adopted by comparatively smaller companies and attempted to find out reasons why or why not they followed gradual incremental pattern while entering new countries. Another stream of studies went on in establishing a methodology for selecting appropriate mode of entry. Many studies were positioned to capture different factors responsible for selecting a particular mode of entry.

Performance studies

Studies under this category originated during 1970s when companies wanted to understand the impact of international expansion on organisational performance. Very soon this topic became a centre of huge attraction amongst the researchers. They contributed articles regularly by considering different financial parameters of multinational corporations representing the dimensions of multinationality as well as company performance. These articles differed greatly in terms of variables used to represent the degree of internationalisation and performance of multinational corporations. Researchers also came out with country specific studies and characterised multinationality-performance relationship in that context. Also articles used different methodologies. Some studies reported a positive relationship between multinationality and corporate performance while others arrived at negative relationship. Some researches went on longitudinally in justifying or not justifying use of certain variables as measures of corporate international expansion and performance.

Other miscellaneous studies

This category belongs to those studies which could not be accommodated under above six categories. Only a few studies delved in understanding the international market research methodologies adopted by the different researchers at different points of time. Amongst the few, notables were Malhotra et al (1996)[6], Okazaki et al (2007)[7] et al and Watkins et al (2010)[8]. A few studies devoted attention on the methodology adopted while doing media research in a cross-cultural setting and commented on the applicability of research tools. A few studies recommended ways to improve the methodology of doing media research so that they can be applied to other countries. Another type of important studies could be noticed related to methodological problems associated with cross cultural marketing research. A few researchers embarked on studying the phenomenon of convergence of taste, preference and behaviour globally[9]. Effect of globalisation on companies was also became a pet subject of study. Globalisation effect and its impact on media advertisement, consumer behaviour, and brand image were taken up as subjects of study by many researchers.

RESEARCH JOURNALS IN INTERNATIONAL MARKETING

There are many scholarly journals concerning international marketing at the international level. These journals publish research-based articles which are good source for readymade knowledge in international marketing. Eminent authors like Tiger Li and S. Tamer Cavusgil categorised these journals into three groups depending upon the concentration of international marketing articles. The first group is exclusive group where only articles related to international marketing are published. The second group is demi-exclusive group which consists of journals whose primary focus is in various facets of international business but not marketing alone. In totality, this group is also quite

---

6 Malhotra, Naresh K. Malhotra, James Agarwal and Mark Peterson (1996), "Methodological issues in cross-cultural marketing research: A state-of-the-art review", *International Marketing Review*, Vol. 13, Issue 5, pp. 7– 43.

7 Okazaki, Shintaro and Barbara Mueller (2007), "Cross-cultural advertising research: Where we have been and where we need to go", International Marketing Review, 24 (5), 499-518.

8 Watkins, Leah (2010), "The cross-cultural appropriateness of survey-based value(s) research: A review of methodological issues and suggestion of alternative methodology", *International Marketing Review*, Vol. 27, Issue 6, pp. 694–716.

9 Douglas, Susan P. and C. Samuel Craig, "Convergence and divergence: Developing a semi-global marketing strategy, *Journal of International Marketing.*

useful for international marketers. The third group is a la carte group which contains many articles with international business orientation and readers require choose and pick those that concentrated on international marketing. These three groups and some journals included in the respective groups are as stated below.

Group 1: Exclusive group

- International Marketing Review
- Advances in International Marketing
- Journal of Global Marketing
- Journal of International Marketing

Group 2: Demi-exclusive group

- Columbia Journal of World Business
- Journal of International Business Studies
- Thunderbird International Business Review
- Multinational Business Review
- Journal of International Business Studies

Group 3: A la carte group

- Journal of Product and Product Brand Management
- Asia-Pacific Journal of Business Administration
- European Journal of Marketing
- Sloan Management Review
- International Journal of Retailing
- International Journal of Advertising
- International Journal of Management Reviews
- Journal of Business Strategy
- Journal of Consumer Research
- Marketing Science
- Journal of Marketing
- Marketing Intelligence and Planning

SOURCES OF DATA FOR INTERNATIONAL MARKETING RESEARCH

Information is the key for executing international market research. Data for international marketing research can come from primary as well as secondary sources. As the basic nature of the research is international, primary sources are often difficult to be used. Secondary source data are generally the starting point of research to understand the basic situation before embarking on primary research. But, basically, the source of data to be involved will be decided by the research requirement. One possible difficulty of secondary data is the problem of possible differential use, i.e., the data could have been collected for some other purpose not exactly matching with the present context at hand. However, use of secondary data is less costly than primary research because of multi-country involvement.

Primary Sources

Primary data has proved to be an essential source for many international marketing researches conducted over the years for various purposes. These data have been used for very purpose-specific and usually make the research more realistic in nature. A researcher may collect data through direct interaction with respondents in the foreign country with or without questionnaire, mail survey, focus group discussions, etc. This method, apart from providing data, allows the researcher to have a close feel of the situation under research. However, in international marketing research since the target group, in respect of whom data to be collected, is from another country, primary data collection through this method is comparatively more difficult, time consuming, and expensive. This is a genuinely acute problem faced by an individual researcher loaded with the responsibility of cross-country primary data collection. The primary data can also be collected through questionnaire mail survey, such as through posting of questionnaires by mail and collecting them back by return mail. This is a less costly process but it usually suffers from poor response rate. However through this process of data collection, it is generally not possible to know the customer's opinion about a product. In a consumer survey through mail the researcher can neither make out the characteristics of the target group nor impress upon the target group the seriousness of the research being undertaken. If the target group consists of company officials or policy makers of another country and the technique adopted by researcher is mail survey then some success may be expected in terms of improved response rate. However, the researcher or some representative needs to follow up closely by telephonic call or regular e mail to ensure quick feedback from the target respondents. Many a time, the questionnaire is not filled by the required person but by some representatives who may not have a good feel of the situation under survey. This dilutes the purpose of the research. Therefore, physical presence of the researcher in the foreign country is desired, if possible, both in case of consumer survey or survey of company officials. Another problem that crops up in the case of direct questionnaire survey in a foreign country is the unwillingness of foreign respondents to face the interviewer of another country. General consumers appear to have less enthusiasm to face a foreign interviewer. This problem is more in Asian countries such as Japan, China, Vietnam, Cambodia, etc. For example, a research study commissioned to understand the competitiveness of Indian handicraft products in Vietnam, launched by Indian Institute of Foreign Trade, required the researcher to question a representative sample of general consumers but the target respondents declined to give interview. A few of them, after lot a persuasion agreed, but they were so reluctant that many questions remained unanswered. In such situations, the spontaneity of information flow becomes erratic, defeating the purpose of the research. Hesitancy of the respondents while confronting a foreigner is another issue noticed in case of countries with high-context culture. A researcher with low-context cultural background will often fail to understand and appreciate this very cultural issue, which may distort information flow. One of the best ways to handle such situations is to involve an interpreter who can effectively communicate with the surveyor and the respondent and ease the situation separated by cultural barrier.

Secondary Sources

Secondary data sources are useful for international marketers as it may be almost readily available. Hence, many international researchers first look at the availability of secondary data before embarking on the task of primary data collection. The cost of obtaining secondary data is significantly less than that for primary data and also they are available, in many cases, in usable format. There are now many internet-based sources that can be explored from any place and at a low cost. Some of the useful sources are mentioned below.

Global edge

Centre for International Business Education and Research (CIBER) at Michigan State University (MSU) created the website "global edge". This is a knowledge web-portal that provides information, insights and learning resources on global business activities. "Global edge" maintains a comprehensive research tool and resources for academics, students and businesspeople. These tools and resources can be used for conducting research in different aspects of international business. It also contains data of about 11 major trading blocs of the world and the participating countries such as APEC, ASIAN, CAFTA-DR, CARCOM, COMESA, ECOWAS, EU, GCC, MERCOSUR, NAFTA and SADC.

FAOSTAT

Food and Agriculture Organisation (FAO) of the United Nations maintains this website. It provides time-series and cross sectional data relating to hunger, food and agriculture for approximately 245 countries and 35 regional areas from 1961 through the present. It also offers an innovative tool, FAOSTAT Analysis, for basic statistical analysis of the data. Researchers can get a comprehensive data based on agriculture, comparative analysis tools of sectors, commodity, country and regions. It is easy to download and use for a particular purpose.

Euromonitor

Euromonitor International has wonderful international coverage with information on most of the countries of the world. Researchers can use it for research undertaken on consumer markets. Global Market Information Database (GMID) of Euromonitor provides updated business and marketing information on over 200 countries, consumers and industries. This data base is ideally suited for organisations such as government departments, export agencies, business schools/universities, consultants and advertising agencies having need for a wide range of updated market data.

Coface

The Coface Group is a trade risk expert and known for credit insurance service coverage. The Group offers credit insurance solutions that aim to protect businesses against the risk of financial default by their customers. It helps to support its clients by assessing and preventing risks, so that they can make the best decision at the most opportune moment. The Website provides a comprehensive analysis of different countries of the world, sectoral data and credit risk analysis. Its online version of Handbook of Country Risk is an important source for assessing country risk.

Lex mundi

Lex Mundi is an organisation of independent law firms but provides various doing business related information which can be useful for international business managers. It provides law-related professional information as well. The 'Guides to Doing Business' is an important publication prepared by Lex Mundi's member firms and provides general information about each jurisdiction's legal and business infrastructures. The guides can serve as a useful resource tool when planning an international business strategy or researching a new business market.

Federation of international trade associations

FITA or Federation of International Trade Associations was founded in 1984 with the objective of strengthening the role of local, regional, national and global associations for development of international trade. As per its Website information, more than 450,000 organisations are linked to FITA through membership, representing a broad cross-section of the international trade and business community. They include manufacturers, trading companies, contractors, freight forwarders, custom house brokers, airlines, shipping companies, port authorities, banks, insurance brokers and underwriters, associations and a wide range of service providers including telecommunications companies, law firms and consultants. FITA also shares resources through GlobalTrade.net, which contains market research reports, market analyses, business tips and a list of over 50,000 qualified international trade service providers.

International trade administration

International Trade Administration (ITA) is a US Website promoting the competitiveness of US industry, trade and investment indicating US trade laws and agreements. ITA works to improve the global business environment and helps US organisations compete at home and abroad. ITA is organised into four distinct but complementary business units:

1. US and Foreign Commercial Service—Promotes US exports, particularly by small and medium-sized enterprises, and provides commercial diplomacy support for US business interests around the world.
2. Manufacturing and Services—Strengthens US competitiveness abroad by helping shape industry-specific trade policy.
3. Market Access and Compliance—Assists US companies and helps create trade opportunities through the removal of market access barriers.
4. Import Administration—Enforces US trade laws and agreements to prevent unfairly traded imports and to safeguard the competitive strength of US businesses.

Its trade statistics section provides US exporters' data base, statistical overview and tables outlining the export activities of US small and medium-sized enterprises.

Trendwatching.com

Trend watching.com, scans the globe for emerging consumer trends, insights and innovations. This data base is useful for consumer surveys performed by individual researchers of companies. The data regarding business and consumerism across 120 countries are updated regularly.

US census bureau

US Census Bureau provides population data and economic data, which are vital for evidence-based decision making in international business. The US Census Bureau conducts applied research on a range of demographic, economic, and health issues and work on a diverse spectrum of on-going and short-term projects, which is quite useful for international marketers. Its International Data Base (IDB) offers a variety of demographic indicators for countries and areas of the world with a population of 5000 or more.

EIU online databases

Economist Intelligence Unit (EIU), an independent business within The Economist Group, actively provides in-depth analysis and forecasts for an individual country's economy and political situation. The business managers can get regular forecast report about business environment of different countries of the world as well as data constituting the reports. The covered areas are economic growth, economic policy, inflation, exchange rates, political stability and effectiveness, elections and international relations. It also regularly published thought provoking articles on events that may impact on the latest forecast and frequent analytical articles on important trends within a country. Economist Intelligence Unit releases The Democracy Index, Government Broadband Index (gBBi), and Quality-of-Life Index, which researchers and analysts use extensively.

Doing business

World Bank launched 'Doing Business Project' during 2002 and shoot in to popularity in terms of use by international business managers instantly. The Doing Business Index of 183 countries allows comparing respective country status every year in terms of business environments prevailing across economies of the world over time. This provides a measurable benchmark to the business managers for understanding the ground situation of the countries of the world in comparative terms. It also serves as a resource for academics, journalists, private sector researchers and others interested in the business climate of each country.

Cornel university law school

International business requires information on legal aspect of doing business abroad so as to frame its strategy on entry, advertisement, recruitment, transfer of profits and various other aspects of business functioning. The legal procedures vary from country to country and information about the formalities is limited in its availability on the internet. This Cornel University

Website endeavours to provide online, digital versions of important legal documents of various countries.

Buy USA.infonet

This Website links to a market research library originally developed as a commercial guide for US companies doing business abroad. The country-wise guide provides information related to political and economic environment, market for US products and services, leading sectors suitable for US export and investment, trade regulations and standards, investment climate, contacts, market research and trade events.

Human development report online

The United Nations Development Programme (UNDP) publishes Human Development Reports. The first Human Development Report came up 1990 with a simply stated premise that people living in a country are its real wealth. The Human Development Reports, since its publication, has been considered as very rich not only because of empirical data and innovative approach towards measuring development but also for its profound impact on development thinking around the world as well. The path breaking Human Development Index (HDI) continued to be published year after year and proved to be the goal setting agenda for the countries of the world. These reports provide a good source of understanding the countries of the world so far as human development is considered.

Index of economic freedom

The Wall Street Journal and the Heritage Foundation of USA created the influential "Index of Economic Freedom" in 1995. Since then, this index is monitoring the progress of economic freedom around the world. The index monitors of the liberty, prosperity and economic freedom of people by creating 10 benchmarks that gauge the economic success of 184 countries around the world. The index covers 10 freedoms – from property rights to entrepreneurship – in 184 countries. Marketing researchers can also explore the data used in creating the index.

Trade port

TradePort is a US-based repository of free information and resources for businesses involved in all aspects of global trade. Created in 1996, TradePort is supported by an alliance of public and private sector trade promotion service organisations in California that assist businesses and their foreign counterparts in bilateral trade and investment opportunities.

Trade map

Trade Map, developed by the International Trade Centre UNCTAD/WTO (ITC), facilitates strategic market research, monitors both national and product-specific trade performance, reveals comparative and competitive advantage, identifies the potential for market or product diversification and helps businesses and trade support institutions to design and prioritise trade development programmes. The Website is free and can be used by a very simple registration process. The time series trade data structured in a six-digit level can be downloaded in MS Word or in Excel easily for further calculations to find answer to the following questions.

- What is the structure of the world market for a product?
- What are the countries with which a given country trades currently?
- Where are opportunities for market diversification?
- What tariff barriers exist in a specific market?
- Which countries are competing in a specific market and globally?
- What are priority markets and products for trade promotion?
- What countries supply the majority of one particular country's imports?
- What alternative sources of supply are available?
- In what areas does a particular country have competitive advantage?
- What is the current trade performance of a country and what are the products in which bilateral trade can be increased?

Management dynamics

Management dynamics (also known as trade wizard) the leading provider of one-stop solutions for global trade. The database has been designed to help companies grow and expand globally by simplifying and accelerating the import, export, and shipping of products between countries. It offers structured data such as those given below, which easily can be used by traders for their business needs.

- Product classification HS codes.
- Landed cost calculator for calculating landed cost of products in different ports.
- Trade party screening services by notifying agency or persons identified as unacceptable trading partners.
- Import and export regulatory compliance requirements.

MARKET RESEARCH ORGANISATIONS

The need for bringing research-based inputs in business decision making has been felt by international companies since the early days of internationalisation. As businesses cross different geographic barriers the uncertainties increase and hence, companies feel the need for updated information to know about what is happening in the competitive space. These researches are undertaken on various issues such as change in the competitive scenario in a specific sector, consumers' taste and preference survey in specific country, brand positioning exercise in target market, consumer segment identification survey for products of interest, etc. However, international market research demands continuity in data collection rather than a one-off study, so that trends can be observed for making strategic decisions at the right time. It may not be possible for all the companies to carryout research on their own. However, it is not uncommon to undertake in-house research on international market trends. Many companies are regular in doing so and many others carry out ad hoc research on some specific requirements only. Citibank does its own research in different countries to stay competitive. KFC carries out consumer preference research continuously. Metro Cash & Carry continues to do in-house market research in search of prospective markets internationally. However, there are companies which do not undertake research at regular intervals and initiate research only when warranted by the situation. These companies generally experience difficulties in conducting research on their own because of lack of in-house experience. Many others feel the requirement of longitudinal research studies to understand certain aspects which are vital for their existence in distant markets but again find themselves handicapped when their in-house personnel are not capable of doing international marketing research. Many a time, companies feel the requirement of fresh data collected through primary survey of foreign consumers so that strategic actions can be initiated. But lack of in-house capability discourages them for undertaking research. To cater to the requirements of such companies there are many market research organisations, small and big, which operate to provide their output, i.e., research based market knowledge as input to the companies striving to perform in the competitive world. There are many market research organisations that professionally work as researchers and carry out research to feed to other companies in need of such data. They are called the market research companies. Jack Honomichl, leading market research industry specialist of the US in association with Laurence N. Gold, the editor of 'Inside Research' of USA, annually ranks the revenue-generating market research companies operating in the United States. The American Marketing Association (AMA) also publishes the 'The Honomichl Top 50 Report' in the summer issue of its Marketing News every year listing the top 50 marketing research organisations. Some of the market research companies that are almost continuously figured in the top 20 Honomichl report during the current years are detailed below.

Market probe inc.

Dr T.R. Rao, a former university professor specialising in marketing and statistics founded the company during 1976 with headquarters in Milwaukee, Wisconsin, USA. The objective of the company was to provide marketing consultancy to the other companies of the world. The company made a beginning by conducting market feasibility studies, consumer research, image research and marketing effectiveness studies for various types of companies. From 1985 onwards, Market Probe involved itself in customer satisfaction and quality studies with the help of refined research methods, improved tools, proprietary software and modelling that generated the customised information. Today, the company is truly globalised and provides market research services to clients across the globe. It operates in countries such as United States, Canada, United Kingdom, India, Dubai, Beijing and Singapore, Belgium, Bahrain, United Arab Emirates, Hong Kong and China. As per the 2012 Honomichl top 50 marketing research listing in the US, Market Probe got the credit of earning 56% of its revenue from non-US clients indicating its global operations.

Nielsen holdings N.V.

Nielsen is the well-known global information and measurement company headquartered at New York and Diemen (Netherlands). The company is actively present in 100 countries around the world and provides clients from the different parts of world, the most complete understanding of what consumers watch and buy. Nielsen Global Consumer Confidence Index, established in 2005, tracks consumer confidence, major concerns and spending intentions among more than 28,000 internet consumers in 56 countries. Consumer confidence levels above and below a baseline of 100 indicate degrees of optimism and pessimism.

Kantar

Kantar is a market research, insight and consultancy organisation headquartered in London (UK), Kantar, founded in 1993, is a network of 13 specialist companies, with around 28,500 employees working in 100 countries across various research and consultancy disciplines. The group serves the marketing research requirements of many Fortune Top 500 companies. It is consistently securing advanced positions in the Honomichl top 50 marketing research listing in the US IMRB International (formerly Indian Market Research Bureau), is a part of Kantar and engaged in multi-country market research, survey and business consultancy in India and abroad. In fact, IMRB is one of the largest providers of market research in India with top clients such as BAT Group, Bharti Group, Cadbury, Ford Group, Frito Lay, GlaxoSmithkline, Heinz, Indian Airlines, ITC Group, Millward Brown, Nestle, Pepsi Group, Reckitt Benckiser, Research International, TVS Motors, Unilever Group, VST and so on.

Ipsos

Ipsos is a 1975 born global market research company, headquartered in Paris, France. Since 1990, the company underwent rapid internationalisation and created or acquired numerous companies throughout the world, and at present, it has presence in as many as 84 countries of the world. In fact during end-2011, Ipsos acquired another London based giant market research company Synovate, resulting in a newly combined Ipsos organisation that ranks as the world's third largest research agency.

J.D. power and associates

J.D. Power and Associates was established in 1968 as a marketing information services company in the US. It has its presence in North America, South America, Europe, and Asia and caters to the requirements of key business sectors across a variety of industries such as automobile, electronics, finance, health care, insurance, telecommunication, etc. The areas of J.D. Power consultancy include customer satisfaction research, market research, automotive forecasting, social media research and performance improvement programs. J.D. Power and Associates is a business unit of the McGraw-Hill Companies. In India, JD power has strong presence in the automobile sector where it conducts studies and provides consulting services.

GfK group

The GfK Group is a worldwide market research organisation headquartered in Nuremberg, Germany. It specialises in providing consultancy services in the three sectors, namely, custom research, retail and technology and media. It has a global presence in over 100 countries of the world. The GfK Group is very active in Asian countries such as Japan, Singapore, Hong Kong (acquired SoHealthAsia), and Thailand through its subsidiaries. In India GfK has made a joint venture with Nielsen India and specialises in retail store audits, consumer electronics, domestic appliances (major and small), telecom, photo and IT.

RESEARCH METHODOLOGY

Research methodology sets the tune of the research undertaken. It allows the research to take a particular direction and achieve the set objectives. It describes, explains and justifies various methods to be utilised in the proposed research to achieve the set objectives of the research scientifically. Therefore, international marketing researchers must frame the research methodology in accordance with the research questions required to be answered through the research. It must contain the research tools and techniques to be used in each step of the research in order to get answers to the research questions framed for the study. For example, if we consider seven broad category of research as relevant to international marketing and several other research areas under each category, then each type of research might have adopted specific methodology. Deciding on the right methodology is important as

Box 12.1 Researching on consumers' spending before entry

International companies with interest in emerging market are eager to know about the spending habits of the consumers living in countries such as India, Indonesia, Malaysia, etc. Information about consumer spending habits is a parameter in deciding entry in to a new country market for the first time since it allows the company to develop a suitable marketing strategy. However, it may be quite difficult for companies to continuously monitor the distant country market through installing research. Here, marketing research companies may be quite useful. For example, Nielsen monitors and publishes the Global Consumer Confidence Index for 56 countries. It reported that consumers' confidence in India had declined during 2012 due to weak employment sentiment, rising inflation, rise in fuel prices, comparatively low GDP and fall of the rupee resulting subdued spending behaviour. "The drop from the top position for India after nine quarters indicates a growing anxiousness amongst consumers today in the matter of job prospects and spending habits", said Nielsen India region president Piyush Mathur in support of the company's research-based findings. The published report of Nielsen noted that India registered a decline of four points in the index to 119 from the first quarter of 2012. The country is now at No 2 in the listing of most-confident countries in the world, along with Indonesia.

Nielsen, as a specialist company, conducted a global survey through polling of 29,000 online consumers in 58 countries across Asia Pacific, Europe, Latin America, the Middle East, Africa and North America and published the trend of consumer confidence and spending intentions.

The findings of the report would be useful for the international marketers to gauge the economic expectations and probable future spending behaviour of consumers of the countries covered under the survey.

Source: The Economic times, July 17, 2012

without it there could be problem in achieving the set objectives. In fact, this is the most critical part, as the outcome of the entire research process will depend on the correctness of the methodology.

However the choice of research methodology in international marketing will depend on the following six points:

(a) Approach for the study: Qualitative or quantitative.
(b) Type of data required to be used to do the research. Availability of secondary information relevant to the problem.
(c) Number and type of countries to be covered under the study and characteristics of these countries such as openness, accessibility to data due to government regulations or otherwise.
(d) Number of countries involved.
(e) The depth of the study: A longitudinal study involving a larger number of populations may require adopting a different methodology than a sample one-time survey.
(f) The researcher's limitation of the time and resources to be utilised for the study.

Selection of methodology

The following point may be helpful in selecting an appropriate methodology to be used in a research.

- Start with a thorough understand of the research questions framed for the study. It is nothing other than the pathways of obtaining, organising and analysing data to answer the research questions.
- Review relevant international marketing literature extensively and understand the methodologies used by the previous researchers. Sort list them in accordance with their applicability to the research in hand.
- Understand the data used by previous researchers in similar kinds of research requirement. Consider the level of difficulties to collect data from the target country of research undertaken.
- Understand the challenges associated with primary data collection and assess the level of ease in collecting data from target group using tools such as questionnaire, focus group discussion, etc.
- Assess secondary data availability and accessibility. Some secondary data may be available but its accessibility may be restricted and highly priced.

Once the exact methodology is finalised then the researcher may write down the sampling plan, geographic units, data collection and analysis techniques, action plan with time frame, financial budget, etc., for the research.

Research Design Equivalence

Research design equivalence occurs when the researchers find that there are no differences between his or her understanding of the tool, techniques, methods, measurement scales or any other elements of research design decided to use in the study and the way they have been used, unfolded or interpreted in the target country environment. In case on non-equivalence there will be problems related to correctness of the outcome achieved through the study.

Hence, the researcher must understand the level of research design equivalence before embarking on the actual study. In case of high degree of non-equivalence there could be two important problems.

1. Reworking on the research design which may require altogether new data set, tools, and techniques.
2. Time and money wasted in the process adds up to the frustrations of not being able to use the findings of the research in new product launching, segmentation or other business purpose in the target country.

The following are examples of the ways in which problems related to research design non-equivalence can present themselves.

- The researcher might have previously used focus group discussion as a research tool in understanding brand appeal in the home country situation and was optimistic of achieving correct result when used in the target country of research. However, in the target country the consumers hesitated to assemble in a place for focus group discussion unlike in the home country. Moreover, they were even reluctant to participate in a discussion because of cultural reasons. In that case, the research tool would fail to deliver expected result.
- The researcher used a Likert 7-point attitudinal scale in a research study previously conducted in the home country and included the same in the questionnaire to be applied in the target country. But when canvassing the questionnaire in the target country it was found that the respondents were uncomfortable with the 7-point scale. The conventional wisdom, in that country, was to use 5-point scale due to cultural reason. As a result, the respondents may either not answered the questions or unwillingly answered them. This disturbed the research outcome.
- The researcher framed questions in the questionnaire using his/ her own understanding but the respondents in the target country could not interpret the questions properly or understood their actual meaning because of cultural/or language translation problems. This resulted in distorted replies that did not fit in the purpose of doing the study.
- The sampling plan selected for the target country was found inadequate. But the same sampling plan provided wonderful result in the home country. This made the study in hand less representative.
- Problems may also arise due to language difference between the two countries. The researcher developed the questionnaire in the English language and then engaged, say, a Thai national to translate it into Thai language to canvass the questionnaire in Bangkok. But the translation was too literal and bookish which almost took away of the exact meaning out of it. So the Thai respondent could not answer it properly resulting distortion in result.

Equivalence checks

All the above examples clearly indicate the complexities associated with research design in a multi country study. Culture and other variables hugely disturb the different elements of research design in a marketing mix oriented study. Under such circumstances the reliability and validity of the research design comes under question mark. Therefore, experts in the field all along suggested that the international marketing researchers need to be extra careful while designing the research. However, in many cases, it becomes difficult for researchers to visualise the distant country culture and commits mistakes of non-equivalence in research design. Therefore, the researcher must ensure the following six types of equivalence checks before embarking on the actual research. Out of the six, the first three are construct equivalence and the other three are measurement equivalence.

Functional equivalence

Different products have different functional utilities in different countries due to socio-economic differences across the countries of the world. National culture and its underpinning in the socio cultural domain are primarily responsible for this to a large extent. For example, tea cups in China do not have handles like that of European countries. In oriental culture tea is not served that hot like that of European countries. In Vietnam, a bicycle serves the basic purpose of transportation in day-to-day life for many people but in Sweden, it will be used for pleasure riding or as an easiest way of doing physical exercise. It is important for international marketing researchers to know the functional utilities of the products in different countries while trying to capture primary data from the target country. For example, a researcher of an Indian bicycle manufacturer was working for positioning its reputed bicycle brand in Vietnam as well as Sweden. A single questionnaire was developed based on the researcher's own understanding of the bicycle's utility in Indian rural condition. When the questionnaires were canvassed in Vietnam as well as Sweden, they failed to elicit the requisite information for brand positioning because of non-functional equivalence in the concerned countries. Therefore, it is the job of the researcher to understand the functional equivalence of the product under study in the concerned countries of research and frame the research tools in accordance with the actual users' definition of the product.

Conceptual equivalence

Conceptual equivalence deals with differential product stimuli originating from products in different countries as a result of impact of culture. National culture and its underpinning on human value system are so strong that consumers accept or reject products based on their interpretation of product stimuli. For example, a packet of fragrant rice would create different stimuli to different people living in different countries. For the Indians it could lead to a thinking of a nice lunch or dinner with Mughal style biryani but for average Thai population it is an item for preparing sticky rice pudding. Milk can differently resonate with Indian mind as they could relate it with some exclusive sweet dish made of milk but it would not be the same with Americans or Japanese. The strong and positive stimuli from products are expected to create greater influence on consumers. While conducting a multi country research, therefore, how culture impacts the target groups value system and resulted interpretation of the products are very important aspects to be understood by the researcher. This understanding is useful for cross-country researchers while designing different research elements.

Category equivalence

Category equivalence deals with how differently or similarly consumers of different countries establish a product category based on their perception. The differences crop up due to socio-cultural differences that exist in the different countries of the world. For example, a person of Swedish origin would tend to categorise a three percent alcoholic beer as soft drink which can surely be consumed during lunch or dinner. But in India, it is neither common to take low alcoholic content beer as substitute for plain water nor would it be considered as soft drink. The culture of Sweden tends to categorise the product under soft drink. Sports Utility Vehicle (SUV) is looked upon by an average American under the category 'life style car' but in India an average individual would rate it as big car for the office goers. A BMW branded car would be immediately categorised by an average Indian people as 'luxury car' but the same car would be categories as 'high official car' in Thailand and 'office car' in Netherland. It is important that cross-country researchers understand the category building tendency of the consumers of the countries under research so that the research design elements are devised in a country-specific way to elicit right information from consumers.

Translation equivalence

Translation equivalence deals with how correctly a pre-designed research tool like questionnaire would perform in a foreign situation. To elicit required information a researcher often use questionnaire survey but the quality of information so gathered depends on how much the questions were intelligible to the target group. In a study plan when a questionnaire is first drafted in the language of the researcher's home country and then translated into the language of respondents' country, the challenge would be in terms of still keeping the same meaning relevant to the research context. Translation non-equivalence occurs when the translated questionnaire fails to be relevant in the foreign country context. To avoid non-equivalence, cross country researchers, traditionally, are using of simple tools such as direct translation, back-translation, parallel translation and committee approach. In direct translation, a bilingual translator may be trained in advance in the matter of translating a questionnaire from one language into another without distorting the originality of expression. In back-translation another bilingual translator may be engaged to translate the translated questionnaire back to the original language to check accuracy. The committee approach is where a committee is constituted with the experts of target country market for addressing translation equivalence problems.

Calibration equivalence

This equivalence is required for ensuring that the different measurement units used in different countries do not create disturbance during data collection. For example, if currency units are used in the questionnaire they are duly converted to the local or internationally accepted units. Similarly, the units of weights and measures are meticulously converted into the units specific to the country where the questionnaire will be used. If the questionnaire contains symbol, shapes, colour, etc., care should be taken to ensure that these convey the relevant meaning in the other countries as well. Indians are used to the unit 'litre' while purchasing fuel for their vehicle but Americans will be more comfortable with the 'gallon' as units of measurement while purchasing fuel for their vehicle. While purchasing egg a person of Indian origin naturally prefer to use dozen as the unit of purchase from shops which is not practiced in Thailand where people prefer to purchase a pack of eight eggs.

Metric equivalence

Often, the questionnaire may contain a scoring procedure to understand the situation on hand. A researcher may use a 7-point scale Likert scale in a questionnaire to understand the liking of Indian urban consumers in respect of brand preference. Now, can the same researcher use the same 7-point scale for a Thai or Vietnamese consumer? A Thai consumer would prefer a shorter scale to answer the questions posed in the questionnaire because of cultural reasons. Therefore, the researcher should understand the different equivalence effective in the countries under research while framing the questionnaire.

Box 12.2 Equivalence problem of a researcher in Vietnam

Mr Tran Thai Bao is the sole owner of the firm Quang Minh Co (QMC) Natural Handicraft Company located in the Thoi Hoa Ward, Ben Cat District, Binh Duong Province of Vietnam. He is also a member of Viet craft organisation, the apex organisation for handicraft product development in the government level. He worked with the Vietnam army after acquiring a law degree from Ho Chi Minh City. The company was set up 2003 and it presently markets its products in the world market. The company has earned good name from its buyers across different parts of the world because of innovative use of natural raw materials in producing quality handicraft products of various styles to meet the demand of interior decoration and outdoor activities. A few researchers from Indian Institute of Foreign Trade researching on the rapid development of Vietnamese handicraft industries approached Mr Tran Thai Bao with a questionnaire developed and tested in the Indian situation. The questionnaire was about ten pages contained about 44 questions. Introductory questions inventoried to elicit information about the identity of the respondent, enterprise size, type of ownership and years in business, etc. The different other questions included in the questionnaire were related to the production process, designing process, marketing mechanism, workers' skill, government support, process of developing relationship with the foreign customer, exporting mechanism with pricing of products, etc. To obtain a greater uniformity of responses and ease of data processing, many questions required the respondent to score on 7-point Likert-type scales, most of them ranging from 'very... to very, very...'. Indian researchers, on reaching Vietnam, contacted and met Mr Tran Thai Bao who was advised by Vietnam Handicraft association to co-operate with the researchers. The initial introduction from both sides took a little more time than expected. The researchers handed over the questionnaire and requested Mr Tran Thai Bao to fill it up. Since it proved impossible to capture so many product lines, the respondent was advised to think of his three most important products while filling up the questionnaire. He took a glance at the lengthy questionnaire written in English and appeared to become perturbed. The researchers noticed it and requested for a question–answer session instead, to which Mr Tran Thai Bao readily agreed. The question–answer session lasted for about two hours. At the end, the researchers thanked Mr Tran Thai Bao and left the place. After coming back to office, the researchers analysed the collected data and tried to fill up the questionnaire with the collected information. However, a number of gaps in information were noticed.

- The name of the finished products and raw material used in the production, as described by Mr Tran Thai Bao, were found difficult to be comprehended as no equivalent English name could be found out.
- The 7-point attitudinal response scale could not be filled up primarily due to difficulty in matching responses of Mr Tran Thai Bao with that of the grading in the scale.
- The finished products' utility for the buyers or product use, as described by Mr Tran Thai Bao, could not be understood.
- Understanding of the product costing was found to be very sketchy. The physical dimensions of many products were expressed in 'dong'. Sometimes the unit of length is also mentioned as the 'thu'ó'c'. The researches got confused while computing.
- The pricing methodology, as expressed by Mr Tran Thai Bao, was found to be based on relationship with the client rather than any cost plus profit system. The questionnaire, which was basically developed in India and tested on Indian handicraft producers before using in Vietnam situation had no scope to capture this peculiar system of pricing.

Source: Author

Questionnaire Length

Questionnaire length is definitely a concern for the international marketing researchers collecting data through canvassing questionnaires in different countries. Long and probing questions may not be entertained by a target group in one country while the reverse may be true for another country. Use of many attitudinal scales in a single questionnaire may make the respondent unwilling to cooperate with the researchers in one country but the opposite may be true in another country. In a particular country where economic activities are comparatively low, consumers with spare time in hand may be willing to accept lengthy questionnaire but in some developed countries people may not be able to spare much time to answer a lengthy questionnaire. Online questionnaire survey may not be a good proposition in many African countries because of low internet access while the same may be a favoured option in developed countries.

Types of Measurement Scales

Often international marketing researchers require understanding the altitude and preference for a certain product, brand, pricing, etc., so that positioning or repositioning can be made in the destination country market. Such researchers endeavour to capture the attitude of the target population by using different scales of measurement. Literally, the term attitude indicates towards a predisposed way of behaving or responding towards a person, thing or situation. Therefore, it is important for the marketers, in general, to understand the altitude and preference of the target population in the foreign country. Capturing the attitude of the target population require using of different scales of measurement. Some responses are required to be captured by assigning a number which is mutually exclusive. For example, a question that asks for 'number of years the brand is in the country market' can fetch a response like 'more than 12 years' or 'less than 12 years'. However, some responses are needed to be captured in a graded scale. For example, questions like 'What is the popularity of the brand in the past 12 years?' can fetch answers in an ordering scale where 1 means most popular and 5 means least popular and 2, 3 and 4 if the respondent desires to choose between most and the least. In this way, the researcher needs to use various scales to understand the exact preference of the consumer. There are four well-known scales of measurement, namely, nominal, ordinal, interval and ratio to capture response of respondents.

Nominal scale

A nominal scale is the simplest scale that allows a number to be assigned to identify or categorise an object but without any order. For example, gender can be categorised as male or female. It is used to record 'Yes' or 'No' types of response. This is very simple to use and categorise objects for further probing by using other higher level of scales to understand the order or distance. The respondents from any country surely would be comfortable in answering questions framed using nominal scale.

Example 1: Do you have professional relations in the neighbouring country?
Answer: Yes/No
Example 2: When you visit them? (Please tick)
Answer: During festival, During official meeting, During vacation, During business season.

Ordinal scale

An ordinal scale extends the information of a nominal scale and arranges or ranks particular objects, individual or attitude. For example, it can be used to rank attitude of the consumer such as' strongly agree', 'agree', 'neutral', 'disagree' and 'strongly disagree'. It provides an understanding of the comparative attitude of customers. Ranking type of ordinal scales are quite commonly used in international marketing research. It can be used easily with target group who are less qualified even. Ordinal scale uses non-parametric statistics.

Example 1: What was your effort for conscious search of professional contacts in the neighbouring country?
Answer: Very strong effort, Strong effort, Neutral, Made an effort for some time, Never made any effort at all.
Example 2: What is your preference order in terms of relationship development?
Answer:

Relationship	As brother	As friend	As partner	As official	As neighbour
Order of preference	1	2	3	4	5

Interval scale

An interval scale is a scale of measurement in which the magnitude of difference between measurements of any two units is same. This allows the researcher to clearly understand distance between them and order as well. Since it has equal units of measurement so calculating arithmetic mean of the scores are also possible. The most cited example of interval scale is Celsius scale of measuring temperature. Here the difference between each value is same. In Celsius scale, the unit of measurement is degree Celsius and in between 60 to 70 degree Celsius there would be interval of 10 degree Celsius. Interval scale is used to measure the attitude of customers in a specific order. Since this type of scale has no true zero so it has only arbitrary zero point. Equal-interval scales of measurement can be used for obtaining the opinion or attitude of individual.

Example 1: What is the level of you happiness when you find in a Lux branded soap?

Answer: 1-10-20-30-40-50-60-80-90-100.

This scale measures the difference at an interval of 10. If someone scores 20 and another 30 then it means the same difference of happiness between someone who score 80 and someone scores 90. Here, ratio of the intervals does not make any sense.

Example 2: Please indicate your acceptance level of Lux as a soap brand by scoring it on a scale of 5 down to 1 where 5 is excellent and 1 poor.

Answer:

Lux as soap brand	Excellent	Very good	Good	Fair	Poor
Your preference	5	4	3	2	1

Ratio scale

This is an interval scale with true zero point. This scale provides deeper meaning to order. An interval scale is a scale of measurement in which the magnitude of difference between measurements of any two units is meaningful. For example, categorising some brand as expensive or inexpensive is nominal. If we categorise brand as 1 = heavily expensive, 2 = moderately expensive, 3 = neither expensive nor inexpensive and 4 = inexpensive, then we have an ordinal level of measurement. If there is a standardised measure of brand and few brands under observation are for measurement, then interval scale is used. The brand may be rated using ratio scale also when one expresses expensiveness of a brand by saying that Brand A is 3 times more expensive than Brand B. Here, the expression in ratio or fraction make would make another sense which could not be captured by other scales described here.

International marketing researchers need to be careful while using different scales in different countries. For example, previous researcher opined that French attitudinal measurement can best be done by using a 20-point scale. However, researchers experienced with such measurements in India, often suggest going with a 5-point or 7-point scale to get the best result. Consequently, therefore, it seems that Indians are more attuned to a shorter scale than the longer scale as in France. Researcher also often reported that longer scale, even a 7-point scale, difficult to be used in Thailand, Cambodia, and Vietnam. The scales can be, therefore, culture-bound and hence require adjustment when used in a different cultural context to get accurate result in a multi-country study. Hence it is essential that the measurement tools used in one country study must be tested for construct equivalence as well as measurement equivalence before being put to actual use in another.

Country Scale Development

How an attitude measurement scale can be developed for a particular country? What alterations/modifications are required to be effected on it while using the same in another country? The answer to these questions came out nicely from the international companies' attempt to know the level of consumer ethnocentrism present in a country. International marketers have always been under the impression that due to prevalence of consumer ethnocentrism in a country, the products of another country are not being accepted. Basically, consumer ethnocentrism is a tendency where people would not like to purchase products produced by foreign companies backed by the thinking that purchasing foreign-made products is unpatriotic. Such 'closed thinking' is detrimental to the international marketing ambition. International companies, therefore, desperately wanted to know the level of consumer ethnocentrism present in a country. Shimp and Sharma[10] lent their wisdom and made a pioneering attempt to support the research requirement of international companies. They presented a scale to measure ethnocentrism of a country and named it as the consumer ethnocentric tendencies scale (CETSCALE). The process for development of the CET scale, described below, amply make the process of attitudinal scale development clear.

Preliminary study

The researchers attempted to understand ethnocentrism of US consumers first. They started eliciting response from about 800 consumers of the US on the subject matter of ethnocentrism. They wanted these target consumers to describe their views on whether it is right and appropriate for American consumers to purchase products that are manufactured in foreign countries.

Content analysis

In the next phase, researchers used a technique called content analysis for making inferences from the views received through the preliminary study. The responses were analysed objectively and systematically to understand the inner meaning of the communications in respect of their feeling of ethnocentrism. At this stage, researchers heavily used insights from existing relevant literature on the subject. In the process, researchers found seven important dimensions attached to consumers' orientations toward ethnocentrism. They were (1) consumer ethnocentric tendencies, (2) price–value perceptions, (3) self-interest concerns, (4) reciprocity norms, and (5) rationalisation of choice, (6) restrictions mentality, and (7) freedom-of-choice views.

Statement generation

Content analysis allowed the researchers to understand the orientation of the respondents correctly in the matter of ethnocentrism under the seven dimensions more intimately. Accordingly, 225 statements were generated to gauge all seven dimensions. These statements were put in a questionnaire

[10] Shimp, T.A. and S. Sharma (1987),"Consumer ethnocentrism: Construction and validation of the CETSCALE", *Journal of Marketing Research*, Vol. 24, Issue 8, pp. 280–289.

format for sending to the target group to elicit their response further. But before that six subject matter experts were engaged to validate each statement. In the process 125 statements were eliminated and 100 statements retained. Subsequently, another 17 statements were added from another research work to make the number of statements to 117.

Sample survey

This phase helped in eliciting response from the actual target group in the field. These 117 statements were mailed to 850 US households who were required to respond to them on a 7-point Likert scale. When the filled up questionnaires were received back, they were subjected to factor analysis. Statements with factor loading below 0.5 were not considered. This resulted in the reduction of statements to 54. These 54 statements found to be concerning five dimensions only.

Final survey

Now, these 54 statements in Likert scale concerning five dimensions formed the new questionnaire which was again circulated to massive 4000 US consumers across the country.

Questionnaire survey

The responses from these 4000 respondents were subjected to second confirmatory factor analysis to judge the five dimensions and the 54 statement structures. The result rejected one of the five dimensions and only 18 statements were found to be reliable and related to the retained four dimensions. The third confirmatory factor analysis was performed by further pooling of data from the four geographic areas into one overall sample. Simultaneously, confirmatory factor analysis was also performed on data from each of the four areas. The results across all the tests consistently indicated that 17 statements satisfied the 0.5 reliability criterion. These 17 statements represent the final CETSCALE as shown in the Table 12.7 below for country USA.

Table 12.7 CETSCALE for a country

S. No.	Items	Item reliability
1.	American people should always buy American-made products instead of imports.	0.65
2.	Only those products that are unavailable in the US should be imported.	0.63
3.	Buy American-made products. Keep America working.	0.51
4.	American products, first, last, and foremost.	0.65
5.	Purchasing foreign-made products is un-American.	0.64
6.	It is not right to purchase foreign products, because it puts Americans out of jobs.	0.72
7.	A real American should always buy American-made products.	0.70
8.	We should purchase products manufactured in America instead of letting other countries get rich off us.	0.67
9.	It is always best to purchase American products.	0.59

(Continued)

Table 12.7 *(Continued)*

S. No.	Items	Item reliability
10.	There should be very little trading or purchasing of goods from other countries unless if it is out of necessity.	0.53
11.	Americans should not buy foreign products because this hurts American businesses and causes unemployment.	0.67
12.	Curbs should be put on all imports.	0.52
13.	It may cost me in the long run but I prefer to support American products.	0.55
14.	Foreigners should not be allowed to put their products on our markets.	0.52
15.	Foreign products should be taxed heavily to reduce their entry into the US	0.58
16.	We should buy from foreign countries only those products that we cannot obtain within our own country.	0.60
17.	American consumers who purchase products made in other countries are responsible for putting their fellow Americans out of work.	0.65

Source: Shimp and Sharma (1987)

CETSCALE development process set a good example of how a country-specific measurement scale can be developed, almost in a textbook-prescribed way, for the use of international marketers. Later, the 17-item CETSCALE was tested by different researchers for cross-cultural validity in countries such as Japan and many European countries, including the East European ones. The result was mixed as some researchers found that a shorter 10-statement structure was valid but not the original one in some countries. Some researchers found that even the ten statements could not pass the tests of validity in the Netherlands.

Etic vs Emic Approach

Emic and Etic were the terms originally used by anthropologists in the context of differential human behaviour due to culture and researchers' possible available approaches to deal with them.

The Emic school of thought is pro adaptation. It favoured that since every country is unique in terms of human behaviour, the cultural variation has to be respected and preserved in the research undertaken. Therefore, researchers' job would be to highlight such differences by developing a research design in accordance with the local requirements. According to this school of thought, high degree of predictive validity of the research findings can be achieved with adaptation only.

Etic school of thought is against any bias due to presence of a particular culture in a country. It argues in favour of maintaining culture free mind by the researchers while doing multi country study. Hence under Etic approach, the researcher is encouraged to devise the international marketing research design, etc., in a culture-free environment. The research methodology, therefore, would be standard and non-deviating even though cultural differences across the target countries have been noticed.

Thus, the Etic and Emic schools of thought in respect of international business research lie on the two extreme ends of a continuum with one end being adaptation and other being standardisation. Researchers would be happier to handle Etic situation as it save time of effecting change in the research design every time a new country is encountered. However, in practical circumstances, the researchers need to have open mind and judiciously trade-off between the two extreme while devising the research design.

Units of Analysis

The unit of analysis, here, refers to the distinct geographic locations considered under the study and from which data will be collected. In international marketing research, deciding on the units of analysis may be a problem for researchers as any part of the globe may be the candidate for research location.

Local study

If the study pertains to a particular location of a country, then the unit of analysis may be considered as local. For example, research issues concerning one part of a country may have different implications for the company installing the research at different levels. In local study, data are collected from a specific part of a country for a certain purpose indicated in the objective of the study. Many foreign companies install such local studies in India in order to understand the specific situation and confine the data collection process to one of the Indian cities such as Pune or Mumbai. The primary benefit will be in terms of minimising the cost of doing the study. At the same time it will be representative of the country and can be extended to whole country situation if such need arises in future. For example, Reckitt Benckiser wanted to understand the brand appeal of Harpic toilet cleaner in India but executed the study only in Pune. KFC wanted to understand the preference of Gujarati population of India before launching its Vegetarian food line hence installed a research only in selected cities of Gujarat.

Country study

International marketing research may be conducted are being conducted where the unit of analysis is country. Many companies from developed countries are installing country-level study to gain an insight into the emerging countries with the understanding that these will be prospective countries of the future in terms of their product sales. American companies of the yester years, in their quest to know culturally dissimilar countries more intimately, opened specialised cells such as 'China research cell' to continue research on various areas in the whole of the country.

Regional study

In these days of regional economic integration, companies are increasingly attempting to shift research attention to the regional level instead of country level. For example, Mekong countries such as Cambodia, Lao People's Democratic Republic (Lao PDR), Myanmar, Thailand, and Vietnam are increasingly becoming the area of market study because of uniform socio-culture situation that can be included in one study frame-work.

Global study

The entire Universe as the unit of study has attracted international marketing researchers over the years. Global companies pursuing global strategies require more such studies to find out global convergence of preference, choice, taste, etc., of the consumers in a global perspective. These findings are helpful for the companies to position their products globally in a similar fashion and enjoy scale economics. McDonald was in need understanding the requirement of standardisation and customisation of products across the globe and hence installed research keeping the consumers across the globe as unit of analysis. The findings helped the company to set a 'gold standard' where in 80% standardisation of products was accepted keeping 20% flexibility for country-specific adaptive requirements.

Sampling Plan

Sampling plan is the most complicated part in international marketing research environment. Research study conducted in another country requires collection of requisite information from the target country to answer the research question. Therefore, first question that come in the mind of researcher is the representativeness and qualitativeness of the sample. The selected sample must have minimised bias, representativeness and size sufficiency. For example, Indian Institute of Foreign Trade (IIFT), an organisation involved in researching on trade and international business issues in India wanted to know competitiveness of the Vietnamese handicraft producers in relation to the Indian made handicraft in the US and other European countries. Specifically, the research objective was to know the Vietnamese products well and then position Indian products in the European and US markets where Vietnamese products are strong competitors. The researchers decided to install primary research in Vietnam for data collection and then bring them back to India for data analysis. The difficulty came in terms of selecting the representative sample of handicraft producers operating in Vietnam. Primarily, there was no existing database describing the handicraft producers on census basis so as to categorise and pick up a representative sample. Also, not much research interest has gone into the sector in Vietnam so as to make secondary sources available to the researchers. On the other hand, keeping in mind the geographic spread of the handicraft producers and the unorganised nature of production set up, it was almost impossible to resort to census type of survey. The decision making on sample plan really seemed to be difficult. The sampling plan selected, therefore, was snowball sampling where one producer identified another for survey and continues till in this fashion till representativeness is achieved. Another problem encountered was related to the literacy level of the respondent producers. Some were well-educated and researchers found that information gathering through questionnaire survey was very easy. But another segment of the sample was found to be illiterate rendering information collection very slow and time consuming. In such situations, researchers reportedly felt biased towards the literate segment. Also, respondents from the literate segment were found be inclined to refer only to a particular handicraft product line which again found against the objective set for the study. There were also vast variations in the demographic pattern and psychographic characteristics of the respondents. The researchers had to increase sample size to neutralise the negative effect of demographic and psychographic variations of the respondents.

CHAPTER SUMMARY

1. The information requirement of an internationalising company can be broadly divided into at least four broad types. These four types are: (1) Information related to foreign market entry (2) Information related to mandatory requirements (3) Information related to the culture of the country and (4) Information related to marketing mix decision. The depth of information required for each of the four types and research requirement thereof depends upon various factors.
2. Research-based articles published in various journals related to international marketing provide good understanding of the problems on hand and solutions achieved by the previous researchers. There are eight broad categories of research studies available in international marketing, which could be quite handy for the researchers to understand a given marketing problem and to find out how the academic world in international marketing has handled such situations and come out with their findings.
3. Data for international marketing research can come from primary as well as secondary sources. As the basic nature of research is international, the primary sources are from more than one country involved in the research. Because of multi-country involvement, it becomes time consuming and expensive. Secondary sources data are comparatively easy to gather but suffer from the problem of possible differential use, i.e., the possibility of the data having been collected for some other purpose that does not match with the present context at hand.
4. It is important to decide on the appropriate methodology for achieving the objective of research. In fact, this is the most critical part as the outcome of the entire research process will depend on the correctness of the methodology. A review of literature and the methods used by the previous researchers helps in identifying the relevant methodology. However, the researcher must take into account the specific research objectives he or she wants to accomplish before making a final decision.
5. When companies are installing cross-cultural research, they are faced with a number of challenges related to the cultural differences across countries. Six types of equivalence issues are required to be addressed by the researchers; the first three are construct equivalence and other three are measurement equivalence. Otherwise, the result of the research gets diminished.
6. Questionnaire, as a tool of primary research in international marketing, is very effective but it needs careful handling. The length of the questionnaire is to be adjusted in accordance with the country-specific requirements. Translation of the questionnaire maintaining the same rhythm and meaning in the foreign language is a must to achieve the desired objective.
7. Deciding on the representative sample is another problem in foreign country research. This is because there may not be an existing database at the secondary level which allows the researcher to pick up a representative sample. Another reason of sample complexity is that the sample which seems to be justified in the home country research situation may prove to be inaccurate or insufficient in the context of foreign country research.

QUESTIONS FOR REVIEW

1. How and where are the following companies required to do international marketing research?
   a. Wall Mart coming to India with 100% ownership.
   b. A day before the US brand opened its first outlet in a south Delhi mall, it put up signboards around the area for a "preview for international travellers" with the telling rider, 'Entry

restricted only to holders of international passports'.

c. Italian fashion brand Diesel is all set to launch its first store in India by the third week of March. The brand is making its India foray in partnership with Reliance Brands, a unit of India's business corporate house Reliance Industries. Earlier, Diesel had tried to enter India through a tie-up with Arvind Brands but its attempts fell through. The new company, Diesel Fashion India Reliance, will initially open five stores. Two of these will be in Mumbai and one each in Delhi, Hyderabad and Bangalore. Though the collection will range from ₹2000 to ₹50,000, the average price of jeans will be in the range of ₹8000 to ₹17,000.

d. Paul Smith is going global. It has a collection that is wholesaled to 66 countries and has 17 shops in England. Paul Smith shops are found in London, Paris, Milan, New York, San Francisco, Los Angeles, Antwerp, Hong Kong, Singapore, Taiwan, Korea, UAE and at over 200 locations throughout Japan. Paul remains fully involved in the Japanese business; designing the clothes, choosing the fabrics, approving the shop locations and overseeing every development within the company. Paul Smith also has impressive and diverse showrooms in London, Paris, Milan, New York, and Tokyo.

2. Red Tape Brand of Mirja International from India became famous in European countries but could not muster up the courage to invade the Chinese market with the brand having a Western image. However, Chinese market is big and the growing craze for Western brands of the Chinese teenagers is a well-known fact. The company officials are thinking of installing an international market research which will give them enough information to make up their plan of China entry. You have been approached by Mirja International to submit a possible area of research. Draft a research plan to be submitted to the company indicating the research areas.

3. What are the different methods of primary data collection in a foreign market? An Indian handicraft company has installed a research in Vietnam to explore the market and send products to the country through export. First, describe the research questions that the company would like to be answered and then indicate the primary data collection method to be employed in the research.

4. What are equivalence problems in international marketing research? Describe the different components of establishing equivalence in international marketing research.

5. What are different types of research in international marketing conducted by academics and published in journals of repute? How can they be of help to other international marketers conducting research? What would be your suggestion towards their practical implication while doing business abroad?

6. You are hired by a medium-sized apparel company of India internationalising for the first time to do some secondary research before sending their products to Latin American countries. The company is looking for information on their market size, tariff barriers and tariff rate, consumer demographics, apparel imports and business regulations. How would you obtain the data on the internet?

7. Diesel brand has just entered in India and is showing early indication of success. Now, the company wants to take the brand to two other Asian countries, Indonesia and Vietnam. Design a questionnaire for brand awareness to be canvassed in both the countries.

8. What are the scales of measurements? What is the process of a country scale development involving attitude measurement of, say for a research theme, "only green brands are selected by consumers"?

9. What is ETIC vs EMIC dilemma in carrying out international marketing research? How can this be resolved?

10. Bundaberg Rum from the Bundaberg distillery of United Distillers Vintners (UDV), Australia, became an icon spirits brand in Australia. In many developed countries UDV command market leadership through well-established global brands. Korea has been identified as a potential market for Bundaberg Rum and hence, it initially planned to enter the market through export even though UDV has some reservations in creating new business at this location. Primarily, Korea is a very culturally sensitive nation. A product's success in Korea can depend on the distribution that is achieved. The company is looking for an established market research agency of repute to which it can handover the research requirement before final entry. But before that, the company wants to draw an outline of research that the company would require at this stage. You are required to draw the outline of the research and introduce

the possible international research agency for carrying out the work.

11. Kraft Foods of USA (It is principally engaged in manufacturing and marketing of packaged food and beverages with world famous brand names of Kraft such as Maxwell House, Oscar Mayer, Oreo, LU, Jacobs Coffee, Tang, Toblerone, etc.) entered China more than 20 years back; but for many years, it was not doing well. This overthrew Kraft's original belief that what was good for one market would also be good for all markets. To win over Chinese customers, Kraft realised that even a global corporation must transform itself, letting local managers make decisions based on their understanding of the market. Kraft learnt that building up a local management team to maintain solid connections with the Chinese distributors is a major part of doing retail business in China. The local team assessed the situation and found that Oreo was too sweet for Chinese consumers. They found that the US price of 5 Yuan (73 cents) for 14 cookies was too heavy for them and the package size was too big. Kraft opened a new facility in Suzhou Industrial Park, near Shanghai, for cookie research and development which allowed Kraft to create new product platforms tailored to suit local tastes. Kraft, thereafter, made a radical move by launching new Oreo products such as Oreo Wafer Sticks, Oreo Wafer Rolls, Oreo Soft Cakes and Oreo Strawberry Creme. The price was reduced and packaging was readjusted to make it small (repacked in a smaller size at 2 Yuan [29 cents] for seven cookies). Kraft then began an extensive advertising and marketing campaign to promote its new range of products. Thanks to these reforms, China is now the world's largest Oreo market outside the United States, with 41.9% growth in measured consumption over the last year, according to ACNielsen. In other words, Chinese consumers ate about 42% more Oreo cookies during the survey period than in the previous year.

    Do you support the localisation effort of Kraft? Why or why not? How it may affect the company's global marketing strategy considering the fact that Kraft Foods operates in over 70 countries and sells its products in over 160 countries across the world?

12. In December 1995, Beverages India released its energy drink, Boosta, in India. This product proved a great success in the Indian market and now dominates the company's sales. In addition to the quality of the product, a major reason for its success has been its eye-catching packaging and effective branding. Boosta is a lightly carbonated, new age beverage containing a uniquely balanced blend of pure spring water, natural amino acid, vitamins and caffeine. Boosta, as a product, provides an immediately discernible boost when an energy lift is needed. The CEO of Beverages India, on his recent tour to South Africa, got attracted to its potential market. His initial research on the market revealed the following: the total value of the South African energy drinks market was AUD 134 million (or 884.4 million South African Rand) during 2008, the total consumption was 204 million litres and total production was 218 litres; disposable income is increasing but this may be within a small segment of the population; black empowerment is a key consideration in South Africa, but there are concerns that this movement will benefit only a certain black elite; unemployment is still rife at approximately 30%; achieving effective distribution in township areas is a key concern, especially as far as physical distribution in the face of criminal activities is concerned; high levels of illiteracy exist in the country. Segmentation is complicated because there are a multitude of black cultures and sub-cultures with no clear regional delineation.

    Evaluate the target market selection process of the company Beverages India. What further market research would be required to consolidate the decision to enter the South African market?

13. Identify a consumer goods company of Indian origin in your locality with subsidiary in another country and visit the company to find out the research requirements to enhance its product marketability. Develop one researchable synopsis on the basis of research requirements indicating literature survey hypotheses and methodology.

14. Today, Indian consumers have wide access to foreign goods. So, a natural question arises about the ethnocentrism of Indian consumers, as it stands today. Choose 100 students of your university through random sampling and run the 17 statement CETSCALE to understand the level of ethnocentrism. Also test the internal consistency of the CETSCALE in the Indian context.

15. Marketing mix decision oriented studies were large in number amongst all the eight categories of international marketing studies mentioned in this chapter. Choose twenty contemporary and important articles from a database like Ebsco/Emerald/Science Direct based on your accessibility level. Understand the research problems

that were taken by each author, the geographic regions covered, mythology used and conclusion arrived. Prepare a comparative chart based on these parameters and present it in the classroom. Repeat the process for the other seven categories of the study as well.

End Case: Amrit Sudha Aqua Water Extends Market to China[11]

The Chinese government has shown active interest in ensuring availability of quality drinking water to its population during 2008. It constituted a research team for the purpose, which carried out spot checks of 148 kinds of bottled drinking water produced by 145 enterprises in 20 provinces and cities such as Beijing, Hebei, Shanxi, Heilongjiang, Shanghai, Jiangsu, Zhejiang and Henan. The result of the checks was satisfactory with the overall quality rate found to be 87.2% (http://www.researchinchina.com). However, with regard to availability of quality water, the research team found that the supply of potable water mainly came from three sources, namely, bottled (barrelled) pure water, household water purifier and pipe direct-drink water supplies. Though government was satisfied with the quality aspect, one finding of the research team raised concern. The team indicated that the demand for quality drinking water supply would be steadily increasing in the years to come with the development of the economy. Bottled (barrelled) pure water demand was for 35 million cubic metres in 2010 and expected to be 150 million cubic metres in 2025. Similarly, the demand for water from household purifiers would be increasing from 11 million cubic metres in 2008 to 240 million cubic metres in 2025. The demand of pipe direct-drink water would also show a similar increase from 7 million cubic metres to 210 million cubic metres during 2025. This was, of course, not at all a bad news for the household water purifier manufacturer as numerous enterprises manufacturing water purifiers in China were competing with each other on the pricing front because of acute competition in the market. Foreign companies such as UK-based Unilever started selling its Pure it brand in Nanjing, Suzhou, Wuxi, Changzhou in Jiangsu province and Shanghai. Amway also entered the market with a bang when it introduced its 6000-Yuan water purifier which attracted the customers instantaneously. Beijing-origin Water Technology Limited claimed to have core competency in membrane technology, attracting Chinese customers with its water purifier product line through an enviable network comprising 100 dealers across the country. According to the China Water Purification Association, there are more than 3000 companies, big and small, in the water purifier business in Beijing with prices ranging from a few hundred to a few thousand Yuan. Interestingly, no brand could claim to have a majority market share in a fragmented market. There was no significant regulation-centric entry barrier for foreign companies and almost no prescribed requirement of quality from Chinese authority. Products could be marketed with certification from other countries such as the US, Japan, India, etc. Recent preference survey has shown clear inclination towards water purifiers using membrane technology, particularly for the rich Chinese segment.

Amrit Sudha Aqua Water Company, a medium-sized home water purifier as well as industry water system manufacturing company located in eastern India, had been doing well in the Indian market. This company targeted customers who were not swayed by big brand names but relied on home-grown companies offering water purification solutions at a low cost. In fact, Amrit Sudha capitalised on the tag line "first fully safe water purifier" and made the brand name acceptable in the Indian market by operating in a niche segment. The product also found customers in Bangladesh and was exported to the country with considerable success. Recently, the company also managed to receive a big export orders for home water purifiers from a local Chinese company that was on the look-out for cheap but effective products. In India, Amrit Sudha had chosen the network marketing business model as a way of creating a recurring revenue structure in the home business.

During the recent visit to China, Mr Kumar, owner manager of the company, noticed that the Chinese importing company simply added local

[11] The case 'Amrit Sudha Aqua Water extends market to China' has been created by the case writer Dr Gautam Dutta of Indian Institute of Foreign Trade as a basis for class room discussion rather than to illustrate either effective or ineffective handling of a business situation.

brand names to the imported products from Amrit Sudha and marketed them through a dealer network. The importer had three different brands, namely, Tanaka, Nongfu and Chimata water filters. Mr Kumar, to his surprise, noted that the original manufacturer's name Amrit Sudha was totally unknown to the Chinese customers. The comparatively low cost of Amrit Sudha was the point of attraction for the Chinese importer as the company was generating comparatively more profit than the original manufacturer of the product. Mr Kumar felt tempted to market his products directly to the Chinese market, particularly when there was no entry barrier imposed by the Chinese authority. He saw that reasonably good profit could be generated by direct marketing in China than exporting its manufactured product almost as a commodity. Backed by this temptation, while in China, Mr Kumar collected the following information.

1. The price of the products is strategically decided by the importing company keeping in view the price of the competitors. In shaping the price of a product, a company should know the reference prices, i.e., what the other brands are charging for the same. The Chinese consumers are fond of price–quality inferences. Many consumers take price as a quality indicator. A more intensive pricing research, therefore, needed to be done before taking a call on direct marketing in China.
2. Water purifiers are needed to be made available through intensive distribution system because it was customary to make these products easily available in the local markets. The company may, in the beginning, opt to choose selected cities to understand the distribution system first before final pushing its products in the market more intensely.
3. There can be zero to 5 levels of intermediaries involved in the supply chain before the product reaches the end consumer. Distributors, wholesalers and retailers constitute the intermediaries involved in the system. The intermediary margins are generally 2% to 5%.
4. Building excitement around the launch of a new water purifier will be difficult in China but it is a requirement. Attracting the attention of the prospective customers through media involvement will be required and just a simple product announcement will not settle the purpose.
5. It will be a challenging task for Amrit Sudha to position the product in the Chinese mind. The product will have to be positioned as 'something new and innovative' to which Chinese consumers would feel attracted. The innovative feature of the product that could be focused on in the media campaign needs to be identified before actual entry into China.
6. Advertising and public relations strategy will be very crucial for the company. The company may use some useful public relation tool for developing people contact. How an effective public relationship development exercise can be developed will, of course, have to be researched out. The local government controlled television may not be very supportive for taking an all-round exercise of appearing constantly on the top of prospective customers mind.
7. With increased levels of affluence, the young Chinese young population is seen inclined to consume fruit juices and flavoured water. Traditionally, tea consumption is also very high in the Chinese market. These two factors can contribute to the decrease the demand for pure water. In fact, various beverage industries foreign origin from USA and Japan are mushrooming, in recent years, in China.
8. While primarily the product requires catering to a segment, the segment in question needs to be defined. Mr Kumar was thinking of the following:
   Geographics: The immediate geographic target is the city of Shanghai, China.
   Demographics: The target would be the married male population. Age: 26–44.
   Behaviour factor: Health-conscious, social and mingling with friends, attends social gathering regularly.
9. Finally, Mr Kumar was thinking of the brand name 'Amrit Sudha'. It might not have acceptability in China. In fact, Chinese were showing inclination to Western brand names than oriental ones. Mr Kumar was not in a mood to adopt either a local name or a Western name. But he was not sure about what needs to be done in this respect because someone told him about Coca Cola's naming problem in China. He was thinking that this issue had to be addressed before launching the products in China.

CASE QUESTION

Q1. You are appointed as consultant of international marketing for Amrit Sudha Aqua Water Company that manufactures and markets home water purifiers in India and right now exports to countries such as Bangladesh, Nepal, and China. The company has a product line of high-quality home water purifiers but maintains a low profile in brand building and marketing in India. The company is deciding to market the home water purifier in China where the company currently exports its unbranded products. The CEO of the company after coming from a short China visit got excited over the possibilities of directly marketing the product by opening a sales office which will also act as the importer and marketer. However, to proceed with the plan he has some queries which need to be answered before making final financial commitments in this direction.

As a consultant, you have been entrusted with the task of developing the international marketing research plan covering the issues the CEO of the company raised in the case. Develop a research plan you will be undertaking on behalf of the company indicating there search issues, objectives, methodologies, details of survey tools and techniques, data availability and sources, time frame, financial involvement, limitations, caveats, etc. Also highlight the requirement of primary information in this case as this may increase the financial involvement, and develop a questionnaire if you require primary data to be collected from China. You are also required to highlight the equivalence issues to be faced while proceeding with the study. Finally, make a power point presentation of your research plan covering all the issues in front of Mr Kumar to get final approval from the company to do the research.

FURTHER READINGS

Okazaki, Shintaro and Barbara Mueller (2007), "Cross-cultural advertising research: Where we have been and where we need to go", *International Marketing Review*, Vol. 24, No. 5.

This is an interesting paper dealing with cross-cultural advertising research. It listed previous cross-cultural advertising research first and then suggested a new directions in understanding the role that culture in cross-national commercial communications. It found that most of researches cultural in cross-cultural advertising research had dealt with cultural value analysis. Content analysis was the most widely used methodology the researchers used. In terms of geographic coverage, North America and the original European Union (EU) member states were the most frequently investigated. However, there are much paucity of research covering countries in Latin American, Middle East, and African markets.

Li Tiger and Cavusgil S. Tamer (1995), "A classification and assessment of research streams in international marketing", *International Business Review*, Vol. 4 (3), pp. 251–277.

This paper categorises and presents six research streams that had been published in different journals related issues in international marketing. The articles also throws light on the main themes that these articles have dealt with. This paper allows the readers to understand different studies took place over the years and their contents and focus areas.

Young, Robert B. and Rajshekhar G. Javalgi (2007), "International marketing research: A global project management perspective", *Business Horizons*, Vol. 50, pp. 113–122.

This paper brings out the important understanding that international marketers should know about the differences between domestic and international marketing research. This paper depicts a framework for conducting international market research. It narrates several challenges that the international marketers must consider while getting engaged in global market research. This paper indicates different operational problems that the researcher encountered during primary data collection and questionnaire construction.

Cadogan, John (2010), "Comparative, cross-cultural, and cross-national research: A comment on good and bad practice", *International Marketing Review*, Vol. 27, Issue 6.

This article deals with problems associated with handling multi-country data while conducting research. This article also provides guideline for those who have data from multiple countries and are planning to write a comparative or cross-cultural/national research paper.

Sinkovics, Rudolf R., Elfriede Penz and Pervez N. Ghauri (2005), "Analysing textual data in international marketing research" *Qualitative Market Research*, Vol. 8, Issue 1.

This article provides guidance for the analysis of qualitative data and observations in order to carry out systematic international marketing research.

Malhotra, Naresh K. (2001), "Cross-cultural marketing research in the twenty-first century", *International Marketing Review*, Vol. 18, Issue 3.

This article comments on the developments that have taken place over the years in the subject area of cross-cultural marketing research. It also narrates methodologies for international marketing research.

Tan, Qun; Sousa, Carlos M.P (2011), "Research on Export Pricing: Still Moving Toward Maturity", *Journal of International Marketing*, Vol. 19, Issue 3.

This paper reviewed 98 articles, published in leading journals, related to export pricing in order to understand the direction of research in this particular area. The authors observed that in the reviewed article, there exists a huge void in terms theoretical underpinning. As a result, the research designs were different in different studies leading to inconsistent findings and conclusions. On the basis of these findings, the authors discuss several implications and consider directions for further research.

Lei, Li (2007), "Multinationality and performance: A synthetic review and research agenda", *International Journal of Management Reviews,* Volume 9, Issue 2.

This paper provides an extensive review of the literature in tabular form on the relationship between a firm's multinationality and performance that drew huge scholarly attention in international business in the past years. The article examined a large number of empirical studies critically and came out with systematic explanation of the main constructs of large number of articles published in the past decades. This paper categorically explained samples used by the past researchers, key intervening variables used, analytical methods used, and control variables taken in order to arrive at the findings and conclusions. In addition, it has proposed a more structurally designed research agenda that endogenises multinationality and takes into account the motivation of firm internationalisation.

Organising for Global Marketing

13

Learning Objectives

After studying this chapter, you should be able to:

- Understand the pattern of organisational development in international business organisation.
- Learn the different forms of global organisation structure and their advantages and disadvantages.
- Understand the effects of an inappropriate organisational structure on marketing effort of international business organisation.
- Understand the different forms of organisational structure available and their right fit with the business.
- Comprehend the international structure stage model of organisation development.
- Appreciate the importance installing right of organisational structure for achieving business excellence.

Chapter Overview

One of the important aspects of international marketing is the existence of an efficient organisation supporting the internationalisation process. As the organisation steps into the internationalisation process, the mode of management continues to behave in a centralised fashion at least for a certain period of time. Then, the situation arises where organisation demands reducing centralisation and increase localisation as well, as the company expands its operations to more number of countries. At this juncture, issues such as redesigning the organisational structure appropriate to manage internationalisation, balancing between centralisation and local autonomy, allocating responsibility of the country heads, etc., gain key importance. Another key issue, at this stage, is to ensure coordination inside the organisational structure, irrespective of its global spread, which allows learning from the different country operations to be effectively ploughed back and disseminated across the organisation. Therefore, the objective of this chapter is to discuss the issues an international company faces as it grows from single country presence to multi-country presence and then spreads its reach globally, and in each stage to show how the organisational structure is required to support the marketing process adequately.

Opening Vignette

Organisational rejig is a must for Himalaya

Today's ₹900–1000 crore multi-country business empire of Himalaya Drug Company actually had a long torturous evolution over a period of 82 years. Mr M Manal, the founder, made a humble beginning with only a hand-cranked tableting machine and a purely entrepreneurial innovative mind as capital. Almost a one-man organisation at that time, the company grew up over the years to have offices in Dubai, Singapore, the US and India. The company continued to innovate herbal-based products to make them brands themselves. Liv 52, a liver formulation that ensures optimum liver function was the first block buster drug from the company followed by Bonnisan, Pilex, Cystone, Septilin and many others from its five product lines, namely, pharmaceuticals, personal care, animal health, baby care and nutrition health. As in the case of many family businesses, the organisation grew under the stewardship of Manal family. The founder's son, Meraj Manal, joined Himalaya in 1964 and put in efforts to modernise the production system and enhance both market and marketability of the products. During 1975, the size of the company grew bigger and the headquarters was shifted to Bengaluru from Dehradun. During 1986, Meraj Manal became Chairman of the company and soon focussed on developing the organisational structure of the company to manage business growth. Another organisational level was created during 1996 with the induction of Mr Ravi Prasad, a highly experienced and professionally qualified manager, as Vice-president of international marketing, who would be reporting to the Chairman of the company. Meraj's visionary influence and Ravi's expertise saw this company marketing its products in countries such as Russia, Commonwealth of Independent States (CIS), Bulgaria and Romania, the Middle East and many other countries including the US. Another level in the organisation structure was created when during 2005 Ravi was promoted as Executive Director reporting to the Chairman of the company. The company further expanded its markets and during 2012, its products were sold in 60 countries across the world including India. The domestic business accounted for 60% of its total revenue and the company expected international business to gather further momentum to account for 50% of the revenue in the next few years. Apart from pharma, Himalaya's two other lines of businesses were personal care and animal health and these were becoming hugely popular in the developed country markets. At that juncture, the company felt further need for an organisation overhaul. The product line based organisational structure soon gave way to area-based organisational structure. Four area-based subsidiaries were created during 2012 and each one was under the leadership of a separate CEO. CEO, Singapore, was entrusted to look after business interests in the Asia–Pacific region; CEO, USA, had America and Latin America under his wings; CEO, India, was in charge of Indian operations and CEO, Dubai, looked after the operations in Europe, the Middle-east and Africa. The CEOs of all areas are to report to Mr Ravi Prasad, Executive Chairman of the company, who in turn, will be reporting to Mr Meraj Manal, Chairman of the company[1].

When this story of evolution of organisational structure was told to the students of international marketing in the classroom the students wondered, "Why did the product-oriented organisational structure had to give way to location based structure? What are its advantages over the others? Who will now have command over the R&D division, which is very essential for this type of company? Will it be shared by all? What will be the flow of command then? What are different types of organisational structure an international company can have? In fact, how does organisational structure evolve in an internationalising organisation? What support must a company get from its organisation structure?"

The new pressures have transformed the global competitive game, forcing the companies to rethink their traditional worldwide strategic approaches, The new strategies, in turn, have raised questions about the adequacy or organisational structures and processes used to manage worldwide operations.

—Christopher A. Bartlett, Sumantra Ghoshal

INTRODUCTION

Nestle, founded in 1886 by Henri Nestle, is now a worldwide business. To run its worldwide business, it has 15 members in the Board of Directors, of which 14 are independent members. Peter Brabeck-Letmathe is the present Chairman of the Board as well as the company. Previously Mr Letmathe was the CEO of Nestlé and in that capacity he gathered huge experience of running the worldwide business. The Board of Directors, for effective corporate

[1] http://www.himalayaglobalholdings.com/abouthimalaya/

FIGURE 13.1 Nestle organisational structure, 2014

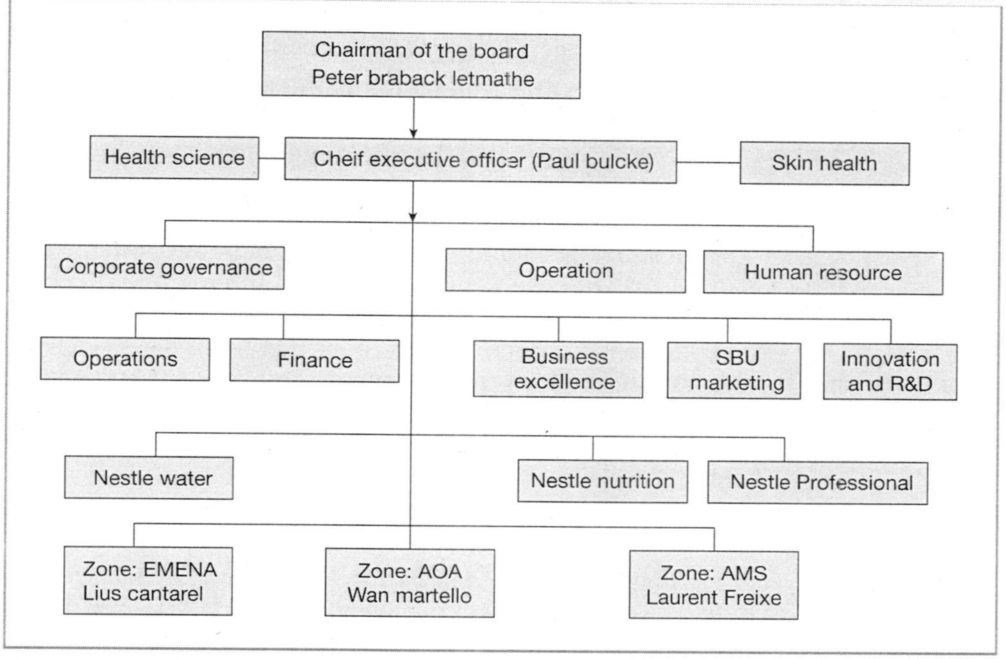

Source: www.nestle.com

governance, is supported by four functional committees, such as Audit Committee, Finance Committee, etc. The company has another Executive Board with 13 designated board members to look after the company operation worldwide and report to the Board of Directors through the Chairman of the company. Paul Bulcke, a Belgian national with Dutch mother tongue, is the current chairman of the executive board. Paul started his career with Nestle in 1979 when he was just a marketing trainee looking after sales in three countries, namely, Switzerland, Spain and Belgium. Paul continuously grew with the organisation and served the company as market head of various countries such as Germany, Peru, Czech and Slovak Republic. Just before becoming the CEO of the company Paul successfully held the post of Executive Vice-president for Zone Americas. The Nestlé Group is managed by geographies, Zone EMENA (Europe, Middle East and North America), Zone AMS (Americas) and Zone AOA (Asia/Oceania/Africa) for most of the food and beverage business. The three zonal heads directly report to the CEO of Board of Executives. However, its business of Nestlé Waters, Nestlé Nutrition, Nestlé Purina Petcare, Nespresso, Nestlé Professional and Nestlé Health Science are managed on a global basis. In general, Nestle keeps a flat and flexible organisation structure with few levels of management (Figure 13.1). The flatness of the organisation structure was quite helpful over the years to bring speed in decision making and act faster in case of any emergency in any part of the world. The Maggi controversy in India and subsequent quick decision making in taking the product off the shelf once again proved this point. Its culture of less bureaucracy and faster decision making has always been appreciated by the international business strategist. It has always given due importance to the requirement of cross-functional communication across the organisation to support each other's cause and most importantly to develop the organisational learning as a whole.

Like many other companies doing business in the food sector, Nestle also could not avoid adaptation altogether. It grew by believing in the viewpoint that every country had specific requirements which may be dissimilar to the others. Therefore, the company delegated total administrative responsibilities to the country heads or product heads to draw their operational strategies for product development, marketing, manufacturing, communications, etc., in accordance with their specific requirements. The corporate headquarter always remained active in making vital decisions such as for acquisition, expansion and financing decisions but not to day to day decisions pertaining to country business management. This localisation strategy of the company continued for a long time. Helmut Maucher, who was the CEO during 1990 to 1997, analysed effectiveness of this strategy for the company seriously. Mr Maucher noticed that the localisation strategy was creating administrative gaps between the thousands of operating divisions and the corporate managers. He understood that localisation strategy, although allowing the company to become market friendly, was creating a vacuum between the top management and operating level management. The company higher ups, for the sake of localisation, entrusted responsibilities of decision making quickly on the divisional managers in the matter of fast changing food business, but retained the system of obtaining administrative approval from the corporate managers of headquarter. This was very much confusing and made the system of organisational communication slower resulting communication delays, overlapping of authorities and responsibilities within the organisational system. As a result, the causes and effects of administrative malfunctioning were eventually affecting the marketing ability of the company. Furthermore, the system was also making the country managers avoiding taking decisions by themselves resulting a pure bureaucratic system engulfing the organisation. The faster cross-divisional interactions and decision making process which for long considered as vital for achieving cost efficiency in sourcing, cross fertilisation of knowledge, etc., were taking the back seat. Mr Maucher realised that the company was operating neither in the multinational mode nor in the global mode, thereby failing to realise the benefits associated with the two systems. Mr Maucher, who joined the company at a very young age, understood the problem correctly and realised fairly well that the organisation structure of the company was also caught in between the two modes. The corporate managers may be global but the country managers did not know their stand exactly. How to address to this situation ensuring that the company's competitiveness in the global market was not harmed but at the same time keeping the localness intact? Mr Maucher understood that application of 'think global act global' principle to a hugely decentralised food business like Nestle was not an easy task. He, therefore, wanted to take up the mammoth task bit by bit and put in place an organisational structure which would be supportive to achieve global efficiency and local responsiveness simultaneously. He started the work by creating seven product groups headed by global managers loaded with responsibilities and authorities to react to the requirements of any part of the world. The products groups were: powdered and milk beverages, water, milk products and ice cream, nutrition and health care, prepared dishes and cooking aids, confectionary and pet care. He dove tailed the task of the product group mangers with the responsibility to deal with the product lines under its command, world over, and position it in such a way that not only creates profit for the country level units but also leverages the benefits of integration. This product grouping allowed the global managers to look at their total responsibilities in a cylindrical way with the benefit of better orchestrating the global business requirements in their respective product line. The divisional managers located in the different geographic regions also received a distinct channel of reporting the local requirements seeking feedback for quick actions. After the product grouping, Mr Maucher looked into geographic grouping to speed up the communication process and strategic decision making. He grouped all divisions within a country or region in to one national or regional strategic business unit (SBU) to be headed by SBU managers. The task of the SBU managers was to link, co-ordinate and oversee the activities of products group managers and the several divisions under them. Once geographic grouping was completed, the result was visible in terms of cost reduction through joint purchasing and joint resource sharing at the country level or at the regional level. The task of Mr Maucher did not end there. He felt the need of introducing the concept of matrix stricture so that activities of product groups, geographic groups and the specialised divisions of the company such as corporate communications, innovation, technology transfer, etc., are integrated. He set the goal of the matrix structure in such a way that the common resources of the organisation could be shared by all. The R&D function of Nestle was required to be strong because of the fast changing nature of its businesses and also because it was required by all SBU heads. The matrix nature of the organisation allowed everybody to take benefits of the 18 decentralised R&D centres strategically located all over the world. All research centres were financed and controlled by the headquarters, receiving the necessary inputs mainly from the strategic business units based upon requests from the markets. For example, a research requirement of Indian market could be researched in an America-based R&D centre.

The above facts of Nestle indicates that when an organisation grows from strength to strength in international business, appropriate organisational design and control system is required to be installed to ensure that it can grow further with effective control on its operations across the countries of the world. Here, in the Nestle case, we have seen that the organisation was in centralisation mode in the initial years but with lack of effective control of the thousands of localised divisions spread in different parts of the world. The organisation was also happy to set the mode of control as centralised at some point of time but later relaxed it on the pretext of localisation strategy. Then the situation came for balancing the requirements of centralisation as well as localisation so as to ensure an optimum level of efficiency. As a result, the company started to address many key issues simultaneously and re-formatted its organisational structure. In the restructuring, it was kept in mind that the organisation is responsive to the market needs, coordination inside the organisational structure was maintained and learning from the different country operations were effectively ploughed back and disseminated across the organisation.

The Nestle ordeal is not unique of its kind. In fact, when business organisations grow from local level and develop multi-country presence, the organisation structure is also required to be evolved strategically so that it can truly play a complementary role to the marketing requirements of the organisation. The synergy between two allows the company to reap maximum benefits in the market place. This chapter, therefore, revolves around the issues an organisation faces as it grows from single-country presence to multi-country internationalisation and then spreads its reach globally and in each stage, shows how the organisational structure is required to support the marketing process adequately.

ORGANISATION AND ORGANISATIONAL STRUCTURE

It is natural that every business organisation, be it one person or a group of people, has a commercial interest. In order to achieve commercial interest it is also essential that people participating in the business organisation are collaborating with each other in a desired way so that the goal is achieved efficiently and competitively. This creates a need to have a compatible organisation with a requisite organisational structure in place. To bring efficiency in the business organisation, it is required that the organisational structure is well-knit and as per the organisational requirements. Organisational structure, in a simple sense, refers to the levels of management and division of responsibilities within the organisation, which the people participating in the organisation will follow. The people running the organisation, both owner and employees of the organisation, set the boundaries or limits of their responsibilities and duties as per requirement. Different hierarchical positions within the organisation are devised and a reporting system framework is developed which nicely depicts who will report to whom within the organisation. An organisational chart is a graphical illustration of the aforesaid collaborative arrangement within the organisation planned to achieve the desired commercial objective. A good organisational structure designed to achieve a pre-determined business objective has the following characteristics.

- *Governance related*: The structure must allow people working within the organisation to be governed and make relevant decisions based on the documented policies and procedures of the organisation.
- *Approach related*: The structure must allow the organisation to tread in the desired direction. For this to happen, the layers, divisions and sub-units of the organisation must be well demarcated. The total organisational tasks are also allocated, divided in the layers, divisions, etc. These are also coordinated and supervised in accordance with the business objectives so that the organisation as a whole moves in the desired direction of the business.
- *Capability utilisation related*: An organisation requires various specialist knowledge and skills in the field of its operation to take the organisational

objective forward. Hence, the organisational structure must accommodate specialised functions along with routine works and practices.

- *Roles and responsibility related*: The organisational structure must allow people to work with clear cut roles and responsibilities. The people working in the organisation must be aware of responsibilities and accountabilities without ambiguity. The structure should be free from creating duplication of roles and responsibilities.
- *Culture related*: The organisation structure must allow developing a unique pattern of doing things, communication and behaviours. In course of time it takes the shape of an organisational culture which is very helpful in keeping the organisational structure healthy.

INTERNATIONALISATION AND ORGANISATIONAL TRANSFORMATION

It is not very difficult to understand that organisation may require some changes due to internationalisation. But what will be the change and how much change need to make in the organisation have been a topic of discussion and research both at the company as well as academic level. What are the efficient forms of organising at different levels of internationalisation? Company managers were seeking an answer to this question for a long period of time. There were many such instances when international company failed because of lack of support from the organisation with right type of organisational structure in place. When companies go international the requirements are varied and complex. To keep competitiveness going in the new situation it should have the support of a strong organisation moulded as per the new requirements. The relationship between internationalisation and organisation vis-à-vis organisational structure is complex and attracted the attention of many researchers in the past. However, there were not enough research-based evidences in literature to establish a clear cut relationship. Therefore, questions related to organisational change, internationalisation, responsiveness, of organisational structure, etc., leading to successful internationalisation remained mostly a grey area. In the early 1980s, a number of great researchers such as Prahalad, Doz, Bartlett and Ghoshal made great attempt in their own way to through some light on this grey but important area. No doubt that these understanding has greatly helped in understanding the impact of organisation structure on international business. From their researches, the following important aspects relating to internationalisation and organisational transformation requirements emerged.

Integration of Activities: Organisational Capabilities

With the spread of business activities beyond national borders many new activities are required to be performed. Interestingly, many of these activities are new for the organisation but require efficient handling at all times to counter competition. International marketing activities pose new challenges which hitherto the company has not faced in the domestic scenario. To handle the different types of complex situations, company managers may be required to assume different types of roles involving different capabilities. Mr Tanti CEO of Suzlon, Indian multinational in wind power business, explained this concept concisely in an interview with Fortune magazine[2]. The Indian company, in order to be competitive in foreign country markets, Suzlon started a new method of sourcing and assembling which it never practiced in the home country. In the new situation, Suzlon had to source the concepts and design for wind turbine from Netherlands, execute engineering jobs from Germany, the commercialisation came from Denmark and assembling executed in India. This very process was needed for the company to be competitive in the new foreign markets. This much higher degree of sourcing and integration practice was never executed before by the company while in domestic market. However, this practice was essential for Suzlon to take the benefits of its presence in multiple countries. The company integrated the specialised jobs carried out at different places to avail economies of scale and scope. The integration also provided the benefit of having technology parity, global sourcing and availing benefits in terms of logistics and transportation. However, it was not an easy task for Suzlon management to handle, as all these were new and counterintuitive activities. The company managers were trying to keep pace with rapid internationalisation requirements. Managing the task of global sourcing and orchestrating the entire process up to marketing in an integrated manner was an absolute requirement. The Suzlon organisational structure might have geared up to manage the culture of worldwide integration efficiently. However for organisations that grew up in a domestic environment, these types of special capabilities were not crafted within their structure because of home country orientation. Although Suzlon could handle it, thanks to the innovative mind of its owner, under such situations the organisational structure of many companies might malfunction if its structure is not aligned to the strategy. The organisational culture might not be ready to take up these types of challenges. An effective organisation structure, therefore, must support development of special knowledge, like global integration of activities, within the organisation and develop capabilities to utilise it while at international arena.

Responsiveness: Organisational Capabilities

Responsiveness is the organisational capacity to respond to the new and existing business related situations cutting across different geographies of organisation presence. Some organisations may remain very active and efficient in organising business in the domestic market only.In course of time they develop proficiency only in a pre-determined way of doing business and stick to that without allowing uncertainties to creep in. People working in such organisations usually develop ethnocentric tendencies and become rigid. The result is obvious in terms of taking time to arrive at decision when confronted with a new situation or act in a new way. A high level of rigidity in the organisational structure does not allow its managers to be flexible enough to react to new requirements.

---

[2] http://money.cnn.com/magazines/fortune/fortune_archive/2007/10/29/100795475/index2.htm

Such a company engaged in domestic marketing would have a problem in international markets when confronted with the requirement of differentiation of marketing programme. An example of flexible organisation is the famous US fast food company McDonald. The flexibility induced in the organisation allows its managers to handle the problem of country-specific marketing differentiation in an exemplary way. It brings changes in its marketing mix and other marketing programmes as per the requirement of the concerned country as and when required to stand up straight in competition. For example, it brought McAloo Tikki for Indian consumers, Bulgogi Burger for the Korean and Chicken Tatsuta for the Japanese with much of operationalisation ease. In addition, the company never forgets to pursue its global character by intelligently devising the marketing mix to great extent and where possible. Maintaining a posture like 'We are global, yet local' is not an easy task. Companies that commence international operations may find it difficult to be flexible enough to react to each country's requirements differently and yet strive to retain a substantial level of standardisation. This balancing is important to retain competitiveness. One important requirement here in the quest of learning the art of balancing standardisation and adaptation is a supportive organisation structure which allows managers to quickly learn and act accordingly.

Worldwide Learning: Organisational Capabilities

An organisation is expected to learn various aspects of doing business from the countries of their presence. These learning are continuous and handsomely contribute to the development of international marketing expertise for an organisation. This is true for all the international business organisations irrespective of their size. Internationalising successfully involves efficient handling of different barriers of doing business such as cultures, distance, languages, etc. Interestingly, various levels of these barriers present in different companies effects different companies differently. Different companies take different approaches to counter the effect of these barriers. How a company overcame certain barriers successfully in one country can become a learning point for its other subsidiaries to follow. Experts say that it is extremely important that the business subsidiaries keep on learning from each other's success stories. Therefore, it is also equally important that success stories are continuously diffused across the different subsidiaries of the entirebusiness so that not only subsidiaries learn but at the same time a knowledge base as a whole is developed within the organisation. The company gets the benefit by utilising them in developing innovative products and marketing processes. International business experts observed that organisations vary in terms of their ability to provide a platform through which subsidiaries to share experience of overcoming barriers. Also subsidiaries vary in terms of inquisitiveness to learn, ability to retain the learning and synthesise them to accrue benefits in the subsequent marketing process. In this matter, the organisationalstructure plays a very important role by allowing the company to be learning sensitive, inquisitive to learn new things, retain the learning in a knitted format and dissemination of such knowledge for further analysis at the headquarter level. Such a learning organisation leverages the benefits of learning through using them in developing future strategy.

ORGANISATIONAL STRUCTURE INADEQUACY

At the first stage of internationalisation the company is engaged in exporting products to only a few countries, then complexities are at a much lower level. It develops products as per the taste and preference of domestic consumers and a part of the produced products are exported. Since the major focus of the company is on the domestic market and export revenue forms only a minor part of the total revenue of the organisation, an export department created for the purpose can manage the internationalisation successfully. However, subsequently when the company grows into a multi-country business with own subsidiaries, the erstwhile export department may not have enough capacity or ability to match up with the management requirements. As more countries are invaded with setting up of own subsidiaries, the complexities are expected to be more now which require efficient and strategic handling by expert international managers. However, the actions and interactions of managers can only be adequately supported by a well-knit organisation where requisite organisational structure is in place. In case of any deficiency towards supportiveness of the organisation inter alia organisational structure, the marketing activities are bound to suffer. The initial symptoms of inadequate organisational support can be inferred from the following events.

- *Information malfunctioning*: Information from different country markets are not adequately captured and are not allowed to be accommodated within the organisation. Hence, international marketing decisions made by the managers are not based on the actual requirements but rather on historical facts or intuitions.
- *Responsiveness rigidity*: The level of responsiveness towards a specific or urgent requirement of a distant country market has been sluggish. It is taking long time to arrive at a decision. The decision making process is centralised and person-specific. The specific person either could not be made aware of the seriousness of the situation correctly or the person's pre occupation consumed long time to arrive at and implement a decision. To make the situation even worse there could be a change of guard who even reversed the already taken decision.
- *Innovation freeze*: The organisational environment is infected with 'wait and see' doctrine. The managers believe in bureaucracy and feel safe by following a tradition in respect of decision making rather than being innovative particularly when make and break types of decisions are to be made concerning competitiveness of different country market operation. The managers may even defer decision making for a long time with the hope that the situation will improve own their own.

- *Decision isolation*: Lack of multi country approach and managers believe in taking business decisions for one country at a time but not in an integrated way. Managers showing tendency to avoid risk and hence averse of making strategic decisions concerning the multi country business as a whole.
- *Imprecise decision*: There is over dependence on ad hoc decision making. Facts and figures are generally being over looked while decision making within the organisation but emphasis is on the intuitive ability of the managers.
- *Impaired management information system*: The system of information collection from different subsidiaries either not in place or lost its relevance. The information collection and dissemination system is weak. The key country level functionaries do not know where to send the important information pertaining to their business operation and corporate managers are not also facilitated by accumulated operational data at the central level. As a result, the management is not strategically oriented to take a decision on standardisation or adaptation based on actual requirements of the country markets.
- *Responsibility authority mismatch*: Either over dependency on the headquarters in decision making irrespective of strategic intent or complete delegation of decision making on the country level managers. Lack of coordination between subsidiaries and headquarters in decision making has made business decisions isolated in nature and different than that of the organisation's strategic intentions. In such situation the country manager think that they are the supreme and independent of any greater organisational goal, mission, vision and objectives.
- *Disconnect feeling*: All-round feeling of isolation at the country level. The managers and staff in the subsidiaries located in different geographical locations do not have any say in the corporate level headquarters leading to a feeling disconnect. Even, there is lack of coordination between line and staff managers resulting frequent stoppage operation. The country levels subsidiaries have also failed to take advantage of the organisation's special or unique expertise adequately.

ORGANISING FOR MARKETING INTERNATIONALLY

Organisation support is essential while internationalising and marketing products or services in different countries of the world. It is just like the support of all the other ten players of a football team to Lionel Messi to score a goal in a very competitive football match in the international level. The geographical expansion of activities increases management complexities that require efficient handling at the requisite level of the company hierarchy depending upon best suitability to the purpose cutting across the country border. In addition, the company organisation must be well-knit for facilitating collection and accumulation of requisite information regarding different host country environment, product and functional knowledge to process them at the requisite level to take correct decisions at the correct time. For example, Nestlé's Maggi noodles caught in to big controversy leading to a blanket ban on product marketing in India and almost immediately its CEO Paul Bulcke announced the decision to make the products off the shelf with reconfirmation of the fact that company maintained same quality standards everywhere in world where India was not an exception. To take such decisions for distant market without much elapse of time, the company used its adequately developed organisational structure which facilitated information flow at different hierarchical levels. The correct decision came at the correct time from the correct hierarchical level. A good compatible organisation structure, therefore, is an absolute necessity to help the company in achieving its objective. However, to have an organisational structure optimally fit in the organisation there are three components on which decisions required to be made by a company.

Organisational Sub-units

The sub-units are the lowest units of an organisation. In organisational parlance, these lowest units are called departments or divisions purposefully created to carry out certain tasks. The tasks may vary in accordance with the requirements of the company. The company requires these sub-units to function under the main organisation structure with definite inter and intra linkage. The organisational sub-units could be of three types such as product based, area based, or function based. For example, an international company may have sub units such as product division, geographical division, or functional division. Products divisions are common in manufacturing organisations and examples of product divisions are valve division, transformer division, etc. Many organisations may create divisions based on areas such as Singapore division, Dubai division, etc. As the name indicates, irrespective of any specific product, area based divisions may handle any number of products desired by the company but within a specific geographical area. Functional divisions such as marketing division or finance division are basically created to perform a type of function. For example, the marketing division will handle marketing related tasks while the finance division will exclusively handle the finance related affairs of the company.

Any organisation design starts with decision making about the number and types of sub units the organisation is likely to create. The guiding factors in these directions are:

- Understand the details of tasks required to be carried out by the organisation and their future requirements as well. Based on the understanding, the departments or the divisions, i.e., the number of sub-units, their types and possible combinations are required to be decided.
- Understand the internal variables such as company objective, geographical spread, product variety, etc., in order to take a decision about the constitution of the organisational sub-units.
- Understand the external variables such as competition, market share, number and type of countries across which the business is spread, etc. The constitution of the organisational sub-units may also be influenced due to the effect of these external variables.

- Understand the organisation's future growth plan internationally and the complexities of marketing abroad. Also understand the long term and short term objectives of the company in the backdrop of competition expected, speed of decision making, product or geographic diversity handled, technology excellence under command, etc. The creation of organisational sub-units must strategically fit the greater plan of the company not only for short-term for long-term as well.

Tasks and Functions

Once the numbers of organisational sub units are strategically planned the next task would be to allot specific tasks and functions to them. While allotting it must be ensured that these tasks and functions, to be performed by the organisational sub-units, are not overlapping in nature. At the same time they are also synchronised enough to drive the organisation to its goal. The tasks and functions are allotted to the organisational sub units keeping the two objectives in mind, i.e , non- overlapping and synchronising. To make the organisational sub units perform up to their capacity necessary responsibilities and authorities are to be allotted to the sub-units. Here, the objective of allotment of responsibilities and authorities would be to ensure that the sub units are in a position to carry out the entrusted tasks and functions independently or with organisational inter-dependence. The principle to be followed here is to ensure that sub-units have responsibilities commensurate with the requisite authorities. That is to avoid responsibility–authority mismatch. In fact, all the organisational sub-units are to be knitted following the same principle to develop a meaningful organisational body. The strings that hold all the sub units to form an organisational structure are the task descriptions coupled with delegated authorities and responsibilities to different sub-units. This is, therefore, a critical stage in which responsibilities and authorities are fixed for different sub units based on the guiding principles of the organisation derived from the company's strategic intent. Based on the responsibilities, authorities, priorities, criticalities, and depth of decision making the hierarchical relationships amongst the different sub units are established.

Reporting and Control

This stage formalises the hierarchy level in the organisational structure. An important aspect at this stage is to decide on the line of control the company wants to place in the organisation. Deciding 'who will report to whom' is an important aspect of ensuring existence of control system in the organisation. It is needless to reiterate that the top management or the CEO of the company must be at one extreme of the hierarchy and be the recipient of reports from different other control nodes down the line. As for control system within the organisation there could be two extreme alternatives: one, the top management may want to retain all the control through centralisation and two, the top management may also like to relax the control system totally and allow the sub-units to take decisions based on their job responsibilities. The former is centralisation and the later one decentralisation of the control system. A centralised organisation structure means that it does not allow the positions, up in the level of hierarchy, to delegate the authority of decision making to the sub-units. On the other hand, a decentralised one would be doing the exact opposite. It is usual to see that an organisation is either fully centralised or fully decentralised. But rather the organisation behave strategically and exercise control through top management on those matters where strategic aspects of doing business are involved and allow the sub-units to exercise their own options on non-strategic ones. For example, most of the international businesses usually delegate the power of decision making to the lower level units on the matter of day to day business issues. These are of repetitive nature hence the top management makes them totally free from centralised control. However, business matters of strategic nature are not put under local control but rather put in the ambit of centralised control. Exception may be there when decision making in some strategic issues is unnecessarily delayed because of geographic distance. In such cases the benefit of quick decision making outweigh the delayed but centralised decision making. Many global organisations follow decentralisation just to allow local level sub-units to be responsive enough to the turbulence in the country environment. However, many global organisations like KFC do not practice the system of decentralisation. They feel that a strong centralised control is absolutely necessary to make all the 8000 franchised business units in 120 countries perform in a standardised manner to the extent possible. Interestingly, in accordance with centralisation and decentralisation of control system, the organisational tallness or flatness also varies. In the parlance of organisation design, a taller organisation structure is one which has multiple layers of hierarchy. Whereas in a flatter organisation structure there will be fewer layers only. A somewhat decentralised organisation, therefore, have the tendency to be flatter which does not require different layers in its ranks for decision making. On the other hand, a considerably centralised business organisation is likely to have a taller structure. A globally spread organisation but with a flatter structure would have lesser reporting and controlling system and hence ideal for reacting to country specific situation more quickly.

ALTERNATIVE ORGANISATIONAL STRUCTURES

In general, an internationalising company has various options for designing its organisational structure, starting with simple to a complex one. The options are used to develop its internal system of administration for accomplishing a pre-determined business objective. The idea is to build the internal system that can match with the external requirements of the organisation in respect of managing its market needs. Hence, the guiding factor for the setting the internal administration framework of an organisation is the type of external market needs and requirements. The organisational structure must, therefore, be built in accordance with the external requirements. Following are the alternative organisational structures available to a company while doing business internationally.

Function Based

As the name indicates, in this type, the organisation uses functional grouping such as marketing, operations, finance, etc., to form the organisational structure. Under the functional departmentalisation people are grouped based on similarity of the functions and activities to be performed by them. For example, marketing department is expected to do marketing related works. The organisation also finds functional departmentalisation very easy to work with and simple in terms of setting the authority and responsibility at a different hierarchical level. The simplicity of this type of organisational structure in terms of monitoring and control also has made it the most favoured organisational structure amongst the small- and medium-sector enterprises. The employees are also able to develop functional specialisation as they continue to work in a single functional area for a longer period of time. The small or medium-sized companies while expanding internationally can also use functional departmentalisation easily to support the new need because of the depth of specialisation developed over the years in the domestic market.

Export Department

This type of organisational structure is very common for a company doing export to a few countries. The company has also primary business interest in the domestic market and hence a major part of the production goes to domestic market. Another part of produce for international market can be handled by creating an export department. The domestic marketing department continues to cater to the requirements of the domestic market and the addition of an export department to the main organisation structure under the marketing department will do the export marketing job nicely as shown in Figure 13.2.

FIGURE 13.2 Export organisational structure

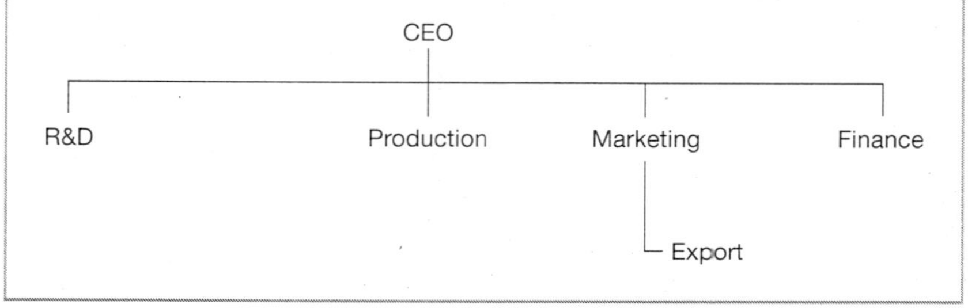

The export department is generally placed below the regular marketing department at least for the initial period of internationalisation. The export head is supposed to report the marketing head under such arrangement. The marketing manager under such an organisation structure gives more emphasis on the company's primary territory, i.e., domestic market and then explores the export marketing requirements. However, problem may come when the marketing head does not knowing much about the export marketing process. Hence, a wrong decision taken by the marketing manager may lead to market failure. Sometimes, to avoid the situation, an additional post is created under the marketing manager and manned by a person who is thorough in dealing with exporting formalities such as market identification, export documentation, etc.

Separate Export Department

This type of organisation structure is common in companies that have attained a fair amount of success in exportation and are earning handsome revenue from external markets. Sometimes, a company management may put a stiff export marketing target for the company requiring a separate export department (Figure 13.3). This type organisation structure is more focussed and can handle more external complexities than the export department functioning under marketing department. The person heading the separate export department is absolutely not dependent on the domestic marketing manager but reports directly to the CEO of the company. This arrangement saves time, allow to frame quick strategies and hence, the model reacts faster to the external market complexities.

This type of organisational structure may be the initiating point to have a full-fledged international division of the company at some point of time when the company expands to many other foreign countries. When the international business matures with time more products are brought in for marketing in different countries of the world and at that time the company wants to put in place an international division to take on the complexities. The international division will operate much like the domestic division and generate profit as independent strategic business unit (SBU) and compete with the domestic division for resources, buying services, strategic input and product design, and other decisions which have implications for their marketing effectiveness.

Geographical/Regional based

An international company enjoying success in the foreign market requires putting more close attention to retain competitiveness. The revenue from

FIGURE 13.3 Separate export department

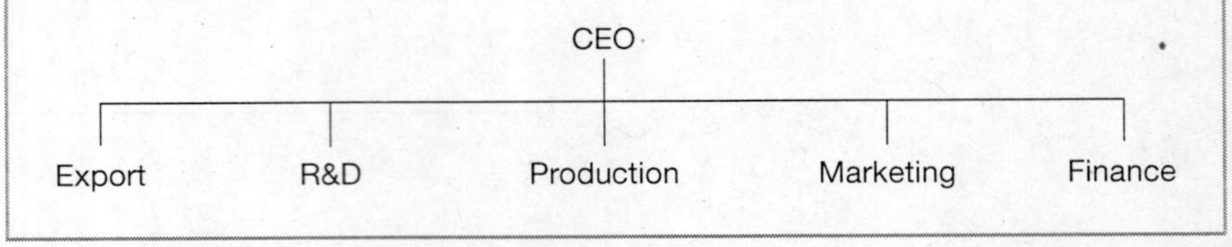

FIGURE 13.4 Geographical/regional structure of Himalaya Drugs Limited

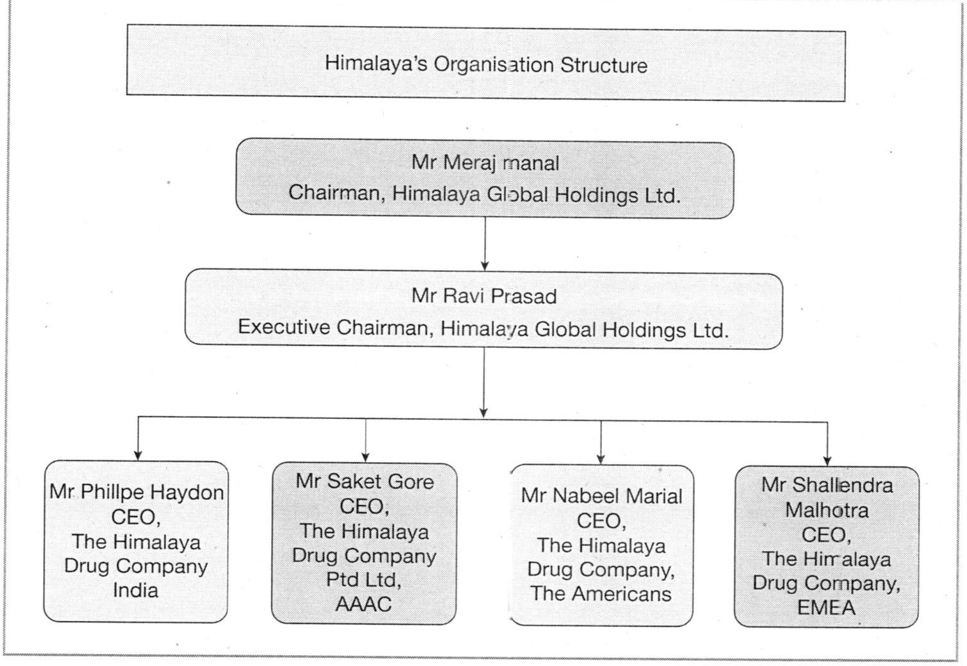

foreign operation may not rise to the level of company expectation unless more attention is paid to the foreign consumers' requirements. This is not possible to handle such intense requirement from a home country based sub ordinate organisational structure. In order to dedicate more time to the foreign markets, an organisational may, therefore, require re-structuring to accommodate geographic or regional organisation structure. Some companies may find a specific foreign country market to be more suitable to do profitable business, and in those circumstances, the company is likely to have a geographic division dedicated for the country or region. Figure 13.4 below depicts the geographically based organisation structure of the Indian company Himalaya Drugs Limited with special attention to regions of the Asia–Pacific, America, India, and Middle-east plus Africa.[3]

Product Division

Product division is the best preferred option for a company producing multiple products, often with unrelated line of business. It is more suitable for a global company where the spread of business is almost in every country. Also the company is emphasising on establishing the supremacy of the products in different country markets. In such situation it does not make sense to manage international business based on geographic organisational structure any more. The companies, therefore, resort to products based structures and find it easy to track market performance through product strings. The decision making also becomes easy for the company managers where the products' performance in different country markets becomes vividly

[3] http://www.himalayahealthcare.com/newsroom/pdf/factsheet.pdf.

FIGURE 13.5 Global product structure of Bayer, Germany

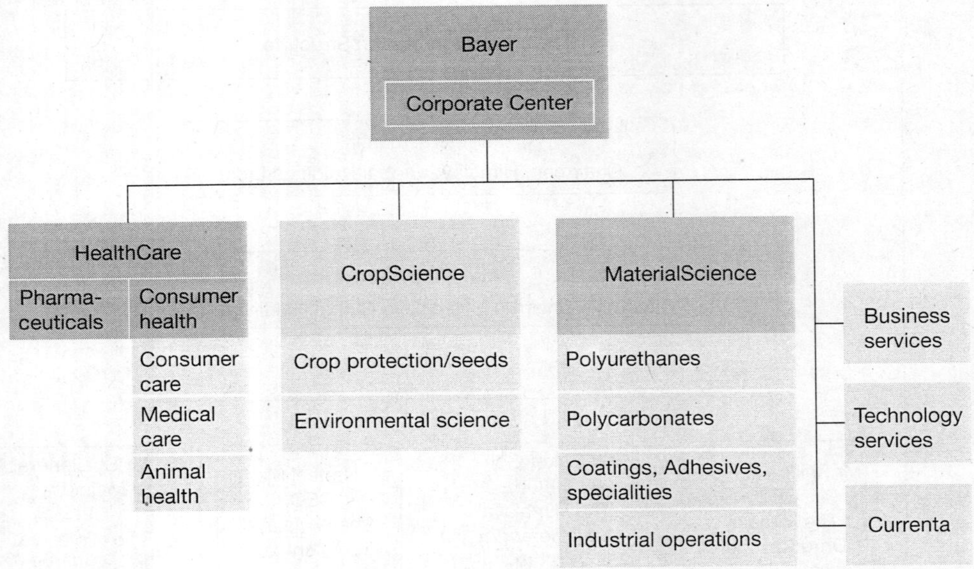

clear following the product strings. The top level managers also prefer rely on such strings rather than relying on geographic units as a unit of performance. It enhances the company's speed of doing business, taking decisions, etc. The product division managers will be allotted responsibilities such as planning, organising, controlling and providing timely feedback in respect of a particular product line across the countries of the world. Any impact of decision regarding standardisation or adaptation of products can also be best understood when the product performance across the globe is analysed. Product division also helps the company to better balance its standardisation/adaptation strategy. The demerit of such organisational structures is that although it enhances coordination of different areas in respect of one product line, it never establishes coordination among the different product lines of a company. The corporate organisation structure of Bayer AG, headquartered in Germany, built on the principle of product structure may be seen in Figure 13.5. The company has built up its organisational structure based on three basic product lines in health care, crop science and material science sub-groups, supported by its three service companies[4].

Matrix Organisation Structure

In a practical sense, operating in the international market requires efficient handling of different complexities in the different country markets where simple forms of organisational structures may not be able to do a good job. Hence, in order to derive maximum benefits from all the simple forms of organisational structure discussed so far, companies often combine them. The matrix structure is such a structure which gives combined benefits of

[4] http://www.annualreport2012.bayer.com/en/corporate-structure.aspx

simplistic forms. More efficient handling of the organisation can be expected from matrix type of organisational structure because of the fact that it can accommodate functional competence-based, geography-based, and product-based structures under one roof so as to provide combined benefits to the organisation. In a sense, therefore, it is all in one. A way to illustrate the matrix organisation structure is by looking at the Nestle case described at the beginning of the chapter. Nestle has seven product categories, namely, powdered and milk beverages, water, milk products and ice cream, nutrition and health care, prepared dishes and cooking aids, confectionary, and pet care. The company supplies these seven groups of products to a large number of markets across the world in Europe, Oceania, Africa, and Asia. In order to be competitive, the organisation requires various functional competencies such as R&D for technology transfer, branding for maintaining its huge 8400 international brand portfolio, media and advertising, etc., to be able to be accessed by the different product groups.

If Nestle was organised only by its product groups, then efforts on market development and customer value creation thrust would tend to be less since it would not be possible for executive in charge of product development to do justice to market development simultaneously as product developers would have exclusive expertise in that line only. Similarly, if the company goes by geographic grouping only and devises its organisational structure accordingly, then it would be closer to the customers of particular cou ntry/countries, and hence, it would appear to be good from the marketing point of view but not from product development point of view. Hence, in that case, the focus on continuous technological development of the products would have suffered. Also, the country or regional manager may be conversant with one or two groups of products and hence may feel biased to develop these product ranges in the geographic area under his command. At the same time, a total functional orientation structure for Nestle would do little justice to the marketing skill that the company wants to hone consistently. A total geography -based structure would not be capable of providing the impetus for continuous product development. A total product-based structure also will be incapable of pushing the marketing agenda of the company in different markets. So, in a sense, all the three options of organisational structure individually fail to deliver the company's objective. Under these circumstances one simply would be required to combine these three types in a suitable way to avail the simultaneous benefits of organisational structuring.

A matrix type of structure would, therefore, be ideally suited for multi-product, multi-country operations of conglomerates like Nestle as shown in Figure 13.6. The different products groups are active in developing state-of-the-art technology for the markets under the supervision of the SBU marketing division of the company, who directly reports to the company's CEO. So, in a way, the thrust on product excellence of the company does not suffer by adopting a totally geography-oriented structure. However, the benefits of geography-oriented structure are also not lost. The geography-based divisions of Europe, Asia, Africa and America contribute in providing market-based knowledge to the products groups as well as to the functional groups such as finance, operation, branding, and HRD. The geographic area heads report the market dynamics of the areas under their respective territories to the

FIGURE 13.6 Matrix structure

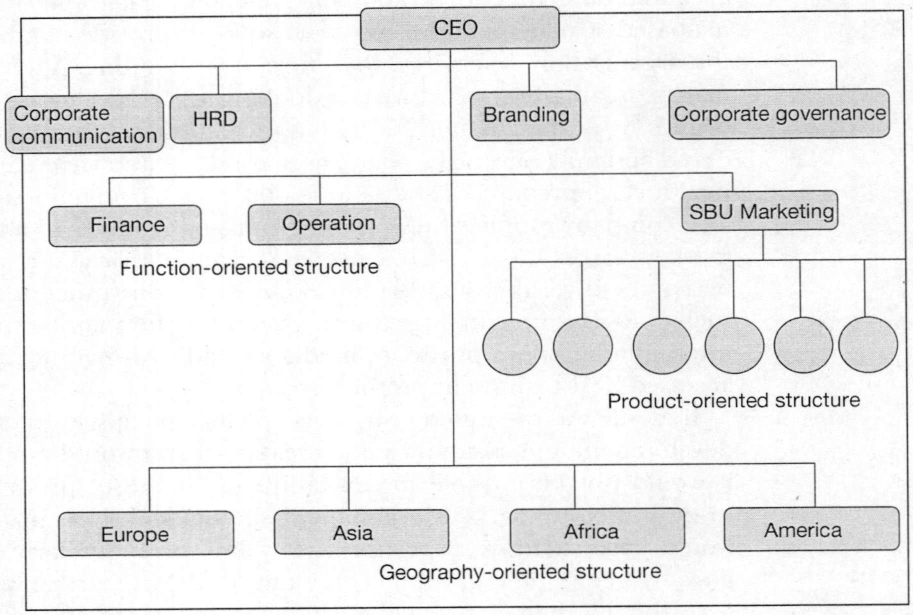

different levels of the organisation. Specialised departments like branding work directly under the supervision of the CEO of the company as it is vital for the company's existence. These departments can be accessed by the product centre head as well as geographic area centre heads. As a result, the matrix organisational structure adopted by the company can excel with product know-how, market-based knowledge, knowledge accumulation and strategy execution thereof, and functional knowledge such as R&D transfer to the required places of the company very efficiently. Effective use of resources is also possible as specialised departments will be accessed by many divisions simultaneously without having the need of creating separate specialised divisions, (say, technology transfer division) for each of the geographic division or product division. The matrix structure also allows the top management to spare more time for deciding the strategic aspects by keeping them away from day-to-day business operation. One of the demerits of the matrix organisation structure is its multi-reporting system. One divisional head will be reporting to two or three superiors, which sometimes hurts the principles of unit of command by abandoning the single line of authority. Another disadvantage is that the managers working in a global company with matrix structure may find it difficult to clarify confusions and resolve conflicts as they are away from headquarters, not only by distance and time but also by language and culture leading to frustration.

Box 13.1 Matrix or no matrix: Decide for yourself

Mr Jay R. Galbraith, as a management consultant, always appreciated an organisational structure which focused on increasing speed, flexibility, agility, quality and customer focus. He was of the opinion that an organisational structure which has rigidity in terms of fixed authority and responsibility is traditional in nature and hence, it will not be good enough to handle the complexities of multi-country business. According to him, therefore, the following characteristics must be there in an organisational structure for it to fit in the present day's international environment.

- It should allow people to freely assemble as a team, purposefully, to achieve the important objectives of the organisation. It should give importance to a person's capability to contribute in a team format rather than follow the organisational dictum expressed by dotted line hierarchy structure.
- The team should plan the tasks at hand and set a goal to achieve the objective and allow purposeful debate to take place to ensure that goal setting has everybody's contribution.
- The team should work with the basic principle of collaboration and each of the members should be ready to collaborate to achieve the mutually set goal.
- It should demonstrate that organisational commands and controls are neither a guide nor the motivator to achieve the goal.
- The team formations should be almost on a voluntarily basis but based on need and people from different streams should participate using cross-functional understanding in a coordinated way to achieve the goal.

According to Mr Galbraith, the above characteristics are possible in the matrix type of organisational structure. In addition, he pointed out that high performers such as Procter & Gamble, IBM, Nokia, Cisco, and Schlumberger have moved beyond the usual debates about dotted lines and reaped maximum benefits by installing matrix type of structure. So, matrix is the future of international business.

Mr Guido Quelle of Mandat GmbH put forth a counter-argument against matrix type of organisational structure:

- Leadership is the key driver to the success of a team. To ensure that leadership is more effective, it requires organisational blessings through clear demarcation of authorities and responsibilities.
- Matrix organisations feature exactly the opposite characteristics, which results in a high degree of complexity, unclear decision paths, unproductive agreement processes, and most worrisome, non-transparent responsibilities. Conflicts of competence are pre-programmed, and it is not clear who is responsible for successes and failures.
- Matrix organisations do not believe in fixing clear responsibilities on the team members. Hence, in case of success there will be a lot of owners and it is difficult to find somebody who could stand up straight for the bad results.
- In the past, companies such as ABB (ABB) and Unilever (UN) have shown that matrix organisations can do more harm than good. It was the matrix that nearly ruined ABB, and Unilever has been oscillating between different organisational designs since 1996.
- Matrix structure is not an end in itself but the starting point of serving the customer better than the competitors through organising in a better way. An organisation structure with properly focussed action, clearly demarcated responsibilities and rigidly set accountabilities in the direction of serving target customer is always better than ambitiously focused, indistinct responsibilities and accountabilities. The former one, i.e., traditional structure can work faster and repetitively while the latter one, i.e., matrix structure is slow because no one is sure about his or her responsibilities.

So, according to Mr Guido Quelle, matrix is not the future of international business, but rather the traditional line organisation with its built-in intelligence that is the key to success.

Source: Bloomsburg Business week debate room (http://www.businessweek.com/debateroom/archives/2009/08/matrix_is_the_ladder_to_success.html

Hub-and-Spoke Structure

Here the term 'hub and spoke' is used as metaphor to describe the organisational structure. Under the hub and spoke system, organisation structure can literally be visualised as is a system of connections arranged like a chariot wheel. In hub-and-spoke organisation structure the 'hub' represents the headquarters and the 'spokes' representing the different country presence of the company. The 'spokes' could be in terms of a distribution subsidiary or a full-fledged international division. The centrally located 'hub' gives out only the objectives of presence in the foreign country to the 'spokes' and the different 'spokes' in different countries carry out the objectives in their own way. The advantage of such a structure is in terms of clear understanding about what is expected out of the 'spokes' and easy evaluation of the outcome.

Team-based Structure

In international markets, a company may face different barriers to marketing that are required to be handled very efficiently. Sometimes the barriers may be related to sudden rise of a major competitor, abrupt change in taste and preference of the target customers, fast technology obsolesce leading to shortening of product life cycle, etc. The international company may have adverse effect on its profitability due to presence of such barriers and their continuation for a long period of time. These barriers may not be permanent but may require immediate attention. So, a company in such a circumstance frames a sub-objective to obviate the barriers. In such situations, a team comprising of few people is set up to attain the objective of bulldosing the barrier faced by the company. Though a project-type philosophy works behind the team formation but the working duration of the team will be intermittent and requirement based. Simply speaking, the duration of the team based organisation will be fixed as per the requirement and could be revived thereafter as and when required. Competent people working in the organisation are generally picked up from different sub-units to form the organisation. The management helps in team formation and provide finance to carry out the task in hand. Generally, the team members derive authorities and responsibilities from the original organisation structure with whom they are permanently attached. It is expected that the team will function synergistically and achieve objective quickly by utilising the individual brilliance of the team members. A slightly modified application of team structure can be seen in the manufacturing and marketing of X Box 360 gaming gadgets by the famous US-based Microsoft Corporation. Here, a Microsoft team was constituted to produce the gaming gadget without having own manufacturing facility. The team successfully selected contract manufacturer, suppliers, R&D experts, etc., for producing the gadgets and markets them all over the world without having a manufacturing facility of its own.

Box 13.2 ABB keeps on realigning organisation structure

ABB, as popularly known to the world, is the abbreviated form of the famous Swedish- Swiss engineering multinational ASEA Brown Boveri. The organisation is headquartered in Zurich, Switzerland. Now, ABB is present in around 100 countries and during 2013 approximately 150,000 worked in the organisation. ABB altered its organisational structure to suit the marketing requirements at different point of time which provided an understanding of requirements of requisite organisational structure at different point of time for a global organisation. ABB changed its organisational structure in a matrix type during 1993 under the tutelage of its high profile CEO Percy Barnevik (1988–1996). There were four major corporate divisions under which about fifty product divisions worked. In this way the products division were accorded due importance in the company. On the other hand the profit centre responsibilities were entrusted on more than 100 country levels local units who were organised under three major regional divisions. The first regional division used to look after European Union, Middle East and Africa followed by the second one in charge of Americas and the third one responsible for the entire Asia. The organisation chart can be seen in the Figure 13.7 (a).

FIGURE 13.7(a) ABB, Organisational structure, 1993: Matrix in nature

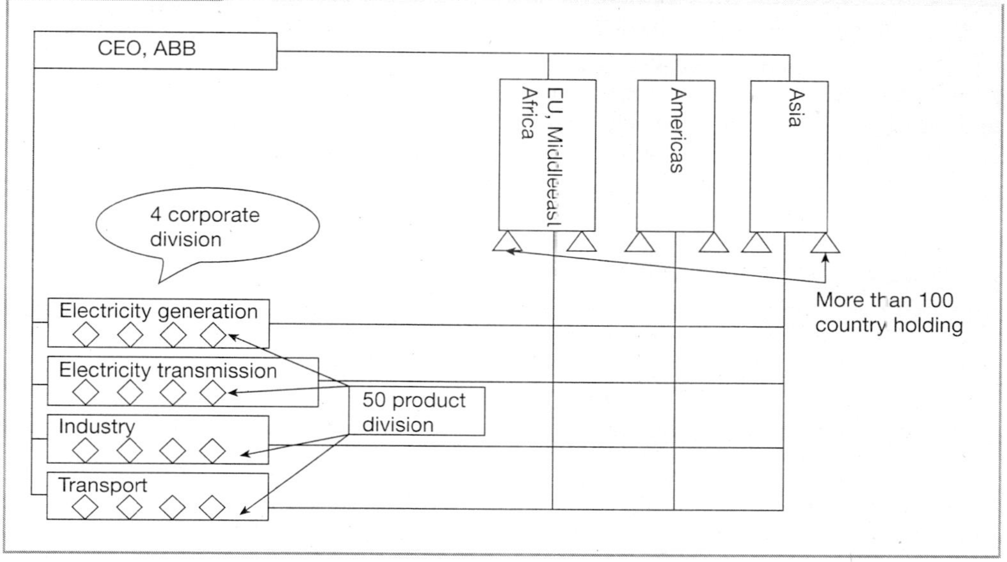

The area based divisions and product based division maintained matrix type of relationship amongst them. The product development and distribution across the globe were the responsibility of the 50 product divisions whereas marketing and sales were the exclusive responsibilities of the 100 country level units. This orthodox matrix structure continued up to 1998 with periodic complains of overlapping jurisdictions causing financial problems. During 1998, ABB effected change in organisational structure in an effort to settle such issues. This time the CEO Goran Lindahl (1997–2001) pushed for product-oriented sector-based organisation, as shown in Figure 13.7 (b). Under this drive six prominent business areas were established such as oil and gas, electricity transmission, etc., top take advantage of global process by abolishing the horizontal area based organisations. The existing country level organisations were retained and more added under each sector to take advantage of multi local situation. Several product oriented units working under each of the sectoral division were given country specific responsibilities with enough decentralisation of power to facilitate entrepreneurial behaviour. To have a strict managerial hierarchy and control an executive member was placed as head of each division who used to report to the CEO of the company directly.

FIGURE 13.7 (b) ABB, Organisational structure, 1998: Product oriented, sector based in nature

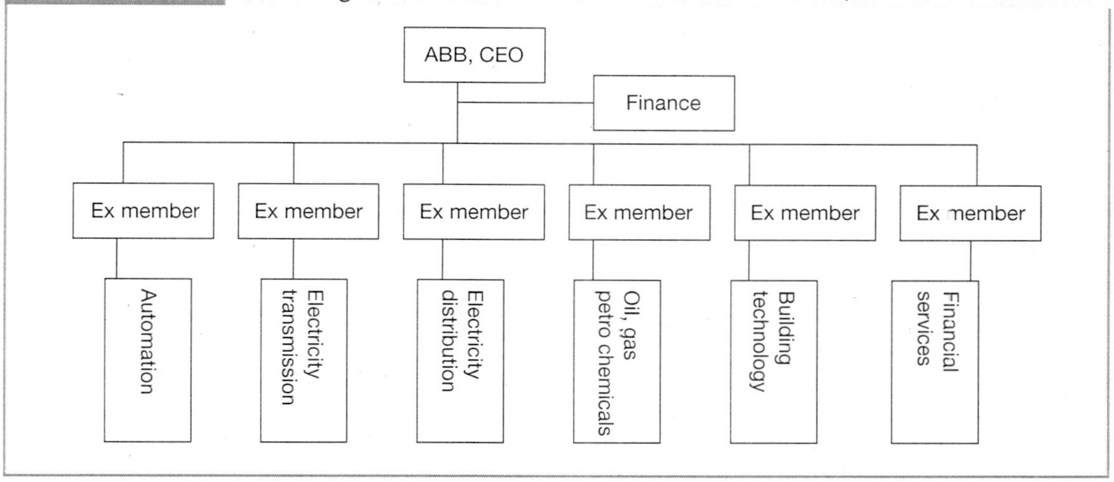

The CEO Jorgen Centerman (2001–2002), who assumed the office during January 2001, announced major reorientation of the organisational structure to make ABB more customers oriented. In order to do that two broad product segments, one based on power technology and another based on automation technology, were created. These two product segments, mandated for solving issues related to product development, production and product related operations, sheltered all the product divisions of ABB. At the same time four application-oriented customer segments were also crafted in ABB to reach out to customers in terms of selling and relationship-building. The customer segments were (1) consumer industries, (2) process industries, (3) oil, gas and petrochemicals and (4) utilities. The basic idea behind the restructuring of the organisation was to ensure that all the products of ABB going out to the customer segments and who, in turn, in close touch with to the buyers all over the world. However, only exception granted for the product segments to be in direct contact with wholesalers, OEMs, etc., by by-passing the customer segments which can be seen in Figure 13.7 (c).

FIGURE 13.7 (c) ABB, Organisational Structure, 2001: Customer oriented, sector based in nature

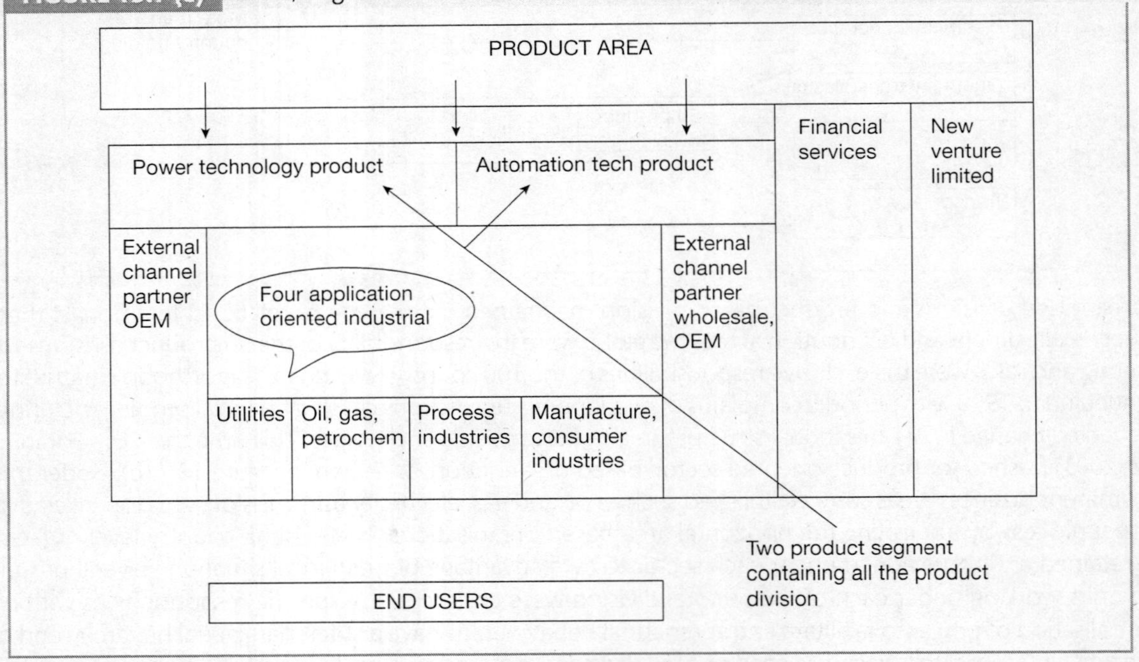

FIGURE 13.7 (d) ABB, Organisational Structure, 2005.

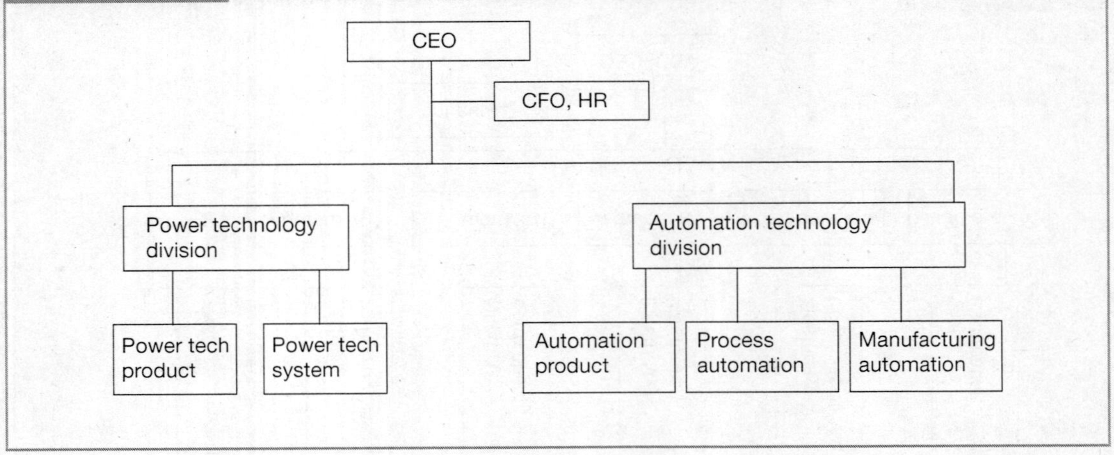

Further, during 2002 the new CEO, Jürgen Dormann (2002–2004), was not happy with the organisational structure because of reported instances of decision failures and hence went on in consolidating divisions and centralising profit-and-loss accountability. He eliminates the front end four customer oriented divisions as well as two channel partner divisions.

The reworked organisation structure, as shown in Figure 13.7 (d), was much simplified and created with the objective of restoring ABB's ability to work on faster decision-making to reach every part of the geographical presence of the business.

Source: www.abb.com

International Structure Stage Model

The rise of multinational corporations in the post-world war era raised curiosity of many business experts about the organisational structure they followed while developing business across the countries of the world. Two well-known researchers Stopford and Well[5] conducted a pioneering research on 187 US MNCs, who figured in the Fortune 500 list of 1963, to understand their organisational development while internationalising from one country to another. The finding of the study later came to known as the international structural stage model. The research indicated that organising structure of multinational companies greatly influenced by two variables, namely, foreign product diversity and foreign sales as a percentage of total sales. This study went on in explaining what would be the organisational structure at different level internationalisation and more importantly when the companies switch over from one structure to another during their internationalisation intensities.

FIGURE 13.8 Right 'fit' between internationalisation and formal management structure

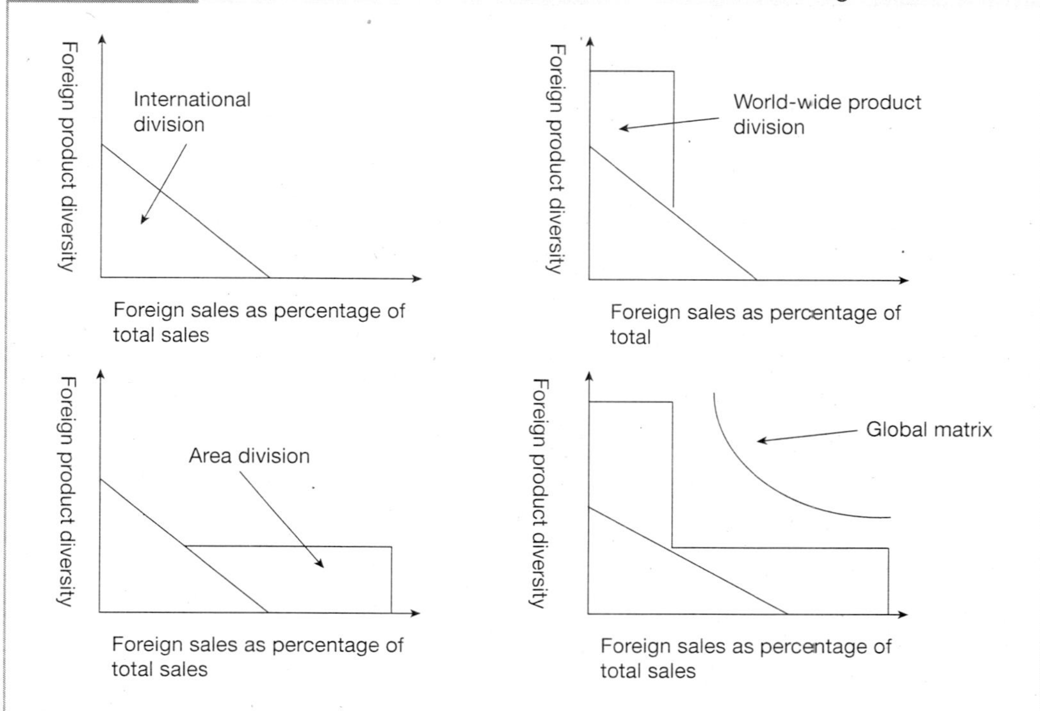

[5] Stopford, J. M. and L. T Wells (1972), *Managing the international enterprise – Organisation of the firms and ownership of the subsidiaries*, Landon, Basic Books.

The findings of the Stopford and Well are depicted in the Figure 13.8. As revealed from the figure that initially the internationalising company would rely on the international division structure in order to manage its international sales. In the study, Stopford and Well found that the companies under study retained their international division up to the point when their foreign sales did not cross 39% of the total sales. However, as the foreign product diversity increases without proportional increase in the foreign sale as percentage of the total sales, the company switches over to the product division structure in order to manage the diversifying product lines. Similarly, if the foreign sale increases without proportional increase in foreign product diversity then the company would switch over to the geographic or area division to manage its multi-country business. However, in case of a company experiencing simultaneous increase in foreign revenue and foreign product diversity there would be switch over to the matrix type of structure to manage the worldwide business operation.

ORGANISATIONAL STRUCTURE AND PERFORMANCE

So far, it has been seen that companies have different options in designing their organisational structure. The Stopford and Well model also well demonstrated that the companies felt the need of organisational structure change to keep pace with its internationalisation. This indicates that company performance in the international market is dependent on organisational structure. This amply suggests that once the organisational structure is designed, then the next objective would be to test the structure against performance expected out of it and establish its adequacy or inadequacy for further action. In terms of performance, it is expected that the organisational structure must be able to support the organisation in achieving its objectives. There could be four types of objectives that a company may want to achieve through designing an optimum organisational structure. These four objectives are described below.

Position objective

This is the most primary objective of having a requisite organisational structure for a company. The management of a company strategically develop a sound organisational structure which is capable of providing the company a certain desired position in the competitive market place. Once this place is attained the company feel less vulnerable to the ever changing competitive dimensions associated with doing business internationally. For example, the Italian fashion company United Colour of Benetton wants to position itself as a company with outstanding ability to roll out new and innovative products. Cadbury, the erstwhile British confectionery multinational, wants to achieve its highest potential by reaching every customer within the shortest possible time at a less cost and hence, it has operational objective to positions itself as an efficient distributor. McDonald, the famous American company, wanted to position itself as a globally accepted fast food producer through dealing with culturally attuned food products. KFC, the American fast food restaurant chain, wanted to position itself as a supplier of high-quality, hygienic and affordable fast food products as well as assortment of complete meals for the entire globe. These varied positional objectives are important for the respective companies to achieve as they can make them less vulnerable to competition. Therefore, while designing an organisational structure its compatibility with the clearly laid down company positioning statement must be taken in to consideration. An adequately designed organisational structure must support the positioning objectives of the company. In case of organisational structure inadequacy, the company will not be successful in attaining the desired position in the international market even though it may be ready with all its resources and even utilise those resources liberally.

Planning and execution objective

An organisation, in order to be successful internationally, must be able to plan its worldwide operation in advance. It is also important that these plans are executed internationally with clinical perfection. However, these tasks are not easy and more so when the company has expanded in to a multi country operation. To perform these difficult tasks the organisational structure not only require to support world-wide planning but also, at the same time, facilitates people working in the organisation to execute the laid-down plan in different country markets. Organisational structure plays a big role here. It must allow continuous information collection from different markets and accumulate the right information at the right place at the right time so that proper planning can be done at the strategic level of the company. The organisation structure also must ensure proper coordination amongst the different vertical levels and horizontal spread so that the plans for distant markets can be articulated for effective implementation at the right time. A sound organisational structure also brings out performance deficiency, both at individual level and collective, to understand the implementation effectiveness of different strategic corporate plans at the country level. The top management at the corporate level must also be able to get the right feedback from different countries about plan deficiency, if any, at the right time so that corrective action can be taken. A compatible organisational structure allows continuous comparison of performance of various departments and benchmarking with the best in the industry or sector to further develop the system as a whole.

Knowledge management objective

International markets are full with challenges and a company needs to successfully confront them in order to market products or services successfully. This requires a quite good understanding of different local markets and different techniques to handle different challenges. It has been observed in the past that organisations prone to manage knowledge accumulation and learning new things are effective in terms of managing challenges effectively. However, knowledge management system practised in an organisation depends on organisational culture and this culture grows up with adequate backing of right organisational structure. The Japanese companies' organisational structure facilitates people working in the organisation to create knowledge by developing a learning environment. Therefore, it is important that organisations should make learning possible within the company and contribute to the personal development of its employees continually so they can update themselves and gear the company to respond to changing demands and needs of international consumers.

Entropy objective

Entropy is concept of thermodynamics and used to measure disorder or uncertainty in a system. In thermodynamics system the entropy can have minimum value when the system in equilibrium, i.e., not subjected to change due to interaction with outside temperature pressure, etc. A business organisation can also be imagined as a system which is not operating in a closed environment but rather interacts with different environmental variables and thereby gain in the way of achieving a definite goal. These environmental variables are technical and technological, cultural, social, political and economic factors present in different country markets. These variables when interacting with the organisation tend to put pressure on the organisation leading to increase in entropy and hence making the system imbalance. The company in an effort to achieve the state of equilibrium uses internal organisational resources for purposeful interaction with various external environmental factors. The internal resource could be the elements such as products, processes, people, information, techniques, facilities, services, and other support elements. It is important for the company that at any point of time, while in international market, the organisational design must be facilitative enough to the system to win over the influence of external environmental variables. The application of its internal resources requires to be such that system maintain equilibrium even when such external factors are turbulent in nature. For example, it may so happen that a product based organisations structure has not been able to withstand the external turbulence and thereby disturbing the system equilibrium which in turn tend to increase the entropy. Such situation is not desirable and may lead to non-achievement of organisational goals. In a sense, therefore, the organisational structure must be geared up so that people working in the organisation understand responsibilities and authorities correctly and engaged effectively to defuse the possible factors creating system unstable. So, another objective of the organisation structure is to keep the entropy low which again indicates that system is working well with greater sustainability.

CHAPTER SUMMARY

1. The question of what makes for more efficient forms of organising in the internationalisation context has attracted attention of many researchers in the past. These academicians have considered three aspects to be of utmost importance while deciding on the organisation structure. These are: integration of activities across the countries of presence, responsiveness to the local needs and ensuring worldwide learning plough back to ensure knowledge dissemination. In this respect a supportive organisation is of utmost importance.
2. When the company is only a few country internationalised and if the mode of entry into foreign market is through export, then it naturally would create a simple type of export division to manage

the exporting process. However, when the company grows into a multi-country business, the export department may not be enough to match up with the complexities of requirements. With multi-country presence, the complexities are expected to be even more and if not adequately supported by requisite organisational structure the marketing activities are bound to suffer.

3. With multi-country presence, the company needs to understand the requirements of creating organisational sub-units diligently based on careful analysis of various factors such as its short-term and long-term objective in the international markets, the key dimensions of maintaining competitiveness, speed of decision making required based on the strategic intents of the company, product or geographic diversity, technology excellence or transfer demanded, etc.
4. In general, a company has various options for designing its organisational structure. The options can be utilised by a company based primarily on the requirement of managing the external market needs through building an internal system of administration. Therefore, external market needs and requirements is the pivotal factor governing the requirements of internal administration and hence, it influences the organisational structure. There are various types of alternative organisational structures available to meet the evolutionary requirements towards multi-country participation of the companies.
5. Initially, the internationalising company would rely on the international division structure in order to manage its international sales. However, as the foreign product diversity increases without proportional increase in the foreign sale as percentage of the total sales, the company switches over to the product division type in order to manage the diversifying product lines.
6. Internationalising companies have different options in designing their organisational structure. Once the organisational structure is designed, the next objective comes is to test the structure against performance and establish its adequacy or inadequacy for further action. In terms of performance, it is expected that the organisational structure must be able to support the organisation in achieving its objectives. There could be four types of objectives that a company may want to achieve through designing an optimum organisational structure, namely, the goals it has set in respect of its position, planning and execution, knowledge management and maintenance of its system stability.

QUESTIONS FOR REVIEW

1. The following is the Asea Brown Boveri (ABB) organisation's structure during 1998–2001. The Group consisted of the President and CEO, the CFO and the heads of global company segments. The regional (continental) dimension was dissolved in order to enable the Group to focus more on exploiting the potential for applying more global processes and programmes throughout the Group. Several business areas have been established under each corporate area. The organisation, at the national level, has been retained in order to further expand the multiple presence in local markets.

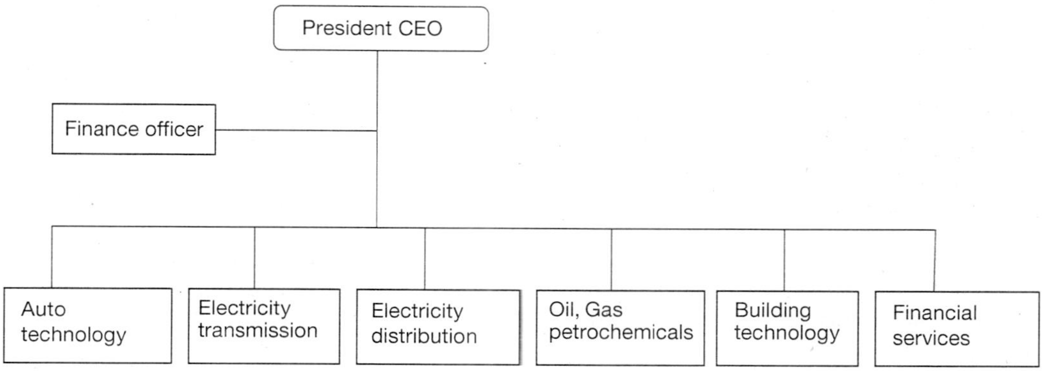

However, during 2001 the company wanted to make it easier for customers to do business with ABB. Hence, the organisation structure was reorganised. The aim of the strategic reorientation was to enhance ABB's relations with customers, thereby boosting its growth. ABB was pursuing a concept that aims at enhancing customer benefits by focusing on customer needs. Visit the ABB Web site at www.abb.com and suggest ways of re-structuring the organisation in the new line.

2. Evaluate the merits and demerits of matrix organisational structure for a global organisation.
3. Describe the Stopford and Well's model for organisational restructuring for internationalising companies. Pick up a growing export-oriented company you are aware of and apply the concept of Stopford and Well's model for predicting structural change.
4. What is product-oriented structure for a multinational company? What are the merits and demerits of such organisational structure? Find out a company from the internet resources where this type of structure is much effective.
5. What is geographic orientation in organisational structure? Do you think this is the right approach for developing organisational structure when a company is practicing localisation strategy? Why or why not? Justify your answer.
6. Visit the Web site of Proctor and Gamble and understand the organisational setting that the company uses to run its global empire. Comment on the involvement of the matrix type of structure in the company.
7. What are the basic objectives that a company would want to achieve by designing a good organisational structure?
8. Study the Bharti Airtel Limited's organisational structure available at www.airtel.in and comment on how internationalisation of the company has been accommodated in the organisation.
9. Visit an international company of Indian origin in your vicinity and study the organisational structure adopted by the company. Interact with the management to understand about their short-term plan (5 years) in respect of international marketing and country coverage. Design a new and revamped organisation structure that can be used by the company in the subsequent years.
10. Collect primary and secondary information about a well-known multinational company to research the validity of Stopford and Well model in the backdrop of the company's internationalisation.

End Case: Suzlon Organising for the World[6]

Sulzer Synthetics Pvt. Ltd or the later-changed name, Suzlon Synthetics Ltd, may be unheard of by many Indians. However, the name Suzlon is not a new name for those who keep tabs on the Indian corporates, for they would immediately relate it to the wind energy business of Tanti family of Rajkot, Gujarat. Mr Tulsi Tanti, along with his two siblings, originally started Sulzer Synthetics P. Ltd., whose name was later changed to Suzlon Synthetics Ltd, but with not much marketing success. The main cause of the collapse was the erratic power supply received by the textile company, which Mr Tanti could not improve in spite of his best efforts. Anyway, there is a saying that once an entrepreneur, always an entrepreneur. During 1990, Mr Tanti was exploring the possibilities of using wind energy as an alternative power supply to his textile factory when he realised that developing wind energy itself in India and abroad could be a very profitable business. By dint of his entrepreneurial trait, he grabbed the opportunity by shifting focus from textile to wind energy during the year 1992. In order to start a company of wind power, Mr Tanti made an invaluable team comprising his two brothers and a couple of his engineering classmates. The initial funding to start the new business came from the sales proceeds of his family property. He then ordered ten wind turbines from Sudwind, a small German company, and started the new business from a rented premise. In order to know the nitty-gritty of wind power business, he hired a German consultant for 90 days. Thereafter, there was no looking back! Suzlon Energy, the new wind power company of India, started with a confident note. Soon, he found that circumstances were favourable to him. Sudwind, from whom he purchased the initial

[6] The case 'Suzlon Organising for the world' has been created by case writer Dr Gautam Dutta of Indian Institute of Foreign Trade as a basis for classroom discussion rather than to illustrate either effective or ineffective handling of a business situation.

turbines, went into liquidation in 1997 and Mt Tanti did not miss the opportunity to take over the ailing company's manpower along with its expertise to strengthen his company. He created a new R&D centre in Germany during 1999 since he realised that continuous research was the key to innovation and becoming successful in the wind power business. Initially, Suzlon Energy started marketing its partly home-grown turbines in the Indian market.

Suzlon Energy internationalised itself very fast. Hansen Transmissions of Belgium was acquired in 2006 for USD 565 million. Hansen was famed as the second largest gearbox maker in the world and Suzlon expected that the acquisition would enhance its wind gearboxes manufacturing and technological development capability. In May 2007, Suzlon acquired a 33.6% stake in REpower, a reputed German wind turbine company for USD 698 million, which was considered as a breakthrough as the acquired company was technology leader with a strong presence in Europe, North America and Australia. Following this foray, Suzlon Energy earned its place among the top five wind energy producers worldwide with sales of over USD 3.4 billion during 2008. Backed by huge marketing success worldwide, Mr Tanti emerged as one of the wealthiest men in the world. Suzlon managed to grab global market share in the wind-turbine business to the extent of about 10.5%. Suzlon projects generated some 15,000 megawatts of wind energy capacity in 25 countries worldwide[7]. The company became global in operation employing about 14,000 people from 15 nationalities. During 2008, about 58% of its revenue came from international operation although it was only 20% about a year back. The company started looking at countries like USA as big potential market, and in fact, USA contributed to about 20% of its total revenues during FY 2008. Europe and China were the other two country markets perceived to be very attractive by the company for wind power business.

By 2011, Suzlon completed the process of acquiring REpower by spending another USD 500 million. REpower's acquisition was expected to add to Suzlon's technological capability, especially in the production of large wind turbines[8]. Suzlon justified its fast internationalisation as it could foresee that revenue would come from developed country markets such as USA, Europe, and China and not from the home country market. In tandem with the internationalisation strategy, it set up its global marketing centre in Amsterdam, Netherlands, and based its international business headquarters in Aarhus, Denmark. The Denmark office was also strengthened to look after its subsidiaries in the USA, Australia, China and Europe. The home country business continued to be operated from Pune, India[9]. In São Paulo, it located the sales and administrative office to serve customers in the Southwest region. Suzlon's wholly-owned subsidiary Suzlon Energy (Tianjin) led Suzlon's marketing ambition in China. Suzlon also made preparations to expand into other East Asian markets – Korea, Vietnam, Philippines and Thailand.

As the business operation grew bigger and bigger, Mr Tanti placed emphasis on building the organisation (Figure 13.9). Mr Tulsi Tanti was the CMD at Suzlon, while Mr Toine van Megen, a Dutch national, was the CEO of the wind energy business at the company during 2008. Mr Sumant Sinha, a finance specialist with experience from Aditya Birla group joined the company as Chief Operating Operator[10]. This was considered as a first step towards appointing professionals, apart from non-promoters, in key posts of the company. However, in a subsequent reorganisation in December 2008, Mr Tulsi Tanti assumed the direct operational control of the company by removing Mr van Megen, who was shifted back to supervisory responsibilities at the Group level[11]. Suzlon, thereafter, created Strategic Business Units (SBUs) and increased decentralisation of power in the company by giving them absolute power. The SBUs were linked with the special skills through creation of a matrix structure where about 70% weight was entrusted to the line manufacturing and about 30% to the functional heads. This change in the organising system was smooth as the heads of the SBUs were experienced enough to understand

[7] India's Suzlon wins $1.28 bn wind power deal, The Economic Times, January 28, 2011.

[8] www.suzlon.com

[9] Suzlon Website, www.suzlon.com – Global Footprint.

[10] http://www.suzlon.com/images/Media_Center_News/56_SEL_COO_Appointment_V1R3_1st_Aug_FINAL.pdf – Accessed on 8th October, 2012.

[11] http://www.suzlon.com/images/Media_Center_News/45_Suzlon_Org_Change_V1_R1.pdf accessed on 8th October, 2012.

the objective of the respective units and honoured them. The SBUs were given the responsibilities and authorities as to hire their own team for the international operations. They were required to set their own target and plan their execution taking into consideration what makes best sense for the business and what makes for the most effective way of working to achieve the targets. In geographic divisions, each country head was made responsible for creating their respective deployment strategy, team, etc., to achieve the organisational goal. Overall, Mr Tanti steadily decentralised decision-making by granting autonomy to the different SBUs. The geographic divisions were also granted a lot of autonomy to facilitate the fast growth which the company desired.

From the marketing point of view, the objective of Suzlon was to satisfy its clients located at different parts of the world, by supplying ready-to-use wind farms. Therefore, Suzlon had to work hard to have full backward integration of the supply chain by developing a comprehensive manufacturing capability for all critical components in wind turbines. No doubt that this allowed the company the economies of scale, quality control and assurance of supplies but at the same time it exerted tremendous pressure on inter-organisational coordination for maintaining the supply chain efficiency. This approach helped the company surge ahead of its competitors who believed in the traditional piecemeal approach.

Mr Tanti explains this concept to Fortune magazine: "Other companies were just equipment vendors. They did give you the turbine, and that was it. Maintenance? 'Not my problem.' Parts? 'That's someone else.' The way we do it, it is like selling a model home. All the customer has to do is pick the model." Mr Tanti further quipped, "We have a business model that is completely counterintuitive. The concepts and design come from the Netherlands, the engineering from Germany, the commercialisation from Denmark and large-scale application comes from India. Only an Indian brain could dream up such a thing". The orchestration in maintaining the inter-country supply chain efficiency required the sound backing of an organisational structure that allowed smooth flow of responsibilities and authorities in the world wide empire of Suzlon. In order to make the company updated with technological status, continuous R&D was planned in strategically located R&D centres. A new 'Innovation Centre' in Denmark and a 'Technology Campus' in Germany were set up exclusively for this purpose. In addition, the

FIGURE 13.9 Suzlon's organisational structure

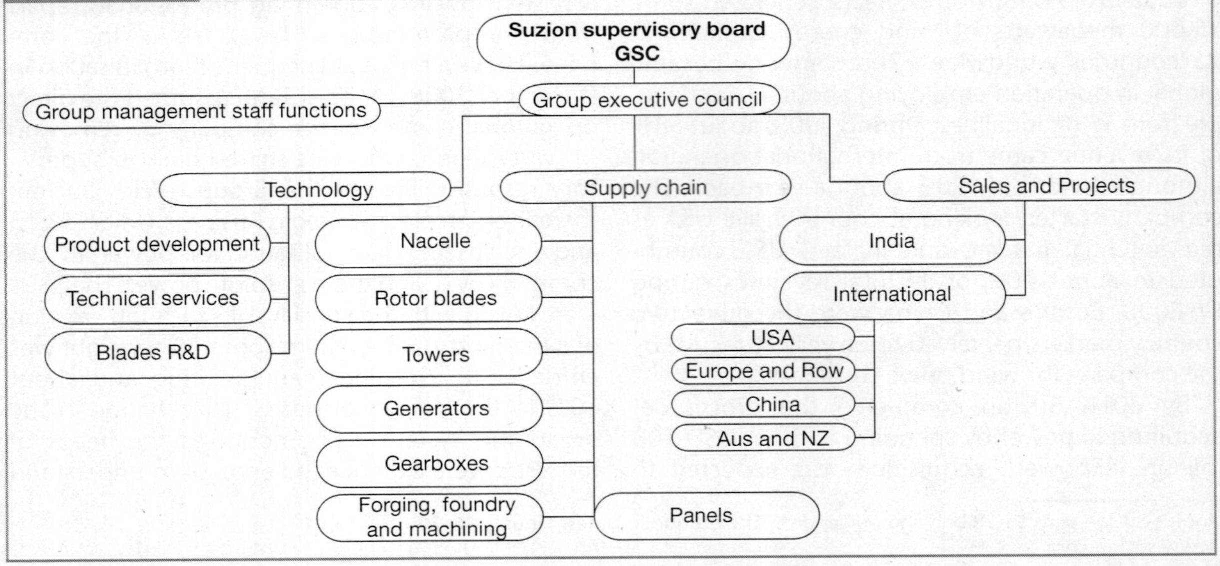

Source: Suzlon group: Powering a greener tomorrow presentation, Suzlon Energy GmbH[12]

12 file.seekpart.com/keywordpdf/2011/3/22/201132281838410.pdf accessed on 8.10.2012.

acquisition of REpower, which was famed to be equipped with cutting-edge R&D capability in the very-large turbine and offshore technology, was expected to provide the entire company the requisite technology back up. Further, the 'Renewable Energy Technology Center GmbH' in Hamburg, Germany, jointly set up by Suzlon and Repower, aimed to conduct research on the technical side of turbine generation and also to start an academy offering high-quality technical training and qualification, initially in collaboration with universities.

The global economic recession was not kind to the company. The empire that was built from a 20-odd men company in 1995 to a 14,000-strong Indian multinational in 2008 was badly hit. Wind energy major Suzlon slipped into red during 2010 as alternative energy had been one of the big casualties of the recession. Suzlon's prospective clients in USA and Europe had drastically cut spending on alternative energy during the crunch. Suzlon's problems were magnified by the debt it had taken to fund its two large European acquisitions in the boom years. The weak demand, high debt in the capital structure and pricing pressure, all started to act on the company and there was also a concern that European governments may further reduce sops to alternative energy to cut fiscal deficits. JP Morgan was entrusted with the responsibilities to chalk out a strategy to bring back the company in to profit. Given the high fixed costs and the weak order outlook, the company is unlikely to become profitable again, said another financial consultancy house.[13]

CASE QUESTIONS

Q1. What type of organisation structure was used by Suzlon during its hay days? What are its benefits and drawbacks?

Q2. Was the organisation adequate in terms of rapid internationalisation of Suzlon?

Q3. Should Suzlon have restructured its organisation in the peaks days of 2008? Why or why not? Redraw and present an ideal organogram for Suzlon with justification.

FURTHER READINGS

Powell, T. (1992), "Organisational alignment as competitive advantage" *Strategic Management Journal*, Vol. 13, Issue 2, pp. 119–134.

The article is an output of an empirical study conducted by the author in two manufacturing industries and found evidence that some organisational alignments could lead to higher profit generation. This increase in profit generation is independent of the profits produced by application of traditional industry and strategy variables. The study confirmed that higher profit can be generated from skill flourished in an organisation, and hence, alignment skills could be considered as a very important strategic resource for generating economic benefits. The article, therefore, concluded that industry requires focusing on the role of organisational factors in producing sustainable competitive advantage which hitherto have not been adequately focussed.

Bartlett, C.A. and S. Ghoshal (1990), "Matrix management: Not a structure, a frame of mind", *Harvard Business Review*, Vol. 68, Issue 4.

This article is the very famous article of these two authors where it has been argued that keeping a company light on its organisational structuring without impairing its ability of coordinating its activities across divisions, functions, even continents, would be rewarding for the multinational companies in terms of elimination of parochialism, improvement of communications, and cross-cultural decision-making process. The authors also did not forget to highlight the benefit of bottom-up communication process practised by companies such as NEC, Philips, and Unilever.

Theuerkauf, Ingo, David Ernst and Amir Mahini (1996), "Think local, organise?", *International Marketing Review*, Vol. 13, No. 3, pp. 7–12, June.

[13] The Asian Age, June 03, 2010.

The article describes how successful US multinational/global consumer goods companies usually maintained a comparatively decentralised structure in order to coordinate international decision-making in a global manner. They took advantage of updated understanding of the managers, which achieved through conducting worldwide manager development programs. The article also observed that a number of firms could not achieve that where there exist, a gap between top management's goals and the organisational systems employed to attain them.

Criscuolo, P., & Narula, R. (2007). Using multi-hub structures for international R&D: Organisational inertia and the challenges of implementation. Management International Review.

This article explores how multinational enterprises (MNEs) are moving away from a 'centralised hub' to a 'multi-hub' network of research and development (R&D) units. The article takes example from European pharmaceutical MNEs and highlights challenges associated with promoting and integrating knowledge flows in multi-hub R&D organisational structures.

Index

A

ABB, 616-619
AB Pharmaceuticals (ABP), 239-244
absolute net shift, 222
ACER, 257
Action Shoes, 387
adaptation approach to marketing programme, 9
Adidas, 525-527
ad valorem (AV), 429
advertisement, culture and, 84
advertising on the Internet, 34
aesthetics, 62-63
American Marketing Association (AMA), 572
Amrit Sudha Aqua Water Company, 591-592
Andean Community, 172-173
antidumping initiations, 1995-2000, 413
anti-grey market alliance, 410
AOL Inc, 135
Aon Corporation, 95
apparel companies internationalisation, 4
Apple iPhone, 340
applied rates, 429
Asian Development Bank (ADB), 186
Aspen, 257
Association of South-east Asian Nations (ASEAN), 175
attitudes, 61-62
Australian Association of National Advertisers (AANA), 140
Australian Competition and Consumer Commission (ACCC), 139-140
Austrian civil law, 120
automobile industry in India, 43-44
Avon, 54

B

Babies "R"Us, 449
barrier-free access, 174
barter trade, 411
Bassi, Peter A., 32
Bata, 387
Bharti Airtel, 5
BMW Group, 150, 255, 280, 342
Borden, Neil, 13
bound rates (tariff binding), 429
brand
  based on geographical coverage, 358-361
  based on product coverage, 361-365
  definition of, 355-356
  in foreign markets, 364
brand architecture, 373-375
brand identity, 356
brand image transfer, 366-368
brand internationalisation, 365-381
  brand image transfer, 366-368
  brand logo transfer, 368-369
  brand name transfer, 369-372
  brand portfolio transfer, 373-375
  communication mix effectiveness, 366
  different expectations, 366
  emotional connect, 366
  foreign country awareness, 366
  level of adaptation, 365-366
  optimum level in brand mix, 375-377
  standardisation or adaptation, 365
brand positioning in foreign countries, 379-381
brand proposition, 356-357
Brazil's population growth, 157
breakeven volume, 418
Business Environment Risk Index (BERI), 233

buyer's personality and purchasing behaviour, 68
Buy US A.infonet, 570
Buzzell, Robert D., 13, 53

C

Cadbury Diary Milk chocolates, 535
Cadillac XTS in China, 52-53
calibration equivalence, 578-579
Canadian Standards Association (CSA), 329
Caribbean Community (CARICOM), 174
Carrefour, 16, 197-201
category equivalence, 578
CBI (Ministry of Foreign Affairs of Netherland), 234
channel performance management, 472-475
  channel alignment, 473-474
  conflict resolution techniques, 480
  cost objective, 473
  customer management, 474
  feedback management, 475
  foreign channels, 475
  harmonisation objective, 473
  product transfer management, 474
  relationship management, 474-475
China
  advertising appeal in, 524-527
  alluring companies with market opportunities, 209-210
  brand names in, 372-373
  component-wise adaptation in international market, 320
  convenience stores or C stores, 467
  departmental stores, 468
  distribution channels, 466-469
  foreign company-FICE combination, 468-469
  foreign company-retailer combination, 469
  GM's local brand in, 359-360
  local brands preparing for a showdown with global brands, 382-383
  luxury sedan market, 323-324
  McDonald's in, 137
  modern retailing formats, 467-468
  Nike footwear advertisement in, 521-522
  product safety and liability, legal restrictions on, 127-128
  regulations on clothing, 332
  retail price maintenance (RPM) in, 130-132
  Revlon distribution system in, case of, 445-446
  super markets and hypermarkets, 468
  water purifiers, 591-592
China Compulsory Certification (CCC), 329
Chinese Advertising Association (CAA), 137
Coca-Cola Co, 9, 22, 525
Coca-Cola Deutschland, 3
Coface Group, 567-568
colour adaptations, 331
colour association, culture and, 82
commitment, 79
Common law (Anglo-American legal system), 119
common market (CM), 171-173
Common Market for Eastern and Southern Africa (COMESA), 172, 209
communication challenges in global marketing, 36
competitive drivers of globalisation, 20
Comprehensive Economic Partnership Agreement (CEPA), 168
conceptual equivalence, 577
Conformité Européne (CE), 329
confrontation, 79
consolidated tariff schedules (CTS), 429
consumer behaviour, relationship between culture and
  Luna and Gupta model, 69-71
  Manrai and Manrai model, 68-69
  Raju's A-B-C-D paradigm model, 67
  Rokeach's value system, 69-70
  Samli model, 67-68
consumer demographics, 152-155
  bases for division of world markets, 162-163
  distribution of global income, 158-161
  distribution of income and wealth, 156-158
  economic dividend from demographic trend, 155-156
  economic integration, 164-166
  inequality within country, 161-163
consumer ethnocentric tendencies scale (CETSCALE), 583-585
contractual manufacturing, 256-260
  benefits, 257-259
  demerits, 259-260
Cornel University, 569-570
corporate brand, 362-363
cost-based export pricing, 417-419
cost competitiveness and internationalisation of business, 4
cost drivers of globalisation, 16-17
cost insurance and freight (CIF) price, 417
counter-purchase, 411
countertrade, 410-411
  forms of, 411

country culture group, 553
country-specific adaptations of marketing programme, 8
country-specific customisation, 55-56
country specific import regulations driven product adaptation, 332
country-specific marketing strategy, 12
country-specific political system, 95-98
cross border marketers, 13
Crown Cork and Seal, 61
cultural dimensions
  culture differences India, Japan, Sweden and UK, 75-76
  Hall's classification, 77-79
  Hofstede's, 71-77, 524
  and marketing implication, 80-84
cultural distance (CD) calculation, 76-77
culture, conceptualising, 56-58
  elements of culture, 59-67
  influence on behaviour, 57
  in marketing, 57-58
customer's perceived benefits of a product, 6
customer value, defined, 6
customer value creation process, 7
customised brand, 357-358
customs duty, 425-428
Customs union (CU), 169-170

D

Daikin, 404
Days Inn, 547
DCM Limited, 20
decision making, culture and, 81
dedicated export department, 255
democracy, 96-97
  measuring, 98-100
  types of, 99
differential pricing, 34
digits, digit-level (tariffs), 429
direct democracy, 96-97
Direct Democracy Index (DDI), 99
direct export, 253-255
  benefits of, 254-255
  drawbacks of, 255
  organisational forms of, 255
distribution channels, 447
  channel performance requirements for the target customer, 477-478
  channel power, 459-460
  channel structure, 451
  channel structure options for the company, 479
  China, 466-469
  choice of, 455-457
  cost-benefit analysis, 479
  designing, 461-462
  developing channel strategy, 479-480
  foreign country target customer, 476-477
  international channel structure design, 475-480
  international distribution, issues with, 457-461
  for international marketing, 452-455
  Japan, 449, 463-466
  performance management, 472-475
  problems with, 451-452
  Russia, 471-472
  structure differences across countries, 462-466
  transportation and logistics, significance of, 450
  Vietnam, 470-471
documentary credit or commercial letter of credit, 194
Doha Development Round, 181
Doing Business Project, 569
domestication, 103
DR CAFTA, 172
Dr Reddy's, 405
dumping, 411-413
Dunning, John, 287
Dynamic Random Access Memory (DRAM) chips, 16

E

East African Community (EAC) Customs Union, 170
eclectic paradigm, 287-288
economic integration, 164-166
  Association of South-east Asian Nations (ASEAN), 175
  benefits of regional integration, 165-166
  Caribbean Community (CARICOM), 174
  common market (CM), 171-173
  cultural factors, 164
  development factors, 164-165
  Economic Union (EU), 173-174
  European Free Trade Association (EFTA), 175
  North American Free Trade Agreement (NAFTA), 175
  proximity factors, 164
  regional, 166-171
economic partnership agreement, 166

Economic Union (EU), 173-174
Economist Intelligence Unit (EIU) databases, 569
education, as a cultural factor, 66-67
Eicher Motor Limited, 20
7-Eleven, 16
e-marketing, 33-34
Emerging Markets Companion, 234
Energy, Export Import bank, 233
English Premiere League matches, 4
enlarged market, 174
entrepreneurship, 5
entry modes
  basic features of, 278-283
  controllability in, 278-279
  country barriers, 282
  exporting as, 249-255
  flexibility in, 279-280
  Goodnow's framework for, 289-295
  marketing control in, 280-282
  resource requirements in, 279
  theories, 283-289
  via contractual agreements, 256-260
  via franchising, 263-266
  via joint ventures, 266-273
  via licensing, 260-263
  via Wholly Owned Foreign Enterprise (WOFE), 273-278
  of Wall-Mart, 289-290
environmental factors, influencing marketing, 31
equivalence checks, 576-577
ESPN Star Sports network, 4
ethnocentric management of an organisation, 217
ethnocentrism, 36
EU regulations on processed food product, 332
Euro Disney Resort, 36, 54
Euromonitor International, 567
European Free Trade Association (EFTA), 175
expected change, 221
expected value, 221
export cell, 255
Export.gov, 233
exporting as entry modes, 249-255
export pricing, 417-430
  chanel used and price variation, 421-422
  cost-based, 417-419
  depth of adaptation and, 422-423
  factors affecting, 419-430
  market-based, 419
  packaging/labelling norms and, 423-425
expropriation risk, 103-104
Extrusion Technology (XTech), 274
Exxon Mobil Corporation, 21

F

factor endowment theory, 178-179
factoring, 195
Fair Packaging and Labeling Act (FPLA), 133
family branding, 362
FAOSTAT Analysis, 567
Federal Anti-Monopoly Service (FAS), 136
Federal Trade Commission Act ("FTC Act"), 133
Federation of International Trade Association (FITA), 234
Federation of International Trade Associations (FITA), 568
Flextronics International Ltd, 259
Ford Motor Company, 3, 21, 306
foreign exchange and exchange market, 186-192
  currency exchange and exchange rate, 188-189
  economic factors, 191-192
  market psychology, 192
  performing countries in Forex reserve, 187
  political stability, 192
franchising, 263-266
  advantages, 264
  disadvantages, 264-265
  exporting combination, 266
  laws across globe, 265
  regulation for Indian franchise sector, 265
  vs licensing, 265-266
free on board price (FOB), 417
free-trade agreement (FTA), 167-168, 205
free trade agreements, 18-19
French civil law, 120
full cost pricing, 417
functional equivalence, 577

G

gaming gadgets, 16
"Gangnam Style" video, 87-89
General Agreement on Tariffs and Trade (GATT), 180, 412
General Electric, 3
Generalised System of Preferences (GSP), 184
General Motor, 21, 364
  in China, 359-360
geocentric approach to marketing, 36
geocentric management of an organisation, 217
German civil law, 120
GfK Group, 574

global brands, 360-361
global corporations, 20-22
globalEDGE, 233
global edge, 567
global income, distribution of, 158-161
  Central and Eastern Europe, 160
  Commonwealth of Independent States, 160
  Developing Asia, 160
  Euro Area, 161
  Low income Countries, 161
  Middle East and North Africa, 160-161
  Western Hemisphere, 160
globalisation, 3
The Globalisation of Markets, 7
global marketing, 13, 25-26
  benefits of, 27-28
  challenges in, 34-38
  communication challenges in, 36
  coordination of activities, 38
  as efficiency point, 32-33
  legal requirements, 37
  limitations of, 38-39
  speed to market products, 37
  targeting customers, 36-37
  tariff and non-tariff barriers, 37-38
global pricing, 434-437
global retail development index, 461
Godrej Industries and Godrej Consumer Products Limited (GCPL), 143-147, 277
  opportunities abroad, 144-146
  political risks for, 145-147
Goldwin Consumer Products Private Ltd, 545-546
Goodnow, James D., 289
government drivers of globalisation, 17-19
  economic policy, 18
  marketing regulations, 18
  technical standards, 18
green products, 332-333
grey marketing, 407-408
  communication process, 409-410
  dealing with, 409-410
growth rate of market, 221
Gulf Cooperation Council (GCC) customs union, 171

H

Haendel, Dan, 113
Hall's classification of culture, 77-79
Harmonised System (HS) codes, 219
headquarter orientation, 23, 25
Heckscher-Ohlin's theory makes, 178-179
Herkovits, Melville J., 56
Hero group of companies, 268-269
high-context culture, 77-78
Himalaya Drug Company, 595-596
Hindustan Semiconductor Manufacturing Corporation (HSMC), 261
Hofstede, Geert, 56
Hofstede's cultural dimensions, 71-77
Honda company, 268-269
Honda Motors, 20
host country market opportunities and competition, 550-551
Howell, Llewellyn D., 102
Human Development Reports, 570
hybrid cars, 8
Hyundai Automobiles, 139-140

I

IFB, 305
iGATE Computer Systems Ltd, 22
IKEA, 548
Imperial Tobacco Company, 63
Index of Economic Freedom, 570
India
  advertisement regulations in, 509-510
  automobile industry in, 43-44
  component-wise adaptation in international market, 320
  culture differences, 75-76
  footwear manufacturing, 385-387
  KFC experience in, 10
  localness or globalness of TV commercial, analysis, 531
  Philips in, 325
  product adaptations, 321
  product safety and liability, legal restrictions on, 124-125
  regulation for Indian franchise sector, 265
  retailing infrastructure, 460
India-Japan CEPA, 168-169
India-Singapore CECA, 169
India-Sri Lanka FTA, 168
indirect democracy, 97
indirect export, 251-253
  benefits of, 252-253
  drawbacks of, 253
Individualism Index (IDV), 73
Indoco Remedies Ltd, 257

industrial network approach (INA) to internationalisation, 288-289
Infineon Technologies AG, 260
influencing factors on marketing variables for a country, 30-31
information exchange, culture and, 82-83
information search, culture and, 80-81
integrated database (IDB), 429
intention formation, culture and, 81
InterGlobe Enterprises, 17
internalised communication, 79
International Commercial Terms or INCO terms, 430-433
International Commodities Agreements (ICA), 184
international companies (ICs), 21
International Country Risk Guide (ICRG), 114
international divisions, 11
internationalisation of business, 2-3, 206-207
- access to emerging markets, 211
- achieving economies of scale, 211
- cost competitiveness and, 4
- to develop global image, 213
- to downplay trade barriers, 214
- due to demand saturation in domestic market, 210
- for global competitive advantage, 213-214
- to grab market opportunities, 208-209
- of Indian companies, 207-208
- lower cost of production, access to, 211-212
- motives for, 4-5
- organisational transformation and, 601-604
- proactive and reactive motives, 208
- raw materials, access to, 212-213
- reasons for international expansion, 208-214
- selection of country markets for expansion, 214-231
- small- and medium-sized companies, benefits of, 5
- technological competence and, 5
- technology changes and, 4
- untapped opportunities and, 5
- by US companies, 3
- *vs* market participation, 26-27

internationalisation of marketing activities
- domestic marketing, 22-23
- international marketing, 23-24
- requirements, 28-29

internationalising company, compatibility of, 551-552
international legal systems, 119-122
- Austrian civil law, 120
- civil law or code law, 119-120
- Common law (Anglo-American legal system), 119
- French civil law, 120
- German civil law, 120
- requirement of, 122
- Scandinavian civil law, 120
- socialist law, 121
- theocratic law (religious legal systems), 120-121

international marketing
- extremes of, 13
- organising for, 605-608
- research plan for, 558-560
- scholarly journals in, 564-565

international markets, 5-6
International Monetary Fund (IMF), 185-186
international product positioning, 341-342
International Telecommunication Union (ITU), 494
international trade, theories of, 175-179
- factor endowment theory, 178-179
- Heckscher-Ohlin's theory makes, 178-179
- mercantilist view, 176
- theory of absolute cost advantage, 176-177
- theory of competititve cost advantage, 177-178

International Trade Administration (ITA), 568
Internet
- effect on marketing, 34
- usage, 33

Ipsos, 573

J

J. Walter Thompson (JWT), 521
Japan
- component-wise adaptation in international market, 319-320
- culture differences, 75-76
- distribution channel system, 449, 463-466
- localness or globalness of TV commercial, analysis, 530
- marketing communications, legal restrictions on, 137-138
- population trend in, 158
- product safety and liability, legal restrictions on, 127

Japan Fair Trade Commission (JFTC), 137-138
J.D. Power and Associates, 573
John Player, 63

joint ventures, 266-273
advantages, 272
disadvantages, 273
in distribution and production
subcontracting, 270
exporting combination, 271
foreign direct investment (FDI)/JV
combination, 272
integrated, 267-268
in production, 269-270

K

Kajaria Ceramics, 203-204
Kantar, 573
Karbonn Mobiles, 494-495
"Keiretsu" network, 464
Kellogg, 62, 303-304, 334
Kellogg Company, 21
Keralite economy and marketing lessons, 149-150
KFC, 32, 503
advertisements and use of media, 515-516
experience in India, 10
Kluckhohn, Clyde, 56
Kotler, Phillip, 13
Krüger GmbH & Co, 434-435
K•Swiss, 247-249

L

label adaptations, 331-332
Lakhani Shoes, 387
La Liga matches, 4
language, as a cultural factor, 65-66
Larsen & Toubro (L&T), 246-247
Lava, 494-495, 497
LED Smart TV, 8
legal environment of the country, 116-118
marketing communications, 132-141
related to product safety & liability, 122-128
retail price maintenance (RPM), 128-132
Levi Strauss & Co, 398
Levitt, Theodore, 7, 307, 310
hypothesis of market homogenisation, 8
Lex Mundi, 568
licensing, 260-263
advantages of entry by, 262
disadvantages of entry by, 262-263
vs franchising, 265-266
Linton, Ralph, 56
local brands, 359
localisation of marketing programme, 13, 29-32
L'Occitane, 299-301, 448
distribution channel for, 483-489
logistics management, 480
L'Oreal, 358, 374-375, 458
localness in advertising, 539-543
low-context culture, 78
Luna and Gupta model of consumer
behaviour, 69-71
Lux soap, 534-535
luxury car market, 149-150

M

3M, 335
MacArthur, Douglas, 11
Mahindra's sports utility vehicle (SUV) in U.S.
market, 41-43, 46-50
Malaysian Communications and Multimedia
Commission Act, 141
management dynamics, 571
management orientation, 23, 25, 35
mandatory requirements group, 552
Manrai and Manrai model of consumer
behaviour, 68-69
Mapplecroft, 95
marginal cost pricing, 418
market-based export pricing, 419
market drivers of globalisation, 15-16
market entry research, 550-552
market homogenisation, 8
marketing communications, legal restrictions
on, 132-141
Australia, 139-140
Brazil, 134-136
Canada, 133-134
China, 137
Hennes & Mauritz AB advertisement in
Dubai, 140
Japan, 137-138
Malaysia, 141
middle east countries, 140-141
Russia, 136
United Kingdom, 134
United State of America, 133
marketing mishaps, 54-55
marketing mix decision group, 553-554
marketing-oriented concept, 13
marketing strategy orientation, 24-25
marketing task of a company
adaptation approach, 9
basic, 6-7

changing concept of, 12-14
identifying segment to target, 7
multinational phase, 10-12
standardisation approach, 7-8
understanding customers' preferences, 6
market participation, 26-27
market place, 5
Market probe inc., 572
market research organisations, 571-574
GfK Group, 574
Ipsos, 573
J.D. Power and Associates, 573
Kantar, 573
Market probe inc., 572
Nielsen holdings N.V., 573
market selection for expansion, 214-231
application of the shift share method for identifying the market, 222-225
assessing market potential, 234-236
countries of possible destination, 220-222
factors affecting, 216-218
final decision on target market, 227
international, 217
level of trade intimacy, 226
niche market specialisation, 218
PESTLE factors, 216
resources, 218
for setting own subsidiary, 227-233
sources of information, 233-236
in terms of management orientation, 217
time factor, 218
trend of importation of the product/products, understanding of, 225-226
market skimming pricing strategy, 420
Masculinity Index (MAS), 73-74
material culture, 64-65
McCarthy, Jerome, 12
McDonald's, 33, 306, 334
advertising adaptation, 335
in China, 137
tag line translation problem, 502
3M Company, 22
Meadow, Robert, 113
MERCOSUR (the Common Market of the South), 171-172
metric equivalence, 579
Metro, 16
METRO Cash and Carry, 215
MFN (most-favoured-nation) tariff, 429
Micromax, 439-443, 494-496
Microsoft Corporation, 4, 258, 399-400, 502
mid-size SUV market in the U.S., 45-46
MIGA (Multilateral Investment Guarantee Assurence), 116
Millennium Development Goals (MDG), 185-186
minilateralism, 38
Mirza International, 387-391
mixed brand, 363-365
Motorola, 447, 526
multi-domestic marketing, 29, 36
multilateralism, 38
multinational corporations (MNCs), 3, 11-12
American, 11
multinationality-performance (MP) group, 554-557
multinational marketing, 13, 24
multinational phase in marketing, 10-12

N

National Counsel of Advertising Self Regulation (Conselho Nacional de Auto Regulamentação Publicitária or CONAR), 135-136
nationalisation, 103
Nestlé, 352-354, 363-364, 596-600
net shift, 221-222
new products launching, 340-343
Nielsen holdings N.V., 573
Nike, 4, 61, 414, 447
footwear advertisement in China, 521-522
marketing strategy of, 17
slogan translation issues, 503
tag line translation problem, 502
Nirula's restaurant, 351-352
Nokia, 21, 495-496
Non-agricultural Market Access (NAMA), 182
non verbal mode of communication, 66
North American Free Trade Agreement (NAFTA), 18-19, 167-168, 172, 175

O

optimum brand mix, 375-377
organisational capabilities
integration of activities, 601-602
responsiveness, 602-603
worldwide learning, 603-604
organisation and organisational structure, 600-601
alternative, 608-620
export department, 609-610
function-based, 609

geographical/regional based structure, 610-611
hub and spoke structure, 615-616
inadequacy, 604-605
international structure stage model, 619-620
matrix organisation structure, 612-615
organisational sub-units, 606-607
organising for marketing internationally, 605-608
performance and, 620-622
product division, 611-612
reporting and control, 607-608
tasks and functions, 607
team-based, 616
transformation of, 601-604
Overseas Private Investment Corporation (OPIC), 233

P

packaging size adaptations, 331
Parsons, Talcott, 56
pegged currency, 421
Peking duck, 15
penetration pricing strategy, 420
Pepsi, 501, 526
perceived risk, culture and, 81-82
percentage net shift, 222
persuasion, culture and, 83-84
PESTLE factors, 216
Philips India, 321, 325
Phoenix International, 387
Pizza Hut, 32, 326
political risk, 102-103
activity-based, 112
assessing and measuring, 111-115
classification of, 103-104
confiscation, 105
currency crisis, 105-106
discriminating tax structure, 107
domestication, 105
event-based, 113
in Indonesia, 145-146
influence on international business operations, 114
insuring, 115-116
labour unrest due to internal politics, 108
local content requirements and import restriction, 106
loss of image due to political transition, 108-109
manifestation in business, 104-110
physical damage to assets from political violence, 106-107
politically motivated cyber attacks, 109-110
pressure groups, 108
restriction on transfer of profit, 107-108
semi-quantitative and risk-ranking approaches, 114-115
system-based, 113
terrorism, 110
Political Risk Atlas of Mapplecroft, 115
Political Risk Services (PRS), 114
political system stability index, 114
political uncertainty
GMR's business in Maldives, case of, 92-93
pharmaceutical industry, 101
Political Risk Map 2011, 100-101
Syrian politics, 93-94
political violence risk, 104
polycentric management of an organisation, 217
polycentric marketing, 36
Power Distance Index (PDI), 72, 76
preferential trading agreements (PTA), 166-167
premium pricing strategy, 419
pre-shipment finance, 195
pricing
company internal factors and, 413-416
competitive structure, 403-406
countertrade, influence on, 410-411
country-of-origin effect, 399-402
dumping, influence on, 411-413
export, 417-430
global, 434-437
government regulations and, 433-434
important in the game plan, 404
income levels, influence on, 406-407
International Commercial Terms or INCO terms and, 430-433
margins and discrimination as source of conflict, 480-481
non price factors, 430-434
objectives pursued by companies in international market, 398
product life cycle and, 402-403
transfer, 414-416
print advertisements, analysis of localness or globalness of, 533-537
Proctor & Gamble (P&G), 162, 305

print advertising campaign, 536
product line and product mix, 339
product adaptation, 308-309, 314-316
advantages, 316
aesthetic adaptation, 319
component-wise adaptation in international market, 319-320
convenience adaptation, 317
country specific import regulations driven, 332
in developed countries, 337
in developing countries, 337
economic adaptation, 317-318
economic factors driven, 327
factors encouraging, 327-333
in least developing countries, 338
local considerations driven, 328-329
mandatory, 324
marketing strategy, 333-335
microwave oven adaptation, case of, 346-348
packaging and labelling restriction driven, 330-332
performance adaptation, 318
social significance adaptation, 318-319
specific regulation driven, 329-330
standards driven, 329
strategy selection, 335-336
timing of entry, 336
trade restrictions driven, 328
tradition driven, 328
usage conditions driven, 327
vs standardisation, 321-324
product and service orientation, 23, 25
product brand, 361
product component mix, 309-327
core component, 311
future component, 312-313
international marketing and, 313-314
packaging component, 311
support service component, 312
product differentiation, 409
product evaluation, culture and, 84
production location orientation, 24, 26
product line and mix, management of, 338-340
alteration of existing product, 340
contraction of product mix in a particular country, 339-340
expansion of product mix in a particular country, 339
product mix strategy, 339-340
product perception, culture and, 83
product safety and liability, legal restrictions on, 122-128
China, 127-128
European Union (EU), 125-127
General Product Safety Directive (GPSD), 125
India, 124-125
Japan, 127
Product Liability Directive (85/374/EEC), 125
Product Warranty Directive (1999/44/EC), 125
product standardisation, 307-308, 314-316
to customised product, 325-327
ethnocentric standardisation, 321-322
geocentric standardisation, 322-323
to global product, 324-327
polycentric standardisation, 322
promotion (marketing communication)
appeal and culture, 523-526
availability of right type of medium, 515-520
benefits of standardisation in, 527-528
economic differences effecting, 522-523
effect of local norms and sentiments in, 520-521
international, 498-500
language differences and, 500-504
model of, 497-498
print advertisements, localness or globalness of, 533-537
prohibitions, 511-515
regulatory control in, 504-511
slogan translation issues, 503-504
tag line translation problem, 501-503
TV advertising in Malaysia, 510-511
TV commercials, localness or globalness of, 528-533
Ps of marketing, 13, 29

R

Raju's A-B-C-D paradigm model, 67
Ravissant, 448
Red Tape, 387
Reebok
case of misleading marketing communication, 134
regiocentric management of an organisation, 217
regional brands, 360
regional economic integrations, 166-171
Comprehensive Economic Partnership Agreement (CEPA), 168

Customs union (CU), 169-170
East African Community (EAC) Customs Union, 170
economic partnership agreement, 166
free-trade agreement (FTA), 167-168
Gulf Cooperation Council (GCC) customs union, 171
India-Japan CEPA, 168-169
India-Singapore CECA, 169
India-Sri Lanka FTA, 168
preferential trading agreements (PTA), 166-167
Southern African Customs Union (SACU), 170-171
registration, evaluation, authorisation and restriction of chemicals (REACH), 330
regulatory chill, 19
regulatory control in communication, 504-511
by advertisers' association, 505-506
by bloggers, 506
by civic groups, 505
country-specific, 506-511
by government agencies, 505
relationships management, 409
religion, as a cultural factor, 60-61
resale price maintenance (RPM), 128
research framework, for international marketing. *see also* research methodology
contemporary research and benefits, 560-564
requirements, 549
research issues, 550-557
research plan, 557-564
scholarly journals in, 564-565
sources of data for international marketing research, 565-571
research methodology, 574-588
country scale development, 583-585
etic *vs* emic approach, 585-586
measurement scales, 580-582
questionnaire survey, 580
research design equivalence, 575-580
sampling, 587-588
unit of analysis, 586-587
responsibility, 79
restriction on hazardous substances (RoHS), 329-330
retail price maintenance (RPM), 128-132
cases from China, 131-132
characteristics of, 128-129
in China, 130-131
in European Commission, 130
in Japan, 130
in Mexico, 130
in USA, 129
right-hand traffic and left-hand traffic regulations, 332
ritualistic behaviour, 70
Robock, Stefan H., 113
Rokeach's value system, 69-70
Royal Philips Electronics, 306
80:20 rule, 32
Russian distribution channel, 471-472
Ryan air Ltd, 135

S

Samli model of consumer behaviour, 67-68
Samsung, 16, 495-496
Scandinavian civil law, 120
Schmidt, David, 102
Schumpeter, Joseph, 110-111
segmentation, targeting and positioning (STP) strategy, 12
Shils, Edward, 56
Siemens AG, 21
Singapore issues, 182
Singer Sewing Machine Company, 3
Skoda, 405
small and medium enterprises (SMEs), factors affecting brand performance, 377-379
Small Business Administration (SBA), 233
Smith, Adam, 176
Smith, Wendell. R., 12
socialism, 98
socialist law, 121
social organisations and culture, 63-64
social orientation, 79
Sojka, Jane, 56
Sony, 8, 306
South Asia Co-operative Environment Programme, 168
South Asian Association for Regional Cooperation (SAARC), 168
South Asian Economic Union and Bay of Bengal Initiative for Multi-Sectoral Technical and Economic Cooperation (BIMSTEC), 168
Southern African Customs Union (SACU), 170-171

Spanish Paella, 15
standard harmonisation, 174
standardisation orientation, 23, 25
standardised brand, 357-358
standardised marketing programme, 7-8
Starbucks, 213
State Administration of Industry and Commerce (SAIC), 137
strategic alliance, 282-283
strategic pricing strategy, 409
subsidiary, market selection for setting, 227-233
  country visit and final choice, 232-233
  decision in terms of opportunities, 231
  decision on country basket, 228
  decision on objective of expansion, 228
  decision on operational issues, 232
  preliminary screening, 228-231
  research of focus countries, 231-232
Sulzer Synthetics Pvt. Ltd, 624-627
sum of net shift, 222
Suzlon, 5
Suzuki Motor Co., Ltd., 215
Suzuki Motor Corporation, 20
Suzuki Wagon R, 319-320
synchronisation orientation, 24-25

T

Taco Bell, 32
Tansuhaj, Patriya S., 56
tariff rate quota (TRQ), 428-429
TATA, 363
team work, 79
technology drivers of globalisation, 19-20
  level of inclination, 20
  level of technological advancements, 20
Tetra Pak, 5
text adaptations, 331
theocratic law (religious legal systems), 120-121
theory of absolute cost advantage, 176-177
theory of competititve cost advantage, 177-178
Tokyo Disneyland, 54
Toshiba, 211
  fixing competitive price for its Kirabook, 394-395
totalitarianism, 97-98
Toyota Motor Corporation, 8, 21, 55, 520
Toys "R"Us, 449, 464
trade across border indicators, 206
trade financing
  counter trade, 194
  documentary credit or commercial letter of credit, 194
  factoring, 195
  instruments, 194-195
  pre-shipment finance, 193-195
Trade Map, 570-571
TradePort, 570
transaction cost approach to internationalisation, 286-288
transfer pricing issues, 414-416
transfer risk, 104
translation equivalence, 578
transnational company, 21
transport infrastructure and delay in export/import clearance, 425
Treaty of Asuncion, 172
Trend watching.com, 569
TÜV Marks, 329
TV commercials, analysis of localness or globalness of, 528-533
Tylor, Sir Edward Burnett, 56

U

UL Marks, 329
Uncertainty Avoidance Index (UAI), 74-76
Unilever, 3
  "Dove Campaign for Real Beauty," 4, 19, 517, 519
United Kingdom
  culture differences, 75-76
  marketing communications, legal restrictions on, 134
United Nation Economic and Social Commission for Asia and the Pacific (UNESCAP) trade finance infrastructure, 193
United Nations Conference on Trade and Development (UNCTAD), 184-185
United Nations Educational, Scientific and Cultural Organisation (UNESCO), 57
United State of America
  advertising guidelines, 506-508
  marketing communications, legal restrictions on, 133
Uppsala model of internationalisation, 283-286
U.S. Census Bureau, 569
U.S. dollar-Indian rupee exchange rate, 190-191
U.S. regulations on processed food product, 332
U.S. Trade and Development Agency (USTDA), 233

V

value added tax (VAT), 429
values, 61-62
variation of marketing programmes, 31-32
Vertu, 314
Vietnamese distribution channel, 470-471
Volkswagen (VW), 502, 504-504

W

Walmart, 16
Walt Disney Company, 36, 54
waste electronic and electronic equipment (WEE), 330
West, Gerald, 113
Whirlpool, 305
Whitelock and Rey's model for TV commercials, 531-533
Wholly Owned Foreign Enterprise (WOFE), 273-278
  by acquisition, 276-277
  advantages, 275
  disadvantages, 275
  exporting combination, 277-278
World Bank, 185-186
  "doing business ranking" system, 205
World Fact book, 233-234
World Trade Organisation (WTO), 180-183
  ministerial conferences, 180-183
  and Shrimp-Turtle Case, 183
  tariff analysis online, 234

X

Xbox 360, 4
Xbox gaming gadget, 4, 37, 258-259, 397, 399, 447, 458
Xerox, 502
Xitong, 466

Y

Yip, George, 14, 26
  drivers of globalisation, 14-20
Yum! Restaurants International, 32